Type Inheritance

and Relational Theory

Subtypes,
Supertypes,
and Substitutability

Inheritance in *The Third Manifesto*

C. J. Date

Revision History:
   2016-08-31 First release.
See *http://oreilly.com/catalog/errata.csp?isbn=0636920051589* for release details.

ISBN: 978-1-491-95999-2
[LSI]

About the Author

C. J. Date is an independent author, lecturer, researcher, and consultant, specializing in relational database technology. He is best known for his book *An Introduction to Database Systems* (8th edition, Addison-Wesley, 2004), which has sold some 900,000 copies at the time of writing and is used in several hundred colleges and universities worldwide. He is also the author of many other books on database management, the following among them:

- From Addison-Wesley: *Databases, Types, and the Relational Model: The Third Manifesto* (3rd edition, with Hugh Darwen, 2007)

- From Trafford: *Logic and Databases: The Roots of Relational Theory* (2007) and *Database Explorations: Essays on The Third Manifesto and Related Topics* (with Hugh Darwen, 2010)

- From Ventus: *Go Faster! The TransRelational^{TM} Approach to DBMS Implementation* (2002, 2011)

- From O'Reilly: *Database Design and Relational Theory: Normal Forms and All That Jazz* (2012); *View Updating and Relational Theory: Solving the View Update Problem* (2013); *Relational Theory for Computer Professionals: What Relational Databases Are Really All About* (2013); *SQL and Relational Theory: How to Write Accurate SQL Code* (3rd edition, 2015); and *The **New** Relational Database Dictionary* (2016)

- From Morgan Kaufmann: *Time and Relational Theory: Temporal Data in the Relational Model and SQL* (with Hugh Darwen and Nikos A. Lorentzos, 2014)

Mr. Date was inducted into the Computing Industry Hall of Fame in 2004. He enjoys a reputation that is second to none for his ability to explain complex technical subjects in a clear and understandable fashion.

Contents

Preface

This book will tell you more than you might have wanted to know about the subject of type inheritance (inheritance for short). Now, if you're reading these remarks, you're already rather special; most people don't bother to read prefaces at all. For that reason, the kind of thing that usually goes into a preface—background material, motivation underlying the work described, reasons for writing the book, "what you will learn," and so forth—I've deliberately deferred, mostly, to the body of the book (to Chapters 1 and 3 in particular). In any case, there's really too much of that general nature that I want to say, and it's too involved and interwoven, to fit comfortably into a conventional preface. But this is still a convenient place to take care of a few boilerplate items.

Right at the outset, I must make it clear that this is a book with an attitude. My friend and colleague, Hugh Darwen, and I have been working for many years on the theory on which this book is based: namely, our inheritance model. As a consequence, we have some very definite opinions about the subject matter, and—speaking purely for myself here—those opinions have had a major influence on the style and content of the writing. In some respects, in fact, the book isn't so much a textbook as it is a plea for the community at large to take a careful look at what we've done: a careful look, in fact, at what we consider to be a logical, sensible, and pragmatically useful approach to the subject. That said, however, the book does resemble a textbook in that most of the chapters include a set of exercises (as well as answers, in most cases); thus, you can test your own understanding of the material as you proceed, if you have a mind to.

Here's what I'll be assuming by way of background on your part:

- First, I assume you have some professional knowledge of data management: what it is, what data itself is, how data can be represented to make it suitable for formal manipulation, what such formal manipulations might look like, and so on. In other words, I assume you're interested in what some people like to call "data modeling"— possibly but not necessarily including comparatively advanced aspects of that subject, such as the notions of generalization and specialization.

- Second, I assume you have a good working knowledge of the relational model. Of course, if you really are interested in data modeling as I've said I assume you are, then this second prerequisite goes (or should go) without saying—though as a matter of fact I think most if not all of the book should make sense even to someone without a detailed background in relational theory.

- Third, I assume you also have some familiarity with at least one conventional programming language—including, preferably, at least one language that's not "object oriented." *Note:* I don't mean to be offensive here; I mean, I don't intend the foregoing remarks to be taken as disparaging object languages as such. Rather, the reason I think it might be desirable for you to be familiar with at least one language that's not an object language is the following. Suppose the only languages you know do in fact happen all to be object languages. Then I'm afraid you might find you need to do some unlearning— and as we all know, unlearning can often be quite difficult to do. For example, in object languages, an object of, say, type NAME typically doesn't contain a name as such; rather, it contains a pointer, or "reference," to such a name. By contrast, in the type theory described in and embraced by the present book, the counterpart of such an object would contain a name as such. (The reasons for this difference in approach are discussed in detail in the body of the book, in Chapters 13 and 21 in particular.)

Here now by contrast are some things I won't be assuming:

- I won't assume you have a deep knowledge of the type system of whatever programming language(s) you do happen to know, nor of type theory in general.

- I won't you assume you know anything about SQL in particular (which is in fact basically just another programming language, though it's not usually described as such). Of course, I don't mean I'm going to be explaining a lot of SQL material that you might already know; rather, I mean that—except for one rather long chapter, Chapter 22, which in any case you can skip if you want—this book isn't really about SQL, as such, at all.

Let me add a couple of further remarks regarding SQL, though. First, please note that throughout the book all references to SQL should be understood as referring to the standard version of that language exclusively, not to some proprietary dialect. The reference document is:

International Organization for Standardization (ISO): *Database Language SQL*, Document ISO/IEC 9075:2008 (2011)

Second, please note that I follow the standard in assuming the pronunciation "ess cue ell," not "sequel" (though this latter pronunciation is common in the field), thereby saying things like *an* SQL table, not *a* SQL table.

Structure of the Book

The book is arranged into five principal parts, as follows:

I. Preliminaries

II. Scalar Types, Single Inheritance

III. Scalar Types, Multiple Inheritance

IV. Tuple and Relation Inheritance

V. Other Approaches

There are also three appendixes and an index. Broadly speaking, the book is meant to be read in sequence as written, except occasionally as noted here and there in the text itself; most of the chapters do rely to some extent on material covered in earlier ones, so you shouldn't jump around too much. (However, let me draw your attention to the glossary in Appendix C; you might find it convenient to refer to that glossary from time to time while reading other parts of the book.)

Now, you might know that Darwen and I have written on this subject before, primarily in our series of books on *The Third Manifesto* (see Chapter 1). However, what follows is much more than just a cobbling together of material from those earlier writings. For one thing, it contains much that's entirely new. For another, it presents a more coherent, and I think much better, perspective on the subject as a whole (I learned a lot myself in putting the book together). Indeed, even when some portion of the text is based on earlier writings by ourselves, the material in question has been totally rewritten and, I trust, improved.

All of that being said, I think I need to say too that the subject of inheritance does seem to involve a certain amount of intrinsic complexity (a fact that accounts in part for the length of the book, of course). Naturally I've done my best to explain the topics as straightforwardly as I can; however, although the basic idea is simple enough, the devil is in the detail—and I do believe you need to be exposed to that detail, even if you don't absorb it all, in order to get a proper sense of the scope of the subject.

Talking of complexity, I'm a little embarrassed at the number of footnotes in this book. I'm only too well aware how annoying footnotes can be—indeed, they can seriously impede readability—but in the present case I think they merely reflect what I referred to in the previous paragraph as the intrinsic complexity of the subject matter. In fact, it occurred to me in writing this preface that I might turn this plague of footnotes to some kind of advantage. To be specific, noting that some chapters certainly seemed to involve rather more than their share, it occurred to me that it might be helpful to the reader if I were to use "average number of footnote lines per page" as a kind of rough and ready measure of relative complexity. To that end, I compiled the following histogram, showing chapters and appendixes along the horizontal axis and "footnote lines per page," measured in units of one tenth, along the vertical axis. For example, the histogram shows that Chapter 1 has an average of 2.5 footnote lines per page. Of course, I make no great claims of either accuracy or precision in this connection, but I do think the histogram gives some overall sense of which chapters might be a little harder, and which a little easier, to come to grips with.

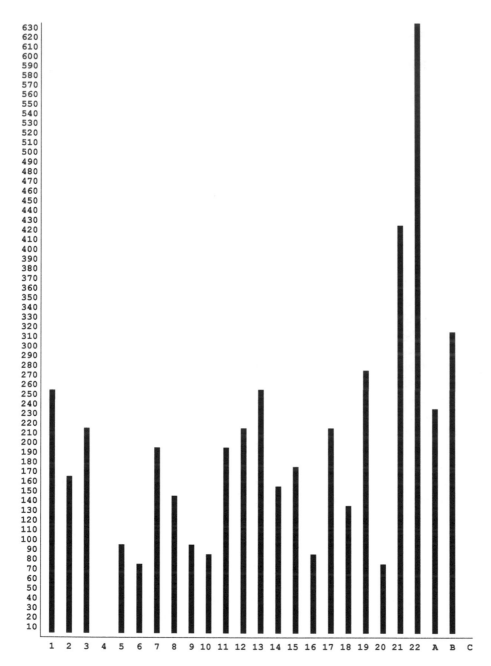

Some of the entries in this histogram deserve a little further explanation. First, the column for Chapter 1 is surprisingly high. Actually I don't think you should find that chapter very difficult at all; it deals with history and other background material, and has more of a narrative feel to it than most of the other chapters. But it does contain several footnotes that give references to other publications, and that fact might account for its comparatively high "relative complexity" score. Similar remarks apply to Appendix B.

Second, the column for Chapter 4 is empty, and yet that chapter is probably the most difficult in the book! But that's because it consists essentially of just a formal statement of the prescriptions of our model of inheritance, with almost nothing by way of further explanation, and no footnotes either. The chapter is provided primarily for purposes of subsequent reference; it's certainly not meant to be read straight through.

Third, the columns for Chapters 21 and (especially) 22 are clearly the highest of all—a state of affairs that doesn't surprise me, because I spent more time on those two chapters than I did on the entire rest of the book put together. And the reason I did so was because, in my opinion, the technical material I was trying to describe in those chapters is rather confusing, and (I'm tempted to say) rather confused as well. Perhaps a kinder way to put it is that the material in question does seem to be ad hoc to a degree, instead of being founded, as we claim our own inheritance model is, on a clear and well thought out set of underlying principles. Be that as it may, I certainly do think those two chapters are quite difficult. Now, I'm sorry that such is the case, and I apologize for it—but I don't think the fault is entirely mine.[1]

Acknowledgments

As I've said, I do believe our model of type inheritance has something truly useful to offer—all the more so, perhaps, because it's so different from other approaches to the subject that have been described in the literature. For that reason, I'd been thinking for some time about a book like this one, one that I hoped could provide a coherent and reasonably complete description of what it was that we were proposing. (After all, those earlier writings by Darwen and myself didn't really do our proposals justice, and in any case those writings were neither complete nor entirely self-contained. At least, so it seemed to me.) But pressure of other work prevented me from getting down to the task until comparatively recently. What finally spurred me into action was a series of relevant technical questions—sometimes quite tricky ones!—from various interested parties, which made me realize that the best way of dealing with such questions was to get on and write the book, once and for all.

So I'm grateful in the first place to everyone who asked such questions, including attendees at live classes, readers of earlier books of mine, and members of the *Third Manifesto* community in general. Talking of classes, incidentally, I'd like to say that almost all of the ideas discussed in this book—in all of my books, as a matter of fact—have been taught and discussed in live classes before being brought to their current documented form. In my opinion this is a very good

---

[1] In my defense here, I'm tempted to invoke what elsewhere I've called *The Principle of Incoherence*. To quote from my book *The New Relational Database Dictionary* (O'Reilly, 2016), *The Principle of Incoherence* (referred to by some, a little unkindly, as *The Incoherent Principle*) is "[a] principle, sometimes invoked in defense of an attempt (successful or otherwise) at criticizing some technical proposal or position, to the effect that it's hard to criticize something coherently if what's being criticized is itself not very coherent in the first place—a state of affairs that goes some way toward explaining why such criticisms can often be longer than what's being criticized."

way to try out ideas to see if they make sense: to make sure that they hang together, as it were, and in particular that they're teachable. I do believe teachability is a good test of the quality of a language. One of the reasons the SQL standard is in the sorry state it's in, I'm convinced, is because the SQL definers seem not to have tried the experiment of teaching what they're defining in a live class. If they had, they would surely have realized what's wrong with it and made appropriate changes to the language. But now I'm getting on a hobby horse ... Let me get back to the acknowledgments.

Second, then, I'm grateful to my technical reviewers Hugh Darwen, Erwin Smout, and Dave Voorhis. Between them, they provided me with the most meticulous reviews a technical writer could possibly wish for. (Mind you, I can't claim to have adopted all of their suggestions!—so, while those suggestions certainly resulted in a vastly improved book, I bear full responsibility for the final text.) Be that as it may, I'm particularly pleased to be able to tell you that Erwin and Dave are responsible for SIRA-PRISE (*SIRA_PRISE@edpnet.be*) and *Rel* (*http://dbappbuilder.sourceforge.net/Rel.html*), respectively; each of these projects consists of a comprehensive implementation of *Third Manifesto* ideas, including in both cases partial support for the inheritance model described in this book. As for Hugh, not only did he very kindly contribute an interesting historical foreword, but his detailed comments on the manuscript, together with much subsequent technical correspondence, led to a number of revisions to the inheritance model itself; thus, that model should most definitely be understood as a joint production by the two of us.

Third, I'd like to thank my wife Lindy, as always, for her support throughout this and all of my other database projects over the years.

Finally, I'm grateful to everyone at O'Reilly for their encouragement, contributions, and support throughout the production of this book.

C. J. Date
Healdsburg, California
2016

Foreword

In this book, Chris Date describes some technical proposals due jointly to him and myself: viz., our proposed model of type inheritance. Those who are familiar with other aspects of our joint work, therefore, might be a little surprised to see that on this occasion I'm not a coauthor. However, I'm more than happy for Chris to have taken on this project *tout seul*, because the fact is—and I'm pleased to have the opportunity to state as much publicly here—it was Chris who came up with the basic ideas on which our inheritance model is based; Chris who proposed the terminology we used for those ideas; and Chris who originally drafted the various prescriptions, as we call them, that formally define that model.

In this foreword, I don't need or even want to say much about our model as such (that's what the book does); however, I do want to give my own recollections of the historical circumstances in which this work arose and certain events that helped both to motivate it and to shape it.

In the mid 1980s my career at IBM suffered for two or three years from an enforced absence from the database scene. (Previously I'd spent some fifteen years as a DBMS software developer, in particular playing a lead role in the development of a relational DBMS for commercial use called Business System 12.) When I returned to that scene in 1987, I found that two important developments had taken place during my absence:

a. SQL, a language that ten years earlier I had confidently predicted would "never catch on" (my very words at the time), was now dominant, and

b. Object oriented (OO) programming—a style that was new to me—had become somewhat à la mode, and had given rise to visions of OO databases and OO DBMSs that its advocates thought should eventually supersede relational databases and SQL.

These two developments—the last two words excepted—filled me with dread. Now able to attend database conferences again, I communicated my concerns to Ted Codd and Chris Date. My collaboration with Chris began shortly thereafter, after some articles by me had been accepted for publication in *The Relational Journal*, a publication of Ted and Chris's company (since defunct) Codd & Date Inc.

Well, it soon became clear that the demise of SQL that I'd predicted was never going to happen (alas!). Moreover, people started to talk about a rapprochement—as Chris himself called it—between relational and object technologies, soon to be known by the generic label "object / relational" (O/R). Key OO features to be included in that rapprochement were (a) user defined types (classes in OO parlance) and (b) type inheritance. Having learned something about those features on a Smalltalk course, I was enthusiastic about both of them. However, my enthusiasm turned to horror when I learned how various pundits at database conferences were proposing to go about incorporating them into a "relational" (or at least SQL) system.

Back in the 1970s many of us had been puzzling over what Codd really meant by the term *domain*, which he'd used to refer to the set of values from which the value of an attribute in a tuple appearing in a relation (or the value of a column in a row appearing in a table, if you prefer) was to be drawn. Eventually it was agreed pretty much all round that it was just another term for a data type (type for short). That said, however, we'd also interpreted—possibly misinterpreted—another aspect of Codd's proposal, viz., *first normal form* (1NF), as meaning that the only types to be supported by a relational DBMS would be simple system defined ones such as those for numbers, character strings, dates and times, and truth values. But that interpretation became widely discredited in the decade that followed, and support for user defined types of arbitrary complexity began to be accepted as both kosher and desirable.

To my astonishment, however, the O/R proposals being advanced at the conferences I mentioned didn't use those arbitrarily complex types as types for attributes of relations; rather, they used them as types for relations themselves (in the way that the type of a relation determines the type of the tuples appearing in it). Thus, a "relation" would be a set of "objects"—meaning, more specifically, so called "encapsulated" objects—of the same type, rather than a set of tuples with the same heading. What made matters worse was that examples of such objects typically quoted were ones representing things like employee records, of a type that had subtypes for special kinds of employees. But we already had perfectly good ways—in fact, demonstrably better ways—of dealing with such situations in relational databases. Also, I wondered how queries might be formulated on such "relations" and combinations thereof: How could they be expressed in a language based on relational algebra? For that matter, how could they be expressed using something like SQL's SELECT – FROM – WHERE and UNION constructs? A telling remark from one of those conference speakers made me chuckle (*wince* might be a better word): "[I have to admit that] we haven't yet figured out how to do joins."

1989 saw the publication of "The Object-Oriented Database System Manifesto," eliciting the appearance the following year of the "Third Generation Database System Manifesto" by way of response. The first of these documents promoted OO as a foundation for future generations of database systems. The second disputed that position and instead proposed staying with SQL but building OO features into that language. Disagreeing rather strongly with both of these positions, Chris and I started to think about producing our own response, in the form of what eventually became *The Third Manifesto* (see below).

By that time I had also established myself as a member of the U.K. delegation to the ISO Working Group responsible for developing and maintaining the SQL international standard. From 1988 to 1992 that U.K. delegation had been focusing its attention entirely on what was to be the next edition of the standard, viz., SQL:1992. At the same time some members of the vendor dominated U.S. delegation had been submitting proposals for certain "advanced" features, having to do (mostly) with O/R support—features that, it had been agreed, wouldn't be part of SQL:1992 but were meant for a follow-on edition, referred to at that time as SQL3. When SQL:1992 was finally put to bed later that year, my U.K. colleagues and I started to scrutinize the SQL3 draft—and I discovered to my dismay that the proposed O/R features were based on the very concept that had so horrified me at those earlier conferences, viz., equating classes to tables instead of types.

I won't say anything here about the controversy that subsequently dominated proceedings in the ISO Working Group, nor about the eventual awful compromise that appeared in SQL:1999 (see Chapter 22). More to the point was that during a weekend in the middle of our January 1994 meeting in Munich, Germany, I was moved to scribble a draft with the title *The Third Manifesto* and fax it to Chris in California. Its nine pages, handwritten in pencil, included the following points, cited verbatim here (please bear in mind that this was only a private memo!):

- **D** shall make no prescriptions, and no proscriptions, concerning the domains over which attributes of relations may be defined. However, **D** shall include some collection of primitive constructs to support the definition of domains and associated operators of arbitrary complexity [i.e., user defined types]. *Note:* We used, and still do use, the name **D** to refer to a hypothetical language conforming to the *Manifesto*.

- [*As a "very strong suggestion":*] Inheritance should be supported.

- Special typing and behavior shall be confined to *domains*, and not applicable to relations.

The second bullet, on type inheritance, was amplified by other points that remain consistent with the model that Chris eventually produced. For example, inheritance was to be multiple (it's not in SQL), and operator binding was to be based on the types of all arguments, not just on one special one as is typically the case in OO languages.

The paper we subsequently worked on, which appeared early the following year in *ACM SIGMOD Record*, continued to use the term *domain* rather than *type* (though it lacked a formal definition of that term). It also used the terms *subdomain* and *superdomain* for what we now call subtypes and supertypes. As for inheritance, apart from stating some of the requirements that Chris elaborates on in this book, such as substitutability, it merely required that "Such a capability shall be in accordance with some clearly defined and generally agreed model." Moreover, although it strongly advocated support for multiple as opposed to single inheritance, it didn't actually insist on such support. Chris was deeply dissatisfied with the lack of specificity in these positions and proposed that we should work on a model of inheritance that would be appropriate for relational databases. That required us first to revise *The Third Manifesto* itself, since we obviously had to be very clear on what we meant by a type as such before we could be equally clear about what we meant by a subtype.

My own ideas about subtypes were pretty vague and somewhat confused at that time. But I had always thought of a type as a named set of values, and I had always accepted the use of constraints to define types. For example, although Business System 12's "domains" weren't really types, user defined domains for proper subsets of system defined ones (think of positive integers, for example) were in common use during the short life of that DBMS in the 1980s.

(The same construct appeared, under that same name *domain*, in SQL:1992. To my knowledge, however, that feature of the standard hasn't been implemented in any of the leading commercial SQL products.) But OO had introduced me to the notion of a subclass being an *extension*, rather than a subset, of its superclass. For example, given class CIRCLE for the geometric shapes of that name, we can define the subclass COLORED_CIRCLE, each value of which has a color component in addition to its circle components. That made sense to me too—every operator defined for circles would work for colored circles also, and additional operators might be defined for colored circles only. Now, I probably imagined that constrained subtypes and extended subtypes could comfortably coexist within the same system, but the two approaches are so different that producing a formal model to embrace both would be daunting to say the least. Furthermore, a model that supported COLORED_CIRCLE as a subtype of CIRCLE would also support PART_TIMER as a subtype of EMPLOYEE, raising questions concerning its appropriateness for use in a relational database. Chris very much wanted to pursue the "subtype = subset" approach only, and he easily persuaded me to go along with that.

Then came a hiccup! While we were still discussing inheritance in the ISO Working Group, we were shown a paper that claimed it's impossible for a system to support type constraints, so long as it does support three other features that our *Manifesto* and SQL both called for—viz., substitutability, compile time type checking, and what the paper called "mutability" (essentially, the ability to update variables and the database). I didn't fully understand at the time how the authors of the paper, Stan Zdonik and David Maier, had arrived at the conclusion they did, nor did Chris when I drew it to his attention. And we remained somewhat baffled even after we'd spent a day discussing it with my IBM colleague Nelson Mattos (who was the person who originally showed that Zdonik and Maier paper to the ISO Working Group).

As we could neither prove nor disprove Zdonik and Maier's claim to our own satisfaction, we felt unable to propose a model that would require the use of constraints for defining subtypes. But we stuck with the "subtype = subset" approach nevertheless, and the result was the model whose definition appeared in the first of the three editions of our book on *The Third Manifesto*, titled *Foundation for Object / Relational Databases*. However, we weren't completely happy with that model, and Chris took it on himself to revise it to include the use of constraints (so that, e.g., circles could be defined as a proper subset of ellipses, the subset in question being precisely those ellipses whose semiaxes are constrained to be of equal length). And he got far enough with that revision without running into any perceived problems for us to include, just in time for the *Manifesto* book's publication, an appendix suggesting that such a revised form of our model might work after all.

Shortly thereafter, it occurred to me that (a) Zdonik and Maier were writing about OO systems specifically, and (b) those OO systems all supported *object identifiers*, or in other words *pointers*. The anomalies that Zdonik and Maier (and Mattos) described arise only when pointers are supported, as Chris explains in Chapter 13. Therefore, so long as we spurn the use of pointers (in the model, that is), type constraints can be used after all without sacrificing any of those other three desiderata. And *The Third Manifesto* does indeed explicitly spurn the use of pointers—by sticking to Codd's original relational model, of course!—and so the revised inheritance model that appeared in the second edition of our book (retitled *Foundation for Future Database Systems*) did fully embrace the use of type constraints. What's more, that model has stood up, so far, to very close scrutiny by others.

In closing, let me add that although I've acknowledged Chris's major role in the development of our model, I've played my own part too as a former software engineer in checking that implementation of our model is computationally feasible (as is my firm belief). Moreover, I've been conscious all along of the care I needed to take in order to justify the model's joint attribution. That awareness applies to all of the revisions that have taken place since that second version, including the very latest ones as documented in the present book (see Chapter 4). Thus, all remaining mistakes are as much mine as Chris's.

Hugh Darwen
Shrewley, England
2016

Part I

PRELIMINARIES

Part I sets the scene for the rest of the book. The first chapter provides some background on *The Third Manifesto* and explains the origins of our inheritance model ("the *Manifesto* model"). Chapter 2 gives an overview of the *Manifesto* theory of types without inheritance. Chapter 3 then takes a preliminary look at the impact of inheritance on that type theory. Finally, Chapter 4 provides, for purposes of subsequent reference, a formal statement of our inheritance model in its entirety.

Chapter 1

Background

Begin at the beginning ...
and go on till you come to the end: then stop.

—Lewis Carroll:
Alice's Adventures in Wonderland (1865)

The foundation of all true general purpose database systems is the relational model of data, first described by E. F. Codd in two landmark papers in 1969 and 1970, respectively:

- "Derivability, Redundancy, and Consistency of Relations Stored in Large Data Banks" (IBM Research Report RJ599, August 19th, 1969)

- "A Relational Model of Data for Large Shared Data Banks" (*CACM 13*, No. 6, June 1970)

These days, of course, it's widely recognized that it was Codd's introduction of the relational model that put the field of database management on a sound theoretical footing. But what still isn't quite so widely recognized, perhaps, is that the relational model implicitly requires a further theoretical footing of its own: namely, a supporting, or underlying, theory of types (or *domains*, as Codd called them in his early papers). The requirement for such a theory arises most obviously—though not exclusively—from the fact that, in the relational model, every attribute of every relation is required to be of some type.

The foregoing state of affairs provides a large part of the motivation for the work my colleague Hugh Darwen and I have been engaged upon ever since the early 1990s. The work in question goes by the generic name of *The Third Manifesto*, or just the *Manifesto* for short (an explanation of that name can be found in the section "A Little History" later in this chapter). The primary objectives of the *Manifesto* are twofold:

1. To provide a careful description of the relational model as such (thereby providing a kind of abstract blueprint for the design of a database language)

2. To provide an appropriate theory of types to support the relational model

Regarding the first of these objectives, it's true that we've taken the opportunity in our *Manifesto* to dot a few *i*'s and cross a few *t*'s that Codd left undotted or uncrossed in his own writings (in other words, we've performed a few minor tidying activities here and there);[1] however, the model as we describe it departs in no essential respects from Codd's original vision as documented in his first two papers. Regarding the second objective, the relational model certainly does assume that types exist, as I've already said; however, nowhere does it say just what those types must be or what properties those types must have. In other words, the relational model and the supporting type theory are to a considerable degree independent of one another (they're *orthogonal*, to use the jargon). Thus, what we've tried to do in the *Manifesto* is define a theory of types that seems to us to be "in the spirit of" the relational model (inasmuch as such a claim makes any sense); more specifically, we've tried to define a theory of types that seems to us to work well with that model.

INHERITANCE ARISES NATURALLY

Basically, a type is just *a named set of values*, where the values in question are all possible values of some specific kind—for example, all possible integers, or all possible character strings, or all possible rectangles, or all possible XML documents, or all possible X rays, or all possible fingerprints (etc., etc.). So, given that "types are sets" (loosely speaking), it seems intuitively obvious and reasonable to say that "subtypes are subsets." More generally, let T and T' be types, such that the set of values constituting T' is a subset of the set of values constituting T; then the notion that T' might be a subtype of T seems reasonable, and in fact intuitively obvious. For example, let T and T' be RECTANGLE (the set of all rectangles) and SQUARE (the set of all squares), respectively. Then, since every square is in fact a rectangle, it surely makes sense to say that type SQUARE is a subtype of type RECTANGLE.

> *Aside:* Please note that, in accordance with standard mathematical practice, throughout this book I take expressions of the form "*B* is a subset of *A*" to include the possibility that sets *B* and *A* might be equal. In other words, every set is a subset of itself. When I want to exclude that possibility, I'll talk in terms of *proper* subsets. For example, the set {*x,y,z*} is certainly a subset of itself, but it isn't a proper subset of itself. (In fact, of course, no set is a proper subset of itself.) Note too that the foregoing remarks apply equally to supersets, mutatis mutandis; for example, the set {*x,y,z*} is a superset of itself, but not a proper superset of itself. *End of aside*.

Now, you might be thinking: So what? Even if it does make sense to say SQUARE is a subtype of RECTANGLE, what's the point? Well—simplifying considerably!—the point is this:

---

[1] Use of the first person plural here, and indeed throughout this book, is intended to refer jointly to Darwen and myself unless the context demands otherwise.

*Any operation that can be applied to values of type RECTANGLE can be applied to values of type SQUARE as well (because squares **are** rectangles).*

For example, suppose we have an operator—actually a function—called AREA_OF that returns the area of a given rectangle. Then we can certainly invoke the AREA_OF operator with an argument of type SQUARE, because (to say it again) squares *are* rectangles. More generally, if type T' is a subtype of type T, then wherever the system expects to see a value of type T, we can always substitute a value of type T' instead. Thus, we can say that operators that apply to values of type T are **inherited by** values of type T'.

I claim, therefore, that the concept of inheritance (which, as I hope you realize, I haven't even begun to define yet in any formal sense) is a logical and natural consequence of the simple notion that types are sets. Thus, if you accept this latter notion—which in itself is hardly novel, and is certainly not controversial, and is the fundamental concept underlying the *Manifesto* theory of types—then I claim that you also have to accept what we're pleased to call our **model of type inheritance**. And, of course, it's that model—referred to hereinafter as "the *Manifesto* model"—that's the principal subject of the present book.

A FUNDAMENTAL CONCEPT

Let T be a type. Then I've claimed, in effect, that every subtype of T is necessarily a subset of T.[2] But—turning this statement around—the obvious question arises: Is every subset of T necessarily a subtype of T?

The *Manifesto* model answers this question in the negative. Rather, it regards type T' as a subtype of type T if, but only if, both of the following conditions are satisfied:

1. Every value of type T' is a value of type T (i.e., "T' is a subset of T").

2. A value of type T is a value of type T' if and only if it satisfies a certain constraint, where the constraint in question is such that it can be tested for any given value of type T by examining just those properties that are intrinsic to values of type T in general.

For example, consider squares and rectangles again (types SQUARE and RECTANGLE, respectively). Condition 1 is certainly satisfied: Every value of type SQUARE is a value of type RECTANGLE. And Condition 2 is satisfied too: A value of type RECTANGLE (i.e., a rectangle) is a value of type SQUARE (i.e., a square) if and only if the sides of the rectangle in question are of equal length—and this latter is a constraint that can be tested for a given

---

[2] I'm being sloppy here: I shouldn't really be talking in terms of types, as such, having subsets (only sets have subsets). In other words, the phrase "subset of T" should really be "subset of the set of values constituting T." In the interest of brevity, however, I'll continue to use this sloppy mode of speaking until further notice.

rectangle by examining just certain intrinsic properties of the rectangle in question, viz., its height and width. So SQUARE is a subtype of RECTANGLE.

By way of a counterexample, consider programmers and employees (types PGMR and EMP, respectively). Again Condition 1 is satisfied: Every value of type PGMR is a value of type EMP (i.e., every programmer is an employee—at least, let's agree as much for the sake of the example). But Condition 2 isn't satisfied: There's no property, intrinsic to employees in general, that can be tested to see whether the employee in question is in fact a programmer. What I mean by this observation is that you can't just look at a given employee and tell whether that employee is a programmer;[3] instead, you'd have to look at certain other information, perhaps information recorded somewhere else in the database, such as a list of employees and their jobs. In the *Manifesto* model, therefore, we wouldn't regard PGMR as a subtype of EMP.[4]

So now I've given a very informal description of what it means in the *Manifesto* model for some type T' to be a subtype of some type T. Please take a moment to make sure you understand it before continuing—not that it's very difficult, of course—because just about everything to be described in later parts of this book is a logical consequence of this simple idea.

THE SUPPLIERS-AND-PARTS DATABASE

If you've read other books of mine, you'll be aware that I almost always use the same basic example to illustrate the various points I want to make: namely, the familiar—not to say hackneyed—suppliers-and-parts database. What's more, I generally go on to say this (quoting now from another recent book of mine, viz., *SQL and Relational Theory: How to Write Accurate SQL Code*, 3rd edition, O'Reilly, 2015):

> I apologize for dragging out this old warhorse yet one more time, but I believe that using the same example in a variety of books and other publications can help, not hinder, learning.

Well, you might be glad to hear that in the present book, by contrast, I won't be using this same old example very much at all. But I will be using it a little! So I want to discuss it, briefly, in the present section. First of all, the database consists of three *relvars*, called S (suppliers), P (parts), and SP (shipments), respectively. (*Note:* If the term *relvar* is unfamilar to you, I'll be explaining it in a few moments.) Fig. 1.1 shows a set of sample values for these relvars; later examples will assume these actual values, where it makes any difference. The semantics are as follows:

---

[3] Some might dispute this claim.

[4] I'll have a lot more to say about the programmers and employees example, and others like it, in Chapter 21.

S

SNO	SNAME	STATUS	CITY
S1	Smith	20	London
S2	Jones	10	Paris
S3	Blake	30	Paris
S4	Clark	20	London
S5	Adams	30	Athens

P

PNO	PNAME	COLOR	WEIGHT	CITY
P1	Nut	Red	12.0	London
P2	Bolt	Green	17.0	Paris
P3	Screw	Blue	17.0	Oslo
P4	Screw	Red	14.0	London
P5	Cam	Blue	12.0	Paris
P6	Cog	Red	19.0	London

SP

SNO	PNO	QTY
S1	P1	300
S1	P2	200
S1	P3	400
S1	P4	200
S1	P5	100
S1	P6	100
S2	P1	300
S2	P2	400
S3	P2	200
S4	P2	200
S4	P4	300
S4	P5	400

Fig. 1.1: The suppliers-and-parts database–sample values

■ *Suppliers*

Relvar S represents *suppliers under contract.* Each supplier has one supplier number (SNO), unique to that supplier; one name (SNAME), not necessarily unique (though the SNAME values in Fig. 1.1 do happen to be unique); one status value (STATUS), representing some kind of ranking or preference level among available suppliers; and one location (CITY).

■ *Parts*

Relvar P denotes *parts used in the enterprise* (more accurately, *kinds* of parts used in the enterprise). Each kind of part has one part number (PNO), which is unique; one name (PNAME); one color (COLOR); one weight (WEIGHT), given in pounds avoirdupois; and one location where parts of that kind are stored (CITY).

■ *Shipments*

Relvar SP represents *shipments* (it shows which parts are shipped, or supplied, by which suppliers). Each shipment has one supplier number (SNO), one part number (PNO), and one quantity (QTY). There's at most one shipment at any given time for a given supplier and given part, and so the combination of supplier number and part number is unique to the shipment in question. Notice that Fig. 1.1 shows one supplier, supplier S5, with no shipments at all.

Now, Fig. 1.1 actually depicts three *relations*, or more precisely three relation *values*: namely, the relation values that happen to appear in the database at some particular time. But if we were to look at that same database at some different time, we would probably see three different relation values appearing in their place. Thus, S, P, and SP in that database are really *variables* (relation variables, to be precise). For example, suppose variable S currently has the value—the relation value, that is—shown in Fig. 1.1, and suppose we delete the set of tuples (actually there's only one) for suppliers in Athens:

```
DELETE S WHERE CITY = 'Athens' ;
```

After this DELETE, relvar S looks like this:

SNO	SNAME	STATUS	CITY
S1	Smith	20	London
S2	Jones	10	Paris
S3	Blake	30	Paris
S4	Clark	20	London

Conceptually, what's happened here is that the old value of variable S has been replaced in its entirety by a new value. Of course, the old value (with five tuples) and the new one (with four) are very similar, in a sense, but they certainly are different values. In fact, the DELETE just shown is logically equivalent to, and indeed shorthand for, the following *relational assignment:*

```
S := S MINUS ( S WHERE CITY = 'Athens' ) ;
```

As usual with assignment, the sequence of events here is that (a) the *source expression* on the right side is evaluated and then (b) the value that results from that evaluation—a relation value in the case at hand, since the expression in question is a relational expression specifically—is then assigned to the *target variable* on the left side—a relation variable, in the case at hand—with the overall effect already explained.

> *Aside:* The foregoing DELETE statement and the relational assignment it's equivalent to are both formulated in a language called **Tutorial D** (note the boldface)—see the section "A Little History" for background explanation—and I'll be using that language as a basis for coding examples throughout this book. Now, **Tutorial D** is intended as far as possible to be pretty much self-explanatory; however, I'll explain specific features of the language as and when we encounter them—basically whenever I feel such further explanation might be needed. *End of aside.*

So DELETE is shorthand for a certain relational assignment. And, of course, an analogous remark applies to INSERT and UPDATE also—they too are basically just shorthand for certain relational assignments. In fact, relational assignment is the only update operator in the relational model as such; indeed, it's the only update operator we need, logically speaking.

So there's a logical difference between relation values and relation variables. The trouble is, the database literature has historically used the same term, *relation*, for both concepts, and that practice has certainly led to confusion. In this book, therefore, I'll distinguish very carefully between the two from this point forward—I'll talk in terms of relation values when I mean relation values, and relation variables when I mean relation variables. However, I'll also abbreviate *relation value*, most of the time, to just *relation* (exactly as we abbreviate *integer value* most of the time to just *integer*). And I'll abbreviate *relation variable* most of the time to **relvar**; for example, I'll say the suppliers-and-parts database contains three *relvars* (three base relvars, to be precise, where a base relvar is a relvar that—unlike a view, for instance—isn't defined in terms of other relvars).

Aside: The foregoing paragraph makes reference to the concept of *logical difference*, a concept that derives from a dictum of Wittgenstein's: ***All logical differences are big differences***. This notion is an extraordinarily useful one; as a "mind tool," it's a great aid to clear and precise thinking, and it can be very helpful in pinpointing and analyzing some of the confusions that are, unfortunately, all too common in the computing world. I'll be appealing to it many times in the pages ahead. *End of aside.*

Here then are **Tutorial D** definitions for relvars S, P, and SP:

```
VAR S BASE RELATION
    { SNO     SNO ,
      SNAME   NAME ,
      STATUS  INTEGER ,
      CITY    CHAR }
    KEY { SNO } ;

VAR P BASE RELATION
    { PNO     PNO ,
      PNAME   NAME ,
      COLOR   COLOR ,
      WEIGHT  WEIGHT ,
      CITY    CHAR }
    KEY { PNO } ;

VAR SP BASE RELATION
    { SNO     SNO ,
      PNO     PNO ,
      QTY     QTY }
    KEY { SNO , PNO }
    FOREIGN KEY { SNO } REFERENCES S
    FOREIGN KEY { PNO } REFERENCES P ;
```

As far as this book is concerned I'll take these definitions (like the language **Tutorial D** itself) to be more or less self-explanatory; in particular, I'll assume you're familiar with the relational key and foreign key concepts. However, please note the following:

- The keyword BASE indicates that the relvar being defined is a base relvar specifically and not some other kind. (As a matter of fact, almost all of the relvars mentioned in this book will be base relvars specifically.)

- Purely for definiteness, I assume that types INTEGER and CHAR are system defined and types SNO, PNO, NAME, COLOR, WEIGHT, and QTY are user defined (see Chapter 2 for further discussion).

- Relvars S, P, and SP have keys {SNO}, {PNO}, and {SNO,PNO}, respectively. *Note:* Fig. 1.1 shows the attributes participating in these keys as being doubly underlined. Such double underlining is usually taken to mean the keys in question are actually the *primary* keys for the pertinent relvars. However, **Tutorial D** deliberately provides no way of—in particular, no syntax for—distinguishing between primary and other keys, referring to them all just as keys.

A LITTLE HISTORY

The first version of *The Third Manifesto* as such was published in March 1995,[5] though we had been thinking about the idea of producing such a document for several years prior to that time. It was quite short, consisting of just eleven pages (and several of those contained only acknowledgments, references, and other boilerplate matter). In essence, it consisted of a series of prescriptions, proscriptions, and what we called "very strong suggestions." The general idea was that, in order to be "*Manifesto* compliant" as it were, a system would certainly have to abide by all of the prescriptions and proscriptions, though it might choose to ignore any or all of the suggestions.

Being so short, the *Manifesto* was of course very terse—so terse, in fact, that we wrote an entire book of nearly 500 pages (!) to explain it:

- C. J. Date and Hugh Darwen: *Foundation for Object / Relational Databases: The Third Manifesto* (Addison-Wesley, 1998)

The title of this book requires some explanation. Note first that, technically speaking, "*The Third Manifesto*" is only the subtitle; the main title, which is to say the title as such, is

---

[5] Specifically, in *ACM SIGMOD Record 24*, No. 1 (March 1995). However, an informal description of what it contained ("Introducing ... *The Third Manifesto*") was published earlier that same year, in *Database Programming & Design 8*, No. 1 (January 1995).

Foundation for Object / Relational Databases. Of course, we would have liked it to have been the other way around—as far as we were concerned, the *Manifesto* as such was what the book was all about—but it was carefully explained to us that bookstores shelve their wares by title, not subtitle, and so our title simply had to contain the crucial word *database* somewhere. That's why *The Third Manifesto* was only the subtitle: essentially just for marketing reasons.[6]

Second, why did we say, or suggest, in our chosen title that the *Manifesto* was a foundation for "object / relational" databases specifically? Well, I'll answer this question in part by quoting from the preface to the book itself:

> *The Third Manifesto* is a detailed proposal for the future direction of data and database management systems (DBMSs). Like Codd's original papers on the relational model, it can be seen as an abstract blueprint for the design of a DBMS and the language interface to such a DBMS. In particular, it lays the foundation for what we believe is the logically correct approach to integrating relational and object technologies—a topic of considerable interest at the present time, given the recent appearance in the marketplace of several "object / relational" DBMS products (sometimes called *universal servers*). Perhaps we should add immediately that we do not regard the idea of integrating relational and object technologies as just another fad, soon to be replaced by some other briefly fashionable idea. On the contrary, we think that object / relational systems are in everyone's future—a fact that makes it even more important to get the logical foundation right, of course, while we still have time to do so.

As this extract says, there was indeed a lot of interest at the time in integrating object and relational technologies. The early 1990s had seen numerous proposals for DBMSs based not on the relational model but rather on some kind of object model. With hindsight, we can see that most of those proposals were never going to go very far; but that fact wasn't so clear at the time, and there were even those who were claiming that "the object model" (whatever that might be) would eventually—possibly even quite soon—replace the relational model. As a consequence, the possibility of a system that got the best of both worlds, as it were, by combining object and relational ideas, did seem an attractive one. The trouble was, it seemed to us that most of the database community were going after this objective in a fatally flawed way. To be specific, they were designing systems on the basis of an incorrect assumption: namely, the assumption that the relational concept that most closely equated to the object concept *class* was the concept of a relation as such—or a *relvar*, really, but this latter term wasn't in wide use at the time.[7] We characterized this mistake at the time, rather rudely, as **The First Great Blunder**.[8] To us, by

---

[6] Actually the book had what might be called a "subsubtitle" too: viz., *a detailed study of the impact of objects and type theory on the relational model of data, including a comprehensive proposal for type inheritance.* What's more, this "subsubtitle" went through a couple of interesting changes in later editions of the book—the reference to objects was dropped, and *comprehensive **proposal for** type inheritance* became *comprehensive **model of** type inheritance* (emphasis added).

[7] Not that it is now, either, but it should be.

[8] There was a second "great blunder" as well: viz., allowing database relations to contain pointers. Both are examined in depth in my book *An Introduction to Database Systems* (8th edition, Addison-Wesley, 2004) and elsewhere, and the second in particular I'll be touching on in passing at several points later in the present book as well (especially in Part V).

contrast, it seemed clear that the true relational analog of an object class was neither a relation nor a relvar, but rather a type. Thus, part of our goal in writing our book was simply to promulgate what we regarded as the right way to go about building object / relational systems, and in particular to help the community avoid that "great blunder," if we could.

All of that being said, I'm sorry to have to say that our chosen title was partly a matter of marketing once again. The term *object / relational* sounds rather quaint now, but as I've indicated object / relational databases were a pretty hot topic at the time (all of the mainstream DBMS vendors were describing their products as, or claiming their products to be, object / relational, to a greater or lesser degree). This state of affairs notwithstanding, it was our opinion at the time (and still is) that a true "object / relational" system would be nothing more nor less than a true relational system[9]—which is to say, it would be a system that supports the relational model, with all that such support entails—and true relational systems were (and still are) what the *Manifesto* is supposed to be a foundation for. So we went along with the idea of using the term *object / relational* in our title, even though it was essentially just a marketing term, dreamt up by the "relational" DBMS vendors at the time to disguise the fact that their original "relational" products weren't really very relational at all.[10]

Be that as it may, what's much more to the point for present purposes is that it was that 1998 book that contained the first published description of our inheritance model. Now, the version of the model described in that book was far from perfect—it suffered from a number of defects, and in particular involved a number of what later turned out to be blind alleys. (I'll have more to say about some of those blind alleys at various points later in the present book.) As a matter of historical record, though, it's true that many of the ideas to be discussed in depth in later chapters of the present book did first see the light of day in that 1998 description. Here's another pertinent quote from the preface to that book:

> [We] should mention one further feature that we believe to be highly significant, and that's our proposal for a model of *subtyping and inheritance*. Many authorities have rightly observed that there's currently no consensus on any such model, and we offer our proposal for consideration in the light of this observation. Indeed, we believe we have some original—and, we also believe, logically sound and correct—thoughts to offer on this important subject.

Of course, there were plenty of languages, and indeed implementations, even back in 1998, that did provide some kind of support for some kind of inheritance. Today, even SQL does so. Yet all of that support was and remains ad hoc to a degree; it's still the case that there's no consensus on any kind of inheritance model as such, and the foregoing remarks are as pertinent today as they were when we first made them.

---

[9] After all, the whole point about an object / relational system from the user's point of view is simply that it allows attributes of relations to be of arbitrarily complex types. In other words, a proper object / relational system is really just a relational system with proper type support (including proper user defined type support in particular)—which just means it's a proper relational system, no more and no less. Thus, what some are pleased to call "the object / relational model" is, likewise, really just the relational model, no more and no less.

[10] They still aren't, but that's another story.

There's another aspect as well of that 1998 book that's relevant to our discussions in this one. To be specific, it was that book that was the original source for the language **Tutorial D**. To elaborate briefly: The main purpose of that book was, of course, to describe and explain *The Third Manifesto* as such. Now, the *Manifesto* as such used the name **D** as a generic name for any language that conformed to *Manifesto* ideas—for example, the very first of the *Manifesto*'s prescriptions reads, in part, "[The language] **D** shall provide facilities for users to define their own scalar types"—and therefore the book did the same. Here's another quote (this one is from Chapter 1 but is very lightly edited here):

> No special significance attaches to our choice of the name **D**—we use it merely to refer generically to any language that conforms to the principles laid down in the *Manifesto*. There could be any number of distinct languages all qualifying as a valid **D**. We define one such language in this book; we call it **Tutorial D**, and we use it as the basis for most of our examples.

In fact, of course, **Tutorial D** was expressly designed to be suitable as a vehicle for illustrating and teaching the ideas of the *Manifesto*. Subsequently, however, we as well as several other people have used it for a variety of related purposes too, including as a basis for various textbooks and live classes in particular—and, as already noted, I'll be using it in the present book as well.

Back to our history. Two years later, we published a second edition of the *Manifesto* book:

■ C. J. Date and Hugh Darwen: *Foundation for Future Database Systems: The Third Manifesto* (2nd edition, Addison-Wesley, 2000)

Here's a quote from the preface:

> The fact that the second edition of this book appears so hot on the heels of its predecessor clearly requires some explanation. In fact, there were several reasons why we felt it desirable to revise the book so soon, but the overriding one had to do with our model of type inheritance. To be specific, the version of the model described in the first edition has been so considerably—though, for the most part, compatibly—extended and improved that we now regard it as a part (albeit an optional part) of the *Manifesto* itself. In the first edition, it was presented merely as a set of somewhat tentative "proposals," with no very definite connection to the *Manifesto* proper; now, by contrast, we present it as a set of firm *prescriptions*, and we require a DBMS that supports the ideas of the *Manifesto*, if it supports type inheritance at all, to support our own inheritance model specifically.
>
> Also, we've taken the opportunity to make a small but significant change to the book's overall title. The title of the first edition characterized the *Manifesto* as a "foundation for object / relational databases." While that characterization was accurate as far as it went, it did not really go far enough. Rather, we now regard (and in fact always did regard) the *Manifesto* as a foundation for future databases in general—including, for example, databases that contain temporal data and databases that are used in connection with the World Wide Web. Moreover, we also regard it as a good foundation on which to build *rule engines* (also known as *business logic servers*), which, as

one of us has tried to show in another recent book,[11] are exactly what [we believe] the next generation of DBMSs really ought to be.

And a few years later we published yet another edition, again with a revised title:

■ C. J. Date and Hugh Darwen: *Databases, Types, and the Relational Model: The Third Manifesto* (3rd edition, Addison-Wesley, 2007)

This time the rewrite was motivated not so much by a change in what was described but rather by a change in our intended audience. (In fact, the same goes for the change in title as well.) The first two editions were aimed primarily at database researchers and DBMS designers and developers. The new edition, by contrast, was aimed more at students and was meant to serve as more of a textbook. From the preface:

> This is a textbook on database management. It's based on our earlier book *Foundation for Future Database Systems: The Third Manifesto* (Addison-Wesley, 2000), but it has been thoroughly revised—indeed, completely rewritten—from start to finish. Part of our reason for wanting to revise it was to make it more suitable as a textbook (the earlier book, by contrast, was quite terse and formal and not very easy to read); in particular, most chapters now include a set of exercises, answers to which can be found on the website *www.thethirdmanifesto.com*. However, we have naturally taken the opportunity to incorporate many other changes as well, including numerous clarifications, a certain amount of restructuring, many more examples, and—we regret to have to say—quite a few corrections also.

Throughout the remainder of the present book, references to "the *Manifesto* book" should be understood as referring to this third edition specifically, unless the context demands otherwise.

Why "The Third" Manifesto?

As I've said, we wrote the original version of the *Manifesto* because we were concerned about certain trends we observed in the database industry at that time; in particular, we were concerned about certain well publicized but ill considered attempts to integrate object and relational technologies. However, we certainly weren't the first to address such matters. In fact, it was precisely one of our aims in writing our original *Manifesto* to respond to two earlier manifestos (hence our choice of title):

---

[11] C. J. Date: *WHAT Not HOW: The Business Rules Approach to Application Development* (Addison-Wesley, 2000).

1. Malcolm Atkinson, François Bancilhon, David DeWitt, Klaus Dittrich, David Maier, and Stanley Zdonik: "The Object-Oriented Database System Manifesto" (Proc. 1st International Conference on Deductive and Object-Oriented Databases, Kyoto, Japan, 1989)

2. Michael Stonebraker, Lawrence A. Rowe, Bruce G. Lindsay, James Gray, Michael Carey, Michael Brodie, Philip Bernstein, and David Beech: "Third Generation Database System Manifesto" (*ACM SIGMOD Record 19*, No. 3, September 1990)

Like our own *Manifesto*, both of these documents proposed a basis on which to build future DBMSs; however, it seemed to us that they both suffered from some very serious defects. Indeed, as we wrote at the time (this is a quote from the first edition of the *Manifesto* book):

■ The first [of the two earlier manifestos] essentially ignored the relational model. In our opinion, this flaw was more than enough to rule it out as a serious contender. In any case, it seemed to us that it failed to give firm direction.

■ The second did correctly embrace the relational model, but failed to emphasize (or indeed even mention) the hopelessness of continuing to follow a commonly accepted perversion of that model—namely, SQL—in pursuit of relational ideals. In other words, it simply assumed that SQL, with all its faults, was (and is) an adequate realization of the relational model and hence an adequate foundation on which to build.[12]

Note: More details on the first two manifestos can be found in Appendix B of the present book.

Let me close this section by saying a little more about the *Manifesto* website *www.thethirdmanifesto.com*. Both the *Manifesto* itself and **Tutorial D** are to some extent "works in progress." In particular, they don't exist (yet) in product form. As a consequence, we have the freedom to make changes from time to time (and we do), without being constrained by what Hugh Darwen has referred to elsewhere as *The Shackle of Compatibility*.[13] But all such changes are documented at the *Manifesto* website; thus, the most recent version of the *Manifesto* as such (including a definition of the inheritance model) and the most recent definition of **Tutorial D** are in principle always to be found at that website.

Note: Much additional relevant material can also be found at that website, including among other things information regarding prototype implementations of **Tutorial D**. In

---

[12] By contrast, we feel (as we also stated in that first edition of the *Manifesto* book) that any attempt to move forward, if it's to stand the test of time, must reject SQL unequivocally. To quote: "Our reasons for taking this position are too many and varied for us to spell them out in detail here; in any case, we have described them in depth in many other places" (and we referred the reader to those other places for more specifics). This state of affairs accounts in part for the lack of emphasis on SQL in the present book as well.

[13] See Hugh's presentation "The Askew Wall" at *www.thethirdmanifesto.com*, also his paper by the same name in our book *Relational Database Writings 1989-1991* (Addison-Wesley, 1992). Perhaps I should add that even though (to repeat) we don't feel ourselves constrained by *The Shackle of Compatibility*, we do generally try to ensure that any changes we might make are evolutionary, not revolutionary, in nature.

particular, the website contains the entire text of another book by Darwen and myself, viz. *Database Explorations: Essays on The Third Manifesto and Related Topics* (originally published by Trafford Publishing Inc. in 2010). Chapter 21 of that book is titled "Extending **Tutorial D** to Support the Inheritance Model." For obvious reasons, I assume for the purposes of the present book that **Tutorial D** has indeed been extended in accordance with the proposals in that earlier book (as well as certain other proposals documented in other writings by ourselves).

EXERCISES

1.1   (*Try this exercise without looking back at the body of the chapter.*) What relvars does the suppliers-and-parts database contain? What attributes do they involve? What keys and foreign keys do they have? (The point of this exercise is simply that it's worth making yourself as familiar as possible with the structure, at least in general terms, of the suppliers-and-parts example. It's not so important to remember the actual data values, though it certainly wouldn't hurt if you did.)

1.2   I showed in the body of the chapter how DELETE can be defined in terms of relational assignment (":=") and relational difference (MINUS). But what about INSERT? And (harder) what about UPDATE?

1.3   Why does the notion of inheritance "arise naturally"?

1.4   What exactly does it mean to say type T' is a subtype of type T?

1.5   Why does the *Manifesto* inheritance model regard SQUARE as a subtype of RECTANGLE but not PGMR (programmers) as a subtype of EMP (employees)?

1.6   What's the difference between **D** and **Tutorial D**?

1.7   Is **Tutorial D** part of *The Third Manifesto*?

1.8   What do you understand by the term *object / relational*?

1.9   The relations depicted in Fig. 1.1 represent sample values for certain relvars, or in other words what some writers refer to as the "state" (or "current state") of the relvars in question. Moreover, that figure shows certain attributes as doubly underlined, and that double underlining is intended to indicate that the attributes in question constitute a key for the pertinent relvar. But consider the following picture, which shows the result of restricting the current value of relvar S to just suppliers in Paris:

SNO	SNAME	STATUS	CITY
S2	Jones	10	Paris
S3	Blake	30	Paris

What this picture shows is just a relation as such, not the relation that happens to be the current value (or "current state") of some relvar. And relations as such don't have keys, relvars do.[14] So what do you think is an appropriate interpretation of that double underlining in pictures like this one?

1.10 Why do you think the incorrect equation "relvar = class" might have seemed—or might still seem!—attractive to some people?

ANSWERS

For answers to Exercises 1.1, 1.3-1.6, and 1.8, please see the body of the chapter.

1.2   I'll answer this exercise in terms of a couple of simple examples. First, the **Tutorial D** INSERT statement

```
INSERT SP
       RELATION { TUPLE { SNO SNO('S5') , PNO PNO('P6') , QTY QTY(250) } } ;
```

(which effectively inserts just a single tuple into relvar SP) is shorthand for the following:

```
SP := SP
      UNION
      RELATION { TUPLE { SNO SNO('S5') , PNO PNO('P6') , QTY QTY(250) } } ;
```

(So what happens if the specified tuple already exists in the target relvar?) *Note:* The expression RELATION {TUPLE {SNO SNO('S5'), PNO PNO('P6'), QTY QTY(250)}}, which appears in both of the code fragments above, is a *relation selector invocation* (see Chapter 2), and it denotes the relation that contains just the tuple to be inserted.
    Second, the **Tutorial D** UPDATE statement

```
UPDATE P WHERE CITY = 'Paris' :
            { CITY := 'Nice' , WEIGHT := 2 * WEIGHT } ;
```

---

[14] Why? Because to say something is a key is to say a certain integrity constraint is in effect—a certain uniqueness constraint, to be specific—and integrity constraints apply to variables, not values. (By definition, integrity constraints constrain updates, and updates apply to variables, not values. See the section "Values vs. Variables" in Chapter 2.)

(which effectively updates all parts in Paris, changing their city to Nice and doubling their weight) is shorthand for the following:

```
WITH ( t1 := P WHERE CITY = 'Paris' ,
       t2 := EXTEND t1 : { CITY := 'Nice' , WEIGHT := 2 * WEIGHT } ) :
P := ( P MINUS t1 ) UNION t2 ;
```

For further explanation—in particular regarding the EXTEND operator in line 2—see, e.g., my book *SQL and Relational Theory: How to Write Accurate SQL Code* (3rd edition, O'Reilly, 2015).

1.7   No, it isn't—it's defined in the *Manifesto* book, but it's not part of the *Manifesto* as such.

1.9   Such pictures can always be regarded as showing a sample value for some relational expression *RX*, where *RX* is something other than a simple relvar reference. (A relvar reference is just a relvar name, syntactically speaking.) Moreover, *RX* in turn can be regarded as defining a possible value for some relvar *R*. So the double underlining indicates that a key *K* could in principle be declared for that relvar *R* and the pertinent attribute is part of *K*.

An alternative but equivalent way of saying the same thing is this: The relation depicted certainly doesn't "have" the indicated key—in fact, it would be logically incorrect to say the relation "has" that key—but it does satisfy the corresponding uniqueness constraint.

1.10   At least part of the reason, it seems to me, is that the terms *class* and *object* have no single, universally agreed meaning. Consider the following. Over the years, there have been several books on object database design.[15] Typically, those books use the terms *object* and *object modeling* to mean what the database community would more usually call an *entity* and *entity / relationship modeling*, respectively, and the term *class* to mean a collection of such objects (or entities). As a consequence, those books go on, in effect, to map those objects to tuples in relvars instead of values in domains (more precisely, they map classes to relvars instead of to domains). Which isn't necessarily a problem, as far as it goes; the problem arises when a change in context occurs and we move into the programming realm, where the terms *class* and *object* take on a different meaning—*class* now being another term for *type*, and *object* now being another term for something that's of such a type. In other words, what happens is that an equation that made sense with one interpretation of the pertinent terms gets carried over unchanged to a context where it doesn't make sense, because the meanings of the terms have changed. That's my guess, anyway.

---

[15] Here are two early examples: (a) *Object-Oriented Modeling and Design for Database Applications*, by Michael Blaha and William Premerlani (Prentice-Hall, 1998); (b) *Object-Oriented Software Engineering*, by Ivar Jacobson (with Magnus Christerson, Patrik Jonsson, and Gunnar Övergaard), revised printing (Addison-Wesley, 1994).

Chapter 2

Types without Inheritance

[Types make] program development and debugging easier
by making program behavior more understandable.

—Andrew Wright:
"On Sapphire and Type-Safe Languages" (*CACM 46*, No. 4, April 2003)

The overall purpose of this book is, of course, to explain the Manifesto model of type inheritance. The present chapter—the longest in the book, unfortunately—lays some necessary groundwork by describing the Manifesto theory of types as such (by which I mean types without inheritance). It's based in part on material from (a) Chapter 2 of my book SQL and Relational Theory: How to Write Accurate SQL Code *(3rd edition, O'Reilly, 2015) and (b) Chapter 5 of my book* An Introduction to Database Systems *(8th edition, Addison-Wesley, 2004); if you're already familiar with either of those references, therefore, you might be able to skip it. But you should probably at least skim it, if only to get some broad sense of what it covers.*

Data types, or just types for short, are fundamental to computer science. As noted in Chapter 1, relational theory in particular requires a supporting type theory, because relations are defined over types—that is, every attribute of every relation is of some type (and so is every attribute of every relvar, of course). For example, with reference to the suppliers-and-parts database from Chapter 1 (see Fig. 1.1 for some sample values), the **Tutorial D** definition for the suppliers relvar S in that chapter shows attribute STATUS of that relvar as being of type INTEGER. What this means is that every relation that's a possible value for that relvar must also have a STATUS attribute that's of type INTEGER—which means in turn that every tuple in such a relation must also have a STATUS attribute that's of type INTEGER, which means further that the tuple in question must have a STATUS value that's an integer.

I'll be discussing relations, tuples, and attributes in much more detail later in the chapter. Before we can get to that discussion, however, I need to cover a lot of material of a rather more fundamental nature. For now, therefore, let me just say that—with certain important exceptions, which I'll also be discussing later—attributes of relations and relvars (or of tuples and "tuplevars," come to that) can be of any type whatsoever, implying among other things that such types can be arbitrarily complex. Importantly, they can even be relation or tuple types in turn. See the answer to Exercise 2.19 at the end of the chapter for examples.

VALUES vs. VARIABLES

The brief discussion in the introduction to this chapter, regarding the fact that attribute STATUS of relvar S is of type INTEGER, touches on the logical difference (discussed in detail in the previous chapter) between relation values and relation variables. In fact, however, that difference is really just a special case of the logical difference between values and variables in general. Before getting into a discussion of types as such, therefore, I'd like to say something about this more general case, because it turns out—perhaps surprisingly—that it's an issue over which there's a great deal of confusion in the literature. Here first are some definitions, based on ones given in *An Introduction to Data Types*, by J. Craig Cleaveland (Addison-Wesley, 1986):

> **Definition:** A *value* is an "individual constant" (to borrow a term from logic), such as the integer 3. A value has no location in time or space. However, values can be represented in memory by means of some encoding, and those representations, or encodings, do have location in time and space; indeed, distinct representations of the same value can appear at any number of distinct locations in time and space, meaning, loosely, that any number of different variables—see the next definition below—can have the same value, at the same time or different times. Observe in particular that, by definition, a value can't be updated, for if it could, then after such an update it wouldn't be that value any longer.

> **Definition:** A *variable* is a holder for a representation of a value. A variable does have location in time and space. Also, variables, unlike values, can be updated; that is, the current value of the variable can be replaced by another value. (After all, that's what "variable" means—to be a variable is to be updatable, to be updatable is to be a variable. Equivalently, to be a variable is to be assignable to, to be assignable to is to be a variable.)

Now, you might find it hard to believe that people can get confused over a distinction as basic and obvious as the one just described between values and variables. In fact, however, it's all too easy to fall into traps in this area. By way of illustration, consider the following extract from a tutorial on object databases (the italicized portions in brackets are comments by myself):

> We distinguish the declared type of a variable from ... the type of the object that is the current value of the variable [*so an object is a value*] ... We distinguish objects from values [*so an object isn't a value after all*] ... [A] mutator [is an operator such that it's] possible to observe its effect on some object [*so in fact an object is a variable*].

So what exactly is an object? Is it a value, or is it a variable? Or is it something else entirely?[1]

---

[1] This lack of clarity as to exactly what an object is accounts for the total lack of mention of objects anywhere in *The Third Manifesto*. Indeed, we found we could formulate everything we wanted to say in the *Manifesto* in terms of values and variables alone, without ever having to appeal to any kind of object notion, as such, at all.

Important: Please note very carefully that it isn't just simple things like the example quoted above—namely, the integer 3—that are legitimate values. On the contrary, values can be arbitrarily complex. For example (as suggested in the previous chapter, in fact), a value might be a supplier number; or a geometric point; or a rectangle; or an X ray; or an XML document; or a fingerprint; or an array; or a relation (etc., etc.). Analogous remarks apply to variables too, of course—or rather, and more generally, they apply to types, as we'll see later.

It's also important to distinguish between a value per se, on the one hand, and an appearance of such a value in some particular context (e.g., as the current value of some variable), on the other. As already explained, the very same value can appear in many different contexts (e.g., as the current value of many different variables) simultaneously. Each of those appearances consists internally of some encoding, or physical representation, of the value in question. Moreover, those encodings aren't necessarily all the same. For example, the integer value 3 occurs exactly once in the set of all integers—there's exactly one integer 3 "in the universe," as it were—but any number of variables might simultaneously contain an appearance of that integer as their current value. What's more, some of those appearances might be physically represented by means of, say, a decimal encoding, and others by means of a binary encoding, of that particular integer. Thus, there's also a logical difference between an appearance of a value, on the one hand, and the internal encoding or physical representation of that appearance on the other. And there might even be a logical difference between the encodings used for different appearances of the same value.

All of that being said, for obvious reasons it's usual to abbreviate *encoding of an appearance of a value* to just *appearance of a value*, or (more often) just *value*, so long as there's no risk of ambiguity. Note, however, that *appearance of a value* is a model concept, while *encoding of an appearance* is an implementation concept. For example, users certainly might need to know whether two distinct variables contain appearances of the same value (i.e., whether they "compare equal"), but they don't need to know whether those two appearances make use of the same physical encoding.

To illustrate the point, let variables N1 and N2 both be declared to be of type INTEGER (see the section "What's a Type?" below). After the following assignments, then, N1 and N2 will both contain an appearance of the integer value 3 and will thus "compare equal," and of course the user needs to understand that these things are so. As for the corresponding physical representations, they might or might not be the same (for example, N1 might use a decimal representation and N2 a binary representation); either way, however, it's of no concern to the user.

```
N1  :=  3  ;

N2  :=  3  ;
```

WHAT'S A TYPE?

With that discussion of values and variables out of the way, I can now move on to discuss types as such. First let me remind you of the loose definition I gave in Chapter 1, to the effect that a type is basically just a named set of values (i.e., all possible values of some particular kind). Now, however, I need to be rather more precise. To be specific:

- First of all, a given type can be either system defined (i.e., built in) or user defined.[2] The relational model prescribes just one system defined type, type BOOLEAN (the most fundamental type of all). That type contains exactly two values: two truth values, to be precise, denoted by the literals TRUE and FALSE, respectively. However, real systems will support a variety of other system defined types as well, of course, and I'll assume for the purposes of this book that types INTEGER (integers), RATIONAL (rational numbers— see the aside below), and CHAR (character strings of arbitrary length) are all available as system defined types in addition to type BOOLEAN.

  Of course, the whole point about a user defined type (from the point of view of a user who is merely using it, that is, as opposed to the user who actually has the job of defining it) is that it's supposed to behave just like a system defined type anyway. In other words, in most contexts the question of whether a given type is system or user defined is largely irrelevant anyway.

- Second, types are always named (and types with different names are different types, so that, e.g., types INTEGER and RATIONAL are different types). Thus, every type has exactly one name.[3]

- Third, I note in the interest of accuracy that, instead of saying (e.g.) that type INTEGER is the set of all possible integers, I ought really to say it's the set of all integers that are capable of representation in the computer system under consideration; obviously there'll always be some integers that are beyond the representational capability of any given system. In other words, the types we have to deal with in practice are always finite, precisely because we're dealing with computers, which are finite by definition.

Aside: I'd like to say a little more here regarding type RATIONAL in particular. By definition, a rational number is a number that can be expressed as the ratio of two

---

[2] I'm making a tacit assumption here that the type in question isn't a generated type (the question of whether a given type is system or user defined doesn't really have any meaning for generated types). See the section "Type Generators" later in the chapter for further explanation.

[3] Elsewhere, however, I've proposed a mechanism by which a type might additionally be allowed to have one or more *synonyms*, so that, e.g., type CHAR might alternatively be referred to by the synonym CHARACTER, or type INTEGER by the synonym INT, or type SNO by the synonym S#. For further details see my paper "The Naming of Types," in *Database Explorations: Essays on The Third Manifesto and Related Topics*, by Hugh Darwen and myself (Trafford, 2010), available free online at the *Manifesto* website *www.thethirdmanifesto.com*.

integers (e.g., 3/8, 593/370, −4/3), while an irrational number is a number that can't be so expressed (e.g., π, √2). Every rational number is such that its fractional part can be represented in decimal notation in one of the following two ways:

a.   As a possibly empty finite sequence of digits followed by an infinite sequence of trailing zeros, which can be ignored without loss (e.g., 3/8 = 0.375000...)

b.   As a possibly empty finite sequence of digits followed by a finite sequence of digits, the first of which is nonzero, that infinitely repeats (e.g., 593/370 = 1.60270270...)

By contrast, the fractional part of an irrational number in decimal notation consists of an infinite, nonrepeating sequence of digits (e.g., π = 3.14159..., √2 = 1.41421...).

Now, many programming languages support a numeric type they call REAL. A real number is a number that's either rational or irrational. Computers being finite, however, the only real numbers they can represent precisely are rational ones, necessarily;[4] hence **Tutorial D**'s choice of the keyword RATIONAL. *End of aside.*

So much for what types are; I turn now to the question of what they're for. The following quote provides one good answer to that question:[5]

> A major purpose of type systems is to avoid embarrassing questions about representations, and to forbid situations in which these questions might come up.

However, a full appreciation of the significance of this answer requires a lot more by way of background knowledge, so let me continue with my explanations. The next point is that, in a properly typed system, just about everything *has*, or *is of*, some type. Let me elaborate:

■   First and foremost, every *value* is certainly of some type. In other words, if *v* is a value, then *v* can be thought of as carrying around with it a kind of flag that announces "I'm an integer" or "I'm a supplier number" or "I'm a rectangle" (etc., etc.).[6] Observe that, by definition, any given value always has exactly one type (except possibly if type inheritance is supported, which as far as this chapter is concerned it isn't), and that type never changes. *Note:* If every value is of exactly one type, then no value is of two or more types, and

---

[4] In fact, if we assume decimal representation, then they can represent precisely (a) only rational numbers of the first kind, such as 3/8, and (b) only a vanishingly small percentage of those (!).

[5] The quote is from "On Understanding Types, Data Abstraction, and Polymorphism," by Luca Cardelli and Peter Wegner (*ACM Comp. Surv. 17*, No. 4, December 1985).

[6] Since tuples and relations are values, these remarks apply to tuples and relations in particular, for which the function of what I'm referring to here as "a kind of flag" is performed by the pertinent *heading* (see the section "Type Generators," later, where I'll have a lot more to say about tuples and relations in general).

distinct types are thus disjoint, absent inheritance. I'll have more to say regarding this particular issue in the answer to Exercise 3.14 in the next chapter.

■ Next, every variable, every attribute of every relvar,[7] every operator that returns a result, every parameter to every operator, and more generally every expression, has what's called a *declared* type.[8] To be specific:

1. Every *variable* is explicitly declared to be of some type, meaning that every possible value of the variable in question is a value of the type in question.

2. Every *attribute* of every relvar is explicitly declared to be of some type, meaning that every possible value of the attribute in question is a value of the type in question.

3. Every *operator* that returns a result is explicitly declared to be of some type, meaning that every possible result that can be returned by an invocation of the operator in question is a value of the type in question. *Note:* Operators in general fall into two disjoint classes, as follows:

    a. Read-only operators,[9] which return a result and thus have a declared type as just explained, and

    b. Update operators, which return no result and thus have no declared type.

    Instead of returning a result, an update operator updates one or more of its arguments. Note that if *A* is such an argument, then *A* is required to be a variable specifically (not just a value), because only variables can be updated.

4. Every *parameter* to every operator is explicitly declared to be of some type, meaning that every possible argument that can be substituted for the parameter in question is a value of the type in question (or a variable of the type in question, if the operator in question is an update operator and will update the argument in question—see point 3 above).

5. More generally, every *expression* denotes some value and is thus implicitly declared to be of some type: namely, the type of the value in question, which is to say the type

---

[7] Or tuplevar—but for simplicity let's agree to ignore tuplevars from this point forward, until further notice.

[8] The difference between declared types and types in general will become extremely important when we get to type inheritance in the next chapter (and in the rest of the book). Without inheritance, however, the declared type of some item reduces to just the type of the item in question, in the sense in which the term *type* is usually understood.

[9] The qualifier *read-only* derives from the fact that such operators simply "read" their arguments and don't update them (in fact they aren't allowed to update anything at all, except possibly for variables that are local to their own implementation code).

of the result returned by the outermost operator in the expression (where by "outermost" I mean the operator that's executed last). For example, the type of the expression

```
( a / b ) + ( x - y )
```

is the type declared for the operator "+", whatever that happens to be. Note in particular that variable references and literals are both considered to be expressions—the operator to be invoked in each case being effectively just "Return the value of"—and thus certainly have a declared type.

Aside: To repeat, variables, relvar attributes, etc., all have a declared type. By contrast, *values* as such aren't declared at all; thus, values can't really be said to have a declared type as such. That being said, however, the only way a value can be referenced within a program is, of course, by means of some expression—possibly just a literal—and such expressions do have a declared type, as we've just seen. So sometimes we have to be rather careful over the logical difference between a value as such, on the one hand, and the expression that's being used to denote that value in some particular context, on the other. *End of aside.*

Now, the fact that parameters in particular are declared to be of some type raises an issue that I've touched on but haven't yet properly discussed—namely:

Associated with every type there's a set of operators for operating on values and variables of the type in question—where to say that operator Op is "associated with" type T basically just means that operator Op has a parameter of type T.[10]

For example, integers have the usual arithmetic operators; dates and times have special calendar arithmetic operators; XML documents have what are called "XPath" and "XQuery" operators; relations have the operators of the relational algebra; and *every* type has the operators of assignment (":=") and equality comparison ("="), where:

- *Regarding ":=":* All assignments are required to abide by *The Assignment Principle*, which states that after assignment of value *v* to variable *V*, the equality comparison *v = V* (see the next bullet item below) must evaluate to TRUE. Of course, this principle—which applies to assignments of all kinds, please note, including relational assignments in particular—is effectively just a somewhat formal definition of the semantics of the assignment operation.

---

[10] It follows that any system that provides proper type support—and "proper type support" here certainly includes the ability for users to define their own types—must provide a way for users to define their own operators, too, because types without operators are useless (see the section "Operators," later).

Note: As the *Manifesto* book explains, the database itself is really a variable—a database variable or "dbvar"—and database updates are really just assignments to that variable. It follows from *The Assignment Principle*, therefore, that such updates aren't allowed to have any hidden side effects.

■ *Regarding "="*: Here's what the *Manifesto* requires of this operator:

D shall support the **equality** comparison operator "=" for every type *T*. Let *v1* and *v2* be values, and consider the equality comparison *v1* = *v2*. The values *v1* and *v2* shall be of the same type *T*. The comparison shall return TRUE if and only if *v1* and *v2* are the very same value.

By way of illustration, consider the system defined type INTEGER. Since the agency responsible for defining this type is the system itself, it's the system that:

■ Will provide an assignment operator ":=" for assigning integer values to integer variables;

■ Will provide comparison operators "=", "≠", "<", etc., for comparing integer values;

■ Will provide arithmetic operators "+", "*", etc., for performing arithmetic on integer values;

■ Will *not* provide operators "||" (concatenate), CHAR_LENGTH (length in characters), etc., for performing string operations on integer values (in other words, string operations on integer values won't be supported).

By contrast, in the case of the user defined type SNO, it's the user responsible for defining the type that:[11]

■ Will provide an assignment operator ":=" for assigning SNO values to SNO variables;

■ Will provide operators "=" and "≠" (and possibly "<" etc.) for comparing SNO values;

■ Will probably not provide arithmetic operators "+", "*", etc., for performing arithmetic on SNO values, and so on, which would mean that arithmetic on supplier numbers wouldn't be supported (why would we ever want to add or multiply two supplier numbers?).

Note: The remarks earlier concerning operators and their parameters need some refinement if the operator in question is *polymorphic*. Speaking a trifle loosely, an operator is said to be

---

[11] I'm talking conceptually here. Even with user defined types, certain operators (for example, assignment) can surely be provided "automatically," in the sense that the system should be able to provide the necessary implementation code without any special effort on the part of the type definer.

polymorphic if it's defined in terms of some parameter *P* and the arguments corresponding to *P* can be of different types on different invocations. The equality operator "=" is an obvious case in point: We can perform equality comparisons between values of any type whatsoever (just so long as the values in question are of the *same* type, of course), and so "=" is polymorphic—it applies to integers, and character strings, and supplier numbers, and in fact to values of every possible type. Analogous remarks apply to the assignment operator ":=", which is also defined for every type: We can assign any value to any variable, just so long as the value and variable in question are of the same type. (Of course, the assignment will fail if it violates some integrity constraint, but it can't fail on a type error as such.)

> *Aside:* What's really going on here, at least in the examples quoted (viz., ":=" and "="), isn't so much that there's a single operator that's associated with many different types; rather, it's that there are many different operators (one for each of many different types), but those different operators all have the same name. In a sense, then, it's the operator names that are polymorphic, rather than the operators as such. But that's because the examples quoted are all examples of what's sometimes called, more specifically, *overloading* polymorphism (also known as ad hoc polymorphism)—and in overloading polymorphism, it really is the operator names that are overloaded, not the operators as such. (Note, however, that the literature almost never admits to this latter fact but does indeed talk as if the overloading applied to the operators themselves.) Later in this chapter, by contrast, we'll meet another kind of polymorphism called generic polymorphism—and in later chapters we'll meet yet another, called inclusion polymorphism—and in these cases it really is the operators as such that are polymorphic. *End of aside.*

SCALAR vs. NONSCALAR TYPES

It's sometimes convenient to draw a distinction between scalar and nonscalar types. Loosely, a type is said to be *scalar* if it has no user visible components and *nonscalar* otherwise; and then values, variables, attributes, operators, parameters, and expressions of some type *T* are said to be scalar or nonscalar according as type *T* itself is scalar or nonscalar. For example:

- Type INTEGER is a scalar type; hence, values, variables, and so on of type INTEGER are also all said to be scalar.

- Tuple and relation types are nonscalar—the pertinent user visible components being the corresponding attributes—and hence tuple and relation values, variables, and so on are also all said to be nonscalar.

That said, I must stress that these notions are quite informal. Indeed, I've explained elsewhere—see, e.g., my book *SQL and Relational Theory: How to Write Accurate SQL Code* (3rd edition, O'Reilly, 2015)—that the concept, frequently appealed to when relational databases are discussed, of *data value atomicity* has no absolute meaning, and "scalarness" is really just that same concept by another name. So the relational model in particular certainly doesn't rely on the scalar vs. nonscalar distinction in any formal sense. In this book, however, I do rely on it informally; I mean, I do find it intuitively useful, on occasion. To be specific:

- I occasionally use the term *nonscalar* to refer to tuple and relation types considered jointly. Of course, there are other nonscalar types in addition to these two—array types are an obvious example—but tuple and relation types are the ones most relevant to the present book.

- I occasionally use the term *scalar* to refer to types that aren't nonscalar in the foregoing sense—in particular, to types that are neither tuple nor relation types.

I also sometimes use the unqualified term *scalar* as a noun to mean a scalar value specifically.

> *Aside:* Another term you'll sometimes hear used to mean "scalarness" is *encapsulation*. Be aware, however, that this term is also used—especially in object contexts—to refer to the physical bundling, or packaging, of code and data (or, rather, operator definitions and data representation definitions, to be more precise about the matter). But to use the term this way is to mix model and implementation concerns; clearly, users shouldn't care, and shouldn't need to care, whether code and data are physically bundled together or are kept separate. See Appendix A for further discussion. *End of aside.*

TYPES vs. REPRESENTATIONS

It should be clear from the section "Values vs. Variables" that there's a logical difference between a type per se, on the one hand, and the physical representation of values of that type inside the system, on the other. In fact, types are a model issue, while physical representations are an implementation issue. For example, supplier numbers might be physically represented as character strings, but it doesn't follow that we can perform character string operations such as "||" (concatenate) on supplier numbers; we can do such things only if appropriate operators have been defined for the type (see the section "What's a Type?"). And the operators we define for a given type will naturally depend on the intended meaning and use of the type in question, not on the way values of that type happen to be physically represented—indeed, those physical representations are, or should be, hidden from the user. In other words, the distinction we draw between type and physical representation is one important aspect of the notion, very familiar from the database world, of *data independence*.

Let *T* be a scalar type. Then the physical representation of values of type *T* can be arbitrarily complex; as explained above, however, that physical representation is hidden from the user. But the *Manifesto* does require that values of type *T* additionally have at least one "possible" representation.[12] Such possible representations are explicitly declared as part of the definition of type *T*, and they're *not* hidden from the user. Moreover, if *PR* is a possible representation for type *T*, then *PR*, unlike *T* as such, does have components, and those components too are visible to the user. Please understand, however, that the components in question aren't components of type *T* as such—rather, they're components of possible representation *PR* (type *T* as such is still scalar in the sense defined in the previous section and has no user visible components). For example, consider the user defined type QTY ("quantities"), whose definition in **Tutorial D** might look like this:[13]

```
TYPE QTY POSSREP QPR ( Q INTEGER ) ;
```

This definition says, in effect, that quantities—i.e., values of type QTY—can possibly be represented by integers. Type QTY has just one declared possible representation ("possrep" for short), called QPR; moreover, that possrep QPR certainly does have user visible components—in fact, it has exactly one such, called Q, of declared type INTEGER—but quantities per se don't.

Important: The fact that quantities can possibly be represented by integers does *not* mean they physically are. They might be; on the other hand, they might be physically represented by rational numbers, or character strings, or indeed anything else you might care to think of. Indeed, distinct QTY values might be physically represented in distinct ways. Even distinct appearances of the *same* QTY value might be physically represented in distinct ways! In other words, there's a logical difference between possible representations and physical representations. (I'd like to say there's a big logical difference, but all logical differences are big by definition.)

Now, I introduced the possrep name QPR in the foregoing example in order to stress the fact that types and possreps are logically distinct constructs. In **Tutorial D** in particular, however, explicit possrep names can be (and often are) omitted, thanks to the following syntax rule: If a possrep is declared for type *T* but has no explicitly declared name, then that possrep is named *T* by default. Here by way of illustration is a simpler definition for type QTY:

```
TYPE QTY POSSREP ( Q INTEGER ) ;
```

In effect, this definition is shorthand for the following:

```
TYPE QTY POSSREP QTY ( Q INTEGER ) ;
```

---

[12] Unless *T* is a dummy type. Dummy types (which are something of a special case) are discussed in Chapter 12; for present purposes, we can ignore them.

[13] The syntax used for TYPE statements in this book differs in certain detailed respects from that documented in the *Manifesto* book and in other books of mine. The reason for this state of affairs isn't important for present purposes, but it's only fair to warn you that the differences in question do exist.

Here now is a more complicated example:

```
TYPE POINT      /* geometric points in two-dimensional space */
       POSSREP CARTESIAN ( X RATIONAL , Y RATIONAL )
       POSSREP POLAR ( RHO RATIONAL , THETA RATIONAL ) ;
```

POINT here is a user defined type with two distinct possible representations, CARTESIAN and POLAR, reflecting the fact that points in two-dimensional space can indeed "possibly be represented" by either cartesian or polar coordinates. Each of those possible representations in turn has two components, both of which happen to be of type RATIONAL. Note carefully, however, that (to say it again) the type per se is still scalar—it has no user visible components.

Selectors and THE_ Operators

Let *PR* be a possrep for scalar type *T*. Then the declaration of *PR* (part of the declaration of *T*) causes "automatic" definition of the following more or less self-explanatory operators:

- A *selector* operator, which allows the user to specify or "select" an arbitrary value of type *T* by supplying a value for each component of possrep *PR*

- A set of *THE_* operators (one for each component of possrep *PR*), which allow the user to access the corresponding *PR* components of an arbitrary value of type *T*

The selector has declared type *T*; each THE_ operator has declared type that of the corresponding component of *PR*. *Note:* When I say the declaration of *PR* causes "automatic definition" of these operators, what I mean is that whatever agency—possibly the system, possibly some human user—is responsible for defining type *T* is also responsible for providing implementation code for the operators in question. I'll come back to this issue in the next section ("The TYPE Statement"). Meanwhile, here are some sample selector and THE_ operator invocations for type POINT, expressed as usual in **Tutorial D**:

```
CARTESIAN ( 5.0 , 2.5 )
/* returns the point with x = 5.0, y = 2.5 */

CARTESIAN ( X1 , Y1 )
/* returns the point with x = X1, y = Y1, where */
/* X1 and Y1 are variables of type RATIONAL     */

POLAR ( 2.7 , 1.0 )
/* returns the point with ρ (rho) = 2.7, θ (theta) = 1.0 */

THE_X ( P )
/* returns the x coordinate of the point in */
/* P, where P is a variable of type POINT    */
```

```
THE_RHO ( P )
/* returns the rho coordinate of the point in P */

THE_Y ( exp )
/* returns the y coordinate of the point denoted  */
/* by the expression exp (which is of type POINT) */

THE_THETA ( exp )
/* returns the theta coordinate of the point denoted */
/* by the expression exp (which is of type POINT)    */
```

Note that, in **Tutorial D** at any rate, (a) selectors have the same name as the corresponding possrep, and (b) THE_ operators have names of the form THE_*C*, where *C* is the name of the corresponding component of the corresponding possrep. Note too that selectors—more precisely, selector invocations—are a generalization of the more familiar concept of a literal.[14] What I mean by this remark is that all literals are selector invocations, but "most" selector invocations aren't literals; in fact, a selector invocation is a literal if and only if all of its arguments are themselves specified as literals in turn. For example, CARTESIAN (X1,Y1) and CARTESIAN (5.0,2.5) are both invocations of the CARTESIAN selector, but only the second is a literal.

It follows that every type has—*must* have—an associated format for writing literals (and for completeness I should add that every value of every type must be denotable by means of some literal of the type in question).

Of course, all of the concepts discussed so far in the present subsection apply to simpler types as well[15]—for example, type QTY. Here are some sample QTY selector invocations:

```
QTY ( 100 )

QTY ( N )

QTY ( N1 - N2 )
```

And here are some sample THE_ operator invocations:

```
THE_Q ( Q1 )

THE_Q ( Q1 - Q2 )

THE_Q ( QTY ( 100 ) )
```

---

[14] The concept might be familiar, but it seems to be quite difficult to find a good definition for it in the literature! See Exercise 2.3 at the end of the chapter.

[15] Including system defined types in particular, though for historical reasons the corresponding selectors and THE_ operators might deviate somewhat from the syntax and other rules described in this section. See the *Manifesto* book for further discussion.

Note: I'm assuming for the sake of these examples that (a) N, N1, and N2 are variables of type INTEGER, (b) Q, Q1, and Q2 are variables of type QTY, and (c) "–" is a polymorphic operator—it applies to both integers and quantities.[16]

Discussion of the QTY selector raises another point, however. Consider attribute QTY of relvar SP ("shipments") in the suppliers-and-parts database, which is of declared type QTY (in this example, the attribute and the type happen to have the same name). As a consequence, it's strictly incorrect to say, for example, that the quantity for a certain shipment is 100. A quantity is a value of type QTY, not a value of type INTEGER! For the shipment in question, therefore, we should more properly say the quantity is QTY(100), not just 100 as such. In informal contexts, however, we usually don't bother to be quite so precise, thus using (e.g.) 100 as a convenient shorthand for QTY(100). Note that I used such shorthands ubiquitously in my picture of the suppliers-and-parts database in the previous chapter (viz., Fig. 1.1).

Here's one more example of a type definition:

```
TYPE LINESEG POSSREP ( BEGIN POINT , END POINT ) ;
```

Type LINESEG denotes line segments. The example shows that a possrep can be defined in terms of user defined types, of course, not just system defined types as in all of the previous examples. In other words, a user defined type is indeed a type.

THE TYPE STATEMENT

New types can be introduced in **Tutorial D** either by means of the TYPE statement, already illustrated in several examples in the previous section, or by means of some type generator. I'll defer discussion of the latter possibility to the section "Type Generators," later; in the present section, I'll discuss the TYPE statement specifically. Here by way of example is a possible definition for type WEIGHT (which was used, recall, in the definition of the parts relvar P in the suppliers-and-parts database):

```
TYPE WEIGHT POSSREP ( L RATIONAL )
          CONSTRAINT L > 0.0 AND L < 5000.0 ;
```

Explanation: Weights can possibly be represented by rational numbers, where the rational number in question (here denoted L) is such that $0.0 < L < 5000.0$.[17]

Now, the preceding sentence in its entirety constitutes an informal statement of the *type constraint* for type WEIGHT. More precisely, the type constraint for any given type *T* is simply a definition of the set of values that constitute that type *T*. In the example, the type constraint

---

[16] Again the kind of polymorphism involved here is overloading polymorphism specifically.

[17] For simplicity I assume that rational numbers in examples throughout this book are accurate to one decimal place (unless the context demands otherwise, of course).

says, in effect, that WEIGHT values are all and only those values that can possibly be represented by a rational number L such that $0.0 < L < 5000.0$. (If a given POSSREP declaration contains no explicit CONSTRAINT specification, then CONSTRAINT TRUE is assumed by default. In the WEIGHT example, therefore, omitting the CONSTRAINT specification would simply mean that anything that can be represented by a rational number—negative values included!—would be a valid weight, and nothing else would be.)

Type constraints are checked whenever some selector is invoked. Assume again that values of type WEIGHT are such that they must be capable of representation as rational numbers L such that $0.0 < L < 5000.0$. Then the expression WEIGHT (250.0) is an invocation of the WEIGHT selector, and it succeeds. By contrast, the expression WEIGHT (6000.0) is also such an invocation, but it fails. In fact, it should be obvious that we can never tolerate an expression that's supposed to denote a value of some type *T* but in fact doesn't; after all, "a value of type *T* that's not a value of type *T*" is a contradiction in terms. Since, ultimately, the only way any expression can ever yield a value of type *T* is via some invocation of some selector for type *T*, it follows in particular that no variable can ever be assigned a value that's not of the right type.

The WEIGHT example raises another point, however. In Chapter 1, I said part weights were given in pounds. In practice, however, it's probably not a good idea to bundle the type notion per se in such a manner with the somewhat separate notion of units of measure. Indeed, we could allow users to think of weights as being measured in either pounds or (say) grams by providing two separate possreps, one for pounds and one for grams, like this:

```
TYPE WEIGHT
    POSSREP LBS ( L RATIONAL )
    POSSREP GMS ( G RATIONAL )
    CONSTRAINT L > 0.0 AND L < 5000.0 AND G = 454 * L ;
```

Note the revised CONSTRAINT specification, which effectively specifies both the set of L values and the set of G values that correspond to legitimate WEIGHT values. (Legal L values are 0.1, 0.2, ..., 4999.9, legal G values are 45.4, 90.8, ..., 2269954.6, and I'm assuming for simplicity that there are 454 grams to the pound.) Now:

■ If W is an expression of type WEIGHT, then THE_L (W) will return a rational number *lbs* denoting the corresponding weight in pounds, while THE_G (W) will return a rational number *gms* denoting that same weight in grams (and *gms* will be equal to 454 * *lbs*).

■ If Z is an expression of type RATIONAL, then the expressions LBS (Z) and GMS (454 * Z) will both return the same WEIGHT value.

By way of another example, let's go back to type POINT, with its cartesian and polar possible representations. Here again is the corresponding TYPE statement, now shown with an appropriate type constraint (I assume for the sake of the example that operators SIN and COS are available and have the obvious semantics):

```
TYPE POINT      /* geometric points in two-dimensional space */
    POSSREP CARTESIAN ( X RATIONAL , Y RATIONAL )
    POSSREP POLAR ( RHO RATIONAL , THETA RATIONAL )
    CONSTRAINT X = RHO * COS ( THETA ) AND Y = RHO * SIN ( THETA ) ;
```

Suppose now for the sake of the discussion that the physical representation of points is in fact cartesian coordinates (though as noted earlier there's no need in general for a physical representation to be identical to any of the declared possible ones). Then the system will provide certain highly privileged and protected operators, denoted in what follows by italic pseudocode, that effectively expose that physical representation, and those operators can then be used to implement the necessary selectors. (Obviously, whoever is responsible for providing those implementations must be an exception to the rule that users in general aren't aware of physical representations.) For example (using a kind of pidgin form of **Tutorial D**):

```
OPERATOR CARTESIAN ( X RATIONAL , Y RATIONAL ) RETURNS POINT ;
    VAR P POINT ;  /* P is a variable of type POINT */
    X component of physical representation of P := X ;
    Y component of physical representation of P := Y ;
    RETURN ( P ) ;
END OPERATOR ;

OPERATOR POLAR ( RHO RATIONAL , THETA RATIONAL ) RETURNS POINT ;
    RETURN ( CARTESIAN ( RHO * COS ( THETA ) , RHO * SIN ( THETA ) ) ) ;
END OPERATOR ;
```

Observe that the POLAR implementation makes use of the CARTESIAN selector. Alternatively, it could be formulated directly in terms of the privileged operators, thus:

```
OPERATOR POLAR ( RHO RATIONAL , THETA RATIONAL ) RETURNS POINT ;
    VAR P POINT ;
    X component of physical representation of P := RHO * COS ( THETA ) ;
    Y component of physical representation of P := RHO * SIN ( THETA ) ;
    RETURN ( P ) ;
END OPERATOR ;
```

Those privileged operators can also be used to implement the necessary THE_ operators, thus (the caret symbol "^"—see the definition of THE_RHO—denotes exponentiation):

```
OPERATOR THE_X ( P POINT ) RETURNS RATIONAL ;
    RETURN ( X component of physical representation of P ) ;
END OPERATOR ;

OPERATOR THE_Y ( P POINT ) RETURNS RATIONAL ;
    RETURN ( Y component of physical representation of P ) ;
END OPERATOR ;

OPERATOR THE_RHO ( P POINT ) RETURNS RATIONAL ;
    RETURN ( SQRT ( THE_X ( P ) ^ 2 + THE_Y ( P ) ^ 2 ) ) ;
END OPERATOR ;
```

```
OPERATOR THE_THETA ( P POINT ) RETURNS RATIONAL ;
   RETURN ( ARCTAN ( THE_Y ( P ) / THE_X ( P ) ) ) ;
END OPERATOR ;
```

Observe that the definitions of THE_RHO and THE_THETA make use of THE_X and THE_Y (I assume for the sake of the example that operators SQRT and ARCTAN are available and have the obvious semantics). Alternatively, of course, THE_RHO and THE_THETA could be defined directly in terms of the privileged operators.

A BNF Grammar

Here for purposes of reference is an abbreviated BNF grammar for scalar type definitions in **Tutorial D** without inheritance. *Note:* When I say the grammar is abbreviated, what I mean is that there are still some issues to be discussed later in this chapter that will have the effect of extending it, though only in comparatively minor ways. Also, when I say the grammar is for scalar type definitions, of course I'm referring to user defined types specifically (note that user defined types are always scalar, by definition, in **Tutorial D**).

```
<scalar type def>
    ::=    TYPE <scalar type name> <possrep def list>
                              [ <possrep constraint def> ]

<possrep def>
    ::=    POSSREP [ <possrep name> ]
                    ( <possrep component def commalist> )

<possrep component def>
    ::=    <possrep component name> <type name>

<possrep constraint def>
    ::=    CONSTRAINT <bool exp>
```

Explanation:

1. Brackets "[" and "]" indicate that the material they enclose is optional, as is usual with BNF notation. By contrast, braces "{" and "}" stand for themselves; i.e., they're symbols in the language being defined, not (as they usually are) symbols of the metalanguage. *Note:* There are no braces in the abbreviated grammar above. In general, however, **Tutorial D** uses braces to enclose a commalist of items (see point 2 below) whenever the commalist in question denotes the elements of a set—or sometimes a bag—of some kind.

2. The grammar makes use of both "lists" and "commalists." The term *commalist* can be defined as follows. Let *xyz* be some syntactic construct (for example, *<possrep component def>* or *<attribute name>*). Then the term *xyz commalist* denotes a sequence of zero or more *xyz*'s in which each pair of adjacent *xyz*'s is separated by a comma (blank spaces

appearing immediately before or after any comma are ignored). For example, if *A*, *B*, and *C* are attribute names, then the following are all *<attribute name commalist>*s:

```
A , B , C

C , A , B , C

B

A , C
```

So too is the empty sequence of attribute names.

In addition, when some commalist is intended to denote the elements of some set and is therefore enclosed in braces, then (a) blank spaces appearing immediately after the opening brace or immediately before the closing brace are ignored; (b) the order in which the elements appear within the commalist is immaterial (because sets have no ordering to their elements); and (c) if an element appears more than once, it's treated as if it appeared just once (because sets don't contain duplicate elements).

The term *list* is defined analogously, the only difference being that each of the separating commas is replaced by at least one blank space.

3. The *<possrep def list>* mustn't be empty. Omitting the *<possrep constraint def>* is equivalent to specifying CONSTRAINT TRUE.

4. Omitting the *<possrep name>* from a *<possrep def>* is equivalent to specifying a *<possrep name>* equal to the *<scalar type name>* of the containing *<scalar type def>*. No two distinct *<possrep def>*s in the same *<possrep def list>* can have the same *<possrep name>*. The *<possrep component def commalist>* will usually not be empty (but see Exercise 2.26 at the end of the chapter).

5. No two distinct *<possrep component def>*s in the same *<possrep def list>* can have the same *<possrep component name>*.

6. In general, a *<bool exp>* ("boolean expression") is any expression that denotes a truth value. In the context at hand, the *<bool exp>* mustn't mention any variables, but *<possrep component name>*s from the associated *<possrep def list>* can be used to refer to the indicated components of the corresponding possible representations of an arbitrary value of the scalar type being defined.

Observe, incidentally, that *<scalar type def>*s quite rightly have nothing to say about physical representations. Observe too that possrep components are defined to have an associated type, but the type in question is specified by means of a *<type name>*, not a *<scalar type name>*.

In other words, the components of a possrep *PR* for some scalar type *T* don't necessarily have to be scalar themselves (see Exercise 2.10 at the end of the chapter).

Here now for future reference are definitions for the user defined scalar types used in the suppliers-and-parts database (apart from types QTY and WEIGHT, which have already been discussed). CONSTRAINT specifications are omitted for simplicity, as are explicit possrep names.

```
TYPE SNO    POSSREP ( SC CHAR ) ... ;
TYPE NAME   POSSREP ( NC CHAR ) ... ;
TYPE PNO    POSSREP ( PC CHAR ) ... ;
TYPE COLOR  POSSREP ( CC CHAR ) ... ;
```

(Recall from Chapter 3 that the supplier STATUS attribute and the supplier and part CITY attributes are defined in terms of system defined types—INTEGER and CHAR, respectively—so no type definitions are shown corresponding to these attributes.)

Of course, it must be possible to get rid of a scalar type if we have no further use for it:

```
DROP TYPE <scalar type name> ;
```

The *<scalar type name>* must identify a user defined type, not a system defined one. After this operation has been executed, the specified type will no longer be known to the system and will hence no longer be available for use.

OPERATORS

So far in this chapter, the only operators for which I've shown definitions have been either selectors or THE_ operators. It's time to look at some more general examples. Here first is a user defined operator, ABS, that applies to values of the system defined type RATIONAL:[18]

```
OPERATOR ABS ( X RATIONAL ) RETURNS RATIONAL ;
   RETURN ( IF X ≥ 0.0 THEN +X ELSE -X END IF ) ;
END OPERATOR ;
```

Operator ABS ("absolute value") is defined in terms of just one parameter, X, of declared type RATIONAL, and it returns a result of that same type (note the RETURNS specification). By definition, therefore, (a) that operator has declared type RATIONAL, and (b) an invocation of that operator—e.g., the invocation ABS (AMT1 + AMT2)—is an expression of declared type RATIONAL as well.

The next example, DIST ("distance between"), takes two parameters both of the same user defined type (POINT) and returns a result of another user defined type (LENGTH):

---

[18] Observe that user defined operators can indeed be defined in association with system defined types as well as user defined ones (or a mixture, of course), as you would surely expect.

```
OPERATOR DIST ( P1 POINT , P2 POINT ) RETURNS LENGTH ;
   RETURN ( WITH ( X1 := THE_X ( P1 ) , Y1 := THE_Y ( P1 ) ,
                   X2 := THE_X ( P2 ) , Y2 := THE_Y ( P2 ) ) :
         LENGTH ( SQRT ( ( X1 - X2 ) ^ 2 + ( Y1 - Y2 ) ^ 2 ) ) ) ;
END OPERATOR ;
```

I'm assuming that the LENGTH selector takes an argument of type RATIONAL. Note the use of a WITH specification in this example to introduce names for the results of certain subexpressions.

Here by way of another example is the required equality comparison operator—for the moment let's call it EQP—for type POINT:

```
OPERATOR EQP ( P1 POINT , P2 POINT ) RETURNS BOOLEAN ;
   RETURN ( THE_X ( P1 ) = THE_X ( P2 ) AND
            THE_Y ( P1 ) = THE_Y ( P2 ) ) ;
END OPERATOR ;
```

Observe that the expression in the RETURN statement here makes use of the system defined "=" operator for type RATIONAL. For simplicity, in fact, I'm going to assume from this point forward that the usual infix notation "=" can be used for the equality operator for all types, including type POINT in particular. I omit consideration here of how such infix names might be specified in practice, since it's basically just a matter of syntax.[19]

Here now is the (presumably required) "<" operator for type QTY:

```
OPERATOR LTQ ( Q1 QTY , Q2 QTY ) RETURNS BOOLEAN ;
   RETURN ( THE_Q ( Q1 ) < THE_Q ( Q2 ) ) ;
END OPERATOR ;
```

The expression in the RETURN statement here makes use of the system defined "<" operator for type INTEGER. In the definition I've shown the operator name as LTQ, but again I'm going to assume from this point forward that the usual infix notation "<" can be used (for all ordered types, that is, including type QTY in particular). *Note:* See the section "Miscellaneous Issues," later, for a discussion of ordered types in general.

Here finally is an example of an update operator definition (all of the previous examples have been of read-only operators, which simply "read" their arguments and don't update them). The operator is called REFLECT. In effect, what it does is move the point with cartesian coordinates (x,y) to the inverse position $(-x,-y)$, and it does this not by returning a result but rather by updating its point argument appropriately (observe that the definition involves an UPDATES specification instead of a RETURNS specification):

---

[19] In any case, the equality comparison operator (as well as certain other operators, possibly)—implementation code included—can surely be provided automatically. I show explicit code here purely for illustrative purposes.

```
OPERATOR REFLECT ( P POINT ) UPDATES { P } ;
   THE_X ( P ) := - THE_X ( P ) ;
   THE_Y ( P ) := - THE_Y ( P ) ;
END OPERATOR ;
```

Points arising:

1. The operator has just one parameter P, of declared type POINT, and—as indicated by the UPDATES specification—that parameter is subject to update, meaning that when the operator is invoked it will update the argument corresponding to that parameter.

2. Since it's going to be updated, the argument in question must be a variable specifically.

3. Since the operator doesn't return anything, (a) it has no declared type, and (b) an invocation doesn't constitute an expression. In particular, therefore, such an invocation can't be used as a subexpression nested inside some expression.[20] Instead, such an invocation has to be done via an explicit CALL statement, as in this example:

```
CALL REFLECT ( ZPT ) ;
```

    Such an invocation will fail on a syntax error at compile time if the argument expression consists of anything other than a simple variable reference.

4. Note that there's no explicit RETURN statement; rather, an implicit RETURN (without any argument) is effectively executed when the END OPERATOR is reached.

    Finally, it must be possible to get rid of an operator if we have no further use for it. **Tutorial D** provides an operator called DROP OPERATOR for this purpose. The operator to be dropped must be user defined, not built in.

THE_ Pseudovariables

The REFLECT operator definition also serves to illustrate, not altogether incidentally, the use of *THE_ pseudovariables*. In essence, a THE_ pseudovariable reference is a THE_ operator invocation that appears on the left side of an assignment. Such an invocation actually *designates*—instead of just returning the value of—the specified possrep component of the specified argument. Within the REFLECT definition, for instance, the assignment

```
THE_X ( P ) := ... ;
```

---

[20] Read-only operator invocations, by contrast, can be used as subexpressions nested inside other expressions; in fact, the terms *expression* and *read-only operator invocation* are effectively synonymous.

assigns a value to the X component of the cartesian possrep of the argument corresponding to the parameter P. (To say it again, any argument to be updated, whether by assignment to a THE_ pseudovariable as in this example or in any other way, must be a variable specifically.)

Pseudovariable references can be nested. Recall this type definition from the very end of the section "Types vs. Representations":

```
TYPE LINESEG POSSREP ( BEGIN POINT , END POINT ) ;
```

Suppose variable LS has been declared to be of type LINESEG. Here then is a possible assignment involving that variable:

```
THE_X ( THE_BEGIN ( LS ) ) := 6.5 ;
```

Now, THE_ pseudovariables are extremely convenient from a usability point of view, but in fact they're logically unnecessary. Consider again the following assignment from the REFLECT operator definition:

```
THE_X ( P ) := - THE_X ( P ) ;
```

This assignment, which uses a THE_ pseudovariable, is logically equivalent to the following one which doesn't:

```
P := CARTESIAN ( - THE_X ( P ) , THE_Y ( P ) ) ;
```

Similarly, the assignment involving nested THE_ pseudovariable references shown above—

```
THE_X ( THE_BEGIN ( LS ) ) := 6.5 ;
```

—is logically equivalent to the following, which involves no such references:

```
LS := LINESEG ( CARTESIAN ( 6.5 , THE_Y ( THE_BEGIN ( LS ) ) ) ,
                THE_END ( LS ) ) ;
```

In other words, THE_ pseudovariables per se aren't strictly necessary in order to support the kind of component level updating I've been discussing. However, using such pseudovariables does seem intuitively more attractive than the alternative (for which it can be regarded as a shorthand); moreover, it also provides a higher degree of imperviousness to changes in the syntax of the corresponding selector.

One last point: It's convenient from a definitional point of view, at least, to treat THE_ pseudovariable references as if they were regular variable references, and this book does so. In other words (but now speaking *very* loosely), pseudovariables are variables.

Multiple Assignment

While I'm on the subject of assignment, I need to say too that *The Third Manifesto* requires support for a *multiple* form of that operation, according to which any number of individual assignments can be performed in parallel ("simultaneously"). For example, the following double DELETE is, logically, a multiple assignment operation:

```
DELETE S  WHERE SNO = SNO('S1') ,
DELETE SP WHERE SNO = SNO('S1') ;
```

Note the comma separator after the first DELETE, which indicates syntactically that the end of the overall statement hasn't yet been reached. That overall statement is logically equivalent to the following "explicit assignment" form:

```
S  := S  MINUS ( S  WHERE SNO = SNO('S1') ) ,
SP := SP MINUS ( SP WHERE SNO = SNO('S1') ) ;
```

In general, the semantics of multiple assignment are as follows: First, all of the source expressions in the individual assignments are evaluated; then all of the individual assignments to the specified target variables are executed in parallel. *Note:* This explanation requires some slight refinement in the case where two or more of the individual assignments specify the same target (see below). Ignoring that refinement for the moment, however, we can say that since the source expressions are all evaluated before any of the individual assignments are done, none of those individual assignments can depend on the result of any other (and so "executing them in parallel" is really only a manner of speaking). In the example, the effect on the database would be exactly the same if the two individual DELETEs were specified in reverse order. Also, since multiple assignment is considered to be an atomic operation, no integrity checking is performed "in the middle of" such an assignment; indeed, this fact is one of the major reasons for supporting multiple assignment in the first place.

As for repeated targets: If two or more of the individual assignments involved in a given multiple assignment do specify the same target variable, then those particular individual assignments are effectively executed in sequence as written (thereby effectively reducing to a single assignment to the variable in question). For example, the double assignment

```
S := S MINUS ( S WHERE SNO = SNO('S1') ) ,
S := S MINUS ( S WHERE SNO = SNO('S2') ) ;
```

is logically equivalent to the following single assignment:

```
S := WITH ( S := S MINUS ( S WHERE SNO = SNO('S1') ) :
                   S MINUS ( S WHERE SNO = SNO('S2') ) ;
```

In this example, the references to "S" in the second line denote the result of executing the parenthesized assignment in the first line; in other words, they can be thought of, loosely, as denoting relvar S after the tuple for supplier S1 has been deleted.

An important special case of repeated targets occurs in connection with assignment via two or more THE_ pseudovariables to the same variable. For example, refer to the REFLECT operator definition once again. That definition contains the following pair of assignments:

```
THE_X ( P ) := - THE_X ( P ) ;
THE_Y ( P ) := - THE_Y ( P ) ;
```

However, we could if we liked replace these two assignments by the following double (and thus multiple) assignment:

```
THE_X ( P ) := - THE_X ( P ) , THE_Y ( P ) := - THE_Y ( P ) ;
```

And now we have an example of exactly the situation we're interested in (viz., assignment via two or more THE_ pseudovariables to the same target variable). The statement overall is logically equivalent to the following:

```
P := WITH ( P := CARTESIAN ( - THE_X ( P ) ,   THE_Y ( P ) ) ) :
                 CARTESIAN (   THE_X ( P ) , - THE_Y ( P ) ) ;
```

Summary So Far

From everything I've said so far (in this section and its immediate predecessor, "The TYPE Statement," in particular), it should be clear that introducing a new scalar type involves at least all of the following:

1. Specifying a name for the type.

2. Specifying the values that make up that type (i.e., defining the corresponding type constraint).

3. Specifying the hidden physical representation for values of that type. As noted earlier, this is an implementation issue, not a model issue, and is thus beyond the scope of this book.

4. Specifying at least one possible representation for values of that type.

5. For each such possible representation, providing a corresponding selector operator for selecting, or specifying, values of that type.[21] *Note:* Here's as good a place as any to spell

---

[21] In the case of a system defined type like INTEGER, however, this point boils down to simply providing appropriate literals (see footnote 23, later); more general selectors aren't needed, nor are THE_ operators.

out the point that a selector for type T isn't "associated with" type T in the sense that it has a parameter of type T; rather, it returns a result of type T.

6. For each component of each such possible representation, providing a corresponding THE_ operator.

7. Providing other read-only and update operators, including in particular assignment (":=") and equality comparison ("=") operators, that apply to values and variables of that type.

8. For those operators that return a result, defining the type of that result.

Observe that points 5-8 taken together imply that (a) the system knows precisely which expressions are legal, and (b) for those expressions that are legal it knows the type of the result—which means in turn that the total collection of available types is a closed set, in the sense that the type of the result of every legal expression is a type that's known to the system. Observe in particular that this closed set must include type BOOLEAN, if comparisons are to be legal expressions! Finally, observe that the fact that the system knows the type of the result of every legal expression means that it knows in particular exactly which assignments are valid, and also which equality comparisons.

> *Aside:* I've used type POINT to illustrate the possibility that a type can have two or more possreps (CARTESIAN and POLAR, in that particular case). For simplicity, however, I'm going to assume from this point forward—for the rest of this book, in fact—that the CARTESIAN possrep has been renamed POINT, implying that, e.g., POINT (5.0,2.5) is a valid point selector invocation. *End of aside.*

TYPE GENERATORS

I turn now to types that aren't defined by means of the TYPE statement but are obtained by invoking some type generator. Basically, a type generator is just a special kind of operator; it's special because (a) it's invoked at compile time instead of run time, and (b) it returns a type instead of, e.g., a simple scalar value. In a conventional programming language, for example, we might write

```
VAR SALES ARRAY INTEGER [1:12] ;
```

to define a variable called SALES whose legal values are one-dimensional arrays of 12 integers. In this example, the specification ARRAY INTEGER [1:12] can be regarded as an invocation of the ARRAY type generator, and it returns a specific array type. That specific array type is a generated type. Points arising:

1. Type generators are referred to by many different names in the literature, including *type constructors*, *parameterized types*, *polymorphic types*, *type templates*, and *generic types*. I'll stay with the term *type generator*.

2. Generated types are indeed types, and can be used wherever ordinary "nongenerated" types can be used; for example, we might define some relvar to have some attribute of type ARRAY INTEGER [1:12]. By contrast, type generators as such are *not* types.

3. Most generated types, though not all, will be nonscalar types specifically (array types are a case in point). Nongenerated types, by contrast, will always be scalar.

    Aside: An example of a scalar generated type is the SQL type CHAR(25). To be specific— and despite what the SQL standard and SQL textbooks and products might have to say about the matter—CHAR in SQL isn't a type at all but a type generator;[22] CHAR(25) constitutes an invocation of that type generator, and the literal 25 denotes the sole argument (actually a length specification) to that invocation. Values of SQL type CHAR(25) are, of course, character strings of length exactly 25 characters.

    One consequence of the foregoing is that, in SQL, the types CHAR(25) and CHAR(26), say, are in fact quite different types. After all, the set of values constituting the type CHAR(25) and the set of values constituting the type CHAR(26) are certainly different sets!—in fact, no value of either is a value of the other. The reason is simple: No string of 25 characters is a string of 26 characters, and no string of 26 characters is a string of 25 characters. In other words, types CHAR(25) and CHAR(26) are indeed disjoint, just as distinct types are supposed to be (absent inheritance). See the last part of the answer to Exercise 2.6 at the end of the chapter for further discussion.

    Note: If the SQL types under discussion had been VARCHAR(25) and VARCHAR(26) instead of CHAR(25) and CHAR(26), respectively, matters would have been rather different. To be specific, types VARCHAR(25) and VARCHAR(26), unlike types CHAR(25) and CHAR(26), are *not* disjoint; in fact, every value of type VARCHAR(25) is also a value of type VARCHAR(26), and it would be legitimate to regard the former as a subtype of the latter. See Chapter 22 for further discussion. *End of aside.*

Now, generated types do have possible representations ("possreps"), but the possreps in question are derived in the obvious way from (a) a generic possrep associated with the type generator in question and (b) the specific possrep(s) of the user visible component(s) of the specific generated type in question. In the case of ARRAY INTEGER [1:12], for example:

---

[22] By contrast, CHAR in **Tutorial D** really is a type as such, not a type generator.

- There'll be some generic possrep defined for one-dimensional arrays in general, probably as a contiguous sequence of array elements that can be identified by subscripts in the range from *lower* to *upper*, where *lower* and *upper* are the applicable bounds (1 and 12, in the example).

- Since arrays of the type in question are indeed one-dimensional, that type as such has just one user visible component; that component is of type INTEGER, and therefore has whatever possrep(s) are defined for type INTEGER. (Of course, the only possrep available for a simple system defined type like INTEGER will very likely be an "identity" possrep, according to which values of the type simply represent themselves.[23])

In like manner, there'll be operators that provide the required selector and THE_ operator functionality. For example, the expression (actually an array literal)

```
ARRAY INTEGER [  2 ,  5 ,  9 ,  9 , 15 , 27 ,
                33 , 32 , 25 , 19 ,  5 ,  1 ]
```

might be used to specify a particular value of type ARRAY INTEGER [12] ("selector functionality"). As for "THE_ operator functionality," the SALES example is really too simple to illustrate it properly. But suppose we're given a variable PTA whose permitted values are one-dimensional arrays of values of type POINT. Then the expression

```
THE_X ( PTA [ 3 ] )
```

might be used to return the *x* coordinate of the point in the third element—see the paragraph immediately following—of the array that happens to be the current value of PTA.

To get back to the SALES example: Of course, the expression

```
SALES [ 3 ]
```

can be used to access the third element of the array that happens to be the current value of the variable SALES (it might also be used as a pseudovariable reference). Assignment and equality comparison operators also apply. For example, here's a valid array assignment:

```
SALES := ARRAY INTEGER [  2 ,  5 ,  9 ,  9 , 15 , 27 ,
                         33 , 32 , 25 , 19 ,  5 ,  1 ] ;
```

---

[23] Here's what the *Manifesto* has to say about such matters: "[For a system defined type *T*], zero or more possible representations for values of type *T* shall be declared and thus made visible in **D**. A possible representation *PR* for values of type *T* that is visible in **D** shall behave in all respects as if *T* were user defined and *PR* were a declared possible representation for values of type *T*. If no possible representation for values of type *T* is visible in **D**, then at least one **selector** operator *S*, of declared type *T*, shall be provided. Each such selector operator shall have all of the following properties: 1. Every argument expression in every invocation of *S* shall be a literal. 2. Every value of type *T* shall be produced by some invocation of *S*. 3. Every successful invocation of *S* shall produce some value of type *T*."

And here's a valid array equality comparison:

```
SALES = ARRAY INTEGER [  2 ,  5 ,  9 ,  9 , 15 , 27 ,
                        33 , 32 , 25 , 19 ,  5 ,  1 ]
```

Next, any given type generator will also have a set of generic type constraints and operators associated with it—generic, in the sense that the constraints and operators in question apply to every specific type obtained via invocation of the type generator in question. For example, in the case of the ARRAY type generator:

■ There might be a generic constraint to the effect that the lower bound mustn't be greater than the upper bound.

■ There might be a generic "reverse" operator that takes an arbitrary one-dimensional array as input and returns as output another such array containing the elements of the given one in reverse order.

   Note: We have here, as promised earlier in the chapter, an example of *generic polymorphism*—"the same" reverse operator is available for use with any one-dimensional array. More generally, generic polymorphism is the kind of polymorphism exhibited by a generic operator, where (loosely speaking) a generic operator in turn is an operator that's available in connection with every type that can be produced by invocation of some given type generator. In fact, the array assignment and equality comparison operators discussed above are also generic operators.

Tuples and Relations

Two type generators that are of particular importance in the database world are (not surprisingly) the TUPLE and RELATION type generators. Before I can discuss them in detail, however, I want to be sure that we all understand exactly what tuples and relations are. Here then are some precise definitions—specifically, for the concepts *heading*, *tuple*, *body*, and *relation*:

Definition: A *heading H* is a set of *n attributes* ($n \geq 0$), each of the form $<Aj,Tj>$, where *Aj* is the *attribute name* and *Tj* is the corresponding *type name* ($0 \leq j \leq n$), and the attribute names *Aj* are all distinct. The value *n* is the *degree* of *H*; a heading of degree one is *unary*, a heading of degree two is *binary*, a heading of degree three is *ternary*, ..., and more generally a heading of degree *n* is *n-ary*.

Definition: Let heading *H* be of degree *n*, and let attribute $<Aj,Tj>$ of *H* be associated with an *attribute value vj* of type *Tj* ($0 \leq j \leq n$), to form the *component* $<Aj,Tj,vj>$. The set—call it *t*—of all *n* components so defined is a *tuple value* (or just a *tuple* for short) over the attributes of *H*. *H* is the *tuple heading* (or just the heading for short) for *t*, and the degree and attributes of *H* are, respectively, the degree and attributes of *t*.

Definition: Given a heading *H*, a *body B* conforming to *H* is a set of *m* tuples (*m* ≥ 0), each with heading *H*. The value *m* is the *cardinality* of *B*.

Definition: Let *H* be a heading, and let *B* be a body conforming to *H*. The pair <*H,B*>— call it *r*—is a *relation value* (or just a *relation* for short) over the attributes of *H*. *H* is the *relation heading* (or just the heading for short) for *r*, and the degree and attributes of *H* and the cardinality of *B* are, respectively, the degree, attributes, and cardinality of *r*.

I'll leave it as an exercise for you to convince yourself that the foregoing definitions do indeed pin down the various notions precisely and do correspond to the constructs in question as you already (possibly only informally) understand them. Let me just make one point, though: Even though tuples and relations do have user visible components—namely, their attributes, and perhaps their tuples as well in the case of a relation—there's no suggestion that those components have to be physically stored as such, in the form in which they're seen by the user. In fact, the physical representation of tuples and relations should generally be hidden from the user, just as it is for scalars.

Tuple Types

Now let's get back to the question of type generators. Here's a **Tutorial D** definition for a tuple variable (or tuplevar) called STV:

```
VAR STV TUPLE { SNO SNO , SNAME NAME , STATUS INTEGER , CITY CHAR } ;
```

Explanation:

- The keyword VAR, which we've already seen in several examples earlier in this chapter as well as in Chapter 1, just means the definition is a variable definition specifically.

- STV ("supplier tuple variable") is the name of the variable being defined.

- The remainder of the definition, from the keyword TUPLE to the closing brace inclusive, specifies the type of that variable. The keyword TUPLE shows it's a tuple type, and the commalist in braces specifies the set of attributes that make up the corresponding heading. No significance attaches to the order in which the attributes are specified. *Note:* Recall that an attribute is an <*Aj,Tj*> pair, and no two distinct attributes in the same heading have the same attribute name. **Tutorial D** doesn't use those angle brackets, however; moreover, it uses spaces instead of a comma to separate the attribute name *Aj* from the type name *Tj*. An analogous remark applies to all uses of the keyword TUPLE in **Tutorial D**, also to all uses of the keyword RELATION (see later); I won't keep on saying as much, therefore, but will instead let this one paragraph do duty for all.

Now let's focus on the tuple type as such. Here again is the pertinent specification:

```
TUPLE { SNO SNO , SNAME NAME , STATUS INTEGER , CITY CHAR }
```

This type is, of course, a tuple type, and it's nonscalar. It's also a generated type, obtained by invoking the TUPLE type generator. More generally, the example illustrates the style used for tuple type names in **Tutorial D**; to be specific, such names take the form TUPLE H, where H is the pertinent heading[24] (and the degree and attributes of H are, respectively, the degree and attributes of the tuple type so named).

Going back to variable STV, the value of that variable at any given time is a tuple with (as you can see) the same heading as that of the suppliers relvar S. Thus, we might imagine a code fragment that (a) extracts a one-tuple relation—say the relation containing just the tuple for supplier S1—from the current value of that relvar, then (b) extracts the single tuple from that one-tuple relation, and finally (c) assigns that tuple to the variable STV. In **Tutorial D**:

```
STV := TUPLE FROM ( S WHERE SNO = SNO('S1') ) ;
```

Next, tuples are, of course, values. Like all values, therefore, they must be returned by some selector invocation (a tuple selector invocation, naturally, if the value is a tuple). Here's an example:

```
TUPLE { SNO SNO('S1') , SNAME NAME('Smith') , STATUS 20 , CITY 'London' }
```

This expression returns the tuple shown first in the picture of the suppliers relation in Fig. 1.1 in Chapter 1. The order in which the tuple components are specified is arbitrary, of course. Note, however, that in **Tutorial D** each component is specified by means of the pertinent attribute name by itself—i.e., without the corresponding type name—separated by blank spaces from an expression denoting the pertinent attribute value. (There's no need to specify the attribute type as such, because it's necessarily equal to the type of the specified expression.)

Here's another example of a tuple selector invocation (unlike the previous one, this one isn't a literal, because not all of its arguments are specified as literals in turn):

```
TUPLE { SNO SV , SNAME NAME('Johns') , STATUS TV + 2 , CITY CV }
```

I'm assuming here that SV, TV, and CV are variables of types SNO, INTEGER, and CHAR, respectively.

---

[24] The reason the *Manifesto* insists on tuple type names being of this specific form, or something logically equivalent to this specific form, has to do with the question of *tuple type inference* (see the *Manifesto* book for further details, also Exercise 21.3 in Chapter 21). An analogous remark applies to relation type names also.

As these examples indicate, a tuple selector invocation in **Tutorial D** consists in general of the keyword TUPLE, followed by—to spell it out again—a commalist of pairs of the form *Aj xj* (where *xj* is an expression denoting the corresponding attribute value *vj*), that whole commalist being enclosed in braces. Note, therefore, that the keyword TUPLE does double duty in **Tutorial D**—it's used in connection with tuple selector invocations as we've just seen, and also with tuple type names as we saw earlier.

So tuple types certainly have selectors. But they don't have, or need, any THE_ operators—at least, not as such; instead, they have operators that provide access to the corresponding attributes of values and variables of the tuple type in question, and those operators provide functionality somewhat analogous to that provided by THE_ operators in connection with scalar types. For example, if TX is a tuple expression denoting a tuple of the same type as tuple variable STV, the **Tutorial D** expression

```
CITY FROM TX
```

extracts the CITY value from the tuple that's the current value of TX.

Finally, tuple assignment and equality comparison operators are also available, with the obvious syntax in each case. (In fact, of course, tuple assignment in particular was illustrated earlier in this subsection.)

A Note on Syntax

I've now explained the **Tutorial D** syntax for tuple type names and tuple selector invocations, and of course I'll be using that syntax throughout this book in coding examples. In the formal prescriptions that make up our inheritance model, however (in Chapter 4 in particular), I'll follow the style used in *The Third Manifesto* as such. Here's what the *Manifesto* has to say in this connection (the following text is lightly edited for present purposes):

> A **heading** *H* is a set of ordered pairs or **attributes** of the form <*A,T*> ... Given some heading *H*, **D** shall support use of the **generated type** TUPLE *H* ... The generated type TUPLE *H* shall be referred to as a **tuple type,** and the name of that type shall be, precisely, TUPLE *H* ... Now let *t* be a set of ordered triples <*A,T,v*>, obtained from *H* by extending each ordered pair <*A,T*> to include an arbitrary value *v* of type *T*, called the **attribute value** for attribute *A* of *t*. Then *t* is a **tuple value** (**tuple** for short) that **conforms** to heading *H*; equivalently, *t* is of the corresponding tuple type.

Note in particular, therefore, that the *Manifesto* as such uses the following style for tuple type names—

```
TUPLE { <A1,T1> , <A2,T2> , ... , <An,Tn> }
```

—and the following style (or something very close to it) for tuple selector invocations:

```
TUPLE { <A1,T1,v1> , <A2,T2,v2> , ... , <An,Tn,vn> }
```

However, it does also say this:

> *Note:* When we say "the name of [a certain tuple type] shall be, precisely, TUPLE *H*," we do not
> mean to prescribe specific syntax. The *Manifesto* does not prescribe syntax. Rather, what we mean
> is that the type in question shall have a name that does both of the following, no more and no less:
> First, it shall specify that the type is indeed a tuple type; second, it shall specify the pertinent
> heading. Syntax of the form "TUPLE *H*" satisfies these requirements, and we therefore use it as a
> convenient shorthand; however, all appearances of that syntax throughout this *Manifesto* are to be
> interpreted in the light of these remarks.

So **Tutorial D** is within its rights in departing from the *Manifesto* style slightly.

Of course, all of the foregoing remarks regarding tuple type and tuple selector syntax apply
equally to relation type and selector syntax also, mutatis mutandis, and I won't bother to spell out
the details, therefore.

Relation Types

I turn now to relation types (the following discussion parallels that of the previous subsection, for
the most part). Here's a **Tutorial D** definition for relvar S from the suppliers-and-parts database
(repeated from Chapter 1 but deliberately reformatted here):

```
VAR S BASE
    RELATION { SNO SNO , SNAME NAME , STATUS INTEGER , CITY CHAR }
    KEY { SNO } ;
```

Explanation:

- Again the keyword VAR means this definition is a variable definition specifically; S is the
  name of the variable being defined, and the keyword BASE means the variable is a base
  relvar specifically.

- The second line of the definition specifies the type of that variable. The keyword
  RELATION shows it's a relation type, and the commalist in braces specifies the set of
  attributes that make up the corresponding heading. Again, of course, no significance
  attaches to the order in which the attributes are specified.

- The last line defines {SNO} to be a key for this relvar.

  Now let's focus on the relation type as such. Here again is the pertinent specification:

```
RELATION { SNO SNO , SNAME NAME , STATUS INTEGER , CITY CHAR }
```

This type is, of course, a relation type, and it's nonscalar. It's also a generated type, obtained by invoking the RELATION type generator. More generally, the example illustrates the style used for relation type names in **Tutorial D**; to be specific, such names take the form RELATION *H*, where *H* is the pertinent heading (and the degree and attributes of *H* are, respectively, the degree and attributes of the relation type so named).

Next, relations are values and must therefore be returned by some selector invocation (a relation selector invocation, naturally, if the value is a relation). Here's an example:

```
RELATION { TUPLE { SNO SNO('S1') , SNAME NAME('Smith') ,
                               STATUS 20 , CITY 'London' } ,
           TUPLE { SNO SNO('S2') , SNAME NAME('Jones') ,
                               STATUS 10 , CITY 'Paris'  } ,
           TUPLE { SNO SNO('S3') , SNAME NAME('Blake') ,
                               STATUS 30 , CITY 'Paris'  } ,
           TUPLE { SNO SNO('S4') , SNAME NAME('Clark') ,
                               STATUS 20 , CITY 'London' } ,
           TUPLE { SNO SNO('S5') , SNAME NAME('Adams') ,
                               STATUS 30 , CITY 'Athens' } }
```

The order in which the tuples are specified is arbitrary. Here's another example (unlike the previous one, this one isn't a literal):

```
RELATION { TX1 , TX2 , TX3 }
```

I'm assuming that TX1, TX2, and TX3 here are tuple expressions, all of the same tuple type. As these examples suggest, a relation selector invocation in **Tutorial D** consists in general[25] of the keyword RELATION, followed by a commalist enclosed in braces of tuple expressions (and those tuple expressions must all be of the same tuple type). Note, therefore, that the keyword RELATION does double duty in **Tutorial D**—it's used in connection with relation selector invocations as we've just seen, and also with relation type names as we saw earlier.

Like tuple types, relation types don't have, or need, any THE_ operators as such. In their place:

- The projection and restriction operators of the relational algebra allow any given relation *r* to be reduced to an arbitrary "subrelation" containing (loosely speaking) just a subset of the attributes and/or a subset of the tuples of *r*.

- The operator TUPLE FROM *RX* allows the single tuple to be extracted from the relation *r* denoted by the relational expression *RX* (relation *r* must have cardinality one).

- The operator *A* FROM *TX* allows the value of attribute *A* to be extracted from the tuple *t* denoted by the tuple expression *TX* (tuple *t* must have an attribute called *A*).

---

[25] But see Exercise 2.22 at the end of the chapter.

Taken together, these operators provide functionality somewhat analogous to that provided by THE_ operators in connection with scalar types.

Finally, relational assignment and equality comparison operators are also available, with the obvious syntax in each case. (In fact, of course, relational assignment in particular was illustrated in an earlier section of this chapter, also at several points in Chapter 1.)

MISCELLANEOUS ISSUES

Initial Values

The *Manifesto* requires all variables, scalar or otherwise, to be assigned an initial value before they're used. If the variable in question, *V* say, is of some user defined (and therefore necessarily scalar) type *T*, this requirement is met in **Tutorial D** by initializing *V* to a value specified via an explicit—and required—INIT clause on the TYPE statement that defines *T*. For example:

```
TYPE QTY POSSREP ( Q INTEGER ) INIT ( QTY ( 0 ) ) ;
```

Now defining a variable to be of type QTY will cause that variable to be set to zero (or QTY(0), rather) before it's used.[26]

The INIT clause on the TYPE statement serves another purpose as well (in fact a more fundamental one). Here's another lightly edited quote from the *Manifesto* (actually it's part of the very first of the *Manifesto*'s various prescriptions):

> With the sole exception of the system defined empty type *omega* (which is defined only if type inheritance is supported), the definition of any given scalar type *T* shall be accompanied by a specification of an **example value** of that type.

The reason for providing such an example value is to guarantee that the type in question is indeed nonempty (i.e., does contain at least one value—see Exercise 2.23 at the end of the chapter). In **Tutorial D**, the INIT clause serves to provide that needed example value.

Note: Although the INIT clause on the TYPE statement is indeed required, I'll omit it from most of my examples from this point forward in order to avoid unnecessary distractions.

Ordered and Ordinal Types

Any given scalar type *T* can be ordered, ordinal, or neither. To elaborate:

---

[26] Except that a variable definition can always contain an INIT specification of its own. If it does (and if the variable in question is scalar, of course), it effectively overrides the INIT specification from the TYPE statement as far as that variable is concerned.

■ *T* is an ordered type if and only if it has a total ordering, meaning that (a) the comparisons *v1* < *v2*, *v1* = *v2*, and *v1* > *v2* are all defined for arbitrary pairs of values *v1* and *v2* of type *T*, and (b) for any such pair of values *v1* and *v2*, one of those comparisons returns TRUE and the other two return FALSE.

■ *T* is an ordinal type if and only if (a) it's an ordered type and (b) the following operators are also defined for it: (a) niladic "first" and "last" operators, which return the first and last value, respectively, of type *T* with respect to the applicable total ordering, and (b) monadic "next" and "prior" operators, which, given a value *v* of type *T*, return the value of type *T* immediately succeeding *v* and the value of type *T* immediately preceding *v*, respectively, again with respect to the applicable total ordering.

INTEGER is an obvious example of an ordinal type (in fact, any ordinal type must be "isomorphic to the integers," meaning it displays ordering behavior that directly parallels that of the integers). RATIONAL is an example of a type that's ordered but not ordinal, because if *p/q* is a rational number, then—in mathematics at least, if not in computer arithmetic—no rational number can be said to be the "next" one, immediately following *p/q*. And type POINT, at least as defined earlier in this chapter, is an example of a type that's not ordered at all (and hence certainly not ordinal either, a fortiori).

In support of the foregoing ideas, **Tutorial D** allows at most one of ORDINAL and ORDERED to be specified as part of the TYPE statement that defines a given type *T*. For example:

```
TYPE QTY ORDINAL POSSREP ( Q INTEGER ) INIT ( QTY ( 0 ) ) ;
```

If ORDERED is specified, associated "<" (etc.) operators must be defined for the type in question. If ORDINAL is specified, the same is true, but corresponding "first," "last," "next," and "prior" operators must be defined as well.

Type Specifications

The BNF grammar for scalar type definitions given in the section "The TYPE Statement" earlier in this chapter includes the following production rule:

```
<possrep component def>
    ::=    <possrep component name> <type name>
```

However, sometimes it can be convenient to specify a particular type not explicitly by its *<type name>* as indicated in this rule but in some more indirect fashion. (This state of affairs perhaps applies not so much in the particular context under discussion here—i.e., within a *<possrep component def>*—as it does in other contexts, but the general point is valid.) For that reason, **Tutorial D** frequently allows a *<type spec>* to appear where a *<type name>* might have been expected, including in the context under discussion. Here's the syntax:

```
<type spec>
    ::=    <scalar type spec>
         | <tuple type spec>
         | <relation type spec>

<scalar type spec>
    ::=    <scalar type name>
         | SAME_TYPE_AS ( <scalar exp> )

<tuple type spec>
    ::=    <tuple type name>
         | SAME_TYPE_AS ( <tuple exp> )

<relation type spec>
    ::=    <relation type name>
         | SAME_TYPE_AS ( <relation exp> )
```

For present purposes I take the semantics of all of the constructs referenced in the foregoing grammar to be intuitively obvious.

CONCLUDING REMARKS

I mentioned in the introduction to this chapter that there were certain important exceptions to the rule that tuple and relation attributes can be of any type whatsoever. In fact, there are two:

■ The first is that if *v* is a tuple or relation with heading *H*, then no attribute of *v* can be defined, at any level of nesting, in terms of any tuple or relation type having that same heading *H*. *Note:* Regarding the idea that tuples and relations might have tuple or relation valued attributes in general, see the answer to Exercise 2.19.

■ The second is that (as is well known) the relational model prohibits any relation in the database from having an attribute of any pointer type.[27]

Let me close this section, and indeed the body of this chapter, by pointing out explicitly something that I rather hope has been obvious throughout, viz.: The operation of defining a type doesn't actually create the corresponding set of values. Rather, those values simply exist, at least conceptually, and always will exist; they're part of the fabric of our universe, as it were, and they can be neither created nor destroyed. Thus, all the "define type" operation—i.e., the TYPE

---

[27] SQL violates this requirement—see Chapter 22—and thus commits what in the first (1998) edition of the *Manifesto* book we referred to, again rather rudely, as **The Second Great Blunder**. It's interesting to note, incidentally, that committing the first "great blunder" seems inevitably to lead to committing the second as well; however, it's possible to commit the second without committing the first.

statement, in **Tutorial D**—really does is introduce a name by which the corresponding set of values can be referenced. Likewise, the DROP TYPE statement doesn't drop the set of values as such, it merely drops the name that was introduced by the corresponding TYPE statement.

EXERCISES

2.1   What's a type?

2.2   Physical representations are always hidden from the user: True or false?

2.3   What do you understand by the term *selector*? And what exactly is a literal?

2.4   What's a THE_ operator?

2.5   This chapter has touched on several logical differences (refer back to Chapter 1 if you need to refresh your memory regarding this important notion), including:

argument	vs.	parameter
generated type	vs.	nongenerated type
ordered type	vs.	ordinal type
physical representation	vs.	possible representation
read-only operator	vs.	update operator
relation	vs.	relvar
relation	vs.	type
scalar	vs.	nonscalar
statement	vs.	expression
type	vs.	representation
user defined type	vs.	system defined type
user defined operator	vs.	system defined operator
value	vs.	variable

What exactly is the logical difference in each case?

2.6   State the type rules for the assignment (":=") and equality comparison ("=") operators.

2.7   What's a polymorphic operator?

2.8   What's a type generator?

2.9   Give some examples of types for which it might be useful to define two or more distinct possible representations. Can you think of an example where distinct possible representations for the same type have different numbers of components?

2.10 Give an example of a scalar type with a nonscalar possrep component.

2.11 Let X be an expression. What's the type of X? What's the significance of the fact that X is of some type?

2.12 Using the definition of the ABS operator as a template (see the section "Operators" in the body of the chapter), define an operator that, given a rational number, returns the cube of that number.

2.13 Let LENGTH be a user defined type, with the obvious semantics. Define an operator that, given the lengths of two adjacent sides of a rectangle, returns the corresponding area.

2.14 Define a read-only operator that, given a point with cartesian coordinates x and y, returns the point with cartesian coordinates $f(x)$ and $g(y)$, where f and g are predefined operators.

2.15 Repeat Exercise 2.14 but make the operator an update operator.

2.16 Define a read-only version of the operator REFLECT (defined as an update operator in the body of the chapter).

2.17 What's a pseudovariable? Why are pseudovariables logically unnecessary?

2.18 Give a type definition for a scalar type called CIRCLE. What selectors and THE_ operators apply to this type? Also, (a) define a set of read-only operators to compute the diameter, circumference, and area of a given circle; (b) define an update operator to double the radius of a given circle (more precisely, to update a given CIRCLE variable in such a way that it now contains a circle value with the same center as before but double the radius). *Note:* Here and throughout this book I follow conventional mathematical usage in using the term *radius* (a) sometimes to mean a line segment connecting the center of a given circle to a point on that circle's perimeter and (b) sometimes, and in fact more frequently, to mean the length of such a line segment (as the context demands).

2.19 Give some examples of (a) tuple types, (b) relation types.

2.20 Suppose we're given a departments-and-employees database in which (a) relvar DEPT ("departments") has attributes DNO, DNAME, BUDGET, and LOCATION and (b) relvar EMP ("employees") has attributes ENO, ENAME, DNO, and SALARY. Suppose further that the attributes are of the following user defined types:

```
DNO          :  DNO
DNAME        :  NAME
BUDGET       :  MONEY
LOCATION     :  CITY
ENO          :  ENO
ENAME        :  NAME
SALARY       :  MONEY
```

Which of the following scalar expressions (or would-be scalar expressions) are valid? For those that are, state the type of the result; for the rest, give an expression that will achieve what appears to be the desired effect.

a. `LOCATION = 'London'`

b. `ENAME = DNAME`

c. `SALARY * 5`

d. `BUDGET + 50000`

e. `ENO > 'E2'`

f. `ENAME || DNAME`

g. `LOCATION || 'burg'`

2.21 It's sometimes suggested that types are really variables, in a sense. For example, employee numbers might grow from three digits to four as a business expands, so we might need to update "the set of all possible employee numbers." Discuss.

2.22 I said in the body of the chapter that a relation selector invocation in **Tutorial D** consists of the keyword RELATION, followed by a commalist enclosed in braces of tuple expressions (and those tuple expressions must all be of the same tuple type)—and I implied, though I didn't actually say as much, that the type of the relation denoted by the overall expression was RELATION *H*, where TUPLE *H* was the common type of all of the specified tuple expressions. But what if that set of specified tuple expressions is empty?—in other words, what if the relation being specified has an empty body?[28] How can its type be determined?

2.23 A type is a (named) set of values and the empty set is a legitimate set; thus, we might define an empty type to be a type where the set in question is empty. Can you think of any uses for such a type?

2.24 A heading is a set of attributes and the empty set is a legitimate set; thus, we might define an empty heading to be a heading where the set in question is empty. Can you think of any uses for such a heading?

---

[28] Such a relation is usually known, a trifle loosely, as an empty relation.

2.25 Does the following represent a legitimate heading?

```
{ A T , A T }
```

2.26 Let *T* be a user defined scalar type, and let *PR* be a declared possrep for *T*. Could the definition of *PR*, within the TYPE statement defining *T*, contain an empty *<possrep component def commalist>*? If so, what would it mean?

2.27 Do you think that types "belong to" databases, in the same sense that database relvars do?

ANSWERS

2.1   A type (also known, especially in early writings on the relational model, as a domain) is a named, and in practice finite, set of values—all possible values of some specific kind: for example, all possible integers, or all possible character strings, or all possible supplier numbers, or all possible XML documents, or all possible relations with a certain heading (etc., etc.). *Note:* In object contexts, a type is often called a *class*.[29] However, that term *class* is also used by some writers to mean (a) the implementation or physical representation of some type, or (b) a type and one of its implementations in combination, or (c) the set of all values of some type currently in use (and (d) possibly other things besides), and for such reasons is probably best avoided. I won't use it much in this book, other than in object contexts.

2.2   True in principle; might not be completely true in practice (but to the extent it isn't, we're talking about a confusion over the logical difference between model and implementation). Incidentally, the quote from Cardelli and Wegner in the body of the chapter is highly pertinent to the present exercise. Here it is again:

> A major purpose of type systems is to avoid embarrassing questions about representations, and to forbid situations in which these questions might come up.

In other words, types are a good idea because they raise the level of abstraction; without a proper type system, everything would be nothing but tedious—and highly error prone—bit twiddling.

---

[29] Or is it? I can't resist throwing the following quote in here (it's from *Object-Oriented Database Systems: Concepts and Architectures*, by Elisa Bertino and Lorenzo Martino, Addison-Wesley, 1993): "Object-oriented systems can be classified into two main categories—systems supporting the notion of *class* and those supporting the notion of *type* ... [Although] there are no clear lines of demarcation between them, the two concepts are fundamentally different" (!). *Note:* I'll have a little more to say about this particular quote in Chapter 21.

2.3   Every type has at least one associated selector; a selector is an operator that allows us to select, or specify, an arbitrary value of the type in question. Let *T* be a type and let *S* be a selector for *T*; then every value of type *T* must be returned by some successful invocation of *S*, and every successful invocation of *S* must return some value of type *T*. *Note:* Selectors are provided "automatically" in **Tutorial D**—since they're required by the relational model, at least implicitly—but not in SQL (at least, not in all cases). In fact, although the selector concept necessarily exists in SQL, SQL doesn't really have a term for it; certainly *selector* as such isn't an SQL term. See Chapter 22 for further discussion.

A literal is a special case of a selector invocation (it's a selector invocation all of whose arguments are themselves specified as literals in turn, implying in particular that a selector invocation with no arguments at all, like the INTEGER selector invocation 4, is a literal by definition). Another way to look at it is this: A literal is a "self-defining symbol" that denotes a value that can be determined at compile time (where the value in question is fixed by the symbol in question, and the type of that value is therefore also fixed and determined by the symbol in question).[30] The *Manifesto* requires every value of every type, tuple and relation types included, to be denotable by means of some literal. Here are some **Tutorial D** examples:

```
4                       /* a literal of type INTEGER  */
'XYZ'                   /* a literal of type CHAR     */
FALSE                   /* a literal of type BOOLEAN  */
2.5                     /* a literal of type RATIONAL */
POINT ( 5.0 , 2.5 )     /* a literal of type POINT    */
```

(The last of these involves the user defined type POINT from the body of the chapter. Note that it relies on the fact that—in accordance with remarks to this effect in the body of the chapter—the CARTESIAN possrep for points has been renamed POINT.)

Note that there's a logical difference between a literal as such and a constant—a constant is a value (no more and no less), while a literal is a symbol that denotes such a value. (By the same token, there's a logical difference between a literal and a value—as just stated, a value is a constant, while a literal is a symbol that denotes such a value, or constant.) That said, however, some languages also support so called "named constants." A named constant denotes a value—the constant in question—that can be referenced by means of a name that's not just a simple literal representation of that value. In other words, a named constant resembles a variable, in that it can be thought of as an abstraction of a storage location that contains a value; however, it differs from a variable in two obvious ways. First, it can never

---

[30] Note, however, that—to jump ahead of ourselves for the moment—the *most specific* type of the value in question might not be known until run time. For example, the system might know at compile time that the literal 4 is of type INTEGER, but then discover at run time that it's actually of type EVEN_INTEGER, where EVEN_INTEGER is a user defined subtype of type INTEGER. See the answer to Exercise 10.5 in Chapter 10 for further discussion of such matters.

serve as the target for an assignment operation. Second, every reference to the pertinent name always denotes the same value.

2.4   A THE_ operator is an operator that provides access (effectively for both retrieval and update purposes) to some component of some "possible representation," or *possrep*, of some specified value of some specified type. *Note:* THE_ operators are effectively provided "automatically" in both **Tutorial D** and SQL, to a first approximation. However, although the THE_ operator concept necessarily exists in SQL, SQL doesn't exactly have a term for it; certainly *THE_ operator* as such isn't an SQL term. See Chapter 22 for further discussion.

2.5   For physical vs. possible representations, see the section "Types vs. Representations," especially the subsection "Selectors and THE_ Operators." For read-only vs. update operators, see the sections "What's a Type?" and "Operators." For relations vs. relvars, see Chapter 1. For scalar vs. nonscalar, see the section "Scalar vs. Nonscalar Types." For types vs. representations, see the section "Types vs. Representations." For values vs. variables, see the section "Values vs. Variables." The remaining logical differences in the list are discussed below.

- A parameter is a formal operand in terms of which some operator is defined. An argument is an actual operand that's substituted for some parameter in some invocation of the operator in question. Be aware, however, that people often use these terms as if they were interchangeable; much confusion is caused that way, and you need to be on the lookout for it. (It might help you remember which is which by noting that *argument* and *actual operand* both begin with *A*.)

  By the way, there's also a logical difference between an argument as such and the expression that's used to specify it. For example, consider the expression $(2 + 3) − 1$, which represents an invocation of the arithmetic operator "−". The first argument to that invocation is the value 5, but that argument is specified by the expression $2 + 3$, which represents an invocation of the arithmetic operator "+". (In fact, of course, *every* expression represents some read-only operator invocation. Even a simple variable reference—*V*, say—can be regarded as representing an invocation of a certain read-only operator: namely, the operator that returns the current value of the specified variable *V*. A similar remark applies to literals also, such as the literal 1 in the example.)

- A generated type is a type obtained by invoking some type generator such as ARRAY, RELATION, or (in SQL) CHAR; specific array, relation, and (in SQL) character string types are thus generated types. A nongenerated type is a type that's not a generated type. Generated types are usually nonscalar, but don't have to be; nongenerated types are always scalar. (It follows, incidentally, that system defined types are always scalar.)

■ An ordered type is a type with a total ordering. An ordinal type is a type that's "isomorphic to the integers"—it's ordered, but additionally has appropriate "first," "last," "next, and "prior" operators associated with it.

■ A relation is a value; it has a type—a relation type, of course—but it isn't itself a type. By contrast (and as noted in the answer to Exercise 2.1), a type is a named, and in practice finite, set of values: viz., all possible values of some particular kind. See the discussion of **The First Great Blunder** in Chapter 1.

■ The logical difference between a statement and an expression wasn't explicitly discussed in the body of the chapter, but it's important. It can be explained as follows. First, an expression represents a read-only operator invocation, and it denotes a value; it can be thought of as a rule for computing the value in question. (Incidentally, the arguments, if any, to that operator invocation are themselves specified as expressions in turn—though the expressions in question might be just simple literals or simple variable references.) By contrast, a statement doesn't denote a value; instead, it causes some action to occur, such as assigning a value to a variable or changing the flow of control. In **Tutorial D**, for example,

```
X + Y
```

is an expression, but

```
Z := X + Y ;
```

is a statement.

    Note: As you can see, statements in **Tutorial D** terminate in a semicolon, and this observation applies to TYPE statements in particular. In other words, a TYPE statement consists of a *<scalar type def>*—see the BNF grammar in the body of the chapter— followed by a semicolon. (That's why that grammar showed no semicolon terminator as part of the production for *<scalar type def>*.)

■ A system defined (or built in) type is a type that's available for use as soon as the system is installed (it "comes in the box the system comes in"). A user defined type is a type whose definition and implementation are provided by some suitably skilled user after the system is installed. (To the user of such a type, however—as opposed to the user who actually defines that type—that type should look and feel just like a system defined type.)

    By the way, I note in passing that there's at least one system defined type (viz., type RATIONAL) that might well have more than one possible representation. For example, the expressions 530.00 and 5.3E2 might well denote the same RATIONAL value—i.e., they might constitute distinct, but equivalent, invocations of two distinct RATIONAL selectors. Likewise, type INTEGER might have (say) both a decimal and a hexadecimal possible representation—perhaps a binary one too.

■ A system defined (or built in) operator is an operator that's available for use as soon as the system is installed (it comes in the box the system comes in). A user defined operator is an operator whose definition and implementation are provided by some suitably skilled user after the system is installed. (To the user of such an operator, however—as opposed to the user who designs and implements that operator—that operator should look and feel just like a system defined operator.) User defined operators can take arguments of either user or system defined types (or a mixture), but system defined operators, obviously enough, can take arguments of system defined types only.

2.6   For assignment, the declared types of the target variable and the source expression must be the same; for equality comparison, the declared types of the comparands must be the same. (Both of these rules will need to be refined somewhat when inheritance is supported.)

Note: Given the foregoing, some obvious questions arise. (The discussion that follows is formulated in terms of assignment for definiteness, but similar considerations apply to equality comparisons also, mutatis mutandis.) Suppose by way of example that variables XINT and XRAT are declared to be of types INTEGER and RATIONAL, respectively, and suppose XINT currently contains the value 4. Surely there must be a way of assigning that current value of XINT to XRAT (even though they're of different types), such that XRAT winds up with current value 4.0? And of course there is, in a sense. Here's how to do it:

```
XRAT := CAST_AS_RATIONAL ( XINT ) ;
```

What happens here is that the CAST_AS_RATIONAL invocation "converts" or "casts" its argument—viz., the current value of the variable XINT—to type RATIONAL (in other words, it "converts" that 4 to 4.0). And that "converted" value can then be assigned to XRAT without violating the type rules for assignment.

Now, some languages allow the necessary type conversion in such a case to be done automatically, thereby allowing the foregoing example to be formulated "more simply" (?) thus:

```
XRAT := XINT ;
```

The type conversion is still being done, but now it's being done implicitly. The technical term for such implicit conversion is *coercion*; thus, what's happening in the "simpler" version of the example is that the current value of XINT is being coerced to type RATIONAL.

All of that being said, it's a widely accepted principle in computing that coercions are best avoided because they're error prone, and **Tutorial D** doesn't support them. (Actually type conversions in general are best avoided, because they can be expensive in performance. But if they must be done, at least they should be done explicitly, via explicit CASTs. **Tutorial D** does support explicit CASTs.)

Note: As you might have realized, the foregoing discussion is touching on what's known in language circles as *strong typing*. Different writers have slightly different definitions for this term, but basically what it means is that (a) everything—in particular, every value and every variable—has a type, and (b) whenever we try to perform some operation, the system checks that the operands are of the right types for the operation in question (or, possibly, that they're coercible to those right types). The *Manifesto* theory of types supports—in fact, requires—strong typing.

More on CAST: If *T* is a scalar type, then invoking the operator CAST_AS_*T* is usually described, as above, as "converting" the argument to the target type *T*. But it doesn't really do anything to that argument as such, of course (after all, it's a read-only operator); all it really does is return the value that corresponds to that argument according to a certain predefined mapping between the pertinent types. In other words, the phrase "type conversion" is rather loose, though convenient as a shorthand.

Observe now that the argument to CAST_AS_*T* can be of different types on different invocations; in other words, we have here another example of overloading polymorphism (see the section "What's a Type?" in the body of the chapter). Observe also that the number of CAST operators actually needed in any given situation can sometimes be reduced by good type design. For example, consider temperatures. A good design will involve a single TEMPERATURE type, together with possreps (and hence selectors and THE_ operators) corresponding to a Celsius representation, a Fahrenheit representation, and so on. A bad design would involve different types—CELSIUS, FAHRENHEIT, and so on—together with a set of CAST operators to convert between them. See the discussion of units of measure in the body of the chapter.

One last point: Consider type QTY from the body of the chapter. That type has a possrep with a single component, Q, of type INTEGER. As a consequence (but now speaking *extremely* loosely!), the QTY selector might be thought of as an operator that converts an integer to a quantity; similarly, the operator THE_Q might be thought of as an operator that converts a quantity to an integer. See the answer to Exercise 2.20 below for several illustrations of this point.

A note on SQL: Let SQL variables C25 and C26 be of types CHAR(25) and CHAR(26), respectively. As explained in the body of the chapter, CHAR(25) and CHAR(26) are different types. So what happens with assignments and comparisons? More specifically, what happens if we try to assign C25 to C26, or C26 to C25, or test C25 and C26 for equality? It turns out that a complete answer to this question is exceedingly complex, and I won't attempt to give anything close to such an answer here. Briefly, however:

- *Assigning C25 to C26:* Before the assignment is done, the value of C25 will be coerced to type CHAR(26) by padding it with a single trailing space.

- *Assigning C26 to C25:* Before the assignment is done, an attempt will be made to coerce the value of C26 to type CHAR(25) by dropping the final character. An error will occur if that final character isn't a space.

- *Testing C25 and C26 for equality:* Depends on the pertinent "collation." If PAD SPACE applies to that collation, the value of C25 will be coerced to type CHAR(26) by padding it with a single trailing space before the comparison is done; otherwise, NO PAD applies, and the comparison will give FALSE—even if the first 25 characters of C26 "compare equal" to C25 and the 26th character is a space.

2.7   Loosely, an operator is said to be polymorphic if it's defined in terms of some parameter *P* and the arguments corresponding to *P* can be of different types on different invocations. There are, however, at least three different kinds of polymorphism (or, rather, three quite different phenomena, all of which happen to be considered by some writers as polymorphism): viz., overloading (or ad hoc), generic, and inclusion polymorphism. The first two of these were explained briefly in the body of the chapter; the third will be discussed, exhaustively, when we get to type inheritance later in this book.

2.8   A type generator is an operator that returns a type instead of a value (and is invoked at compile time instead of run time).

2.9   A triangle can possibly be represented by (a) its three vertices or (b) the midpoints of its three sides or (c) the three line segments constituting its sides or (d) the line segments constituting two of its sides together with the corresponding included angle (etc., etc.). A line segment can possibly be represented by (a) its begin and end points or (b) its midpoint, length, and angle of inclination.

2.10   A polygon can possibly be represented by a relation containing one tuple for each of its vertices, each such tuple containing the number of the pertinent vertex and the corresponding point in two-dimensional space:

```
TYPE POLYGON
      POSSREP ( VERTICES RELATION { VNO INTEGER , VERTEX POINT } )
      CONSTRAINT ... ;
```

The CONSTRAINT specification might look like this:

```
CONSTRAINT
    WITH ( N := COUNT ( VERTICES ) ) :
          COUNT ( VERTICES { VNO } ) = N
          AND
          COUNT ( VERTICES { VERTEX } ) = N
          AND
          IS_EMPTY ( VERTICES WHERE VNO < 1 OR VNO > N )
```

Explanation: This CONSTRAINT specification involves three separate conditions all ANDed together. Let *p* be an arbitrary value of type POLYGON. Then the first condition ensures that no two tuples in the VERTICES relation for *p* have the same vertex number; the second ensures that no two tuples in the VERTICES relation for *p* have the same vertex; and the first and third together ensure that if *p* has *n* vertices, then the *n* tuples in the VERTICES relation for *p* contain exactly the VNO values 1, 2, ..., *n*.

Note: Actually the foregoing possrep is incomplete in several respects. One is as follows. Suppose for simplicity that the polygon is in fact a triangle. Clearly, then, the very same triangle can be specified by giving its three vertices in any of six different orders. Now, you might be thinking such a state of affairs surely doesn't matter, but in fact it does (in a right triangle, for example, we might want to be sure it's the "first" vertex that corresponds to the right angle). In general, then, we'd need a way of pinning down the precise order in which the vertices are to be specified. E.g., in terms of polar coordinates, we might say they're specified in terms of increasing values of θ (but even then we'd need a way of breaking ties).

2.11 The type of expression *X* is the type, *T* say, specified as the type of the result of the operator to be executed last—"the outermost operator"—when *X* is evaluated. That type is significant because it means the expression can be used in exactly (that is, in all and only) those positions where a literal of type *T* can appear.

2.12
```
    OPERATOR CUBE ( X RATIONAL ) RETURNS RATIONAL ;
        RETURN ( X ^ 3 ) ;
    END OPERATOR ;
```

2.13
```
    OPERATOR AREA_OF_R ( H LENGTH , W LENGTH ) RETURNS AREA ;
        RETURN ( H * W ) ;
    END OPERATOR ;
```

I'm assuming here, not unreasonably, that (a) it's legal to multiply a value of type LENGTH by another such value, and (b) the result of such a multiplication is a value of type AREA (another user defined type).

```
2.14  OPERATOR FG ( P POINT ) RETURNS POINT ;
          RETURN ( POINT ( F ( THE_X ( P ) ) , G ( THE_Y ( P ) ) ) ) ;
      END OPERATOR ;

2.15  OPERATOR FG ( P POINT ) UPDATES { P } ;
          THE_X ( P ) := F ( THE_X ( P ) ) ,
          THE_Y ( P ) := G ( THE_Y ( P ) ) ;
      END OPERATOR ;

2.16  OPERATOR REFLECT ( P POINT ) RETURNS POINT ;
          RETURN ( POINT ( - THE_X ( P ) , - THE_Y ( P ) ) ) ;
      END OPERATOR ;
```

2.17 A pseudovariable reference is the use of an operational expression instead of a regular variable reference to denote the target for some assignment or other update operation (of course, all update operations are logically equivalent to some assignment anyway). In the body of the chapter I discussed THE_ pseudovariables in particular, but THE_ pseudovariables aren't the only kind. For example, let CS be a variable of declared type CHAR, with current value the string 'Middle', and consider the following assignment statement:

```
SUBSTR ( CS , 2 , 1 ) := 'u' ;
```

SUBSTR here is the substring operator, and the effect of the assignment is to "zap" the second character position within CS, replacing the 'i' by a 'u' (after the update, therefore, the current value of CS is the string 'Muddle'). The expression on the left side of the assignment symbol is a pseudovariable reference.

Pseudovariables are logically unnecessary because they're just shorthand—any assignment involving a pseudovariable is logically equivalent to one that doesn't. *Subsidiary exercise:* Give an assignment statement that's logically equivalent to the one shown above but doesn't use any pseudovariables.

```
2.18  TYPE CIRCLE POSSREP ( R LENGTH , CTR POINT ) ;
          /* R represents the radius of the circle */
          /* and CTR represents the center        */
```

The sole selector that applies to type CIRCLE is as follows:

```
CIRCLE ( r , ctr )
/* returns the circle with radius r and center ctr */
```

THE_ operators:

```
THE_R ( c )
/* returns the radius of circle c (a length) */
THE_CTR ( c )
/* returns the center of circle c (a point)  */
```

a.
```
OPERATOR DIAMETER_OF ( C CIRCLE ) RETURNS LENGTH ;
    RETURN ( 2 * THE_R ( C ) ) ;
END OPERATOR ;

OPERATOR CIRCUMFERENCE_OF ( C CIRCLE ) RETURNS LENGTH ;
    RETURN ( 3.14159 * DIAMETER ( C ) ) ;
END OPERATOR ;

OPERATOR AREA_OF ( C CIRCLE ) RETURNS AREA ;
    RETURN ( 3.14159 * ( THE_R ( C ) ^ 2 ) ) ;
END OPERATOR ;
```

I'm assuming here that (a) multiplying a length by an integer or a rational number returns a length and (b) multiplying a length by a length returns an area.

b.
```
OPERATOR DOUBLE_R ( C CIRCLE ) UPDATES { C } ;
    THE_R ( C )  := 2 * THE_R ( C ) ;
END OPERATOR ;
```

2.19 The following examples are deliberately a little complicated. First, here's a tuple type with a relation valued attribute (RVA):

```
TUPLE { SNO SNO ,
        PNO_REL RELATION { PNO PNO } }
```

And here's a corresponding selector invocation (actually it's a literal):

```
TUPLE { SNO SNO('S2') ,
        PNO_REL RELATION { TUPLE { PNO PNO('P1') } ,
                           TUPLE { PNO PNO('P2') } } }
```

Second, here's a relation type with a tuple valued attribute (TVA):

```
RELATION { NAME NAME ,
           ADDR TUPLE { STREET CHAR ,
                        CITY   CHAR ,
                        STATE  CHAR ,
                        ZIP    CHAR } }
```

(A corresponding selector invocation is left as a subsidiary exercise.) Finally, here's a relation type involving two RVAs:

```
RELATION { CNO      CNO ,
           TEACHER RELATION { TNO TNO } ,
           TEXT    RELATION { XNO XNO } }
```

And here's a possible sample value (as another subsidiary exercise, you might try writing out in longhand, as it were, a relation selector invocation—in fact, a relation literal—representing this specific sample value):

CNO	TEACHER	TEXT
C1	TNO T2 T4 T5	XNO X1 X2
C2	TNO T4	XNO X2 X4 X5

A relvar of the foregoing type might have the following predicate:[31]

Course CNO can be taught by every teacher TNO in TEACHER (and no other teachers) and uses every textbook XNO in TEXT (and no other textbooks).

Subsidiary exercise: Type generators are supposed to have generic possreps, operators, and constraints associated with them—so what possreps, operators, and constraints are associated with the RELATION and TUPLE type generators? (*Answer:* The possreps are implicit in the formats for the corresponding selectors. The operators are basically (a) the operators of the relational algebra for relations and (b) tuple analogs of those operators for tuples. As for constraints, see Chapter 17.)

2.20 I assume throughout the following answers that each of the types involved has a selector with the same name. a. Not valid; LOCATION = CITY('London'). b. Valid; BOOLEAN.

---

[31] A *relvar predicate* is, loosely, just a reasonably precise, but informal, statement of how the relvar in question is meant to be understood by the user. See, e.g., my book *SQL and Relational Theory: How to Write Accurate SQL Code* (3rd edition, O'Reilly, 2015) for a detailed discussion of this important notion.

c. Presumably valid; MONEY (I'm assuming that multiplying a money value by an integer returns another money value). d. Not valid; BUDGET + MONEY(50000). e. Not valid; ENO > ENO('E2'). f. Not valid; NAME(THE_NC(ENAME) || THE_NC(DNAME)) (recall from the body of the chapter that type NAME has a possrep with a single component, called NC, of type CHAR). g. Not valid; CITY(THE_CC(LOCATION) || 'burg') (I'm assuming here that type CITY has a possrep with a single component, called CC, of type CHAR).

2.21 Such an operation logically means replacing one type by another, not "updating a type" (types aren't variables and hence can't be updated, by definition). The following observations are pertinent. First, as pointed out in the body of the chapter, the operation of defining a type doesn't actually create the corresponding set of values; all the "define type" operation—the TYPE statement, in **Tutorial D**—really does is introduce a name by which that set of values can be referenced. Likewise, the DROP TYPE statement doesn't actually drop the corresponding values, it merely drops the name that was introduced by the corresponding TYPE statement. It follows that "updating an existing type" really means dropping the existing type name as such and then redefining that same name to refer to a different set of values. Of course, there's nothing to preclude the use of some kind of "alter type" shorthand to simplify such an operation (as SQL does, in fact, at least in connection with what it calls "structured types"—see Chapter 22).

2.22 The complete syntax for a relation selector invocation in **Tutorial D** is as follows—

```
RELATION [ <heading> ] <body>
```

—where (a) the syntax for *<heading>* is as explained in the body of the chapter, and (b) a *<body>* in turn consists of a *<tuple exp commalist>* enclosed in braces, such that the tuple expressions in question all denote tuples with that specified *<heading>*. Moreover, there's a syntax rule to the effect that the *<heading>* must be specified if the *<tuple exp commalist>* is empty (it can be omitted otherwise, as indeed it was in all of the examples I've shown so far). By way of example, therefore, the empty suppliers relation can be specified as follows:

```
RELATION { SNO SNO , SNAME NAME , STATUS INTEGER , CITY CHAR } { }
```

As an aside, I note that TABLE_DUM and TABLE_DEE—see the answer to Exercise 2.24—can be thought of as shorthand for the relation selector invocations RELATION { } { } and RELATION { } { TUPLE { } }, respectively. They can also be thought of as named relation constants.

2.23 The empty scalar type is certainly a valid type; however, it wouldn't make much sense to define a variable to be of such a type, because no value could ever be assigned to it! Despite this fact, the empty scalar type—there's exactly one such, and we call it *omega*—turns out to be critically important in connection with our inheritance model. See Part II of this book (Chapter 12 in particular) for further discussion.

2.24 Yes! There's exactly one tuple with an empty heading, and we call it the empty tuple or 0-tuple. In **Tutorial D**, we write it thus: TUPLE { }. Its type is also written TUPLE { }.
    As for relations, there are exactly two relations with an empty heading; one has an empty body as well, and we call it TABLE_DUM (DUM for short); the other has a body containing exactly one tuple (viz., the empty tuple), and we call it TABLE_DEE (DEE for short). For further discussion, I refer you to my book *SQL and Relational Theory: How to Write Accurate SQL Code* (3rd edition, O'Reilly, 2015).
    Note: If a relvar (as opposed to a relation) has an empty heading, then it must have just one key, and that key must be empty too. However, a relvar doesn't have to have an empty heading to have an empty key; in fact, a relvar will have an empty key if and only if it's constrained never to contain more than just one tuple (though it's true that the empty key will certainly be the *only* key for such a relvar). For further discussion of such matters, again I refer you to my book *SQL and Relational Theory: How to Write Accurate SQL Code* (3rd edition, O'Reilly, 2015).

2.25 Technically speaking, yes, it does (at least in **Tutorial D**), because if an element appears more than once in a commalist denoting a set, as in the case at hand, then it's treated as if it appeared just once. Please note, however, that I'll never exploit this fact in this book. Thus, if I show (e.g.) a heading looking like this—

   { *A1 T1* , *A2 T2* , ..., *An Tn* }

—you can assume that the *Ai*'s (*i* = 1, 2, ..., *n*) are all distinct.

2.26 It would mean that *T* has at most one value—in fact, exactly one value, since there are no user defined empty scalar types. That value would be denoted by the only legal invocation of the corresponding selector, viz., *PR* ( )—which is in fact a literal, and indeed the only legal literal, corresponding to possrep *PR*.

2.27 No! (Which database does type INTEGER belong to?) In an important sense, the whole subject of types and type management is orthogonal to the subject of databases and database management. We might even imagine the need for a "type administrator," whose job it would be to look after types in a manner analogous to that in which the database administrator looks after databases.

Chapter 3

Types with Inheritance

Ruinous inheritance

—Gaius:
The Institutes (c. 175 CE)

This chapter provides a preliminary overview of some of the basic ideas of our inheritance model, in order to pave the way for a much more complete treatment of the material in subsequent chapters. It's based in part on Chapter 12 of the Manifesto book (i.e., Databases, Types, and the Relational Model: The Third Manifesto, *by Hugh Darwen and myself, 3rd edition, Addison-Wesley, 2007).*

As noted in Chapter 1, there's no consensus in the community at large on a formal, rigorous, and abstract type inheritance model. In our work on *The Third Manifesto*, therefore, Darwen and I were more or less forced to develop an inheritance model of our own—and of course it's that model that's the principal subject of the present book. Moreover, we were, and still are, very serious about our work in connection with that model. As we wrote in the *Manifesto* book:

> We would like this effort on our part *not* to be seen as just an academic exercise. Rather, we would like our proposal to be considered by the community at large as a serious contender for filling the gap alluded to above (i.e., as a candidate for the role that *is* "formal, rigorous, and abstract" and can be generally agreed upon by that "community at large"). We offer it here in that spirit.

As I said in Chapter 1, these remarks remain just as applicable today as they were when we first wrote them.

WHY INHERITANCE?

Why is this topic worth investigating in the first place? There seem to be at least two answers to this question:

- First, the ideas of subtyping and inheritance do seem to arise naturally in the real world. That is, it's not at all unusual to encounter situations in which all values of a given type have certain properties in common, more or less by definition, while some of those values have certain additional properties of their own. For example, all ellipses have an area, while some ellipses—namely, those that happen to be circles—have a radius as well. Thus, we might say that type ELLIPSE has a *subtype* CIRCLE; further, we might say that type CIRCLE *inherits* the property of having an area from its *supertype* ELLIPSE, but that circles also have certain properties of their own that ellipses in general don't have, such as a radius. Thus, subtyping and inheritance do look as if they might be useful tools for "modeling reality."

■ Second, if we can recognize such general patterns—patterns of subtyping and inheritance, that is—and build intelligence regarding them into our application and system software, we might be able to achieve certain practical economies. For example, a program that works for ellipses might work for circles too, even if it was originally written with no thought for circles at all (perhaps type CIRCLE hadn't even been defined at the time the program in question was written).

That said, I should say too that most of the existing literature seems more concerned—I'm tempted to say, *much* more concerned—with the second of these goals than it is with the first; in other words, it seems to be principally interested in inheritance as a mechanism for designing, building, and (re)using *programs*. Our own focus, by contrast, is more on the first than the second; that is, we're interested in inheritance as a conceptual tool for designing, building, and (re)using *data structures*.[1] In other words, what we're looking for is an inheritance model that can be used to "model reality"—certain aspects of reality, at any rate—much as the relational model itself can also be used to model certain aspects of reality. To put it yet another way, we're concerned (as always) with the possibility of constructing an abstract model, not so much with matters of implementation. That said, however, please note that the discussions and explanations that follow, both here and in later chapters, do sometimes touch on implementation matters, if only for purposes of clarification.

Before going any further, I should warn you that this whole topic is considerably more complex than you might expect. The trouble is, although "the basic idea of inheritance is simple,"[2] the devil is in the detail—you have to study the topic in its entirety (and, I might add, extremely closely and carefully) in order to come properly to grips with it: in particular, to appreciate the fact that it's not at all as straightforward as it might seem at first sight. All of which perhaps helps to justify the possibly rather surprising length of this book, and in particular to explain why this overview chapter is needed.

There's another point I need to warn you of, too. The fact is, there isn't even consensus in the literature on the meanings of such basic terms as *subtype* and *inheritance*, let alone on an entire inheritance model. In fact, it has been suggested that there are many different kinds of

---

[1] Reasonably enough, I think, since we're "database people" and therefore took the relational model as the starting point for our investigations. By contrast, it's probably fair to say that most of the existing inheritance literature approaches the problem much more from a software engineering or application development perspective.

[2] The quote is from "On the Notion of Inheritance," by Antero Taivalsaari (*ACM Comp. Surv. 28*, No. 3, September 1996).

inheritance, and hence many sets of concepts and many definitions of terms, that are all distinct from one another and yet overlap in a variety of ways. For example:

■ From "The Object-Oriented Database System Manifesto," by Malcolm Atkinson, François Bancilhon, David DeWitt, Klaus Dittrich, David Maier, and Stanley Zdonik, Proc. 1st International Conference on Deductive and Object-Oriented Databases (Kyoto, Japan, 1989, published by Elsevier Science, 1990):

[There] are at least four types of inheritance: *substitution* inheritance, *inclusion* inheritance, *constraint* inheritance, and *specialization* inheritance ... Various degrees of these four types of inheritance are provided by existing systems and prototypes, and we do not prescribe a specific style of inheritance.[3]

■ From *An Introduction to Data Types*, by J. Craig Cleaveland (Addison-Wesley, 1986):

[Inheritance can be] based on [a variety of] different criteria and there is no commonly accepted standard definition.

The book then goes on to give eight possible interpretations. (Bertrand Meyer, in "The Many Faces of Inheritance: A Taxonomy of Taxonomy," *IEEE Computer 29*, No. 5, May 1996, gives twelve.)

■ From technical correspondence by Kenneth Baclawski and Bipin Indurkhya in *CACM 37*, No. 9, September 1994:

[A language merely] provides a set of [inheritance] mechanisms. While these mechanisms certainly restrict what one can do in that language and what views of inheritance can be implemented [in that language], they do not by themselves validate some view of inheritance or other. [Types,] specializations, generalizations, and inheritance are only concepts, and ... they do not have a universal objective meaning ... This [state of affairs] implies that how inheritance is to be incorporated into a specific system is up to the designers of [that] system, and it constitutes a policy decision that must be implemented with the available mechanisms.

And so on. Taken together, I think such quotes go a long way toward justifying my claim that there really is no consensus on any kind of inheritance model as such.[4] *Caveat lector.*

As I've said, therefore, Darwen and I were more or less forced to introduce our own definitions—and while we naturally did our best to do so in a manner that made sense to us, you

---

[3] Incidentally, I think it can be argued (and I think it's worth noting, too) that our own model supports all four of the various kinds of inheritance mentioned in this quote.

[4] In this connection, one of my reviewers drew my attention to two further papers, the first titled "Inheritance Is Not Subtyping" and the second "Inheritance *Is* Subtyping" (*https://www.researchgate.net/publication/220997250/Inheritance_Is_Not_Subtyping* and *https://www.cs.rice.edu/~javaplt/papers/Inheritance.pdf*, respectively). The titles say it all.

need to be aware that different definitions can be found in the literature. We defend our definitions—and our entire model, come to that—on the grounds that (among other things, and indeed as noted in Chapter 1) they're mostly just a logical consequence of our type theory as described in Chapter 2. In other words, we think it would be inconsistent to agree with the *Manifesto*'s approach to types in general but not to agree with our inheritance model in particular. But you must be the judge of this claim, of course.

  One last introductory point: The subject of type inheritance has a lot to do with data in general, of course, but I don't think there's anything about it that has to do with persistent or database data only. For simplicity, therefore, most though not all of the examples in this chapter (and indeed in the rest of this book) are formulated, not in terms of database data in particular, but rather just in terms of data in general.

TOWARD A MODEL OF INHERITANCE

As noted in the previous section, the term *type inheritance* (inheritance for short) refers to that phenomenon according to which we can sensibly say, for example, that every circle is an ellipse,[5] and hence that all properties that apply to ellipses in general apply to—i.e., *are inherited by*—circles in particular. For example, every ellipse has an area, and therefore every circle has an area also. More precisely, we can say that:

  a. Types ELLIPSE and CIRCLE are such that ELLIPSE is a supertype of CIRCLE and CIRCLE is a subtype of ELLIPSE.

  b. There's an operator—AREA_OF, say—that returns the area of a given ellipse, and that operator can be invoked with an argument of type CIRCLE, because circles are ellipses.

  Of course, the converse is false—the subtype will have properties of its own that don't apply to the supertype. For example, circles have a radius, but ellipses in general don't; in other words, there's an operator that returns the radius of a given circle, but that operator can't be invoked with an argument that's "just an ellipse," because such ellipses aren't circles.

  So operators are inherited. (*Note:* By *operators* here, I really mean read-only operators specifically, as I'll explain in the section "Scalars, Tuples, and Relations," later.) But constraints are properties too, of a kind, and are therefore inherited too—where by the term *constraints*, unqualified, I mean type constraints specifically (see Chapter 2), a convention I'll adhere to throughout this book unless the context demands otherwise. Thus, e.g., any constraint that applies to ellipses in general also applies, necessarily, to circles in particular (for if it didn't, then some circles wouldn't be ellipses). For example, if ellipses are subject to the constraint that the

---

[5] I need to add immediately that some people would dispute even this apparent truism, as we'll see in Chapter 13. Nothing can be taken for granted! Thus, many remarks presented here or in subsequent chapters as statements of fact must be understood as carrying with them some kind of silent qualification along the lines of "at least in our model."

length *a* of their major semiaxis is greater than or equal to the length *b* of their minor semiaxis, then this same constraint must be satisfied by circles also. (For circles, of course, the semiaxes coincide in the radius, and this particular constraint is satisfied trivially.) Once again, however, the converse is false—there'll be constraints that apply to circles but not to ellipses in general. In fact, the specific constraint just mentioned, to the effect that $a = b$, is an example of one that applies to circles in particular but not to ellipses in general.

> *Aside:* A point arises here that beginners sometimes find a little confusing: namely, that a subtype has a subset of the values but a superset of the properties ("properties" here meaning, to repeat, operators and constraints). For example, the subtype CIRCLE contains a subset of the values of the supertype ELLIPSE, but an individual circle has all of the properties of an ellipse and more besides. For exactly such reasons, in fact, some writers prefer to avoid the "sub and super" terminology and talk of *descendants* and *ancestors* instead.[6] We think this latter nomenclature has problems of its own, however, and prefer to stay with the "sub and super" terminology. *End of aside*.

A Note on Possible Representations

In the section "The Running Example" later in this chapter, I'm going to declare a possible representation (or possrep) for type ELLIPSE as consisting of the combination of the major semiaxis length *a*, the minor semiaxis length *b*, and the center point *ctr*. Now, I hope it's obvious that this same possrep would at least be adequate for type CIRCLE as well because, as I keep saying, circles are ellipses. By definition, in fact, every possrep for ellipses is necessarily, albeit implicitly, a possrep for circles as well. (Of course, the converse is false—a possrep for circles isn't necessarily a possrep for ellipses.) Thus, possreps might be thought of as further "properties" that are inherited by subtypes from supertypes. As far as our model is concerned, however, we don't regard such inherited possreps as *explicitly declared* ones.[7] Thus, to say that type CIRCLE inherits a possrep from type ELLIPSE is only a manner of speaking—it doesn't carry any formal weight. Accordingly, from this point forward I'll take the unqualified term *possible representation*, or the abbreviated form *possrep*, to mean an explicitly declared possrep specifically, not an implicitly inherited one, unless the context demands otherwise.

---

[6] See, for example, Ivar Jacobson (with Magnus Christerson, Patrik Jonsson, and Gunnar Övergaard): *Object-Oriented Software Engineering* (revised printing, Addison-Wesley, 1994).

[7] Here's why, in outline: If we were to regard such an inherited possrep as an explicitly declared one, we would run into a contradiction concerning inheritance of update operators (inheritance of THE_ pseudovariables, to be specific). This point is explained in detail in Chapter 11. See also Exercise 3.9 at the end of the chapter.

Values vs. Variables Again

It's important in the inheritance context—as in all others!—to distinguish very carefully between values and variables. When I say that, e.g., every circle is an ellipse, what I mean, more precisely, is that every circle *value* is an ellipse *value*. I certainly don't mean that every circle *variable* is an ellipse *variable*—i.e., that a variable of declared type CIRCLE is a variable of declared type ELLIPSE, and hence can contain a value that's an ellipse and not a circle.[8] In other words, and speaking somewhat loosely once again, *inheritance applies to values, not variables* (though naturally there are implications for variables too, as we'll see). Indeed, we conjecture that much of the confusion we observe in this field—and there's a lot of it—is due precisely to a failure to distinguish properly between values and variables.

SINGLE vs. MULTIPLE INHERITANCE

As I'm sure you know, there are two broad "flavors" of type inheritance, single and multiple. Loosely speaking, single inheritance means each subtype has just one supertype and inherits properties from just that one supertype, while multiple inheritance means a subtype can have any number of supertypes and inherits properties from all of them. Obviously the former (single) is a special case of the latter (multiple).

Now, we do believe that support for multiple inheritance is desirable; in fact, we believe that if inheritance is supported at all, it has to be multiple. Despite this fact, our strategy when we first began to investigate this topic was (a) to construct a sound model of single inheritance first, and then (b) to extend that model to incorporate multiple inheritance subsequently. Our reason for adopting this perhaps rather cautious approach was that even single inheritance raises numerous tricky questions; thus, it seemed reasonable to us to try to find good answers to those questions first, before having to concern ourselves too much with the additional complexities that multiple inheritance might bring in its wake. Of course, we did try not to build anything into our single inheritance model that might preclude later extension to deal with the multiple inheritance case, and it's a measure of our cautious optimism regarding our model overall that the single inheritance version does seem to extend gracefully to cover this latter case.

Be that as it may, the structure of Parts II and III of the book reflects this history:

■ Part II discusses and illustrates a series of detailed prescriptions ("IM prescriptions") that together constitute a basis for the kind of robust inheritance model we seek, at least for the case of single inheritance only.[9]

---

[8] The converse is true, though (i.e., a variable of declared type ELLIPSE can certainly contain a value that's a circle).

[9] The *Manifesto* model of inheritance and the *Manifesto* as such both involve a set of prescriptions. In an attempt to avoid confusion, therefore, throughout this book I'll refer to prescriptions of our inheritance model as such as "IM prescriptions" and prescriptions of *The Third Manifesto* as such as "*TTM* prescriptions."

■ Part III then goes on to extend the model discussed in Part II to incorporate support for multiple inheritance as well.

SCALARS, TUPLES, AND RELATIONS

I said earlier that inheritance applies to values, not variables. At that point, however, I was making a tacit assumption that "values" meant scalar values specifically. (Of course, scalar values can have an arbitrarily complex physical, or internal, structure—see Chapter 2—but that physical structure is part of the implementation, not the model, and it's hidden from the user.) But inheritance clearly has implications for nonscalar values as well—for tuple and relation values in particular—since, ultimately, such nonscalar values are built out of scalar values. However, we obviously can't even begin to talk sensibly about those implications until we've pinned down what subtyping and inheritance mean for scalar values specifically.

Please note carefully, therefore, that throughout Parts II and III of this book (i.e., Chapters 5-13) I take the unqualified term *value* to mean a scalar value specifically. By the same token, throughout the discussions in those chapters I take the unqualified terms *type, subtype,* and *supertype* to mean scalar types, subtypes, and supertypes specifically, and I take the unqualified terms *variable, operator, expression,* and *result* to mean scalar variables, operators, expressions, and results specifically.[10] Note, however, that formal statements in those chapters—in particular, the IM prescriptions themselves—are worded, most of the time, in such a way as to allow, e.g., the term *value* to be taken to mean a scalar value or a tuple value or a relation value, as the context demands. They're also worded in such a way as to apply to multiple inheritance as well as single, barring explicit statements to the contrary.

Now, scalar values by definition have no user visible structure. So when I talk, in the context of our model, of such values inheriting "properties," I don't mean inheritance of structure, because as far as the model is concerned there *is* no structure to inherit. Rather, as noted earlier, I mean inheritance of constraints and operators.[11] For the moment, however, I want to ignore the constraints and focus on the operators, partly because the literature does so too (in fact, it typically ignores constraints altogether). *More terminology:* Inheritance of operators is often referred to in the literature as *behavioral* inheritance, mainly because:

    a. The literature in question is, typically, the object literature—most reported investigations into inheritance do seem to assume an object context—and

---

[10] By *operators* here, I mean read-only operators, of course, since update operators don't have any type at all.

[11] Following on from footnote 10, you can take *inheritance of operators* here to refer to read-only operators specifically, thanks to the fact that inheritance applies to values, not variables—but there are implications for update operators too, to be discussed in detail in Chapter 11.

b. Objects in the object literature are often said, rather anthropomorphically, to display "behavior." For example, to quote *Object-Oriented Methods: A Foundation*, by James Martin and James J. Odell (Prentice-Hall, 1998):[12] "[Behavior is a] metaphor referring to the way objects are accessed or are changed over time."

And the literature then typically goes on to contrast behavioral inheritance with *structural* inheritance. This latter term refers to inheritance of physical representations;[13] as such, it's properly an implementation matter, not part of the model. Of course, we certainly don't preclude such inheritance; to repeat, however, if it's supported at all, then it's a matter of concern to the implementation only, and it has, or should have, no effect on the model. Unfortunately, much of the literature, especially the object literature, does tend to assume that inheritance means—or at least includes—inheritance of physical representations; it further tends to assume that some operators, at least, depend on those physical representations. I regard this state of affairs simply as evidence of confusion over the logical difference between model and implementation, and choose not to discuss it further in the present chapter.

Turning now to tuple and relation types: As noted earlier, the notions of scalar subtyping and inheritance do have implications for tuples and relations, because tuples and relations are ultimately constructed out of scalar components. For example, a relation with an attribute of type ELLIPSE might include some tuples in which the value corresponding to that attribute is specifically a circle and not "just an ellipse." Part IV of the book considers the question of extending our inheritance model for scalar types—for both single and multiple inheritance, as discussed in Parts II and III—to take tuple and relation types into account as well.

THE RUNNING EXAMPLE

I now introduce a running example that I'll be using as a basis for examples and discussions in much of the rest of the book (especially Part II). The example is based on a collection of geometric types—PLANE_FIGURE, ELLIPSE, POLYGON, and so on (see Fig. 3.1). *Note:* I assume for simplicity, here and throughout this book, that the only plane figures we're interested in are either ellipses or polygons; thus, every value of type PLANE_FIGURE is either a value of type ELLIPSE or a value of type POLYGON (and never both, of course).

---

[12] The term *method* is basically just an object term for operator. By the way, note the reference in the extract quoted to objects "changing over time." In other words, (a) the term *objects* in that quote is clearly meant to include variables and (b) the corresponding operators are clearly meant to include update operators (if the quote really means what it says, that is; to me, however, it just looks like a typical confusion).

[13] Some might dispute this claim (see the brief explanation of "the EXTENDS relationship" in the section "Concluding Remarks" at the end of this chapter). I stand by it, however, so long as the types under discussion are scalar types specifically. The true state of affairs is too complicated to deal with adequately here, but part of the problem is precisely that the literature doesn't always distinguish properly between scalar and nonscalar types. Chapter 21 discusses the situation in depth.

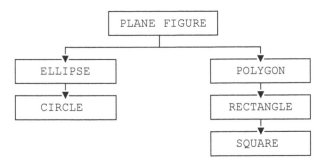

Fig. 3.1: Example of a type hierarchy

Each of the types in the figure is a named set of values; for example, there's a set of values named ELLIPSE, and every value in that set is some specific ellipse.[14] The various types are arranged into what's called a *type hierarchy*, with type PLANE_FIGURE serving as the *root* of that hierarchy and types CIRCLE and SQUARE as the *leaves*. *Note:* Type hierarchies as such will certainly be inadequate when we get to multiple inheritance, when they'll have to be replaced by more general type *graphs*. However, they're sufficient for present purposes.

Aside: Please note that my choice of a slightly academic example is deliberate. While it might be objected that geometric figures aren't the kind of thing we usually expect to have to deal with in a typical database or typical application, in fact there are several advantages to such an example, the main one being that the semantics of the various types involved are (or should be) crystal clear to everyone. We can therefore avoid the kind of unproductive debate that tends to arise when "fuzzier" examples are chosen. For instance, suppose I had chosen an example involving a type BOOK. OK: So what's a book? Is it a single bound volume, or is it all copies of "the same" book produced in a single print run? Or in consecutive print runs? What about ebooks? What about different editions of "the same" book? What about translations? Is a journal a book? Is a magazine? Etc., etc., etc. *End of aside.*

Back to Fig. 3.1. Now, the type hierarchy in that figure is meant to be self-explanatory, more or less; it shows, for example, that type RECTANGLE is a subtype of supertype POLYGON, which means that all rectangles are polygons but some polygons aren't rectangles. As a consequence, all properties that apply to polygons in general apply to—i.e., are inherited by—rectangles in particular, but rectangles have properties of their own that don't apply to polygons in general.

---

[14] More precisely, it's an ellipse at some specific location in two-dimensional space. In other words, ellipses that occupy different locations in space but are otherwise identical are assumed for the sake of the example to be distinct (and similarly for circles, rectangles, etc.).

Of course, the running example deliberately involves scalar types only and single inheritance only. As I've said, our model does include support for both nonscalar types and multiple inheritance, but scalar types and single inheritance are what Part II of the book is all about. Scalar types and single inheritance also suffice to illustrate most of the points I need to make in the remainder of the present chapter. However, if I do need to say something that (a) applies to scalar and not nonscalar types (or the other way around), or (b) applies to single and not multiple inheritance (or the other way around), then I'll do my best to make it clear that such is indeed the case.

I turn now to **Tutorial D**. **Tutorial D** as originally defined didn't include any support for inheritance at all; however, you'll recall from Chapter 1 that Darwen and I have proposed a set of extensions to the language to take care of that omission, and of course I assume for the purposes of the present book that those extensions have been accepted and incorporated into the language. For example, we obviously need a way of telling the system which types are subtypes of which other types (in other words, we need a way of defining type hierarchies). With that aim in mind:

■ The syntactic category *<scalar type def>*—see the grammar in Chapter 2—is extended to cover both root and nonroot types. For a root type, the *<scalar type def>* contains a *<possrep def list>* and (usually) a *<possrep constraint def>*, more or less as explained in Chapter 2 (note that all scalar types are root types, absent inheritance support).[15] See the section "A BNF Grammar" for further explanation.

■ For a nonroot type, by contrast, the *<scalar type def>* contains an *<is def>* ("IS definition"), the detailed content of which depends on whether the nonroot type in question has a regular type or a dummy type as immediate supertype (again, see the section "A BNF Grammar" for further explanation). Here by way of example are *<scalar type def>*s for the nonroot types ELLIPSE and CIRCLE:

```
TYPE ELLIPSE
     IS { PLANE_FIGURE
          POSSREP ( A LENGTH , B LENGTH , CTR POINT )
          CONSTRAINT A ≥ B } ;

TYPE CIRCLE
     IS { ELLIPSE
          CONSTRAINT THE_A ( ELLIPSE ) = THE_B ( ELLIPSE )
          POSSREP ( R   = THE_A   ( ELLIPSE ) ,
                    CTR = THE_CTR ( ELLIPSE ) ) ;
```

Now the system knows that (a) ELLIPSE is a subtype of PLANE_FIGURE (loosely, every ellipse "is a" plane figure), and hence that (b) operators and constraints that apply to plane figures in general apply to ellipses in particular. It also knows that (a) CIRCLE is a

---

[15] Of course, they're all leaf types, too.

subtype of ELLIPSE (loosely, every circle "is a" ellipse), and hence that (b) operators and constraints that apply to ellipses in general apply to circles in particular.

Let's take a closer look at these definitions. First of all, I assume throughout this book that ellipses are always oriented such that their major axis is horizontal and their minor axis vertical (in other words, they're always "short and fat," not "tall and thin"). Thus, they might indeed have a possrep consisting of their semiaxis lengths a and b and their center. By contrast, circles might have a possrep consisting just of their radius r and their center. Observe now that:

- For type ELLIPSE, I've specified the (a,b,ctr) possrep in the usual way, together with a constraint to the effect that $a \geq b$. *Note:* I'm assuming for the sake of the example that types LENGTH and POINT have already been defined. Also, to keep the example simple, I've omitted the constraint $b > 0$ that ought by rights to be specified as well (and I'll continue to omit this latter constraint throughout the rest of this book).

- For type CIRCLE, by contrast, I've specified that every circle "is a" ellipse—in fact, an ellipse satisfying the constraint $a = b$. Along with that constraint, I've specified how the (r,ctr) possrep for circles is derived from the (a,b,ctr) possrep for ellipses. Note the use of the supertype name ELLIPSE, in both the constraint and the definition of the derived possrep, to denote an arbitrary value of the supertype in question (i.e., an arbitrary ellipse).

Let me also draw your attention to the difference in syntax between the two constraint specifications in this example (once again, see the section "A BNF Grammar" for further explanation):[16]

- For type ELLIPSE, the constraint $a \geq b$ is specified via what in Chapter 2 I called a *<possrep constraint def>*. That *<possrep constraint def>* immediately follows the *<possrep def list>* for the type, and it's formulated directly in terms of the possreps—actually the sole possrep, in the case at hand—for that type ELLIPSE itself.

- For type CIRCLE, by contrast, the constraint $a = b$ is specified via what's called an *<additional constraint def>* (part of the *<is def>*). That *<additional constraint def>* immediately precedes what's called a *<derived possrep list>*, and it's formulated in terms of a possrep, not for type CIRCLE as such, but rather for an immediate supertype (viz., type ELLIPSE) of that type.

There are a couple more things I need to say regarding possreps. Let type T' be a subtype of type T. Then:

---

[16] The difference derives from the fact that PLANE_FIGURE is a dummy type (see Chapter 12).

■ It'll often be the case in practice, just as it is in the example of circles and ellipses, that *T'* has a possrep—an explicitly declared and derived possrep, that is, not just an "inherited" one—that's similar (possibly identical) to some possrep for *T*. This fact suggests that it might be convenient in practice to have some syntactic shorthand for declaring a possrep for *T'*, perhaps along the lines of "same as possrep *PR* for *T* but subtracting component(s) *A*, *B*, ..., *C* and adding component(s) *X*, *Y*, ..., *Z*." However, the issue is a purely syntactic one, secondary to my main purpose of describing our abstract model, and I don't propose to discuss it any further here.

■ At the same time, it's certainly possible for *T* and *T'* to have possreps that differ quite markedly from each other. For example, let *T* and *T'* be PENTAGON and REGULAR_PENTAGON, respectively. Then *T* might have a possrep consisting of five points (the five vertices), while *T'* has one consisting of just two points (the center and one vertex). However, it's always the case—in fact, it must always be the case—that every possrep (declared or otherwise) for the subtype *T'* is expressible in terms of, and is thus derivable from, each of the possreps (declared or otherwise) for the supertype *T*.

Finally, observe that—precisely because I haven't specified any explicit possrep names in the example—the sole selector for type ELLIPSE is called ELLIPSE and the sole selector for type CIRCLE is called CIRCLE.[17]

A Note on Physical Representations

Although we're primarily concerned in this book with an inheritance model and not with implementation issues, there are as noted earlier certain aspects of implementation that do need to be appreciated if the overall concept of inheritance is to be properly understood, and now we come to one such (and this one will turn out to be important at several points in later chapters):

> *The fact that T' is a proper subtype of T does not imply that the physical representation of T' values is the same as that of T values (it might be or it might not).*

For example, ellipses and circles might be *physically* represented by their center and semiaxis lengths and their center and radius, respectively (although as we know from Chapter 2 there's no logical reason, in general, why a physical representation needs to be the same as any declared possrep). In fact we already know, also from Chapter 2, that there's also no logical reason why distinct appearances of values of the same type—or even distinct appearances of the same value—need have the same physical representation. For example, some points might be physically represented in cartesian coordinates and some in polar; some temperatures might be

---

[17] By the phrase "selector for type *T*," of course, I mean a selector whose declared or target type is *T*.

physically represented in degrees Celsius and some in Fahrenheit; some integers might be physically represented in decimal and some in binary; and so on.

MORE TERMINOLOGY

I now introduce a number of further terms and concepts, most of them fairly self-explanatory (in any case, they'll all be amplified in later chapters):

- A subtype of a subtype of T is a subtype of T (e.g., SQUARE is a subtype of POLYGON).

- Every type is a subtype of itself (e.g., ELLIPSE is a subtype of ELLIPSE).

- If T' is a subtype of T and T' and T are distinct, then T' is a *proper* subtype of T (e.g., SQUARE is a proper subtype of POLYGON).

Analogous remarks apply to supertypes, of course. Thus:

- A supertype of a supertype of T is a supertype of T (e.g., POLYGON is a supertype of SQUARE).

- Every type is a supertype of itself (e.g., ELLIPSE is a supertype of ELLIPSE).

- If T is a supertype of T' and T and T' are distinct, then T is a *proper* supertype of T' (e.g., POLYGON is a proper supertype of SQUARE).

Moreover:

- If T' is a proper subtype of T and there's no type that's both a proper supertype of T' and a proper subtype of T, then T' is an *immediate* subtype of T and T is an *immediate* supertype of T' (e.g., SQUARE is an immediate subtype of RECTANGLE, and RECTANGLE is an immediate supertype of SQUARE).

- As I've more or less already said, a *root* type is a type with no proper supertype (e.g., PLANE_FIGURE is a root type), and a *leaf* type is a type with no proper subtype (e.g., SQUARE is a leaf type).[18] Of course, a given type can be said to be a root or leaf type only in the context of some specific type hierarchy (or specific type graph). For example, if we were to remove type SQUARE from the hierarchy of Fig. 3.1, then type RECTANGLE

---

[18] More correctly, a scalar root type has no proper supertype except *alpha* and a scalar leaf type has no proper subtype except *omega* (see the discussion of IM Prescription 6 in Chapter 5).

would be a leaf type in the hierarchy that results. Informally, however, we usually take the context as understood.

By the way, I can now give a precise characterization of single inheritance: Single inheritance means, precisely, that *every proper subtype has exactly one immediate supertype.*

The Disjointness Assumption

It's convenient, at least for tutorial purposes, to adopt the following simplifying assumption:

> **Definition** (*the disjointness assumption*): If and only if types *T1* and *T2* are such that neither is a subtype of the other, then they're disjoint—i.e., no value is of both type *T1* and type *T2*.

Now, this assumption certainly holds so long as we limit our attention to single inheritance only; for example, no value is both an ellipse and a rectangle. It won't hold any longer when we get to multiple inheritance. As already noted, however, the emphasis in this book until further notice is on single inheritance only, and so we can take it as holding for the time being. Here are some immediate consequences of adopting the assumption:

■ Distinct root types are disjoint, and hence distinct type hierarchies are disjoint also (i.e., no value is of two distinct types *T1* and *T2* such that *T1* and *T2* belong to two distinct type hierarchies).

■ Distinct subtypes of the same supertype are disjoint unless one's a subtype of the other. In particular, distinct leaf types are disjoint.

■ (*Important!*) Every value has exactly one *most specific* type. For example, a given value might be "just an ellipse" and not a circle, meaning its most specific type is ELLIPSE (in the real world, some ellipses aren't circles).

■ In fact, following on from the previous point, if value *v* is of most specific type *T*, then the set of types possessed by *v* is, precisely, the set consisting of all supertypes of *T* (a set which has *T* itself as a member, of course). In other words, *v* is of every type that's a supertype of *T* and is of no other type.

Finally, I said the disjointness assumption applies to single inheritance only. As we'll see in Part III of this book, however, there are situations, even with multiple inheritance, in which certain types are required to be (or are at least assumed to be) disjoint. Unfortunately, it's always possible that the type designer could make a mistake and define types that are supposed to be disjoint but aren't. For example, the designer might define types RECTANGLE and

RHOMBUS both as proper subtypes of type PARALLELOGRAM, and forget that some parallelograms are both a rectangle and a rhombus.[19] Neither of RECTANGLE and RHOMBUS is a subtype of the other, of course, and so the disjointness assumption will say they're disjoint. The consequences of such a violation of the prescriptions of the model will be unpredictable, in general. Although this fact need not concern us from the point of view of the model—a violation is simply a violation, and there's no need *within the model* to spell out what the consequences might be—in practice I would hope that some kind of mechanical aid would be available to help the designer avoid such errors.

Type Hierarchy Defined

Although I've mentioned them several times, it's important to understand that type hierarchies aren't part of our inheritance model as such[20]—they're merely an intuitively convenient way of depicting certain subtype / supertype relationships, which are. (In fact, type hierarchies play a role in our inheritance model analogous to that played by tables in the relational model: Tables aren't part of the relational model as such, they're merely an intuitively convenient way of depicting relations, which are.) For the record, however, here's a more precise definition:

> **Definition:** A *type hierarchy* is a directed acyclic graph (*TH*, say), consisting of a finite set *N* of nodes and a finite set *D* of directed arcs that together satisfy the following properties:
>
> 1.   *TH* is empty if and only if *N* is empty (in which case *D* is necessarily empty too, thanks to point 4 below).
>
> 2.   Each node is given the name of a type.
>
> 3.   No two nodes have the same name. Also, no node is named either *alpha* or *omega*; by convention, the types with these names (which are primarily conceptual in nature anyway—see Chapter 12) aren't represented in the graph at all.
>
> 4.   Each arc connects exactly two distinct nodes and represents a directed path from one of those two nodes (the *parent*) to the other (the *child*). There's an arc from parent *T* to child *T'* if and only if type *T* is an immediate supertype of type *T'*.
>
> 5.   Each parent is connected to one or more children. Each child is connected to exactly one parent.

---

[19] In case your memory needs jogging, a rhombus is a parallelogram whose sides are all the same length, and a parallelogram that's both a rectangle and a rhombus is in fact a square. I'll be discussing this example in detail in Part III of this book.

[20] A good thing, you might think, since as you'll see their formal definition is a little complicated.

6. Node *T* is an *ancestor* of node *T′* if and only if it's the parent of node *T′* or the parent of an ancestor of node *T′* (i.e., if and only if type *T* is a proper supertype of type *T′*). Node *T′* is a *descendant* of node *T* if and only if node *T* is an ancestor of node *T′*.

7. Node *T* is a *root* node if and only if it's connected to no parent (i.e., if and only if type *T* is a root type). *Note:* If *TH* is nonempty, it has exactly one root node, otherwise it has no root node at all.

8. Node *T* is a *leaf* node if and only if it's connected to no children (i.e., if and only if type *T* is a leaf type).

Note: Type hierarchies are known in the literature by a variety of different names, the following among them:

- Class hierarchies (on the grounds that types are sometimes called classes, especially in the object world)

- Generalization hierarchies (on the grounds that, e.g., an ellipse is a generalization of a circle)

- Specialization hierarchies (on the grounds that, e.g., a circle is a specialization of an ellipse)

- Inheritance hierarchies (on the grounds that, e.g., circles inherit properties from ellipses)

- "IS A" hierarchies (on the grounds that, e.g., every circle "is a" ellipse)

And so on (this isn't an exhaustive list).

SUBSTITUTABILITY

By definition, if *T′* is a subtype of *T*, then all of the operators that apply to values of type *T* apply to values of type *T′* too. For example, if AREA_OF (*e*) is valid, where *e* is an ellipse, then AREA_OF (*c*), where *c* is a circle, must be valid too. In other words, wherever the system expects a value of type ELLIPSE, we can always substitute a value of type CIRCLE (because, to say it one more time, circles are ellipses).

Now, this matter of *substitutability* is in many ways the whole point of inheritance. I suggested earlier that one reason for wanting to support inheritance in the first place is that (for example) a program that works for ellipses might work for circles too, even if the program in question was originally written with no thought for circles. Well, it should be clear now that, to the extent that such an objective might be achievable, it's substitutability that makes it so.

Incidentally, the foregoing paragraph touches once again on one of the logical differences discussed briefly in Chapter 2: viz., that between arguments and parameters. This particular difference becomes especially significant in the inheritance context. To spell the point out, we need to be very careful over the difference between the parameters in terms of which an operator is defined, with their *declared* types, and the corresponding arguments to some invocation of that operator, with their *actual*—i.e., *most specific*—types. In the AREA_OF example, for instance, the operator is presumably defined in terms of a parameter of declared type ELLIPSE, but the most specific type of the argument *c* in the invocation AREA_OF (*c*) is CIRCLE. (Indeed, the declared type of the expression *exp* denoting that argument *c* might be CIRCLE too.)[21]

A BNF GRAMMAR

User defined types—which are necessarily scalar, remember—are defined in **Tutorial D** by means of a TYPE statement, which consists of a *<scalar type def>* followed by a semicolon. In this section I give a BNF grammar for *<scalar type def>*s, for purposes of future reference. Note in particular that the grammar takes inheritance into account (multiple as well as single) and thereby subsumes the grammar already given in Chapter 2. Detailed explanations are given in Parts II and III of this book; here I just note that in practice it might be necessary to allow several distinct *<scalar type def>*s to be bundled up into a single statement, in order to allow all of the types involved in a given type schema to be defined "simultaneously," as it were.[22] *Note: Type schema* is a term sometimes used to refer to a collection of related type definitions. For example, the definitions for the six types shown in Fig. 3.1 could together be regarded as constituting a type schema.

```
<scalar type def>
    ::=    TYPE <scalar type name> [ ORDERED | ORDINAL ] [ UNION ]
                    <possrep def list> [ <possrep constraint def> ]
                                [ <is def> ] INIT ( <literal> )
```

Let *T* be the scalar type being defined. If and only if ORDERED is specified, then *T* is an ordered type; if and only if ORDINAL is specified, then *T* is an ordinal type (see Chapter 2). If and only if UNION is specified, then *T* is a union type (see Chapter 12). The *<possrep def list>* must be empty if *T* (a) is a dummy type (again, see Chapter 12) or (b) has a regular—i.e., nondummy—immediate supertype; otherwise it must be nonempty. The *<possrep constraint def>* can be specified if and only if a nonempty *<possrep def list>* is specified. The *<is def>*

---

[21] More generally, if operator *Op* is defined in terms of a parameter *P* of declared type *T*, and *Op* is invoked with an argument *A* corresponding to *P* that's of most specific type *T'* (where *T'* is a subtype of *T*), then the declared type of the expression *Ax* denoting *A* in that invocation can be any type that's both a supertype of *T'* and a subtype of *T*.

[22] Certain aspects of such bundling are explored further in the answer to Exercise 12.10 in Chapter 12.

must be specified if *T* (a) is a regular type and (b) the *<possrep def list>* is empty (in which case *T* is a nonroot type by definition); otherwise it must be omitted. The declared type of *<literal>* must be some nonunion subtype of *T*. *Note:* The syntactic categories *<possrep def>* and *<possrep constraint def>* were defined in Chapter 2.

```
<is def>
    ::=    IS { <scalar type name commalist>
                         [ <possrep and constraint specs> ] }
```

Let *T* be the nonroot type being defined; then the *<scalar type name commalist>* contains the names of all of the immediate supertypes of *T*. The *<possrep and constraint specs>* must be specified if *T* is a regular type; otherwise it must be omitted. *Note:* An extension to the syntactic category *<is def>*—viz., a NOT specification—is discussed in Chapters 5 and 14.

```
<possrep and constraint specs>
    ::=    <possrep def list> [ <possrep constraint def> ]
         | [ <additional constraint def> ] <derived possrep def list>
```

Let *T* be the regular nonroot type being defined. If *T* has just one immediate supertype *IST*, then (a) if *IST* is a dummy type, a nonempty *<possrep def list>* must be specified, and a *<possrep constraint def>* can optionally be specified, just as if *T* were a root type; (b) if *IST* is a regular type, then an *<additional constraint def>* and a nonempty *<derived possrep def list>* must both be specified. If *T* has two or more immediate supertypes, then the *<additional constraint def>* must be omitted and a nonempty *<derived possrep def list>* must be specified.[23]

```
<additional constraint def>
    ::=    CONSTRAINT <bool exp>
```

Let *T* be the regular nonroot type being defined, and let *IST* be the (unique and regular) immediate supertype of *T*. The boolean expression *<bool exp>* mustn't mention any variables, but the name *IST* can, and in fact must, be used in that expression to denote an arbitrary value of that type. *Note:* In practice, we would expect all such appearances of that name *IST* to occur in the context of a THE_ operator invocation in which the argument expression is, precisely, *IST*.

```
<derived possrep def>
    ::=    POSSREP [ <possrep name> ]
                 ( <derived possrep component def commalist> )
```

Let *T* be the regular nonroot type being defined. Omitting the *<possrep name>* from a given *<derived possrep def>* is equivalent to specifying the *<possrep name>* *T*. No two distinct

---

[23] The grammar presented in this section has been designed on the basis of a certain reasonable assumption: namely, that if *T* has a dummy type *IST* as an immediate supertype, then *IST* is *T*'s *only* immediate supertype. Under single inheritance, of course, that assumption is valid by definition; under multiple inheritance, it might not be. Further research might be required.

*<derived possrep def>*s in the same *<derived possrep def list>* can have the same *<possrep name>*. The *<derived possrep component def commalist>* will usually not be empty.

```
<derived possrep component def>
    ::=    <possrep component name> = <exp>
```

Let *T* be the regular nonroot type being defined, and let *IST* be the immediate supertype of *T* in terms of which a given *<derived possrep component def>* is being formulated.[24] The expression *<exp>* mustn't mention any variables, but the name *IST* can, and in fact must, be used in that expression to denote an arbitrary value of that supertype. (*Note:* In practice, we would expect *<exp>* to take the form of a THE_ operator invocation in which the argument expression is, precisely, *IST*.) No two distinct *<derived possrep component def>*s in the same *<derived possrep def list>* can have the same *<possrep component name>*.

MORE TERMINOLOGY *bis*

As you know by now, (a) if *v* is a value of most specific type *T*, then *v* has every supertype of *T* as one of its types as well; also, (b) if *V* is a variable—or a relvar (or tuplevar) attribute, or a parameter, or an expression (i.e., a read-only operator invocation)—of declared type *T*, then the value denoted by *V* at any given time can have as its most specific type any subtype of *T*. In order to avoid a certain amount of circumlocution, therefore, throughout this book from this point forward I'll adopt the following terminological simplifications:

a. I'll take the phrase "the type," unqualified, when applied to a value *v*, to mean the most specific type of *v* specifically, unless the context demands otherwise.

b. I'll take the phrase "the type," unqualified, when applied to a variable, relvar (or tuplevar) attribute, read-only operator, parameter, or expression *V*, to mean the declared type of *V* specifically, unless the context demands otherwise.

I turn now to the term *type constraint*. Let scalar type *T* be a root type, with possrep *PR*; then any given value of type *T* (a) is constrained to be such that it can be possibly represented as specified by *PR*, and (b) is usually constrained further by an explicit CONSTRAINT specification. Alternatively, let scalar type *T* be a nonroot type; then any given value of type *T* (a) is constrained to be a value of each of type *T*'s immediate supertypes and—at least in the case of single inheritance—(b) is constrained further by an explicit CONSTRAINT specification. In both cases, it's the combination of (a) and (b) that, formally speaking,

---

[24] There's a tacit assumption here that even if type *T* has two or more immediate supertypes, any given possrep for *T* will be defined in terms of exactly one of them (in fact, in terms of exactly one possrep for exactly one of them). See Chapter 14 for further discussion.

constitutes the type constraint for *T*. In both cases, however, the term *type constraint* is often used informally to refer to just the (b) portion—i.e., the CONSTRAINT specification—by itself. This informal usage is strictly incorrect but very, very common, and I'll follow it myself in this book occasionally—but, please note, only in informal contexts.

CONCLUDING REMARKS

Preceding sections have presented an introduction to some of the basic ideas of our own inheritance model ("the *Manifesto* model"). As noted earlier in the chapter, however, many alternative approaches to inheritance have been described in the literature, and I'd like to mention a couple of them briefly here:

■ First, some writers discuss what they call *the EXTENDS relationship*, typically defined[25] as "a single inheritance relationship between two classes whereby the subordinate class inherits all of the properties and all of the behavior of the class that it extends" (*class* and *properties* here referring to type and structure, respectively). For example, class *EmployeePerson* might extend class *Person* by adding "attributes" *hireDate* and *payRate* to the ones it inherits from class *Person* (viz., *name* and *birthDate*). Clearly, the EXTENDS relationship has something to do with structural inheritance (see the section "Scalars, Tuples, and Relations" earlier in this chapter)—but it's a form of structural inheritance in which the structure concerned consists of "attributes" that are most definitely visible to the user. *Note:* C++, Java, and SQL all support the EXTENDS relationship in some shape or form. Our model, by contrast, doesn't (at least, not directly, but Chapter 21 shows how it can provide equivalent functionality).

■ Second, some writers discuss *subtables and supertables* (not always by that name, however).[26] This concept might be thought of as an application of the EXTENDS relationship concept to tables specifically; the basic idea is that some table *T'* can be defined to have all of the columns of some other table *T*, together with certain additional columns of its own. (I deliberately use the SQL terminology of tables and columns here instead of relational terminology, because SQL supports the "subtables and supertables" concept and the relational model doesn't.) For example, the STUDENT table might inherit all of the columns of the PERSON table but might also add a GPA column ("grade point average") of its own. Chapter 21 discusses this idea in more detail as well.

---

[25] See, e.g., *The Object Data Standard: ODMG 3.0*, by R. G. G. Cattell and Douglas K. Barry (eds.), Morgan Kaufmann (2000), from which this definition and the subsequent *EmployeePerson* example are taken.

[26] See, e.g., *Object-Relational DBMSs: Tracking the Next Great Wave* (2nd edition), by Michael Stonebraker and Paul Brown (with Dorothy Moore), Morgan Kaufmann (1999), from which the subsequent GPA example is taken.

One last point: Regardless of whether we're talking about our own inheritance model or one of the other approaches mentioned above, it would be remiss of me not to point out that inheritance can give rise to some thorny practical problems. For example, given the type hierarchy of Fig. 3.1, what do you think should happen if we try to drop type ELLIPSE? Should there be a way to "alter" or rename type ELLIPSE without dropping it? Should we be able to introduce a new type as an immediate supertype of an existing type? What if that existing type is system defined? And so on. Such questions must clearly be answered in any real implementation, but they don't affect our model per se, and for that reason I won't discuss them further in this book.

EXERCISES

3.1 Explain the *type inheritance* and *subtype* concepts in your own words.

3.2 Distinguish between immediate and proper subtypes.

3.3 What do you understand by the term *most specific type*?

3.4 What do you understand by the term *substitutability*?

3.5 With reference to the type hierarchy of Fig. 3.1, consider a value *e* of type ELLIPSE. The most specific type of *e* is either ELLIPSE or CIRCLE. What's the *least* specific type of *e*?

3.6 Define the terms *root type* and *leaf type*.

3.7 State the disjointness assumption. What are some of the implications of that assumption? What do you think should replace that assumption if multiple inheritance is supported? *Note:* This latter question wasn't answered in the body of the chapter; the point of the question is simply to get you thinking about the issue, should you feel so inclined, before we get to the detailed discussions in later chapters.

3.8 Give as precise a definition as you can of the term *type hierarchy*. (You might like to try giving a recursive definition, different from the one given in the body of the chapter.) Why are type hierarchies strictly not part of our inheritance model?

3.9 Are possreps inherited? If not, why not?

3.10 Use the syntax defined in this chapter to give definitions for types RECTANGLE and SQUARE from Fig. 3.1. Assume for simplicity that all rectangles are centered on the origin, but don't assume that all sides are either vertical or horizontal. What about types POLYGON and PLANE_FIGURE?

3.11 Given your answer to Exercise 3.10, define a read-only operator that, given a particular rectangle centered on the origin, returns a rectangle identical to the given one except that it's rotated through 90° about its center.

3.12 (*This exercise will probably take longer to read than to answer!*) A derived type hierarchy is a type hierarchy that's derived from another. Here's a precise definition. Let *TH* be a type hierarchy. Then:

- *TH* itself is considered to be a type hierarchy derived from *TH*.

- Let *DH* be a graph obtained from *TH* by choosing the node corresponding to some type *T* and removing (a) all nodes not corresponding to some subtype *T'* of *T* and (b) all arcs emanating from those nodes. Then *DH* is a derived type hierarchy, with *T* as its root—specifically, a type hierarchy derived from *TH*.

- Let *DH* be a type hierarchy derived from *TH*. Then any graph obtained from *DH* by removing the node corresponding to some type *T* is a derived type hierarchy, with the root of *DH* as its root (unless the node corresponding to the root of *DH* was the one removed)—specifically, a type hierarchy derived from *TH*—provided that removal of a node is always accompanied by removal of (a) the arc, if any, entering into that node and (b) all corresponding immediate subtype nodes. *Note:* It follows that the empty graph can be regarded as a type hierarchy derived from *TH*.

By contrast, if (a) *TH* is a type hierarchy with root *T*, and if (b) type *T* is an immediate supertype of type *T'* and type *T'* is an immediate supertype of type *T''* (and if—let's assume for simplicity—type *T'* is an immediate supertype of no type other than type *T''*), and if (c) *XH* is the graph derived from *TH* by removing node *T'* and coalescing the arc connecting nodes *T* and *T'* and the arc connecting nodes *T'* and *T''* into a single arc connecting nodes *T* and *T''*, then (d) *XH* isn't a derived type hierarchy (at least, it's not one that can be derived from *TH*), because it causes *T''* to lose some of its inheritance, as it were.

Given the foregoing definition, how many distinct type hierarchies can be derived from that of Fig. 3.1?

3.13 In the body of the chapter I said that if inheritance is supported at all, it must be multiple. Why do you think this is? *Note:* As with the second part of Exercise 3.7, this question wasn't answered in the body of the chapter; again, the point is simply to get you thinking about the issue, if you feel so inclined.

3.14 In Chapter 2, I said the system defined types INTEGER and RATIONAL were different types. But wouldn't it be more accurate to say that type INTEGER is a proper subtype of type RATIONAL?

ANSWERS

3.1 The term *type inheritance* refers to that phenomenon according to which we can sensibly say, for example, that every circle is an ellipse, and hence that all properties that apply to ellipses in general apply to circles in particular (where "properties" means, basically, read-only operators and type constraints). Note carefully, however, that the foregoing loose definition refers only to *values* (ellipse and circle values, in the example quoted); inheritance does have implications for variables too, but this book hasn't yet explained them.

A subtype *T'* of a given type *T* is a type whose values are defined to be a certain specific subset of the values constituting *T*. Values of type *T'* inherit operators that apply to values of type *T* (because values of type *T' are* values of type *T*), but additionally have operators of their own that don't apply values of type *T* in general. Likewise, values of type *T'* satisfy the type constraint for values of type *T* (because, again, values of type *T'* are values of type *T*), but additionally satisfy a type constraint of their own that doesn't apply to values of type *T* in general.

Note: Of course, the foregoing answers do assume our own inheritance model as context; given a different context, the answers might be different. Please note too that a similar remark applies to this book as a whole—not just to answers to exercises—from this point forward!

3.2 *T'* is a proper subtype of *T* if and only if it's a subtype of *T* and *T'* ≠ *T*. *T'* is an immediate subtype of *T* if and only if it's a proper subtype of *T* and there's no type *T''* such that *T'* is a proper subtype of *T''* and *T''* is a proper subtype of *T*.

3.3 Type *T* is the most specific type of value *v* if and only if *v* is of type *T* and not of any proper subtype of *T*.

3.4 Substitutability refers to the ability for a value of type *T'* to appear wherever a value of type *T* is permitted (i.e., a value of type *T'* can be "substituted for" a value of type *T*). Such substitutions are certainly permitted if type *T'* is a subtype of type *T*. Note carefully, however, that the foregoing definition refers specifically to values; a certain degree of substitutability can sometimes apply to variables too, but this book hasn't yet discussed this latter possibility.

Note: An expression of type *T'* might sometimes be allowed to appear wherever an expression of type *T* is permitted even if *T'* isn't a subtype of *T*, if the system supports coercions (see Chapter 2). However, we saw in the answer to Exercise 2.6 in Chapter 2 that coercions are generally deprecated; for that reason (and also to avoid confusion), in this book I choose not to regard the foregoing possibility as an example of substitutability as such.

3.5   PLANE_FIGURE, the pertinent root type—or, if type *alpha* is taken into consideration, then type *alpha* (see footnote 18).

3.6   A root type is a type that has no immediate supertype (other than as noted in footnote 18); a leaf type is a type that has no immediate subtype (again, other than as noted in footnote 18).

3.7   The disjointness assumption says that if types *T1* and *T2* are such that neither is a subtype of the other, then they're disjoint—i.e., no value is of both type *T1* and type *T2*. Some of the implications of this assumption are that (a) distinct root types are disjoint, and hence distinct type hierarchies are disjoint also; (b) distinct leaf types are disjoint; and (c) importantly, every value has a unique most specific type.

Now, I think it's reasonable to require that properties (a), (b), and (c) hold with single inheritance; in fact, however, as we'll see in Chapters 14 and 15, they hold with multiple inheritance as well, even though the disjointness assumption as such doesn't. In particular, therefore, they hold for tuple and relation types as well as for scalar types (see Part IV of this book), even though, again, the disjointness assumption doesn't.

A multiple inheritance version of the disjointness assumption might look like this: If types *T1* and *T2* are such that (a) neither is a subtype of the other and (b) they have no nonempty common subtype, then they're disjoint. A simpler version might be just: If types *T1* and *T2* are distinct root types, then they're disjoint. See Chapters 14 and (especially) 15 for further discussion.

3.8   Here's a recursive definition: A type hierarchy is a graph that either is empty or consists of a node (the root node, representing a type) with zero or more outgoing arcs, such that:

a.   Each outgoing arc connects that root node to a nonempty type hierarchy.

b.   Starting from a given node, every path that can be traced by following an outgoing arc from that node, then following an outgoing arc from the node the previous arc connects to, and so on, eventually reaches a node with no outgoing arcs (a leaf node).

Type hierarchies aren't part of the inheritance model because they're just pictures—i.e., they're merely an intuitively convenient way of depicting certain subtype / supertype relationships (and in any case they're inadequate in the case of multiple inheritance, when more general type graphs become necessary).

3.9 Yes and no! If scalar type *T'* is an immediate subtype of scalar type *T*, then every possrep for *T* is necessarily a possrep for *T'* as well, but only implicitly. As far as our model is concerned, the only *declared* possreps for type *T'* are the ones explicitly defined in the TYPE statement for *T'* (and the unqualified term *possrep* is always taken to refer to an explicitly declared possrep specifically, unless the context demands otherwise). Consider ellipses and circles, for example. If the (*a*,*b*,*ctr*) possrep for ellipses were considered a declared possrep for circles, then the system would be required to allow assignments of the form

```
THE_A ( C ) := ... ;
```

for a variable C of declared type CIRCLE. But after such an assignment, THE_A(C) and THE_B(C) would, in general, denote different values—meaning that C would violate its own type constraint (viz., the type constraint for circles)—and the assignment would therefore fail at run time. See Exercise 11.9 in Chapter 11 for further discussion.

3.10 The following solutions aren't the only ones possible, but they're perhaps the most straightforward. First of all, assume for simplicity that POLYGON is a dummy type (because if it were a regular type instead, we'd have to define a possrep for it, and then define the RECTANGLE possrep(s) in terms of that possrep). Now let *ABCD* be a rectangle, with vertices *A*, *B*, *C*, and *D*. If *ABCD* is centered on the origin *O*, the line segments *OA*, *OB*, *OC*, and *OD* will all be the same length. Also, there'll be two adjacent vertices with a positive *x* coordinate and two with a negative *x* coordinate. (For definiteness, I assume we can talk about the vertices of *ABCD* in terms of a possrep consisting of cartesian coordinates.) Let *A* and *B* be the vertices with a positive *x* coordinate and let *C* and *D* be the other two. Either of these pairs will serve to pin down the entire rectangle precisely. Suppose we choose the (*A*,*B*) pair. But the (*B*,*A*) pair would do just as well! In order to distinguish between these two possibilities, therefore, let's insist, arbitrarily, that *A* is the one with the larger *y* coordinate (note that the *y* coordinates of *A* and *B* are necessarily different). So we have:

```
TYPE RECTANGLE
     IS { POLYGON
          POSSREP ( A POINT , B POINT )
          CONSTRAINT WITH ( AX := THE_X ( A ) ,
                            AY := THE_Y ( A ) ,
                            BX := THE_X ( B ) ,
                            BY := THE_Y ( B ) ) :
                   AX > 0.0 AND BX > 0.0 AND AY > BY
                   AND AX ^ 2 + AY ^ 2 = BX ^ 2 + BY ^ 2 } } ;
```

Note that the sole possrep here, and hence the sole selector, are both named RECTANGLE by default.

Note: In case you're wondering why it's necessary to distinguish between the two possibilities—(*A,B*) vs. (*B,A*)—consider what happens if we don't. If we don't, then invoking the RECTANGLE selector with *A* = *a* and *B* = *b*, say, will return the same rectangle, *r* say, as invoking it with *A* = *b* and *B* = *a*. So given that rectangle *r*, what does THE_A(*r*) return—*a* or *b*?

Now suppose *ABCD* is actually a square. Then it's easy to see that if *A* is the point (*x,y*), then *B* must be the point (*y,-x*). So we have:

```
TYPE SQUARE
     IS { RECTANGLE
          CONSTRAINT WITH ( RA := THE_A ( RECTANGLE ) ,
                            RB := THE_B ( RECTANGLE ) ) :
              THE_X ( RB ) =   THE_Y ( RA ) AND
              THE_Y ( RB ) = - THE_X ( RA )
          POSSREP ( A = THE_A ( RECTANGLE ) ) } ;
```

The sole possrep here, and hence the sole selector, are both named SQUARE by default.

Turning to type POLYGON (and now dropping our previous assumption that it's a dummy type), one possible representation was sketched in outline in the answer to Exercise 2.10 in Chapter 2. Specifying such a possrep would have certain knock-on effects on the definition of type RECTANGLE, however. To be specific (and as noted above, in fact), the RECTANGLE possrep would now have to be defined in terms of the POLYGON possrep, just as the SQUARE possrep is defined in terms of the RECTANGLE possrep. I omit further consideration of such matters here.

As for type PLANE_FIGURE, it's virtually certain that that type *would* be a dummy type and thus would have no possrep. Indeed, it's hard to think of a sensible possrep that could work for an arbitrary plane figure.

3.11 Observe first that vertices *C* and *D* are the "reflections" of *A* and *B*, respectively (in the sense that if *A* is the point (*x,y*), *C* is the point (*-x,-y*), and similarly for *B* and *D*). Assume for definiteness that the rotation is anticlockwise (does it make any difference if it's clockwise?). After that rotation, then, the vertices with a positive *x* coordinate will be *C* and *D*; *C* will be the reflection of the old *B* in the *x* axis(i.e., if the old *B* is the point (*x,y*), the new *C* will be the point (*x,-y*)), and similarly for *D* and *A*. So:

```
OPERATOR QUARTER_TURN ( R RECTANGLE ) RETURNS RECTANGLE ;
     RETURN ( RECTANGLE ( POINT (   THE_X ( THE_B ( R ) ) ,
                                  - THE_Y ( THE_B ( R ) ) ) ,
                          POINT (   THE_X ( THE_A ( R ) ) ,
                                  - THE_Y ( THE_A ( R ) ) ) ) ) ;
     END OPERATOR ;
```

Or if you prefer an update operator (which I rather hope you don't!):

```
OPERATOR QUARTER_TURN ( R RECTANGLE ) UPDATES { R } ;
   R := RECTANGLE ( POINT (    THE_X ( THE_B ( R ) ) ,
                          -  THE_Y ( THE_B ( R ) ) ) ,
                   POINT (    THE_X ( THE_A ( R ) ) ,
                          -  THE_Y ( THE_A ( R ) ) ) ) ) ;
END OPERATOR ;
```

3.12 There are 22 derived type hierarchies in all. To spell them out:

1. The empty graph
2. PLANE_FIGURE
3. PLANE_FIGURE and ELLIPSE
4. PLANE_FIGURE, ELLIPSE, and CIRCLE
5. ELLIPSE
6. ELLIPSE and CIRCLE
7. CIRCLE
8. PLANE_FIGURE and POLYGON
9. PLANE_FIGURE, POLYGON, and RECTANGLE
10. PLANE_FIGURE, POLYGON, RECTANGLE, and SQUARE
11. POLYGON
12. POLYGON and RECTANGLE
13. POLYGON, RECTANGLE, and SQUARE
14. RECTANGLE
15. RECTANGLE and SQUARE
16. SQUARE
17. PLANE_FIGURE, ELLIPSE, and POLYGON
18. PLANE_FIGURE, ELLIPSE, POLYGON, and RECTANGLE
19. PLANE_FIGURE, ELLIPSE, POLYGON, RECTANGLE, and SQUARE
20. PLANE_FIGURE, ELLIPSE, CIRCLE, and POLYGON
21. PLANE_FIGURE, ELLIPSE, CIRCLE, POLYGON, and RECTANGLE
22. PLANE_FIGURE, ELLIPSE, CIRCLE, POLYGON, RECTANGLE, and SQUARE

3.13 I'm not going to answer this question in depth here—I'll just give an example for you to think about. Given scalar types CIRCLE, ELLIPSE, SQUARE, and RECTANGLE as in Fig. 3.1, consider these three tuple types:

```
TUPLE { E CIRCLE  , R SQUARE }
TUPLE { E ELLIPSE , R SQUARE }
TUPLE { E CIRCLE  , R RECTANGLE }
```

It should be clear that (a) every tuple of the first type is also a tuple of both the second type and the third, while (b) each of the second and third types is such that some tuples are of that type and not the other. Thus, the first type is a proper subtype of the second and also of the third, while neither of these latter two is a subtype of the other. It follows that, for tuple types at least, multiple inheritance is a logical necessity. For further discussion, see Part IV of this book.

3.14 Well, it might be or it might not. The important point to note is that rational numbers are normally defined in terms of integers—by definition, a rational number is a number that can be expressed as the ratio of two integers—and if they are, then to say an integer "is a" rational number would be to go round in circles; in effect, it would be defining integers in terms of themselves. (A detailed analysis of this example and others like it can be found in my paper "Toward a Better Understanding of Numeric Data Types," in *Database Explorations: Essays on The Third Manifesto and Related Topics*, by Hugh Darwen and myself, available free online at the website *www.thethirdmanifesto.com*.) In order to be able to claim legitimately that INTEGER is a subtype of RATIONAL, therefore, it would first be necessary to come up with a definition of rational numbers that makes no mention of the concept of an integer. *Note:* It's relevant to mention here that examples of this same general nature ("INTEGER is a subtype of RATIONAL") are frequently used to illustrate the basic idea of inheritance in the literature. *Caveat lector.*

The foregoing discussion of types INTEGER and RATIONAL raises another question, however (nothing to do with inheritance as such). In Chapter 2 I said this (approximately):

> Any given value always has exactly one type (except possibly if type inheritance is supported) ... If every value is of exactly one type, then no value is of two or more types, and distinct types are thus disjoint, absent inheritance.

Now, you might have raised an eyebrow at these remarks. Surely the value 3, for example—to use decimal notation—is both an integer and a rational, and is thus a value of both types. Isn't it? Or, to take another example, what about the value zero?

To answer such questions properly requires a very clear understanding of the way the types concerned are defined. I said above that a rational number is a number that can be expressed as the ratio of two integers. In fact, we might more properly say that values of type RATIONAL are *ordered pairs* of integers (n,d), where n is the numerator and d is the denominator and $d \neq 0$. For example, the rational number "five eighths" is the pair (5,8). By contrast, values of type INTEGER are just integers. And there's certainly a logical difference between a pair of integers and an integer! In particular, the integer pair (3,1) isn't the same as the integer 3. It's true that an isomorphism can be established between integer pairs of the form $(n,1)$ and integers n—but to say two things are isomorphic is not the same as saying they're the same. *Note:* For an explanation of what an isomorphism is, I refer you to my book *The **New** Relational Database Dictionary* (O'Reilly, 2016).

Chapter 4

The Inheritance Model

O England! model to thy inward greatness,
Like little body with a mighty heart,
What mightst thou do, that honour would thee do,
Were all thy children kind and natural!

—William Shakespeare:
King Henry the Fifth (1598-1599)

This chapter provides, for purposes of subsequent reference, a precise statement of the 28 IM prescriptions that make up our inheritance model. It's based on Chapter 19 of the book Database Explorations: Essays on The Third Manifesto and Related Topics, *by Hugh Darwen and myself (available free online at the website* **www.thethirdmanifesto.com**). *However, I've found it necessary, or at least convenient, to perform a certain amount of revision on some of the prescriptions, as will be made clear in subsequent chapters. I've also added two new ones (numbers 23 and 26, according to the numbering below). Note: Whenever there's a technical discrepancy between the present chapter—or anything else in this book, come to that—and previous publications by Darwen and myself on this topic, the present text should be taken as superseding. At the same time, please note that it's my intention that any such discrepancies be called out explicitly and justified.*

Throughout this chapter, as well as elsewhere in this book, I use the symbols T and T' as generic names for a pair of types such that T' is a subtype of T (equivalently, such that T is a supertype of T'). You might find it helpful to think of T and T' as ELLIPSE and CIRCLE, respectively; however, keep in mind that they're not limited to being scalar types specifically, barring explicit statements to the contrary (moreover, the various prescriptions are all worded in such a way as not to be limited to single inheritance only, either). Note too that distinct types have distinct names; in particular, if T' is a proper subtype of T, then their names will be distinct, even if the set of values constituting T' isn't a proper subset of the set of values constituting T. (Conversely, if their names aren't distinct, then T' and T are the very same type and the corresponding sets of values will be identical.) Also, I assume that all of the types under discussion, including the maximal and minimal types discussed in IM Prescriptions 20 and 25, are members of some given set of available types *GSAT* (though the only explicit mention of that set is in IM Prescription 20, q.v.); in particular, the definitions of the terms *root type* and *leaf type* in IM Prescription 6 are to be understood in the context of that set. For example, given the type hierarchy of Fig. 3.1 in Chapter 3, the set of available types consists of:

a. PLANE_FIGURE, ELLIPSE, CIRCLE, POLYGON, RECTANGLE, and SQUARE

b. The types in terms of which the possreps for the types listed under point a. are defined

c. The types in terms of which the possreps for the types included under point b., such as LENGTH and POINT, are defined (and so on, recursively, all the way down to and including the pertinent primitive types—see below)

d. The maximal scalar type *alpha* and the minimal scalar type *omega* (see IM Prescription 20)

e. Tuple and relation types that can be generated using any of the types mentioned in any of these five points a.-e.

Note: The term *primitive type*, mentioned under point c. above, refers to a system defined type (scalar by definition) with no declared possrep. The qualifier *primitive* derives from the fact that all of the types available in any given context are ultimately defined in terms of such types. Typical examples of such primitive types include the types INTEGER, RATIONAL, CHAR, and BOOLEAN.

By the way, it's worth stating explicitly that type PLANE_FIGURE is *not* the only root type with respect to the foregoing set of types. It's not even the only scalar root type. By way of example, consider type POINT. Since it's the type of (among other things) a possrep component for type CIRCLE, type POINT is certainly a member of the given set of types; however, it's not a subtype of PLANE_FIGURE, and so it must be part of some distinct type hierarchy—possibly one consisting of type POINT only—and, by definition, that distinct type hierarchy has a distinct root type of its own.

THE IM PRESCRIPTIONS

1. *T* and *T'* shall each be types; i.e., each shall be a named set of values.

2. Every value in *T'* shall be a value in *T*; i.e., the set of values constituting *T'* shall be a subset of the set of values constituting *T* (in other words, if a value is of type *T'*, it shall also be of type *T*).

3. *T* and *T'* shall not necessarily be distinct; i.e., every type shall be both a subtype and a supertype of itself.

4. Every subtype of T' shall be a subtype of T. Every supertype of T shall be a supertype of T'.

5. Let T and T' be scalar types. Then:

   a. If and only if T and T' are distinct, then T shall be a **proper** supertype of T' and T' shall be a **proper** subtype of T.

   b. Let T be a proper supertype of T', and let S be a sequence of types $T1$, $T2$, ..., Tm such that T is a proper supertype of $T1$, $T1$ is a proper supertype of $T2$, ..., and Tm is a proper supertype of T' ($m \geq 0$). Then either (a) no such sequence S shall exist (i.e., every such sequence shall be such that $m = 0$), in which case (and in which case only) T shall be an **immediate** supertype of T', or (b) every such sequence S shall be such that $m > 0$, in which case (and in which case only) T shall be a **nonimmediate** supertype of T'. Also, T' shall be an **immediate** subtype of T if and only if T is an immediate supertype of T', and T' shall be a **nonimmediate** subtype of T if and only if T is a nonimmediate supertype of T.

   c. If and only if T is an immediate supertype of T' and T' is neither a root type nor type *omega*—see IM Prescription 20—then the definition of T' shall be accompanied by a specification of an **example value** that is of type T and not of type T'.

6. A scalar type that has type *alpha*—see IM Prescription 20—as its sole immediate supertype shall be a (scalar) **root** type. A scalar type that has type *omega*—again, see IM Prescription 20—as its sole immediate subtype shall be a (scalar) **leaf** type.

7. Types $T1$ and $T2$ shall be **disjoint** if and only if no value is of both type $T1$ and type $T2$. Types $T1$ and $T2$ shall **overlap** if and only if there exists at least one value that is common to both. Distinct root types shall be disjoint. If types $T1$ and $T2$ are distinct immediate subtypes of the same scalar type T, there shall exist at least one value that is of type $T1$ and not of type $T2$.

8. Let $T1$, $T2$, ..., Tm ($m \geq 0$), T, and T' be scalar types. Then:

   a. Type T shall be a **common supertype** for, or of, types $T1$, $T2$, ..., Tm if and only if, whenever a given value is of at least one of types $T1$, $T2$, ..., Tm, it is also of type T. Further, that type T shall be the **most specific** common supertype for $T1$, $T2$, ..., Tm if and only if no proper subtype of T is also a common supertype for those types.

   b. Type T' shall be a **common subtype** for, or of, types $T1$, $T2$, ..., Tm if and only if, whenever a given value is of type T', it is also of each of types $T1$, $T2$, ..., Tm.

Further, that type T' shall be the **least specific** common subtype—also known as the **intersection type** or **intersection subtype**—for $T1, T2, ..., Tm$ if and only if no proper supertype of T' is also a common subtype for those types.

Note: Given types $T1, T2, ..., Tm$ as defined above, it can be shown (thanks in particular to IM Prescription 20) that a unique most specific common supertype T and a unique least specific common subtype T' always exist. In the case of that particular common subtype T', moreover, it can also be shown that whenever a given value is of each of types $T1, T2, ..., Tm$, it is also of type T' (hence the alternative term *intersection type*). And it can further be shown that every scalar value v has both a unique least specific type and a unique most specific type (regarding this latter—which elsewhere in these prescriptions is denoted $MST(v)$—see also IM Prescription 9).

9. Let scalar variable V be of declared type T. Because of value substitutability (see IM Prescription 16), the value v assigned to V at any given time can have any nonempty subtype T' of type T as its most specific type. We can therefore model V as a named ordered triple of the form $<DT,MST,v>$, where:

   a.   The name of the triple is the name of the variable, V.

   b. DT is the name of the declared type for variable V.

   c. MST is the name of the **most specific type**—also known as the **current** most specific type—for, or of, variable V.

   d. v is a value of most specific type MST—the **current value** for, or of, variable V.

   We use the notation $DT(V)$, $MST(V)$, $v(V)$ to refer to the DT, MST, v components, respectively, of this model of scalar variable V. *Note:* Since $v(V)$ uniquely determines $MST(V)$—see IM Prescription 8—the MST component of V is strictly redundant. We include it for convenience.
   Now let X be a scalar expression. By definition, X represents an invocation of some scalar operator Op. Thus, the notation $DT(V)$, $MST(V)$, $v(V)$ just introduced can be extended in an obvious way to refer to the declared type $DT(X)$, the current most specific type $MST(X)$, and the current value $v(X)$, respectively, of X—where $DT(X)$ is the declared type of the invocation of Op in question (see IM Prescription 17) and is known at compile time, and $MST(X)$ and $v(X)$ refer to the result of evaluating X and are therefore not known until run time (in general).

10. Let T be a regular type (see IM Prescription 20) and hence, necessarily, a scalar type, and let T' be a nonempty immediate subtype of T. For each such immediate supertype T of T',

the definition of *T'* shall specify a **specialization constraint** *SC*, formulated in terms of *T*, such that a value shall be of type *T'* if and only if it satisfies all such constraints *SC*.

11. Consider the assignment

    ```
    V := X
    ```

    (where *V* is a variable reference and *X* is an expression). *DT(X)* shall be a subtype of *DT(V)*. The assignment shall set *v(V)* equal to *v(X)*, and hence *MST(V)* equal to *MST(X)* also.

12. Consider the equality comparison

    ```
    Y = X
    ```

    (where *Y* and *X* are expressions). *DT(Y)* and *DT(X)* shall overlap. The comparison shall return TRUE if *v(Y)* is equal to *v(X)* (and hence if *MST(Y)* is equal to *MST(X)* also), and FALSE otherwise.

13. Let *RX* and *RY* be relational expressions. In accordance with IM Prescription 28, each of *RX* and *RY* has a declared type. Let those declared types have headings

    ```
    {  <A1,TX1> ,  <A2,TX2> ,  ... ,  <An,TXn> }
    {  <A1,TY1> ,  <A2,TY2> ,  ... ,  <An,TYn> }
    ```

    respectively, where (a) $n \geq 0$ and (b) for all *j* (*j* = 1, 2, ..., *n*), types *TXj* and *TYj* have most specific common supertype *Tj* and least specific common subtype *Tj'*. Further, let the values denoted by *RX* and *RY* be relations *rx* and *ry*, respectively. Then:

    a. An expression of the form (*RX*) UNION (*RY*), or logical equivalent thereof, shall be supported and shall denote the **union** of *rx* and *ry*. The declared type of that expression shall have heading

       ```
       {  <A1,T1> ,  <A2,T2> ,  ... ,  <An,Tn> }
       ```

    b. An expression of the form (*RX*) INTERSECT (*RY*), or logical equivalent thereof, shall be supported and shall denote the **intersection** of *rx* and *ry*. The declared type of that expression shall have heading

       ```
       {  <A1,T1'> ,  <A2,T2'> ,  ... ,  <An,Tn'> }
       ```

Note: Intersection is a special case of join; given the prescriptions of paragraph d. below, therefore, the present paragraph b. is strictly redundant. We include it for convenience.

c.   An expression of the form (*RX*) MINUS (*RY*), or logical equivalent thereof, shall be supported and shall denote the **difference** between *rx* and *ry*, in that order. The declared type of that expression shall have heading

```
{ <A1,TX1> , <A2,TX2> , ... , <An,TXn> }
```

Now let the declared types of relational expressions *RX* and *RY* have headings

```
{ <A1,TX1> , <A2,TX2> , ... , <An,TXn> , <B1,TB1> , ... , <Bp,TBp> }
{ <A1,TY1> , <A2,TY2> , ... , <An,TYn> , <C1,TC1> , ... , <Cq,TCq> }
```

where (a) $n \geq 0$, $p \geq 0$, and $q \geq 0$, and (b) for all j ($j = 1, 2, ..., n$), types TXj and TYj have least specific common subtype Tj'. Further, let the values denoted by *RX* and *RY* be relations *rx* and *ry*, respectively. Then:

d.   An expression of the form (*RX*) JOIN (*RY*), or logical equivalent thereof, shall be supported and shall denote the **join** of *rx* and *ry*. The declared type of that expression shall have heading

```
{ <A1,T1'> , <A2,T2'> , ... , <An,Tn'> ,
          <B1,TB1> , ... , <Bp,TBp> , <C1,TC1> , ... , <Cq,TCq> }
```

Note: Intersection is a special case of join; thus, the prescriptions of the present paragraph d. degenerate to those for intersection (see paragraph b. above) in the case where $p = q = 0$.

14.   Let *X* be an expression, let *T* be a type, and let *DT(X)* and *T* overlap. Then an operator of the form

```
TREAT_AS_T ( X )
```

(or logical equivalent thereof) shall be supported, with semantics as follows: If $v(X)$ is not of type *T*, then a type error shall occur; otherwise, the declared type of the invocation TREAT_AS_T(X) shall be *T*, and the result of that invocation, *r* say, shall be equal to $v(X)$ (hence, *MST(r)* shall be equal to *MST(X)* also).

15. Let *X* be an expression, let *T* be a type, and let *DT*(*X*) and *T* overlap. Then an operator of the form

    ```
    IS_T ( X )
    ```

    (or logical equivalent thereof) shall be supported. The operator shall return TRUE if *v*(*X*) is of type *T*, FALSE otherwise.

16. Let *Op* be a read-only operator, let *P* be a parameter to *Op*, and let *T* be the declared type of *P*. Then the declared type of the argument expression (and therefore, necessarily, the most specific type of the argument as such) corresponding to *P* in an invocation of *Op* shall be allowed to be **any subtype** *T'* of *T*. In other words, the read-only operator *Op* applies to values of type *T* and therefore, necessarily, to values of type *T'*—*The Principle of* **Read-Only Operator Inheritance**. It follows that such operators are *polymorphic*, since they apply to values of several different types—*The Principle of* **Read-Only Operator Polymorphism**. It further follows that wherever a value of type *T* is permitted, a value of any subtype of *T* shall also be permitted—*The Principle of* **Value Substitutability**.

17. Let *Op* be an operator. Then *Op* shall have a *specification signature* and a set of *invocation signatures*. Let the parameters of *Op* and the argument expressions involved in any given invocation of *Op* each constitute an ordered list of *n* elements ($n \geq 0$), such that the *j*th argument expression corresponds to the *j*th parameter ($j = 1, 2, ..., n$). Further, let $PDT = <DT1, DT2, ..., DTn>$ be the declared types, in sequence, of those *n* parameters, and let $PDT' = <DT1', DT2', ..., DTn'>$ be a sequence of types such that *DTj'* is a nonempty subtype of *DTj* ($j = 1, 2, ..., n$). Then:

    a. If *Op* is a read-only operator, the **specification signature** shall consist of the operator name, the sequence *PDT*, and a type (the **declared type** *DT*(*Op*) for, or of, operator *Op*). Also, for each possible sequence *PDT'*, let *OpI* be an invocation of *Op* with argument expressions of declared types as specified by *PDT'*; then there shall exist an **invocation signature** for *OpI*, consisting of that sequence *PDT'* and a type (the **declared type** *DT*(*OpI*) for, or of, invocation *OpI*). *DT*(*OpI*) shall be a subtype of *DT*(*Op*), and the type of the result of *OpI* shall be a subtype of *DT*(*OpI*).

    b. If *Op* is an update operator, the **specification signature** shall consist of the operator name, the sequence *PDT*, and an indication as to which parameters are subject to update. Also, let the sequence *PDT'* be such that an invocation *OpI* of *Op* with argument expressions of declared types as specified by *PDT'* is legitimate (see IM Prescription 19). For each such sequence *PDT'*, there shall exist an **invocation signature** consisting of that sequence *PDT'*.

If two distinct operators (either both read-only or both update operators) have the same name and the same number n of parameters, then for some j ($1 \le j \le n$) the declared types of their jth parameters, as given by their respective specification signatures, shall be disjoint.

Note: Ordered lists or sequences are used in the text of this prescription purely as a convenient basis for defining the various correspondences (e.g., between parameters and their declared types) that the prescription requires. They are not an intrinsic part of the prescription as such. Rather, the implementation is free to establish those correspondences by whatever means it deems suitable, just so long as the overall effect is functionally equivalent to that defined by the foregoing text.

18. Let *Op* be an update operator and let *P* be a parameter to *Op* that is not subject to update. Then *Op* shall behave as a read-only operator as far as *P* is concerned, and all relevant aspects of IM Prescription 16 shall apply, mutatis mutandis.

19. Let *Op* be an update operator, let *P* be a parameter to *Op* that is subject to update, and let *T* be the declared type of *P*. Then it might or might not be the case that the declared type of the argument expression (and therefore, necessarily, the most specific type of the argument as such) corresponding to *P* in an invocation of *Op* shall be allowed to be some proper subtype *T'* of type *T*. It follows that for each such update operator *Op* and for each parameter *P* to *Op* that is subject to update, it shall be necessary to state explicitly for which proper subtypes *T'* of the declared type *T* of parameter *P* operator *Op* shall be inherited—*The Principle of* **Update Operator Inheritance**. (And if update operator *Op* is not inherited in this way by type *T'*, it shall not be inherited by any proper subtype of type *T'* either.) Update operators shall thus be only conditionally polymorphic—*The Principle of* **Update Operator Polymorphism**. If *Op* is an update operator and *P* is a parameter to *Op* that is subject to update and *T'* is a proper subtype of the declared type *T* of *P* for which *Op* is inherited, then by definition it shall be possible to invoke *Op* with an argument expression corresponding to parameter *P* that is of declared type *T'*—*The Principle of* **Variable Substitutability**.

20. Type *T* shall be a **union type** if and only if it is a scalar type and there exists no value that is of type *T* and not of some immediate subtype of *T* (i.e., there exists no value v such that $MST(v)$ is *T*). Moreover:

   a. A type shall be a **dummy type** if and only if either of the following is true:

      1. It is one of the types *alpha* and *omega* (see below).

2.   It is a union type, has no declared possible representation (and hence no selector), and no regular supertype. *Note:* Type *alpha* in fact satisfies all three of these conditions; type *omega* satisfies the first two only.

A type shall be a **regular type** if and only if it is a scalar type and not a dummy type.

b.   Conceptually, there shall be a system defined scalar type called *alpha*, the **maximal type** with respect to every scalar type. That type shall have all of the following properties:

1.   It shall contain all scalar values.

2.   It shall have no immediate supertypes.

3.   It shall be an immediate supertype for every scalar root type in the given set of available types *GSAT*.

No other scalar type shall have any of these properties.

c.   Conceptually, there shall be a system defined scalar type called *omega*, the **minimal type** with respect to every scalar type. That type shall have all of the following properties:

1.   It shall contain no values at all. (It follows that, as RM Prescription 1 in fact states, it shall have no example value in particular.)

2.   It shall have no immediate subtypes.

3.   It shall be an immediate subtype for every scalar leaf type in the given set of available types *GSAT*.

No other scalar type shall have any of these properties.

d.   The given set of available types *GSAT* shall contain at least one regular scalar type *T* such that *T* is neither a subtype nor a supertype of the required (and system defined) scalar type **boolean**.

21. Type *T* shall be an **empty type** if and only if it is either an empty scalar type or an empty tuple type. Scalar type *T* shall be empty if and only if *T* is type *omega*. Tuple type *T* shall be empty if and only if *T* has at least one attribute that is of some empty type. An empty

type shall be permitted as the type of (a) an attribute of a tuple type or relation type; (b) nothing else.

22. Let T and T' be both tuple types or both relation types. Then type T' shall be a **subtype** of type T, and type T shall be a **supertype** of type T', if and only if (a) T and T' have the same attribute names $A1, A2, ..., An$ and (b) for all j ($j = 1, 2, ..., n$), the type of attribute Aj of T' is a subtype of the type of attribute Aj of T. Tuple t shall be of tuple type T if and only if t has a heading that is that of some subtype of T. Relation r shall be of relation type T if and only if r has a heading that is that of some subtype of T (in which case every tuple in the body of r shall also have a heading that is that of some subtype of T).

23. Let T and T' be both tuple types or both relation types, with headings

    ```
    {  <A1,T1>  ,  <A2,T2>  ,  ...  ,  <An,Tn>  }

    {  <A1,T1'> ,  <A2,T2'> ,  ...  ,  <An,Tn'> }
    ```

    respectively. Then T' shall be a **proper** subtype of T, and T shall be a **proper** supertype of T', if and only if (a) for all j ($j = 1, 2, ..., n$), type Tj' is a subtype of Tj and (b) there exists at least one j ($j = 1, 2, ..., n$) such that Tj' is a proper subtype of Tj. Also, T' shall be an **immediate** subtype of T, and T shall be an **immediate** supertype of T', if and only if (a) there exists some j ($j = 1, 2, ..., n$) such that Tj' is an immediate subtype of Tj and (b) for all k ($k = 1, 2, ..., n, k \neq j$), $Tk' = Tk$. If and only if T' is a proper but not an immediate subtype of T, then T' shall be a **nonimmediate** subtype of T and T shall be a **nonimmediate** supertype of T'.

24. Let $T1, T2, ..., Tm$ ($m \geq 0$), T, and T' be all tuple types or all relation types, with headings

    ```
    {  <A1,T11>  ,  <A2,T12>  ,  ...  ,  <An,T1n>  }
    {  <A1,T21>  ,  <A2,T22>  ,  ...  ,  <An,T2n>  }

    ...................................

    {  <A1,Tm1>  ,  <A2,Tm2>  ,  ...  ,  <An,Tmn>  }
    {  <A1,T01>  ,  <A2,T02>  ,  ...  ,  <An,T0n>  }
    {  <A1,T01'> ,  <A2,T02'> ,  ...  ,  <An,T0n'> }
    ```

    respectively. Then:

    a.   Type T shall be a **common supertype** for, or of, types $T1, T2, ..., Tm$ if and only if, for all j ($j = 1, 2, ..., n$), type $T0j$ is a common supertype for types $T1j, T2j, ..., Tmj$.

Further, that type T shall be the **most specific** common supertype for $T1$, $T2$, ..., Tm if and only if no proper subtype of T is also a common supertype for those types.

b. Type T' shall be a **common subtype** for, or of, types $T1$, $T2$, ..., Tm if and only if, for all j ($j = 1, 2, ..., n$), type $T0j'$ is a common subtype for types $T1j$, $T2j$, ..., Tmj. Further, that type T' shall be the **least specific** common subtype—also known as the **intersection type** or **intersection subtype**—for $T1$, $T2$, ..., Tm if and only if no proper supertype of T' is also a common subtype for those types.

Note: Given types $T1$, $T2$, ..., Tm as defined above, it can be shown (thanks in particular to IM Prescription 25) that a unique most specific common supertype T and a unique least specific common subtype T' always exist. In the case of that particular common subtype T', moreover, it can also be shown that whenever a given value is of each of types $T1$, $T2$, ..., Tm, it is also of type T' (hence the alternative term *intersection type*)— in which case, for all j ($j = 1, 2, ..., n$), type $T0j'$ is the intersection type for types $T1j$, $T2j$, ..., Tmj. And it can further be shown that every tuple value and every relation value has both a unique least specific type and a unique most specific type (regarding the latter, see also IM Prescription 27).

25. Let T, T_alpha, and T_omega be all tuple types or all relation types, with headings

```
{ <A1,T1>         , <A2,T2>         , ... , <An,Tn>         }
{ <A1,T1_alpha> , <A2,T2_alpha> , ... , <An,Tn_alpha> }
{ <A1,T1 omega> , <A2,T2_omega> , ... , <An,Tn_omega> }
```

respectively. Then (a) type T_alpha shall be the **maximal type with respect to type T** if and only if, for all j ($j = 1, 2, ..., n$), type Tj_alpha is the maximal type with respect to type Tj; (b) type T_omega shall be the **minimal type with respect to type T** if and only if, for all j ($j = 1, 2, ..., n$), type Tj_omega is the minimal type with respect to type Tj.

26. A **root type** shall be a scalar root type (see IM Prescription 6), a tuple root type, or a relation root type. A type shall be a **tuple** root type if and only if it is a tuple type TT such that every attribute of TT is of a root type. A type shall be a **relation** root type if and only if it is a relation type RT such that every attribute of RT is of a root type.

    A **leaf type** shall be a scalar leaf type (see IM Prescription 6), a tuple leaf type, or a relation leaf type. A type shall be a **tuple** leaf type if and only if it is a tuple type TT such that every attribute of TT is of a leaf type. A type shall be a **relation** leaf type if and only if it is a relation type RT such that every attribute of RT is of a leaf type.

    A **superroot type** shall be a scalar superroot type, a tuple superroot type, or a relation superroot type. A type shall be a **scalar** superroot type if and only if it is type *alpha*. A type TT shall be a **tuple** superroot type if and only if it is a proper supertype of some tuple root type (in which case at least one attribute of *TT* must be of some superroot type). A type *RT* shall be a **relation** superroot type if and only if it is a proper supertype of some relation root type (in which case at least one attribute of *RT* must be of some superroot type).

A **subleaf type** shall be a scalar subleaf type, a tuple subleaf type, or a relation subleaf type. A type shall be a **scalar** subleaf type if and only if it is type *omega*. A type *TT* shall be a **tuple** subleaf type if and only if it is a proper subtype of some tuple leaf type (in which case at least one attribute of *TT* must be of some subleaf type). A type *RT* shall be a **relation** subleaf type if and only if it is a proper subtype of some relation leaf type (in which case at least one attribute of *RT* must be of some subleaf type).

27. Let *H* be a heading defined as follows:

    ```
    { <A1,T1> , <A2,T2> , ... , <An,Tn> }
    ```

    Then:

    a. If *t* is a tuple of type TUPLE *H*, meaning *t* shall take the form

        ```
        TUPLE { <A1,MST1,v1> , <A2,MST2,v2> , ... , <An,MSTn,vn> }
        ```

        where, for all *j* ($j = 1, 2, ..., n$), type *MSTj* is a subtype of type *Tj* and is the most specific type of value *vj*, then the **most specific** type of *t* shall be

        ```
        TUPLE { <A1,MST1> , <A2,MST2> , ... , <An,MSTn> }
        ```

    b. If *r* is a relation of type RELATION *H*, let the body of *r* consist of tuples *t1, t2, ..., tm* ($m \geq 0$). Tuple *ti* ($i = 1, 2, ..., m$) shall take the form

        ```
        TUPLE { <A1,MSTi1,vi1> , <A2,MSTi2,vi2> , ... , <An,MSTin,vin> }
        ```

        where, for all *j* ($j = 1, 2, ..., n$), type *MSTij* is a subtype of type *Tj* and is the most specific type of value *vij* (note that *MSTij* is different for different tuples *ti*, in general). Then the **most specific** type of *r* shall be

        ```
        RELATION { <A1,MST1> , <A2,MST2> , ... , <An,MSTn> }
        ```

        where, for all *j* ($j = 1, 2, ..., n$), type *MSTj* is the most specific common supertype of those most specific types *MSTij*, taken over all tuples *ti*.

28. Let *V* be a tuple variable or relation variable of declared type *T,* and let *T* have attributes *A1, A2, ..., An.* Then we can model *V* as a named set of named ordered triples of the form <*DTj,MSTj,vj*> (*j* = 1, 2, ..., *n*), where:

   a. The name of the set is the name of the variable, *V.*

   b. The name of each triple is the name of the corresponding attribute.

   c. *DTj* is the name of the declared type of attribute *Aj.*

   d. *MSTj* is the name of the **most specific type**—also known as the **current** most specific type—for, or of, attribute *Aj.* (If *V* is a relation variable, then the most specific type of *Aj* is the most specific common supertype of the most specific types of the *m* values in *vj*—see the explanation of *vj* below.)

   e. If *V* is a tuple variable, *vj* is a value of most specific type *MSTj*—the **current value** for, or of, attribute *Aj.* If *V* is a relation variable, then let the body of the current value of *V* consist of *m* tuples (*m* ≥ 0); label those tuples (in some arbitrary sequence) "tuple 1," "tuple 2," ..., "tuple *m*"; then *vj* is a sequence of *m* values (not necessarily all distinct), being the *Aj* values from tuple 1, tuple 2, ..., tuple *m* (in that order). Note that those *Aj* values are all of type *MSTj.*

We use the notation *DT*(*Aj*), *MST*(*Aj*), *v*(*Aj*) to refer to the *DTj*, *MSTj*, *vj* components, respectively, of attribute *Aj* of this model of tuple variable or relation variable *V.* We also use the notation *DT*(*V*), *MST*(*V*), *v*(*V*) to refer to the overall declared type, overall current most specific type, and overall current value, respectively, of this model of tuple variable or relation variable *V.*

Now let *X* be a tuple expression or relation expression. By definition, *X* specifies an invocation of some tuple operator or relation operator *Op.* Thus, the notation *DTj*(*V*), *MSTj*(*V*), *vj*(*V*) just introduced can be extended in an obvious way to refer to the declared type *DTj*(*X*), the current most specific type *MSTj*(*X*), and the current value *vj*(*X*), respectively, of the *DTj*, *MSTj*, *vj* components, respectively, of attribute *Aj* of tuple expression or relation expression *X*—where *DTj*(*X*) is the declared type of *Aj* for the invocation of *Op* in question (see IM Prescription 17) and is known at compile time, and *MSTj*(*X*) and *vj*(*X*) refer to the result of evaluating *X* and are therefore not known until run time (in general).

Part II

SCALAR TYPES,
SINGLE INHERITANCE

As explained in Chapter 4, our inheritance model consists of a total of 28 IM prescriptions. Part II of the book (nine chapters) discusses the first 20 of those prescriptions and explains their significance for what might be called "the base case," involving scalar types only and single inheritance only.

Chapter 5

Basic Definitions

*A definition is the enclosing [of] a wilderness of idea
within a wall of words.*

—Samuel Butler:
Notebooks (1912)

I hate definitions.

—Benjamin Disraeli:
Vivian Grey (1826)

For convenience I repeat below in Fig. 5.1 the sample type hierarchy from the section "The Running Example" in Chapter 3.

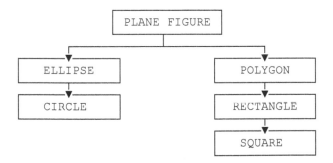

Fig. 5.1 (same as Fig. 3.1): Example of a type hierarchy

The rest of this chapter considers the first seven IM prescriptions, using Fig. 5.1 as a basis for examples. Let me remind you from Chapter 3 that, in an attempt to avoid confusion, throughout this book I refer to prescriptions of the *Manifesto* as such as "*TTM* prescriptions" and prescriptions of our inheritance model as "IM prescriptions." Let me also repeat the following from the preamble to Chapter 4:

Throughout this chapter, as well as elsewhere in this book, I use the symbols T and T' as generic names for a pair of types such that T' is a subtype of T (equivalently, such that T is a supertype of T'). You might find it helpful to think of T and T' as ELLIPSE and CIRCLE, respectively; however, keep in mind that they're not limited to being scalar types specifically, barring explicit statements to the contrary (moreover, the various prescriptions are all worded in such a way as not to be limited to single inheritance only, either). Note too that distinct types have distinct names; in particular, if T' is a proper subtype of T, then their names will be distinct, even if the set of values constituting T' isn't a proper subset of the set of values constituting T. (Conversely, if their names aren't distinct, then T' and T are the very same type and the corresponding sets of values will be identical.) Also, I assume that all of the types under discussion, including the maximal and minimal types discussed in IM Prescriptions 20 and 25, are members of some given set of available types *GSAT* (though the only explicit mention of that set is in IM Prescription 20, q.v.); in particular, the definitions of the terms *root type* and *leaf type* in IM Prescription 6 are to be understood in the context of that set. For example, given the type hierarchy of Fig. 3.1 in Chapter 3, the set of available types consists of:

a.   PLANE_FIGURE, ELLIPSE, CIRCLE, POLYGON, RECTANGLE, and SQUARE

b.   The types in terms of which the possreps for the types listed under point a. are defined

c.   The types in terms of which the possreps for the types included under point b., such as LENGTH and POINT, are defined (and so on, recursively, all the way down to and including the pertinent primitive types—see Chapter 4)

d.   The maximal scalar type *alpha* and the minimal scalar type *omega* (see IM Prescription 20)

e.   Tuple and relation types that can be generated using any of the types mentioned in any of these five points a.-e.

    Note: The term *primitive type*, mentioned under point c. above, refers to a system defined type (scalar by definition) with no declared possrep. The qualifier *primitive* derives from the fact that all of the types available in any given context are ultimately defined in terms of such types. Typical examples of such primitive types include the types INTEGER, RATIONAL, CHAR, and BOOLEAN.

    By the way, it's worth stating explicitly that type PLANE_FIGURE is *not* the only root type with respect to the foregoing set of types. It's not even the only scalar root type. By way of example, consider type POINT. Since it's the type of (among other things) a possrep component for type CIRCLE, type POINT is certainly a type in the given set; however, it's not a subtype of PLANE_FIGURE, and so it must be part of some distinct type hierarchy—possibly one consisting of type POINT only—and, by definition, that distinct type hierarchy has a distinct root type of its own.

    In fact the foregoing preliminary remarks are applicable not just to this chapter but also to the next few chapters, but I won't bother to repeat them again, instead allowing this single (re)statement to do duty for all.

IM PRESCRIPTION 1: TYPES ARE SETS

T and *T'* shall each be types; i.e., each shall be a named set of values.

IM Prescription 1 simply asserts that subtypes and supertypes are indeed types, in the full sense of that term as prescribed by *The Third Manifesto*. One consequence of this requirement is that, in general, subtypes can have lower level subtypes of their own and supertypes can have higher level supertypes of their own, as of course we already know.

    Note: Prior to this writing, the most recent version of our inheritance model was the one documented in our book *Database Explorations: Essays on The Third Manifesto and Related Topics* (available free online at *www.thethirdmanifesto.com*). For the purposes of this book, I'll refer to that version from this point forward as "the *Explorations* version." In the case of IM Prescription 1 in particular, the *Explorations* version actually said that each of *T* and *T'* shall be a named, *finite* set of values (emphasis added). The reason for the slight discrepancy is that when IM Prescription 1 was first written, one of the *TTM* prescriptions explicitly required scalar types (and hence, implicitly, nonscalar types as well) to be finite. Although there can be no doubt that, in practice, types indeed always are finite, some researchers questioned the need to say so in the *Manifesto* as such; the requirement was therefore dropped, and so I've dropped it from IM Prescription 1 accordingly.

    Another consequence of IM Prescription 1 is this: Since types are named, and since the only way a scalar type in particular can acquire a name is by being explicitly declared, it follows that all scalar types referenced in any of the IM prescriptions must be explicitly declared ones.

    By the way, note that I've characterized this prescription as saying "types are sets" (see the section title). Well, so they are—they're sets of values. But sometimes we need to be a little careful about the logical difference between type *T* as such, on the one hand, and the set of values that constitute type *T* on the other. To that end, I'll introduce some notation: From this point forward, I'll occasionally use the symbol $|T|$ to denote the set of values that constitute type *T*. That said, however, I won't always bother to distinguish between *T* and $|T|$, unless I'm trying to be formal or especially explicit.

IM PRESCRIPTION 2: SUBTYPES ARE SUBSETS

Every value in *T'* shall be a value in *T*; i.e., the set of values constituting *T'* shall be a subset of the set of values constituting *T* (in other words, if a value is of type *T'*, it shall also be of type *T*).

If types are sets, it obviously makes good intuitive sense to say that subtypes are subsets; thus, to say that value *v* is of type *T'* means among other things that *v* is certainly also of type *T*. It follows that if *v* is of type *T'*, the read-only operators that apply to *v* include, by definition, all of the operators—necessarily read-only operators specifically—that apply to values of type *T*. For example, if the read-only operator AREA_OF ("return the area of") applies to values of type ELLIPSE, then it certainly applies to values of type CIRCLE. In other words: *Read-only operators associated with type T are inherited by type T'*.

Here in outline are some of the read-only operators I'll assume apply to values of type ELLIPSE, and hence to values of type CIRCLE also. (I'll show later, however, that some of these operators might be *reimplemented* for type CIRCLE, implying that two distinct *implementation versions* of the operator in question, an ELLIPSE version and a CIRCLE version, might exist under the covers. See Chapters 7 and 11 for further discussion.)

```
OPERATOR THE_A ( E ELLIPSE ) RETURNS LENGTH ;
   /* "the length of the a semiaxis of" */ ... ;
END OPERATOR ;

OPERATOR THE_B ( E ELLIPSE ) RETURNS LENGTH ;
   /* "the length of the b semiaxis of" */ ... ;
END OPERATOR ;

OPERATOR THE_CTR ( E ELLIPSE ) RETURNS POINT ;
   /* "the center of" */ ... ;
END OPERATOR ;

OPERATOR AREA_OF ( E ELLIPSE ) RETURNS AREA ;
   /* "the area of" */ ... ;
END OPERATOR ;
```

And here's a read-only operator that applies to values of type CIRCLE but not to values of type ELLIPSE:

```
OPERATOR THE_R ( C CIRCLE ) RETURNS LENGTH ;
   /* "the radius of" */ ... ;
END OPERATOR ;
```

Of course, as we saw in Chapter 2, the operators THE_A, THE_B, and THE_CTR (for type ELLIPSE) and THE_R and THE_CTR (for type CIRCLE) are all required by *The Third Manifesto* as such, and they're provided "automatically." In the case of THE_CTR for type CIRCLE in particular, it's precisely inheritance from type ELLIPSE that serves as the required "automatic" provision of that operator, though again it's possible—albeit unlikely, perhaps—that some reimplementation might be involved. As for THE_A and THE_B for type CIRCLE, these operators are required, not by *The Third Manifesto* as such, but rather by the very notion of inheritance (though once again it's possible that there might be some reimplementation involved).

Moreover, it follows from all of the above that if *v* is of type *T'*, then *v* must satisfy all of the constraints that apply to values of type *T*, as well as all of the constraints that apply to values of type *T'* specifically. To repeat an example from Chapter 3, if *c* is a circle (and hence an ellipse), and if ellipses are subject to the constraint that the length *a* of their major semiaxis must be greater than or equal to the length *b* of their minor semiaxis, then that same constraint must be satisfied by *c*—as indeed it is, trivially, because in the case of a circle the semiaxes coincide in the radius. In other words: *Constraints associated with type T are inherited by type T'.*

Now, in Chapter 2 I said that if *v* is a scalar value, it can be thought of as carrying around with it a kind of flag that announces "I'm an integer" or "I'm a supplier number" or "I'm a rectangle" (etc., etc.). Now we see that, conceptually speaking, it might have to carry around several distinct flags—e.g., "I'm an ellipse" *and* "I'm a circle." (Of course, a flag that specifies just the most specific type is all that's logically required. See IM Prescription 8 in Chapter 6 for further discussion.)

I also said in Chapter 2 that distinct types are disjoint "except possibly if type inheritance is supported"—but now it's clear that two types are definitely not disjoint if one's a subtype of the other. And there are other cases of nondisjointness, too, which we'll encounter in Parts III and IV of this book. As far as the present part (i.e., Part II) is concerned, however, two types *T1* and *T2* are disjoint if and only if neither is a subtype of the other; in other words, we can stay with the disjointness assumption (see Chapter 3), and I will, until further notice.

> *Aside:* To repeat, to say that value *v* is of type *T'* means among other things that *v* is certainly also of type *T*. On the other hand, to say that value *v* is of type *T* doesn't in general preclude the possibility that *v* is also of type *T'*. For example, to say that *e* is an ellipse doesn't preclude the possibility that *e* is also a circle. In fact, to say that *v* is of type *T* means, precisely, that the most specific type of *v* (see IM Prescription 8 in Chapter 6) is some subtype of *T* (see IM Prescriptions 3-5 below). *End of aside.*

(*Important!*) Note that it's an obvious corollary of IM Prescription 2 that there can't be more values of type *T'* than there are of type *T*. This apparently trivial observation can be very helpful in pinpointing errors and clearing up confusions. For example, it would be an error according to our model to suggest that colored circles (type COLORED_CIRCLE) might be regarded as a subtype of circles in general (type CIRCLE)—a state of affairs that might come as something of a surprise to you, if you happen to be familiar with object systems. The reason is this: If circles as such are "plain" or uncolored, then there are clearly more colored circles than there are just plain circles. (I'm assuming here that, e.g., a red circle and a blue circle of the same size and at the same location are different colored circles.) What's more, there's clearly no CIRCLE selector invocation that could possibly yield a value of type COLORED_CIRCLE (the CIRCLE selector has parameters corresponding to the radius and center but no "color" parameter). And so the proposed subtype / supertype relationship, as such, does not in fact exist. *Note:* I'll have quite a lot more to say regarding this particular example in Chapter 21.

Finally, the *Explorations* version of IM Prescription 2 had a note attached to it, having to do with proper subtypes and supertypes. I've deleted that note as such, replacing it by an extension to IM Prescription 5 that takes care of the issue raised by the note in question.

IM PRESCRIPTION 3: "SUBTYPE OF" IS REFLEXIVE

T and *T'* shall not necessarily be distinct; i.e., every type shall be both a subtype and a supertype of itself.

IM Prescriptions 3-7 mostly have to do with matters of terminology (basically they just elaborate on certain of the terms and concepts introduced in Chapter 3). IM Prescription 3 in particular recognizes that, just as in mathematics it's convenient to regard any set *S* as both a subset and a superset of itself, so in our inheritance model it's convenient to regard any type *T* as both a subtype and a supertype of itself. Thus, for example, "ELLIPSE is a subtype of ELLIPSE" is a true statement, and so is "ELLIPSE is a supertype of ELLIPSE." This convention has the effect of simplifying both (a) many of the discussions we'll be having later and (b) the formulation of many of the IM prescriptions in particular.

Note: To say that a given dyadic boolean or truth valued operator *Op* is reflexive—see the title of the present section—is merely to say that, for all *x*, *x Op x* evaluates to TRUE. Thus, e.g., "=" is reflexive, and so is "is a subtype of." By contrast, "<" and "is a proper subtype of" aren't reflexive.

IM PRESCRIPTION 4: "SUBTYPE OF" IS TRANSITIVE

Every subtype of *T'* shall be a subtype of *T*. Every supertype of *T* shall be a supertype of *T'*.

This prescription (which was IM Prescription 5 in the *Explorations* version) simply says, loosely, that a subtype of a subtype is a subtype and a supertype of a supertype is a supertype. Thus, for example, RECTANGLE is a subtype of PLANE_FIGURE, and PLANE_FIGURE is a supertype of RECTANGLE.

Note: To say that a given dyadic boolean operator *Op* is transitive—see the title of this section—is merely to say that, for all *x*, *y*, and *z*, if *x Op y* and *y Op z* both evaluate to TRUE, then so does *x Op z*. Thus, e.g., "=" is transitive, and so is "is a subtype of." By contrast, "≠" and "is disjoint from" aren't transitive.

IM PRESCRIPTION 5: PROPER AND IMMEDIATE SUBTYPES AND SUPERTYPES

Let T and T' be scalar types. Then:

a. If and only if T and T' are distinct, then T shall be a **proper** supertype of T' and T' shall be a **proper** subtype of T.

b. Let T be a proper supertype of T', and let S be a sequence of types $T1, T2, ..., Tm$ such that T is a proper supertype of $T1$, $T1$ is a proper supertype of $T2$, ..., and Tm is a proper supertype of T' $(m \geq 0)$. Then either (a) no such sequence S shall exist (i.e., every such sequence shall be such that $m = 0$), in which case (and in which case only) T shall be an **immediate** supertype of T', or (b) every such sequence S shall be such that $m > 0$, in which case (and in which case only) T shall be a **nonimmediate** supertype of T'. Also, T' shall be an **immediate** subtype of T if and only if T is an immediate supertype of T', and T' shall be a **nonimmediate** subtype of T if and only if T is a nonimmediate supertype of T.

c. If and only if T is an immediate supertype of T' and T' is neither a root type nor type *omega*—see IM Prescription 20—then the definition of T' shall be accompanied by a specification of an **example value** that is of type T and not of type T'.

This prescription has been tightened up considerably, in part because the Explorations version failed to deal adequately with the multiple inheritance case. Basically, however, it consists of a combination of the Explorations versions of IM Prescriptions 4 and 6, tailored to scalar types specifically. The nonscalar aspects of those prescriptions now form the new IM Prescription 23.

IM Prescription 5 does a couple of related things:

■ *Proper subtypes and supertypes:* First, it introduces some terminology for talking about subtypes and supertypes—at least, scalar subtypes and supertypes—when the types in question are distinct. To be specific, it recognizes that, much as in mathematics (where "set S' is a proper subset of set S" means that (a) S' is a subset of S and (b) S' and S are distinct), it's useful to define T' as being a proper subtype of T if and only if (a) T' is a subtype of T and (b) T' and T are distinct. (Recall that types are distinct if and only if they have distinct names.) Thus, for example, CIRCLE is a proper subtype of both ELLIPSE and PLANE_FIGURE (note that, like "subtype of," "proper subtype of" is transitive). CIRCLE is also a subtype of CIRCLE, but not a proper one. Likewise, PLANE_FIGURE is a proper supertype of both ELLIPSE and CIRCLE; it's also a supertype of PLANE_FIGURE, but not a proper one.

■ *Immediate subtypes and supertypes:* Second, the prescription also introduces some terminology for talking about scalar subtypes and supertypes when the types in question are adjacent to each other, as it were, or in other words have no types coming between them. The wording of the prescription in this connection might look a little complicated, but what it boils down to—at least in the single inheritance case—is that, for example, CIRCLE is an immediate subtype of ELLIPSE, and ELLIPSE is an immediate supertype of CIRCLE. CIRCLE is also a subtype of PLANE_FIGURE, but not an immediate one; equivalently, PLANE_FIGURE is a supertype of CIRCLE, but not an immediate one.

Note: In view of the first of the two bullet items above, you might feel the informal characterization given earlier for IM Prescription 2 ("subtypes are subsets") could better be stated—in fact, strengthened—thus: *Proper* subtypes are *proper* subsets. Consider the following argument:

If T and T' are distinct, there must exist at least one value of type T that's not a value of type T'. Because suppose not. Then every value of type T would be a value of type T' (so $|T'|$ and $|T|$ would be equal); hence, (a) every operator that applied to values of type T' would apply to values of type T, and (b) every constraint that applied to values of type T' would apply to values of type T. Thus, T' and T would effectively be identical except for their names, and there wouldn't be any logical reason to distinguish between them.

In fact this argument is valid for scalar types.[1] However, it's not valid—not quite—for tuple or relation types, as we'll see in Chapter 17. But scalar types are what we're supposed to be concentrating on in this part of the book, so I'm going to ignore tuple and relation types until further notice. In the case of scalar types, then, that stronger characterization (viz., that proper subtypes are proper subsets) does in fact apply, thanks to part c. of IM Prescription 5: *If and only if T is an immediate supertype of T' and T' is neither a root type nor type omega—see IM Prescription 20—then the definition of T' shall be accompanied by a specification of an* **example value** *that is of type T and not of type T'.* For example:

```
TYPE CIRCLE
     IS { ELLIPSE
          CONSTRAINT THE_A ( ELLIPSE ) = THE_B ( ELLIPSE )
          POSSREP ( R  = THE_A    ( ELLIPSE ) ,
                    CTR = THE_CTR ( ELLIPSE ) )
          NOT { ELLIPSE ( LENGTH ( 2.0 ) ,
                          LENGTH ( 1.0 ) ,
                          POINT  ( 0.0 , 0.0 ) ) } } ;
```

---

[1] Note, however, that it does rely—somewhat indirectly—on part d. of IM Prescription 20 (discussed in Chapter 12).

The intent of the NOT specification here is to say that the specified value is a value of type ELLIPSE that's not a value of type CIRCLE. (It might be nice to find a better keyword than NOT for this purpose.)[2] Note that, by definition, the example value specified in connection with type T' must satisfy the type constraint for type T and not the type constraint for type T'. See the discussion of IM Prescription 10 in Chapter 8 for further discussion.

Incidentally, it follows immediately from the fact that, at least with scalar types, proper subtypes are proper subsets that the most specific type of a given value isn't necessarily a leaf type. For example, some ellipses are "just ellipses" and not circles. Of course, it would be possible to set up the type schema[3] in such a way as to ensure that most specific types are all leaf types, if desired. With reference to Fig. 5.1, for example, introducing types NONCIRCLE, NONRECTANGLE, and NONSQUARE (all with the intuitively obvious semantics) as immediate subtypes of types ELLIPSE, POLYGON, and RECTANGLE, respectively, would have such an effect. The *Manifesto* model doesn't assume such an arrangement, but neither does it prohibit it.

It also follows from the fact that proper subtypes are proper subsets that type hierarchies can't contain any cycles (i.e., such hierarchies are indeed hierarchic). For suppose, contrariwise, that there existed some sequence of types $T1, T2, T3, ..., Tn$ such that $T1$ was an immediate supertype of $T2$, $T2$ was an immediate supertype of $T3$, ..., and Tn was an immediate supertype of $T1$. Then every one of these types $T1, T2, T3, ..., Tn$ would be a proper supertype, and hence a proper superset, of itself!

To close this section, I remind you from Chapter 3 that if T' is a proper subtype of T, there's no requirement that their physical representations be the same. Of course, there's no requirement that they be different, either.

IM PRESCRIPTION 6: SCALAR ROOT AND LEAF TYPES

A scalar type that has type *alpha*—see IM Prescription 20—as its sole immediate supertype shall be a (scalar) **root** type. A scalar type that has type *omega*—again, see IM Prescription 20—as its sole immediate subtype shall be a (scalar) **leaf** type.

IM Prescription 6 has to do with root and leaf types (in essence, it consists of what remains of the *Explorations* version after the material having to do with immediate subtypes and supertypes is removed; however, it has also been reworded—in fact, reduced in scope slightly—to make it clear that the new version applies to scalar types specifically). Loosely, a root type is a type such

---

[2] But what would be a suitable NOT specification for type ELLIPSE? I'll discuss this question in Chapter 12 also.

[3] Recall from Chapter 3 that the term *type schema* refers to a collection of related type definitions. For example, the collection of type definitions for the six types shown in Fig. 5.1 could be regarded as constituting a type schema.

as PLANE_FIGURE that has no immediate supertype, and a leaf type is a type such as CIRCLE or SQUARE that has no immediate subtype. Recall, however, that these terms are context dependent and must always be understood in the context of the given set of available types, *GSAT*. For example, if type *T* is a leaf type but then we add some proper subtype *T'* of *T* to the type hierarchy, clearly *T* won't be a leaf type any longer. When we were defining our original model, however, there was some debate over how the terms *root* and *leaf* should be interpreted when the special types *alpha* and *omega*—or, rather, what we now call *superroot* and *subleaf* types in general (see the discussion of IM Prescription 26 in Chapter 19)—were taken into account. After much consideration, we decided that it made better sense to define the terms in such a way as to exclude those special types, and IM Prescription 6 does so.

Note: It follows from the foregoing that the type hierarchy concept itself is also context dependent (and the same goes for the more general type graph concept, to be discussed in Chapter 14). Of course, those concepts aren't part of our formal inheritance model anyway. However, it's worth noting that the set of types *GSAT* available in any given situation can always be partitioned into a set of disjoint *lattices* (see the next subsection), as follows:[4]

■ The set of all scalar types is a lattice; for any given pair of such types, the least upper bound and the greatest lower bound are, respectively, the most specific common supertype and the least specific common subtype for the pair in question (see IM Prescription 8). The least upper and greatest lower bounds for the lattice as a whole are the maximal scalar type *alpha* and the minimal scalar type *omega*, respectively.

■ Let *T* be a tuple type, with corresponding maximal and minimal types *T_alpha* and *T_omega*, respectively (see IM Prescription 25). Then the set of all subtypes of *T_alpha* down to and including *T_omega* is a lattice;[5] for any given pair of such types, the least upper bound and the greatest lower bound are, respectively, the most specific common supertype and the least specific common subtype for the pair in question (see IM Prescription 24). The least upper and greatest lower bounds for the lattice as a whole are *T_alpha* and *T_omega*, respectively. Note that, by definition, all types belonging to a given tuple type lattice have the same attribute names.

■ Let *T* be a relation type, with corresponding maximal and minimal types *T_alpha* and *T_omega*, respectively (again, see IM Prescription 25). Then the set of all subtypes of *T_alpha* down to and including *T_omega* is a lattice;[6] for any given pair of such types, the least upper bound and the greatest lower bound are, respectively, the most specific common

---

[4] The material in the rest of this section is included primarily for purposes of future reference—it relies on numerous concepts I haven't had a chance to discuss yet and thus might not make much sense on a first reading. You can skip it for now if you like.

[5] The phrase "the set of all subtypes of *T_alpha* down to and including *T_omega*" could be replaced here by the phrase "the set of all supertypes of *T_omega* up to and including *T_alpha*" without changing the meaning, since the two sets are identical.

[6] The previous footnote applies here also.

supertype and the least specific common subtype for the pair in question (see IM Prescription 24). The least upper and greatest lower bounds for the lattice as a whole are *T_alpha* and *T_omega*, respectively. Note that, by definition, all types belonging to a given relation type lattice have the same attribute names.

The foregoing lattices are pairwise disjoint, in the sense that every type in the given set of available types *GSAT* belongs to exactly one of them. Moreover, no type in any of those lattices overlaps any type in any other (see IM Prescription 7).

Lattices

In case you're not familiar with the concept of a lattice, let me elaborate briefly. First we need some definitions. Let S be a set, and let a partial ordering "≤" be defined on S, where:

> **Definition:** A *partial ordering* "≤" on set S is a dyadic truth valued operator such that for all x, y, and $z \in S$, (a) $x \leq y$ or $y \leq x$ or both, or possibly neither; (b) $x \leq x$ (reflexivity); (c) if $x \leq y$ and $y \leq z$, then $x \leq z$ (transitivity); and (d) if $x \leq y$ and $y \leq x$, then $x = y$ (antisymmetry). *Note:* The symbol "∈" denotes the set membership operator; it can be read as "in" or "is an element of" or "belongs to." As for the symbol "≤", it can be read as "less than or equal to," of course, but it doesn't necessarily represent the usual arithmetical "less than or equal to" operator as such.

Given this definition, I hope you can see that "is a subtype of" is a partial ordering on the set of types shown in Fig. 5.1.

Now let S' be a subset of S (the possibility that S' might be equal to S isn't excluded, of course). Then:

> **Definition:** The element x is a *lower bound* for S' if and only if $x \in S$ and x is less than or equal to every element of S' with respect to the specified ordering (note that x might or might not be an element of S' as such, as opposed to S). Likewise, the element x is an *upper bound* for S' if and only if $x \in S$ and x is greater than or equal to every element of S' with respect to the specified ordering (again x might or might not be an element of S' as such, as opposed to S).[7]

For example, given "is a subtype of" as a partial ordering on the set of types shown in Fig. 5.1, SQUARE and RECTANGLE are both lower bounds for the subset consisting of POLYGON and RECTANGLE, and PLANE_FIGURE and POLYGON are both upper bounds for that same subset.

---

[7] I'm taking a slight liberty with terminology here, since "greater than" hasn't technically been defined. For the record, then: We define "x is greater than or equal to y" (in symbols, "$x \geq y$") to be logically equivalent to "y is less than or equal to x" ("$y \leq x$").

Definition: If the subset S' has any lower bounds x at all, then it's easy to see there must be a largest one, and that largest x is the *greatest lower bound* (GLB) for S' with respect to the specified ordering. Likewise, if the subset S' has any upper bounds x at all, then it's easy to see there must be a smallest one, and that smallest x is the *least upper bound* (LUB) for S' with respect to the specified ordering.[8]

For example, given "is a subtype of" as a partial ordering on the set of types shown in Fig. 5.1, RECTANGLE is the GLB for the subset consisting of POLYGON and RECTANGLE, and POLYGON is the LUB for that same subset.

Now I can define the term *lattice*:

Definition: Let S be a set and let a partial ordering be defined on S. Then the combination of S and that ordering is a *lattice* if and only if every pair of elements of S has both a least upper bound and a greatest lower bound with respect to that ordering.

Note, therefore, that strictly speaking it's not a set as such that constitutes a lattice; rather, it's a set together with some partial ordering. But it's usual to say things like "set S is (or forms) a lattice," without explicitly mentioning the ordering, when the ordering in question is understood. As far as we're concerned in this book, of course, the pertinent ordering will always be "is a subtype of," so I won't usually bother to mention it explicitly.

Note too, incidentally, that it follows from the foregoing definition that a set of cardinality either one or zero can always be regarded as a lattice.

Now, I've already said that the set of available types *GSAT* in any given situation can be partitioned into a set of disjoint lattices, and I've explained in outline what I mean by that observation. Now I'd like to add the following:[9]

- Let T be any type. Then the set of all subtypes of T, including both type T itself and type T_omega, can be regarded as a lattice in its own right, with least upper bound and greatest lower bound T and T_omega, respectively.

- Likewise, the set of all supertypes of T, including both type T itself and type T_alpha, can also be regarded as a lattice in its own right, with least upper bound and greatest lower bound T_alpha and T, respectively.

---

[8] Again I'm taking some slight liberties with terminology, since "largest" and "smallest" haven't been defined. This time, however, I'll leave the formal definitions to you.

[9] Note that the types T_alpha and T_omega, mentioned earlier in this chapter and mentioned again several times in what follows, reduce to just *alpha* and *omega*, respectively, if type T is scalar. See Part IV of this book for further explanation.

- The set of all subtypes and supertypes of *T* can also be regarded as a lattice in its own right, with least upper bound and greatest lower bound *T_alpha* and *T_omega*, respectively.

- Finally (*important!*): Let *T* be a type, with corresponding maximal and minimal types *T_alpha* and *T_omega*, respectively. Then the set of all subtypes of *T_alpha* down to and including *T_omega* is a lattice, with least upper bound and greatest lower bound *T_alpha* and *T_omega*, respectively. *Please note that from this point forward in this book, the unqualified term* **type lattice** *should always be taken to refer to a lattice of this particular kind, unless the context demands otherwise.*

IM PRESCRIPTION 7: DISJOINT AND OVERLAPPING TYPES

Types *T1* and *T2* shall be **disjoint** if and only if no value is of both type *T1* and type *T2*. Types *T1* and *T2* shall **overlap** if and only if there exists at least one value that is common to both. Distinct root types shall be disjoint. If types *T1* and *T2* are distinct immediate subtypes of the same scalar type *T*, there shall exist at least one value that is of type *T1* and not of type *T2*.

The last sentence of this prescription is new. See Chapter 14 for further discussion.

This prescription provides explicit definitions for (a) the concept of disjoint types in general—for root types in particular—and (b) the converse concept of overlapping types. Certain of the prescriptions to be discussed in later chapters appeal explicitly to these concepts. But let me say a little more, in connection with scalar types specifically, concerning the requirement that distinct root types must be disjoint. (Actually, the argument that follows applies in all essential respects to nonscalar types as well.)

Let *RT1* and *RT2* be distinct root types (i.e., roots for distinct type hierarchies). Clearly, neither of *RT1* and *RT2* is a subtype of the other, because otherwise they'd be part of the same type hierarchy, and so at least one wouldn't be a root type after all. By the disjointness assumption, therefore, *RT1* and *RT2* are disjoint. So, at least in the case of scalar types and single inheritance, distinct root types are necessarily disjoint. And it follows immediately that distinct type hierarchies are disjoint as well—no value *v* is of two distinct types *T1* and *T2* such that *T1* is part of type hierarchy *TH1* and *T2* is part of type hierarchy *TH2* (because that value *v* would then necessarily be a value of the roots of both hierarchies, in which case those roots wouldn't be disjoint after all). For example, suppose we were to drop type PLANE_FIGURE (only) from Fig. 5.1; then we would have two distinct type hierarchies, one rooted at type ELLIPSE and the other at type POLYGON, that are necessarily disjoint (no value is both an ellipse and a polygon).

Note further that, at least in the context of scalar types and single inheritance, distinct immediate subtypes of the same supertype are disjoint as well (this is another consequence of the disjointness assumption). Given that the subtypes in question are also necessarily nonempty (see the section "Miscellaneous Issues," subsection "Initial Values," in Chapter 2), the requirements of the final sentence of IM Prescription 7 are thus satisfied a fortiori.

Here for the record are some further consequences of IM Prescription 7:

- Let *T1* and *T2* be scalar types. Then they're certainly disjoint if they're distinct leaf types or if either one is type *omega*. (Note in particular that type *omega* is disjoint from itself! Certainly there's no value that's of both type *omega* and type *omega*.)

- Let *TT1* and *TT2* be tuple types from the same type lattice. Then they're certainly disjoint if they're distinct leaf types (see the discussion of IM Prescription 24 in Chapter 18). They might or might not be disjoint—though in practice they usually will be—if one is the pertinent minimal type (see the discussion of IM Prescription 25 in Chapter 19).

- Let *RT1* and *RT2* be relation types from the same type lattice. Then they're certainly *not* disjoint, even if they're distinct leaf types (again see the discussion of IM Prescription 24 in Chapter 18), and even if one is the pertinent minimal type (again see the discussion of IM Prescription 25 in Chapter 19). For example, let *RT1* and *RT2* be the relation types RELATION {PF CIRCLE} and RELATION {PF SQUARE}, respectively. Then *RT1* and *RT2* overlap, because the empty relation RELATION {PF *omega*} is a value of both types. In fact, every type in the pertinent type lattice, even the pertinent minimal type RELATION {PF *omega*}, contains that same empty relation as a value. Note, therefore, that minimal relation types are never empty.

Note: The *Explorations* version of IM Prescription 7 additionally stated that two types overlap if they're the same type, implying in particular that type *omega* was considered to overlap with itself (as well as being disjoint from itself). However, this part of the prescription seems never to have had a good logical basis; it seems to have been included purely because of a vague feeling on the part of Darwen and myself at the time that allowing a type not to overlap with itself was somehow counterintuitive.

EXERCISES

5.1   Distinguish between *T* and |*T*|.

5.2   Why doesn't it make sense to think of "colored circles" as constituting a subtype of the type "circles in general"?

5.3   Explain how it can be definitionally guaranteed that some rectangles aren't squares (i.e., that some values of type RECTANGLE aren't also values of type SQUARE).

5.4   What's a type schema?

5.5   What's a lattice? Show that the set of types in Fig. 5.1, together with types *alpha* and *omega*, can indeed be regarded as a lattice.

5.6   If type *T'* is an immediate subtype of type *T*, do you think it could make sense for *T'* to be user defined and *T* to be system defined?

ANSWERS

5.1   The symbol |*T*| denotes the set of values that constitute type *T*.

5.2   Informally, because there are more colored circles than there are just plain circles. See the discussion of IM Prescription 2 in the body of the chapter, also (and more especially) the more extensive discussion of this same example in Chapter 21.

5.3   By explicitly specifying as part of the definition of type SQUARE—thereby demonstrating the existence of—a value that's of type RECTANGLE and not of type SQUARE.

5.4   A type schema is a collection of related type definitions.

5.5   For an explanation of what a lattice is, see the body of the chapter. To show that the set of types in Fig. 5.1 (plus types *alpha* and *omega*) can be regarded as a lattice, we need to show that every pair of types from that set has both a least upper bound (LUB) and a greatest lower bound (GLB) with respect to "is a subtype of." Well, there are eight types in total, so there are 8+7+6+5+4+3+2+1 =36 pairs of types altogether (including pairs for which the two types are identical, but treating pairs of the form (*T1*,*T2*) and (*T2*,*T1*) as one and the same). Let (*T1*,*T2*) be one such pair. Then:

 ■   Any pair such that *T1* is *alpha* or *T2* is *omega* has LUB *T1* and GLB *T2*.

For the remainder of this discussion, therefore, let's ignore pairs with either *T1* or *T2* equal to either *alpha* or *omega*. Next:

 ■   Any pair such that *T1* is PLANE_FIGURE has LUB *T1* and GLB *T2*.

For the remainder of this discussion, therefore, let's ignore pairs with either *T1* or *T2* equal to PLANE_FIGURE. Next:

■   Any pair such that *T2* is a subtype of *T1* has LUB *T1* and GLB *T2*.

The only remaining pairs are of the form (*T1*,*T2*) where one of *T1* and *T2* is either ELLIPSE or CIRCLE and the other is either POLYGON, RECTANGLE, or SQUARE. All such pairs have LUB PLANE_FIGURE and GLB *omega*.

5.6   If *T* is system defined but has an explicitly declared possrep, there's no problem—*T'* can be defined in this case exactly as if *T* were user defined. But what if *T* is system defined and has no explicitly declared possrep? In such a case, *T'* obviously can't have a possrep that's derived from some explicitly declared possrep for *T*. However, one of the *TTM* prescriptions *requires T'* to have a declared possrep; moreover, the BNF grammar in Chapter 3 requires that possrep to be explicitly derived from some possrep for *T*. This state of affairs suggests that the *Manifesto* itself might need some minor extension in this area—perhaps an extension according to which type *T* does have a possrep after all, albeit one that's provided automatically. By way of example, suppose, not unreasonably, that the system defined type INTEGER has no explicitly declared possrep. Given the suggested *Manifesto* extension, then, we might define type EVEN_INTEGER as a subtype of INTEGER like this (to invent some syntax on the fly):

```
TYPE EVEN_INTEGER IS { INTEGER
                       CONSTRAINT IS_FACTOR_OF ( INTEGER , 2 )
                       POSSREP ( SAME_AS ( INTEGER ) )
                       NOT { 1 } } ;
```

    Note the type constraint: A given value is defined to be of type EVEN_INTEGER if and only if it's of type INTEGER *and* it has 2 as a factor. (I'm assuming the availability of an operator called IS_FACTOR_OF that returns TRUE if and only its second argument divides its first exactly *n* times, where *n* is an integer.) That type constraint overall is an example of what IM Prescription 10 calls a *specialization* constraint. See Chapter 8 for further explanation.

Chapter 6

Scalar Values with Inheritance

The tragedy of the commons
—William Forster Lloyd (attrib.):
Two Lectures on the Checks to Population (1833)

The scalar value concept needs some extension if type inheritance is supported, basically because such values are no longer limited to being of just one type. As we'll see, IM Prescription 8 addresses this issue, though it does so in a rather roundabout way. In particular, that prescription has the important consequence that every scalar value has exactly one most specific type. Of course, we already know this—I mean, we already know that scalar values always have a unique most specific type, at least in the single inheritance context—because it's a logical consequence of the disjointness assumption (see Chapter 3). However, the fact that this same state of affairs holds as a logical consequence of IM Prescription 8 as well is more significant, in a way, because the disjointness assumption applies only to single inheritance, while IM Prescription 8 applies to multiple inheritance as well as single.

That said, I won't attempt to prove my claim in this chapter (my claim, that is, that the uniqueness of most specific types is a logical consequence of IM Prescription 8); instead, I'll defer that proof to Chapter 15, where I'll show that the claim does hold for multiple inheritance and hence for single as well, a fortiori. (As a matter of fact, it holds for tuple and relation inheritance too, as we'll see in Part IV of this book. But first things first.)

Of course, IM Prescription 8 is deliberately worded in such a way as to apply to inheritance in general, not just to single inheritance in particular (though only to scalar types in both cases; as already noted, tuple and relation inheritance is dealt with elsewhere). Partly as a consequence of this generality, the prescription might look a little complicated at first sight. However, in the degenerate case we're concerned with in the present chapter (single inheritance only), it does become somewhat simpler than it might initially appear.

IM PRESCRIPTION 8: COMMON SUBTYPES AND SUPERTYPES

Let $T1$, $T2$, ..., Tm ($m \geq 0$), T, and T' be scalar types. Then:

a. Type T shall be a **common supertype** for, or of, types $T1$, $T2$, ..., Tm if and only if, whenever a given value is of at least one of types $T1$, $T2$, ..., Tm, it is also of type T.

Further, that type *T* shall be the **most specific** common supertype for *T1*, *T2*, ..., *Tm* if and only if no proper subtype of *T* is also a common supertype for those types.

b.   Type *T'* shall be a **common subtype** for, or of, types *T1*, *T2*, ..., *Tm* if and only if, whenever a given value is of type *T'*, it is also of each of types *T1*, *T2*, ..., *Tm*. Further, that type *T'* shall be the **least specific** common subtype—also known as the **intersection type** or **intersection subtype**—for *T1*, *T2*, ..., *Tm* if and only if no proper supertype of *T'* is also a common subtype for those types.

Note: Given types *T1*, *T2*, ..., *Tm* as defined above, it can be shown (thanks in particular to IM Prescription 20) that a unique most specific common supertype *T* and a unique least specific common subtype *T'* always exist. In the case of that particular common subtype *T'*, moreover, it can also be shown that whenever a given value is of each of types *T1*, *T2*, ..., *Tm*, it is also of type *T'* (hence the alternative term *intersection type*). And it can further be shown that every scalar value *v* has both a unique least specific type and a unique most specific type (regarding this latter—which elsewhere in these prescriptions is denoted *MST(v)*—see also IM Prescription 9).

Before discussing IM Prescription 8 as such, I need to say a little more about the special scalar types *alpha* and *omega* (I've mentioned these types several times in passing in earlier chapters, but it's time to get a little more specific). So:

■   First, type *omega*. Type *omega* is the empty scalar type—it contains no values at all. And, since the empty set is a subset of every set, it follows that type *omega* is a subtype of every scalar type (itself included, of course). *Note:* There's a lot more that can and needs to be said about type *omega* in general, but I'll defer detailed discussion to IM Prescription 20 in Chapter 12. For present purposes, it's sufficient to understand just that (a) such a type does exist (at least conceptually; I mean, I wouldn't expect it to have to be explicitly declared), and (b) it's unique, meaning it's the *only* empty scalar type (see Exercise 6.6 at the end of the chapter).

■   As for type *alpha*, it's type *omega*'s polar opposite; in other words, where type *omega* contains no values at all, type *alpha* contains *all* values (all scalar values, that is), and it's a supertype of every scalar type, itself included. *Note:* As with type *omega*, there's a lot more that can and needs to be said about type *alpha* in general, but I'll defer detailed discussion to IM Prescription 20 in Chapter 12. For present purposes, it's sufficient to understand just that (again as with type *omega*) (a) such a type does exist, at least conceptually, and (b) it's unique.

COMMON SUBTYPES

Now I turn to IM Prescription 8 as such. It's convenient to deal with part b. of this prescription first, which asserts among other things that any given set of *m* scalar types *T1*, *T2*, ..., *Tm* ($m \geq 0$) has a common subtype *T'*. In order to show that this proposition is reasonable, I'll begin by considering the case *m* = 2. In this case we're dealing with precisely two types *T1* and *T2* (and we can assume that these two types are distinct, for otherwise we're dealing with the case *m* = 1). Thus:

- If one of *T1* and *T2*, say *T2*, is a subtype—necessarily a proper subtype—of the other (i.e., *T1*), then (a) every subtype of *T2* is necessarily a common subtype for *T1* and *T2*, and (b) of those common subtypes, *T2* itself is clearly the one that's the least specific. In other words, *T2* itself is the unique least specific common subtype in this case. For example, the least specific common subtype for types PLANE_FIGURE and RECTANGLE is RECTANGLE.

- If neither of *T1* and *T2* is a subtype of the other, then, by virtue of the disjointness assumption,[1] they're disjoint and have no values in common. So in this case the only type that's a common subtype for *T1* and *T2* is necessarily type *omega*—and since it's the only one, it's clearly also the least specific common subtype of *T1* and *T2* a fortiori. For example, the least specific common subtype for types ELLIPSE and POLYGON is *omega*.

  Aside: To repeat, *omega* is a subtype of every scalar type; e.g., given the type hierarchy of Fig. 5.1, *omega* is a subtype of both of the leaf types CIRCLE and SQUARE. It follows that we're already moving into the realm of multiple inheritance, albeit in a very limited kind of way. Nevertheless, I'll continue to assume throughout most of this chapter, and most of the rest of this part of the book, that it still makes sense to talk in terms of single inheritance only. Note in particular, therefore, that the disjointness assumption still holds, even given type *omega*. For example, types CIRCLE and SQUARE are still disjoint, even though they have a common subtype. The point is, of course, that the subtype in question is empty. (If they had a nonempty common subtype, then every value of that subtype would be both a circle and a square, and the types would thus not be disjoint.) *End of aside.*

---

[1] This is where the proof of part b. of the prescription relies on the fact that we're dealing with single inheritance specifically.

In both cases, therefore, scalar types *T1* and *T2* do have a unique least specific common subtype. Let that type be *T'*. Then it should be clear in both cases that the set of values $|T'|$ is precisely the set theory intersection $|T1| \cap |T2|$ of the sets of values $|T1|$ and $|T2|$.[2] The alternative name *intersection type*, or (more specifically) *intersection subtype*, is thus reasonable, and in some ways intuitively preferable to the more formal name *least specific common subtype*.

Now consider the case *m* = 3 (so we have three distinct types *T1*, *T2*, and *T3*). Choose any pair of types in this set, say *T1* and *T2*, and replace them by their intersection subtype, *T12* say. By our previous argument, *T12* and *T3* in turn have a unique intersection subtype of their own, say *T123*. By definition, then, the set of values $|T123| = |T12| \cap |T3|$. But $|T12| = |T1| \cap |T2|$, and so we have $|T123| = |T1| \cap |T2| \cap |T3|$. (Note that "$\cap$" is associative, so this latter expression doesn't need any parentheses.) It follows that:

- First, *T123* is uniquely defined—it doesn't matter which pair of types we choose initially.

- Second, it's clearly a common subtype for *T1*, *T2*, and *T3*—every value in *T123* is a value of each of *T1*, *T2*, and *T3*.

- Third, no proper supertype of *T123* can possibly be a common subtype for *T1*, *T2*, and *T3*, because any such proper supertype will necessarily contain at least one value that's not a value of all three of *T1*, *T2*, and *T3*, thanks to IM Prescription 5.

Thus, *T123* is clearly the unique least specific common subtype, or intersection subtype, for *T1*, *T2*, and *T3*.

It should be clear without going into detail that the foregoing argument can readily be extended to the case of arbitrary *m* > 2. So what about the remaining possibilities, *m* = 1 and *m* = 0? Well, for *m* = 1 there's just one type, *T1*, and the corresponding unique least specific common subtype is thus clearly *T1* itself. As for *m* = 0 ...Well, here I'm afraid you're just going to have to trust me, at least for the time being; all I'm going to do right now is state what the situation is, without attempting to justify it (I'll give that justification in the answer to Exercise 6.2 at the end of the chapter). You can skip the rest of this subsection if you like, at least on a first reading.

I'll begin by reminding you that, as we saw in the discussion of IM Prescription 6 in Chapter 5, the set *S* of all scalar types (types *alpha* and *omega* included) forms a lattice, with *alpha* and *omega* as least upper and greatest lower bound, respectively. Consider some subset *S'* of *S*, consisting of types *T1*, *T2*, ..., *Tm*, say. Then:

- If *m* = 0 (i.e., if *S'* is empty), then every type in *S*, including both *alpha* and *omega* in particular, is a common subtype for the types in that subset *S'*.

---

[2] The set theory intersection symbol "$\cap$" can conveniently be pronounced "cap."

■ It follows that the unique, least specific, common subtype (or intersection subtype) for an empty set of scalar types is—believe it or not—type *alpha*. (By contrast, the unique most specific common subtype is type *omega*. Of course, type *omega* is the unique most specific common subtype of *any* set of scalar types *T1, T2, ..., Tm* ($m \geq 0$). See the section "Intersection Types vs. Union Types," later.)

COMMON SUPERTYPES

Now I turn to part a. of IM Prescription 8, which says among other things that any given set of *m* scalar types *T1, T2, ..., Tm* ($m \geq 0$) has a common supertype *T*. In order to show that this proposition too is reasonable, again I'll begin by considering the case *m* = 2 (and so again we have precisely two types *T1* and *T2*, which we can assume are distinct). Thus:

■ If one of *T1* and *T2*, say *T1*, is a supertype—necessarily a proper supertype—of the other (i.e., *T2*), then (a) every supertype of *T1* is necessarily a common supertype for *T1* and *T2*, and (b) of those common supertypes, *T1* itself is clearly the one that's the most specific. In other words, *T1* itself is the unique most specific common supertype in this case. For example, the most specific common supertype for types RECTANGLE and SQUARE is RECTANGLE.

■ If neither of *T1* and *T2* is a supertype of the other, then there are two possibilities:[3]

1. *T1* and *T2* belong to the same type hierarchy, *TH* say. In this case, by virtue of the fact that it's indeed a hierarchy that we're dealing with, there'll be some nonempty sequence of types *Ta, Tb, ..., Tz* in *TH* such that (a) *Ta* is the root type for *TH*, *Tb* is an immediate subtype of *Ta*, *Tc* is an immediate subtype of *Tb*, and so on; (b) the last type *Tz* in the sequence is a supertype (not necessarily immediate) for both *T1* and *T2*; and (c) no type not in that sequence is a supertype for both *T1* and *T2*. Thus, every type in that sequence *Ta, Tb, ..., Tz* is necessarily a common supertype for *T1* and *T2*, and (b) of those common supertypes, *Tz* is clearly the one that's the most specific. In other words, *Tz* is the unique most specific common supertype in this case. For example, the most specific common supertype for types ELLIPSE and RECTANGLE is PLANE_FIGURE.

2. *T1* and *T2* belong to distinct type hierarchies (in particular, they might happen to be the root types for their respective hierarchies). In this case the only type that's a common supertype for *T1* and *T2* is clearly type *alpha*—and since it's the only one, it's clearly also the most specific common supertype, a fortiori. For example, if we

---

[3] And this is where the proof of part a. of the prescription relies on the fact that we're dealing with single inheritance specifically.

had another type hierarchy (rooted in type SOLID_OBJECT, say, and corresponding to geometric objects in three-dimensional space) in addition to the one shown in Fig. 5.1, the most specific common supertype for types PLANE_FIGURE and SOLID_OBJECT would be *alpha*.

Now consider the case $m = 3$ (so we have three distinct types *T1*, *T2*, and *T3*):

■   If *T1*, *T2*, and *T3* aren't all part of the same type hierarchy, then their sole (and therefore their unique, most specific) common supertype is type *alpha*.

■   So assume *T1*, *T2*, and *T3* are all part of the same type hierarchy *TH*. Observe that, by definition, the root type *RT* of *TH* is certainly a common supertype for *T1*, *T2*, and *T3*. Now consider the set of values |*T1*| ∪ |*T2*| ∪ |*T3*| (note that "∪" is associative, so this expression doesn't need any parentheses).[4] Then there are two possibilities:

1.   A type *T* with exactly this set of values exists within *TH*. In this case, that type *T* is clearly the unique most specific common supertype for *T1*, *T2*, and *T3*, because (a) it's uniquely defined; (b) it's clearly a common supertype for *T1*, *T2*, and *T3* (every value of type *T1*, *T2*, or *T3* is a value of type *T*); and (c) no proper subtype of *T* can possibly be a common supertype for *T1*, *T2*, and *T3*, because any such proper subtype will fail to contain at least one value that's a value of at least one of *T1*, *T2*, and *T3*.

2.   Alternatively, no such type *T* exists within *TH*. In this case, let me conduct a little thought experiment. Suppose we explicitly define that type *T* (just for the sake of the argument) and introduce it into *TH* at the appropriate point. Note that (a) that "appropriate point" will necessarily be somewhere below the root type *RT*, and hence that (b) the new type *T* will necessarily have an immediate supertype within *TH*, *T** say. Then that type *T** will be the unique most common supertype for *T1*, *T2*, and *T3*.

Again I think it should be clear without going into detail that the arguments given above can readily be extended to the case of arbitrary $m > 2$. So what about the remaining possibilities, $m = 1$ and $m = 0$? Well, for $m = 1$ there's just one type, *T1*, and the corresponding unique most specific common supertype is clearly *T1* itself. As for $m = 0$, however, I'm going to have to ask you to trust me again, because again I'm just going to state what the situation is, without trying to justify it (again I'll give the justification in the answer to Exercise 6.2 at the end of the chapter). Again you can skip these details for now, if you want.

---

[4] The set theory union symbol "∪" can conveniently be pronounced "cup."

First recall again that the set *S* of all scalar types (types *alpha* and *omega* included) forms a lattice, with *alpha* and *omega* as least upper and greatest lower bound, respectively. Consider some subset *S'* of *S*, consisting of types *T1*, *T2*, ..., *Tm*, say. Then:

- If *m* = 0 (i.e., if *S'* is empty), then every type in *S*, including both *alpha* and *omega* in particular, is a common supertype for the types in that subset *S'*.

- It follows that the unique, most specific, common supertype for an empty set of scalar types is type *omega*. (By contrast, the unique least specific common supertype is type *alpha*. Of course, type *alpha* is the unique least specific common supertype of *any* set of scalar types *T1*, *T2*, ..., *Tm* (*m* ≥ 0). See the section "Intersection Types vs. Union Types" immediately following.)

INTERSECTION TYPES vs. UNION TYPES

To summarize thus far, then, every set *T1*, *T2*, ..., *Tm* (*m* ≥ 0) of scalar types has both a unique most specific common supertype and a unique least specific common subtype. Note, however, that there's some asymmetry here, at least with respect to nomenclature. For simplicity, let's focus on the case *m* = 2. Let *T1* and *T2* have most specific common supertype *T* and least specific common subtype *T'*. Then, while type *T'* is referred to as the corresponding intersection type, type *T* is *not* referred to as the corresponding union type. The reason is that *T* isn't necessarily a union type as this latter term is defined within our inheritance model (see the discussion of IM Prescription 20 in Chapter 12). That is, while the set of values |*T*| is precisely the intersection |*T1*| ∩ |*T2*| of the sets of values |*T1*| and |*T2*|, the set of values |*T*| by contrast is a superset—in general, a *proper* superset—of the union |*T1*| ∪ |*T2*| of those sets. In general, in other words, there'll be values of type *T* that aren't values of either type *T1* or type *T2*. For example, *T*, *T1*, and *T2* might be PARALLELOGRAM, RECTANGLE, and RHOMBUS, respectively. Type PARALLELOGRAM here is—let's agree for the sake of the example—the most specific common supertype of types RECTANGLE and RHOMBUS, but some parallelograms are neither rectangles nor rhombi.[5]

Next, it should be clear that any given set of scalar types also has both a unique *least* specific common *supertype* and a unique *most* specific common *subtype*. (I mention this point mainly for completeness; it's probably not very important in practice, as will quickly become obvious.) To be specific:

- The least specific common supertype of any set of scalar types (the empty set included) is type *alpha*. *Note:* Informally, however, scalar least specific common supertypes are often defined to exclude type *alpha*, in which case (a) the term has meaning only if the types in

---

[5] As noted in Chapter 3, I'll be discussing this example in much more detail in Part III of this book.

question all belong to the same type hierarchy, and then (b) it's taken to refer to the pertinent root type. With reference to Fig. 5.1, for example, the least specific common supertype for types ELLIPSE and SQUARE is either type *alpha* or (if *alpha* is excluded) type PLANE_FIGURE.

■ The most specific common subtype of any set of scalar types (the empty set included) is type *omega*. *Note:* Informally, however, scalar most specific common subtypes are often defined to exclude type *omega*, in which case the term has meaning only if the types in question all overlap. With reference to Fig. 5.1, for example, (a) the most specific common subtype for types POLYGON and SQUARE is either type *omega* or (if *omega* is excluded) type SQUARE; (b) the most specific common subtype for types ELLIPSE and SQUARE either is type *omega* or (if *omega* is excluded) doesn't exist.

CONCLUDING REMARKS

To say it one more time, I've shown in this chapter that every set $T1$, $T2$, ..., Tm ($m \geq 0$) of scalar types has both a unique most specific common supertype and a unique least specific common subtype. And I've claimed, though I haven't yet shown, that—at least with single inheritance—every scalar value has a unique most specific type (indeed, the note attached to IM Prescription 8 makes that same claim).[6] I've also claimed (and again the note to IM Prescription 8 does the same) that even with multiple inheritance the "unique most specific type" property—which I'll abbreviate from this point forward to just "MST uniqueness"—still holds; that is, it's still the case that every scalar value does have a unique most specific type. With multiple inheritance, however, it's not because of the disjointness assumption that MST uniqueness holds, because (as we'll see in Chapter 14) the disjointness assumption itself doesn't hold in that context. Rather, MST uniqueness holds in that context because of IM Prescription 8.[7] Now, I haven't covered enough groundwork to demonstrate the truth of this claim yet, so you'll just have to take it on trust for now. I'll come back and explain it in detail in Chapter 15.

As mentioned in Chapter 3, to say value v is of most specific type T is to say the set of types possessed by v is, precisely, the set consisting of all supertypes of T (a set with T itself as a member, of course); in other words, v is of every type that's a supertype of T and is of no other type. For example, a value of most specific type RECTANGLE is of types RECTANGLE, POLYGON, PLANE_FIGURE, *alpha*, and no others (in particular, it's not of type SQUARE).

Finally, it's obvious that (as that same note to IM Prescription 8 also claims) every scalar value also has a unique *least* specific type: namely, type *alpha*, or, if *alpha* is excluded, the

---

[6] I've revised the final sentence of that note slightly (the fact that the most specific type of value v is referred to elsewhere in the IM prescriptions as $MST(v)$ was inadvertently omitted from the *Explorations* version).

[7] Of course it holds as a consequence of IM Prescription 8 in the single inheritance context as well, as previously noted.

pertinent root type. For example, a value of any of the types shown in Fig. 5.1 has as its least specific type either *alpha* or (if *alpha* is excluded) PLANE_FIGURE.

EXERCISES

6.1   Let scalar types *T1, T2, ..., Tm* be such that at least two of those types are disjoint. What common supertypes and common subtypes does that set possess?

6.2   Try and justify in your own words the rules regarding common subtypes and supertypes for an empty set of types.

6.3   Does it make sense for a variable to have declared type *omega*?

6.4   Does it make sense for an attribute of some tuple or relation type to have declared type *omega*?

6.5   With reference to Fig. 5.1, complete the following table (MS = most specific, LS = least specific):

set of types	common sub types	MS common subtype	LS common subtype	common super types	MS common supertype	LS common supertype
ELLIPSE CIRCLE						
ELLIPSE RECTANGLE						
CIRCLE SQUARE POLYGON						
(empty)						

6.6   Consider the following type definition. Can you see anything wrong with it?

```
TYPE BETA  ... POSSREP ( X alpha ... ) ... ;
```

What about this one?

```
TYPE GAMMA ... POSSREP ( X omega ... ) ... ;
```

Or this one?

```
TYPE DELTA ... POSSREP ( ... ) CONSTRAINT FALSE ... ;
```

ANSWERS

6.1   The sole, and hence both least and most specific, common subtype is type *omega*. As for common supertypes, type *alpha* is certainly one, and if it's the only one—which it will be if and only if the types in question don't all belong to the same type hierarchy—then it's clearly both least and most specific; otherwise the pertinent root type will also be a common supertype, and there could be others too, depending on the specifics of the types in question. *Note:* In fact, it's largely to guarantee the validity of IM Prescription 8 in general, even when the types in question are all disjoint, that we insist on the uniqueness of types *alpha* and *omega*. See the discussion of IM Prescription 20 in Chapter 12.

6.2   In general, type *T'* is a common subtype for types *T1, T2, ..., Tm* if and only if the predicate

```
FORALL v ( IF v ∈ |T'| THEN v ∈ INTERSECT { |T1| , |T2| , ..., |Tm| } )
```

is satisfied by *T'*. Now, if *m* = 0, the set of types *T1, T2, ..., Tm* is empty, and the specified intersection becomes the intersection of no sets at all, which by definition is the universal set. In this case, therefore, the overall predicate evaluates to TRUE for all types *T'* in the pertinent type lattice, and so every type in the pertinent type lattice is a common subtype; hence the least specific of those common subtypes, if we're talking about scalar types specifically, is *alpha*. (The most specific is, of course, *omega*.)

Similarly, in general type *T* is a common supertype for types *T1, T2, ..., Tm* if and only if the predicate

```
FORALL v ( IF v ∈ UNION { |T1| , |T2| , ..., |Tm| } THEN v ∈ |T| )
```

is satisfied by *T*. If *m* = 0, the set of types *T1, T2, ..., Tm* is empty, and the specified union becomes the union of no sets at all, which by definition is the empty set. In this case, therefore, the overall predicate evaluates to TRUE for all types *T* in the pertinent type lattice, and so every type in the pertinent type lattice is a common supertype; hence the most specific of those common supertypes, if we're talking about scalar types specifically, is *omega*. (The least specific is, of course, *alpha*.)

Note: The foregoing arguments don't rely on the pertinent lattice being the scalar type lattice specifically but are actually more general. Thus, if the lattice in question is the type lattice corresponding to some tuple or relation type *T*, the least specific common subtype and the most specific common supertype for the empty subset of the types in that lattice are *T_alpha* and *T_omega*, respectively. See Chapter 19 for further discussion.

6.3   No, because no value—no initial value in particular (see Chapter 2)—could ever be assigned to the variable in question.

6.4   (a) A tuple type can have an attribute of declared type *omega*, but the tuple type in question will necessarily be empty. (b) A relation type can have an attribute of declared type *omega* too; in this case, however, the relation type won't be empty but will contain exactly one value: namely, the empty relation of that type. *Note:* In each of the foregoing cases (a) and (b), "*omega*" could be replaced by "an arbitrary empty type" without invalidating the claim being made. For further discussion, see the discussion of IM Prescription 21 in Chapter 17.

6.5

set of types	common sub types	MS common subtype	LS common subtype	common super types	MS common supertype	LS common supertype
ELLIPSE CIRCLE	CIRCLE omega	omega	CIRCLE	ELLIPSE PLANE_ FIGURE alpha	ELLIPSE	alpha
ELLIPSE RECTANGLE	omega	omega	omega	PLANE_ FIGURE alpha	PLANE_ FIGURE	alpha
CIRCLE SQUARE POLYGON	omega	omega	omega	PLANE_ FIGURE alpha	PLANE_ FIGURE	alpha
(empty)	(all)	omega	alpha	(all)	omega	alpha

6.6   Type BETA is surely illegal, because by definition *alpha* is a supertype of every scalar type, and BETA is a scalar type; so in effect BETA is being defined in terms of itself. As for type GAMMA, it's illegal too, because if it were permitted it would be empty, and we require type *omega* to be the sole empty scalar type. (Recall the following text from *The Third Manifesto*, quoted in Chapter 2:

> With the sole exception of the system defined empty type *omega* (which is defined only if type inheritance is supported), the definition of any given scalar type *T* shall be accompanied by a specification of an **example value** of that type.

But no such value can be defined for type GAMMA.)
       For essentially similar reasons type DELTA is illegal as well.

Chapter 7

Scalar Variables with Inheritance

That mysterious independent variable

—T. H. Huxley:
Universities, Actual and Ideal (1874)

Like the concept of a scalar value (see Chapter 6), the scalar variable concept needs some extension if type inheritance is supported, basically because such variables are permitted to have a value whose most specific type is any nonempty subtype of the declared type of the variable in question. IM Prescription 9 addresses this issue.

 Note: Of course, IM Prescription 9, like IM Prescription 8 in Chapter 6, is deliberately worded in such a way as to apply to multiple inheritance as well as single inheritance (though only to scalar types in both cases; tuple and relation types are dealt with separately in IM Prescription 28—see Chapter 20).

IM PRESCRIPTION 9: MODEL OF A SCALAR VARIABLE

Let scalar variable V be of declared type T. Because of value substitutability (see IM Prescription 16), the value v assigned to V at any given time can have any nonempty subtype T' of type T as its most specific type. We can therefore model V as a named ordered triple of the form $<DT,MST,v>$, where:

a. The name of the triple is the name of the variable, V.

b. DT is the name of the declared type for variable V.

c. MST is the name of the **most specific type**—also known as the **current** most specific type—for, or of, variable V.

d. v is a value of most specific type MST—the **current value** for, or of, variable V.

We use the notation $DT(V)$, $MST(V)$, $v(V)$ to refer to the DT, MST, v components, respectively, of this model of scalar variable V. *Note:* Since $v(V)$ uniquely determines $MST(V)$—see IM Prescription 8—the MST component of V is strictly redundant. We include it for convenience.

Now let *X* be a scalar expression. By definition, *X* represents an invocation of some scalar operator *Op*. Thus, the notation *DT*(*V*), *MST*(*V*), *v*(*V*) just introduced can be extended in an obvious way to refer to the declared type *DT*(*X*), the current most specific type *MST*(*X*), and the current value *v*(*X*), respectively, of *X*—where *DT*(*X*) is the declared type of the invocation of *Op* in question (see IM Prescription 17) and is known at compile time, and *MST*(*X*) and *v*(*X*) refer to the result of evaluating *X* and are therefore not known until run time (in general).

Consider the following code fragment:

```
VAR E ELLIPSE ;
VAR C CIRCLE ;

E := C ;
```

Clearly, the *declared type DT*(E) of scalar variable E here is ELLIPSE. Equally clearly, however, the value of E at run time can have as its most specific type any nonempty subtype of ELLIPSE (possibly just ELLIPSE itself, of course). For example, after the assignment shown (of C to E), that value will be a circle instead of "just an ellipse." Thus, we can say that the *current most specific type*—or, more usually, just the *most specific type*—*MST*(E) of E at the time in question is CIRCLE,[1] and the current value *v*(E) of E at that same time is the specific circle in question. In other words, the situation after the assignment is as follows:

■ *DT*(E) is ELLIPSE. Actually, of course, it's always ELLIPSE; indeed, the fact that it's ELLIPSE is known at compile time as well as at run time.

■ *MST*(E) is CIRCLE. This fact isn't known until until run time.

■ *v*(E) is whatever circle happens to be the current value of E at run time.

Observe, therefore, that we must be very careful in the inheritance context over the logical difference between the two important types that apply to any given variable: viz., the *declared* type, which doesn't change over time, vs. the *current most specific* type, which does (in general). Observe further that if type *T'* is the current most specific type of variable *V*, then every proper supertype of type *T'* is also a "current type" of variable *V*, in a sense. However, the term "current type" is usually used, informally, to mean the *most specific* current type specifically, barring explicit statements to the contrary.

Note: By virtue of IM Prescription 8, every value has a unique most specific type; thus, *MST*(*V*) is in fact implied by *v*(*V*), and is therefore logically unnecessary as a component of the

---

[1] Recall that type CIRCLE in our running example (Fig. 5.1) has no proper subtype apart from type *omega*.

model of *V*. We include it for reasons of convenience and explicitness. Also, recall from Chapter 2 that the *Manifesto* requires all variables to be assigned an initial value before they're used; as a consequence of this fact, *DT(V)* can never be *omega*. Nor can *MST(V)*, of course, because there simply *is* no value of type *omega*.

Model of a Scalar Expression

It should be clear that—as IM Prescription 9 in fact says—the foregoing definitions can readily be extended to apply to arbitrary scalar expressions instead of just to scalar variables as such. Let *X* be such an expression, and let *v(X)* be the result of evaluating that expression at run time. Then:

- *X* has a *declared type DT(X)*, viz., the declared type of the operator invocation at the outermost level of *X* (i.e., the operator invocation that occurs last in the evaluation of *X*). *DT(X)* is known at compile time; in fact, it's determined by the pertinent *invocation signature*, as we'll see in the discussion of IM Prescription 17 in Chapter 11.

- *X* also has a *current most specific type MST(X)*, viz., the type that's the most specific type of *v(X)*. *MST(X)* is not known until run time, in general. (Of course, *MST(X)* is implied by *v(X)* and is therefore logically unnecessary as a component of this model of *X*; again we include it for reasons of convenience and explicitness.)

INCLUSION POLYMORPHISM

I've now laid enough groundwork to be able to discuss an important concept that pervades the entire topic of type inheritance: *polymorphism*. (Of course, we've met this concept before, in Chapter 2 in particular, but there's a lot more to be said about it in the present context.) As we've seen, if *T'* is a subtype of *T*, then all operators—all read-only operators, that is—that apply to values of type *T* apply to values of type *T'* as well. Thus, to repeat a by now familiar example, if AREA_OF (*e*) is valid, where *e* is an ellipse, then AREA_OF (*c*), where *c* is a circle, must be valid as well. It follows that the AREA_OF operator is polymorphic: It can take arguments of different types on different invocations. And the kind of polymorphism involved is called *inclusion* polymorphism specifically, on the grounds that the relationship between *T* and *T'* is basically that of set inclusion—the set of values |*T*| constituting type *T* is a superset of, or includes, the set of values |*T'*| constituting type *T'*.

Note: As the foregoing paragraph suggests (and despite the title of this chapter), inclusion polymorphism as discussed here does have to do with values specifically. But there are implications for variables too, some of which we'll get to toward the end of the chapter.

IMPLEMENTATION VERSIONS

Recall now that ellipses and circles, at least as we defined them in Chapter 3, have different possreps. Just to remind you, here are those definitions again (in outline):

```
TYPE ELLIPSE ...
     POSSREP ( A ... , B ... , CTR ... ) ... ;
TYPE CIRCLE  ...
     POSSREP ( R ... , CTR ... ) ... ;
```

It's conceivable, therefore, that two different implementation versions of the AREA_OF operator will exist under the covers, one for type ELLIPSE that makes use of the ELLIPSE possrep and one for type CIRCLE that makes use of the CIRCLE possrep. To repeat, it's conceivable—but it's *not* absolutely necessary; so long as the code that implements AREA_OF for type ELLIPSE is written in terms of the ELLIPSE possrep, that code will work for circles too, because the ELLIPSE possrep is necessarily a possrep for CIRCLE too (even though, as explained in Chapter 3, it might not be an explicitly declared one). To be specific, the area of a general ellipse is πab, while that of a circle is πr^2; thus, the code that implements the ellipse version of AREA_OF will presumably invoke THE_A and THE_B, and that code will certainly work for a circle.

Observe now, however, that the ellipse AREA_OF code will definitely not work for circles if it's written in terms of a *physical* representation instead of a possible one, and the physical representations for types ELLIPSE and CIRCLE differ. The practice of implementing operators in terms of physical representations is thus clearly contraindicated. Code defensively! In fact, I'd like to recommend that access to physical representations be limited to code that implements the following operators *only:*

- Selectors

- THE_ operators

- IS_*T* operators (see the discussion of IM Prescription 15 in Chapter 10, and the section "Code Reuse" below for some examples)

Of course, many of these operators—possibly all of them—will have system provided implementations anyway.

On the other hand, the type implementer might want to provide distinct versions of some operator at the supertype and subtype levels anyway, even when there's no logical need to do so. Consider polygons and rectangles, for example. Let the AREA_OF operator apply to polygons and rectangles as well as to ellipses and circles. Then whatever complicated algorithm is used to compute the area of a general polygon will certainly work for a rectangle; for rectangles, however, a much more efficient algorithm—just multiply the height by the width—is available.

At least for performance reasons, therefore, it might be desirable to have two distinct implementation versions of the AREA_OF operator, thus (in outline only, but note the VERSION specifications in particular):

```
OPERATOR AREA_OF VERSION AREA_OF_P ( P POLYGON ) RETURNS AREA ;
   RETURN ( ... ) ;
END OPERATOR ;

OPERATOR AREA_OF VERSION AREA_OF_R ( R RECTANGLE ) RETURNS AREA ;
   RETURN ( ... ) ;
END OPERATOR ;
```

The net of the foregoing discussion is that what appears to be a single operator above the covers can have any number n ($n > 0$) of implementation versions—versions for short—under the covers. Of course, it makes no difference to the user how many such versions exist; in the case of AREA_OF, for example, the user knows the operator works for, say, ellipses, and therefore it works for circles too, by definition, because circles are ellipses. That's what inclusion polymorphism is all about.

A Remark on THE_ Operators

Consider the operators THE_A, which applies to values of type ELLIPSE and hence to values of type CIRCLE as well, and THE_R, which applies only to values of type CIRCLE (for simplicity, let's agree to ignore the operator THE_B throughout this subsection). Now suppose ellipses and circles have the same physical representation and—in accordance with the remarks above concerning such matters—THE_A for type ELLIPSE is implemented in terms of that physical representation. Then that same implementation code can clearly serve as the implementation of THE_A for type CIRCLE too, and THE_R for type CIRCLE can then be implemented as follows, without accessing the physical representation at all:

```
OPERATOR THE_R ( C CIRCLE ) RETURNS LENGTH ;
   RETURN ( THE_A ( C ) ) ;
END OPERATOR ;
```

Of course, it could also be implemented directly in terms of the physical representation if desired.

Now suppose instead that ellipses and circles have different physical representations, but THE_A for type ELLIPSE is still implemented in terms of the ELLIPSE physical representation. Then THE_R for type CIRCLE might be implemented in terms of the CIRCLE physical representation, and THE_A for type CIRCLE could then be implemented as follows:

```
OPERATOR THE_A ( C CIRCLE ) RETURNS LENGTH ;
   RETURN ( THE_R ( C ) ) ;
END OPERATOR ;
```

Of course, it could also be implemented directly in terms of the CIRCLE physical representation if desired.

The net of the foregoing discussion is just this: For type CIRCLE, at most one[2] of THE_A and THE_R needs to be implemented in terms of the physical representation, and then the other can be implemented in terms of that one. Either way, of course, it makes no logical difference so far as the user is concerned.

CODE REUSE

One important consequence of the notion of inclusion polymorphism is the possibility of code reuse. Suppose with reference to our running example that we need to write a program to display some diagram, made up of squares, circles, ellipses, etc. Without inclusion polymorphism, the code for this task will involve an expression looking something like this:[3]

```
FOR EACH x ∈ DIAGRAM
    CASE
        WHEN IS_SQUARE ( x ) THEN DISPLAY_SQUARE ( ... )
        WHEN IS_CIRCLE ( x ) THEN DISPLAY_CIRCLE ( ... )
        WHEN     .......................................
    END CASE
```

With such support, by contrast, the code will be much simpler and more succinct:

```
FOR EACH x ∈ DIAGRAM DISPLAY ( x )
```

Explanation: The operator DISPLAY in this second version of the code is (let's assume for the sake of the example) defined for values of type PLANE_FIGURE—i.e., the sole parameter to that operator is of declared type PLANE_FIGURE—and is therefore inherited by types SQUARE, CIRCLE, etc. For generality, let's assume a different implementation version of DISPLAY is defined for each of those types. (If indeed it does turn out to be desirable to define an implementation version that's specific to some given subtype, then that version can be defined when that subtype is defined or at some later time.) Then, at run time,[4] when the system encounters the operator invocation DISPLAY (x), it will determine the version of DISPLAY that's appropriate to the most specific type of x at that time, and will invoke that version accordingly (see the discussion of *run time binding* in Chapter 11). Thus, inclusion

---

[2] It'll be none at all if the THE_A implementation code for ellipses works for circles too.

[3] The expressions denoting the arguments to the various DISPLAY invocations are omitted to avoid distracting irrelevancies. For the record, however, they would most likely take the form TREAT_AS_*T* (*x*), where *T* is the pertinent most specific type; e.g., the argument expression in the case of DISPLAY_SQUARE would probably take the form TREAT_AS_SQUARE (*x*). See Chapter 10 for further explanation.

[4] Or possibly compile time (see Chapter 11).

polymorphism effectively leads to certain CASE expressions, and/or CASE statements, that would otherwise have had to appear in the user's source code being moved under the covers: in effect, being performed by the system on the user's behalf.

Observe the implications of the foregoing for program maintenance in particular. For example, suppose a new type TRIANGLE is defined as another subtype of PLANE_FIGURE— in fact, as an immediate subtype of POLYGON. Suppose also for generality that a corresponding new implementation version of DISPLAY is defined as well. Without inclusion polymorphism, it would be necessary to examine every source program to see whether any CASE expression or statement needed to be modified to include something like the following:

```
WHEN IS_TRIANGLE ( x ) THEN DISPLAY_TRIANGLE ( ... )
```

With inclusion polymorphism, however, no such modifications will be needed.

Because of examples like the foregoing, inclusion polymorphism is sometimes characterized, a little colorfully, as allowing "old code to invoke new code"; that is, a program *P* is effectively able to invoke some version of an operator *Op* that didn't exist—the version, that is—when *P* was written. Thus, we have, at least potentially, what's called *code reuse*: The very same program *P* might be usable on data of a type that wasn't defined when *P* was written. (Certainly the code of program *P* is being reused here. The code that implements operator *Op* under the covers might or might not be reused; for example, the code that implements the AREA_OF operator for polygons might or might not be reused for rectangles, as previously discussed.)

OVERLOADING POLYMORPHISM

Polymorphism as discussed in this chapter so far, meaning inclusion polymorphism specifically, is a logical consequence of the very notion of type inheritance. Now, we've already seen several examples of polymorphic operators in this book (in Chapter 2 in particular): "=", ":=", "<", "-", and so on. But there's no inheritance, as such, involved in these examples—they're all examples of *overloading* polymorphism (also known as ad hoc polymorphism, or just *overloading* for short).[5]

Unfortunately, these two kinds of polymorphism are frequently confused in the literature (especially, it seems, in the object literature). But they're not the same thing. A helpful way to characterize the logical difference between them is as follows:

■ Inclusion polymorphism means there's just one operator, with several distinct implementation versions under the covers (but the user doesn't need to know the versions

---

[5] Actually, "=" and ":=" in particular might be inherited from type *alpha* (see the discussion of IM Prescription 20 in Chapter 12), in which case they'll be examples of inclusion polymorphism after all. However, the general point here regarding overloading polymorphism is valid nonetheless.

in question are in fact distinct—to the user, to say it again, there's just the one operator). AREA_OF is an example.

■ Overloading polymorphism, by contrast, means there are several distinct operators with the same name (and the user does need to know the operators in question are in fact distinct, with distinct—though preferably similar—semantics). For example, in many languages the "+" operator is overloaded: There's one "+" operator for integers, another for rational numbers, and so on.[6]

These matters are explained more fully under IM Prescriptions 16-19 in Chapter 11, but I'll elaborate on them very briefly here for purposes of future reference (despite the fact that such elaboration might not make very much sense at this juncture). Briefly, then:

■ For overloading polymorphism, each of the distinct operators will have its own distinct *specification signature* (because otherwise invocations of the operators in question would be ambiguous), and those specification signatures will be visible to the user.

■ For inclusion polymorphism, by contrast, the single operator will have just one specification signature (visible to the user),[7] but each distinct implementation version of that operator will have its own distinct *version* signature (hidden under the covers and not visible to the user).

Note: For obvious reasons, I'll take the unqualified term *polymorphism* throughout the remainder of this book to mean inclusion polymorphism specifically, barring explicit statements to the contrary.

Changing Semantics

Unfortunately, there's a fly in the ointment. To be specific, let *Op* be a polymorphic operator (meaning, to repeat, an operator such as AREA_OF that displays inclusion polymorphism specifically). Then there can be no guarantee that the various implementation versions of *Op* all implement the same semantics! If they don't, then we don't have true inclusion polymorphism any more, we have overloading polymorphism instead; such a state of affairs constitutes a violation of the model (the *Manifesto* model, that is), and the consequences are unpredictable. Regrettably, however, the requirement that all versions of a given operator implement the same

---

[6] Some languages overload the "+" operator still further and use it to mean both numeric addition and string concatenation. However, this particular overloading violates the goal of "preferably similar semantics" because, in such a language, if A and B are numbers, then $A+B = B+A$, but if they're strings then (in general) $A+B \neq B+A$.

[7] As noted at the end of the discussion of IM Prescription 9 earlier, each specification signature in turn—regardless of whether we're talking about overloading or inclusion polymorphism—will be accompanied by a set of *invocation* signatures, and those invocation signatures will also be visible to the user. See Chapter 11 for further explanation.

semantics is unenforceable. What's more, some writers even claim, in effect, that the ability to change semantics is desirable! To quote *The Object Data Standard: ODMG 3.0* (R. G. G. Cattell and Douglas K. Barry, eds.; Morgan Kaufmann, 2000):

> For example, the Employee type might have an operation for calculate_paycheck. The Salaried_Employee and Hourly_Employee class implementations might each refine that behavior to reflect their specialized needs.[8]

Refine that behavior here means, precisely, changing the semantics. Note, however, that there does seem to be a tacit assumption in the example cited that the "subtypes" Salaried_Employee and Hourly_Employee aren't really subtypes at all (at least, not in the sense of that term as defined in our model) but are, rather, what are sometimes called *derived* types. See the discussion of "the EXTENDS relationship" in Chapter 21 for further explanation.

A Note on Overriding

There's another concept that's frequently confused in the literature with either overloading or inclusion polymorphism or both: viz., operator *overriding*. Operator overriding can be defined as the replacement of an operator by another operator having the same specification signature but different semantics. For example, suppose there exists an operator called LOG (perhaps built in) that returns natural logarithms; then it might be possible to override that operator by one that returns logarithms to base ten instead.

Here's an example of confusion over the use of this term (it's from *The Object Database Handbook: How to Select, Implement, and Use Object-Oriented Databases*, by Douglas K. Barry, Wiley Publishing, 1996—italics as in the original):

> The object model allows ... multiple use of the same method, which is called *overloading*. The overloaded definition of Display in the [subclass] *overrides* the definition of Display in the [superclass] because it is lower in the class hierarchy.

And elsewhere in the same book:

> *Overriding:* Where a method for a subclass adds to or replaces a method of its superclass.

Incidentally, note that these quotes seem also to embrace the idea that the ability to change semantics is a good thing (see the previous subsection). They also seem to be confused over the difference between a model and its implementation, though in fact this latter criticism can justifiably be leveled at object writings in general.

---

[8] I can't help pointing out, for what it's worth, that the first sentence of this quote uses the term *type* and the second *class*.

SUBSTITUTABILITY

Recall now the concept of *substitutability*, which I said in Chapter 3 was "in many ways the whole point of inheritance." Just to remind you, substitutability means among other things that, e.g., wherever the system expects a value of type ELLIPSE, we can always substitute a value of type CIRCLE instead, because circles are ellipses. Here are a couple of important specific manifestations of this phenomenon:

- If relvar *R* has an attribute *A* of declared type ELLIPSE, some of the *A* values in the value of *R* at some given time might in fact be circles rather than "just ellipses."

- If scalar expression *X* has declared type *T* and *T* has a possrep component *A* of declared type ELLIPSE, then the operator invocation THE_*A*(*X*) might sometimes return a circle instead of "just an ellipse."

More generally, wherever the system expects a value of type *T*, we can always substitute a value of some subtype *T'* of *T*—*The Principle of Value Substitutability* (see the discussion of IM Prescription 16 in Chapter 11). But it should be clear by now that substitutability as explained above is really just the by now familiar notion of inclusion polymorphism in a different guise. I mention it here principally because it's widely recognized as the sine qua non of type inheritance, and no discussion of that topic would be complete without such a mention.

Now, I said earlier in this chapter that the concept of inclusion polymorphism had implications for variables as well as values. It's time to get more specific. By way of example, consider the following read-only operator definition:[9]

```
OPERATOR MOVE ( E ELLIPSE , R RECTANGLE ) RETURNS ELLIPSE ;
   RETURN ( ELLIPSE ( THE_A ( E ) , THE_B ( E ) , CTR ( R ) ) ) ;
END OPERATOR ;
```

Loosely speaking, operator MOVE moves a specified ellipse such that it becomes centered on the center of a specified rectangle (CTR is, let's assume, a read-only operator that returns the center of its rectangle argument).

To repeat, MOVE as just defined is a read-only operator (neither of its parameters is subject to update). Thanks to value substitutability, therefore, (a) the argument that's substituted for the first parameter in a MOVE invocation can be a value of any nonempty subtype of type ELLIPSE; similarly, (b) the argument that's substituted for the second parameter in such an invocation can be a value of any nonempty subtype of type RECTANGLE. Thus, for example, the following is a legal MOVE invocation—

---

[9] Now we know that operators can have several different implementation versions, it would be more accurate to regard operator definitions like the one shown here as defining just one particular implementation version of the operator in question, out of possibly several such. For simplicity, however, I'll continue to talk in terms of operator definitions per se and not "operator implementation version definitions" (unless the context is such that it's really important to stress the difference).

```
MOVE ( C , S )
```

—where C is a variable of declared type CIRCLE and S is a variable of declared type SQUARE. Now suppose by contrast that we define MOVE as an update operator instead:

```
OPERATOR MOVE ( E ELLIPSE , R RECTANGLE ) UPDATES { E } ;
    THE_CTR ( E ) := CTR ( R ) ;
END OPERATOR ;
```

With this revised definition, the argument that's substituted for the second parameter in a MOVE invocation can still be a value of any nonempty subtype of type RECTANGLE. However, the first parameter is now subject to update, so the argument that's substituted for that parameter must be a variable specifically, and that variable will be updated as a result of the invocation in question. Hence, the declared type of that variable must be such that assignment to THE_CTR of that variable makes sense, and so that declared type can be ELLIPSE (of course), and it can also be CIRCLE.[10] But suppose type CIRCLE has a proper subtype O_CIRCLE (where an "O-circle" is a circle with center the origin):

```
TYPE O_CIRCLE
    IS { CIRCLE
          CONSTRAINT THE_CTR ( CIRCLE ) = POINT ( 0.0 , 0.0 )
          POSSREP ( R = THE_R ( CIRCLE ) )
          NOT { CIRCLE ( LENGTH ( 2.0 ) , POINT ( 1.0 , 0.0 ) ) } } ;
```

Then it doesn't make sense for the argument that's substituted for the first MOVE parameter to have declared type O_CIRCLE, because the center of an O-circle is always the origin and can't be changed (see the CONSTRAINT specification in the foregoing type definition). As far as the first parameter is concerned, therefore—i.e., the one that's subject to update—the update form of MOVE is defined for type ELLIPSE, is inherited by type CIRCLE, but probably isn't inherited by type O_CIRCLE. (And if it isn't, it won't be inherited by any proper subtype of type O_CIRCLE either, a fortiori.)

We see, therefore, that update operators are only conditionally polymorphic; that is, an update operator that applies to variables of type *T* might or might not apply to variables of some nonempty proper subtype *T'* of *T*—*The Principle of Variable Substitutability*. If it does apply, then it too is said to exhibit inclusion polymorphism, of a kind. Note, however, that this whole issue is examined in much more detail in the discussion of IM Prescription 19 in Chapter 11.

Let me close this chapter by pointing out that the notions of polymorphism and substitutability, important though they are in practice, are both logically implied by the notion of type inheritance—they're not, logically speaking, completely separate concepts. In other words,

---

[10] It can be CIRCLE because of a phenomenon known as *specialization by constraint*, S by C (discussed in detail in the next chapter). To spell out the details: By definition, THE_CTR(E) := CTR(R) is shorthand for E := ELLIPSE (THE_A(E), THE_B(E), CTR(R)). But if THE_A(E) is equal to THE_B(E)—which it will be, if E currently contains a circle—then the ELLIPSE selector invocation just shown in fact returns a circle, thanks to S by C.

if the system supports type inheritance, it *must* support polymorphism and substitutability as well (because if it didn't it wouldn't be supporting type inheritance, by definition).

EXERCISES

7.1   In the model of scalar variable *V* as a named ordered triple of the form <*DT,MST,v*>, the *MST* component is logically redundant. Why?

7.2   Which components in the model of scalar variable *V* as a named ordered triple of the form <*DT,MST,v*> are known at compile time and which at run time?

7.3   In the model of scalar variable *V* as a named ordered triple of the form <*DT,MST,v*>, the *DT* and *MST* components can never be *omega*. Why not? And is the same true of the analogous model of scalar expression *X*?

7.4   Let variable E have declared type ELLIPSE, and let expression *X* be THE_A(E). What's the declared type of *X*? What's its most specific type?

7.5   Consider the following expression:

```
ELLIPSE ( LENGTH ( 5.0 ) , LENGTH ( 5.0 ) , POINT ( 0.0 , 0.0 ) )
```

What's the declared type of this expression? What's its most specific type?

7.6   Distinguish between inclusion polymorphism, overloading, and overriding. What do any of these concepts have to do with substitutability?

7.7   "Implementation version" is purely an implementation notion and not part of the model: True or false?

7.8   The body of the chapter recommended that access to physical representations be limited to the code that implements certain operators. Which ones? And why?

7.9   What do you understand by the term *code reuse*?

7.10   What do you understand by the term *run time binding*?

7.11   State *The Principle of Value Substitutability* and *The Principle of Variable Substitutability* as you understand them.

7.12 Does your solution to Exercise 3.11 in Chapter 3 work if the rectangle in question is actually a square?

ANSWERS

7.1   Because it's necessarily equal to the most specific type of the *v* component, and—as we know from Chapter 6—the most specific type of any given value *v* is unique.

7.2   All three are known at run time; only *DT(V)* is known at compile time (in general).

7.3   First, no variable can ever have declared type *omega*, because no value could ever be assigned to it. (In fact, such a declaration would be in conflict with one of the prescriptions of *The Third Manifesto*, which—as we saw in Chapter 2—requires all variables to be assigned an initial value before they're used.) Second, no variable can ever have most specific type *omega*, because to say *MST(V)* is *omega* for some *V* at some time would be to say that *V* has no value at all at the time in question. Third, since any given scalar expression is supposed to denote some scalar value, yes, it's true more generally that neither *DT(X)* nor *MST(X)* can ever be *omega* for any such expression *X*.

7.4   The declared type is the declared type of component A of the ELLIPSE possrep, which is LENGTH. The most specific type could in principle be any nonempty subtype of LENGTH; since we haven't in fact defined any such subtype, however, the most specific type is LENGTH also.

7.5   The given expression is, of course, an ELLIPSE selector invocation (in fact, it's a literal), and the declared type of the expression is thus ELLIPSE by definition. However, the ellipse it denotes is in fact a circle, and indeed an O-circle also (if such a type has in fact been defined, as in the final section in the body of the chapter). So the most specific type is CIRCLE, or possibly O_CIRCLE. See Chapter 8 for further explanation.

7.6   Inclusion polymorphism is a logical consequence of inheritance (in effect, it's just substitutability by another name). To be specific, if *Op* is a read-only operator that applies to values of type *T*, then *Op* also applies to values of every subtype *T'* of *T*. (Several distinct implementation versions of *Op* might exist under the covers, but whether or not they do is of no concern to the model, or to the user.) *Note:* Inclusion polymorphism can have implications for update operators as well. For the specifics, see the body of the chapter, also Chapter 11.

Overloading polymorphism has nothing to do with inheritance or substitutability. Loosely, what it means is that there are several distinct operators with the same name (and the user does need to know that the operators in question are in fact distinct). For example, the "+"

operator will very likely be overloaded, in that there'll be one "+" for integers, another for rational numbers, and so on.

Operator overriding is a totally different phenomenon. It can be defined as the replacement of a given operator by another operator having the same specification signature but different semantics. It has nothing to do with inheritance or substitutability, nor indeed with polymorphism of any kind.

7.7   Well, it should be true, but it might not be completely so in some systems (especially object systems). To the extent it's not, however, we're talking about a failure on the part of the system in question to distinguish adequately between model and implementation.

7.8   Selectors, THE_ operators, and IS_*T* operators. The reason is to increase the potential for code reuse and decrease the need for code maintenance.

7.9   (*Of implementation versions*) Using the type *T* implementation version of some operator *Op* to operate without change on values or variables of declared type some proper subtype of *T*. (*Of application programs*) Using an application program that operates on values or variables of declared type *T* to operate without change on values or variables of declared type some proper subtype of *T*.

Note: Of course, code reuse doesn't imply type inheritance, but the kinds of reuse that aren't related to inheritance aren't new. The following quote is worth pondering in this connection. It's taken from *Object-Oriented Modeling and Design for Database Applications*, by Michael Blaha and William Premerlani (Prentice-Hall, 1998; the italics are mine):

> DBMSs are intended to provide generic functionality for a wide variety of applications ... *You are achieving reuse when you can use generic DBMS code, rather than custom written application code.*

I agree with this observation, and would add that such reuse is supported very well by relational DBMSs, rather less well by object DBMSs.

7.10 Run time binding is the process of determining at run time the particular implementation version of some given operator to be invoked. For further discussion, see Chapter 11.

7.11 See the body of the chapter; see also Chapter 11 for further discussion.

7.12 The following solution from Chapter 3—

```
OPERATOR QUARTER_TURN ( R RECTANGLE ) RETURNS RECTANGLE ;
    RETURN ( RECTANGLE ( POINT (   THE_X ( THE_B ( R ) ) ,
                                 - THE_Y ( THE_B ( R ) ) ) ,
                         POINT (   THE_X ( THE_A ( R ) ) ,
                                 - THE_Y ( THE_A ( R ) ) ) ) ) ;
END OPERATOR ;
```

—clearly does work if the rectangle in question is actually a square. But the following code clearly works too, and is obviously more efficient (in fact all it does is return its input):

```
OPERATOR QUARTER_TURN ( S SQUARE ) RETURNS SQUARE ;
    RETURN ( S ) ;
END OPERATOR ;
```

However, there's a logical difference between these two solutions (i.e., they're not logically equivalent), because if *s* is a square—and considering just the specific vertex *A*, for definiteness—then the result returned by THE_A (QUARTER_TURN (*s*)) will depend on which version of the QUARTER_TURN operator is invoked.[11]

An analogous remark applies to the update operator solutions also, which I now turn to. Here first is the update operator solution from Chapter 3:

```
OPERATOR QUARTER_TURN ( R RECTANGLE ) UPDATES { R } ;
    R := RECTANGLE ( POINT (   THE_X ( THE_B ( R ) ) ,
                             - THE_Y ( THE_B ( R ) ) ) ,
                     POINT (   THE_X ( THE_A ( R ) ) ,
                             - THE_Y ( THE_A ( R ) ) ) ) ;
END OPERATOR ;
```

This one also works if the rectangle is actually a square. But the following code clearly works too, and is obviously more efficient (in fact it's a "no op," and the sole effect of the UPDATES specification is to ensure that the argument to an invocation is a variable specifically):

```
OPERATOR QUARTER_TURN ( S SQUARE ) UPDATES { S } ;
END OPERATOR ;
```

Again, however, there's a logical difference between the two solutions.

---

[11] Of course, if operator QUARTER_TURN does have two implementation versions as suggested, then those versions will need some appropriate distinguishing version names (see the section "Implementation Versions" in the body of the chapter). An analogous remark applies to the update operator solutions also.

Chapter 8

Specialization by Constraint etc.

Expression X has value v
And value v has MST
Determined, thanks to S by C

—Anon.:
Where Bugs Go

In this chapter I propose to examine an aspect of our inheritance model that we regard as both crucial and fundamental, despite the fact that it (or something very like it) has been the subject of much controversy in the literature: viz., the concept we call *specialization by constraint*. In terms of our running example, the basic point is this: In our model (and indeed in accordance with mathematical reality), an ellipse is a circle if and only if its semiaxis lengths a and b are equal. In other words, if and only if (a) value e is of type ELLIPSE, but also (b) THE_A(e) is equal to THE_B(e), then (c) e is additionally of type CIRCLE—*and the system is aware of this fact*. And that, in effect, is exactly what IM Prescription 10 says.

IM PRESCRIPTION 10: SPECIALIZATION BY CONSTRAINT

Let T be a regular type (see IM Prescription 20) and hence, necessarily, a scalar type, and let T' be a nonempty immediate subtype of T. For each such immediate supertype T of T', the definition of T' shall specify a **specialization constraint** SC, formulated in terms of T, such that a value shall be of type T' if and only if it satisfies all such constraints SC.

I need to get a few preliminary matters out of the way before I can get to the substance of this prescription, as follows:

- First of all, the prescription, like IM Prescription 8 in Chapter 6 and IM Prescription 9 in Chapter 7, is deliberately worded in such a way as to apply to multiple as well as single inheritance (though only to scalar types in both cases).[1] *Note:* The notion of specialization

---

[1] By contrast, the *Explorations* version of the prescription was worded in such a way as to apply single inheritance only.

by constraint does apply to tuple and relation types as well as scalar types; as we'll see in Chapter 17, however, it does so only implicitly. What I mean by "only implicitly" here is this: If specialization by constraint occurs as described in this chapter for scalar types, it'll happen automatically for tuple and relation types as well, and nothing more needs to be said about the matter. What's more, the same goes for generalization by constraint also, mutatis mutandis (see later in the chapter).

■ Of course, in this chapter we're limiting ourselves to single inheritance anyway. For present purposes, therefore, we can simplify the prescription slightly as follows:

Let *T* be a regular type (see IM Prescription 20) and hence, necessarily, a scalar type, and let *T'* be a nonempty immediate subtype of *T*. Then the definition of *T'* shall specify a **specialization constraint** *SC*, formulated in terms of *T*, such that a value shall be of type *T'* if and only if it satisfies constraint *SC*.

Please note that all references to IM Prescription 10 in this chapter from this point forward should be understood as applying to this simpler version specifically.

■ Pleas note too that the prescription has to do, not just with scalar types specifically, but (even more specifically) with scalar types that are *regular* types. A regular type is a scalar type that's not a dummy type. Dummy types are discussed under IM Prescription 20 in Chapter 12; for the purposes of the present chapter, we can ignore them, and I will.

■ The *Explorations* version of the prescription actually said "a value shall be of type *T'* if and only if *it is of type T and* it satisfies constraint *SC*." This phrasing is misleading, however, inasmuch as it suggests, incorrectly, that the fact that the value is required to be of type *T* isn't part of constraint *SC* as such. For that reason I've dropped that italicized text.

■ The *Explorations* version of the prescription also had a note attached to it, to the effect that there should be at least one value of type *T* that fails to satisfy constraint *SC*. However, this requirement is subsumed by part c. of IM Prescription 5—which requires the definition of *T'* to be accompanied by a specification of an example value that's of type *T* and not of type *T'* (see Chapter 5)—and so I've dropped that note as well.

SPECIALIZATION CONSTRAINTS

IM Prescription 10 is tightly bound up with the notion of a "specialization constraint." Let's look at an example. Here once again are the type definitions for types ELLIPSE and CIRCLE (irrelevant details omitted):

```
TYPE ELLIPSE
     IS { PLANE_FIGURE
          POSSREP ( A LENGTH , B LENGTH , CTR POINT )
          CONSTRAINT A ≥ B
          NOT { ... } } ;    /* see Chapter 12 for further explanation * /

TYPE CIRCLE
     IS { ELLIPSE
          CONSTRAINT THE_A ( ELLIPSE ) = THE_B ( ELLIPSE )
          POSSREP ( R   = THE_A   ( ELLIPSE ) ,
                    CTR = THE_CTR ( ELLIPSE ) )
          NOT { ELLIPSE ( LENGTH ( 2.0 ) ,
                          LENGTH ( 1.0 ) ,
                          POINT  ( 0.0 , 0.0 ) ) } } ;
```

Now let's focus on the IS specification—i.e., the *<is def>*, as the BNF grammar in Chapter 3 called it—for type CIRCLE.[2] That specification does the following (among other things):

■ It defines a *specialization constraint* for type CIRCLE. The specialization constraint in question says that a value e is of type CIRCLE if and only if IS_ELLIPSE(e) and THE_A(e) = THE_B(e) both evaluate to TRUE (in other words, if and only if e is of type ELLIPSE and has equal semiaxis lengths).

■ It defines a *derived possrep* for type CIRCLE in terms of (one of the possreps for) its sole immediate supertype ELLIPSE. The derived possrep in question says that circles can possibly be represented in terms of their radius and their center, where the radius is equal to the length a of the major semiaxis[3] of the pertinent ellipse and the center is equal to the center of that same ellipse. However, possreps, derived or otherwise, are irrelevant as far as the present discussion is concerned, and I'll ignore them for the rest of this chapter.

So let's take a closer look at the "specialization constraint" concept. Here's a precise definition:

Definition: Let T be a regular type (and hence, necessarily, a scalar type), and let T' be a nonempty immediate subtype of T. Then the type constraint for type T' will specify that, in order for some given value to be of type T', that value must be of type T and must additionally satisfy some further constraint. That type constraint—i.e., the constraint that the value must be of type T and must additionally satisfy that further constraint—is the *specialization constraint* for type T'.

---

[2] It might help if I remind you from Chapter 3 that all nonroot types have an associated *<is def>* and no root type does. (Of course, all scalar types are root types, and indeed regular types, in the absence of inheritance support.)

[3] I could have used the minor semiaxis here in place of the major semiaxis, of course—it would have made no difference.

And now I can also give a precise definition of the notion of "specialization by constraint" (S by C for short):

Definition: Let S be a selector of declared type T,[4] and let X be an expression denoting an invocation of S (thus $DT(X) = T$). Let the value returned by X be x. By definition, then, $v(X) = x$ and $MST(X) = MST(x)$. Further, let x satisfy the specialization constraint for proper subtype T' of T and not for any proper subtype of T'. Again by definition, then, $MST(X) = MST(x) = T'$. This effect on $MST(X)$—i.e., the fact that $MST(X)$ is now not T but T'—is referred to as *specialization by constraint* (S by C).

By way of example, with reference to Fig. 5.1 from Chapter 5, let expression X be as follows:

```
ELLIPSE ( LENGTH ( 5.0 ) , LENGTH ( 5.0 ) , POINT ( 0.0 , 0.0 ) )
```

This expression is, of course, an ELLIPSE selector invocation—in fact it's an ELLIPSE literal—and its declared type $DT(X)$ is thus ELLIPSE by definition. However, the ellipse denoted by that expression satisfies the specialization constraint for type CIRCLE, so the most specific type $MST(X)$ of X at run time is CIRCLE.

Moreover, suppose type CIRCLE had additionally been defined to have a proper subtype O_CIRCLE (where an "O-circle" is a circle with center the origin):

```
TYPE O_CIRCLE
     IS { CIRCLE
          CONSTRAINT THE_CTR ( CIRCLE ) = POINT ( 0.0 , 0.0 )
          POSSREP ( R = THE_R ( CIRCLE ) )
          NOT { CIRCLE ( LENGTH ( 2.0 ) , POINT ( 1.0 , 0.0 ) ) } } ;
```

(irrelevant details omitted as usual). Then the circle denoted by X would additionally satisfy the specialization constraint for type O_CIRCLE, and the most specific type $MST(X)$ of X at run time would therefore be O_CIRCLE, not CIRCLE.

SPECIALIZATION BY CONSTRAINT

So much for the basic idea; now let's take a closer look. Assume for simplicity that the only types we have to deal with are ELLIPSE and CIRCLE. Here once again are the type definitions (irrelevant details omitted as usual):

---

[4] As noted in Chapter 2, the declared type of a selector is, of course, the specified target type. For example, the declared type of the ELLIPSE selector is ELLIPSE.

```
TYPE ELLIPSE
     IS { PLANE_FIGURE
          POSSREP ( A LENGTH , B LENGTH , CTR POINT )
          CONSTRAINT A ≥ B
          NOT { ... } } ;    /* see Chapter 12 for further explanation */

TYPE CIRCLE
     IS { ELLIPSE
          CONSTRAINT THE_A ( ELLIPSE ) = THE_B ( ELLIPSE )
          POSSREP ( R   = THE_A   ( ELLIPSE ) ,
                    CTR = THE_CTR ( ELLIPSE ) )
          NOT { ELLIPSE ( LENGTH ( 2.0 ) ,
                          LENGTH ( 1.0 ) ,
                          POINT  ( 0.0 , 0.0 ) ) } } ;
```

Now, the CONSTRAINT specification for type CIRCLE here says the semiaxis lengths are supposed to be equal for a circle. Or does it? What *exactly* does it say? Well, let *e* be a value of type ELLIPSE, and let *a* and *b* be the corresponding semiaxis lengths. Then there are four possibilities—four possible ways, that is, in which the CONSTRAINT specification might be interpreted by the system:[5]

1. If $a = b$, then *e* is of type CIRCLE.
2. If *e* is of type CIRCLE, then $a = b$.
3. Neither 1 nor 2.
4. Both 1 and 2.

I'll consider each possibility in turn.

1. Clearly, possibility 1 permits—or at least fails to prohibit—"noncircular circles" (i.e., values of type CIRCLE that don't have $a = b$). *Note:* By the term *noncircular circle*, I mean something the system thinks is a circle but actually isn't. In other words, it's a value whose most specific type as far as the system is concerned is CIRCLE and yet has different semiaxis lengths, and thus logically ought to have most specific type ELLIPSE. Clearly, noncircular circles are a contradiction in terms—but they're typical of the logical absurdities that can and do occur if S by C isn't supported.

2. Likewise, possibility 2 permits "circular noncircles" (i.e., values of type ELLIPSE and not type CIRCLE that do have $a = b$). *Note:* By the term *circular noncircle*, I mean something the system thinks isn't a circle but actually is. In other words, it's a value whose most specific type as far as the system is concerned is ELLIPSE and yet has equal semiaxis

---

[5] Or so it might be thought. However, along with the fact that the type being defined—viz., type CIRCLE—is an immediate subtype of type ELLIPSE, that CONSTRAINT specification basically just serves to define the type constraint for type CIRCLE. And as we know from Chapter 2, a type constraint is nothing more or less than a definition of the set of values that constitute the type in question—from which it follows that the only valid "possible interpretation" has to be number 4. But I think detailed consideration of the other three apparent possibilities is a worthwhile exercise nonetheless.

lengths, and thus logically ought to have most specific type CIRCLE. Like noncircular circles, circular noncircles are clearly a contradiction in terms, but they too are typical of the logical absurdities that can and do occur if S by C isn't supported.

3. Possibility 3 permits both "noncircular circles" and "circular noncircles," in which case there doesn't seem to be any point in specifying the constraint at all.

4. Thus, possibility 4 appears to be the only sensible option. Certainly it's the only one that corresponds to mathematical reality, which is why it's the one adopted in the *Manifesto* model. And it follows immediately that the system must support S by C. Here again by way of example is the ELLIPSE selector invocation from the previous section:

```
ELLIPSE ( LENGTH ( 5.0 ) , LENGTH ( 5.0 ) , POINT ( 0.0 , 0.0 ) )
```

The value denoted by this expression is an ellipse with $a = b$ and is thus a circle, and is therefore—at least in the *Manifesto* model—of type CIRCLE. Thus, S by C implies, as the definition near the end of the previous section in fact states, that certain selector invocations will produce results whose most specific type is some proper subtype of the specified target type.

   Note: In fact, of course, S by C applies to expressions in general, not just to selector invocations. As pointed out in Chapter 2, however, the only way any expression can yield any value at all is, ultimately, via some selector invocation; hence, the effect of S by C on the most specific type of any expression depends, ultimately, on the effect defined earlier of S by C on the most specific type of some selector invocation. It follows that S by C can be thought of as being implemented as part of the implementation of the pertinent selector operators (conceptually, at any rate, though various optimizations are possible in practice, as we'll see in the section "Implementation Considerations" in Chapter 13).

To repeat, then, S by C means in particular that certain selector invocations will produce results whose most specific type is some proper subtype of the specified target type. Note, however, that this effect occurs at run time, *not* at compile time. For example, the selector invocation shown above—

```
ELLIPSE ( LENGTH ( 5.0 ) , LENGTH ( 5.0 ) , POINT ( 0.0 , 0.0 ) )
```

—has declared type ELLIPSE (known at compile time) but most specific type CIRCLE (not known until run time).

   Note: I've said that S by C can be thought of as being implemented inside selector implementation code. The following recursive procedure ("FIND_*MST*"), expressed in pseudocode, gives some idea as to what such an implementation might look like:

```
OPERATOR FIND_MST ( v value , T type ) RETURNS type ;
   let T1 , T2 , ..., Tn be all of the immediate subtypes of T
      in some arbitrary order ;
   let the corresponding specialization constraints be
      SC1 , SC2 , ..., Scn , respectively ;
   DO j := 1 TO n ;
      IF v satisfies SCj
         THEN RETURN ( FIND_MST ( v , Tj ) ) ;
      END IF ;
   END DO ;
   RETURN ( T ) ;
END OPERATOR ;
```

Procedure FIND_*MST* is initially invoked with arguments the selected value and the declared type of the pertinent selector; for example, in the case of the ELLIPSE selector invocation discussed earlier—

```
ELLIPSE ( LENGTH ( 5.0 ) , LENGTH ( 5.0 ) , POINT ( 0.0 , 0.0 ) )
```

—the initial arguments are the indicated ellipse value and type ELLIPSE. However, I must stress that the procedure as shown is purely conceptual in nature; as I've already said, various optimizations are possible in practice, as we'll see in Chapter 13.

So much for S by C, at least until further notice; now I want to turn to the companion notion of generalization by constraint (G by C). In order to discuss this latter notion, I first need to say something about IM Prescription 11, which has to do with the rules for assignment in the inheritance context.

IM PRESCRIPTION 11: ASSIGNMENT WITH INHERITANCE

Consider the assignment

```
V := X
```

(where *V* is a variable reference and *X* is an expression). *DT(X)* shall be a subtype of *DT(V)*. The assignment shall set *v(V)* equal to *v(X)*, and hence *MST(V)* equal to *MST(X)* also.

The model of a scalar variable introduced in IM Prescription 9 (see Chapter 7) is useful in pinning down the precise semantics of various operations, and this remark is true of assignment operations in particular. Now, without inheritance, the type rule for the assignment

```
V := X
```

is very simple: It just says the types of *V* and *X* must be the same (in effect, it can be thought of as saying their *declared* types must be the same, since their declared types are the only types they'll have if there's no inheritance). IM Prescription 11 extends that rule—actually it weakens it, in a way—by requiring only that the declared type of *X* be some subtype (not necessarily a proper subtype, of course) of the declared type of *V*. By way of example, let E and C be scalar[6] variables of declared types ELLIPSE and CIRCLE, respectively. Then the assignment

```
E := C ;
```

is clearly valid; it has the effect of setting the current value *v*(E) of E equal to the current value *v*(C) of C (and therefore setting the most specific type *MST*(E) equal to *MST*(C) also).

Note: When I say the foregoing assignment is clearly valid, I'm actually appealing to the notion of substitutability, which says in the case at hand that (a) a value of type ELLIPSE would be acceptable as the source of the assignment, and therefore (b) a value of type CIRCLE can legitimately appear in its place.

By the way, it's important to understand that what does *not* happen in an assignment like the one just shown is that the value of the source expression on the right side gets "converted up" to the declared type of the target variable on the left side. For if such a conversion did occur, the value in question would lose its most specific properties, as it were.[7] In the case at hand, for example, we wouldn't be able to ask for the radius of E—more precisely, the radius of the circle that's now the current value of E—because the circle would have been converted to "just an ellipse," and ellipses that are "just ellipses" don't have a radius.

Note: You might possibly see a problem here, and indeed there is one. To be specific, the operator THE_R ("the radius of") can't validly be applied to a variable such as E whose declared type is ELLIPSE and not CIRCLE, because, to say it again, ellipses that are "just ellipses" don't have a radius. Thus, the expression

```
THE_R ( E )     /* warning: compile time type error! */
```

will fail at on a type error at compile time.

The solution to this problem is to use the operator TREAT. That is, while the expression THE_R(E) fails at compile time as just explained, the following extended version of that expression—

```
THE_R ( TREAT_AS_CIRCLE ( E ) )
```

---

[6] IM Prescription 11 applies to tuple and relation assignments as well as scalar ones, but all assignments, and therefore all variables and all expressions, discussed in the present section are scalar ones specifically.

[7] In fact, of course, IM Prescriptions 8 and 10 both imply that any such "conversion up" is logically impossible. For if it were possible, it would mean that the very same value could have most specific type CIRCLE *and* most specific type ELLIPSE, thereby violating IM Prescription 8; it would also mean that, after the assignment, the target variable would contain an ellipse that could be "S by C'd" to a circle but hasn't been, thereby violating IM Prescription 10.

—will satisfy the compile time type checking; moreover, it'll succeed at run time as well—i.e., it'll return the corresponding radius—if (but only if) the current value of E is indeed of type CIRCLE. See Chapter 10 for further explanation.

So much for the (valid) assignment of C to E. But what about assigning E to C?—

```
C := E ;    /* warning: compile time type error! */
```

In accordance with IM Prescription 11, this one will fail on a type error at compile time, (even if the current value of E would have been a circle at run time), because *DT*(E) = ELLIPSE and *DT*(C) = CIRCLE, and ELLIPSE isn't a subtype of CIRCLE.

Of course, if variable E does have a circle as its current value at run time, there must surely be some way of assigning that circle to variable C, and so there is; the solution, again, is to use TREAT (again see Chapter 10). To be specific, the following revised form of the foregoing assignment—

```
C := TREAT_AS_CIRCLE ( E ) ;
```

—will satisfy the compile time type checking, and will succeed at run time as well if (but only if) the current value of E is indeed of type CIRCLE.

Following on from this point, the assignment

```
C := ELLIPSE ( LENGTH ( 5.0 ) , LENGTH ( 5.0 ) , POINT ( ... ) ) ;
                        /* warning: compile time type error! */
```

will also fail on a type error at compile time, even though the ELLIPSE selector invocation on the right side would clearly return a circle at run time. (Recall again that S by C happens at run time, not compile time.) Instead, the assignment needs to be written like this:

```
C := TREAT_AS_CIRCLE
     ( ELLIPSE ( LENGTH ( 5.0 ) , LENGTH ( 5.0 ) , POINT ( ... ) ) ) ;
```

Of course, it could also be written like this:

```
C := CIRCLE ( LENGTH ( 5.0 ) , POINT ( ... ) ) ;
```

To summarize: Assignment without inheritance simply requires the source expression and target variable to be of the same type. By contrast (and thanks to substitutability), the rules for assignment with inheritance are as follows:

■ The declared type *DT*(X) of the source expression *X* on the right side can be any subtype of the declared type *DT*(V) of the target variable *V* on the left side (this is a compile time check).

- The most specific type *MST(X)* of the source expression *X* on the right side can be any subtype of the declared type *DT(V)* of the target variable *V* on the left side. (In fact, of course, *MST(X)* will necessarily be some subtype of *DT(X)*; thus, it'll be some subtype of *DT(V)* a fortiori.)

- The target variable *V* on the left side acquires its new value, and hence its new most specific type, from the value denoted by the source expression *X* on the right side.

Now suppose again that variable E, of declared type ELLIPSE, has a circle as its current value, and consider the following code:

```
VAR A AREA ;

A := AREA_OF ( E ) ;
```

What happens here is the following:

- The system performs a compile time type check on the expression AREA_OF (E); that check succeeds, because E is of declared type ELLIPSE and the single parameter to AREA_OF is of declared type ELLIPSE also (or let's assume so for the sake of the example, at any rate).

- The system discovers at run time that the current value of E is of type CIRCLE.

- The system also discovers at run time that an implementation version of AREA_OF exists that applies to circles—or, again, let's assume so for the sake of the example—and it therefore invokes that version. (In other words, it performs the run time binding process discussed briefly in the section "Code Reuse" in Chapter 7. See Chapter 11 for further explanation.)

- The result of that invocation is then assigned to the variable A.

Note finally that IM Prescription 11 concludes by saying this: *The assignment shall set v(V) equal to v(X), and hence MST(V) equal to MST(X) also.* In other words, the prescription explicitly requires the assignment to satisfy *The Assignment Principle.* (Just to remind you from Chapter 2, *The Assignment Principle* states that after assignment of value *v* to variable *V*, the comparison *v* = *V* must evaluate to TRUE.)

GENERALIZATION BY CONSTRAINT

Again let E be a variable of declared type ELLIPSE, and let its current value be an ellipse with $a = 4$ and $b = 3$. Consider the following assignment:

```
THE_A ( E )  := LENGTH ( 3.0 ) ;
```

The expanded form of this assignment is:

```
E := ELLIPSE ( LENGTH ( 3.0 ) , THE_B ( E ) , THE_CTR ( E ) ) ;
```

And since THE_B(E) = LENGTH(3.0), S by C occurs; the selector invocation on the right side returns a circle, not "just an ellipse," and that circle is then assigned to the variable E. Loosely, we can say that the type—meaning, more precisely, the most specific type *MST*(E)—of variable E has been "changed down," or *specialized*, from ELLIPSE to CIRCLE.

Now suppose the foregoing assignment is followed by this one:

```
THE_B ( E )  := LENGTH ( 2.0 ) ;
```

Here's the expanded form:

```
E := ELLIPSE ( THE_A ( E ) , LENGTH ( 2.0 ) , THE_CTR ( E ) ) ;
```

Since THE_A(E) = LENGTH(3.0), the selector invocation on the right side here returns "just an ellipse" (i.e., an ellipse that's not a circle), and that ellipse is then assigned to the variable E. Thus, it should be clear that the most specific type *MST*(E) of variable E is now ELLIPSE again (because THE_A(E) is now greater than THE_B(E)). We refer to this effect as *generalization by constraint* (G by C for short); loosely, we can say that the type—meaning, more precisely, the most specific type *MST*(E)—of variable E has been "changed up," or *generalized*, from CIRCLE to ELLIPSE. In fact, it should be obvious that a system that supports S by C needs to support G by C as well. What's more, the algorithm FIND_*MST* given earlier in this chapter for implementing S by C can in fact be used for G by C as well, as should also be obvious—though perhaps I should add that, unlike S by C, which occurs on the invocation of some selector, G by C occurs on the execution of some assignment, as the foregoing example illustrates.

Here then is a precise definition:

> **Definition:** Let types *T″*, *T′*, and *T* be such that *T″* is a proper subtype of *T′* and *T′* is a subtype of *T*, and let *v′* be a value that satisfies the type constraint for type *T′* and not for any proper subtype of *T′* (thus *MST*(*v′*) = *T′*). Also, let *V* be a variable of declared type *T*, and let the current most specific type *MST*(*V*) of *V* be *T″*. Finally, let the value *v′* be assigned to *V*. By definition, then, *MST*(*V*) = *MST*(*v′*) = *T′*. This effect on *MST*(*V*)—i.e.,

the fact that $MST(V)$ is now not T'' but T'—is referred to as *generalization by constraint* (G by C).

So S by C and G by C together support changing types both "up" and "down"—and it follows that they support changing types "sideways," too. For example, suppose type ELLIPSE has another immediate subtype NONCIRCLE, with the obvious semantics (i.e., ELLIPSE is now a union type—see Chapter 12—and every ellipse is either a circle or a noncircle, and no ellipse is both). Let the current value of variable E be an ellipse with $a = 4$ and $b = 3$, and hence in fact a value of type NONCIRCLE. Then the assignment

```
THE_A ( E ) := LENGTH ( 3.0 ) ;
```

will assign a circle of radius three to E, and will thus effectively also change the type—meaning, more precisely, the most specific type $MST(E)$—of variable E "sideways," from NONCIRCLE to CIRCLE. Moreover, the assignment

```
THE_B ( E ) := LENGTH ( 2.0 ) ;
```

will then assign to E an ellipse with $a = 3$ and $b = 2$, and will thus effectively change the most specific type of variable E "sideways" from CIRCLE back to NONCIRCLE again.

CONCLUDING REMARKS

This brings me to the end of my explanation of the basics of S by C and G by C. As I hope you'll agree, these concepts not only make good logical sense but are in fact quite straightforward and easy to understand. As noted at the beginning of the chapter, however, S by C at least is widely regarded as controversial.[8] In fact, this entire subject seems to be surrounded by a very great deal of muddle and confusion. In view of this state of affairs:

- Regarding the controversy, I do want to try and explain what it's all about and why it exists. However, to do that properly means I need to appeal to a number of concepts that I haven't had a chance to explain in detail (or at all, in some cases) in this book so far. For that reason, I'll defer detailed discussion of the controversy as such to Chapter 13; as far as this chapter is concerned, I'll content myself simply with claiming that, so far as I'm aware, no other approaches to inheritance described in the literature support either S by C or G by C at all.

---

[8] The reason I say "S by C at least" here is that critics of these concepts tend to focus on S by C specifically and ignore, or at any rate overlook, the companion notion of G by C—despite the fact that, as I said earlier, it's obvious that a system that supports S by C must support G by C as well.

■ Regarding the "muddle and confusion," however, I would at least like to try to clarify matters somewhat, and that's what the remainder of this final section is about.

I'll begin by distinguishing—or trying to distinguish!—between *specialization* as such, on the one hand, and *specialization by constraint* (i.e., S by C), on the other. By way of example, consider our usual variables E and C, with their declared types ELLIPSE and CIRCLE, respectively. Let their current most specific types be ELLIPSE and CIRCLE, respectively, as well. Now consider this assignment:

```
E := C ;
```

This assignment has the effect of changing ("specializing") the most specific type of E—or, loosely, just specializing E as such—"down" from ELLIPSE to CIRCLE. In other words, *MST*(E) is now CIRCLE. More precisely, after the assignment, *MST*(E) is the same as *MST*(C), which in principle might be some nonempty proper subtype of CIRCLE—though not in the case at hand, because type CIRCLE doesn't have any proper subtypes apart from type *omega*. (However, if as in Chapter 7, and indeed elsewhere in the present chapter, type CIRCLE had a proper subtype O_CIRCLE, where an "O-circle" is a circle with center the origin, and if C currently contained an O-circle, then after the foregoing assignment *MST*(E) would be O_CIRCLE.)

Now, the foregoing example shouldn't come as a surprise to you in any way—it's in full accord with how our inheritance model works, and (as far as I know) with how other systems work as well.[9] But note very carefully that the foregoing process of specialization, unlike the process of S by C, happens not as part of some selector invocation, but rather as part of some assignment. In other words, it happens in the same way as G by C does in our model. So the point is this: Languages that support inheritance, even ones that don't support S by C (which I believe is all of them), might still provide some mechanism for changing types "down"—but if they do, then that mechanism will come into play not as part of some selector invocation (as is the case with S by C in our model), but rather as part of some assignment (as is the case with G by C in our model). Hence we have the following definition:

Definition: Let types T'', T', and T be such that T'' is a proper subtype of T' and T' is a subtype of T, and let v'' be a value of most specific type T'' (thus $MST(v'') = T''$). Also, let V be a variable of declared type T, and let the current most specific type $MST(V)$ of V be T'. Finally, let the value v'' be assigned to V. By definition, then, $MST(V) = MST(v'') = T''$. This effect on $MST(V)$—i.e., the fact that $MST(V)$ is now not T' but T''—is referred to as *specialization* (sometimes *further* specialization, for emphasis).

---

[9] Of course, if they don't, the result will be that E now contains a "circular noncircle" (see earlier in this chapter).

So much for specialization; what about generalization? Well, the obvious definition looks like this (please note the subtle differences between this definition and that given for G by C in the previous section):

Definition: Let types T'', T', and T be such that T'' is a proper subtype of T' and T' is a subtype of T, and let v' be a value of most specific type T' (thus $MST(v') = T'$). Also, let V be a variable of declared type T, and let the current most specific type $MST(V)$ of V be T''. Finally, let the value v' be assigned to V. By definition, then, $MST(V) = MST(v') = T'$. This effect on $MST(V)$—i.e., the fact that $MST(V)$ is now not T'' but T'—is referred to as *generalization*.

Now, I'm sure you realize that this definition of generalization is 100 percent compatible with the way our own inheritance model works. In some systems, however, it seems that generalization as such might not happen at all. By way of example, let variable E be of declared type ELLIPSE, and consider the following sequence of events. First, a value of most specific type CIRCLE is assigned to E; the most specific type of E thus becomes CIRCLE (at least, let's assume so for the sake of the discussion). Next, E is updated in such a way that, after the update, THE_A(E) is greater than THE_B(E). In our model, the most specific type of E now becomes ELLIPSE again; but if it doesn't—if it remains unchanged and is still CIRCLE—then the result will be that E now contains a "noncircular circle."

Specialization via Constraints

The final confusion factor I want to mention in this chapter is a notion called "specialization via constraints." This notion, which is found in the object literature, might or might not be related to—but, as far as I can see (?), is certainly not the same thing as—S by C. Here's a definition (it's taken from "Fundamentals of Object-Oriented Databases," by Stanley B. Zdonik and David Maier, in *Readings in Object-Oriented Database Systems*, Zdonik and Maier, eds., Morgan Kaufmann, 1990):

Specialization via constraints happens whenever the following is permitted:

B subtype_of A and T subtype_of S and
$f(...b:T...)$ returns $r:R$ in Ops(B) and
$f(...b:S...)$ returns $r:R$ in Ops(A) and [*sic*]

That is, specialization via constraints occurs whenever the operation redefinition on a subtype constrains one of the arguments to be from a smaller value set than the corresponding operation on the supertype.

Well, I don't know about you, but I don't find this definition very clear. As near as I can tell, however, "operator redefinition on a subtype" seems to mean (to use terminology defined elsewhere in the present book) nothing more than definition of a new implementation version of the operator in question for the subtype in question. "Specialization via constraints" thus seems to mean—to take a concrete example—that if AREA_OF is an operator that's defined to work on ellipses, and a version of AREA_OF is defined to work on ellipses that happen to be circles, then the argument to an invocation of that version of AREA_OF must be a circle specifically and not just an ellipse. It's not really clear, therefore, that "specialization via constraints" has anything to do with an inheritance *model* (as opposed to the implementation of such a model) at all.[10]

EXERCISES

The following exercises all appeal to a family of types called CHAR_n ($n \geq 0$), where (a) a value is of type CHAR_n if and only if it's a character string of at most n significant characters and (b) a character is *significant* if and only if it's not a trailing space. *Note:* It's worth pointing out that this family of types is very similar, though not identical, to the SQL family of types VARCHAR(n). In other words, CHAR_ can be regarded as a type generator, just as VARCHAR is in SQL.

8.1   Is it true that type CHAR_n' is a subtype of type CHAR_n if and only if $n' \leq n$?

8.2   Does value substitutability apply?

8.3   Are there any operators that apply to values of type CHAR_n' and not to values of type CHAR_n?

8.4   Do S by C and G by C apply?

8.5   Is there a nonempty type that's a subtype of all possible types in the family?

8.6   Consider the literal 'ABC ' (note the trailing space). What's the declared type of that literal?

8.7   What's the most specific type of that same literal?

8.8   What's the root type corresponding to type CHAR_n?

---

[10] See the discussion of "the three out of four rule" in Chapter 13 for further speculation as to what the term *specialization via constraints* might possibly mean.

ANSWERS

8.1   Yes, it is. For example, every value of type CHAR_3 is also a value of type CHAR_5 (and the converse is false, of course).

8.2   Yes, it does (by definition, in fact, given the answer to Exercise 8.1).

8.3   In principle, yes—any operator with a parameter of declared type CHAR_n' (in other words, any operator for which some character string operand is constrained to consist of at most n' significant characters) is such an operator.

8.4   Yes, by definition.

8.5   Yes, CHAR_0. CHAR_0 is nonempty, because every string consisting of nothing but spaces—including the empty string in particular—is of type CHAR_0 (and no other string is of that type). Note that CHAR_0 might have proper subtypes of its own (e.g., constrained according to length), but no such subtype is a member of the CHAR_n family as such.

8.6   We don't really have enough information to answer this question—it's a matter of how the pertinent language is defined. But it's probably reasonable to assume that the declared type of a character string literal of length n characters is CHAR_n (i.e., CHAR_4 in the case of 'ABC ')—although it might be more useful in practice if that particular literal were defined to have declared type CHAR_3, for then it could be assigned to a variable of type CHAR_3, which a value of declared type CHAR_4 can't be. On the other hand, we don't usually expect compilers to have to evaluate expressions at compile time with a view to determining their declared types, so we might be required to assign CAST_AS_CHAR_3 ('ABC ') instead. *Note:* The declared type can't be CHAR_n where $n < 3$, because the value denoted by the literal is certainly of type CHAR_3 (as well as some user defined proper subtype thereof, possibly, if any such exists), and the declared type of an expression can't possibly be a proper subtype of the value it denotes.

8.7   CHAR_3, or possibly some proper subtype thereof, if any such exists (see the answer to Exercise 8.6).

8.8   Presumably the root type is CHAR_N, where N is the maximum value for n supported by the implementation in question. *Note:* I said in Chapter 2 that I'd assume support for type CHAR as a system defined type. Type CHAR is clearly a supertype for type CHAR_n for all possible n (including $n = N$ in particular). However, type CHAR isn't itself a member of the CHAR_n family as such.

Chapter 9

Equality Comparisons etc.

The defect of equality is that we only desire it with our superiors.
—Henry Becque:
Querelles Littéraires (1890)

All animals are equal, but some animals are more equal than others.
—George Orwell:
Animal Farm (1945)

This chapter considers the question of how the fundamental operation of equality comparison needs to be revised to take account of inheritance. It also looks at the implications of inheritance for the dyadic relational operators union, intersection, difference, and join, all of which are crucially dependent on that notion of equality (tuple equality, to be precise)—though there's quite a bit more to discuss in connection with those operators than just the issue of equality as such.

IM PRESCRIPTION 12: EQUALITY WITH INHERITANCE

Consider the equality comparison

    Y = X

(where *Y* and *X* are expressions). *DT(Y)* and *DT(X)* shall overlap. The comparison shall return TRUE if *v(Y)* is equal to *v(X)* (and hence if *MST(Y)* is equal to *MST(X)* also), and FALSE otherwise.

Without inheritance, the type rule for the equality comparison

    Y = X

is very simple: It just says the types of *Y* and *X* must be the same (in effect, it can be thought of as saying their *declared* types must be the same, since their declared types are the only types they'll have if there's no inheritance). IM Prescription 12 extends that rule—actually it weakens it, in a way—by requiring only that the declared types of *Y* and *X* overlap, or in other words have a nonempty common subtype (not necessarily a proper subtype, of course). By way of example, let E and C be scalar[1] variables of declared types ELLIPSE and CIRCLE, respectively. Then the comparison

```
E = C
```

is clearly valid, and will evaluate to TRUE if and only if the current value of E is a circle—i.e., is of type CIRCLE—and is in fact the same circle as the current value of C.

Note: When I say the foregoing comparison is clearly valid, I'm actually appealing to the notion of substitutability once again, which says in the case at hand that (a) a value of type ELLIPSE would be acceptable as the right comparand, and therefore (b) a value of type CIRCLE can legitimately appear in its place.

So the rules for equality comparison with inheritance are as follows:

- The declared types $DT(X)$ and $DT(Y)$ of the expressions on the right and left side of the comparison, respectively, must have a nonempty common subtype (this is a compile time check). *Note:* We'll see in Chapter 15 that if two types do have a nonempty common subtype, then they must also have a common supertype, and that's something else that can be checked at compile time. But having a common supertype, though necessary, is obviously not sufficient to guarantee the existence of a nonempty common subtype (think of types ELLIPSE and RECTANGLE, for example).

- The most specific type $MST(X)$ of the expression *X* on the right side can be any subtype of the declared type $DT(X)$ of that expression *X*; likewise, the most specific type $MST(Y)$ of the expression *Y* on the left side can be any subtype of the declared type $DT(Y)$ of that expression *Y*. (It follows that those most specific types must have a common supertype, a fortiori.)

- If we're dealing with single inheritance only and we can rely on the disjointness assumption, then the compile time checking mentioned in the first bullet item above can be simplified. To be specific, if the disjointness assumption holds, then $DT(X)$ and $DT(Y)$ can have a nonempty common subtype if and only if one is a nonempty subtype of the other; thus, if this condition isn't satisfied, the comparison will fail on a compile time type error. For example, if $DT(X)$ and $DT(Y)$ are ELLIPSE and RECTANGLE, respectively, the comparison will fail at compile time.

---

[1] IM Prescription 12 applies to tuple and relation equality comparisons as well as scalar ones, but the comparisons (and therefore the variables and expressions as well) discussed in this section are all scalar ones. (Of course, the prescription is also worded in such a way as to apply to multiple as well as single inheritance, but the focus in the present chapter is on single inheritance only, where it makes any difference.)

■ Assuming the compile time type checking succeeds, the comparison will give FALSE if the most specific types of the comparands are different—a difference in type is certainly a logical difference—but will give TRUE if those most specific types are the same and the values are the same as well. *Note:* I remind you once again that the most specific type of any value is implied by the value in question. It follows that if $v(Y)$ and $v(X)$ are the same, then $MST(Y)$ and $MST(X)$ must be the same as well, and there's no need to say as much in so many words; I do so here only for explicitness.

A note on "<" etc.: The rules for ordered types (see Chapter 2) for comparisons of the form "$Y < X$" and "$Y > X$" are similar to, but not quite the same as, the rules for equality comparisons. Certainly the declared types of the comparands, and hence the corresponding most specific types as well, need to have a common supertype; this is a compile time check. However, those most specific types don't necessarily have to be the same in order for the comparison to give TRUE. By way of example, let 5 and 8 be values of most specific type ODD_INTEGER and EVEN_INTEGER, respectively, where ODD_INTEGER and EVEN_INTEGER have the intuitively obvious semantics. Note in particular that those types have INTEGER as a common supertype; note too that they don't overlap. Nevertheless, the comparison 5 < 8 can and surely should be defined in such a way as to give TRUE.

> *Aside:* The foregoing paragraph is perhaps a little oversimplified, in the sense that the literals 5 and 8 will probably not be of declared types ODD_INTEGER and EVEN_INTEGER, respectively; instead, they'll almost certainly both be of declared type INTEGER, and 5 < 8 will thus be a straightforward integer comparison. Thanks to value substitutability, however, we can replace those literals 5 and 8 by the literals ODD_INTEGER(5) and EVEN_INTEGER(8), respectively,[2] and then—assuming a sensible definition for "<"—the comparison will still give TRUE. Note that, by contrast, analogous remarks do *not* apply to the equality comparisons 5 = 8 and ODD_INTEGER(5) = EVEN_INTEGER(8). To be specific, while the first of these latter comparisons is legal (though it gives FALSE), the second is in violation of IM Prescription 12 and should fail at compile time. *End of aside*.

IM PRESCRIPTION 13: JOIN ETC. WITH INHERITANCE

Let *RX* and *RY* be relational expressions. In accordance with IM Prescription 28, each of *RX* and *RY* has a declared type. Let those declared types have headings

```
{ <A1,TX1> , <A2,TX2> , ... , <An,TXn> }
```

---

[2] Regarding the syntax of those literals, see the answer to Exercise 10.5 in Chapter 10.

```
{ <A1,TY1> , <A2,TY2> , ... , <An,TYn> }
```

respectively, where (a) $n \geq 0$ and (b) for all j ($j = 1, 2, ..., n$), types TXj and TYj have most specific common supertype Tj and least specific common subtype Tj'. Further, let the values denoted by RX and RY be relations rx and ry, respectively. Then:

a. An expression of the form (RX) UNION (RY), or logical equivalent thereof, shall be supported and shall denote the **union** of rx and ry. The declared type of that expression shall have heading

```
{ <A1,T1> , <A2,T2> , ... , <An,Tn> }
```

b. An expression of the form (RX) INTERSECT (RY), or logical equivalent thereof, shall be supported and shall denote the **intersection** of rx and ry. The declared type of that expression shall have heading

```
{ <A1,T1'> , <A2,T2'> , ... , <An,Tn'> }
```

Note: Intersection is a special case of join; given the prescriptions of paragraph d. below, therefore, the present paragraph b. is strictly redundant. We include it for convenience.

c. An expression of the form (RX) MINUS (RY), or logical equivalent thereof, shall be supported and shall denote the **difference** between rx and ry, in that order. The declared type of that expression shall have heading

```
{ <A1,TX1> , <A2,TX2> , ... , <An,TXn> }
```

Now let the declared types of relational expressions RX and RY have headings

```
{ <A1,TX1> , <A2,TX2> , ... , <An,TXn> , <B1,TB1> , ... , <Bp,TBp> }
{ <A1,TY1> , <A2,TY2> , ... , <An,TYn> , <C1,TC1> , ... , <Cq,TCq> }
```

where (a) $n \geq 0$, $p \geq 0$, and $q \geq 0$, and (b) for all j ($j = 1, 2, ..., n$), types TXj and TYj have least specific common subtype Tj'. Further, let the values denoted by RX and RY be relations rx and ry, respectively. Then:

d. An expression of the form (RX) JOIN (RY), or logical equivalent thereof, shall be supported and shall denote the **join** of rx and ry. The declared type of that expression shall have heading

```
{ <A1,T1'> , <A2,T2'> , ... , <An,Tn'> ,
        <B1,TB1> , ... , <Bp,TBp> , <C1,TC1> , ... , <Cq,TCq> }
```

Note: Intersection is a special case of join; thus, the prescriptions of the present paragraph d. degenerate to those for intersection (see paragraph b. above) in the case where $p = q = 0$.

This prescription has been fairly drastically reworded vis-à-vis the *Explorations* version, though the general intent hasn't changed much. The fact is, however, the *Explorations* version was unfortunately confused on several points. In particular, it was formulated in terms of the "declared types" of attributes of relations—but since a relation is a value, it doesn't have a declared type, and neither do its attributes! Rather, as we saw in Chapter 2, a relation has a heading, and that heading in turn is made up of attributes of the form $<A,T>$, where A is the name of the attribute in question and T is the name of the type of that attribute—*the* type, please note, not the declared type; to repeat, there *is* no declared type as such.

Pictures of Relations

The foregoing fact—the fact, that is, that attributes of relations as such don't have declared types—raises another issue, though, having to do with the way we depict relations as tables (on paper, for example). In the answer to Exercise 1.9 in Chapter 1, I said, in effect, that such pictures can always be regarded as showing a sample value for some relvar. Now, attributes of relvars (as opposed to relations) do have declared types—viz., the types declared when the relvar in question is itself declared. For example, let relvar ERV be defined as follows:

```
VAR ERV BASE RELATION { E ELLIPSE , R RECTANGLE } KEY { E , R } ;
```

Then attributes E and R of this relvar have declared types ELLIPSE and RECTANGLE, respectively.

Now let *e1* and *e2* be values of most specific type ELLIPSE and let *r3* and *r4* be values of most specific type RECTANGLE (where *e1* ≠ *e2* or *r3* ≠ *r4* or both). Then the following picture shows a possible value for relvar ERV:

ERV

E	R
e1	r3
e2	r4

Note in particular that it's usual to omit the type names and show just the attribute names in pictures like this one. But it wouldn't be wrong to include such type names as shown here:

```
ERV
  ┌─────────────────┬───────────────────┐
  │  E : ELLIPSE    │  R : RECTANGLE    │
  ╞═════════════════╪═══════════════════╡
  │      e1         │       r3          │
  │      e2         │       r4          │
  └─────────────────┴───────────────────┘
```

To spell out the situation precisely, ELLIPSE and RECTANGLE in this picture denote the declared types of attributes E and R, respectively, of relvar ERV.

Now, thanks to value substitutability, the E and R values in any given tuple of ERV can be of any subtype of types ELLIPSE and RECTANGLE, respectively. For example, let $c5$ and $c6$ be values of most specific type CIRCLE and let $s7$ and $s8$ be values of most specific type SQUARE ($c5 \neq c6$ or $s7 \neq s8$ or both). Then the following picture—I deliberately don't show any type names for the moment—shows another possible value for relvar ERV:

```
ERV
  ┌───────┬───────┐
  │   E   │   R   │
  ╞═══════╪═══════╡
  │  c5   │  s7   │
  │  c6   │  s8   │
  └───────┴───────┘
```

For the sake of the discussion, let's agree to refer to this relation as "relation *cs*."

So what about those type names? Well, since every E value in relation *cs* is of most specific type CIRCLE and every R value in that same relation is of most specific type SQUARE, I think it's intuitively obvious that the most specific type of the value that's relation *cs* as such—i.e., just considering it as an independent value, not necessarily as a possible value for relvar ERV—is this:

```
RELATION { E CIRCLE , R SQUARE }
```

Here's the picture:[3]

```
cs
  ┌─────────────────┬─────────────────┐
  │  E : CIRCLE     │  R : SQUARE     │
  ╞═════════════════╪═════════════════╡
  │      c5         │      s7         │
  │      c6         │      s8         │
  └─────────────────┴─────────────────┘
```

---

[3] *A note on the double underlining in this picture*: To repeat another point from the answer to Exercise 1.9 in Chapter 1, relation *cs* certainly doesn't have the key indicated by that double underlining—relations as such don't have keys—but it does satisfy the corresponding key uniqueness constraint. (In the case at hand, of course, the constraint in question isn't much of a constraint, since it boils down merely to saying that the tuples in relation *cs* are all distinct! But the general point is valid.)

On the other hand, suppose we want to draw a picture showing relation *cs* as a sample value for relvar ERV. In this case, the picture is really a picture of ERV as such (a possible picture, anyway), and it thus seems appropriate to show the attribute type names as ELLIPSE and RECTANGLE instead of CIRCLE and SQUARE, as here:

```
ERV

┌─────────────────┬─────────────────┐
│  E : ELLIPSE    │  R : RECTANGLE  │
╞═════════════════╪═════════════════╡
│     c5          │     s7          │
│     c6          │     s8          │
└─────────────────┴─────────────────┘
```

And I'll follow these conventions throughout the remainder of this book. That is, when I show a picture of a relation and I explicitly want to show appropriate attribute type names along with the pertinent attribute names, then:

■ When the picture is meant to show some relation as a possible value for some relvar—or, more generally, as a possible value for some expression—I'll show the declared type names for the attributes of that relvar or expression.

■ When the picture is meant to show some relation as such—that is, just as a relation value, independent of any specific relvar or expression—I'll show the attribute type names that are appropriate to the most specific type of that relation.

   Of course, the obvious question arises immediately: What *is* the most specific type of a relation, in general? Well, I'm afraid I'm going to have to defer detailed discussion of that question to Part IV of this book; suffice it to say for now that in the case of our example relation *cs*, the most specific type is indeed as stated above, viz., RELATION {E CIRCLE, S SQUARE}. For further explanation, see the discussion of IM Prescription 27 in Chapter 20 (and the answer to Exercise 20.2 in that chapter in particular).

Dyadic Relational Operators

Now I can get back to IM Prescription 13 as such. By way of a simple introductory example, let relational expressions *RX* and *RY* have declared types RELATION {E ELLIPSE} and RELATION {E CIRCLE}, respectively. (For the sake of the discussion, let's assume that ELLIPSE and CIRCLE are the only scalar types we have to deal with; in fact, let's stay with that assumption throughout the rest of this chapter, barring explicit statements to the contrary.) Now let the relations *rx* and *ry* currently denoted by expressions *RX* and *RY*, respectively, be as follows:

```
rx                              ry
┌─────────────────┐     ┌─────────────────┐
│ E   : ELLIPSE   │     │ E   : CIRCLE    │
├─────────────────┤     ├─────────────────┤
│ e1  : ellipse   │     │ c2  : circle    │
│ c2  : circle    │     │ c3  : circle    │
└─────────────────┘     └─────────────────┘
```

I'm assuming here that *e1* is an ellipse that's not a circle and *c2* and *c3* are circles (and *c2* ≠ *c3*). For reasons of explicitness I've tagged each attribute value in the picture with its most specific type (shown in lowercase italics).

Given these sample values, then, *rx* UNION *ry*, *rx* INTERSECT *ry*, *rx* MINUS *ry*, and *ry* MINUS *rx* are as shown here (*rx* JOIN *ry* is identical to *rx* INTERSECT *ry* in this simple example):[4]

```
rx UNION ry          rx INTERSECT ry    rx MINUS ry         ry MINUS rx
┌─────────────────┐  ┌─────────────────┐ ┌─────────────────┐ ┌─────────────────┐
│ E   : ELLIPSE   │  │ E   : CIRCLE    │ │ E   : ELLIPSE   │ │ E   : CIRCLE    │
├─────────────────┤  ├─────────────────┤ ├─────────────────┤ ├─────────────────┤
│ e1  : ellipse   │  │ c2  : circle    │ │ e1  : ellipse   │ │ c3  : circle    │
│ c2  : circle    │  └─────────────────┘ └─────────────────┘ └─────────────────┘
│ c3  : circle    │
└─────────────────┘
```

Note the attribute types in particular in these results. Indeed, given that:

a. The value of attribute E in some tuples of *rx* is "just an ellipse" and not a circle, while

b. The value of attribute E in every tuple in *ry* is a circle specifically,

it's intuitively obvious that the type of attribute E with respect to *rx* UNION *ry* (or whichever case it is we're dealing with) must be as follows:

■ *rx* UNION *ry*   :   ELLIPSE

■ *rx* INTERSECT *ry*   :   CIRCLE

■ *rx* MINUS *ry*   :   ELLIPSE

■ *ry* MINUS *rx*   :   CIRCLE

■ *rx* JOIN *ry*   :   CIRCLE

Observe now that IM Prescription 13 does indeed concern itself with types, and therefore headings, only; the corresponding bodies are assumed to be well understood. For the record,

───────────────

[4] I'm adopting an obvious shorthand notation here, writing *rx* UNION *ry* for the result of (*RX*) UNION (*RY*) and so on.

however, let me spell out the rules regarding the bodies as well (I deliberately state these rules in such a way as to emphasize their reliance on the notion of tuple equality):

- `rx UNION ry`

  The body consists of all tuples *t* such that *t* is equal to some tuple that appears in at least one of *rx* and *ry*.

- `rx INTERSECT ry`

  The body consists of all tuples *t* such that *t* is equal to some tuple that appears in each of *rx* and *ry*.

- `rx MINUS ry`

  The body consists of all tuples *t* such that *t* is equal to some tuple that appears in *rx* and not in *ry* (and conversely for *ry* MINUS *rx*, of course).

- `rx JOIN ry`

  The body consists of all tuples *t* such that *t* is equal to the set theory union of some tuple from *rx* and some tuple from *ry*.

Further Points

Now, the state of affairs as so far described is surely quite straightforward and easy to understand. However, there are a few points that are worth discussing further. First of all, the rules regarding the declared types of the expressions (*RX*) UNION (*RY*), (*RX*) INTERSECT (*RY*), and (*RX*) MINUS (*RY*)—though not (*RX*) JOIN (*RY*)—can be formulated more concisely by appealing to the notion of the declared type of a relational expression as such (as opposed to the notion of the declared types of individual attributes of such an expression). I'll give the rules here for the record; for further explanation, however, again I'll have to refer you to Part IV of this book.

For union, intersection, and difference, then, the declared types $DT(RX)$ and $DT(RY)$ of *RX* and *RY*, respectively, must have a common supertype.[5] Then the declared types of the various expressions are as follows:

- `( RX ) UNION ( RY )`

  The most specific common supertype of $DT(RX)$ and $DT(RY)$.

---

[5] Equivalently, those declared types must belong to the same type lattice (see Chapter 5).

- ■   (*RX*) INTERSECT (*RY*)

  The least specific common subtype—i.e., the intersection type—of *DT(RX)* and *DT(RY)*.

- ■   (*RX*) MINUS (*RY*)

  DT(RX).

Turning now to join: In general, the join of relations *rx* and *ry* is defined if and only if *rx* and *ry* are *joinable*. Now, in the absence of inheritance, *rx* and *ry* are joinable if and only if attributes with the same name are of the same type—equivalently, if and only if the set theory union of their headings is a legal heading. But this definition needs to be extended somewhat if type inheritance is supported:

> **Definition:** Relations *rx* and *ry* are *joinable* if and only if attributes with the same name are such that their types have a common supertype.

So let relational expressions *RX* and *RY* denote relations *rx* and *ry*, respectively, and let *rx* and *ry* be joinable in the foregoing sense. Then, for each pair of attributes <*A,TX*> of *RX* and <*A,TY*> of *RY* having the same attribute name *A*, the declared type of attribute *A* in (*RX*) JOIN (*RY*) is the least specific common subtype *T'*—the intersection type, in fact—of *TX* and *TY*. (And if *RX* has an attribute called *Z* but *RY* doesn't, or vice versa, then attribute *Z* simply becomes an attribute of the result in the usual way, of course.)

Now let relational expressions *RX* and *RY* have declared types RELATION {PF ELLIPSE} and RELATION {PF RECTANGLE}, respectively. Then according to both the foregoing definition of joinability and IM Prescription 13, the expression (*RX*) JOIN (*RY*) is legal; however, the result of that join is necessarily empty (and the declared type of that expression is RELATION {PF *omega*}). Thus, while the join is indeed legal, it might be advisable for the implementation to warn the user of this latter state of affairs, just in case he or she might have made a mistake. More generally, in fact, the implementation might want to flag any attempt to evaluate an expression of the form (*RX*) JOIN (*RY*) if the declared type of any attribute of that expression is some empty type (see the discussion of IM Prescription 21 in Chapter 17)—or possibly if it's merely some subleaf type (see the discussion of IM Prescription 26 in Chapter 19 for an explanation of this latter concept). Similar remarks apply to intersection also, of course.

As for union, suppose relational expressions *RX* and *RY* have declared types RELATION {A ELLIPSE} and RELATION {A CUBE}, where ELLIPSE and CUBE belong to distinct (and hence disjoint) type hierarchies. According to IM Prescription 13, then, the expression (*RX*) UNION (*RY*) is legal; however, that union is necessarily a disjoint union (and the declared type of that expression is RELATION {A *alpha*}). Thus, while the union is indeed legal, it might be advisable for the implementation to warn the user of this latter state of affairs, just in case he or she might have made a mistake. More generally, in fact, the implementation might want to flag any attempt to evaluate an expression of the form (*RX*) UNION (*RY*) if the declared type of any attribute of that expression is some superroot type (see the discussion of IM Prescription 26 in Chapter 19 for an explanation of this latter concept).

My last point is the following. As you can see, IM Prescription 13 has a lot to say about declared types, but it doesn't have anything to say about corresponding *most specific* types. But that's because the whole question of types, most specific or otherwise, of relations hasn't been properly discussed in this book yet (that discussion appears under IM Prescription 27 in Chapter 20). Here, therefore, I'll just content myself with the following brief remarks.

Let relational expression *RX*, of declared type RELATION {E ELLIPSE}, have current value *rx* as shown here:

```
rx

 E   : ELLIPSE
 e1 : ellipse
 c2 : circle
```

Then I think it's "obvious"—well, fairly obvious!—that the most specific type of this relation is the same as the declared type of *RX*: viz., RELATION {E ELLIPSE}.

Now consider the expression (*RX*) MINUS (*RX*). In accordance with IM Prescription 13, the declared type of that expression is RELATION {E ELLIPSE}. Of course, evaluating that expression produces an empty relation as a result:

```
rx MINUS rx

 E   : omega
```

As we'll see in Chapter 20, therefore (and indeed as the picture indicates), the most specific type of that result is RELATION {E *omega*}.

What's more, a similar remark applies whenever some expression evaluates to an empty relation. For example, the expressions

- (*RX*) JOIN TABLE_DUM

- (*RX*) WHERE E ≠ E

- (*RX*) WHERE FALSE

all have declared type RELATION {E ELLIPSE} and all produce as a result an empty relation, of most specific type RELATION {E *omega*}.

EQUIVALENCE OF EXPRESSIONS

Once again let relational expressions *RX* and *RY* have declared types RELATION {E ELLIPSE} and RELATION {E CIRCLE}, respectively. Then:

- First of all, it's well known that intersection can be defined in terms of difference. That is, the equivalence—

```
X INTERSECT Y  ≡  X MINUS ( X MINUS Y )
```

—holds for all sets *X* and *Y*, as can easily be confirmed using Venn diagrams.

- It follows that the relational expression (*RX*) INTERSECT (*RY*) ought by rights—but see below—to be logically equivalent to the relational expression (*RX*) MINUS ((*RX*) MINUS (*RY*)).

- Consider the subexpression—let's call it *RD*—(*RX*) MINUS (*RY*). As we've seen, this expression has declared type RELATION {E ELLIPSE}.

- Now consider the expression (*RX*) MINUS (*RD*). This expression also has declared type RELATION {E ELLIPSE}.

- It follows that (*RX*) INTERSECT (*RY*), because it's logically equivalent to (*RX*) MINUS (*RD*), ought by rights to have declared type RELATION {E ELLIPSE} as well. But it doesn't! According to IM Prescription 13, it has declared type RELATION {E CIRCLE}. What's more, I said earlier that this latter fact was "intuitively obvious," "quite straightforward," and "easy to understand." So what exactly is going on here?

Well, what the foregoing argument really shows is that the expression (*RX*) INTERSECT (*RY*) is *not* logically equivalent to the expression (*RX*) MINUS ((*RX*) MINUS (*RY*)) after all—at least, not in the formal system we're developing here (viz., our inheritance model). Rather, it's logically equivalent to a version of this latter expression that's been "treated" to the appropriate type (viz., type RELATION {E CIRCLE}, in the example), perhaps like this:[6]

```
TREAT_AS_SAME_TYPE_AS ( ( RX ) INTERSECT ( RY ) ,
                        ( RX ) MINUS ( ( RX ) MINUS ( RY ) ) )
```

This expression and the expression (*RX*) INTERSECT (*RY*) *are* logically equivalent, and they're logically interchangeable (either one can be replaced by the other).

---

[6] See Chapter 20 for an explanation of the TREAT_AS_SAME_TYPE_AS construct used in this example.

The message of the foregoing discussion is that certain expressions that are logically equivalent in the absence of inheritance aren't necessarily guaranteed to remain so when support for inheritance is introduced. However, such guarantees can be reinstated, as it were, by judicious use of the TREAT operator (see Chapters 10, 16, and 20).

EXERCISES

9.1   Given the code fragment—

```
VAR E ELLIPSE ;
VAR C CIRCLE ;

E := ELLIPSE ( LENGTH ( 5.0 ) , LENGTH ( 5.0 ) , POINT ( 0.0 , 0.0 ) ) ;
C := CIRCLE  ( LENGTH ( 5.0 ) , POINT ( 0.0 , 0.0 ) ) ;
```

—what happens with the equality comparison E = C?

9.2   Let relational expressions *RX* and *RY* denote relations *rx* and *ry*, respectively, where *rx* and *ry* are as follows (you can assume attribute values *c2* and *c3* are distinct):

rx

E : ELLIPSE	P : POLYGON
e1 : ellipse	*r4 : rectangle*
c2 : circle	*s5 : square*
c3 : circle	*p6 : polygon*

ry

E : ELLIPSE	P : RECTANGLE
e1 : ellipse	*r4 : rectangle*
c3 : circle	*r4 : rectangle*
c2 : circle	*s5 : square*

Show the results produced by evaluating the expressions (*RX*) UNION (*RY*), (*RX*) INTERSECT (*RY*), (*RX*) MINUS (*RY*), and (*RY*) MINUS (*RX*).

9.3   Let relational expressions *RX* and *RY* (each of which is of declared type RELATION {PF PLANE_FIGURE}) denote relations *rx* and *ry*, respectively, where *rx* and *ry* are as follows:

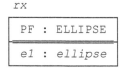

rx

PF : ELLIPSE
e1 : ellipse

ry

PF : RECTANGLE
r2 : rectangle

Then the expression

```
( RX ) JOIN ( RY )
```

is legal, while the expression (a would-be scalar equality comparison)

```
PF FROM TUPLE FROM RX = PF FROM TUPLE FROM RY
```

isn't.[7] How do you account for the discrepancy?

9.4   IM Prescription 13 specifies the rules regarding declared types (in the context of inheritance) for the dyadic relational operators UNION, INTERSECT, MINUS, and JOIN. But there are other dyadic relational operators too—TIMES, D_UNION, I_MINUS, XUNION, MATCHING, and NOT MATCHING (see my book *SQL and Relational Theory: How to Write Accurate SQL Code*, 3rd edition, O'Reilly, 2015). Are there any analogous rules for these operators?

9.5   IM Prescription 13 specifies the rules regarding declared types (in the context of inheritance) for the dyadic relational operators UNION, INTERSECT, MINUS, and JOIN. But what about the monadic relational operators—rename, restrict, project, and extend? Are there any analogous rules for these operators?

ANSWERS

9.1   It returns TRUE. The reason is, of course, that the value of E at run time is a circle (the same circle as the one that's the value of C at run time, in fact), thanks to specialization by constraint on the result of the expression—a selector invocation (actually a literal)—on the right side of the assignment to E.

9.2   Note the attribute types in particular in the following results:

```
rx UNION ry
```

E : ELLIPSE	P : POLYGON
e1 : ellipse	r4 : rectangle
c2 : circle	s5 : square
c3 : circle	p6 : polygon
c3 : circle	r4 : rectangle

---

[7] In fact the would-be tuple equality comparison TUPLE FROM *RX* = TUPLE FROM *RY* isn't legal either, come to that.

`rx INTERSECT ry`

E : ELLIPSE	P : RECTANGLE
e1 : ellipse c2 : circle	r4 : rectangle s5 : square

`rx MINUS ry`

E : ELLIPSE	P : POLYGON
c3 : circle	p6 : polygon

`ry MINUS rx`

E : ELLIPSE	P : RECTANGLE
c3 : circle	r4 : rectangle

9.3   (*Note:* You might want to come back and revisit this answer after reading Chapter 18.) Observe first that the (relational) equality comparison *RX* = *RY* is legal, because *DT*(*RX*) and *DT*(*RY*) do overlap—they have a nonempty common subtype, viz., RELATION {PF *omega*}. (Even though the sole attribute of that common subtype is of an empty type, that subtype itself isn't empty—it contains just one value, viz., the empty relation of type RELATION {PF *omega*}.) Thus, since *RX* = *RY* is legal, it makes sense to say *RX* JOIN *RY* is legal too. (Note, however, that *RX* = *RY* gives FALSE, and *RX* JOIN *RY* gives an empty result. Note too that the declared type of that expression *RX* JOIN *RY* and the most specific type of the result of evaluating that expression are both RELATION {PF *omega*}.)

Now consider the expressions PF FROM TUPLE FROM *RX* and PF FROM TUPLE FROM *RY*, which evaluate to *e1* (an ellipse) and *r2* (a rectangle), respectively. Since types ELLIPSE and RECTANGLE don't overlap—i.e., they don't have a nonempty common subtype—the scalar equality comparison *e1* = *r2* is illegal (it fails on a compile time type error).

9.4   TIMES: The rules are as they are for TIMES without inheritance. D_UNION and XUNION: The rules are as for UNION. I_MINUS: The rules are as for MINUS. MATCHING and NOT MATCHING: The rules for the operands are as for JOIN; the expression denoting the MATCHING or NOT MATCHING invocation has declared type the same as that of the first operand.

9.5   The rules are the same as they are without inheritance in all cases.

Chapter 10

Treating and Type Testing

Talk about a treat

—Charles Collins:
Any Old Iron (1911)

One, two, three, testing

—20th century catchphrase

The topics of this chapter—treating and type testing, and the associated operators TREAT and IS_*T*—have been touched on, and indeed illustrated, several times in earlier chapters. However, it's time to get more specific. In fact, there's quite a lot more to be said about these matters, as will quickly become clear.

Note: Once again the pertinent prescriptions—here, IM Prescriptions 14 and 15—are deliberately worded in such a way as to apply to multiple as well as single inheritance, and to tuple and relation types as well as scalar types. As usual, however, the present chapter discusses single inheritance and scalar types only; multiple inheritance is discussed in Part III of this book and tuple and relation types are discussed in Part IV.

IM PRESCRIPTION 14: TREAT

Let *X* be an expression, let *T* be a type, and let *DT*(*X*) and *T* overlap. Then an operator of the form

```
TREAT_AS_T ( X )
```

(or logical equivalent thereof) shall be supported, with semantics as follows: If *v*(*X*) is not of type *T*, then a type error shall occur; otherwise, the declared type of the invocation TREAT_AS_T(*X*) shall be *T*, and the result of that invocation, *r* say, shall be equal to *v*(*X*) (hence, *MST*(*r*) shall be equal to *MST*(*X*) also).

Compared to the Explorations version, IM Prescription 14 as stated here involves several cosmetic revisions and one substantial one. The substantial revision is this: The Explorations version allowed a TREAT invocation to be used as a pseudovariable; the present version

doesn't. There are several reasons for this change, but the most significant one is simply that TREAT pseudovariables didn't seem to add much by way of useful functionality.

Consider the following code fragment:

```
VAR E ELLIPSE ;
VAR C CIRCLE ;

C := CIRCLE ( ... ) ;
E := C ;
```

After the first assignment here, variable C contains a circle, *c* say. Then, in the second assignment, what does not (and in fact could not) happen, as explained in Chapter 8 under IM Prescription 11, is that circle *c* gets converted to "just an ellipse"—because if such a conversion were to occur, then among other things we wouldn't be able to ask for the radius of the circle that's the current value of variable E.

Suppose we do now want to ask for that radius. We might try:

```
VAR L LENGTH ;

L := THE_R ( E ) ;    /* warning: compile time type error! */
```

As the comment indicates, the expression on the right side of the assignment here raises a compile time type error, because variable E is of declared type ELLIPSE and THE_R is defined in terms of a parameter of declared type CIRCLE. (In other words, THE_R doesn't apply to ellipses, loosely speaking.) Of course, if that compile time type check weren't done, we'd get a run time type error instead—which is worse—if the current value of E at run time turned out to be just an ellipse and not a circle. In the case at hand, of course, we do know the value at run time will be a circle; the trouble is, we know this, but the compiler doesn't.

TREAT is intended to address such situations. The correct way to obtain the radius in the example is as follows:

```
L := THE_R ( TREAT_AS_CIRCLE ( E ) ) ;
```

Intuitively speaking, the expression TREAT_AS_CIRCLE (E) tells the compiler we believe E will contain a circle when that expression is evaluated at run time. In particular, the expression is defined to have declared type CIRCLE, so the compile time type checking succeeds. Then at run time:

■ If the current value of E is indeed of type CIRCLE, then the overall expression does return the radius of that circle as desired. More precisely, if *MST*(E) is some subtype of CIRCLE (not necessarily a proper subtype, of course), then the TREAT invocation yields a result, *res* say, that (a) is equal to *v*(E) and hence (b) has most specific type equal to *MST*(E) also.

In the case at hand, therefore, *MST*(*res*) is CIRCLE; so THE_R can be applied to *res* to obtain the desired radius, and that radius can then be assigned to the variable L.

■ But if *MST*(E) is some proper supertype of CIRCLE—in particular, if it's type ELLIPSE—then the TREAT invocation fails on a run time type error.

In other words, the expression TREAT_AS_CIRCLE (E) is logically equivalent to an IF – THEN – ELSE expression along the following lines (note the appeal in the first line of this expansion to the type testing operator IS_CIRCLE—see later in this chapter):

```
IF IS_CIRCLE ( E )
   THEN CIRCLE ( THE_A ( E ) , THE_CTR ( E ) )
   ELSE type error
END IF
```

So the broad intent of IM Prescription 14 is twofold: First, defining a given type should cause "automatic" provision of a corresponding TREAT operator; second, TREAT operators in general allow a tight boundary to be drawn around those situations in which a run time type error might occur. To be specific, the only possible way a run time type error can ever occur in our inheritance model is on an attempt to TREAT a value to a type it doesn't possess.

Suppose now as we did in Chapters 7 and 8 that CIRCLE has a proper subtype O_CIRCLE, where an "O-circle" is a circle that's centered on the origin. Then the current value of variable E at some given time might be of most specific type O_CIRCLE instead of just CIRCLE. If it is, then the TREAT invocation

```
TREAT_AS_CIRCLE ( E )
```

will succeed, and will yield a result, *res* say, with most specific type *MST*(*res*) equal to O_CIRCLE, because O_CIRCLE is the most specific type of E, and value equal to *v*(E). (The *declared* type of that TREAT invocation is CIRCLE, of course, because of that "..._AS_CIRCLE" specification.) In other words, TREAT always leaves the most specific type alone—it never "pushes it up" to make it less specific than it was before.[1]

Another Example

Here's another example (actually a simpler example), repeated from Chapter 8, that involves the use of TREAT. Suppose again that the current value of variable E is of type CIRCLE. Then the assignment

---

[1] Of course, it *must* leave the specific type alone, precisely because it leaves the value alone. In any case, IM Prescriptions 8 and 10 both imply that any such "pushing up" is logically impossible. For if it were possible, it would mean that the very same value could have most specific type CIRCLE *and* most specific type O_CIRCLE, thereby violating IM Prescription 8; it would also mean that, after the "pushing up," the result would be a circle that could be "S by C'd" to an O-circle but hasn't been, thereby violating IM Prescription 10.

```
C := E ;    /* warning: compile time type error! */
```

will fail on a compile time type error, because $DT(E)$ = ELLIPSE and $DT(C)$ = CIRCLE and ELLIPSE isn't a subtype of CIRCLE (see IM Prescription 11). However, the following revised form of the assignment—

```
C := TREAT_AS_CIRCLE ( E ) ;
```

—will satisfy the compile time type checking, and will succeed at run time as well if the value of E at run time is indeed of type CIRCLE.

A Remark on Single Inheritance

Given the expression TREAT_AS_T (X), IM Prescription 14 requires only that T and $DT(X)$ overlap, or in other words that they have a nonempty common subtype (this is a compile time check). In the examples we've seen so far, however, T has actually been a proper subtype of $DT(X)$—in fact, T has been CIRCLE and $DT(X)$ has been ELLIPSE—and the nonempty common subtype in question has thus just been T itself (i.e., CIRCLE, in those examples). And in practice T frequently will be a proper subtype of $DT(X)$; the examples have been completely realistic in this respect. But there's no reason to insist on this state of affairs, and with multiple inheritance, in fact, it would be counterproductive to do so (see Chapter 16). With single inheritance, however, to say that T and $DT(X)$ have a nonempty common subtype is merely to say that one must be a nonempty subtype of the other (not necessarily a proper subtype, of course). In terms of our usual variables E and C, therefore, the expression

```
TREAT_AS_CIRCLE ( E )
```

is certainly valid syntactically, as we already know (though it might fail at run time). More to the point, the expression

```
TREAT_AS_ELLIPSE ( C )
```

is also valid syntactically; what's more, it can't possibly fail at run time. (The expression has declared type ELLIPSE, but the most specific type of the value it denotes is some subtype of CIRCLE.)

Now, I don't mean to suggest that TREAT expressions in which T is a supertype of $DT(X)$ are particularly useful; however, IM Prescription 14 does permit them, mainly because there seems little reason not to—also because general purpose applications have a tendency to come up with requirements that might look a little surprising on their face, such as a requirement to support TREAT expressions like the ones under discussion here. A similar remark applies to code produced by code generator products.

Generalizing TREAT

In practice, it turns out to be desirable to support an additional, slightly more general form of TREAT that allows one scalar expression to be "treated" to the declared type of another instead of to some explicitly named type, thus:

```
TREAT_AS_SAME_TYPE_AS ( Y , X )
```

Here X and Y are scalar expressions such that $DT(Y)$ and $DT(X)$ have a nonempty common subtype, and the overall expression is defined to be equivalent to

```
TREAT_AS_T ( X )
```

where T is $DT(Y)$.

　　Note: Since T is known at compile time, this more general form of TREAT is logically unnecessary, because it can always be replaced by the equivalent simpler form. Support for it is still desirable, however, for reasons of generality, convenience, and—perhaps most important—consistency with the tuple and relation versions of TREAT to be discussed in Chapter 20.

A New Relational Operator

It also turns out to be desirable to support a new relational operator[2] of the following form:

```
RX : TREAT_AS_T ( A )
```

Here RX is a relational expression; T is a scalar type; A is an attribute, of some scalar type, of the relation r denoted by RX (and hence can be regarded—see the discussion of IM Prescription 28 in Chapter 20—as an attribute of the expression RX as such); and the overall expression is defined to be equivalent to the following:[3]

```
EXTEND RX : { A := TREAT_AS_T ( A ) }
```

　　In other words, if there's at least one tuple in r in which the A value isn't of some subtype of type T, the expression overall raises a run time type error; otherwise it returns a result identical to r, except that attribute A of the expression denoting that result—unlike attribute A of the original expression RX, probably—has declared type T. For example, suppose the current value of relvar RV, of declared type RELATION {E ELLIPSE}, looks like this:

---

[2] And a tuple analog as well.

[3] The definition makes use of the relational EXTEND operator. If you're unfamiliar with that operator, please see, e.g., my book *Relational Theory for Computer Professionals* (O'Reilly, 2013).

```
RV
┌─────────────────┐
│ E   : ELLIPSE   │
├─────────────────┤
│ c1  : circle    │
│ c2  : circle    │
│ c3  : circle    │
└─────────────────┘
```

(*c1*, *c2*, and *c3* all distinct). Then the expression

```
RV : TREAT_AS_CIRCLE ( E )
```

produces a result relation *r* looking like this (note the heading in particular):

```
r
┌─────────────────┐
│ E   : CIRCLE    │
├─────────────────┤
│ c1  : circle    │
│ c2  : circle    │
│ c3  : circle    │
└─────────────────┘
```

Note, incidentally, that the declared type of attribute E of the specified expression RV : TREAT_AS_CIRCLE(E) would still be CIRCLE, even if every tuple currently appearing in RV had an E value of some proper subtype of CIRCLE. On the other hand, if (say) *c1* had been of most specific type ELLIPSE and not CIRCLE, then that same expression would have failed on a run time type error.

The obvious generalized form should be supported too:

```
RX : TREAT_AS_SAME_TYPE_AS ( Y , A )
```

Here *Y* is a scalar expression such that *DT*(*A*) and *DT*(*Y*) have a nonempty common subtype, and the overall expression is equivalent to

```
RX : TREAT_AS_T ( A )
```

where *T* is *DT*(*Y*).

Note: Once again, since *T* is known at compile time, this more general form of the operator is logically unnecessary; it's supported for reasons of generality, convenience, and consistency with the tuple and relation versions to be discussed in Chapter 20.

IM PRESCRIPTION 15: TYPE TESTING

Let X be an expression, let T be a type, and let $DT(X)$ and T overlap. Then an operator of the form

```
IS_T ( X )
```

(or logical equivalent thereof) shall be supported. The operator shall return TRUE if $v(X)$ is of type T, FALSE otherwise.

The general intent of IM Prescription 15 is simply that defining a given type T should cause "automatic" provision of a boolean operator IS_T for testing values to see whether they're of the type in question. Note that the declared type $DT(X)$ of the argument expression X and the type T being tested for are required to overlap (this is a compile time check). Thus, for example, if E is of declared type ELLIPSE, the expression

```
IS_SQUARE ( E )    /* warning: compile time type error! */
```

is invalid (it'll fail on a compile time type error). By contrast, the expression

```
IS_CIRCLE ( E )
```

will satisfy the compile time type checking, and will return TRUE if the current value of variable E at run time is in fact of type CIRCLE, or FALSE if it's only of type ELLIPSE.

> *Aside:* Another approach—which we did consider but quickly rejected—to this same general problem could be to provide an operator of the form TYPE (X), which returns the type of the value denoted by the argument expression X. That returned type could then be tested to see whether it is, for example, equal to type SQUARE. However, this approach raises certain obvious questions. For example, what type would the result of the TYPE operator be? If it's TYPE, can we declare variables of type TYPE? What are the implications? Also, what would happen if the argument denoted by X in TYPE (X) is of several types—both CIRCLE and ELLIPSE, say—"at the same time," as it were? Not to mention the question of what should happen if X isn't scalar, and numerous other problems. *End of aside.*

A Remark on Single Inheritance

Given the expression IS_T (X), IM Prescription 15 requires only that T and $DT(X)$ overlap, or in other words have a nonempty common subtype (this is a compile time check). In practice, however, T will often be a proper subtype of $DT(X)$, in which case the nonempty common subtype in question will just be T itself. But there's no reason to insist on this state of affairs, and with multiple inheritance, in fact, it would be counterproductive to do so (see Chapter 16). With single inheritance, however, to say that T and $DT(X)$ have a nonempty common subtype is merely to say that one must be a nonempty subtype of the other (not necessarily a proper subtype, of course). In terms of our usual variables E and C, for example, the expression

```
IS_CIRCLE ( E )
```

is certainly valid syntactically, as we already know (though it might give FALSE). More to the point, the expression

```
IS_ELLIPSE ( C )
```

is also valid syntactically; what's more, it can't possibly give FALSE.

Note: I don't mean to suggest that IS_T expressions in which T is a supertype of $DT(X)$ are particularly useful; however, IM Prescription 15 does permit them, just as IM Prescription 14 permits expressions like TREAT_AS_ELLIPSE (C), and for essentially similar reasons.

Generalizing IS_T

In practice, it turns out to be desirable to support an additional, slightly more general form of IS_T that looks like this:

```
IS_SAME_TYPE_AS ( Y , X )
```

Here X and Y are scalar expressions such that $DT(Y)$ and $DT(X)$ have a nonempty common subtype, and the overall expression is defined to be equivalent to

```
IS_T ( X )
```

where T is $DT(Y)$.

Note: Since T is known at compile time, the foregoing more general form of IS_T is logically unnecessary, because it can always be replaced by the equivalent simpler form. Support for it is still desirable, however, for reasons of generality, convenience, and—probably most important—consistency with the tuple and relation versions of IS_T to be discussed in Chapter 20.

Another New Relational Operator

Consider the following example. Let relvar RV have an attribute E of declared type ELLIPSE, and suppose we want to query the current value of RV to find those tuples where the E value is in fact a circle and the radius of that circle is greater than two. Now, we might try an expression of the following form:

```
RV WHERE THE_R ( E ) > LENGTH ( 2.0 )
        /* warning: compile time type error! */
```

But this expression will fail on a compile time type error, because THE_R requires an argument of type CIRCLE and the declared type of attribute E of RV is ELLIPSE, not CIRCLE. (If that compile time type check weren't done, we'd get a run time type error instead—which is worse—as soon as we encountered a tuple in RV in which the E value was just an ellipse and not a circle.) So what we clearly need to do is filter out and eliminate those tuples in which the E value is just an ellipse before we even attempt to obtain the radius. And that's exactly what happens with the following formulation:

```
RV : IS_CIRCLE ( E ) WHERE THE_R ( E ) > LENGTH ( 2.0 )
```

Loosely speaking, this expression returns those tuples of RV in which the E value is a circle with radius greater than two.[4] More precisely, the expression is defined to have

  a. Heading the same as that of RV, except that the declared type corresponding to attribute E is CIRCLE instead of ELLIPSE,

and it yields a relation with

  b. Body consisting of just those tuples from the current value of RV in which the E value is of type CIRCLE and the radius for the circle in question is greater than two.

In other words, what we're talking about here is a new relational operator, of the form

```
RX : IS_T ( A )
```

where *RX* is a relational expression; *T* is a scalar type; *A* is an attribute, of some scalar type, of the relation *r* denoted by *RX* (and hence can be regarded—see the discussion of IM Prescription 28 in Chapter 20—as an attribute of the expression *RX* as such); and the overall expression is defined to have

---

[4] I'm assuming for simplicity that the operator precedence rules are such that the subexpression RV:IS_CIRCLE(E) is evaluated before the WHERE clause is applied.

a. Heading the same as that of *r*, except that the type of attribute *A* in that heading is *T*,

and it yields a relation with

b. Body consisting of just those tuples of *r* in which attribute *A* contains a value of type *T*.

By the way, you might be thinking the following expression could have served as a valid formulation of the original query:

```
RV WHERE IS_CIRCLE ( E ) AND THE_R ( E ) > LENGTH ( 2.0 )
                        /* warning: compile time type error! */
```

But of course this expression still fails on a compile time type error. The point is, we need to get rid of the noncircles before we even *attempt* to apply THE_R, and that's what the correct formulation, using the new relational operator, does.

And by the way again, note that the correct formulation

```
RV : IS_CIRCLE ( E ) WHERE THE_R ( E ) > LENGTH ( 2.0 )
```

is almost but not quite equivalent to the following:

```
RV WHERE
     CASE
        WHEN IS_CIRCLE ( E )
             THEN THE_R ( TREAT_AS_CIRCLE ( E ) ) > LENGTH ( 2.0 )
        WHEN NOT ( IS_CIRCLE ( E ) )
             THEN FALSE
     END CASE
```

The difference is that this latter expression has heading the same as that of RV. More generally, however, the expression

```
RX : IS_T ( A )
```

is equivalent to, and is therefore shorthand for, the following expression:

```
( RX WHERE IS_T ( A ) ) : TREAT_AS_T ( A )
```

Moreover, this latter expression is itself shorthand (see the discussion of IM Prescription 14 earlier in the chapter).

The obvious generalized form of the "*RX*:IS_*T*(*A*)" operator should be supported too:

```
RX : IS_SAME_TYPE_AS ( Y , A )
```

Here Y is a scalar expression such that $DT(A)$ and $DT(Y)$ have a nonempty common subtype, and the overall expression is equivalent to

```
RX : IS_T ( A )
```

where T is $DT(Y)$.

Note: Once again, since T is known at compile time, this more general form of the operator is logically unnecessary; it's supported for reasons of generality, convenience, and consistency with the tuple and relation versions to be discussed in Chapter 20.

EXERCISES

10.1 Let E be a variable of declared type and current most specific type both ELLIPSE. State the result of each of the following expressions:

  a. `IS_PLANE_FIGURE ( E )`

  b. `IS_ELLIPSE ( E )`

  c. `IS_CIRCLE ( E )`

  d. `IS_RECTANGLE ( E )`

  e. `IS_alpha ( E )`

  f. `IS_omega ( E )`

10.2 Let E be a variable of declared type and current most specific type both ELLIPSE. State the result of each of the following expressions:

  a. `TREAT_AS_PLANE_FIGURE ( E )`

  b. `TREAT_AS_ELLIPSE ( E )`

  c. `TREAT_AS_CIRCLE ( E )`

  d. `TREAT_AS_RECTANGLE ( E )`

  e. `TREAT_AS_alpha ( E )`

  f. `TREAT_AS_omega ( E )`

10.3 Can the implementation of TREAT_AS_T and IS_T be automated?

10.4 Do TREAT_AS_T and IS_T apply to system defined types?

10.5 Let *T'* be an immediate subtype of type *T*. It has been conjectured that if the only operators that apply to values and variables that are of type *T'* and not of type *T* are those provided "automatically"—THE_ operators, selectors, "=", ":=", TREAT_AS_*T'*, and IS_*T'* operators—then type *T'* was probably not worth defining in the first place. Discuss.

10.6 Let C be a variable of declared type CIRCLE. What does the following expression return?

```
THE_R ( TREAT_AS_ELLIPSE ( C ) )
```

10.7 Show that out of all of the various treat and type testing operators defined in the body of this chapter, there's really only one that's primitive—all of the others can be defined in terms of that single one.

10.8 Do you think it could be useful to provide an operator of the form IS_NOT_*T* (*X*)?

10.9 It has been suggested that "most specific type" counterparts to all of the various type testing operators could also be provided if desired. For example, the operator

```
IS_MS_T ( X )
```

could be defined to give TRUE if the most specific type of *X* is *T* and FALSE otherwise. (It might help to observe that, e.g., whereas the operator IS_ELLIPSE is perhaps best rendered into natural language as "is an ellipse," the operator IS_MS_ELLIPSE might better be rendered as "is *most specifically* an ellipse"). Other possible "most specific type" testing operators include the following (the semantics are meant to be obvious in every case):

- `IS_SAME_MS_TYPE_AS ( Y , X )`
- `r : IS_MS_T ( A )`
- `r : IS_SAME_MS_TYPE_AS ( Y , A )`

However, it's easy to see that these operators are logically unnecessary. Show that this is so.

ANSWERS

10.1 a. TRUE. b. TRUE. c. FALSE. d. Compile time type error. e. TRUE (in fact, of course, IS_*alpha*(X) returns TRUE for all possible scalar expressions X). f. FALSE (in fact, of course, IS_*omega*(X) returns FALSE for all possible scalar expressions X).

10.2 Throughout these answers, let *X* be the expression (i.e., the specified TREAT invocation) in question. a. A result *r* = *v*(E) with *MST*(*r*) = ELLIPSE; *DT*(*X*) = PLANE_FIGURE. b. A result *r* = *v*(E) with *MST*(*r*) = ELLIPSE; *DT*(*X*) = ELLIPSE. c. Run time type error. d. Compile time type error. e. A result *r* = *v*(E) with *MST*(*r*) = ELLIPSE; *DT*(*X*) = *alpha*. f. Compile time type error (I'm assuming here that the compiler recognizes that there aren't any values of type *omega*; otherwise the result will be a run time type error).

10.3 Yes—given the type constraint for type *T*, the system can always determine whether a given value is of that type.

10.4 Yes. Note that there's nothing in our inheritance model that prohibits a system defined type from having proper supertypes or proper subtypes; what's more, such proper subtypes, though possibly not such proper supertypes, might even be user defined. *Note:* In fact, of course, our model requires (a) every scalar root type to be a proper subtype of type *alpha* and (b) every scalar leaf type to be a proper supertype of type *omega*, and *alpha* and *omega* are certainly system defined. But these are special cases. A more typical system defined type, such as INTEGER, might well have user defined proper subtypes (see the answer to Exercise 10.5 below, also the answer to Exercise 5.6 in Chapter 5, for further discussion of such a possibility), but whether it could have any user defined proper supertypes is another question.

10.5 The following might be an example of such a type *T'* (compare the answer to Exercise 5.6 in Chapter 5):

```
TYPE POSINT
     IS { INTEGER
          CONSTRAINT INTEGER > 0
          POSSREP ( SAME_AS ( INTEGER ) )
          NOT { -1 } } ;
```

Of course, if some user defines some operator with a parameter of type POSINT, then the condition stated in the exercise (i.e., that the only operators defined for type *T'* and not type *T* are the ones provided "automatically") will no longer be satisfied. But assume no such operator is defined. Might not POSINT still prove useful as, for example, the declared type of certain attributes of certain relvars? Or as the declared type of certain components of certain possreps? If the answer to either of these questions is *yes*, then it does seem that declaring the type might be a useful way of "factoring out" a certain commonly required constraint.

By the way, notice that even given type POSINT as defined above, the declared type of an integer literal such as 4 is likely to be just INTEGER, not POSINT, even if the integer in question happens to be positive (recall from Chapter 8 that specialization by constraint happens at run time, not compile time). Thus, it might sometimes be necessary to use an explicit TREAT on such a literal, thereby writing (e.g.) TREAT_AS_POSINT (4), in order to avoid certain compile time type errors that might otherwise occur. Now, having to write an expression like TREAT_AS_POSINT (4) might be regarded as a trifle user hostile. For that reason, Darwen and I have proposed elsewhere[5] that defining type POSINT as above should cause an operator with the same name to be provided automatically, with the following conceptual definition:

```
OPERATOR POSINT ( I INTEGER ) RETURNS POSINT ;
   RETURN ( TREAT_AS_POSINT ( I ) ) ;
END OPERATOR ;
```

Now the expression TREAT_AS_POSINT (4) can be replaced by the simpler expression POSINT (4). More generally, the expression POSINT(*x*), where *x* is an expression of type INTEGER, can be regarded as—in fact, is—a selector invocation for type POSINT, and it returns a positive integer (unless the integer denoted by *x* is less than or equal to zero, of course, in which case it fails on a type constraint error). As a consequence, the expressions 4, POSINT(4), POSINT(POSINT(4)), and so on, all denote the very same value. Such an approach could be used with any proper subtype of a system defined type that has no explicitly defined possrep of its own. Also, it could (and for consistency probably should) be used with such system defined types themselves, as in this example:

```
OPERATOR INTEGER ( I INTEGER ) RETURNS INTEGER ;
   RETURN ( I ) ;
END OPERATOR ;
```

Now the expressions 4, INTEGER(4), INTEGER(INTEGER(4)), and so on, all denote the very same value; in fact, they're all valid selector invocations, and indeed literals, of type INTEGER.

10.6 It doesn't return anything at all—rather, it fails on a compile time type error, because the TREAT subexpression is of declared type ELLIPSE, and THE_R isn't defined for arguments of declared type ELLIPSE.

10.7 TREAT_AS_*T* is defined in terms of IS_*T*. TREAT_AS_SAME_TYPE_AS is defined in terms of TREAT_AS_*T*. The relational expression *RX* : TREAT_AS_*T* is defined in terms of TREAT_AS_*T*. The relational expression *RX* : TREAT_AS_SAME_TYPE_AS is defined in terms of TREAT_AS_SAME_TYPE_AS. IS_SAME_TYPE_AS is defined in terms of IS_*T*. The relational expression *RX* : IS_*T* is defined in terms of IS_*T* and TREAT_AS_*T*. The relational expression *RX* : IS_SAME_TYPE_AS is defined in terms of *RX* : IS_*T*. It follows from all of this that the only new primitive operator is IS_*T*.

---

[5] In our book *Database Explorations: Essays on The Third Manifesto and Related Topics* (Trafford, 2010), available free online at the *Manifesto* website *www.thethirdmanifesto.com*.

10.8 Well, I think it could, so long as there aren't any surprises in the way it's defined. To be specific, I would define IS_NOT_*T* (*X*) to be logically equivalent to NOT (IS_*T* (*X*)). In other words, I would require *DT*(*X*) and *T* to overlap, and then I would define IS_NOT_*T* (*X*) to give TRUE if and only if *MST*(*X*) is some proper supertype of *T*. (IS_*T* (*X*), of course, gives TRUE if and only if *DT*(*X*) and *T* overlap and *MST*(*X*) is some subtype of *T*.)

Of course, if IS_NOT_*T* (*X*) is supported, then I think IS_NOT_SAME_TYPE_AS (*Y,X*), *RX* : IS_NOT_*T* (*A*), and *RX* : IS_NOT_SAME_TYPE_AS (*Y,A*) should all be supported as well (and I'll assume for definiteness from this point forward that these operators are indeed all supported). *Subsidiary exercise:* What do you think the declared type of the expression *RX* : IS_NOT_*T* (*A*) should be? (In particular, what do you think the type of attribute *A* within that declared type should be?)

10.9 Let types *T1*, *T2*, and *T3* be such that *T3* is both a leaf type and an immediate subtype of *T2* and *T2* is an immediate subtype of *T1*. Let *X* be an expression of declared type *T1*. Then the following equivalences hold:

- ■   IS_MS_*T1* (*X*) is TRUE if and only if IS_*T2* (*X*) is FALSE.

- ■   IS_MS_*T2* (*X*) is TRUE if and only if IS_*T2* (*X*) is TRUE and IS_*T3* (*X*) is FALSE.

- ■   IS_MS_*T3* (*X*) is TRUE if and only if IS_*T3* (*X*) is TRUE.

The foregoing argument can clearly be generalized to show that IS_MS_*T* is logically unnecessary. It follows that the other suggested operators are logically unnecessary as well.

Chapter 11

Substitutability

There is no substitute for hard work.

—Thomas Alva Edison:
Life (1932)

One's style is one's signature always.

—Oscar Wilde:
Letter to the *Daily Telegraph* (1891)

This rather lengthy chapter is concerned with a series of interconnected prescriptions, all of them having to do with the notion of substitutability and its numerous ramifications.

IM PRESCRIPTION 16: VALUE SUBSTITUTABILITY

Let *Op* be a read-only operator, let *P* be a parameter to *Op*, and let *T* be the declared type of *P*. Then the declared type of the argument expression (and therefore, necessarily, the most specific type of the argument as such) corresponding to *P* in an invocation of *Op* shall be allowed to be **any subtype** *T'* of *T*. In other words, the read-only operator *Op* applies to values of type *T* and therefore, necessarily, to values of type *T'*—*The Principle of **Read-Only Operator Inheritance***. It follows that such operators are *polymorphic*, since they apply to values of several different types—*The Principle of **Read-Only Operator Polymorphism***. It further follows that wherever a value of type *T* is permitted, a value of any subtype of *T* shall also be permitted—*The Principle of **Value Substitutability***.

The main purpose of IM Prescription 16 is (a) to pin down precisely the notion of value substitutability—which by now should be very familiar to you—and (b) more specifically, to define three interrelated principles: *The Principle of Read-Only Operator Inheritance*, *The Principle of Read-Only Operator Polymorphism*, and *The Principle of Value Substitutability*. Now, we know from discussions in earlier chapters that value substitutability implies that a reference to a variable of declared type *T* can denote a value of any subtype *T'* of *T*. However, it also implies something I haven't emphasized prior to this point: namely, that an invocation of a read-only operator of declared type *T* can likewise denote a value of any subtype *T'* of *T*.[1] Here's a trivial example:

```
OPERATOR COPY ( E ELLIPSE ) RETURNS ELLIPSE ;
   RETURN ( E ) ;
END OPERATOR ;
```

Clearly, an invocation of COPY (which is certainly a read-only operator) returns either a circle or "just an ellipse," depending on whether the argument corresponding to its sole parameter E is a circle or "just an ellipse" in turn.

Result Covariance

Now, the foregoing property—i.e., that if *Op* is a read-only operator, then the most specific type of the value returned by an invocation of *Op* can be any subtype *T'* of the declared type *T* of *Op*—has been referred to in the literature as *result covariance*. It's not a good term, though. For one thing, it's presumably intended to reflect the idea that the most specific type of the result "covaries" with the most specific type of the argument (which indeed it does, in the COPY example). But there seems to be a tacit assumption that there's just one argument! By way of a counterexample, recall the read-only operator MOVE from the discussion of substitutability in Chapter 7:

```
OPERATOR MOVE ( E ELLIPSE , R RECTANGLE ) RETURNS ELLIPSE ;
   RETURN ( ELLIPSE ( THE_A ( E ) , THE_B ( E ) , CTR ( R ) ) ) ;
END OPERATOR ;
```

Loosely speaking, operator MOVE moves a given ellipse such that it becomes centered on the center of a given rectangle (CTR here is a read-only operator that returns the center of its rectangle argument). And it should be clear in this example that the most specific type of the result "covaries" with that of the first argument but not with that of the second. To be specific, if the first argument is a circle, then the result is a circle; if it's just an ellipse, then the result is just an ellipse.

> *Aside:* To jump ahead of ourselves for a few moments, what's going on in the MOVE example—at least conceptually—is this. First, the operator has a *specification signature* (see the discussion of IM Prescription 17 later in this chapter) that looks like this:
>
> ```
> MOVE ( ELLIPSE , RECTANGLE ) RETURNS ELLIPSE
> ```

---

[1] Though we do know from Chapter 8 that this observation is true of selectors in particular, thanks to S by C.

This signature represents the user's overall perception of the operator (viz., that the operator is called MOVE; that it takes two parameters, of declared types ELLIPSE and RECTANGLE, respectively; and that its declared type is ELLIPSE, meaning it returns an ellipse when it's invoked). *Note:* The keyword RETURNS shown in this and other signatures in this book is just a noiseword, included to improve readability.

Second, the MOVE operator also has four corresponding *invocation signatures* (again see the discussion of IM Prescription 17 later in this chapter) that look like this:

```
( CIRCLE  , SQUARE    ) RETURNS CIRCLE
( CIRCLE  , RECTANGLE ) RETURNS CIRCLE
( ELLIPSE , SQUARE    ) RETURNS ELLIPSE
( ELLIPSE , RECTANGLE ) RETURNS ELLIPSE
```

As you can see, there's one invocation signature for each possible combination of argument declared types;[2] thus, any given invocation of MOVE must have arguments whose declared types match the argument types as specified in exactly one of these invocation signatures. And the result of that invocation is defined to be of the type indicated in the pertinent invocation signature, so the declared type of that invocation is that particular type. *End of aside.*

Anyway, here for the record is a definition (note, however, that it does rely on that concept of an invocation signature, which is something that won't be fully explained until we get to that promised discussion of IM Prescription 17 later in the chapter):

Definition: Let *Op* be a read-only operator and let *T* be the declared type of some invocation of *Op*, as specified in the pertinent invocation signature. Then the *result covariance* property states that an invocation of *Op* whose arguments are of declared types as specified in that invocation signature can return a result whose most specific type is any nonempty subtype of *T*.

Now, this definition does capture the essence of the "result covariance" concept, but there's quite a lot more to be said about that concept in general. First, here for interest is another definition (this one is from the object literature—specifically, from Elisa Bertino and Lorenzo Martino: *Object-Oriented Database Systems: Concepts and Architectures*, Addison-Wesley, 1993, though I've paraphrased it somewhat here):

---

[2] I'm being sloppy here: Arguments as such (meaning argument *values*) don't have declared types—rather, the expressions denoting those arguments do. For reasons of brevity, however, throughout this chapter (at least in informal contexts) I'll use *argument declared type*, or some simple variation on that phrase, as a convenient shorthand for what should more correctly be referred to as the declared type of the expression denoting the argument in question.

A type *T'* is a subtype of a type *T* if ... for each method *M* of *T* there is a corresponding method *M'* of *T'* such that ... if there is a result, then the type of the result of *M'* is a subtype of the type of the result of *M* (*rule of covariance in results*).

(As noted in Chapter 7 and elsewhere, *method* is basically just an object term for an operator.) Now, this definition can certainly be criticized on a number of grounds. For instance:

- First of all, it seems to be circular—it defines what it means for some type to be a subtype of another in terms of some type being a subtype of another.

- Second, it seems to be saying that an operator *Op* that applies to values of type *T must* have a distinct implementation version that applies to values of type *T'* (certainly that word "corresponding" does suggest rather strongly that *M* and *M'* are distinct).[3]

- Third, if such a distinct implementation version does exist, then the definition seems to be saying that the type of the result of that *T'* version *must* be a (proper?) subtype of the type of the result of the *T* version.[4] And if it is (but only if it is?), then once again there's some kind of "result covariance" going on.[5]

- Fourth, it seems to be saying that *T'* is a subtype of *T* if substitutability applies, whereas we say that substitutability applies if *T'* is a subtype of *T*.

Anyway, let's get back to our examples. We've seen that the most specific type of the result of operator COPY "covaries" with that of its sole argument, and the most specific type of the result of operator MOVE "covaries" with that of its first argument but not its second. So far, so good, then (?). But now consider the following example (which is admittedly somewhat contrived but suffices to illustrate the point I want to make):

---

[3] In other words, it seems to me that the term *method* in the extract quoted refers not so much to an operator per se but rather to an implementation version of the operator in question. Or is it talking about invocation signatures? Frankly, it's hard to be sure. *Note:* The notion of implementation versions was discussed briefly in Chapter 7 and is discussed in more detail under IM Prescription 17 later in the present chapter. As already noted, invocation signatures are also discussed in detail under that same prescription.

[4] Though I do have to ask: By "the" type here, does the extract quoted mean the declared type or the most specific type? And note too that the definition does seem to allow the type of the result of *M'* *not* to be a subtype of the type of the result of *M* (?)—though in that case perhaps *T'* isn't considered to be a subtype of *T* after all (?).

[5] Implementation versions are purely an implementation notion, of course, not part of the model (to say it one more time, there's just one operator as far as the user is concerned, no matter how many implementation versions of that operator might exist under the covers). So if different implementation versions of the same operator do produce results of different types, this fact must be explained to the user without any recourse to the implementation version notion. But that's easily done. For example, the semantics of COPY are simply that it returns a copy of its argument (if it's passed a circle, it returns a circle, and if it's passed just an ellipse, it returns just an ellipse)—and this explanation is valid regardless of whether the effect in question is produced by distinct implementation versions or otherwise. *Note:* More generally, the notion of invocation signatures is intended, in part, to help deal with this issue of explaining operator semantics. Once again, see IM Prescription 17.

```
OPERATOR EORC ( B BOOLEAN ) RETURNS ELLIPSE ;
    RETURN ( IF B THEN ELLIPSE ( LENGTH ( 5.0 ) , LENGTH ( 4.0 ) ,
                                              POINT ( ... ) )
                    ELSE CIRCLE  ( LENGTH ( 5.0 ) , POINT ( ... ) )
            END IF ) ;
END OPERATOR ;
```

Note that I'm certainly within my rights here, thanks to value substitutability, when I specify (in the ELSE portion of the IF – THEN – ELSE expression) that a circle is to be returned instead of "just an ellipse." Clearly, then, an invocation of EORC will return either just an ellipse (with semiaxis lengths $a = 5$ and $b = 4$) if the argument corresponding to the sole parameter B is TRUE, or a circle (with radius $r = 5$) if it's FALSE. So in this example the most specific type of the result depends on the value, not the type, of the argument. And it would surely be a little odd to think of result *types* "covarying" with argument *values*, since of course the mapping between the two could be arbitrarily complex—much more complex, surely, than the simple term *covarying* might reasonably be expected to signify, or bear.

To summarize, let *Op* be a read-only operator. Then:

- First, if *Op* has several distinct implementation versions, then *Op* might produce results of different most specific types on different invocations.

- Second, however, note that our examples COPY, MOVE, and EORC all manage to illustrate the "result covariance" phenomenon without involving distinct implementation versions at all.[6] In other words, the result of *Op* can "covary" even if *Op* has just a single implementation version under the covers.

- Third, the result of *Op* can "covary" even if no argument has a most specific type that's a proper subtype of the declared type of the corresponding parameter—i.e., even if every argument type is the same as the declared type of the corresponding parameter on every invocation (e.g., see EORC).

- Fourth, the result can "covary" even if there are no explicit arguments at all (imagine an operator that returns a circle on weekdays but just an ellipse on weekends).

The net of all this is that, while the *concept* of "result covariance" (of some kind or other) is both necessary and desirable—in fact, it's nothing but *The Principle of Read-Only Operator Polymorphism* by another name—the *term* "result covariance" is really inappropriate, and logically unnecessary, and in some ways quite misleading.

---

[6] So do selectors, incidentally.

Argument Contravariance

There's another concept, *argument contravariance*, that's also discussed in the literature and seems to be vaguely related to the concept of result covariance. It's not part of our own inheritance model, but I do think it's worth trying to explain exactly what the concept is, if only to show why we reject it. Though I think I also need to say up front that the concept is in fact quite difficult to explain—more so than "result covariance," even—because it seems to be based on (a) a confusion between model and implementation, and (b) a confusion between arguments and parameters, and quite possibly (c) a flawed definition of the subtype concept as well. (Regarding points (b) and (c) here, see the further remarks near the end of the present subsection.)

Now, *The Principle of Value Substitutability* requires that if (a) *Op* is a read-only operator, (b) *P* is a parameter to *Op*, and (c) *T* is the declared type of *P*, then (d) the declared type *T'* of the argument expression—and therefore the most specific type of the argument as such—corresponding to *P* in any given invocation of *Op* must be some nonempty subtype of *T* (not necessarily a proper subtype, of course). Unfortunately, some systems not only fail to abide by this requirement but, in effect, claim that failure as a feature! Here's an example. Consider a variant form of the read-only operator MOVE from the previous subsection, with specification signature as follows:

```
MOVE ( ELLIPSE , SQUARE ) RETURNS ELLIPSE
```

The difference between this and the previous form of the example is that the declared type of the second parameter is now SQUARE instead of RECTANGLE. Thus, what the operator does is this: It returns a result just like its first argument (an ellipse) except that it's centered on the center of its second (a square).

Now suppose distinct implementation versions of this operator—call them CMOVE and EMOVE—are provided for the case where the first argument is a circle and the case where it's just an ellipse, respectively, and consider what happens if MOVE is invoked with first argument a circle. At run time, then, the system will invoke CMOVE, not EMOVE.[7] Since, by definition, the second argument to that invocation is of type SQUARE, it follows that the declared type of the second *parameter* to CMOVE could have been any proper supertype of SQUARE, say RECTANGLE,[8] and the type checking, at both compile time and run time, would still work. And this property (*warning! complicated text coming up!*)—the property, that is, that if (a) *Op* is an operator with a parameter *P* that (according to the pertinent specification signature) is of declared type *T*, and (b) *Op* is invoked with an argument corresponding to *P* that's of some proper subtype of *T*, then (c) the declared type of some other parameter *Q* to the pertinent

---

[7] This effect occurs thanks to the binding process, to be discussed in the section on IM Prescription 17 later in this chapter. What's more, as that same section also explains, it can occur either at compile time or at run time, depending on circumstances.

[8] But if so, this state of affairs would have to be made known to the user somehow.

implementation version, and hence the declared type of the argument corresponding to Q in that invocation, might be allowed to be some proper supertype of the declared type of Q as specified in the pertinent specification signature—is the "argument contravariance" property.

However, the notion of allowing an operator to be invoked with an argument of type some proper supertype of the pertinent parameter declared type, as given by the pertinent specification signature, is surely more than a little suspect. In the case at hand, surely it would be better just to define MOVE as having a specification signature that looks like this (note the revised declared type of the second parameter):

```
MOVE ( ELLIPSE , RECTANGLE ) RETURNS ELLIPSE
```

Now the user knows, because of value substitutability, that the arguments to any given MOVE invocation can be of any nonempty subtypes of ELLIPSE and RECTANGLE, respectively. In particular, of course, they can be of most specific types ELLIPSE and RECTANGLE as such, because every type is a subtype of itself. By contrast, the "argument contravariance" property seems to be saying—in the case at hand, and now going back to the earlier specification signature

```
MOVE ( ELLIPSE , SQUARE ) RETURNS ELLIPSE
```

—that MOVE can be invoked (a) with arguments of most specific types ELLIPSE and SQUARE, respectively, and (b) with arguments of most specific types CIRCLE and RECTANGLE, respectively (and therefore (c) with arguments of most specific types CIRCLE and SQUARE, respectively), but not (d) with arguments of most specific types ELLIPSE and RECTANGLE, respectively! As already noted, this state of affairs violates value substitutability—it could be argued that it violates orthogonality too—and it's therefore very strongly deprecated. In other words, it seems to me there'd be no need to mention the concept of argument contravariance at all, if only value substitutability were taken seriously. And by "taking value substitutability seriously" here, all I mean is requiring that if argument A is denoted by expression Ax, then the declared type of Ax should be some subtype of the declared type of the corresponding parameter, as given by the pertinent specification signature.[9] After all, *not* requiring such a thing is surely nonsense—isn't it?

A few further observations to wind up this subsection:

- The term *argument contravariance* is presumably meant to reflect the fact that the (declared? most specific?) type of one argument "contravaries" with that of another. But in a sense it's really parameters that "contravary," not arguments, so at the very least the term ought really to be *parameter* contravariance (?).

---

[9] In the example, this would entail reverting to the specification signature MOVE (ELLIPSE,RECTANGLE) RETURNS ELLIPSE, thereby legitimizing an invocation with arguments of most specific types ELLIPSE and RECTANGLE, respectively.

■ There seems to be a tacit assumption underlying the terminology to the effect that there are exactly two parameters. In the case of MOVE, there are indeed two parameters, which do "contravary" (or so it might be argued, at least)—but what if there had been three?

■ Earlier in this subsection I mentioned what I said was "a flawed definition of the subtype concept." The definition in question is in fact another part of that definition, quoted in the previous subsection, from Elisa Bertino and Lorenzo Martino: *Object-Oriented Database Systems: Concepts and Architectures* (Addison-Wesley, 1993), and it goes like this:

A type T' is a subtype of a type T if ... for each method M of T there is a corresponding method M' of T' such that ... the ith argument type of M is a subtype of the ith argument type of M' (*rule of contravariance in arguments*).

To those earlier criticisms of this definition, I think we can now add that it's confused over the logical difference between arguments and parameters.

■ Here for interest is another definition from the object literature (this one is from Stanley B. Zdonik and David Maier: "Introduction to Object-Oriented Fundamentals," in *Readings in Object-Oriented Database Systems* (Zdonik and Maier, eds.; Morgan Kaufmann, 1990):

[The] important contravariance rule ... If function signatures are viewed as types for functions, then a function type **G** can be viewed as a subtype of a function type **F** if and only if the inputs to **F** are subtypes of the inputs to **G** and the result type of **G** is a subtype of the result type of **F**.[10]

Whether this definition is consistent with the explanations given previously is left as an exercise for the reader. *Note: Function* as used here is just another word for operator, of course—though whether it means a read-only operator specifically isn't entirely clear.[11]

Note finally that IM Prescription 16 does indeed require that read-only operators be defined in such a way as to allow the most specific type of any given argument to any given invocation of any given operator to be the same as the declared type of the corresponding parameter. (What it actually says, in essence, is this: "The declared type of the argument expression—and therefore, necessarily, the most specific type of the argument as such—corresponding to parameter P in an invocation of [the read-only operator] Op shall be allowed to be any subtype of the declared type of P.") Indeed, it seems perverse in the extreme, as well as logically incorrect, to do otherwise. And if this simple discipline is followed, then we can forget about the "argument contravariance" concept entirely.

---

[10] Incidentally, note the sloppy phrasing here—inputs aren't types, they have types.

[11] Functions in mathematics are read-only by definition, but functions in programming languages, even if basically read-only, are unfortunately sometimes allowed to have side effects. Such is the case in SQL, for example.

Note: The foregoing paragraph needs a tiny refinement to take care of the possibility that the declared type of a parameter might be a *union* type. A union type can't be the most specific type of anything, by definition (see the discussion of IM Prescription 20 in Chapter 12). Hence, if parameter *P* has declared type *T* and *T* is a union type, the most specific type of any argument corresponding to *P* must be some subtype of *T'*, where *T'* is a proper subtype of *T* that (a) isn't a union type and (b) has no nonunion type as a proper supertype. See Chapter 12 for further explanation.

IM PRESCRIPTION 17: OPERATOR SIGNATURES

Let *Op* be an operator. Then *Op* shall have a *specification signature* and a set of *invocation signatures*. Let the parameters of *Op* and the argument expressions involved in any given invocation of *Op* each constitute an ordered list of *n* elements ($n \geq 0$), such that the *j*th argument expression corresponds to the *j*th parameter ($j = 1, 2, ..., n$). Further, let $PDT = \langle DT1, DT2, ..., DTn \rangle$ be the declared types, in sequence, of those *n* parameters, and let $PDT' = \langle DT1', DT2', ..., DTn' \rangle$ be a sequence of types such that DTj' is a nonempty subtype of DTj ($j = 1, 2, ..., n$). Then:

a. If *Op* is a read-only operator, the **specification signature** shall consist of the operator name, the sequence *PDT*, and a type (the **declared type** $DT(Op)$ for, or of, operator *Op*). Also, for each possible sequence *PDT'*, let *OpI* be an invocation of *Op* with argument expressions of declared types as specified by *PDT'*; then there shall exist an **invocation signature** for *OpI*, consisting of that sequence *PDT'* and a type (the **declared type** $DT(OpI)$ for, or of, invocation *OpI*). $DT(OpI)$ shall be a subtype of $DT(Op)$, and the type of the result of *OpI* shall be a subtype of $DT(OpI)$.

b. If *Op* is an update operator, the **specification signature** shall consist of the operator name, the sequence *PDT*, and an indication as to which parameters are subject to update. Also, let the sequence *PDT'* be such that an invocation *OpI* of *Op* with argument expressions of declared types as specified by *PDT'* is legitimate (see IM Prescription 19). For each such sequence *PDT'*, there shall exist an **invocation signature** consisting of that sequence *PDT'*.

If two distinct operators (either both read-only or both update operators) have the same name and the same number *n* of parameters, then for some *j* ($1 \leq j \leq n$) the declared types of their *j*th parameters, as given by their respective specification signatures, shall be disjoint.

Note: Ordered lists and sequences are used in the text of this prescription purely as a convenient basis for defining the various correspondences (e.g., between parameters and their declared types) that the prescription requires. They are not an intrinsic part of the prescription as such. In other words, the implementation is free to establish those correspondences by whatever means it deems suitable, just so long as the net effect is functionally equivalent to that defined by the foregoing text.

———— ◆◆◆◆◆ ————

There are quite a few differences between IM Prescription 17 as stated here and the corresponding Explorations version. It's not worth discussing all of those differences in detail; I'll limit myself to saying just that the Explorations version (a) was a little confused over exactly what a specification signature was; (b) had nothing to say about update operators at all; (c) omitted the note at the end; and (d) omitted the sentence immediately preceding that note entirely.[12]

Let *Op* be an operator. Then there are three related but logically separate concepts arising in connection with *Op* that need to be clearly distinguished. First of all, there's operator *Op* itself; second, there are implementation versions of *Op*; third, there are invocations of *Op*. The concept of *signatures* is intended to help make and clarify these important distinctions. In essence:

■ Operator *Op* as such has a *specification signature*.

■ Each implementation version of *Op* has its own *version signature*.

■ For each possible combination of argument declared types for invocations of *Op*, there's a corresponding *invocation signature*.

Let's take a closer look. First of all, let's assume until further notice that the operators we're talking about are all read-only operators specifically. Thus, let *Op* be a read-only operator, with parameters *P1*, *P2*, ..., *Pn* (only). Also, let parameter *Pj* have declared type *DTj* (j = 1, 2, ..., *n*)—but note immediately that a large part of the point of the discussion that follows is to make this notion of parameter declared types, and corresponding argument types, much more precise. Thanks to value substitutability, then, the argument *Aj* corresponding to parameter *Pj* in an invocation of *Op* can have as its most specific type *MSTj* any nonempty subtype of *DTj*. (*Note:* It follows a fortiori that the expression *Axj* denoting argument *Aj* can have as its declared type any type that's both a subtype of *DTj* and a supertype of *MSTj*.) Conceptually, then, *Op* has a specification signature, denoting the user's overall perception of the operator in question, and a set of invocation signatures, where:

■ The specification signature consists of the operator name, the parameter declared types *PDT1*, *PDT2*, ..., *PDTn*, and the operator declared type *DT(Op)*.

---

[12] Which is a little odd, incidentally, given that the issue addressed by that sentence *was* addressed (albeit in different words, and not entirely correctly) by an earlier version of the prescription. The issue in question is explained in Chapter 14, in the section "Two Remarks on Operator Inheritance."

■ There's one invocation signature for each possible combination of argument declared types *ADT1, ADT2, ..., ADTn.* Each such signature consists of the pertinent combination *ADT1, ADT2, ..., ADTn,* together with the declared type *DT(OpI)*—necessarily a subtype of *DT(Op)*—of an invocation *OpI* of *Op* with arguments of most specific types equal to the declared types *ADT1, ADT2, ..., ADTn,* respectively, as specified in the invocation signature in question. *Note:* Under the covers, each distinct invocation signature will be associated with exactly one implementation version of *Op* (but the same implementation version might be associated with any number of distinct invocation signatures). See later in this section for further explanation.

Aside: The foregoing definitions and explanations notwithstanding, you need to be aware that different writers and different languages define the term *signature* in a variety of different ways. For example, the term is sometimes taken to include parameter names. Note further that this remark applies regardless of whether the signature in question is a specification signature or some other kind; in fact, writers generally seem not to distinguish between specification signatures and other kinds. Here's a typical quote: "The signature [*note the definite article*] specifies the name of the method, the names and classes of the arguments [*sic*], and the class of the result, if the method returns one" (from Elisa Bertino and Lorenzo Martino: *Object-Oriented Database Systems: Concepts and Architectures*, Addison-Wesley, 1993). *End of aside.*

So, to repeat, operator *Op* has exactly one specification signature, plus exactly one invocation signature for each possible combination of argument declared types (at least, that's what the model says, though certain obvious shorthands are likely to be available in concrete syntax—see further discussion below). By way of example, consider the read-only operator MOVE once again, which moves a specified ellipse such that it becomes centered on the center of a specified rectangle. The specification signature looks like this:

```
MOVE ( ELLIPSE , RECTANGLE ) RETURNS ELLIPSE
```

Generally speaking, in other words, MOVE takes an ellipse and a rectangle as arguments and returns an ellipse as result—and the following implementation code supports that understanding (once again I'm assuming the availability of a read-only operator called CTR that returns the center of its rectangle argument):

```
OPERATOR MOVE ( E ELLIPSE , R RECTANGLE ) RETURNS ELLIPSE ;
   RETURN ( ELLIPSE ( THE_A ( E ) , THE_B ( E ) , CTR ( R ) ) ) ;
END OPERATOR ;
```

Thanks to value substitutability, however, a given invocation of MOVE can have a value of any nonempty subtype of ELLIPSE as its first argument and a value of any nonempty subtype of RECTANGLE as its second argument. In other words, the first argument can have most specific type either CIRCLE or ELLIPSE, and the second argument can have most specific type either SQUARE or RECTANGLE. Moreover, if the first argument is in fact a circle and not just an ellipse, the result will clearly be a circle too. At least abstractly, therefore—indeed, as previously noted in the discussion of result covariance earlier in this chapter—MOVE will have four distinct invocation signatures, as follows:

```
( CIRCLE  , SQUARE     ) RETURNS CIRCLE
( CIRCLE  , RECTANGLE ) RETURNS CIRCLE
( ELLIPSE , SQUARE     ) RETURNS ELLIPSE
( ELLIPSE , RECTANGLE ) RETURNS ELLIPSE
```

Thus, e.g., if C and R are variables of declared types CIRCLE and RECTANGLE, respectively, then the declared type of the expression MOVE (C,R) is CIRCLE.

In **Tutorial D**, invocation signatures are defined by means of the RETURNS clause on the operator definition. For example, here again is the definition of MOVE as a read-only operator, now shown complete:

```
OPERATOR MOVE ( E ELLIPSE , R RECTANGLE )
   RETURNS
      CASE
         WHEN IS_CIRCLE  ( E ) AND IS_SQUARE    ( R ) THEN CIRCLE
         WHEN IS_CIRCLE  ( E ) AND IS_RECTANGLE ( R ) THEN CIRCLE
         WHEN IS_ELLIPSE ( E ) AND IS_SQUARE    ( R ) THEN ELLIPSE
         WHEN IS_ELLIPSE ( E ) AND IS_RECTANGLE ( R ) THEN ELLIPSE
      END CASE ;
   RETURN ( ELLIPSE ( THE_A ( E ) , THE_B ( E ) , CTR ( R ) ) ) ;
END OPERATOR ;
```

Aside: In our previous definitions of MOVE, the RETURNS clause has taken a much simpler form: viz., just RETURNS ELLIPSE. As you can now see, however, that simpler form isn't sufficient. (Well, it's sufficient to define the specification signature—see below—but not the invocation signatures, at least not in general.) In fact, that simpler formulation must now be regarded as shorthand for a RETURNS clause that looks like this—

```
RETURNS
   CASE
      WHEN IS_CIRCLE  ( E ) AND IS_SQUARE    ( R ) THEN ELLIPSE
      WHEN IS_CIRCLE  ( E ) AND IS_RECTANGLE ( R ) THEN ELLIPSE
      WHEN IS_ELLIPSE ( E ) AND IS_SQUARE    ( R ) THEN ELLIPSE
      WHEN IS_ELLIPSE ( E ) AND IS_RECTANGLE ( R ) THEN ELLIPSE
   END CASE
```

—in other words, a RETURNS clause that says that every possible MOVE invocation has declared type ELLIPSE (which is, of course, not quite what we want). *End of aside.*

As for the specification signature, that signature is now effectively defined by means of the combination of the operator name, the parameter declared types, and that particular one of the invocation signatures that has argument declared types the same as the corresponding parameter declared types—in other words, the last of the invocation signatures shown, in the example.

There's a slightly tricky point here, however. To be specific, observe that:

- The CASE expression in the RETURNS specification is evaluated (in effect) at compile time, not at run time. (More precisely, it's evaluated, in effect, whenever the compiler processes a MOVE invocation.)

- Hence, the various "IS_" operator invocations in that CASE expression are also effectively evaluated at compile time, not at run time.

- Those "IS_" operator invocations therefore return TRUE if and only if the corresponding *declared* types are as indicated.

In other words, those "IS_" operators aren't the usual operators of those names, which return TRUE if and only if their operands have the indicated types at run time.[13]

Now, I've said that if C and R are variables of declared types CIRCLE and RECTANGLE, respectively, then the declared type of the expression MOVE (C,R) is CIRCLE. Moreover, the specifications in the RETURNS clause mean the compiler is aware of this fact, as just explained. As a consequence, various TREAT invocations (see Chapter 10) that might otherwise have been needed won't be needed after all. For example, given C and R as above, we can write

```
C := MOVE ( C , R ) ;
```

instead of what we would otherwise have had to have written:

```
C := TREAT_AS_CIRCLE ( MOVE ( C , R ) ) ;
```

Aside: As mentioned in passing earlier in this chapter, few writers (or languages or systems, come to that) seem to distinguish properly—or at all—between specification and invocation signatures. As the foregoing example suggests, languages and systems that do fail to make this distinction will probably require more explicit TREAT invocations (or equivalents) than ones that do make it. *End of aside.*

---

[13] Certain of my reviewers were quite critical of the proposals of this section—in particular, of the "tricky point" discussed in these bullet items. One even said those proposals would eventually lead to a need for "an entire full blown expression-evaluating language for directing the compiler." But I disagree; I think those proposals are reasonable, and I'll stand by them until someone comes up with a clearly superior alternative (which my reviewers didn't do).

To return to the question of concrete syntax: As noted earlier, certain obvious shorthands are likely to be possible in practice. For example, the RETURNS clause in the MOVE example might reasonably be abbreviated to just:

```
RETURNS IF IS_CIRCLE ( E ) THEN CIRCLE ELSE ELLIPSE END IF
```

Another possible shorthand is illustrated by the following self-explanatory example:

```
RETURNS SAME_TYPE_AS ( E )
```

However, this latter shorthand obviously won't work in general. To see why not, consider an operator that returns a square if its sole argument has most specific type CIRCLE, but "just a rectangle" and not a square if its argument has most specific type ELLIPSE instead.

Now suppose once again (as we've done several times previously in this book) that type CIRCLE has a proper subtype O_CIRCLE, where an "O-circle" is a circle with center the origin:

```
TYPE O_CIRCLE
    IS { CIRCLE
         CONSTRAINT THE_CTR ( CIRCLE ) = POINT ( 0.0 , 0.0 )
         POSSREP ( R = THE_R ( CIRCLE ) )
         NOT { CIRCLE ( LENGTH ( 2.0 ) , POINT ( 1.0 , 0.0 ) ) } } ;
```

Conceptually, then, the read-only version of MOVE will now require six invocation signatures instead of four, thus:

```
( O_CIRCLE , SQUARE    ) RETURNS CIRCLE
( O_CIRCLE , RECTANGLE ) RETURNS CIRCLE
( CIRCLE   , SQUARE    ) RETURNS CIRCLE
( CIRCLE   , RECTANGLE ) RETURNS CIRCLE
( ELLIPSE  , SQUARE    ) RETURNS ELLIPSE
( ELLIPSE  , RECTANGLE ) RETURNS ELLIPSE
```

Here's a possible RETURNS clause shorthand:

```
RETURNS
   CASE
      WHEN IS_CIRCLE  ( E ) THEN CIRCLE
      WHEN IS_ELLIPSE ( E ) THEN ELLIPSE
   END CASE
```

Here I'm assuming, reasonably enough, that the compile time version of IS_CIRCLE (like its run time counterpart) will return TRUE if the declared type of E is *any subtype of* CIRCLE, including type O_CIRCLE in particular. *Note:* The second of these WHEN clauses might be simplified to just ELSE ELLIPSE—see the paragraph immediately following. Alternatively, the entire RETURNS clause might once again be replaced by the following:

```
RETURNS IF IS_CIRCLE ( E ) THEN CIRCLE ELSE ELLIPSE END IF
```

I'd like to consider one final example, in order to illustrate yet another possibility. Suppose that (a) read-only operator *Op* has a specification signature involving two parameters E1 and E2, both of declared type ELLIPSE; (b) invocation declared types are explicitly defined (via appropriate invocation signatures) corresponding to the argument declared type combinations CIRCLE / CIRCLE, CIRCLE / ELLIPSE, and ELLIPSE / CIRCLE (only); and (c) *Op* is invoked with the argument declared type combination ELLIPSE / ELLIPSE. That invocation doesn't correspond to any of the specified invocation signatures exactly—so what's its declared type? The simplest solution to this problem (perhaps not the only one) is to allow the CASE expression that specifies the various invocation signatures to include an appropriate ELSE clause, as here:

```
CASE
    WHEN IS_CIRCLE  ( E1 ) AND IS_CIRCLE  ( E2 ) THEN ...
    WHEN IS_CIRCLE  ( E1 ) AND IS_ELLIPSE ( E2 ) THEN ...
    WHEN IS_ELLIPSE ( E1 ) AND IS_CIRCLE  ( E2 ) THEN ...
    ELSE ...
END CASE
```

Caveat: It would be remiss of me not to point out that there's a trap for the unwary in the scheme as sketched above. To be specific, it's important that the WHEN clauses be specified in the right sequence. By way of example, consider the following example (a possible shorthand form of the RETURNS clause for the MOVE operator) once again:

```
RETURNS
    CASE
        WHEN IS_CIRCLE  ( E ) THEN CIRCLE
        WHEN IS_ELLIPSE ( E ) THEN ELLIPSE
    END CASE
```

Suppose we were to switch the WHEN clauses, thus:

```
RETURNS
    CASE
        WHEN IS_ELLIPSE ( E ) THEN ELLIPSE
        WHEN IS_CIRCLE  ( E ) THEN CIRCLE
    END CASE
```

Then if C and R are variables of declared types CIRCLE and RECTANGLE, respectively, the declared type of the expression MOVE (C,R) will be ELLIPSE, not CIRCLE!—because the expression IS_ELLIPSE(C) will be evaluated first, and it'll return TRUE. (In fact, of course, the expression IS_CIRCLE(C) won't be evaluated at all in this example.)

Analogously, the shorthand form

```
RETURNS IF IS_CIRCLE ( E ) THEN CIRCLE ELSE ELLIPSE END IF
```

must be written as shown and not as

```
RETURNS IF IS_ELLIPSE ( E ) THEN ELLIPSE ELSE CIRCLE END IF
```

Update Operators

So much for read-only operators; I turn now to the question of signatures for update operators. Here repeated from the section "Substitutability" in Chapter 7 is MOVE as an update operator:

```
OPERATOR MOVE ( E ELLIPSE , R RECTANGLE ) UPDATES { E } ;
    THE_CTR ( E ) := CTR ( R ) ;
END OPERATOR ;
```

Now there's no question of specifying either invocation declared types or an overall (specification signature) declared type, because update operator invocations don't return a result. But invocation signatures and a specification signature are still required for purposes of type checking and binding (see the subsection following this one), as well as for defining the user's overall perception of the operator. In the example, the specification signature might look like this:

```
MOVE ( *ELLIPSE , RECTANGLE )
```

(The asterisk is an ad hoc syntactic trick for showing that the corresponding parameter is subject to update.) And the invocation signatures might look like this:

```
( CIRCLE  , SQUARE    )
( CIRCLE  , RECTANGLE )
( ELLIPSE , SQUARE    )
( ELLIPSE , RECTANGLE )
```

Note that the specification signature does need to specify somehow that MOVE invocations update the argument corresponding to the first parameter; however, the invocation signatures don't need anything analogous. More to the point, note that even if circles have "O-circles" as a proper subtype, the argument corresponding to that first parameter can't be of type O_CIRCLE (at least, let's assume as much for the sake of the example), because the center of an O-circle is always the origin and can't be changed. Thus, there are no invocation signatures (not even purely conceptual ones) showing the type of the first parameter as O_CIRCLE. As far as the first parameter is concerned, in other words—i.e., the one that's subject to update—the update form of MOVE is defined for type ELLIPSE, is inherited by type CIRCLE, but isn't inherited by type O_CIRCLE.[14] Some syntactic construct for specifying such a state of affairs is thus necessary—perhaps as illustrated here:

---

[14] And if O_CIRCLE had any nonempty proper subtypes, it wouldn't be inherited by those either, a fortiori. See the discussion of IM Prescription 19 later in this chapter.

```
OPERATOR MOVE ( E ELLIPSE , R RECTANGLE )
                             UPDATES { E IS_NOT_O_CIRCLE ( E ) } ;
   THE_CTR ( E ) := CTR ( R ) ;
END OPERATOR ;
```

So let *Op* be an update operator, with parameters *P1*, *P2*, ..., *Pn* (and no others), and let parameter *Pj* have declared type *PDTj* (*j* = 1, 2, ..., *n*). If *Pj* isn't subject to update, then *Op* behaves as if it were a read-only operator as far as *Pj* is concerned, and the earlier discussion of the read-only case applies directly, mutatis mutandis. But if *Pj* is subject to update, then the argument *Aj* corresponding to *Pj* in an invocation of *Op* must be a variable specifically, and it might or might not be allowed to have some given proper subtype of *PDTj* as its most specific type (and a fortiori as its declared type, too). As in the read-only case, therefore, *Op* has a specification signature and a set of invocation signatures—but in this case:

a. The specification signature consists of the operator name, the parameter declared types *PDT1*, *PDT2*, ..., *PDTn*, and an indication as to which parameters are subject to update.

b. There's one invocation signature for each legitimate combination of argument declared types *ADT1*, *ADT2*, ..., *ADTn*. Each such signature consists simply of the pertinent combination *ADT1*, *ADT2*, ..., *ADTn*.

The Binding Process

As noted in Chapter 3, there are certain implementation issues that need to be understood if the overall concept of inheritance is to be properly understood in turn, and the binding process is one of them. In essence, the binding process is simply the process of determining which implementation version of a given operator is to be executed in response to some given invocation of the operator in question. For example, consider the following code fragment (I've numbered the lines for purposes of subsequent reference):

```
1.  VAR C CIRCLE ;
2.  VAR R RECTANGLE ;

3.  C := CIRCLE ( ... ) ;
4.  R := RECTANGLE ( ... ) ;
5.  C := MOVE ( C , R ) ;
```

Explanation:

■ Lines 1 and 2 simply define two variables, C and R, with declared types CIRCLE and RECTANGLE, respectively.

- Lines 3 and 4 assign values to those variables, of (let's assume) most specific types CIRCLE and RECTANGLE, respectively.

- Line 5 then invokes the read-only operator MOVE, with arguments the current values of C and R, respectively, and assigns the result of that invocation to C.

But what *exactly* happens in line 5? Well, at this point I need to make a couple of assumptions:

- First, for the sake of the example, I'll assume there's a distinct implementation version of the MOVE operator for each possible combination of argument most specific types: viz., CSMOVE, CRMOVE, ESMOVE, and ERMOVE, for the combinations CIRCLE / SQUARE, CIRCLE / RECTANGLE, ELLIPSE / SQUARE, and ELLIPSE / RECTANGLE, respectively. (I choose to ignore the fact that, given the implementation code shown for the MOVE operator in the next bullet item below, these four separate implementation versions are clearly unnecessary. The reason is that the code in question—which in fact consists of just a single RETURN statement—is clearly sufficient, in and of itself, to handle all four cases correctly anyway.)

- Second, I'll assume (in accordance with the suggestions of the previous subsection) that the complete definition of the MOVE operator looks like this:

```
OPERATOR MOVE ( E ELLIPSE , R RECTANGLE )
   RETURNS
      CASE
         WHEN IS_CIRCLE  ( E ) AND IS_SQUARE     ( R ) THEN CIRCLE
         WHEN IS_CIRCLE  ( E ) AND IS_RECTANGLE  ( R ) THEN CIRCLE
         WHEN IS_ELLIPSE ( E ) AND IS_SQUARE     ( R ) THEN ELLIPSE
         WHEN IS_ELLIPSE ( E ) AND IS_RECTANGLE  ( R ) THEN ELLIPSE
      END CASE ;
   RETURN ( ELLIPSE ( THE_A ( E ) , THE_B ( E ) , CTR ( R ) ) ) ;
END OPERATOR ;
```

Among other things, then, the compiler knows that the specification signature for MOVE is this:

```
MOVE ( ELLIPSE , RECTANGLE ) RETURNS ELLIPSE
```

It also knows that the first argument to the invocation MOVE (C,R) is of declared type CIRCLE and the second is of declared type RECTANGLE. As a consequence:

- The line 5 compile time type checking on the invocation MOVE (C,R) succeeds, because the declared types of C and R are some subtype of ELLIPSE and some subtype of RECTANGLE, respectively.

■ Also, the compiler knows, from the second WHEN clause in the operator definition, that the declared type of that invocation is CIRCLE. Hence, the line 5 compile time checking on the assignment operation as such (as opposed to the MOVE invocation on the right side of that assignment) also succeeds.

Aside: It wouldn't have been wrong to write that assignment as follows:

```
C := TREAT_AS_CIRCLE ( MOVE ( C , R ) ) ;
```

However, that TREAT would effectively be a "no op"; if it's specified, therefore, it can and should be optimized away by the compiler. *End of aside.*

■ Moreover, if the compiler is aware of the existence of the four MOVE implementation versions—and there's no logical reason why it shouldn't be—then it can determine that the implementation version to be invoked at run time is version CRMOVE specifically. And if it does make that determination, then what we have is an example of *compile time binding*. Here's the definition:

Definition: Given an expression *OpI* denoting an invocation of some operator *Op*, *compile time binding* is the process of finding, at compile time, the unique invocation signature for *Op* for which the declared types of the parameters exactly match the declared types of the corresponding argument expressions in *OpI*, thereby causing the unique corresponding implementation version of *Op* to be invoked at run time (unless the compiler's decision is overridden at run time by run time binding—see further discussion below).

In the example, then, if the compiler does make the appropriate determination as suggested, it will bind the MOVE invocation MOVE (C,R) to the implementation version CRMOVE.

Aside: The process of binding a given invocation to a given implementation version is often described as a process of comparing the pertinent invocation signature with the version signatures of the available implementation versions, looking for the best match. (Generally speaking, the version signature for a given version will in fact look very like an invocation signature.) However, all that's really necessary is for each invocation signature to have associated with it an identification—perhaps just the name—of the implementation version to be executed when an invocation with that invocation signature is encountered. *End of aside.*

Now suppose once again that type CIRCLE has a proper subtype O_CIRCLE, and suppose there's yet another implementation version of MOVE, OMOVE, that's intended for the case where the most specific type of the first argument is O_CIRCLE. Suppose further that the most specific type of variable C at run time (i.e., in the invocation MOVE (C,R) in line 5) is in fact O_CIRCLE. At run time, then, the system can effectively override the compiler's decision to invoke CRMOVE and invoke OMOVE instead: an example of *run time binding*.[15] Here's the definition:

> **Definition:** Given some invocation *OpI* of some operator *Op*, *run time binding* is the process of finding, at run time, the unique invocation signature for *Op* for which the declared types of the parameters exactly match the most specific types of the corresponding arguments to *OpI*, thereby causing the unique corresponding implementation version of *Op* to be invoked.

More on Binding

The foregoing discussion shows that the binding process can be done at compile time or run time or both. In principle, however, it can "almost always" be done at compile time!—and if it can, then run time binding is logically unnecessary (though it might lead to better performance). Let me explain:

■ Let scalar type T be a proper supertype of scalar type T', and let PR and PR' be possreps for T and T', respectively ($PR \neq PR'$).

■ Let Op be a read-only operator that applies to values of type T and hence, by definition, to values of type T' also.

■ Let OpV and OpV' be implementation versions of Op that apply to values of type T and values of type T', respectively. Further, let OpV be implemented in terms of PR and let OpV' be implemented in terms of PR'.

By definition, then, PR is an inherited possrep for type T'.[16] As a consequence, OpV will certainly work—perhaps not as efficiently as OpV' does—for values of type T'; hence, compile time binding will always work too. In fact, the compiler could simply bind every invocation of Op to the implementation version OpV, without paying any attention to argument declared types at all. (On the other hand, such an approach would mean that the compiler would no longer be aware that, e.g., the expression MOVE (C,R), where C is of declared type CIRCLE, denotes a circle instead of "just an ellipse," and additional explicit TREATs would therefore be required.)

---

[15] Of course, the invocation signature for OMOVE will necessarily talk in terms of the *declared* type of the first parameter (viz., O_CIRCLE). Thus, since the declared type of variable C is just CIRCLE, not O_CIRCLE, the binding of the invocation MOVE (C,R) to OMOVE can't possibly be done at compile time but has to wait until run time.

[16] See Chapter 3 if you need to refresh your memory regarding inherited possreps.

Aside: Of course, the foregoing explanation does assume (a) to repeat, that implementation versions are written in terms of possreps, not physical representations, and (b) that distinct implementation versions of the same operator implement the same semantics (see the discussion of changing semantics in Chapter 7). It also assumes, obviously enough, that *OpV* exists!—in other words, it does rely on there being an implementation version of *Op* for type *T*. But if *T* is a union type (see the discussion of IM Prescription 20 in Chapter 12), *OpV* might not exist after all, even if that operator *Op* is defined for type *T*. For example, suppose type ELLIPSE has another immediate subtype NONCIRCLE, with the intuitively obvious semantics (so ELLIPSE is now a union type, meaning every ellipse is either a circle or a noncircle and no ellipse is both). Suppose further, not all that unrealistically, that the operator AREA_OF is defined at the level of type ELLIPSE, and that implementation versions of AREA_OF are defined for CIRCLE and NONCIRCLE but not for type ELLIPSE as such. Finally, let E be a variable of declared type ELLIPSE, and consider the expression AREA_OF (E). Obviously, which implementation version of AREA_OF is to be executed in response to this invocation can't be determined at compile time, because whether the value of E at run time will be a circle or just an ellipse can't be known at compile time. Thus, the concept of union types implies that some binding, at least, will probably have to be done at run time after all. *End of aside*.

Here are some further relevant considerations:

- Compile time binding means the run time overhead of searching for implementation versions is avoided. However, it also means that programs might need to be recompiled if new implementation versions are defined (or existing ones dropped).

- In some cases it's not only possible to do the binding at compile time, it's actually better— run time binding adds nothing except overhead. For example, consider MOVE once again (and assume for simplicity that there's no type O_CIRCLE). If the user invokes MOVE with arguments of declared types CIRCLE and SQUARE, respectively, then the compiler should clearly be able to determine that the implementation version CSMOVE is the one to invoke, because CIRCLE and SQUARE are both leaf types and no "lower" implementation version of MOVE can possibly exist.

- Even if some run time binding is required, it still might not involve as much overhead as you might think. Suppose types *T1*, *T2*, *T3*, *T4*, and *T5* are such that *T1*, *T2*, *T3*, and *T4* are immediate supertypes of *T2*, *T3*, *T4*, and *T5*, respectively; suppose operator *Op* has implementation versions corresponding to types *T1* and *T3* (only); finally, suppose the most specific type of the argument *x* in some invocation of *Op* is *T5*. Then there's no need for the system to determine this latter fact; all it needs to do is ascertain that *x* is certainly of type *T3* and therefore invoke the *T3* version of *Op*.

A note on terminology: Be aware that numerous other terms are used in the literature in connection with what I've been calling binding. Binding as such is sometimes called *dispatching* (sometimes spelled *despatching*) or *function resolution* or *subject routine determination* (this last is the SQL term). Compile time binding is sometimes referred to as *static* or *early* binding (or dispatching, etc.). Run time binding is sometimes referred to as *dynamic* or *late* binding (or dispatching, etc.). And so on.

No "Distinguished Parameters"

By definition, implementation versions are an implementation concern, and so binding is too.[17] Despite this state of affairs, we (i.e., Darwen and I) do have some opinions about it! To be specific, we believe—and, in effect, in our model we insist—that all arguments to a given operator invocation should participate equally in the binding process. In other words, we don't much care for the notion, typically supported by object systems, that operators might have a specially distinguished parameter such that the corresponding argument plays a controlling role in the binding process. To elaborate:

- Treating one parameter as the controlling one has the obvious advantage that it makes the binding process simpler—simpler for the system, that is—because that process involves determining the type of just one argument (viz., the argument corresponding to that special parameter).

However, it has certain obvious disadvantages too, not the least of which is that it can make it harder for the implementer to write the implementation code. For example:

- Consider the MOVE example once again. Suppose the first parameter to that operator (i.e., the one of declared type ELLIPSE) is the controlling one. Then there can be at most two distinct implementation versions of MOVE, one for moving a circle and one for moving just an ellipse; in effect, what I referred to earlier—in the subsection "The Binding Process"—as versions CSMOVE and CRMOVE would have to be combined into a single version (CMOVE, say), and what I referred to earlier as versions ESMOVE and ERMOVE would also have to be combined into a single version (EMOVE, say).

- So if we wanted different implementation code depending on whether the second argument is a square or just a rectangle, then we'd have to include explicit type testing and branching operations within both CMOVE and EMOVE. What's more, we might have to include both the square code and the rectangle code within both of those versions.

---

[17] Assuming once again, that is, that distinct implementation versions of the same operator do implement the same semantics.

■ Alternatively, and perhaps more likely in practice, CMOVE and EMOVE could both invoke a "square or rectangle?" subroutine. But even with this minor simplification, the fact remains that we'll still have had to do a certain amount of work that would and could be much better done by the system.

So we reject the object concept of a distinguished or controlling parameter. It follows that we also reject the concepts of "selfish methods" and the related concept of "messages"; these concepts too we find to be neither necessary nor desirable.

> *Aside:* In case you're not familiar with the foregoing terminology, let me elaborate briefly. First, a "selfish method" is a method, in the object sense of that term, for which one parameter—variously known as the *subject, distinguished, controlling, receiver,* or *target* parameter—is singled out for special semantic treatment (and special syntactic treatment also, necessarily), instead of all parameters being treated equally. The special semantic treatment consists in using the argument corresponding to the distinguished parameter, and no other arguments, to control the binding process. The term *selfish method* derives from the fact that the distinguished parameter is typically unnamed and thus has to be referenced within the method's implementation code in some ad hoc way, typically by means of the keyword SELF (sometimes *this*). Note that object methods are almost always assumed in practice to be selfish in the foregoing sense. For example, here's a quote from Douglas K. Barry, *The Object Database Handbook: How to Select, Implement, and Use Object-Oriented Databases*, Wiley Publishing, 1996 (emphasis added):

> [Polymorphism is a] mechanism that selects a method *based on the type of the target operand*.

> As for the term *message*, a "message" in object contexts is basically just an operator invocation. However, messages are usually considered as being "sent" to a specific object: viz., the object—the subject object?—that's the argument that corresponds, in the invocation in question, to the subject or distinguished parameter (see above). *End of aside.*

Changing Semantics Revisited

As noted in Chapter 7, the fact that there can be several implementation versions for the same operator opens up the possibility of changing the semantics of the operator in question. The following sequence of events illustrates the point:

1. Suppose type ELLIPSE and operator AREA_OF have both been defined but type CIRCLE hasn't, yet. Variable E, of declared type ELLIPSE, is assigned an ellipse value for which $a = b$. The operator AREA_OF is then invoked on E, giving a result *area1*, say.

2. Suppose type CIRCLE is now defined as an immediate subtype of type ELLIPSE and a new version of AREA_OF is implemented for this new type. Variable E is assigned the same ellipse value as before, but S by C now comes into play and *MST*(E) becomes CIRCLE. The operator AREA_OF is now invoked on E, giving a result *area2*, say.

At this point we'd surely like to be able to say that the comparison *area1* = *area2* must give TRUE—but we can't. That is, there's little to stop AREA_OF from being reimplemented for circles in such a way as to return, e.g., the diameter instead of the area.[18]

As also noted in Chapter 7, some writers actually claim that it's desirable to be able to change semantics in such a manner. Here's an example of a situation in which such a claim might be made:

1. A type called HIGHWAY is defined, together with an operator called TRAVEL_TIME that computes the time it takes to travel between two points *a* and *b* on highway *h*, using the formula *d/s* (where *d* = distance between *a* and *b* and *s* = speed). The highway value *h* is assigned to a variable H of declared type HIGHWAY, and TRAVEL_TIME is invoked on H (and points *a* and *b* on *h*) and returns a result, *tt1* say.

2. Type TOLL_HIGHWAY is now defined as an immediate subtype of type HIGHWAY and a new implementation version of TRAVEL_TIME is defined for this new type using the formula (*d/s*)+(*n**t), where *n* = number of tollbooths, *t* = time spent at each tollbooth, and *d* and *s* are as before.

3. Variable H is assigned the same highway value *h* as before. Assume for the moment that *h* isn't a toll highway. Then invoking TRAVEL_TIME on H with the same points *a* and *b* as before gives the same result *tt1* as before.

4. By contrast, suppose *h* is a toll highway after all. Then S by C comes into play,[19] *MST*(H) becomes TOLL_HIGHWAY, and invoking TRAVEL_TIME on H with the same points *a* and *b* as before gives a different result *tt2*.

Now, of course it's true that the presence or absence of tollbooths does affect travel time, and an advocate of the idea that changing semantics can be desirable might therefore claim that the foregoing state of affairs (in particular, the fact that *tt1* ≠ *tt2*) is reasonable. But consider the following counterargument:

---

[18] Careful type design can alleviate this problem somewhat. For example, if AREA_OF is defined to return a result of type AREA, obviously the implementation can't return a result of type LENGTH. However, it can still return the wrong area.

[19] Or does it? What's the constraint a value of type HIGHWAY has to satisfy in order to be a value of type TOLL_HIGHWAY? Careful consideration of this question should suffice to show what's wrong with this example. See also the counterargument that follows almost immediately.

- If TOLL_HIGHWAY truly is a subtype of HIGHWAY, it means by definition that every individual toll highway is a highway.

- Thus, some values of type HIGHWAY are toll highways and do have tollbooths. So type HIGHWAY isn't "highways without tollbooths," it's "highways with *n* tollbooths," where *n* might be zero (and type TOLL_HIGHWAY is "highways with *n* tollbooths" where *n* is greater than zero).

- So the operator TRAVEL_TIME for type HIGHWAY isn't "compute the travel time for a highway *without* tollbooths," it's "compute the travel time for a highway *ignoring* tollbooths." Note the logical difference here!

- By contrast, the operator TRAVEL_TIME for type TOLL_HIGHWAY is "compute the travel time for a highway *not* ignoring tollbooths." So the two TRAVEL_TIMEs are truly different operators[20] (another logical difference here). The confusion arises because those two different operators have been given the same name; in fact, the example is an example of overloading, not of inclusion polymorphism at all.

In other words, we reject the suggestion that changing operator semantics can ever be a good idea, and we define our model to say that if a change in semantics occurs, then the implementation is in violation—i.e., it's not an implementation of the model, and the implications are unpredictable. Indeed, it could be argued that the ability to change operator semantics (or, rather, the fact that some writers seem to regard that ability as a virtue) is—like that business of argument contravariance discussed earlier in this chapter—a case of *the implementation tail wagging the model dog*.

IM PRESCRIPTION 18: READ-ONLY PARAMETERS TO UPDATE OPERATORS

Let *Op* be an update operator and let *P* be a parameter to *Op* that is not subject to update. Then *Op* shall behave as a read-only operator as far as *P* is concerned, and all relevant aspects of IM Prescription 16 shall apply, mutatis mutandis.

Given all of the discussions in earlier sections of this chapter, this prescription doesn't seem to need any further explanation—except perhaps to note that (a) the concept of a read-only

---

[20] Though (a) they do return the same result if their highway argument has no tollbooths (i.e., if *n* = 0), and (b) the invocation TRAVEL_TIME (H) does always return the actual travel time, regardless of whether or not H denotes a toll highway.

parameter (see the title of this section) is, I hope, self-explanatory, and (b) since update operators don't return a result, the property of "result covariance" is obviously irrelevant.

IM PRESCRIPTION 19: VARIABLE SUBSTITUTABILITY

Let *Op* be an update operator, let *P* be a parameter to *Op* that is subject to update, and let *T* be the declared type of *P*. Then it might or might not be the case that the declared type of the argument expression (and therefore, necessarily, the most specific type of the argument as such) corresponding to *P* in an invocation of *Op* shall be allowed to be some proper subtype *T'* of type *T*. It follows that for each such update operator *Op* and for each parameter *P* to *Op* that is subject to update, it shall be necessary to state explicitly for which proper subtypes *T'* of the declared type *T* of parameter *P* operator *Op* shall be inherited—*The Principle of **Update Operator Inheritance***. (And if update operator *Op* is not inherited in this way by type *T'*, it shall not be inherited by any proper subtype of type *T'* either.) Update operators shall thus be only conditionally polymorphic—*The Principle of **Update Operator Polymorphism***. If *Op* is an update operator and *P* is a parameter to *Op* that is subject to update and *T'* is a proper subtype of the declared type *T* of *P* for which *Op* is inherited, then by definition it shall be possible to invoke *Op* with an argument expression corresponding to parameter *P* that is of declared type *T'*—*The Principle of **Variable Substitutability***.

────── ◆◆◆◆◆ ──────

The main purpose of IM Prescription 19 is to pin down the notion of variable substitutability (distinguishing it carefully from the more familiar notion of value substitutability), and more specifically to define three interrelated principles: *The Principle of Update Operator Inheritance*, *The Principle of Update Operator Polymorphism*, and *The Principle of Variable Substitutability*.

First let me give an example to show why it doesn't make much sense for update operators to be inherited unconditionally. Let variables R and S have declared types RECTANGLE and SQUARE, respectively. Then—speaking *very* loosely—it's obviously possible to change the height of R without changing its width; more precisely, it's possible to update R in such a way as to replace its current rectangle value *r1* by a new rectangle value *r2* that has the same width as *r1* but a different height. However, it's certainly not possible to do the same kind of thing to S, because squares must always have equal height and width. Thus, a certain update operator, "change the height but not the width," might effectively be defined for type RECTANGLE but not for type SQUARE (i.e., the RECTANGLE operator won't be inherited by type SQUARE).

In contrast to the foregoing, here's an example of an update operator that does make sense for variables of type SQUARE as well as of type RECTANGLE (i.e., it's defined for type RECTANGLE and inherited by type SQUARE): "double both the height and the width."

For a slightly more probing example, let's consider our MOVE operator once again. This time, however, let's make it an update operator:

```
OPERATOR MOVE ( E ELLIPSE , R RECTANGLE ) UPDATES { E } ;
    THE_CTR ( E ) := CTR ( R ) ;
END OPERATOR ;
```

This revised MOVE operator updates its first argument, and so that argument must be a variable specifically; moreover, the code, like the read-only code shown in earlier discussions of the MOVE example, works for circles as well as ellipses, and the variable in question can thus have declared type either ELLIPSE or CIRCLE.[21] However, that same code doesn't work for O-circles, because updating a variable of declared type O_CIRCLE to change its center is clearly invalid (the center for such a variable must be the origin and can't be changed); thus, the variable in question can't have declared type O_CIRCLE. What's more, it's not just this particular code that doesn't work for O-circles; *no* code that attempts to update the center of a variable of declared type O_CIRCLE can possibly work.[22]

From all of the above it follows that it does make sense for certain update operators not to be inherited by certain subtypes. Essentially, what this means is that *which update operators are inherited by which subtypes must be specified explicitly.* For example, we might reasonably specify the following:

■ The update operators that apply to variables of declared type ELLIPSE are:

1. Assignment to THE_A, THE_B, and THE_CTR

2. MOVE (update form)

■ The update operators that apply to variables of declared type CIRCLE are:

1. Assignment to THE_CTR and THE_R

2. MOVE (update form)

---

[21] I remind you from the subsection "The Binding Process" in the section on IM Prescription 17 that distinct implementation versions (CSMOVE, CRMOVE, ESMOVE, ERMOVE) were introduced in the read-only case only for the sake of the example—they weren't strictly necessary, because the MOVE implementation code shown in that subsection was sufficient, in and of itself, to handle all possible cases correctly.

[22] Unless the update is a "no op," perhaps. In other words, we could allow the update form of MOVE to be inherited by type O_CIRCLE after all if we really wanted to, but any attempt to update an O-circle to make its center something other than the origin would then have to fail at run time on a type constraint error. Thus, the advantage of not having the operator be inherited is that it effectively causes a certain *type constraint* error (caught at run time) to be replaced by a certain *type* error (caught at compile time). Analogous remarks apply to update operators in general, which is precisely why IM Prescription 19 allows them not to be inherited in the first place.

Observe in particular that, given these specifications, THE_A and THE_B can't be used as pseudovariables in connection with variables of declared type CIRCLE. Let me elaborate. Consider the following code fragment:

```
VAR C CIRCLE ;
VAR L LENGTH ;

L := THE_A ( C ) ;
```

This assignment is valid, because the read-only operator THE_A *is* inherited by type CIRCLE from type ELLIPSE. By contrast, the following attempted assignment—

```
THE_A ( C ) := L ;     /* warning: compile time type error! */
```

—is shorthand for the following:

```
C := ELLIPSE ( L , THE_B ( C ) , THE_CTR ( C ) ) ;
```

It thus fails on a compile time type error (the declared type of the expression on the right side is ELLIPSE, which isn't a subtype of the declared type, CIRCLE, of the variable reference on the left side).

■ The update operators that apply to variables of declared type O_CIRCLE are:

1.   Assignment to THE_R

Given this specification, the update form of MOVE and the THE_CTR pseudovariable can't be used in connection with variables of declared type O_CIRCLE.

Note: I remind you from the earlier section on IM Prescription 17 that one way of specifying in concrete syntax that the update form of MOVE applies to ellipses and circles but not to O-circles might be as illustrated here:[23]

```
OPERATOR MOVE ( E ELLIPSE , R RECTANGLE )
                          UPDATES { E IS_NOT_O_CIRCLE ( E ) } ;
    THE_CTR ( E ) := CTR ( R ) ;
END OPERATOR ;
```

I remind you too that—as in fact should be obvious—if update operator *Op* applies to type *T* but isn't inherited by type *T'* (where *T'* is an immediate subtype of *T*), then it can't be inherited by any proper subtype *T''* of type *T'* either.

Let's consider a few examples. Suppose variables E, C, and O are declared as follows:

---

[23] For a THE_ pseudovariable not to be usable, of course, it's sufficient that there be no corresponding possrep component.

```
VAR E ELLIPSE ;
VAR C CIRCLE ;
VAR O O_CIRCLE ;
```

Also, let the variables be assigned values as follows:

```
E := ELLIPSE ( LENGTH ( 6.0 ) , LENGTH ( 5.0 ) , POINT ( 4.0 , 3.0 ) ) ;
C := CIRCLE  ( LENGTH ( 5.0 ) , POINT ( 4.0 , 3.0 ) ) ;
O := O_CIRCLE ( LENGTH ( 5.0 ) ) ;
```

Now consider the following updates, which I assume to be executed in sequence as shown (where it makes any difference). I've numbered them for convenience.

1. `THE_A ( E ) := LENGTH ( 5.0 ) ;`

MST(E) is now CIRCLE, thanks to S by C. However, if we now try the following—

2. `THE_R ( E ) := LENGTH ( 4.0 ) ;   /* warning: compile time type error! */`

—we'll get a compile time error, because no declared possrep for type ELLIPSE has an R component, and hence no THE_R operator or pseudovariable is defined for that type. By contrast, the following *will* work:

3. `E := CIRCLE ( LENGTH ( 4.0 ) , THE_CTR ( E ) ) ;`

The following will also work:

4. `THE_A ( E ) := LENGTH ( 6.0 ) ;`

MST(E) is now ELLIPSE again, thanks to G by C.

5. `THE_CTR ( C ) := POINT ( 0.0, 0.0 ) ;`

MST(C) is now O_CIRCLE. However, we *can* now invoke the MOVE operator (update form) on variable C; the effect—unless the update is a "no op"—will be to set *MST*(C) back to CIRCLE again, thanks to G by C. By contrast, if we try to invoke the MOVE operator (update form) on the variable O, we'll get a compile time type error (obviously we can't "G by C" a variable to some proper supertype of its declared type).

So much for the examples. For completeness, let me remind you that (as noted under IM Prescription 18) the property of "result covariance" doesn't apply to update operators, since update operators don't return a result. However, all of the remarks in the section on IM

Prescription 17—regarding implementation versions, signatures, binding, and so forth—do apply to update operators as well as to read-only ones, mutatis mutandis.

Values vs. Variables Once Again

Like S by C and G by C, update operator inheritance is an area where our thinking might be regarded as a little controversial (some might say heretical). To be specific, some writers—in fact, probably most writers, in this particular field—would say that update operators, like read-only operators, should be inherited unconditionally. By contrast, we think they should be inherited only where they make sense.[24] Indeed, it seems to us that those who want such unconditional inheritance run into a variety of logical problems and other undesirable consequences that our model avoids. For example:

- In some cases, they allow update operators to return a value—"they allow read-only operators to have side effects" might be a better way of putting it—thereby allowing (among other things) what would otherwise be read-only operations to have the side effect of updating the database.

- Or they allow (e.g.) a value of most specific type SQUARE to have sides of different lengths and/or a value of most specific type RECTANGLE to have sides of the same length, thereby undermining the database "as a model of reality" and causing programs to produce nonsensical results such as "nonsquare squares" and "square nonsquares."

- Or they don't support S by C or G by C.

- Or they simply don't support type constraints at all (see Chapter 13, also Chapter 22, for a detailed discussion of this particular—and important—issue).

Of course, these points aren't all unrelated. Indeed, the common thread running through all of them, it seems to us, is *a failure to make a clear distinction between values and variables*. To us, by contrast, that distinction is both crucial and fundamental; indeed, as explained in Chapter 2, we regard it as one of the great logical differences—one that underlies and buttresses our thinking throughout both *The Third Manifesto* itself and the inheritance model that's based on it (this latter, of course, being the subject of the present book).

---

[24] Actually our position here isn't as controversial as it might seem. Nobody wants ":=" to be inherited unconditionally; e.g., assignment of a value of most specific type ELLIPSE to a variable of declared type CIRCLE is never valid (at least, not in any inheritance scheme that we're aware of). And assignment is the only update operator that's logically necessary! Thus, those who want update operators to be inherited unconditionally might be accused of a certain lack of consistency.

EXERCISES

11.1 Explain the "result covariance" and "argument contravariance" concepts in your own words.

11.2 Give specification signatures for our usual ELLIPSE and CIRCLE selectors.

11.3 Distinguish between specification, invocation, and version signatures.

11.4 In the discussion of the read-only MOVE operator in the section on IM Prescription 17, in the subsection "The Binding Process," I noted that we didn't really need all those different implementation versions (CSMOVE, CRMOVE, and so on), because the code given was sufficient, in and of itself, to handle all possible cases correctly. But does it correctly handle the case where the first argument is of most specific type O_CIRCLE?

11.5 Suppose the type hierarchy of Fig. 5.1 in Chapter 5 is extended as follows: Type POLYGON has two new immediate subtypes, PENTAGON and TRIANGLE; PENTAGON has REGULAR_PENTAGON as an immediate subtype; TRIANGLE has ISOSCELES_TRIANGLE as an immediate subtype; and ISOSCELES_TRIANGLE has EQUILATERAL_TRIANGLE as a further immediate subtype of its own. Suppose further that PTX is a read-only operator that takes two parameters P and T of declared types PENTAGON and TRIANGLE, respectively, and returns a polygon, and PTX invocations have declared types as follows:

a. If the argument corresponding to P is a regular pentagon and the argument corresponding to T is an isosceles triangle, then SQUARE

b. If the argument corresponding to P is a regular pentagon and the argument corresponding to T is "just a triangle," then RECTANGLE

c. If the argument corresponding to P is "just a pentagon," then POLYGON

Give an appropriate specification signature and a corresponding set of invocation signatures.

11.6 Distinguish between compile time and run time binding. Is it true that, at least in principle, binding can always be done at compile time?

11.7 The section on IM Prescription 19 in the body of the chapter included the following text:

> I remind you too that—as in fact should be obvious—if update operator *Op* applies to type *T* but isn't inherited by type *T′* (where *T′* is an immediate subtype of *T*), then it can't be inherited by any proper subtype of type *T′* either.

But why exactly is this fact "obvious"?

11.8 Here are some of the inheritance concepts we've been discussing at considerable length in this and previous chapters: *inclusion polymorphism*; *value substitutability*; *result covariance*; *argument contravariance*; *code reuse*; *implementation versions*; *specification signatures*; *version signatures*; *invocation signatures*; *variable substitutability*; and *binding*. Which of these are truly features of the model as such?

11.9 If C is a variable of declared type CIRCLE, assignment to THE_A(C) and THE_B(C) is probably not supported. What's the formal reason for this state of affairs?

ANSWERS

11.1 The term *result covariance* is used, not very appropriately, to refer to that phenomenon according to which, if *Op* is a read-only operator, then the most specific type of the value returned from an invocation of *Op* can be any subtype of the declared type of *Op* as defined in the pertinent specification signature. *Note:* A more precise definition was given in the body of the chapter.

The term *argument contravariance*, by contrast, seems to reflect nothing but muddle. (Certainly it seems to be hard to define precisely!) It's replaced in our model by a rule—a rather obvious rule, it might be thought—to the effect that argument expressions are required to have declared type some subtype of that of the corresponding parameter, as defined by the pertinent specification signature.

11.2 `ELLIPSE ( LENGTH , LENGTH , POINT ) RETURNS ELLIPSE`

`CIRCLE ( LENGTH , POINT ) RETURNS CIRCLE`

11.3 See the body of the chapter.

11.4 Yes, it does.

11.5 Specification signature:

`PTX ( PENTAGON , TRIANGLE ) RETURNS POLYGON`

Invocation signatures:

```
( REGULAR_PENTAGON , EQUILATERAL_TRIANGLE ) RETURNS SQUARE
( REGULAR_PENTAGON , ISOSCELES_TRIANGLE )   RETURNS SQUARE
( REGULAR_PENTAGON , TRIANGLE )             RETURNS RECTANGLE
( PENTAGON         , EQUILATERAL_TRIANGLE ) RETURNS POLYGON
( PENTAGON         , ISOSCELES_TRIANGLE )   RETURNS POLYGON
( PENTAGON         , TRIANGLE )             RETURNS POLYGON
```

Subsidiary exercise: How might the foregoing specification and invocation signatures be specified in concrete syntax? *Answer* (for definiteness I'll show the entire operator definition, at least in outline, but note that this answer isn't the only one possible):

```
OPERATOR PTX ( P PENTAGON , T TRIANGLE )
    RETURNS
        CASE
            WHEN IS_REGULAR_PENTAGON ( P ) AND
                 IS_ISOSCELES_TRIANGLE ( T ) THEN SQUARE
            WHEN IS_REGULAR_PENTAGON ( P ) THEN RECTANGLE
            ELSE POLYGON
        END CASE ;
    RETURN ( ... ) ;
END OPERATOR ;
```

11.6 For compile time vs. run time binding, see the body of the chapter. As for the second part of the exercise, the answer is *no*, but "almost" *yes*—see the aside (regarding union types etc.) in the subsection "More on Binding," in the section discussing IM Prescription 17.

11.7 Let *T″* be a proper subtype of *T′*. Let *V″* and *V′* be variables of declared types *T″* and *T′*, respectively. Obviously, every possible value of *V″* is also a possible value for *V′*; thus, if there's a "state" (i.e., a value) of *V″* that permits a certain update to be applied to that variable, there's also a state of *V′* that permits that same update to be applied to *that* variable. Thus, to say a certain update operator (inherited from type *T*) can be used to update variables of declared type *T″* but not variables of declared type *T′* is a contradiction in terms.

11.8 *Inclusion polymorphism* is implied by the very notion of type inheritance. *Value substitutability* is basically just inclusion polymorphism in a different guise. *"Result covariance"* (such as it is) is implied by value substitutability. *"Argument contravariance"* is a muddled concept, but the unmuddled analog—viz., that argument expressions must have declared type some subtype of that of the corresponding parameter—is also implied by value substitutability. *Implementation versions* are an implementation concept (obviously); they're likely to exist in any real system, but one such version per operator is all that's logically required by the model. *Specification signatures* and *invocation signatures* certainly exist, at least implicitly, by virtue of value and variable substitutability; *version signatures* are an implementation concept (but will exist in any real system that allows several implementation versions per operator). *Variable substitutability* (to the extent such a notion makes sense) is implied by the notion of update operators. *Binding* is an implementation concept (but will be found in any real system that allows several implementation versions per operator).

The net of all this seems to be: Everything to do with implementation versions is an implementation concept, the rest are model concepts. But those model concepts are all, in the final analysis, just a logical consequence of the fact that if T' is a subtype of T, then operators that apply to values of type T apply to values of type T' also. Everything else follows from this simple fact.

11.9 The formal reason is that type CIRCLE has no declared possrep with components called A and B; hence, no selector for type CIRCLE has A and B parameters, and no THE_A and THE_B pseudovariables are defined for that type. (By contrast, THE_A and THE_B read-only operators *are* defined—they're inherited from type ELLIPSE.)

Note: If we were to make (a,b,ctr) an explicitly declared possrep for type CIRCLE—which we could, if we wanted to—then THE_A and THE_B pseudovariables would be available for variables of declared type CIRCLE after all. However, any attempt to use them would fail at run time if it violated the constraint $a = b$.

Chapter 12

Union and Dummy Types

Here the impossible union ... is actual

—T. S. Eliot:
The Dry Salvages (1941)

dummy *adj. artificial, bogus, dry, fake, false, imitation, mock, phoney,*
practice, sham, simulated, trial
—*Chambers 20th Century Thesaurus* (1986)

This chapter is primarily concerned with the classification of scalar types into (a) union vs. nonunion types and (b) dummy vs. regular types. Note carefully, therefore, that all of the types mentioned in this chapter will be scalar types specifically, barring explicit statements to the contrary. Now, I've mentioned the special types *alpha* and *omega* several times in earlier chapters; what I haven't mentioned prior to this point, however, is that these types are actually union types, and indeed dummy types as well. (To be more specific, they're important special cases of these latter constructs.) Fig. 12.1 summarizes the situation.

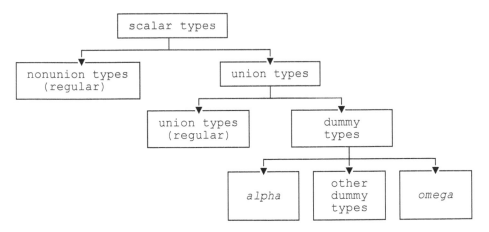

Fig. 12.1: Classification of scalar types

To elaborate briefly:

- A scalar type is either a nonunion type or a union type, and can't be both. All nonunion types are regular types.

- A union type is either a regular union type or a dummy type, and can't be both. All regular union types are union types, and so are all dummy types.

- *Alpha* and *omega* are dummy types, and therefore union types too (but in practice there'll probably be other dummy types in addition to *alpha* and *omega* per se).

- A regular type is either a nonunion type or a regular union type, and can't be both; in other words, a regular type is a scalar type that's not a dummy type. (These points aren't directly illustrated in the figure.)

- A regular type always has at least one explicitly declared possrep, at least if it's user defined. A dummy type has no possrep. (These points aren't directly illustrated in the figure either.)

This chapter explains these matters in depth.

IM PRESCRIPTION 20: UNION AND DUMMY TYPES ETC.

Type *T* shall be a **union type** if and only if it is a scalar type and there exists no value that is of type *T* and not of some immediate subtype of *T* (i.e., there exists no value *v* such that *MST*(*v*) is *T*). Moreover:

a. A type shall be a **dummy type** if and only if either of the following is true:

1. It is one of the types *alpha* and *omega* (see below).

2. It is a union type, has no declared possible representation (and hence no selector), and no regular supertype. *Note:* Type *alpha* in fact satisfies all three of these conditions; type *omega* satisfies the first two only.

A type shall be a **regular type** if and only if it is a scalar type and not a dummy type.

b. Conceptually, there shall be a system defined scalar type called *alpha*, the **maximal type** with respect to every scalar type. That type shall have all of the following properties:

1. It shall contain all scalar values.

2.   It shall have no immediate supertypes.

3.   It shall be an immediate supertype for every scalar root type in the given set of available types *GSAT*.

No other scalar type shall have any of these properties.

c.   Conceptually, there shall be a system defined scalar type called *omega*, the **minimal type** with respect to every scalar type. That type shall have all of the following properties:

1.   It shall contain no values at all. (It follows that, as RM Prescription 1 in fact states, it shall have no example value in particular.)[1]

2.   It shall have no immediate subtypes.

3.   It shall be an immediate subtype for every scalar leaf type in the given set of available types *GSAT*.

No other scalar type shall have any of these properties.

d.   The given set of available types *GSAT* shall contain at least one regular scalar type *T* such that *T* is neither a subtype nor a supertype of the required (and system defined) scalar type **boolean**.

In the Explorations version of this prescription, (a) the word "possible" was inadvertently omitted from part a., point 2; (b) the given set of available types—see Chapters 4 and 5 for further explanation—was denoted GST, not GSAT; and (c) the sentence beginning "No other scalar type" at the end of part b. read as follows: "No other scalar type shall have any of these properties (unless the given set of types GST contains just one regular type—necessarily type **boolean**—*in which unlikely case that type will of course satisfy the first property)." The situation described in parentheses in that sentence can't now occur, however, thanks to part d. of the prescription, which is new (see Exercise 12.2 at the end of the chapter).*

When I was discussing generalization by constraint in Chapter 8 (in the section on IM Prescription 11), I briefly considered the possibility of introducing an additional immediate

---

[1] RM Prescription 1 is the very first *TTM* prescription. The pertinent text from that prescription (which I've quoted a couple of times in this book already, in Chapters 2 and 6, respectively) reads as follows: "With the sole exception of the system defined empty type *omega* ... the definition of any given scalar type *T* shall be accompanied by a specification of an **example value** of that type."

subtype of type ELLIPSE called NONCIRCLE, with the intuitively obvious semantics. By way of an introduction to some of the issues raised by IM Prescription 20, let's examine that possibility a little more closely. Refer to Fig. 12.2.

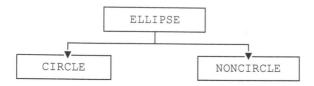

Fig. 12.2: ELLIPSE as a union type (possibly a dummy type)

Type ELLIPSE is now a union type: Every ellipse is either a circle or a noncircle—i.e., there's no value of type ELLIPSE that's not a value of some immediate subtype of that type—and so the set of values |ELLIPSE| constituting type ELLIPSE is the union of the sets of values |CIRCLE| and |NONCIRCLE| constituting types CIRCLE and NONCIRCLE, respectively.[2] *Note:* Actually the union in question is a *disjoint* union, because no ellipse is both a circle and a noncircle. Indeed, it must be a disjoint union as far as the present chapter is concerned, for otherwise we'd be in violation of the disjointness assumption (I remind you once again that we're still in the context of single inheritance only).

> *Aside: Union type* is the traditional term for this concept (see, e.g., *An Introduction to Data Types*, by J. Craig Cleaveland, Addison-Wesley, 1986). Be aware, however, that other terms are found in the literature, including *abstract* type, *noninstantiable* type (on the grounds, presumably, that such a type has no "instances"),[3] or occasionally just *interface*. A type that's not a union type is then referred to as a *concrete* type, an *instantiable* type, or just a *type* (unqualified), respectively. *End of aside.*

UNION TYPES

A union type is a type that's not the most specific type of any value at all. Unless it's type *omega*, therefore—a pathological case, which I'll ignore until further notice—such a type must have immediate subtypes, and every value of the type in question must be a value of one of those immediate subtypes. Moreover, the specialization constraints for those immediate subtypes (see the discussion of IM Prescription 10 in Chapter 8) must be such as to guarantee that this

---

[2] Recall from Chapter 5 that the symbol |*T*| denotes the set of values constituting type *T*.

[3] The term *instance* is used a lot in the object literature, but its meaning isn't always entirely clear. Depending on context, in fact, it seems it can denote any or all of the following: a value; a variable; an occurrence, or appearance, of a value (or even of a variable?); and possibly other things besides. See Chapters 21 and 22 for further discussion.

requirement is met.[4] Note that union types don't make sense outside of the inheritance context, because they rely on the concept, and indeed existence, of certain proper (in fact, immediate) subtypes.

Why might it be desirable to define a union type? The principal reason is that such a definition provides a way of defining operators—or defining the pertinent specification and invocation signatures, at any rate—that apply to values and variables of several different types, all of them immediate subtypes of the union type in question. Appropriate implementation versions of the operator in question can then be defined, if necessary, at each of the applicable subtype levels. By way of illustration, here are type definitions and one operator definition for the types shown in Fig. 12.2 in the previous section:

```
TYPE ELLIPSE UNION
     IS { PLANE_FIGURE
          POSSREP ( A LENGTH , B LENGTH , CTR POINT )
          CONSTRAINT A ≥ B
          NOT { RECTANGLE ( ... ) } } ;

TYPE CIRCLE
     IS { ELLIPSE
          CONSTRAINT THE_A ( ELLIPSE ) = THE_B ( ELLIPSE )
          POSSREP ( R   = THE_A   ( ELLIPSE ) ,
                    CTR = THE_CTR ( ELLIPSE ) )
          NOT { NONCIRCLE ( LENGTH ( 2.0 ) ,
                            LENGTH ( 1.0 ) , POINT ( 0.0 , 0.0 ) ) } } ;

TYPE NONCIRCLE
     IS { ELLIPSE
          CONSTRAINT THE_A ( ELLIPSE ) > THE_B ( ELLIPSE )
          POSSREP ( A   = THE_A   ( ELLIPSE ) ,
                    B   = THE_B   ( ELLIPSE ) ,
                    CTR = THE_CTR ( ELLIPSE ) )
          NOT { CIRCLE ( LENGTH ( 1.0 ) , POINT ( 0.0 , 0.0 ) ) } } ;

OPERATOR AREA_OF ( E ELLIPSE ) RETURNS AREA ;
     /* declared type of parameter E is a union type, */
     /* but the following implementation code works   */
     /* for both circles and noncircles               */
     RETURN ( 3.14159 * THE_A ( E ) * THE_B ( E ) ) ;
END OPERATOR ;
```

Points arising:

■ Union types are explicitly declared as such—note the UNION specification in the definition of type ELLIPSE. The <*is def*> for that union type ELLIPSE (a) defines that type to be an immediate subtype of type PLANE_FIGURE; (b) specifies the (*a,b,ctr*) possrep in the usual way; (c) specifies the constraint $a \geq b$, also in the usual way; and

---

[4] Assuming such specialization constraints exist, that is, which will be the case so long as the union type in question isn't a dummy type (see the next section).

(d) gives an example via the NOT specification—see the next bullet item below—to show that there's at least one value of type PLANE_FIGURE that's not a value of type ELLIPSE. *Note:* Actually, that type PLANE_FIGURE, which I deliberately don't want to discuss in detail until the next section, is also a union type; in fact, it's a dummy type.

■ To repeat, the purpose of the NOT specification for type ELLIPSE is to show that there's at least one value of type PLANE_FIGURE that's not a value of type ELLIPSE; in other words, it guarantees that the set of values |ELLIPSE| is a proper subset of the set of values |PLANE_FIGURE|. The PLANE_FIGURE value in question happens to be a rectangle (and thus a plane figure a fortiori), and it's specified by means of a RECTANGLE selector invocation. (The argument expressions are omitted from that invocation simply because I haven't discussed an appropriate possrep for type RECTANGLE in this book prior to this point.) Note that what we can't do here is specify a plane figure "directly"—i.e., by means of a PLANE_FIGURE selector invocation—because, as noted above, PLANE_FIGURE is a dummy type and thus has no possrep and no selectors (see the next section).

■ Similarly, the purpose of the NOT specifications for types CIRCLE and NONCIRCLE is to guarantee that the sets of values |CIRCLE| and |NONCIRCLE| are proper subsets of the set of values |ELLIPSE|. Of course, any noncircle will do as the example value for type CIRCLE and any circle will do as the example value for type NONCIRCLE; I show the particular values I do just for definiteness.

Other aspects of the *<is def>*s (for all three types shown) are more or less as explained in earlier chapters. Note in particular, however, that ellipses are constrained to have $a \geq b$ while circles and noncircles are constrained to have $a = b$ and $a > b$, respectively. It follows that, first, types CIRCLE and NONCIRCLE are disjoint (which, as noted earlier, is consistent with the disjointness assumption, of course); second, those types together "span" type ELLIPSE, in the sense that every ellipse is either a circle or a noncircle. Taken together, therefore, these constraints guarantee that (as required) there's no value of type ELLIPSE that's not a value of one of its immediate subtypes.

Aside: The *Manifesto* book says the constraint $a \geq b$ for type ELLIPSE "seems to be redundant," but it isn't. For suppose it weren't specified, and consider an attempt to select an ellipse with $a < b$. That attempt has to fail—but how? What constraint does it violate? It can't be the constraint for type ELLIPSE, because (by default) that one would just be TRUE. What this thought experiment shows is that if the constraint $a \geq b$ weren't specified for type ELLIPSE, then either that type would need another immediate subtype, with constraint $a < b$, or (perhaps more likely in practice) the constraint $a > b$ for type NONCIRCLE would have to be replaced by $a \neq b$ (which is, of course, shorthand for $a > b$ OR $a < b$). *End of aside.*

Here are some further points:

■ Since type ELLIPSE does have a declared possrep, it also has a selector (of declared type ELLIPSE), but invoking that selector will never return a value of most specific type ELLIPSE, because there aren't any values of most specific type ELLIPSE.

■ A variable of declared type ELLIPSE will always have most specific type some proper subtype of ELLIPSE because, again, there aren't any values of most specific type ELLIPSE.

■ Operator AREA_OF is defined at the ELLIPSE level. That is, its sole parameter E is of declared type ELLIPSE, and its specification signature looks like this:

```
AREA_OF ( ELLIPSE ) RETURNS AREA
```

The corresponding (albeit implicit) invocation signatures look like this:

```
( CIRCLE     ) RETURNS AREA
( NONCIRCLE  ) RETURNS AREA
( ELLIPSE    ) RETURNS AREA
```

However, the argument to an invocation of AREA_OF will never have most specific type ELLIPSE. To say it one more time, there aren't any such values.

■ The fact that ELLIPSE is now a union type doesn't mean that operators can't have ELLIPSE as their declared type. For example, the specification signature for our read-only MOVE operator (see Chapters 7 and 11) will still specify ELLIPSE as the declared type of that operator—but, of course, no MOVE invocation will now ever return a result of most specific type ELLIPSE.

Finally, a union type obviously can't be a leaf type. As noted in the discussion of IM Prescription 5 in Chapter 5, however (albeit not in these words), it would be possible to set up the type hierarchy in such a way that all types other than leaf types are union types; in terms of our running example, introducing type NONCIRCLE as above, together with types NONRECTANGLE and NONSQUARE (with the obvious semantics) as immediate subtypes of POLYGON and RECTANGLE, respectively, would have such an effect. *All most specific types must be leaf types* might thus be regarded as the extreme form of the union types idea, and some writers have indeed advocated such a notion. Our model doesn't prohibit such an arrangement, but it doesn't insist on it, either; in other words, we do allow values to exist whose most specific type is, say, RECTANGLE and not SQUARE (as of course we already know).

DUMMY TYPES

A dummy type is a union type that has no possrep, and therefore no possrep constraint in particular[5] (and any scalar type that's not a dummy type is a regular type). By way of example, let me revise types ELLIPSE, CIRCLE, and NONCIRCLE from the previous section to make ELLIPSE a dummy type, thus:

```
TYPE ELLIPSE UNION
     IS { PLANE_FIGURE
          NOT { RECTANGLE ( ... ) } } ;

TYPE CIRCLE
     IS { ELLIPSE
          POSSREP ( R LENGTH , CTR POINT )
          NOT { NONCIRCLE ( LENGTH ( 2.0 ) ,
                            LENGTH ( 1.0 ) , POINT ( 0.0 , 0.0 ) ) } } ;

TYPE NONCIRCLE
     IS { ELLIPSE
          POSSREP ( A LENGTH , B LENGTH , CTR POINT )
          CONSTRAINT A > B
          NOT { CIRCLE ( LENGTH ( 1.0 ) , POINT ( 0.0 , 0.0 ) ) } } ;
```

Points arising:

- Type ELLIPSE is still a union type as it was in the previous section, but now it's a dummy type as well: It has no possrep, and hence no possrep constraint either. Note that the fact that it has no possrep means that, unlike type ELLIPSE in the previous section, it also has no selector and no THE_ operators (at least, no automatically defined ones, but see further discussion below).

- No *additional constraint def*s—see the section "A BNF Grammar" in Chapter 3—have been specified for types CIRCLE and NONCIRCLE, since type ELLIPSE has no possrep in terms of which such additional constraints might be formulated. Thus, specialization by constraint, as such, no longer applies to those types; that is, circles and noncircles can no longer be obtained from ellipses via S by C. (By contrast, note that S by C did apply to those types when ELLIPSE was a union type but not a dummy type.)

- Type CIRCLE does have a possrep—though, for simplicity, no associated possrep constraint[6]—and a selector. It also has some THE_ operators (THE_R and THE_CTR).

---

[5] Recall from Chapters 2 and 3 that a possrep constraint is a constraint that's explicitly formulated in terms of the possrep(s) declared for the type whose definition the constraint in question is defined as part of. The constraint specified for type ELLIPSE in the previous section (to the effect that $a \geq b$) is an example.

[6] In any case, the only such constraint that would seem to make any sense is the rather obvious one R > LENGTH (0.0)—and even that would be unnecessary if type LENGTH is subject to a type constraint saying that lengths must be positive.

Note that THE_A and THE_B now no longer apply to type CIRCLE (nor do they apply to type ELLIPSE, of course—see the next bullet item but one).

- Type NONCIRCLE also has a possrep and a selector; unlike type CIRCLE, it also has an associated possrep constraint. It also has some THE_ operators (THE_A, THE_B, and THE_CTR).

- Operators THE_A and THE_B no longer apply to expressions of declared type ELLIPSE, since that type has no corresponding possrep (indeed, to repeat, it has no possrep at all). *Note:* By contrast, the operator THE_CTR might still apply (see further discussion below).[7]

- The implementation version of the AREA_OF operator shown in the previous section won't work any longer (basically because that version was defined at the ELLIPSE level, and type ELLIPSE now has no possrep in terms of which such a version might be defined).[8] Instead, we'll effectively have to give just a specification signature (and invocation signatures as well, at least implicitly) at the ELLIPSE level and then provide appropriate implementation versions at the CIRCLE and NONCIRCLE levels, perhaps as follows:

```
OPERATOR AREA_OF ( E ELLIPSE ) RETURNS AREA ;
    /* declared type of parameter E is a dummy type; */
    /* no implementation code provided at this level */
END OPERATOR ;

OPERATOR AREA_OF VERSION AREA_OF_C ( C CIRCLE ) RETURNS AREA ;
    /* implementation version for type CIRCLE */
    RETURN ( 3.14159 * ( THE_R ( C ) ^ 2 ) ) ;
END OPERATOR ;

OPERATOR AREA_OF VERSION AREA_OF_NC ( NC NONCIRCLE ) RETURNS AREA ;
    /* implementation version for type NONCIRCLE */
    RETURN ( 3.14159 * THE_A ( NC ) * THE_B ( NC ) ) ;
END OPERATOR ;
```

- Note finally that I'm assuming for the sake of the example that PLANE_FIGURE too is a dummy type and thus has no possrep and no selectors. (As mentioned in the answer to Exercise 3.10 in Chapter 3, it's hard to think of a sensible possrep that could work for an

---

[7] Actually THE_A and THE_B could be made to apply to type ELLIPSE if desired, using the same scheme as for THE_CTR (see that same "further discussion below")—in which case they'd apply to type CIRCLE after all, because they'd be inherited.

[8] Two points here: First, these remarks shouldn't be construed as meaning that we can never specify implementation code at a dummy type level (see the discussion of DOUBLE_AREA_OF, later in this section, for a counterexample). Second, if we were to *force* THE_A and THE_B to apply to type ELLIPSE—see the previous footnote—then the implementation code shown for AREA_OF in the previous section would work after all.

arbitrary plane figure. And in any case, Exercise 12.6 at the end of the chapter shows that if ELLIPSE is a dummy type, then PLANE_FIGURE must be too.)

Now, the foregoing example isn't very realistic, because we've already seen in the previous section that if we were to make ELLIPSE a regular union type—i.e., one with a possrep—instead of a dummy type, then we could define an implementation version of AREA_OF at the ELLIPSE level that would work for both circles and noncircles. But consider type PLANE_FIGURE, which as I've just said would almost certainly be a dummy type. Given that fact, it surely does make sense to give just the pertinent signatures for AREA_OF at the PLANE_FIGURE level and corresponding implementation versions at, say, the ELLIPSE and POLYGON levels.

Despite the foregoing, let's stay with the example of ELLIPSE as a dummy type, for simplicity. In particular, let's focus on the operator THE_CTR ("the center of"). Observe now that THE_CTR is "automatically" defined for types CIRCLE and NONCIRCLE but not for type ELLIPSE. In other words, the expression THE_CTR(E) is valid if E has declared type either CIRCLE or NONCIRCLE, but not if it has declared type ELLIPSE. But such a state of affairs is clearly absurd! To say every ellipse is either a circle or a noncircle, and circles and noncircles both have a center but ellipses as such don't, is an affront to common sense. After all, compare the situation with areas: Every ellipse has an area, because every ellipse is either a circle or a noncircle and circles and noncircles both have an area, and so we do allow AREA_OF to be applied to expressions of declared type ELLIPSE. By analogy, therefore, we should surely be allowed to do the same with THE_CTR, if we wanted to. (Indeed, if we didn't, then THE_CTR would be overloaded—I mean, there'd be two distinct operators with that name, one for type CIRCLE and one for type NONCIRCLE—and we wouldn't be talking about inclusion polymorphism any more.)

The anomaly is easily fixed, however—we simply assert, by fiat as it were, that THE_CTR does apply at the ELLIPSE level after all, thus:[9]

```
OPERATOR THE_CTR ( E ELLIPSE ) RETURNS POINT ;
   /* declared type of parameter E is a dummy type; */
   /* no implementation code provided at this level */
END OPERATOR ;
```

Thus, for example, the assignment

```
P := THE_CTR ( E ) ;
```

---

[9] Note that implementation versions of this operator will certainly be provided for both circles and noncircles. Note too, however, that THE_CTR here is indeed a THE_ operator in the usual sense of that term (meaning among other things that it has prescribed semantics, and those semantics mustn't be changed). In particular, as we'll see in a moment, it can be used as a pseudovariable—a fact that suggests that simply providing a specification signature at the ELLIPSE level might not quite be adequate as a mechanism for "asserting that THE_CTR does apply," since other operators defined in such a fashion are generally not usable as pseudovariables. Perhaps more research is required.

(where P is of declared type POINT and E is of declared type ELLIPSE) is effectively shorthand for something like the following:

```
P := CASE
        WHEN IS_CIRCLE ( E ) THEN
                THE_CTR ( TREAT_AS_CIRCLE ( E ) )
        WHEN IS_NONCIRCLE ( E ) THEN
                THE_CTR ( TREAT_AS_NONCIRCLE ( E ) )
     END CASE ;
```

Likewise, the assignment

```
THE_CTR ( E ) := P ;
```

(where P and E are as before and THE_CTR is being used as a pseudovariable) is effectively shorthand for something like the following:

```
E := CASE
        WHEN IS_CIRCLE ( E ) THEN
                CIRCLE ( THE_R ( TREAT_AS_CIRCLE ( E ) ) , P )
        WHEN IS_NONCIRCLE ( E ) THEN
                NONCIRCLE ( THE_A ( TREAT_AS_NONCIRCLE ( E ) ) ,
                            THE_B ( TREAT_AS_NONCIRCLE ( E ) ) , P )
     END CASE ;
```

Now, I don't mean to suggest by anything I've said so far that implementation code for operators defined at the level of some dummy type *must* be provided at the level of the pertinent subtypes. By way of a trivial counterexample, we might define an operator called DOUBLE_AREA_OF, with the intuitively obvious semantics, at the ELLIPSE level or even (more strikingly) at the PLANE_FIGURE level, thus:

```
OPERATOR DOUBLE_AREA_OF ( PF PLANE_FIGURE ) RETURNS AREA ;
    RETURN ( 2 * AREA_OF ( PF ) ) ;
END OPERATOR ;
```

I'll close this section with a couple of miscellaneous observations. First, certain system defined types resemble dummy types in that they're allowed by *The Third Manifesto* to have no explicitly declared possrep (type INTEGER is a case in point). Such types aren't dummy types, however, because (a) values do exist, in general, whose most specific type is the type in question, and (b) in any case there's a *TTM* prescription—see footnote 23 in Chapter 2—that requires the type in question to have at least one associated selector that permits the specification of literals whose most specific type is the type in question.[10]

---

[10] See also the answer to Exercise 5.6 in Chapter 5, which contains some further considerations that might possibly be relevant to this issue.

Second, I note that some systems and languages use dummy types as a way of providing what might be regarded as a kind of type generator functionality. For example, RELATION might be a dummy type in such a system (with generic operators JOIN, UNION, and so forth), and every specific relation type would then be a proper subtype of that dummy type. We don't adopt such an approach in our model, however, because we certainly don't want support for type generators in general, and support for the RELATION type generator in particular, to rely on support for inheritance. (Note among other things that such an approach would make support for inheritance a mandatory part of *The Third Manifesto*, which it currently isn't.) What's more, such an approach would seem to imply that specific implementation code must be provided for each specific join, each specific union, and so forth—surely not a very desirable state of affairs. (Contrast the situation with a relational DBMS, where all such operations are done by means of generic, optimized, system provided code.) Finally, the kind of relation type inheritance—if any (?)—that such an approach to relation types seems to entail isn't the kind of relation type inheritance we think we need; in particular, it doesn't provide the kind of substitutability we think we need. See Part IV of this book for a detailed discussion of our own approach to relation type inheritance.

TYPES *alpha* AND *omega*

As noted in the introduction to this chapter, I've mentioned types *alpha* and *omega* several times in this book already—in Chapter 6 in particular, where I said this:

■ Type *omega* is the empty scalar type—it contains no values at all. And, since the empty set is a subset of every set, it follows that type *omega* is a subtype of every scalar type (itself included, of course) [...].

■ Type *alpha* [is] type *omega*'s polar opposite; in other words, where type *omega* contains no values at all, type *alpha* contains *all* values (all scalar values, that is), and it's a supertype of every scalar type, itself included [...].

Now it's time to get more specific.

Recall first that distinct root types, and hence distinct scalar root types in particular, are necessarily disjoint. However, we can always invent some kind of "system" type that's an immediate supertype for those scalar root types, thereby effectively tying all of the corresponding type hierarchies together into one. In fact, some object systems come ready equipped with such a type, often called OBJECT (on the grounds that "everything's an object"). In our model, we address this issue by introducing a special scalar type that we call *alpha* (or α, if you prefer Greek letters). *Alpha* is the *maximal* scalar type: It contains all scalar values and is a supertype of every scalar type (more precisely, it's an immediate supertype of every scalar root type, and it's a proper supertype of every scalar type except itself).[11]

> *Aside:* Actually, IM Prescription 20 doesn't say *alpha* is an immediate supertype of *every* scalar root type, it says it's an immediate supertype of every scalar root type *in the given set of available types GSAT.* (Of course, an analogous remark applies to *omega* also, mutatis mutandis.) In practice, we don't usually bother to mention *GSAT* at all but simply take it as understood—and indeed IM Prescription 20 is the only one of the IM prescriptions to make any explicit reference to it. In any given situation, however, *GSAT* must necessarily exist, at least conceptually. See the introductory remarks in either Chapter 4 or Chapter 5 if you need to refresh your memory regarding this notion. *End of aside.*

Analogously, we introduce another special scalar type that we call *omega* (or ω). *Omega* is the *minimal* scalar type: It contains no values at all and is a subtype of every scalar type (more precisely, it's an immediate subtype of every scalar leaf type, and it's a proper subtype of every scalar type except itself).

Here are some more specifics regarding type *alpha*:

- *Alpha* is indeed a dummy type—it has no possrep and hence no selector.

- The corresponding type constraint is just TRUE.

- IS_*alpha* (...) always gives TRUE.

- TREAT_AS_*alpha* (...) always succeeds.

As for type *omega* (which, perhaps surprisingly, turns out to be more important than type *alpha* in certain respects, as we'll see in Part IV):

- *Omega* is also a dummy type—it has no possrep and hence no selector. Observe, incidentally, that *omega* genuinely is a union type (as all dummy types must be) because, by definition, there's no value of type *omega* that's not a value of some immediate subtype of *omega*. (You might want to read that sentence again.)

- The corresponding type constraint is just FALSE.

---

[11] Recall that (in accordance with IM Prescription 6) *alpha* itself isn't regarded as a root type, nor is *omega* regarded as a leaf type. Recall too from Chapter 6 that *alpha* and *omega* are primarily conceptual in nature anyway, meaning among other things that we wouldn't expect the user to have to declare them. *Note:* Also, in accordance with part c. of IM Prescription 5, scalar root types need no NOT specification.

■ IS_*omega* (...) always gives FALSE.

■ TREAT_AS_*omega* (...) always fails (or would always fail, perhaps, since the expression is clearly a contradiction in terms and might well be rejected at compile time).

■ No variable, no operator, and in fact no expression can have either declared or most specific type *omega*.

■ Type *omega* inherits all possible read-only operators, but vacuously so, since they can never be invoked on any value of the type.

Finally, let me remind you from Chapter 6 that, since it's a subtype of every scalar type, the introduction of type *omega* takes us, by definition, into the realm of multiple inheritance. (This is one reason why it really makes little logical sense to consider single inheritance only—despite the fact that I've been doing exactly that for most of this book, prior to this point! But I was doing so for pedagogical reasons, not logical ones.) Indeed, the introduction of *omega* into any given type hierarchy has the effect of converting that hierarchy into a lattice. See Chapter 14 for further discussion.

EXERCISES

12.1 Fig. 12.1 shows the relationships between union, dummy, and regular types (or some of those relationships, at any rate). (a) Try reproducing that figure from memory. (b) Do you think that figure might be regarded as representing a type hierarchy? Explain your answer.

12.2 Our inheritance model requires that *alpha* and *omega* be unique, in the sense that *alpha* is the only universal scalar type and *omega* is the only empty scalar type. But how are these requirements enforced? *Note:* The term *universal scalar type* wasn't used in the body of the chapter, but the intended meaning is surely clear.

12.3 What's the point of defining a (regular, or in other words nondummy) union type? What's the point of defining a dummy type?

12.4 Is it true that any given union type must have at least two immediate subtypes? If so, why? Also, can such subtypes be union types in turn? Can they be dummy types? Do they have to be disjoint?

12.5 Can a type that's not a union type have an immediate subtype that is?

12.6 Can a dummy type have a regular supertype?

12.7 Can a type that has a union type as an immediate supertype have any other immediate supertypes (union or otherwise)?

12.8 Suppose we drop all types from Fig. 5.1 except for type CIRCLE. Suppose further, not very realistically, that we make type CIRCLE a (regular) union type, with immediate subtypes O_CIRCLE and NON_O_CIRCLE, with the intuitively obvious semantics. Show some appropriate type definitions. Also show how we might define the AREA_OF operator in this situation.

12.9 Repeat Exercise 12.8 but make CIRCLE a dummy type. This time, show also how we might define the THE_R operator.

12.10   It has been suggested that the syntax of a union type definition might profitably be extended to include the names—and further details, perhaps—of the immediate subtypes of the union type in question. Discuss.

ANSWERS

12.1 (a) *No answer provided.* (b) Well, it's certainly true that the figure represents what might be regarded as a set of subtype / supertype relationships. However, if that figure is to be understood as representing a type hierarchy, then the nodes in the figure must be understood as representing types, where the values constituting those types are themselves types.[12] For example, if *S* and *U* are types whose constituent sets of values are the set of all scalar types and the set of all union types, respectively, then *U* is clearly a subtype of *S*. So: If we agree to interpret the node labeled *alpha* as representing not type *alpha* as such, but rather a type whose sole value is type *alpha* (and similarly for the node labeled *omega*), then yes, the figure might be regarded as representing some kind of type hierarchy—or a "meta" type hierarchy, perhaps (?).

That said, observe that the figure doesn't show all of the subtype / supertype relationships we might wish it to. In particular, it doesn't show that "nonunion types" and "regular union types" are both subtypes of "regular types" (note that there's no "regular types" node). Moreover, if we tried to add such a node, then (a) "nonunion types" and "regular union types" would both have two distinct immediate supertypes, meaning the graph would no longer be a hierarchy as such, and (b) "regular types" and "union types" together would violate

---

[12] Note that it might certainly be argued that types as such are indeed values, albeit values of rather a special kind (values of type TYPE, perhaps?). More specifically, a type is a pair of the form <*N*,*S*>, where *N* is a name and *S* is a set of values—and such a pair in turn is certainly a value.

the disjointness assumption, since they certainly wouldn't be disjoint, and yet neither would be a subtype of the other.

12.2 The uniqueness of *omega* is guaranteed because the definition of every other scalar type is required to be accompanied by an example value of the type in question (hence, the type in question must be nonempty). As for *alpha*, so long as there are at least two distinct type hierarchies, then no type—in particular, no root type—can possibly contain all scalar values, since distinct root types are disjoint (and nonempty). But there *will* be at least two distinct type hierarchies, thanks to part d. of IM Prescription 20. Thus, the uniqueness of *alpha* is guaranteed as well.

12.3 A (nondummy) union type serves as a basis for specifying operators that apply to values and variables of several different types, all of them immediate subtypes of the union type in question. A dummy type[13] does the same, but in situations where it doesn't make sense (for some reason) to specify a possrep at the level of the union type—i.e., the dummy type, in this case—in question.

12.4 Let *T* be a union type other than *omega*.[14] Then *T* must have at least two immediate subtypes because if it had just one or none at all, then—since "proper subtypes are proper subsets"—there'd be some values of type *T* that weren't values of any immediate subtype of *T*. But there can't be any such values, by definition of the very concept of a union type.

An immediate subtype of a union type can be a union type. For example, suppose as in the examples in the body of the chapter that ELLIPSE is a union type. ELLIPSE has CIRCLE as an immediate subtype. But CIRCLE might be a union type in turn, with immediate subtypes the regular types O_CIRCLE and NON_O_CIRCLE (see Exercise 12.8).

An immediate subtype of a union type can be a dummy type, but only if the union type in question is also a dummy type. See the answer to Exercise 12.6 for further discussion. *Note:* Type *omega* is a special case here, however. Type *omega* is a dummy type, but it's a subtype of every scalar type, regular types included; so *omega* is an example (actually the only one) of a dummy type with regular types as proper supertypes.

There's no intrinsic reason why the immediate subtypes of a union type have to be disjoint, but if they're not they'll violate the disjointness assumption, and we'll be moving into the realm of multiple inheritance (see Part III of this book).

---

[13] Other than type *omega*, that is (see the next footnote).

[14] Type *omega* is excluded because it has no immediate subtypes at all, of course (as I said in the body of the chapter, it's really a pathological case).

12.5 A type that's not a union type can have an immediate subtype that is. For example, type RECTANGLE, which isn't a union type, has SQUARE as an immediate subtype. Suppose every square is either a "large square" or a "small square," and no square is both. Then we could define LARGE_SQUARE and SMALL_SQUARE as immediate subtypes of SQUARE, and SQUARE itself would be a union type.

12.6 Unless it's type *omega*—which is a very special case, discussed in the answer to Exercise 12.4—a dummy type can't have a regular supertype. In fact, IM Prescription 20 explicitly states as much. But it's worth taking a moment to think about why it does so. Let type *T'* be an immediate subtype of type *T*, and let *T'* and *T* be a dummy type and a regular type, respectively. Since it's a regular type, *T* has a possrep and a selector, and so there's a way to select any given value of type *T*. In particular, therefore, there's a way to select any given value of type *T'*. But a dummy type has no possrep and no selector, and so there isn't supposed to be a way to select a given value of type *T'* after all. There seems to be some kind of contradiction here.

Another way to think about the matter is this: If *T* has a possrep, then *T'* at least has an inherited possrep, even if it doesn't have a declared one. But of course we could always make that inherited possrep an explicitly declared one if we wanted to. However, it's of the essence of the dummy type idea that there's no possrep that makes sense (think of type PLANE_FIGURE, for example); indeed, if there were such a possrep, there'd be no point in making the type a dummy type in the first place—we might as well make it a regular type.

The net of all the foregoing (speaking very loosely!) is that as we travel up the type hierarchy, once we encounter a dummy type, it's dummy types all the way, from that point to the very top (i.e., up to and including the root, and in fact including type *alpha* as well).

12.7 There's no intrinsic reason why a type that has a union type as an immediate supertype can't have any other immediate supertypes, but if it does they'll violate the disjointness assumption and we'll be moving into the realm of multiple inheritance (see Part III of this book).

12.8 Here's type CIRCLE as a regular union root type:

```
TYPE CIRCLE UNION POSSREP ( R LENGTH , CTR POINT )
                          CONSTRAINT R > LENGTH ( 0.0 ) ;
```

Here's the rest of the type hierarchy:

```
TYPE O_CIRCLE
     IS { CIRCLE
          CONSTRAINT THE_CTR ( CIRCLE ) = POINT ( 0.0 , 0.0 )
          POSSREP ( R = THE_R ( CIRCLE ) )
          NOT { CIRCLE { LENGTH ( 1.0 ) , POINT ( 1.0 , 1.0 ) ) } } ;
```

```
TYPE NON_O_CIRCLE
    IS { CIRCLE
         CONSTRAINT THE_CTR ( CIRCLE ) ≠ POINT ( 0.0 , 0.0 )
         POSSREP ( R   = THE_R ( CIRCLE ) ,
                   CTR = THE_CTR ( CIRCLE ) )
         NOT { CIRCLE ( LENGTH ( 1.0 ) , POINT ( 0.0 , 0.0 ) ) } } ;
```

Here's the definition of operator AREA_OF:

```
OPERATOR AREA_OF ( C CIRCLE ) RETURNS AREA ;
    /* declared type of parameter C is a union type, */
    /* but the following implementation code works   */
    /* for both O-circles and non O-circles:         */
    RETURN ( 3.14159 * ( THE_R ( C ) ^ 2 ) ) ;
END OPERATOR ;
```

12.9 Here's type CIRCLE as a dummy root type:

```
TYPE CIRCLE UNION ;
```

Here's the rest of the type hierarchy:

```
TYPE O_CIRCLE
    IS { CIRCLE POSSREP ( R LENGTH )
         CONSTRAINT R > LENGTH ( 0.0 )
         NOT
         { NON_O_CIRCLE { LENGTH ( 1.0 ) , POINT ( 1.0 , 1.0 ) ) } } ;

TYPE NON_O_CIRCLE
    IS { CIRCLE POSSREP ( R LENGTH , CTR POINT )
         CONSTRAINT R > LENGTH ( 0.0 ) AND
                    CTR ≠ POINT ( 0.0 , 0.0 ) }
         NOT { O_CIRCLE ( LENGTH ( 1.0 ) ) } } ;
```

Operator definitions:

```
OPERATOR AREA_OF ( C CIRCLE ) RETURNS AREA ;
    /* declared type of parameter C is a dummy type; */
    /* no implementation code provided at this level */
END OPERATOR ;

OPERATOR AREA_OF VERSION O_AREA ( O O_CIRCLE ) RETURNS AREA ;
    /* implementation version for type O_CIRCLE */
    RETURN ( 3.14159 * ( THE_R ( O ) ^ 2 ) ) ;
END OPERATOR ;

OPERATOR AREA_OF VERSION N_AREA ( N NON_O_CIRCLE ) RETURNS AREA ;
    /* implementation version for type NON_O_CIRCLE */
    RETURN ( 3.14159 * ( THE_R ( N ) ^ 2 ) ) ;
END OPERATOR ;
```

Of course, the implementation code here for types O_CIRCLE and NON_O_CIRCLE is essentially the same. We can simplify the situation by defining THE_R to apply at the dummy type level:

```
OPERATOR THE_R ( C CIRCLE ) RETURNS LENGTH ;
    /* declared type of parameter C is a dummy type; */
    /* no implementation code provided at this level */
END OPERATOR ;
```

Then, e.g., the assignment

```
L := THE_R ( C ) ;
```

(where L is of declared type LENGTH and C is of declared type CIRCLE) will effectively be shorthand for something like the following:

```
L := CASE
        WHEN IS_O_CIRCLE ( C ) THEN
              THE_R ( TREAT_AS_O_CIRCLE ( C ) )
        WHEN IS_NON_O_CIRCLE ( C ) THEN
              THE_R ( TREAT_AS_NON_O_CIRCLE ( C ) )
     END CASE ;
```

Now we can drop the two implementation versions of AREA_OF for types O_CIRCLE and NON_O_CIRCLE and replace the AREA_OF specification at the CIRCLE level by the following:

```
OPERATOR AREA_OF ( C CIRCLE ) RETURNS AREA ;
    RETURN ( 3.14159 * ( THE_R ( C ) ^ 2 ) ) ;
END OPERATOR ;
```

12.10 Consider the example from the body of the chapter in which ELLIPSE is a union type—not a dummy type—with CIRCLE and NONCIRCLE as nonunion immediate subtypes. Since type ELLIPSE can't sensibly be said to exist until types CIRCLE and NONCIRCLE have been defined, in practice it seems likely that all three type definitions would have to be bundled up into a single statement.[15] (All we might need to do, syntactically speaking, to achieve such a bundling is replace the first two semicolons by commas.)

Suppose, however, that (a) the suggested syntactic solution—i.e., using commas instead of semicolons—isn't supported, and (b) the system therefore requires CIRCLE and NONCIRCLE to be mentioned in the ELLIPSE definition. We might try:

---

[15] I note in passing that another reason why distinct type definitions might need to be bundled up into a single statement is the fact that, as we saw several times in the body of the chapter, the definition of type *T1* might refer in its NOT specification to some type *T2* that's not a supertype of *T1*.

```
TYPE ELLIPSE UNION { CIRCLE , NONCIRCLE } ...
     POSSREP ( A LENGTH , B LENGTH , CTR POINT ... ) ;
```

But the very fact that it mentions CIRCLE and NONCIRCLE lends further weight to the idea that the ELLIPSE definition needs to be bundled with the CIRCLE and NONCIRCLE definitions—for otherwise we're faced with the possibility that a type definition might be allowed to complete execution even if it includes a reference to something that doesn't yet exist, and in fact might never exist. And if we do bundle the three definitions into a single statement, then allowing CIRCLE and NONCIRCLE to be mentioned in the ELLIPSE definition doesn't seem to achieve very much.

Despite the foregoing, let's stay for the moment with the assumption that three separate statements are required. What happens if we work bottom up, as it were, and define the subtypes first?—

```
TYPE CIRCLE IS { ELLIPSE ...
```

Well, we run into a problem right away: namely, we have a reference, again, in the definition of one type to another that hasn't yet been defined, and might never be defined. So that won't work.

Perhaps we could define the subtypes first, without mentioning the supertype at all?—

```
TYPE CIRCLE     POSSREP ( R LENGTH , CTR POINT ) ;
TYPE NONCIRCLE POSSREP ( A LENGTH , B LENGTH , CTR POINT ... ) ;
TYPE ELLIPSE    UNION   { CIRCLE , NONCIRCLE } ... ;
```

But now what do we do about the possrep for type ELLIPSE? Note that we do want it to have a possrep (it's not a dummy type, and we don't want it to be a dummy type). But if we do specify a possrep, then at best there'll be some kind of redundancy (i.e., repetition of specifications that have already been given—and *must* already have been given—for types CIRCLE and NONCIRCLE); at worst, there'll be some kind of inconsistency (what happens if there's a conflict with the specifications already given for types CIRCLE and NONCIRCLE?).

Finally, even if we can resolve the foregoing issues satisfactorily, it doesn't seem easy (or possible?) to make this "bottom up" style conform to the requirement of IM Prescription 10 that types CIRCLE and NONCIRCLE be defined by constraining type ELLIPSE.

From such considerations, I conclude that there doesn't seem to be an easy way to make the original suggestion—i.e., that if *T* is a union type, then the definition of *T* should mention *T*'s immediate subtypes—work, nor does there seem to be much point in trying. By contrast, what definitely does seem to be desirable is to find a way of bundling several type definitions up into a single statement.

Chapter 13

Interlude:

The S by C Controversy

*When men understand what each other mean, they see, for the most part,
that controversy is either superfluous or hopeless.*

—Cardinal Newman:
Sermon at Oxford (1839)

*This chapter is heavily based on Appendix F ("A Closer Look at Specialization by Constraint")
of the Manifesto book. However, it does also contain quite a lot of new material.*

Over the past few chapters, I've relied heavily on our ellipses and circles example; in particular,
I've relied on the mathematical fact that an ellipse is a circle if and only if its semiaxis lengths *a*
and *b* are equal. In terms of our inheritance model, what this means is that if an invocation of the
ELLIPSE selector produces an ellipse with *a* = *b*, then specialization by constraint (S by C)
comes into play and the result of that invocation is in fact of type CIRCLE.

As noted in Chapter 8, however, not everyone agrees with us on these matters. In fact,
arguments have raged for years in the literature (especially the object literature) over exactly the
ellipses and circles example. By way of illustration, consider the following quote from Section
23.4.3.1 of Bjarne Stroustrup's book *The C++ Programming Language* (3rd edition, Addison-
Wesley, 1997):

> [In] mathematics a circle is a kind of an ellipse, but in most programs a circle should not be derived
> from an ellipse or an ellipse derived from a circle. The often-heard arguments "because that's the
> way it is in mathematics" and "because the representation of a circle is a subset of that of an
> ellipse" are not conclusive and most often wrong. This is because for most programs, the key
> property of a circle is that it has a center and a fixed distance to its perimeter. All behavior of a
> circle (all operations) must maintain this property (invariant; [*here Stroustrup gives a reference to
> Section 24.3.7.1 of his book, which explains the concept of invariants*]). On the other hand, an
> ellipse is characterized by two focal points that in many programs can be changed independently of
> each other. If those focal points coincide, the ellipse looks like a circle, but it is not a circle because
> its operations do not preserve the circle invariant. In most systems, this difference will be reflected
> by having a circle and an ellipse provide sets of operations that are not subsets of each other.

Now, the obvious response to such claims, it seems to me, is that if someone wants to work with constructs that look a bit like ellipses and circles but manifestly aren't ellipses and circles, then clearly they must be allowed to—but if they then go on to insist on calling those constructs ellipses and circles as such, I would have to question their wisdom in doing so. At the very least they're going to run the risk of causing a great deal of confusion.[1]

Be that as it may, perhaps you can begin to see why I said in Chapter 8 that the concept of S by C (and G by C) was controversial—so controversial, in fact, that (somewhat against our own better judgment) we omitted it entirely from the first version of our model.[2] Why? Essentially because everyone else seemed to have done the same thing (or so we were told, at any rate)—not a very good reason, you might think. In this chapter, I'd like to offer some observations in this connection and review a little of the related history.

So why was there this broad sentiment against S by C?—indeed, why does that sentiment persist to this day? (*Note:* For simplicity, throughout what follows I'll use "S by C" as a convenient shorthand label, most of the time, for specialization by constraint and generalization by constraint considered in combination.) The answer seems to have something to do with performance; there seems to be a widespread belief that S by C must be difficult to implement efficiently and must therefore perform badly. Now, performance isn't a model concern, by definition—we'd always rather get the model right first and worry about the implementation afterward—but we do have some thoughts on the performance issue, which I'll discuss in the section "Some Implementation Considerations" later in this chapter. First, however, I want to take a closer look at S by C as such. Thus, the chapter overall is structured as follows:

- The next two sections, immediately following this introductory material, offer a brief historical overview.

- The two sections following that overview summarize the benefits of S by C and suggest that the reason it typically hasn't been supported in the past is because most of the work on inheritance seems to have been done in an object context specifically.

- The final section offers the promised thoughts on implementation and performance.

There's a postscript, too, having to do with the logical difference between object IDs and foreign keys.

---

[1] I've elaborated on these arguments—in particular, on the quote from Stroustrup's book—in my paper "Is a Circle an Ellipse?" in the book *Date on Database: Writings 2000-2006* (Apress, 2006). Now, I apologize for the self-advertisement here; however, if you're interested in this topic, then I do think that paper is worth reading, if only for its "Technical Correspondence" section, which gives some idea of the truly amazing amount of confusion that's out there on questions like the one at hand.

[2] I refer to the version documented in the first edition of the *Manifesto* book, viz., C. J. Date and Hugh Darwen: *Foundation for Object / Relational Databases: The Third Manifesto* (Addison-Wesley, 1998). *Note:* Hugh Darwen's foreword to the present book has more to say regarding the backdrop for our original lack of support for S by C.

THE THREE OUT OF FOUR "RULE"

It's instructive to begin by taking a look at a historical issue that's related (or appears to be related, at any rate) to the S by C controversy. The issue in question is known informally as "the three out of four rule,"[3] and it turns out that S by C—or G by C, rather, which is part of the same overall phenomenon, of course—is the key to resolving it.

I've said that S by C is controversial. To say it one more time, S by C means among other things that the system should be aware that, e.g., if an ellipse has equal semiaxes, then it's really a circle. Now, I've assumed throughout preceding chapters, somewhat tacitly perhaps, that the inverse notion—i.e., that the system should be aware that, e.g., if an ellipse is really a circle, then its semiaxes must be equal—isn't controversial at all;[4] taking both notions together, in fact, what we have is basically just the type constraint for circles (a given value is a circle *if and only if* it's an ellipse with equal semiaxes). Note, incidentally, that without type constraints we don't even have a way of specifying the values that go to make up a given type; after all, that's exactly what a type constraint is—viz., a specification of the values that constitute the type in question.

Not everyone agrees with the foregoing, however (in other words, our position on type constraints is controversial too). By way of example, consider the following lightly edited extract from Stanley B. Zdonik and David Maier: "Fundamentals of Object-Oriented Databases," in *Readings in Object-Oriented Database Systems* (Zdonik and Maier, eds.; Morgan Kaufmann, 1990):

> We can list four features of a subtyping mechanism that all seem to be desirable, yet ... it is not possible to combine them in a single type system. The four features are:
>
> - Substitutability
> - Static type checking
> - Mutability
> - Type constraints
>
> [*Let me break in at this point in order to explain a few things. First of all, "static type checking" is just another term for compile time type checking. Second, "mutability" just means updatability, "mutator" being the object term for an update operator (the object term for a read-only operator is "observer"). Third, Zdonik and Maier refer to the last item in their list not as type constraints but rather as "specialization via constraints." But this latter term doesn't refer to S by C as such; rather, it refers to the more fundamental (?) notion that some type T' might be defined as a "constrained" form of a given type T. In other words, it really is talking about type constraints. (What Zdonik and Maier actually say is this: "Specialization via constraints occurs whenever the operation redefinition on a subtype constrains one of the arguments to be from a smaller value set than the corresponding operation on the supertype." As I said in Chapter 8, I don't find this*

---

[3] I call your attention to the deliberately different positioning of the quotation marks in the title to this section.

[4] Though I did point out in Chapter 8 that if this is *all* the system knows, then "circular noncircles" can occur.

*definition very clear, but "constraining one of the arguments to be from a smaller value set" surely requires there to be some kind of constraint in effect in order to do the constraining—and what else can that constraint be, if not a type constraint? Moreover, Zdonik and Maier then go on to claim, in effect (see the example below), that specialization via constraints implies that if we assign a circle value to an ellipse variable, one thing we subsequently can't do is assign a value to that variable that's "just an ellipse" and not a circle, and this state of affairs certainly has **something** to do with type constraints.) To continue:]*

All four of these properties seem to be desirable ... We submit, however, that it is impossible to have all four of them in the same type system. This conflict can be illustrated with the following example. [*I've replaced Zdonik and Maier's example by one that's essentially similar to theirs but conforms to our own notation and our own running example.*]

```
VAR E ELLIPSE ;
VAR C CIRCLE ;

C := CIRCLE ( LENGTH ( 3.0 ) , ... ) ;
E := C ;
THE_A ( E ) := LENGTH ( 4.0 ) ;
```

[The first assignment assigns to C a circle of radius three.] The [second] assignment must be allowed ... if we have substitutability and mutability ... The [third assignment] would type check at compile time ... Of course, [that assignment] ... will fail [at run time] even though the compile time check determined that it was all right.

[*And the extract concludes:*]

We observe that any three of the four features seem to work just fine. No one of them is obviously the one that must be discarded, but in any type system, at least one of them must be sacrificed to achieve consistency with the others.

Now, perhaps you can see right away what's wrong with this argument. To be specific, in our model, G by C would occur on the third assignment, *MST*(E) would become ELLIPSE again, and everything would indeed "work just fine." However, Zdonik and Maier don't consider the possibility of G by C, so let's agree to ignore that possibility ourselves for the time being and see where the argument takes us. I'll begin by taking a closer look at the four features and seeing how each relates to the example at hand:

- *Substitutability:* As explained in Chapter 7, type inheritance implies substitutability (value substitutability, at any rate), so this feature can't possibly be discarded. The second assignment in the example appeals to value substitutability.

- *Static type checking:* Zdonik and Maier define static type checking to mean that there's "no need to insert expensive run time [type] checks [into the compiled] code," and also that "the coder can be assured that [run time type] errors can never occur." In our inheritance model, by contrast, run time type errors certainly can occur in the context of TREAT (see Chapter 10), even if static type checking is performed.[5] So perhaps it might be argued that static type checking is the feature we've discarded.

However, I would argue that to insist that everything be fully type checkable at compile time is to throw the baby out with the bathwater. For example, consider the following code fragment (as usual, the declared types of variables E and C are ELLIPSE and CIRCLE, respectively):

```
VAR L LENGTH ;

E := C ;
L := THE_R ( E ) ;
```

The expression THE_R(E) in the last line here will fail on a compile time type check, of course. So now we have no way to obtain the radius of the circle that's the current value of E (we can't use TREAT, because TREAT *intrinsically* can't be fully type checked at compile time). So there's really no point in saying that the current value of E is of type CIRCLE; we might as well convert that circle to make it "just an ellipse" when we do the assignment of C to E.[6] And so we've lost substitutability!—and hence the whole idea of type inheritance, in fact.

■ *Mutability:* As noted earlier, mutability just means updatability. Updatability in turn implies support for variables and assignment (and the example does involve variables and assignment, clearly). Now, I could certainly be persuaded—indeed, it's obvious, as we saw in Chapters 1 and 2—that assignment as such is the only update operator (or "mutator") that's logically necessary. But that still leaves us with mutability as a sine qua non.

Now, it's possible that what Zdonik and Maier mean by the term *mutability* isn't assignment as such, but rather the idea that certain mutators work in such a way as to assign to *some component of* their target while leaving other components unchanged (as in the assignment to THE_A(E) in the example). If so, then I agree that such operators are very desirable in practice, but it's still the case that they're logically unnecessary, in the final analysis. Thus, the possibility in question—the possibility, that is, that Zdonik and Maier are really talking about some piecemeal kind of "mutability"—doesn't seem to be germane to the bigger issue.

■ *Type constraints:* As I've said, Zdonik and Maier don't consider the possibility of generalization by constraint. As a consequence, they claim that if type constraint checking is done, then the assignment to THE_A(E) will fail at run time. To be more specific, they claim that the assignment to THE_A(E) will fail because the most specific type of the

---

[5] They can't occur anywhere else, though.

[6] Of course, such a conversion couldn't be done in our model (and if it could, the result would be a "circular noncircle").

target is CIRCLE, and assignment to THE_A for a circle will, in general, violate the constraint on circles that the semiaxis lengths a and b must be equal. (I don't agree with this argument, of course—I'm just doing my best to explain Zdonik and Maier's point of view.) According to Zdonik and Maier, then, it follows that if we want the assignment not to fail at run time, *the system mustn't be informed of the constraint.* But this conclusion is surely unacceptable; surely, the more constraints the system is aware of and can enforce, the better. After all, we surely we want our data to be as correct as possible at all times. Don't we?

In fairness to Zdonik and Maier, let me now add that they're not alone in coming to the conclusion they do; two other writers, Nelson Mattos and Linda G. DeMichiel, examine the foregoing claims in their paper "Recent Design Trade-Offs in SQL3" (*ACM SIGMOD Record 23*, No. 4, December 1994)[7] and come to the same conclusion: viz., that type constraints are the feature that must be discarded. Their analysis goes somewhat as follows:

■ *Can we discard substitutability?* Well, no: As we've already seen, substitutability—value substitutability, that is—can't possibly be thrown away without undermining the whole idea, and point, of type inheritance.

■ *Can we discard static type checking?* Well, no: Discarding static type checking is highly undesirable, of course, and in any case it solves nothing—in the example, the assignment to THE_A(E) will still fail at run time (absent support for G by C, that is).

■ *Can we discard mutability?* Well, no: We must have assignment, at least, and component level update operators too are highly desirable in practice. (I note in passing that Mattos and DeMichiel do in fact assume that the term *mutability* refers to the idea of component level updating specifically, not just to wholesale assignment.)

Mattos and DeMichiel thus conclude that "the most appropriate [solution] is to not permit specialization via constraints" (meaning, to say it again, that they advocate not enforcing, and therefore not even declaring, type constraints). They claim that to do otherwise would mean "[forcing] the overloading of all [operators] defined on supertypes." What this claim means in terms of our example is that assignment to THE_A would have to be overloaded for a circle in such a way as to have the side effect of assignment to THE_B as well, so that the circle still satisfies the constraint $a = b$ after the update.[8] And they go on to say:

---

[7] "SQL3" was the working title at the time for what ultimately became the 1999 version of the SQL standard (viz., SQL:1999).

[8] Note that this really is overloading, not merely defining different implementation versions (because assignment to THE_A for an ellipse and assignment to THE_A for a circle will now have different semantics, and the user will need to understand the difference).

This option [*i.e., of forcing overloading*] seems to be unacceptable because we believe that ... users are not likely to define type hierarchies themselves, but to buy them as class libraries from third party vendors. It is an important requirement that users be able to define ... subtypes of these type hierarchies [*sic*] ... If we force all operators to be overloaded, users will have to redefine every [operator] provided by the class libraries whenever they need to [define such a subtype].

Now, I certainly agree that "forcing overloading" in the sense described is unacceptable in general. In the particular case of assignment via a THE_ pseudovariable such as THE_A, in fact, I would argue that the semantics of such an assignment are—for very good reasons—prescribed by the model and simply mustn't be changed, or overloaded, in the manner suggested (not in any other manner either, come to that). And even if those semantics weren't prescribed by the model, I would still argue that (a) changing the semantics of an operator in arbitrary ways is a bad idea in general, and (b) changing the semantics of an operator in such a way as to cause arbitrary side effects is an even worse one; it's a good general principle to insist that operators have exactly the requested effect, no more and no less.[9] What's more, I note that the option of changing the semantics in the manner suggested isn't always available, anyway. For example, let type ELLIPSE have another immediate subtype NONCIRCLE, with the intuitively obvious semantics; let the constraint $a > b$ apply to noncircles; and consider an assignment to THE_A for a noncircle that, if accepted, would set a equal to b. What would be an appropriate overloading for that assignment?—i.e., exactly what side effect would be appropriate in order to ensure that the result is still of type NONCIRCLE and not CIRCLE?[10]

On the face of it, therefore, the conclusion that type constraints have to be rejected might seem to be inescapable (if there's no G by C, that is). But observe the following implications of adopting that position:

- As already explained, assignment to THE_A is *not* reimplemented (or overloaded) for circles.

- The fact that the current value of E in the example is a circle does *not* cause the assignment to THE_A to fail.

- But the result is that after that assignment, variable E contains a "noncircular circle"—that is, it contains a value of type CIRCLE for which $a > b$. (The type is still CIRCLE because, according to the scheme under consideration, nothing has been done to change it.)

- Even worse, the fact that assignment to THE_A is supported (without any type checking) for a variable of declared type ELLIPSE but current most specific type CIRCLE suggests

---

[9] In fact it's basically just *The Assignment Principle* (see Chapter 2).

[10] Actually, and despite Mattos and DeMichiel's claims, no overloading as such would be required at all if the system did support type constraints!—an assignment to a variable of declared type NONCIRCLE that attempts to set a equal to b will simply fail on a type constraint violation.

rather strongly that assignment to THE_A should be supported (again without any type checking) for a variable of *declared* type CIRCLE.

- So let C be such a variable of declared type CIRCLE. After such an assignment, then, variable C will (in general) contain a "noncircular circle"—that is, a value of type CIRCLE for which $a > b$.

- So the constraint $a = b$ isn't being enforced for type CIRCLE.

- More generally, type constraints won't and can't be enforced—and there's no point in even letting them be stated, therefore—*even if inheritance is currently not supported at all*, just in case such support might be added at some future time![11]

To me, these implications, the last one in particular, seem even more unacceptable than the option of "forcing overloading."

So what's to be done? Well, let's step back a moment and take stock. It seems to me that the system should indeed support all four of the features mentioned (substitutability, static type checking, mutability, and type constraints). More precisely, it seems to me that:

- The system should support *The Principle of Value Substitutability* 100 percent.

- It should also support static type checking to the maximum extent possible (the only place where run time type checking is needed being in the context of TREAT).

- It should also support mutability—meaning not only that it should support assignment per se, but also that it should support component level update operators as a shorthand.

- It should also support type constraints—meaning in particular that it should be aware of the fact that circles are subject to the constraint $a = b$, and meaning further that assignment to THE_A(C) fails at compile time if the declared type of C is CIRCLE.

- *But it should additionally support S by C and G by C!* In particular, if the declared type of E is ELLIPSE, then it should always permit assignment to THE_A(E)—subject of course to the constraint $a \geq b$—and it should be prepared for *MST*(E) to change on such an assignment, either "down" from ELLIPSE to CIRCLE or "up" from CIRCLE to ELLIPSE, as and when appropriate.

---

[11] This is the way the SQL standard is, incidentally. See Chapter 22 for further discussion.

In other words, S by C and G by C are the solution to "the three out of four problem." In fact, we can now see that the three out of four "rule" isn't really a rule at all, so long as S by C and G by C are supported—as I believe they should be.

WHAT DOES INHERITANCE REALLY MEAN?

This section is partly a repeat of material from various earlier chapters. But the material is important, and I think it bears some repetition.

As explained in Chapter 11, update operators are inherited only conditionally in our model. For example, assume that assignment via THE_A isn't inherited by type CIRCLE from type ELLIPSE. Doesn't this state of affairs raise an obvious question (some might say it's *the* question): namely, what does inheritance really mean? A good model of inheritance must surely have a good answer to this question. But does such a model even exist? If assignment via THE_A applies to variables of type ELLIPSE but not to variables of type CIRCLE, is it reasonable to regard type CIRCLE as a subtype of type ELLIPSE? After all, to say that type CIRCLE is a subtype of type ELLIPSE means that all operators that apply to type ELLIPSE apply to type CIRCLE too, doesn't it?

Well, no, it doesn't. As I said in Chapter 3:

> It's important in the inheritance context—as in all others!—to distinguish very carefully between values and variables. When I say that, e.g., every circle is an ellipse, what I mean, more precisely, is that every circle *value* is an ellipse *value*. I certainly don't mean that every circle *variable* is an ellipse *variable*—i.e., that a variable of declared type CIRCLE is a variable of declared type ELLIPSE, and hence can contain a value that's an ellipse and not a circle. In other words, and speaking somewhat loosely once again, *inheritance applies to values, not variables* (although naturally there are implications for variables too, as will be seen). Indeed, we conjecture that much of the confusion we observe in this field—and there's a lot of it—is due precisely to a failure to distinguish properly between values and variables.

Thus, it seems to me that the key to what I referred to above as *the* question is to recognize

■ The logical difference between values and variables, and hence

■ The logical difference between read-only and update operators, and hence

■ The logical difference between value and variable substitutability,

and, of course, to act appropriately upon such recognition.

It further seems to me that the positions argued in the papers discussed in the previous section[12]—I refer to the papers by Zdonik & Maier and Mattos & DeMichiel—stem from a failure to make these crucial distinctions. And it seems still further to me that such failures are at least partly responsible for the lack of consensus, noted earlier in this book, on a formal, rigorous, and abstract inheritance model. By contrast, our own position is as follows: First, we do believe there's such a thing as a good inheritance model; we believe further that any such model must pay careful attention to the logical differences (values vs. variables and the rest) articulated in this book; and we believe still further that any such model must support S by C and G by C. And yes, we do believe a circle is an ellipse!—see the discussions in the next two sections.

BENEFITS OF S BY C

I've shown that one advantage of S by C and G by C is that together they solve the three out of four "problem." But of course they bring many other advantages with them as well, and those advantages are the subject of this section.

First, however, I ought to consider whether there are any *dis*advantages. The obvious one is as follows. Recall from Chapter 8 that S by C has the fundamental consequence that—at least as far as the model is concerned—a selector invocation might return a value of some proper subtype of the specified target type. For example, the ELLIPSE selector invocation

```
ELLIPSE ( LENGTH ( ... ) , LENGTH ( ... ) , POINT ( ... ) )
```

will return a value of type CIRCLE, not just ELLIPSE, if the two LENGTH invocations happen to return the same value at run time. Thus, it follows that—at least conceptually—S by C must be implemented *inside selector implementation code*. Note immediately, however, that I do say "at least conceptually." In fact, I'll argue in the section "Some Implementation Considerations" later that it's never actually necessary to compute the most specific type of the result of a selector invocation—not at the time of that invocation, at any rate. Nevertheless, suppose for the moment that the implementation does in fact have to determine the most specific type of the result of a selector invocation as soon as that result is computed. Let's consider some of the implications.

First of all, then, every time we define a new proper subtype T', the selector(s) for each proper supertype[13] T of T' will need to be reimplemented, or at least revised, because those selectors might now return values of that new type T' as their most specific type. But those revisions can clearly be automated! In the case of ellipses and circles, for example, the system knows exactly *when* an ellipse is in fact a circle, and it also knows exactly *which* circle the ellipse in question is. Note in particular, therefore, that what we don't have to do is what Mattos

---

[12] Argued also in a host of similar writings.

[13] Or perhaps (depending on the implementation) just for each *immediate* supertype.

and DeMichiel said we'd have to do: viz., "redefine every [operator] provided by the class libraries whenever [we] need to [define a subtype]." In other words, the possible need to revise certain selectors—which, let me stress, is the only disadvantage to the S by C idea as far as I can see—is perhaps a minor burden on the system, but it's no burden at all on any human user.[14]

Now I turn to the advantages. I've numbered them for convenience.

1. The first is simply the overriding point that S by C means the model is a better model of reality. "The more the system knows, the better" is surely a good general principle.

2. It's a direct consequence of S by C that values of most specific type ELLIPSE correspond to noncircles—i.e., to ellipses that definitely aren't circles in the real world. By contrast, in other approaches (i.e., without S by C), values of most specific type ELLIPSE can have $a = b$ and can thus correspond to circles in the real world (the "circular noncircles" phenomenon). Hence, defining CIRCLE as a subtype of ELLIPSE in such approaches partitions the set of ellipses, not into circles vs. noncircles, but rather into circles vs. "maybe circles"—intuitively not a very satisfactory state of affairs.[15]

3. Following on from the previous point, it's also a direct consequence of S by C that values of most specific type CIRCLE correspond to ellipses that are definitely circles in the real world. In other words, "noncircular circles" and similar nonsenses can't occur.

4. More compile time type checking can be done and fewer run time type errors can occur; in fact, run time type errors can occur solely on an attempt to TREAT a value to a type it doesn't possess. (By contrast, in our original model, which didn't support S by C, additional run time type errors could occur—for example, on an attempt to assign via THE_A to a variable of declared type ELLIPSE but current most specific type CIRCLE, as in the example earlier illustrating "specialization via constraints.")

5. Assignments are logically simpler (especially assignments to THE_ pseudovariables, which in our original model involved a complicated CASE expression on the right side in their expansion). In particular, changing types "up" or "down" is easy. That is, given variable E of declared type ELLIPSE, in order to change the most specific type of E from ELLIPSE to CIRCLE or the other way around, it's sufficient just to update E appropriately.

6. Changing types "sideways" is also easy. That is, given (say) type ELLIPSE with subtypes CIRCLE and NONCIRCLE, in order to change the most specific type of variable E (of

---

[14] It's not even a performance burden. Again, see the section "Some Implementation Considerations," later.

[15] In some systems, moreover (including SQL systems, incidentally), it can also be the case—point 3 notwithstanding—that values of most specific type CIRCLE have $a \neq b$ (the "noncircular circles" phenomenon). If so, then defining CIRCLE as a subtype of ELLIPSE partitions the set of ellipses not into "circles vs. maybe circles" but—what seems to me to be worse—into "maybe circles vs. maybe circles" (if you see what I mean).

declared type ELLIPSE) from CIRCLE to NONCIRCLE or the other way around, it's sufficient just to update E appropriately. (In our original model, by contrast, changing types "sideways" in such a manner was a considerably more complex process, involving a "TREAT UP" operation on E—see points 7 and 8 below—to force it to be "just an ellipse" first, followed by an assignment with a complicated CASE expression on its right side second. What's more, the overall process didn't work properly anyway if ELLIPSE was a union type, as in fact it is in the foregoing example. All of these complications go away with S by C.)

7. Equality comparisons are easy. For example, given our usual variables E and C of declared types ELLIPSE and CIRCLE, respectively, we can test them for equality as follows:

```
E = C
```

In our original model, by contrast, we would have had to have written something like this:

```
TREAT_UP_AS_ELLIPSE ( E ) = TREAT_UP_AS_ELLIPSE ( C )
```

(This expression can be read as "treat both comparands as just ellipses and then compare the two ellipses.")

8. In fact, the TREAT UP operator mentioned in points 6 and 7, which was included in our original model for a variety of reasons, becomes completely unnecessary with S by C and G by C and so can be dropped. (Actually it was only shorthand anyway, but any simplification is generally to be desired.) *Note:* Perhaps I should point out that our model does still support "treating up" as well as "treating down," but only in a harmless kind of way. Given our usual variable C, for example, the expression TREAT_AS_ELLIPSE (C) is valid, but it can never fail; in fact, it's almost a "no op."

9. With S by C and G by C, the rules regarding conditional inheritance of update operators apply to declared types. In our original model, by contrast, they applied to most specific types instead, a fact that made them harder to understand and harder to implement and led to more run time type checking and more run time type errors.

10. More code reuse is achievable, and programs are more immune to the introduction of new subtypes. For example, a program that assigns to THE_A(E) will still work after type CIRCLE is introduced (which it might not have done under our original model).

11. There's never any logical need to CAST—i.e., convert—a value of type ELLIPSE to type CIRCLE, because an ellipse that can logically be "converted to" type CIRCLE will in fact be of type CIRCLE already, under S by C. The operator itself thus becomes unnecessary (which wasn't the case, under our original model).

12. S by C can also have the effect of making certain implementation versions of certain operators logically unnecessary. For example, the update version of MOVE discussed in Chapter 7 for ellipses and rectangles will work for any combination of most specific argument types—ELLIPSE or CIRCLE for the first argument and RECTANGLE or SQUARE for the second argument—whereas such was not the case with our original model.

In fact, I'd like to go further; I'd like to argue that *S by C is the only conceptually valid way of defining subtypes!*—so long as the supertype is a regular type, at any rate (S by C from a dummy type makes no sense, as we saw in Chapter 12). I justify this strong claim as follows. Let scalar type T' be a proper subtype of (regular) scalar type T. Then:

- Loosely, T' and T are both sets (more precisely, the set of values $|T'|$ constituting T' is a subset of the set of values $|T|$ constituting T).

- Therefore T and T' both have membership predicates—predicates, that is, such that a given value is of the type in question if and only if it satisfies the corresponding predicate. Let those predicates be P and P', respectively.

- Since we're dealing with finite sets only, we can for simplicity regard predicates P and P' as effectively just enumerating the values in $|T|$ and $|T'|$, respectively.

- Since every value of type T' is also a value of type T, it follows that predicate P' can be formulated in terms of values of type T (not T') only.

- And that predicate P', formulated in terms of values of type T, is precisely the constraint that values of type T have to satisfy in order to be values of type T'. In other words, a value of type T is specialized to type T' precisely if it satisfies the constraint P'. *Note:* P' is what IM Prescription 10 calls the *specialization constraint* for T'. In **Tutorial D,** it's specified via the *<is def>* on the definition of that type T'.

Thus, to repeat, we see S by C as the only conceptually valid way of defining subtypes. In particular, therefore (as noted a couple of sections back), our answer to the notorious question "Is a circle an ellipse?" is a very firm *yes*.

WHAT ABOUT OBJECTS?

The *Manifesto* book includes the following very strong claim: *Support for objects in the object oriented sense is incompatible with support for a good model of inheritance*—and I've now laid sufficient groundwork to be able to justify that claim. Let me explain.

I begin by reminding you that object languages typically make heavy use of object IDs, or in other words pointers,[16] and variables in such languages typically contain such pointers instead of regular nonpointer values. Thus, for example, the analog of our usual variables E and C in such a language would typically be variables—let's call them XE and XC—that contain pointers to ellipses and circles instead of ellipses and circles as such. Furthermore, when I say pointers to ellipses and circles, I really mean pointers to ellipse and circle *variables*,[17] because by definition it's variables, not values, that have addresses.

Next, I remind you that support for pointers necessarily includes support for associated referencing and dereferencing operators as well (or something equivalent to those operators, at any rate). Here are loose definitions:

- *Referencing*: Given a variable V, the referencing operator applied to V returns a pointer to V.

- *Dereferencing*: Given a variable P containing a pointer, the dereferencing operator applied to P returns the variable the pointer in P points to.

So consider the following code fragment:

```
VAR E   ELLIPSE ;
VAR XE PTR_TO_ELLIPSE ;

E  := CIRCLE ( LENGTH ( 5.0 ) , POINT ( 1.0 , 1.0 ) ) ;
XE := PTR_TO ( E ) ;
```

I'm assuming here that:

- If T is a type, then PTR_TO_T is a type too, and its values are pointers to, or object IDs for, variables of type T. In other words, PTR_TO_ is a type generator (a scalar type generator, in fact).

- If V is a variable of type T, then the operator invocation PTR_TO (V) returns a pointer to V. In other words, PTR_TO is the referencing operator mentioned above.

---

[16] See Chapter 22 for arguments in support of my claim here that object IDs really are just pointers.

[17] An object language would say they're pointers to ellipse and circle *objects*.

The effect of the code fragment is thus to set the variable E to contain a circle of radius five and then to set the variable XE to contain a pointer to E. Note the appeal to substitutability in the first of these assignments.

Now let's introduce another variable:

```
VAR XC PTR_TO_CIRCLE ;
```

If we assume, not unreasonably, that type PTR_TO_CIRCLE is a proper subtype of type PTR_TO_ELLIPSE,[18] we can now perform the following assignment:

```
XC := TREAT_AS_PTR_TO_CIRCLE ( XE ) ;
```

Now XC also contains a pointer to E—in fact, it contains the same pointer as XE does.

Finally, we attempt the following assignment (let's call it Assignment Z):

```
THE_A ( DEREF ( XE ) ) := LENGTH ( 6.0 ) ;
```

DEREF here is the dereferencing operator—it takes a variable of some pointer type as argument and returns the variable that the pointer variable in question currently points to.[19] Thus, the intent of Assignment Z is, loosely, to update the length of the *a* semiaxis of the ellipse variable E that XE currently points to, setting it to six. So what happens? Well, it seems there are three possibilities, all of them bad. I'll consider each in turn.

1. Assignment Z fails on a run time type error, because *MST*(E) is CIRCLE and assignment to THE_A isn't supported for type CIRCLE (again as in the "specialization via constraints" discussion earlier in this chapter). In this case, the model is bad because (a) it leads to run time type errors in a context other than TREAT, and (b) more important, it doesn't support G by C and so isn't "a good model of reality."

2. Assignment Z "succeeds" (i.e., there's no run time type error and the update is done), but G by C doesn't occur. In this case, the model is bad because (a) it fails to support G by C and so isn't "a good model of reality"; (b) variable XC now points to a "noncircular circle"; and (c) more generally, type constraints can't be supported (see that "specialization via constraints" discussion once again).

---

[18] Such would certainly be the case for the SQL analogs of these types, incidentally (see Chapter 22).

[19] Note that the DEREF invocation in the example appears on the left side of the assignment and is thus being used as a kind of pseudovariable (I say a "kind of" pseudovariable, because the overall assignment isn't just shorthand for something else, as it would have to be if the DEREF invocation were a true pseudovariable—see Exercise 2.17 in Chapter 2). It follows that support for pointers implies a need to extend the syntax and semantics of assignment somewhat. I omit the details here, since the whole point of the example under discussion is to bolster the argument that pointers as such shouldn't be supported in the first place.

3. Assignment Z "succeeds" (i.e., there's no run time type error and the update is done), and G by C does occur. In this case, the model is bad because (a) variable XC, of declared type PTR_TO_CIRCLE, now points to a variable of current most specific type ELLIPSE, and hence (b) type constraints can't be supported. *Note:* In practice, this option is probably a nonstarter, precisely because of point (a); thus, G by C probably does *not* occur, and we're back with Case 2.

Conclusion: Whichever option we choose, the model is bad. And the culprit, at least in this particular example, is the concept of "shared variables": Pointer variables XE and XC "share" the ellipse variable E. Furthermore, it's pointers (i.e., object IDs) that permit that sharing in the first place. It follows that *object IDs—at least if they permit shared variables—and a good model of inheritance are incompatible.*

As a matter of fact, we don't even need to invoke the concept of shared variables in order to illustrate the problem. Consider the following simpler version of the example:

```
VAR E   ELLIPSE ;
VAR XC PTR_TO_CIRCLE ;

E := CIRCLE ( LENGTH ( 5.0 ) , POINT ( 1.0 , 1.0 ) ) ;
XC := TREAT_AS_PTR_TO_CIRCLE ( PTR_TO ( E ) ) ;
THE_A ( E ) := LENGTH ( 6.0 ) ;
```

The first assignment here sets E to contain a circle of radius five. The second sets XC to point to E. The third ("Assignment Z") attempts to update the length of the *a* semiaxis of the ellipse variable E to six. What happens? Without going into details, it should be clear that there are the same three possibilities as before, again all of them bad, and the overall conclusion is the same as before as well: *Object IDs and a good model of inheritance are incompatible.*

For a third and final example, consider the following still simpler code fragment:

```
VAR C   CIRCLE ;
VAR XE PTR_TO_ELLIPSE ;

C  := CIRCLE ( LENGTH ( 5.0 ) , POINT ( 1.0 , 1.0 ) ) ;
XE := PTR_TO ( C ) ;
THE_A ( DEREF ( XE ) ) := LENGTH ( 6.0 ) ;
```

Here S by C and G by C have no part to play (variable C can never have most specific type ELLIPSE), but the final assignment still either raises a run time type error or produces a noncircular circle. Once again, therefore, I conclude that object IDs and a good model of inheritance are incompatible.

Darwen and I conjecture that examples like those above, and in particular the conclusions arising from such examples, go some way toward explaining why there haven't been any good inheritance models in the past so far as we know. To be specific, all of the prior work on inheritance that we're aware of has been done in an object context specifically, and the object world generally seems to take it as a sine qua non that object IDs must be supported. As we've just seen, however, object IDs imply that the model must be bad. In other words, (a) objects imply object IDs; (b) object IDs and a good model of inheritance are incompatible; (c) hence, objects per se and a good model of inheritance are incompatible!

What's more, since it's clearly an assumption underlying Zdonik and Maier's claims regarding "the three out of four rule" that object support is a desideratum, it's tempting to suggest that we should really have been talking all along about "a four out of five rule" instead, where the fifth element—and clearly the one to be discarded—was *objects themselves*.

SOME IMPLEMENTATION CONSIDERATIONS

To summarize to this point: S by C (including G by C) is an area where our approach to inheritance differs markedly from what's found in a typical object language. The following quote from a paper by James Rumbaugh[20] illustrates the point very well:

> Is SQUARE a subclass of RECTANGLE? ... Stretching the *x* dimension of a rectangle is a perfectly reasonable thing to do. But if you do it to a square, then the object is no longer a square. This is not necessarily a bad thing conceptually. When you stretch a square you *do* get a rectangle ... But ... most object-oriented languages do not want objects to change class ... [This] suggests [a] design principle for classification systems: *A subclass should not be defined by constraining a superclass.*

Observe that Rumbaugh's conclusion—i.e., his "design principle for classification systems"—is the diametric opposite of our own, which is that S by C is the only conceptually valid way of defining a subtype (or subclass, to use Rumbaugh's term). Note too, however, that one of Rumbaugh's reasons for taking the position he does is that "[object] languages do not want objects to change class." Our own model, by contrast, was deliberately not constrained by existing languages or implementations;[21] we wanted to define the abstract model first and leave implementation concerns till later. In particular, we included S by C because we found it useful, as well as being logically correct (or so it seemed to us). But we would certainly drop it if it turned out to be impossible to implement, or impossible to implement efficiently.

So can it be implemented efficiently? Well, it's relevant here to observe that Rumbaugh buttresses his conclusion with the following argument:

---

[20] James Rumbaugh: "A Matter of Intent: How to Define Subclasses," *Journal of Object-Oriented Programming* (September 1996). Incidentally, this paper is one of many we've seen that fail to distinguish properly between values and variables. Here's a direct quote: "Barbara Liskov is responsible for the Liskov Substitution Principle that an instance [*sic*] of a subclass must be substitutable and usable wherever a variable [*sic!*] of one of its ancestor classes is allowed. This principle has helped to avoid a lot of confusion in forming class hierarchies and affects most discussions of [object] classification."

Perhaps I should add that it was precisely because of this quote that I felt I needed to take a careful look at the Liskov Substitution Principle (LSP). I wanted to know whether LSP was the same thing as substitutability, as this latter term is understood in our model. I reported on what I found in another paper—"What Does Substitutability Really Mean?"—in the book already mentioned in an earlier footnote, *Date on Database: Writings 2000-2006* (Apress, 2006). This isn't the place to discuss the conclusions of that paper in detail; let me just say that one thing that (it seemed to me) LSP most definitely did *not* do was distinguish adequately—or indeed at all—between values and variables.

[21] Actually the first version was, as previously noted (and it was defective for that very reason).

> It would be computationally infeasible to support a rule based, intensional definition of class membership, because you would have to check the rules after each operation that affects an object.

(The phrase "rule based, intensional definition of class membership" here refers to S by C and G by C; it means, for example, that a given ellipse is defined to be a member of the class of circles if—and only if?—it satisfies the rule that $a = b$. As for "operation[s] that affect an object," the operations in question are update operations, of course, or more fundamentally just assignments.)

However, we reject the foregoing argument; that is, we believe the computational aspects of S by C can be handled both simply and efficiently. To be more specific, we reject both

a. The suggestion that S by C is "computationally infeasible" (i.e., that it imposes intolerable computational overhead), and

b. The suggestion that the most specific type has to be (re)computed "after each operation that affects an object."

Let me elaborate. Let X be an expression. Then the first and overriding point is that it's *never* necessary to compute the current most specific type $MST(X)$, as such, of that expression X; it's only necessary to determine in certain contexts whether the current value $v(X)$ of X is of some particular type—or, to be more specific, whether it's of some particular proper subtype of the declared type $DT(X)$ of X. By way of illustration, consider the simple type graph shown in Fig. 13.1, which shows (a) type PARALLELOGRAM as having two immediate subtypes, RECTANGLE and RHOMBUS, and (b) each of these latter types as having type SQUARE as an immediate subtype:[22]

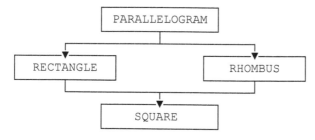

Fig. 13.1: Example of a type graph

---

[22] As you can see, the example involves multiple inheritance, which I haven't yet discussed in detail. So if you want to skip this section for now and come back to it later, please feel free to do so.

Now let expression *X* have declared type PARALLELOGRAM, and consider the expression TREAT_AS_RECTANGLE (*X*). In order to evaluate that expression, we clearly don't need to compute *MST(X)* as such—all we need to do is check whether IS_RECTANGLE (*X*) evaluates to TRUE. In particular, if *MST(X)* happens to be SQUARE, there's no need to determine that fact in order to evaluate IS_RECTANGLE (*X*).

Observe next that the remarks of the preceding paragraph apply if *X* is a selector invocation in particular. To revert for a moment to our usual example of ellipses and circles: As we know, the selector invocation

```
ELLIPSE ( LENGTH ( 5.0 ) , LENGTH ( 5.0 ) , POINT ( ... ) )
```

is defined by our model to return a value at run time of most specific type CIRCLE, not ELLIPSE. But there's no need for the implementation to perform S by C, as such, at the time that selector invocation is evaluated; all it has to do, to repeat, is to be able to ascertain subsequently that the value in question is indeed a circle, if and when some expression—for example, the expression TREAT_AS_CIRCLE (*X*)—is evaluated that depends in some way on that fact.

As a basis for a more searching discussion, refer to Fig. 13.1 again. Suppose again that *DT(X)* is PARALLELOGRAM, and suppose we need to determine whether *v(X)* is of type SQUARE. Now, there are two paths in the graph from PARALLELOGRAM to SQUARE, via RECTANGLE and RHOMBUS respectively, and the system needs to choose one in order to make that determination. Suppose it chooses the one via RHOMBUS. If *v(X)* fails to satisfy the constraint for RHOMBUS, then it's certainly not of type SQUARE; however, if it does satisfy the constraint for RHOMBUS, then it needs to be tested against the constraint for SQUARE. On the face of it, therefore, it seems that no more than two nodes of the graph need be visited in order to discover whether *v(X)* is a square: two if it's a rhombus, otherwise just one.

As we'll see in Chapter 14, however, the *<is def>* for type SQUARE looks like this:

```
IS { RECTANGLE , RHOMBUS }
```

(irrelevant details omitted). What this specification means is that a given value is of type SQUARE if and only if it's of type RECTANGLE *and* of type RHOMBUS. Thus, it looks as if it might be necessary to traverse the path from PARALLELOGRAM to RECTANGLE, as well as the one from PARALLELOGRAM to RHOMBUS, in order to determine whether *v(X)* satisfies the constraint for type RECTANGLE as well as the one for type RHOMBUS. However, we can avoid this apparent need to visit additional nodes by labeling the arc from RHOMBUS to SQUARE with the constraint for type RECTANGLE.[23] Then, if the

---

[23] If there were any intervening nodes between PARALLELOGRAM and RECTANGLE, the constraint in question would have to be the logical AND of all constraints on the path from PARALLELOGRAM to RECTANGLE. And if there were more than one such path, the system would have to choose one, just as it had to choose whether to follow the RECTANGLE or RHOMBUS path to SQUARE in the previous discussion.

implementation discovers that $v(X)$ is a rhombus, it can immediately check to see whether it's a rectangle (and hence a square) too, without having to visit any additional nodes.

Here then is a pseudocode algorithm ("TEST_S") that embodies the foregoing ideas and can be used to test whether some specified value v of some known type T is of some specified type S. Note in particular that S isn't necessarily a subtype of T (observe in Fig. 13.1 that neither of RECTANGLE and RHOMBUS is a subtype of the other). Nor does the algorithm rely on the disjointness assumption holding, so it works for multiple as well as for single inheritance.

```
OPERATOR TEST_S ( v value , T type , S type ) RETURNS BOOLEAN ;
    IF S = T THEN RETURN ( TRUE ) ;
    ELSE BEGIN ;
            let T' be some immediate subtype of T
                        that's also a supertype of S ;
            let IC be the constraint on the arc from T to T' ;
            IF v satisfies IC
                THEN RETURN ( TEST_S ( v , T' , S ) ) ;
                ELSE RETURN ( FALSE ) ;
            END IF ;
        END ;
    END IF ;
END OPERATOR ;
```

This algorithm is certainly "computationally feasible," and it should be clear that it doesn't impose any intolerable overhead. Of course, we do have to consider how often it's invoked; could it be that it's invoked so frequently that those invocations in themselves constitute an excessive burden? In order to examine this question, we first need to pin down the contexts in which such invocations occur. Careful examination of the *Manifesto* model shows there are precisely three such contexts:

1. *TREAT:* The expression TREAT_AS_S (X), where S is a proper subtype of $DT(X)$, is evaluated by raising a type error if TEST_S $(X, DT(X), S)$ returns FALSE.

2. *Type testing:* The expression IS_S (X), where S is a proper subtype of $DT(X)$, is logically equivalent to TEST_S $(X, DT(X), S)$.

3. *Binding:* As explained under IM Prescription 17 in Chapter 11 (subsection "The Binding Process"), (a) operators are allowed to have several implementation versions, each with a different version signature, and (b) the system is generally expected to bind a given invocation to what might be described as the "most appropriate" implementation version.[24] Let *Op* be an operator, then, and let *OpI* be some invocation of *Op*. If the most specific types of the arguments are all known (which won't be the case until run time, in general), then the binding problem for *OpI* reduces to one already solved in existing systems. However, determining those most specific types itself clearly does involve overhead, so

---

[24] As also noted in Chapter 11, however, there's usually no requirement in the model per se that it actually do so.

let's focus for the moment on the corresponding declared types instead (which are known at compile time). If any of those types is a proper subtype of that of the corresponding parameter and an implementation version specific to that proper subtype is available, then at least part of the binding process can be done at compile time. At run time, the system will need to know which implementation versions are available to suit the declared types of the arguments. And if there are several such, and if at least one has a parameter whose declared type is a proper subtype of that of the corresponding argument, then the system does have to do some type testing (i.e., it does need to invoke TEST_*S* at run time). I'll have more to say in connection with this point in the very last sentence of this section.

Nothing else requires TEST_*S* to be invoked. In particular, equality comparisons don't; on the contrary, in order to evaluate the comparison $X = Y$, it's sufficient (a) to determine the most specific common supertype of $DT(X)$ and $DT(Y)$ (which can be done at compile time) and then (b) to invoke the "=" operator for that common supertype. (Actually, any common supertype that's not a dummy type can be chosen for this purpose.)

I offer one further argument to justify my claim that S by C doesn't entail excessive overhead: Whenever the assignment $X := Y$ is executed, either explicitly or implicitly, the system knows the declared type of Y and can thus flag X internally as being of that type. Such a flag could allow subsequent invocations of TEST_*S* on X to be performed on a smaller portion of the type graph, or even to be eliminated entirely in some cases. In the same kind of way, whenever X is specified as an argument to some operator invocation that requires run time examination of the types of its arguments, the system can take the opportunity to "remember" any types it discovers.

I turn now to the suggestion that the most specific type has to be (re)computed "after each operation that affects an object" (quoting Rumbaugh once again). In fact, of course, we've already seen that there's no need to compute the most specific type, as such, at all. In particular, if variable V is updated by some invocation of some update operator, there's no need to determine $MST(V)$ after that invocation (not at the time of the invocation, at any rate). All that's needed is to be able to determine subsequently whether V is of some specified type—and I've already discussed that requirement at length.

Finally, I return to the question of how often TEST_*S* needs to be invoked, in order to consider whether those invocations in themselves might constitute a serious performance burden. By way of a thought experiment, suppose the system doesn't support inheritance at all (and so certainly doesn't support S by C in particular), and suppose we have a user defined type POLYGON. Then there are two possibilities: (a) We might want, on certain occasions, to execute different code depending on whether a given polygon is in fact a rectangle or "just a polygon," or (b) we might not. For example, suppose we want to implement an AREA_OF operator for polygons. Then we might or might not want to test whether the argument to a given AREA_OF invocation is in fact a rectangle, and use the simple "height times width" formula when it is.

a. Suppose we do want to perform such a test. In effect, then, we'll have to include our own implementation of the IS_RECTANGLE operator—in effect, our own implementation of TEST_RECTANGLE—inside the AREA_OF code. Clearly, support for inheritance and S by C would make our task a little easier in this case, because there wouldn't be any need for us to provide that implementation after all. Moreover, the effect on overall system performance will be more or less the same either way; the main difference is just that the type testing will be done by the system instead of the application, if S by C is supported.

b. By contrast, suppose we don't want to perform such a test. In that case, support for S by C (and TEST_*S*) would clearly impose no overhead at all, because the type testing simply wouldn't be done.

Analogous remarks apply to TREAT operations and the binding process (these being the other areas requiring invocation of TEST_*S*, if S by C is supported). Let's consider the binding process briefly. To continue with the AREA_OF example, the question is: Would we include code in the AREA_OF implementation, not only to test whether the argument to a given AREA_OF invocation is a rectangle, but also to use the simple "height times width" formula when it is?

a. Suppose we would include such code. In effect, then, we'll be providing code for two separate versions of the AREA_OF operator bundled together inside the AREA_OF implementation, as well as code to perform the run time binding process. In this case, direct support for inheritance with S by C would (again) surely make our task a little easier, and the effect on overall system performance will be more or less the same either way.

b. By contrast, suppose we wouldn't include such code. In that case, support for S by C clearly imposes no overhead at all.

In conclusion, it's worth pointing out that (as the foregoing discussion indicates) what overhead S by C does impose is a function of the number of distinct implementation versions that have been defined, not a function of the number of subtypes as such.

POSTSCRIPT: A NOTE ON FOREIGN KEYS

In the object world, object IDs are used to identify and reference objects. In the relational world, somewhat analogous functionality is provided by key and foreign key values.[25] Now, in the body of the chapter, we saw that object IDs and a good model of inheritance are incompatible.

---

[25] Note, however, that those key and foreign key values are used to identify tuples, not objects, and tuples and objects are most certainly not the same thing (logical difference!)—in part because objects are supposed to be "encapsulated" and tuples aren't.

So why don't those problems with object IDs occur in connection with key and foreign key values as well? Or do they occur?

In fact they don't. By way of illustration, consider this example once again (the second of the examples discussed in the section "What about Objects?" earlier):

```
VAR E  ELLIPSE ;
VAR XC PTR_TO_CIRCLE ;

E := CIRCLE ( LENGTH ( 5.0 ) , POINT ( 1.0 , 1.0 ) ) ;
XC := TREAT_AS_PTR_TO_CIRCLE ( PTR_TO ( E ) ) ;
THE_A ( E ) := LENGTH ( 6.0 ) ;
```

Ignoring irrelevant aspects, a relational analog of this example might involve relation variables (i.e., relvars) that look something like this:

```
VAR R1 BASE RELATION { K ELLIPSE , ... } KEY { K } ;

VAR R2 BASE RELATION { K CIRCLE , ... }  KEY { ... }
       FOREIGN KEY { K } REFERENCES R1 ;
```

For simplicity, assume no referential actions—cascade update, etc.—are specified (this simplifying assumption doesn't affect the argument in any material respect). Assume also that both relvars are initially empty.

Observe now that every value of K in R1 that matches some value of K in R2 must be of type CIRCLE, not just of type ELLIPSE. So let's insert a tuple into each of the two relvars:

```
INSERT R1 RELATION { TUPLE
      { K CIRCLE ( LENGTH ( 5.0 ) , POINT ( 1.0 , 1.0 ) ) } , ... } ;

INSERT R2 RELATION { TUPLE
      { K CIRCLE ( LENGTH ( 5.0 ) , POINT ( 1.0 , 1.0 ) ) } , ... } ;
```

Finally, let's try to update the tuple (forgive the sloppy manner of speaking here) in R1:

```
UPDATE R1 WHERE K = CIRCLE ( LENGTH ( 5.0 ) , POINT ( 1.0 , 1.0 ) ) :
      { THE_A ( K ) := LENGTH ( 6.0 ) } ;
```

This UPDATE attempts to "G by C" the circle in the single tuple in R1 so that its most specific type becomes just ELLIPSE. That attempt fails, however (and the overall UPDATE fails), on a referential integrity violation. So we do get a run time error. But the error in question is an integrity constraint violation, not a type error as such (integrity constraint violations are always possible, of course). What we don't get is a noncircular circle, nor a G by C failure as such. Overall, in fact, we have a system in which noncircular circles can't occur, type constraints can be supported, and in particular S by C and G by C can be supported too.

Part III

SCALAR TYPES,

MULTIPLE INHERITANCE

Part III of this book consists of three chapters. It revisits the concepts introduced in Part II for scalar types and single inheritance and considers what happens to those concepts under multiple inheritance (albeit still for scalar types only).

Chapter 14

An Overview of

Multiple Inheritance

[The] insane root
That takes the reason prisoner

—William Shakespeare:
Macbeth (1606)

This chapter and the next two explain what happens to our inheritance model when multiple inheritance is taken into account. In fact, it turns out that IM Prescriptions 1-20 as defined and discussed in Part II need no revision or reformulation at all, although some of them do have implications that aren't always immediately obvious, and one in particular—number 8, on common subtypes and supertypes—needs especially careful discussion. I'll deal with that one in the next chapter. In this chapter, by contrast, I just want to lay some general groundwork.

As you know, single inheritance means every proper subtype has exactly one immediate supertype, from which it inherits operators and constraints; by contrast, multiple inheritance means a proper subtype can have several immediate supertypes, and it inherits operators and constraints from all of them. Fig. 14.1, a repeat of Fig. 13.1 from Chapter 13, shows a simple example. Note in particular that type SQUARE in that figure has two immediate supertypes, and hence that the example is indeed an example of multiple inheritance as such.

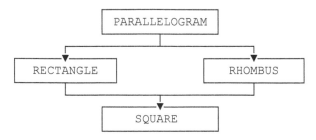

Fig. 14.1 (same as Fig. 13.1): Example of a type graph

Fig. 14.1 will serve as the basis for discussions and explanations throughout this part of the book. First, however, I need to make a few further preliminary remarks:

■ To repeat something I said in Chapter 3, multiple inheritance support isn't just desirable, it's logically required. Other writers agree with this position, too. For example:[1]

> Most modern ... systems allow [multiple inheritance] ... A generally accepted view is that a modern ... language should support [multiple inheritance], despite the fact that [it] introduces many conceptual and technical intricacies.

We'll be taking a look at some of those "conceptual and technical intricacies" in this part of the book (also in the next, Part IV).

■ For simplicity, throughout this part of the book (as in Part II) I'll take the unqualified terms *type*, *subtype*, and *supertype* to refer to scalar types, subtypes, and supertypes specifically; the unqualified terms *value*, *variable*, *(read-only) operator*, *expression*, and *result* to refer to scalar values, variables, operators, expressions, and results specifically; and the unqualified term *constraint* to refer to a type constraint specifically (barring explicit statements to the contrary in every case).

■ I'll continue to assume that all of the types under discussion are members of some given set of available types *GSAT*, and that the root and leaf type concepts in particular are to be understood in terms of that set.

■ Finally, I'll continue to use the symbols T and T' to refer generically to a pair of types such that T' is a subtype of T—equivalently, such that T is a supertype of T'.

THE RUNNING EXAMPLE

Like the running example in Part II of this book, the example of Fig. 14.1 involves a set of geometric types. The types in question are PARALLELOGRAM, RECTANGLE, RHOMBUS, and SQUARE, where, as the figure shows, PARALLELOGRAM is a root type; SQUARE is a leaf type; and SQUARE has two immediate supertypes, RECTANGLE and RHOMBUS, each of which has PARALLELOGRAM as its sole immediate supertype.

As the caption indicates, the structure in Fig. 14.1 is actually an example of a *type graph*. Of course, type graphs, like type hierarchies before them, aren't part of our inheritance model as such—they're merely an intuitively convenient way of depicting subtype / supertype

---

[1] The quote is from "On the Notion of Inheritance," by Antero Taivalsaari (*ACM Comp. Surv. 28*, No. 3, September 1996).

relationships, which are. And the following observations should suffice to show that the relationships depicted in Fig. 14.1 in particular do make good intuitive sense:

- Every parallelogram has a "long" diagonal of length *ld* and a "short" one of length *sd*, where $ld \geq sd$ (and those diagonals intersect at the parallelogram's center and bisect each other).

- Every parallelogram also has two "long" sides of length *ls* and two "short" ones of length *ss*, where $ls \geq ss$ (and the long sides are opposite each other and parallel, and so are the short sides).

- A rectangle is a parallelogram for which $ld = sd$. Unlike parallelograms in general, every rectangle has a unique circumscribed circle (i.e., a circle that passes through each of that rectangle's four vertices); hence, every rectangle has a property that's unique to those parallelograms that happen to be rectangles, viz., that circumscribed circle. Of course, it also has a unique diagonal length, which parallelograms in general don't have.

- A rhombus is a parallelogram for which $ls = ss$.[2] Unlike parallelograms in general, every rhombus has a unique inscribed circle (i.e., a circle that touches each of that rhombus's four sides); hence, every rhombus has a property that's unique to those parallelograms that happen to be rhombi, viz., that inscribed circle. Of course, it also has a unique side length, which parallelograms in general don't have.

- A square is a parallelogram that's both a rectangle and a rhombus.[3] Unlike rectangles and rhombi in general, every square has a unique associated annulus that's defined by the difference between the corresponding circumscribed and inscribed circles; hence, every square has a property that's unique to those parallelograms that happen to be both rectangles and rhombi, viz., that annulus. Moreover, every square has both a unique side length, which rectangles in general don't have, and a unique diagonal length, which rhombi in general don't have.

---

[2] I note in passing that a parallelogram that's not a rhombus is sometimes called a *rhomboid*—a rather unfortunate term, perhaps, given that one of the dictionary definitions of *rhomboid* is "like a rhombus"!

[3] Note in particular, therefore, that the disjointness assumption doesn't hold—types RECTANGLE and RHOMBUS overlap, yet neither is a subtype of the other.

POSSIBLE REPRESENTATIONS

This section has little or nothing to do with type inheritance as such—it has to do with with issues that are specific to the choice of running example—but I think it's necessary. At least it gives some idea of the kind of thing a type designer might need to give careful consideration to in practice.

It's instructive to consider the question of what possreps we might want to define in the running example. First let's consider the root type, type PARALLELOGRAM. Let *p* be a parallelogram, with vertices (in clockwise sequence) *A*, *B*, *C*, *D*, and let the center of *p* be *E*, as illustrated in Fig. 14.2.

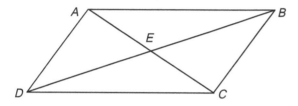

Fig. 14.2: Parallelogram *p*

Now, it should be clear that there are many different ways of "possibly representing" *p*.[4] The first and most obvious one is surely just to use the four vertices *A*, *B*, *C*, and *D*. Of course, it's not the case that every set of four points defines a parallelogram, so we'll need to impose some appropriate constraints on the points *A*, *B*, *C*, *D*. There are several different ways to state those constraints, too. For example, we might say that sides *AB* and *DC* must be of equal length and sides *BC* and *AD* must be of equal length also; alternatively, we might say that sides *AB* and *DC* must be parallel and sides *BC* and *AD* must be parallel also; and there are clearly other possibilities as well. Note too that *A*, *B*, *C*, and *D* must all be distinct—in fact, no three of them can be collinear, which implies that they must all be distinct a fortiori. (*Exercise:* Check this latter claim!) So here's a first attempt at defining type PARALLELOGRAM:

```
TYPE PARALLELOGRAM    /* first attempt */
     POSSREP ( A POINT , B POINT , C POINT , D POINT )
     CONSTRAINT NOT COLLINEAR ( A , B , C )
            AND NOT COLLINEAR ( B , C , D )
            AND NOT COLLINEAR ( C , D , A )
            AND NOT COLLINEAR ( D , A , B )
            AND DIST ( A , B ) = DIST ( D , C )
            AND DIST ( B , C ) = DIST ( A , D ) ;
```

---

[4] In contrast to type PLANE_FIGURE (the root type in the running example in Part II of this book), type PARALLELOGRAM is—in fact, *must* be, as we'll see in Chapter 15—a regular type, not a dummy type, and so it certainly does need a possrep. (Actually, not only isn't it a dummy type, it isn't even a union type, because some parallelograms are neither rectangles nor rhombi.)

I'm assuming here that:

- COLLINEAR returns TRUE if and only if its three POINT arguments lie on a straight line.

- DIST returns the distance between its two POINT arguments as a value of type LENGTH.

However, there's at least one problem with the $A - B - C - D$ possrep, as you might have already realized: namely, that the vertices A, B, C, and D aren't all independent of one another—as soon as any three of them are pinned down, the fourth is fully determined.[5] What's more, using just three of the vertices, say A, B, and C, as a possrep would simplify the type constraint considerably:

```
TYPE PARALLELOGRAM    /* second attempt */
    POSSREP ( A POINT , B POINT , C POINT )
    CONSTRAINT NOT COLLINEAR ( A , B , C ) ;
```

Note in particular that we no longer need to say that AB and DC must be of equal length and that BC and AD must be of equal length as well.

Of course, if we do go with a three-vertex possrep as just suggested, there's the problem that there are four different vertex triples we could use, without there being any obvious reason to choose any particular triple over the other three. There's also the problem that whichever triple we do choose, the vertex left out will necessarily "look and feel" different from the other three; for example, if we choose the $A - B - C$ triple, then THE_A, THE_B, and THE_C operators will "automatically" be defined, but a THE_D operator won't be. Partly for such reasons, let's assume until further notice that we do go with the $A - B - C - D$ possrep despite the redundancy, and let's see what some of the implications of that decision might be.

Note: It's worth mentioning that choosing the $A - B - C - D$ possrep doesn't violate the *The Third Manifesto* in any way; that is, the *Manifesto* book doesn't actually require possrep components to be mutually independent, or in other words to be fully orthogonal to one another. However, the book does at least say that such orthogonality might be desirable, and the arguments in the subsection immediately following tend to support that position rather strongly.

How to "Update a Parallelogram"

Choosing the $A - B - C - D$ possrep for type PARALLELOGRAM has the obvious advantage that all four operators THE_A, THE_B, THE_C, and THE_D are available for parallelograms

---

[5] This statement is slightly oversimplified. For example, if we're given A, B, and C, *and we also know that AC is a diagonal* (equivalently, that A and C represent opposite vertices), then D is indeed fully determined, as can easily be seen from Fig. 14.1. But if AC is not a diagonal but a side, then either AB or BC could be a diagonal, and each of these possibilities corresponds to a different D (so given only A, B, and C, there are three different possible D's altogether). I'll come back to such matters later; for now, please take it on trust that we can indeed use just three vertices as the basis for a possrep if we want to.

(and hence for rectangles, rhombi, and squares as well). But what about the corresponding pseudovariables? Well, it should be obvious that any attempt to "update a parallelogram"—if you'll forgive such a sloppy manner of speaking—via just one of the four pseudovariables will necessarily fail. Why? Because if it didn't, the result wouldn't be a parallelogram any longer (unless the update was a "no op," I suppose). On the face of it, then, any such updating would seem to require some kind of multiple assignment.[6]

Let's consider an example. To be specific, let P be a variable of declared type PARALLELOGRAM; let *p* be a value of most specific type PARALLELOGRAM;[7] and let *p* be assigned to P. Now suppose we want to update P in such a way that, after the update, P contains a parallelogram obtained from *p* by extending side *AB* by one unit of length at the "*B*" end and simultaneously extending side *DC* by one unit of length at the "*C*" end (thereby ensuring that the result is still a parallelogram as such). So we might try a multiple assignment looking something like this:

```
THE_B ( P ) := SHIFT ( THE_B ( P ) ) ,     /* warning -   */
THE_C ( P ) := SHIFT ( THE_C ( P ) ) ;     /* invalid !!! */
```

I'm assuming for the sake of the example that SHIFT is a read-only operator that does whatever's necessary to "shift" its point argument as required (or, rather, to return the point that marks the position that would be reached if its point argument had been so shifted). *Note:* Further details of SHIFT as such—for example, a parameter (presumably needed in practice) to specify the direction of shifting—are irrelevant to the present discussion, and I'll ignore them to avoid undesirable distractions.

Of course, the individual assignments in the foregoing multiple assignment both have the same target variable, viz., P. According to the discussion of such matters in Chapter 2, therefore, the assignment overall is shorthand for the following:

```
P :=
WITH ( P := PARALLELOGRAM ( THE_A ( P ) , SHIFT ( THE_B ( P ) ) ,
                            THE_C ( P ) , THE_D ( P ) ) ) :
          PARALLELOGRAM ( THE_A ( P ) , THE_B ( P ) ) ,
                          SHIFT ( THE_C ( P ) ) , THE_D ( P ) ) ;
```

But now there's another problem! Here again, but deliberately reformatted, is the first of the two foregoing PARALLELOGRAM selector invocations (i.e., the one inside the WITH specification):

---

[6] Refer to Chapter 2 if you need to refresh your memory regarding the concept of multiple assignment.

[7] I assume here and elsewhere in this chapter that it's still legitimate to talk about "the"—i.e., the unique—most specific type of a value, even in the multiple inheritance context. I'll show in the next chapter that such an assumption is justified (at least in the case of scalar types, which is what we're talking about here).

```
PARALLELOGRAM ( THE_A ( P ) ,
                SHIFT ( THE_B ( P ) ) ,
                THE_C ( P ) ,
                THE_D ( P ) )
```

And this invocation will clearly fail—because if it didn't, whatever it returned certainly wouldn't be a parallelogram, because it would violate the constraint on parallelograms that sides *AB* and *DC* are supposed to be of equal length.[8]

In order to get around this problem, what we need to do is perform the entire update en bloc, using a single assignment and an explicit selector invocation instead of a multiple assignment and pseudovariables:

```
P := PARALLELOGRAM ( THE_A ( P ) , SHIFT ( THE_B ( P ) ) ,
                SHIFT ( THE_C ( P ) ) , THE_D ( P ) ) ;
```

What this example shows, in other words, is that if we do go for the $A - B - C - D$ possrep, then we probably won't be able to make much use of THE_A etc. as pseudovariables at all!—which does tend to suggest that choosing such a possrep isn't a very good idea. In other words, it probably is a good idea after all to choose a possrep in which the components are all orthogonal, even though the *Manifesto* doesn't actually require us to do so. For example, if we choose the $A - B - C$ possrep, we can at least still use THE_A, THE_B, and THE_C as pseudovariables,[9] even if we no longer have THE_D available. From this point forward, therefore, I'll assume just to be definite that the $A - B - C$ possrep is the one to go for.

Resolving Ambiguities

Even if we agree to use the $A - B - C$ possrep, however, there's still another problem: namely, which vertex is which? Let me elaborate. Let i, j, and k be any three noncollinear points. At first blush, then, it might appear that any permutation of i, j, and k could be used as the A, B, and C arguments to an invocation of the PARALLELOGRAM selector, and the result produced would be the same parallelogram—call it p—in every case. But then what would the value of, say, THE_A(p) be? What this thought experiment shows is that choosing $A - B - C$ as a possrep is insufficient by itself; we need a way of saying which of A, B, and C is which.[10]

Well, actually the foregoing paragraph doesn't quite state the problem accurately (nor is the problem quite as bad as that paragraph might suggest). Whichever three vertices we choose, it

---

[8] Recall from Chapter 2 that type constraints are checked on selector invocations. (Indeed, they must be; to repeat from that chapter, we can never tolerate an expression that's supposed to denote a value of some type *T* but in fact doesn't—even if we're immediately going to go on and remedy the situation, as it were, as indeed we are in the case at hand. As Chapter 2 also says, "a value of type *T* that's not a value of type *T*" is a contradiction in terms.)

[9] Of course, use of these pseudovariables will still be subject to the pertinent type constraint (i.e., updating via any of them must be such as to ensure that the points *A, B, C* remain noncollinear).

[10] The situation here is reminiscent of the one discussed in connection with type RECTANGLE in the answer to Exercise 3.10 in Chapter 3.

must be the case that two of them are opposite one another. To be definite, let's agree that *A* and *C* are the opposite ones—so *AC* is a diagonal and not a side—and hence that *B* is the odd one out, as it were; in other words, let's require that the argument corresponding to parameter *B* always be that "odd one out." So now we need to find a way of distinguishing between the *A* and *C* vertices. The following will do the trick. Let *V1* and *V2* be the *A* and *C* vertices (not necessarily in that order), and let their cartesian coordinates be (*x1,y1*) and (*x2,y2*), respectively. Then:

■ If *x1* = *x2*, then let *A* be that one of *V1* and *V2* with the smaller *y* coordinate.

■ Otherwise, let *A* be that one of *V1* and *V2* with the smaller *x* coordinate.

Of course, all I've done here is define a simple ordering according to which, given any two distinct points, one of those points is first with respect to that ordering and the other is second.

> *Aside:* Another and possibly slightly better solution would be to use a possrep consisting not of the three vertices *A*, *B*, and *C* as such but rather just of vertex *B* together with a *line segment* representing the diagonal *AC*. Recall from Chapter 2 that line segments are defined to have a specific begin point and specific end point, and thus have a direction to them; so, to say that diagonal *AC* is the line segment from *A* to *C* (rather than from *C* to *A*) is to say that *A* is the begin point and *C* is the end point with respect to that diagonal, and all ambiguities are thereby removed. That said, however, for definiteness I'll stay with the *A* – *B* – *C* possrep as previously described. *End of aside.*

But we're still not done!—we've pinned down *A* and *C* precisely, but there are still two choices for *B*, one on either side of the *AC* diagonal. So here I'll appeal to the mathematical result that says that the point with cartesian coordinates (*x,y*) is on one side of diagonal *AC* if it makes the expression (*x2−x1*)*(*y−y1*) − (*y2−y1*)*(*x−x1*) positive and on the other side if it makes that same expression negative. Let's take *B* to be the vertex that makes it positive. Then the final version of the PARALLELOGRAM type definition looks like this:

```
TYPE PARALLELOGRAM    /* third and final attempt */
     POSSREP ( A POINT , B POINT , C POINT )
     CONSTRAINT NOT COLLINEAR ( A , B , C )
          AND WITH ( X1 := THE_X ( A ) , Y1 := THE_Y ( A ) ,
                     X  := THE_X ( B ) , Y  := THE_Y ( B ) ,
                     X2 := THE_X ( A ) , Y2 := THE_Y ( C ) ) :
             IF X1 = X2 THEN Y1 < Y2 ELSE X1 < X2 END IF
             AND ( X2 - X1 ) * ( Y - Y1 ) > ( Y2 - Y1 ) * ( X - X1 ) ;
```

More Possreps

I said earlier that there were many different ways of possibly representing the parallelogram *p* from Fig. 14.2. I've considered a couple in some detail, but here in outline are several more:

- We could use any two adjacent vertices (*A* and *B*, say) and the center *E*. There are four possible choices for the pair of adjacent vertices.

- We could use any two adjacent sides (*AB* and *BC*, say). There are four possible choices for the pair of adjacent sides.

- We could use a pair of opposite sides (*AB* and *DC*, say). There are two choices here.

- We could use the diagonals *AC* and *BD*.

- We could use a pair of adjacent half-diagonals (EA and EB, say). Four choices here.

- We could use one vertex, the interior angle at that vertex, and the lengths of the sides that meet at that vertex (for example, the point *A*, the angle *DAB*, and the lengths of sides *AB* and *AD*). Four choices.

And so on, probably. I'll leave it as an exercise (if you're interested) to think about what type constraints would be required in each of the foregoing cases.

POSSIBLE REPRESENTATIONS CONTINUED

So much for type PARALLELOGRAM; what about the other three types in Fig. 14.1? Given our choice of an *A* – *B* – *C* possrep for type PARALLELOGRAM, the obvious possrep for type RECTANGLE—at least, so it seems to me—is one that involves those same three vertices plus an additional constraint. That additional constraint in turn can be specified in several different ways; one simple one is just to say that the diagonals must be of equal length. So here's a plausible type definition:

```
TYPE RECTANGLE
    IS { PARALLELOGRAM
         CONSTRAINT LD ( PARALLELOGRAM ) = SD ( PARALLELOGRAM )
         POSSREP ( A = THE_A ( PARALLELOGRAM ) ,
                   B = THE_B ( PARALLELOGRAM ) ,
                   C = THE_C ( PARALLELOGRAM ) )
         NOT { PARALLELOGRAM ( POINT ( 0.0 , 2.0 ) ,
                               POINT ( 4.0 , 2.0 ) ,
                               POINT ( 3.0 , 0.0 ) ) } } ;
```

I've assumed the availability of operators LD and SD that return the length of the long diagonal and that of the short diagonal, respectively, of a given parallelogram (see the section "Operators," later). The purpose of the NOT specification is to show that there's at least one value that's a parallelogram and not a rectangle, thereby ensuring that types RECTANGLE and PARALLELOGRAM are in conformance with the requirement—see IM Prescription 5—that, for scalar types at least, proper subtypes shall be proper subsets.

> *Aside:* The fact that the declared possreps for type RECTANGLE and its immediate supertype PARALLELOGRAM are identical[11] does have one small consequence that's worth spelling out explicitly. By way of example, consider the (read-only) operator THE_A, which applies to values of type PARALLELOGRAM because one of the components of the sole possrep for that type has a component called A. Normally, then, that same operator would apply to values of type RECTANGLE as well, thanks to inheritance. In fact, however, we've effectively *overridden* that operator by specifying a possrep for type RECTANGLE that also has a component called A. Of course, we've also specified that this latter component is equal to "THE_A (PARALLELOGRAM)," so the two THE_A operators are effectively one and the same anyway. *End of aside.*

Next, type RHOMBUS. Here the obvious possrep involves the three vertices *A*, *B*, and *C* once again, plus a constraint to say that the sides must all be of the same length. So we have:

```
TYPE RHOMBUS
     IS { PARALLELOGRAM
          CONSTRAINT LS ( PARALLELOGRAM ) = SS ( PARALLELOGRAM )
          POSSREP ( A = THE_A ( PARALLELOGRAM ) ,
                    B = THE_B ( PARALLELOGRAM ) ,
                    C = THE_C ( PARALLELOGRAM ) )
          NOT { PARALLELOGRAM ( POINT ( 0.0 , 2.0 ) ,
                                POINT ( 4.0 , 2.0 ) ,
                                POINT ( 4.0 , 0.0 ) ) } } ;
```

I've assumed the availability of operators LS and SS that return the length of the long side and the short side, respectively, of a given parallelogram (again see the section "Operators," later).

Finally, type SQUARE. Given that any particular square is both a rectangle and a rhombus (and therefore satisfies the constraints that the diagonals are of equal length and the sides are all of equal length as well),[12] two opposite vertices are sufficient to determine the square in question uniquely. Hence:

---

[11] Indeed, the type definitions in this section all lend weight to the suggestion from Chapter 3 (section "The Running Example") to the effect that if *T'* is an immediate subtype of *T*, then it might be convenient to have some syntactic shorthand for defining a possrep for *T'* that's similar, or even identical, to some possrep for *T*.

[12] In fact, type SQUARE is the intersection type for types RECTANGLE and RHOMBUS (see Chapter 15).

```
TYPE SQUARE
    IS { RECTANGLE , RHOMBUS
         POSSREP ( A = THE_A ( RECTANGLE ) ,
                   C = THE_C ( RECTANGLE ) )
         NOT { RECTANGLE ( POINT ( 0.0 , 2.0 ) ,
                           POINT ( 4.0 , 2.0 ) ,
                           POINT ( 4.0 , 0.0 ) ) ,
               RHOMBUS   ( POINT ( 3.0 , 4.0 ) ,
                           POINT ( 8.0 , 4.0 ) ,
                           POINT ( 5.0 , 0.0 ) ) ) } } ;
```

Points arising:

- The specialization constraint here says a given value s is of type SQUARE if and only if IS_RECTANGLE (s) and IS_RHOMBUS (s) both evaluate to TRUE. No additional CONSTRAINT specification is stated, or indeed allowed. *Note:* Such an additional specification is allowed—in fact it's required—if and only if (a) the subtype being defined has exactly one immediate supertype (which is always the case with single inheritance, of course) and (b) that supertype is a regular type, not a dummy type.

- Note that the possrep for type SQUARE is defined in terms of the possrep for its immediate supertype RECTANGLE. However, it could equally well have been defined in terms of the possrep for its immediate supertype RHOMBUS instead—it would have made no difference. (The slight degree of arbitrariness involved in such cases might be considered a little unsatisfactory. Perhaps more study is required.)

- Following on from the previous point, however, I now observe that the <*is def*>

```
IS { RECTANGLE , RHOMBUS }
```

—irrelevant details omitted for simplicity—can be regarded as shorthand for either or both[13] of the following:

```
IS_RECTANGLE ( s ) AND LS ( s ) = SS ( s )

IS_RHOMBUS   ( s ) AND LD ( s ) = SD ( s )
```

(where s denotes an arbitrary value of the type being defined, viz., type SQUARE). In other words, the specified <*is def*> does conform, albeit implicitly, to that part of IM Prescription 10 that requires the definition of a type such as SQUARE to include an appropriate specialization constraint for each of the type in question's immediate supertypes.

---

[13] By "both" here, I mean the logical AND, of course.

■ Finally, note the NOT specification, which guarantees that the set of values constituting type SQUARE is a proper subset of the set of values constituting type RECTANGLE *and* a proper subset of the set of values constituting type RHOMBUS.

OPERATORS

In this section I show definitions (some just in outline) for a set of operators that would surely prove useful in practice in connection with the running example. Note that several of these definitions make use of type LINESEG ("line segment"), which was defined in Chapter 2 as follows:

```
TYPE LINESEG POSSREP ( BEGIN POINT , END POINT ) ;
```

Now to the operators as such. The first few just return the sides of a parallelogram as line segments (note that, e.g., *AB* and *BA* are the same side but distinct line segments):

```
OPERATOR AB ( P PARALLELOGRAM ) RETURNS LINESEG ;
   RETURN ( LINESEG ( THE_A ( P ) , THE_B ( P ) ) ) ;
END OPERATOR ;

OPERATOR BA ( P PARALLELOGRAM ) RETURNS LINESEG ;
   RETURN ( LINESEG ( THE_B ( P ) , THE_A ( P ) ) ) ;
END OPERATOR ;
```

Similarly for operators BC and CB, of course (I'll skip the details). But CD and DC, and AD and DA, all involve vertex *D*, and of course we don't have a THE_D operator for type PARALLELOGRAM. Now, we can define an operator that provides the functionality—at least the read-only functionality—of such a hypothetical "THE_D" operator, but I don't think it would be a good idea to call it THE_D as such. Let's call it DVX instead (for "*D* vertex"):

```
OPERATOR DVX ( P PARALLELOGRAM ) RETURNS POINT ;
   RETURN ( some expression that computes the location of vertex D ) ;
END OPERATOR ;
```

Now I can define CD and DC:

```
OPERATOR CD ( P PARALLELOGRAM ) RETURNS LINESEG ;
   RETURN ( LINESEG ( THE_C ( P ) , DVX ( P ) ) ) ;
END OPERATOR ;

OPERATOR DC ( P PARALLELOGRAM ) RETURNS LINESEG ;
   RETURN ( LINESEG ( DVX ( P ) , THE_C ( P ) ) ) ;
END OPERATOR ;
```

And similarly for AD and DA, of course (again I'll skip the details).

Now let's do for the diagonals the same kind of thing we've just done for the sides (i.e., define operators that return the corresponding line segments):

```
OPERATOR AC ( P PARALLELOGRAM ) RETURNS LINESEG ;
   RETURN ( LINESEG ( THE_A ( P ) , THE_C ( P ) ) ) ;
END OPERATOR ;

OPERATOR CA ( P PARALLELOGRAM ) RETURNS LINESEG ;
   RETURN ( LINESEG ( THE_C ( P ) , THE_A ( P ) ) ) ;
END OPERATOR ;

OPERATOR BD ( P PARALLELOGRAM ) RETURNS LINESEG ;
   RETURN ( LINESEG ( THE_B ( P ) , DVX ( P ) ) ) ;
END OPERATOR ;

OPERATOR DB ( P PARALLELOGRAM ) RETURNS LINESEG ;
   RETURN ( LINESEG ( DVX ( P ) , THE_B ( P ) ) ) ;
END OPERATOR ;
```

Now, we're probably going to need to work with the actual lengths of these various sides and diagonals from time to time. To that end, let me define an auxiliary operator (LEN) that returns the length of an arbitrary line segment:

```
OPERATOR LEN ( LSG LINESEG ) RETURNS LENGTH ;
   RETURN ( DIST ( THE_BEGIN ( LSG ) , THE_END ( LSG ) ) ) ;
END OPERATOR ;
```

Hence:

```
OPERATOR LS ( P PARALLELOGRAM ) RETURNS LENGTH ;
   /* "length of long side of" */
   RETURN ( MAX { LEN ( AB ( P ) ) , LEN ( BC ( P ) ) } ) ;
END OPERATOR ;

OPERATOR SS ( P PARALLELOGRAM ) RETURNS LENGTH ;
   /* "length of short side of" */
   RETURN ( MIN { LEN ( AB ( P ) ) , LEN ( BC ( P ) ) } ) ;
END OPERATOR ;

OPERATOR LD ( P PARALLELOGRAM ) RETURNS LENGTH ;
   /* "length of long diagonal of" */
   RETURN ( MAX { LEN ( AC ( P ) ) , LEN ( BD ( P ) ) } ) ;
END OPERATOR ;

OPERATOR SD ( P PARALLELOGRAM ) RETURNS LENGTH ;
   /* "length of short diagonal of" */
   RETURN ( MIN { LEN ( AC ( P ) ) , LEN ( BD ( P ) ) } ) ;
END OPERATOR ;
```

Next I'll define some operators to return the interior angles at the vertices of a given parallelogram:

```
OPERATOR DAB ( P PARALLELOGRAM ) SYNONYMS { BAD , BCD , DCB }
   RETURNS ANGLE ;
   RETURN ( WITH LAB := LEN ( AB ( P ) ) ,
                 LAD := LEN ( AD ( P ) ) ,
                 LDB := LEN ( DB ( P ) ) ) :
      ARCCOS ( ( LAB ^ 2 + LAD ^ 2 - LDB ^ 2 ) / ( 2 * LAB * LAD ) ) ;
END OPERATOR ;
```

Operator DAB returns the interior angle at vertex *A*. Note the SYNONYMS specification, which defines some alternative names for that same operator. (More precisely, BAD really is that same operator; BCD and DCB ought by rights to return the interior angle at vertex *C*, not *A*, but of course the interior angles at *C* and *A* are equal.) ABC is similar:

```
OPERATOR ABC ( P PARALLELOGRAM ) SYNONYMS { CBA , ADC , CDA }
   RETURNS ANGLE ;
   RETURN ( WITH LBA := LEN ( BA ( P ) ) ,
                 LBC := LEN ( BC ( P ) ) ,
                 LAC := LEN ( AC ( P ) ) ) :
      ARCCOS ( ( LBA ^ 2 + LBC ^ 2 - LAC ^ 2 ) / ( 2 * LBA * LBC ) ) ;
END OPERATOR ;
```

A couple of obvious further operators:

```
OPERATOR AREA_OF ( P PARALLELOGRAM ) RETURNS AREA ;
   /* "area of" */
   RETURN ( some expression that computes the area of P ) ;
END OPERATOR ;

OPERATOR CTR_OF ( P PARALLELOGRAM ) SYNONYMS { CTR } RETURNS POINT ;
   /* "center of" */
   RETURN ( some expression that computes the center E of P ) ;
END OPERATOR ;
```

All of the foregoing operators apply to parallelograms, and hence to rectangles and rhombi, and hence to squares as well (note in particular that type SQUARE inherits all of these operators from both of its immediate supertypes RECTANGLE and RHOMBUS, a point I'll return to in the section "Two Remarks on Operator Inheritance," later). The following operators, by contrast, don't apply to parallelograms in general:

```
OPERATOR DIAG ( R RECTANGLE ) RETURNS LENGTH ;
   /* "diagonal of" */
   RETURN ( LD ( R ) ) ;
END OPERATOR ;
```

```
OPERATOR SIDE ( R RHOMBUS ) RETURNS LENGTH ;
   /* "side of" */
   RETURN ( LS ( R ) ) ;
END OPERATOR ;

OPERATOR CIRCUM_CIRCLE ( R RECTANGLE ) RETURNS CIRCLE ;
   /* "circumscribed circle of" */
   RETURN ( some expression that computes the required circle ) ;
END OPERATOR ;

OPERATOR IN_CIRCLE ( R RHOMBUS ) RETURNS CIRCLE ;
   /* "inscribed circle of" */
   RETURN ( some expression that computes the required circle ) ;
END OPERATOR ;

OPERATOR ANNULUS ( S SQUARE ) RETURNS ANNULUS ;
   /* "annulus of" */
   RETURN ( some expression that computes the required annulus ) ;
END OPERATOR ;
```

TYPE GRAPHS

In our running example, types RECTANGLE and RHOMBUS each have one immediate supertype, PARALLELOGRAM, and type SQUARE has two, RECTANGLE and RHOMBUS. The obvious question arises: Could we additionally define PARALLELOGRAM as an immediate supertype of SQUARE? In terms of Fig. 14.1, such a definition would involve an additional arc from type PARALLELOGRAM to type SQUARE (see Fig. 14.3). So could we add such an arc?

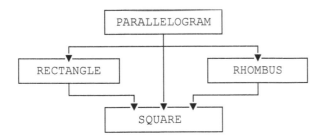

Fig. 14.3 (modified version of Fig. 14.1): A graph that's not a valid type graph

Well, observe that if we did add that extra arc, we'd be in violation of IM Prescription 5. Paraphrasing considerably, that prescription says among other things that:

■ First, type *T* is an immediate supertype of type *T′* if there's just one path in the graph from *T* to *T′* and that path contains no type that's both a proper subtype of *T* and a proper supertype of *T'*—so PARALLELOGRAM is definitely not an immediate supertype of SQUARE according to Fig. 14.3 (not according to Fig. 14.1 either, come to that).

■ Second, type *T* is a nonimmediate supertype of type *T'* if every path in the graph from *T* to *T'* contains at least one type that's both a proper subtype of *T* and a proper supertype of *T'* [14]—so PARALLELOGRAM isn't a nonimmediate subtype of SQUARE either, again according to Fig. 14.3 (though it is according to Fig. 14.1).

■ But, third, every proper supertype of type *T'* is supposed to be either an immediate or a nonimmediate supertype of *T'*—and that's why the prescription is violated, because PARALLELOGRAM, though clearly it *is* a supertype of SQUARE, is apparently neither an immediate one nor a nonimmediate one (once again, according to Fig. 14.3, that is).

At the very least, then, we'd have to revise IM Prescription 5 if we wanted to permit that additional arc. So do we want to permit it?

We answer this question in the negative. First, permitting such an arc doesn't provide any additional functionality, because all of the operators and constraints that type SQUARE would then inherit "immediately" from type PARALLELOGRAM it already inherits anyway, transitively, via the intermediate types RECTANGLE and RHOMBUS. Second, permitting such an extension to our understanding of the term *immediate supertype* certainly has the potential to complicate certain other concepts and definitions unduly. We therefore reject such an extension. As already indicated, we don't need to change our model in any way to achieve this result—IM Prescription 5 already takes care of matters for us.

Now, multiple inheritance clearly implies that we can no longer talk about type hierarchies as such; instead, we need to introduce the more general concept of a type graph. Here's a definition: [15]

Definition: A *type graph* is a directed acyclic graph (*TG*, say), consisting of a finite set *N* of nodes and a finite set *D* of directed arcs that together satisfy the following properties:

1. *TG* is empty if and only if *N* is empty (in which case *D* is necessarily empty too).

2. Each node is given the name of a type.

---

[14] In principle, this condition would be satisfied if there were no paths from *T* to *T'* at all. However, IM Prescription 5 guarantees that at least one such path does exist, because it requires *T* to be a proper supertype of *T'*.

[15] Of course, a type hierarchy is a special case of a type graph as here defined.

3.   No two nodes have the same name. Also, no node is named either *T_alpha* or *T_omega* for any possible type *T*; by convention, the types with these names—which are primarily conceptual in nature anyway—aren't represented in the graph at all.[16]

4.   There's an arc from node *T* to node *T'* if and only if type *T* is an immediate supertype of type *T'*.

5.   If there's an arc from node *T* to node *T'*, then node *T'* isn't reachable from node *T* via any other path, where (a) a path from node *T* to node *T'* is a sequence of *n* arcs *A1* (from *T* to *T1*, say), *A2* (from *T1* to *T2*, say), ..., *An* (from *T(n−1)*, say, to *T'*) such that $n \geq 0$, and $n = 0$ implies $T = T'$ (i.e., there's always a path from node *T* to itself); (b) a node *T'* is reachable from a node *T* if and only if there's a path from node *T* to node *T'*.

6.   If the graph includes any nodes at all, then—because it's directed and acyclic—it necessarily contains at least one node that has no immediate supertype node. Such a node is called a root node, and the type corresponding to that node is called a root type.

7.   If the graph includes any nodes at all, then—again because it's directed and acyclic—it necessarily contains at least one node that has no immediate subtype node. Such a node is called a leaf node, and the type corresponding to that node is called a leaf type.

8.   If nodes *T1* and *T2* are distinct root nodes, then no node is reachable from both *T1* and *T2*.

9.   If nodes *T1*, *T2*, *T'*, and *T''* are such that there exist paths from both *T1* and *T2* to both *T'* and *T''*, then there must exist a node *T* that's common to every such path.

Explanation:

■ Points 1, 2, and 3 are self-explanatory, except for the remark concerning types *T_alpha* and *T_omega*. Since this part of the book is concerned with scalar types only, the only "*T_alpha* and *T_omega*" types we need concern ourselves with for present purposes are the scalar types *alpha* and *omega*, respectively, and so point 3 reduces just to saying that *alpha* and *omega* aren't represented in the graph. The more general terms *T_alpha* and *T_omega* will be explained in Part IV of this book (see Chapter 19).

---

[16] More generally, in the case of tuple and relation types, no type that has an attribute of some superroot or subleaf type—see the discussion of IM Prescription 26 in Chapter 19—is represented in the graph.

- Point 4 is also self-explanatory. Point 5 reflects the fact that no type *T* can be both an immediate and a nonimmediate supertype of the same type *T'*.

- Points 6 and 7 are obvious generalizations of the corresponding portions of the "type hierarchy" definition for the single inheritance case (see Chapter 3). Note that a root type can be regarded as an entry point into the overall type graph. Note too that we don't assume that there's exactly one root type.

- Point 8 is discussed in the next section but one.

- Finally, point 9 is discussed in the next chapter (see Exercise 15.5 in that chapter).

Observe now that it follows from the foregoing definition that any given type graph *TG* can be divided into a set of disjoint partitions *P1, P2, ..., Pr*—a nonempty set, unless *TG* itself is empty—such that (a) each *Pi* (*i* = 1, 2, ..., *r*) contains exactly one root node and one or more leaf nodes, and (b) no type in *Pi* (*i* = 1, 2, ..., *r*) overlaps any type in *Pj* (*j* = 1, 2, ..., *r*; *j* ≠ *i*). Moreover, if *Pi* contains just one leaf node, then that partition forms a lattice, with least upper bound the pertinent root node and greatest lower bound that leaf node. *Note:* Refer to Chapter 5 if you need to refresh your memory regarding the concept of lattices in general, and the concept of type lattices in particular.

Of course, in this part of the book we're concerned with scalar types only, in which case:

- Even if *Pi* doesn't contain just one leaf node, it can always be converted into a lattice by violating point 3 and introducing the minimal scalar type (viz., type *omega*).

- However, the lattices in question aren't type lattices as such—at least, not as this latter term is usually understood (again see Chapter 5)—because they don't contain the maximal scalar type (viz., type *alpha*).

- On the other hand, if again we violate point 3 by introducing both types *alpha* and *omega*, then the entire graph becomes a single type lattice, with *alpha* and *omega* as least upper bound and greatest lower bound, respectively.

TWO REMARKS ON OPERATOR INHERITANCE

Consider the read-only operator AREA_OF, which is defined for type PARALLELOGRAM and is inherited from that type by type RECTANGLE and also by type RHOMBUS. As a consequence, type SQUARE inherits that operator from both of its immediate supertypes. What are the implications of this state of affairs?

Well, if there's an implementation version of AREA_OF that's specific to squares, there's no problem: The invocation AREA_OF (*s*), where *s* is of most specific type SQUARE, will unambiguously refer to that particular version. But if there's no such specific version, then there are two possibilities:

■ Types RECTANGLE and RHOMBUS have no implementation versions of their own. In this case, the PARALLELOGRAM version must necessarily be used, and again there's no problem.

■ At least one of RECTANGLE and RHOMBUS does have an implementation version of its own. For generality, in fact, we can assume they both do, because if either one doesn't then the PARALLELOGRAM version will apply to that one anyway.

Now there are two further possibilities:

■ If those two versions implement the same semantics—i.e., if the expression AREA_OF (*s*) gives the same result, no matter which version is invoked—then again there's no problem. (No problem so far as the model's concerned, that is. However, whoever defines the invocation signature for AREA_OF corresponding to an argument of type SQUARE—see the discussion of IM Prescription 17 in Chapter 11—will certainly have to decide, and will have to specify at "operator definition time," which of the two versions is the one to be invoked. In practice, of course, such decisions will be guided by performance concerns or other such pragmatic considerations. But these matters are of no concern to a user who just wants to obtain the area of some specific square.)

■ However, if the semantics of those two versions differ, then it matters very much which version is inherited by type SQUARE. But now the situation is absurd! To say that SQUARE is a subtype of both RECTANGLE and RHOMBUS is to say that any given square is both a rectangle and a rhombus. But then to go on and say that the area of that square depends on whether we think of it as a rectangle or as a rhombus is surely nonsense. Thus, to repeat something I said at the end of the discussion of IM Prescription 17 in Chapter 11, we reject the suggestion that changing operator semantics can ever be a good idea; further, we define our model to say simply that if a change in semantics occurs, the implementation is in violation—i.e., it's not an implementation of the model—and the implications are unpredictable.

Now I turn to another issue, related to the previous one but different. Suppose some read-only operator *Op* has been defined for rectangles and another operator with the same name *Op* has been defined for rhombi. Suppose further that these operators aren't inherited from parallelograms—i.e., there's no operator called *Op* for type PARALLELOGRAM—and so the two operators named *Op* really are different operators (in other words, we're talking about overloading, not inclusion polymorphism). Suppose further for simplicity that each of these operators takes just one parameter (of type RECTANGLE and type RHOMBUS, respectively). What do we do about the inheritance of *Op* by type SQUARE?

On the face of it, there *is* a problem here: By the very notion of type inheritance, both operators must indeed be inherited by type SQUARE, and it appears, therefore, that an invocation *Op* (*s*), where *s* is of declared type SQUARE, will be ambiguous. Clearly, then, what we have to do is prevent such a situation from arising. But that's exactly what the following rule (part of IM Prescription 17) does for us:

> If two distinct operators (either both read-only or both update operators) have the same name and the same number *n* of parameters, then for some *j* ($1 \leq j \leq n$) the declared types of their *j*th parameters, as given by their respective specification signatures, shall be disjoint.

In the example, the two operators do have the same name and the same number of parameters (viz., one).[17] Moreover, their sole parameter has declared type RECTANGLE in the one case and RHOMBUS in the other, and these types aren't disjoint. The example thus clearly violates the foregoing rule.

Note: We wouldn't expect that rule to cause any significant hardship in practice, because the system should be able to detect violations as soon as they occur (i.e., at "operator definition time" once again).

IM PRESCRIPTIONS 1 - 7 REVISITED

In Part II of this book I discussed IM Prescriptions 1-20 as they applied to scalar types and single inheritance. Now we need to review those prescriptions to see what additional discussion, if any, is needed to cater for multiple inheritance (though still for scalar types only). This section considers IM Prescriptions 1-7, which were originally discussed in Chapter 5.[18] In fact, it's mostly concerned with IM Prescription 7 in particular, since there really isn't very much to say regarding IM Prescriptions 1-6. But just for the record:

- IM Prescription 1 (types are sets): No further discussion needed.

- IM Prescription 2 (subtypes are subsets): No further discussion needed.

- IM Prescription 3 ("subtype of" is reflexive): No further discussion needed.

---

[17] If they had the same name but different numbers of parameters, then they would certainly have different specification signatures and there wouldn't be any ambiguity.

[18] Of the remainder, numbers 8 and 9 are discussed in Chapter 15 and the rest in Chapter 16.

- IM Prescription 4 ("subtype of" is transitive): No further discussion needed.

- IM Prescription 5 (proper and immediate subtypes and supertypes): This prescription still applies 100 percent. Note, however, that it does require among other things that if T and T' are scalar types and T' is a nonempty immediate subtype of T (and isn't a root type), then the definition of T' must be accompanied by a specification of an example value that's of type T and not of type T'. It follows that if (scalar, nonempty, nonroot) type T' has n distinct immediate supertypes $T1$, $T2$, ..., Tn—and with multiple inheritance, n can be greater than one—then its definition must be accompanied by specifications of an example value that's of type $T1$ and not of type T', an example value that's of type $T2$ and not of type T', ..., and an example value that's of type Tn and not of type T'. For an illustration of this point, see the definition of type SQUARE earlier in this chapter.

- IM Prescription 6 (scalar root and leaf types): No further discussion needed.

As for IM Prescription 7 (disjoint and overlapping types), here repeated from Chapter 5 is the text of that prescription:

> Types $T1$ and $T2$ shall be **disjoint** if and only if no value is of both type $T1$ and type $T2$. Types $T1$ and $T2$ shall **overlap** if and only if there exists at least one value that is common to both. Distinct root types shall be disjoint. If types $T1$ and $T2$ are distinct immediate subtypes of the same scalar type T, then there shall exist at least one value that is of type $T1$ and not of type $T2$.

Now, with single inheritance, this prescription was tightly bound up with the disjointness assumption, which says that types $T1$ and $T2$ are disjoint if and only if neither is a subtype of the other. With multiple inheritance, however, that assumption no longer holds. For example, types RECTANGLE and RHOMBUS certainly aren't disjoint, even though neither is a subtype of the other, because some rectangles aren't rhombi and some rhombi aren't rectangles. Of course, those values that are both rectangles and rhombi are, precisely, squares; but until such time as we actually define type SQUARE, we still don't have multiple inheritance as such. Thus, in order to support multiple inheritance, it's necessary but not sufficient that we relax the disjointness assumption. (More precisely, if we relax it for leaf types only, we still don't have multiple inheritance; if we relax it for nonleaf types, we do.)

We don't have to drop that assumption in its entirety, however, nor do we wish to. Rather, what we do, in effect, is simplify it to say just that distinct *root* types must be disjoint—which is, of course, guaranteed by virtue of IM Prescription 7 anyway, but let's take a closer look.

First, you might recall the term *least specific type*, which was mentioned in a note attached to IM Prescription 8 and was briefly discussed in Chapter 6 (see also Exercise 3.5 in Chapter 3). One of the things that note said was that the least specific type for, or of, any given scalar value is unique. In fact this point is surely obvious, but let me spell out the details:

Definition: Let value *v* be of type *T* and not of any proper supertype of *T*; then *T* is the *least specific* type of *v*. Note that *T* is necessarily a maximal type and is thus unique; hence, if *v* is a scalar value in particular, the least specific type of *v* is *alpha*. Informally, however, least specific types are often defined to exclude the pertinent maximal type, thus: Let *v* be of type *T* and not of any proper supertype of *T* apart from the pertinent maximal type; then *T*—which is necessarily a root type—is the least specific type of *v*.[19]

Note: Throughout the rest of this book, I'll use the term *least specific type* in this latter, informal sense (that is, I'll take the least specific type of any given value to be a root type), barring explicit statements to the contrary.

To see that least specific types must be unique, consider the example represented by the graph shown in Fig. 14.4 (note that I don't refer to that graph as a type graph, because it isn't one):

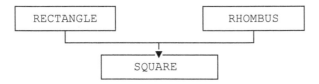

Fig. 14.4: Another graph that's not a valid type graph

As the figure suggests, no type PARALLELOGRAM has been defined. Apparently, then, type SQUARE has two immediate supertypes, RECTANGLE and RHOMBUS, both of which are root types; thus, if *v* is a value of type SQUARE, it's also a value of both of those root types. But such a state of affairs violates IM Prescription 7, which requires that distinct root types be disjoint; so we don't allow it.

Now, it should be obvious that the same simple analysis applies even if additional types appear in the graph between SQUARE and RECTANGLE and/or between SQUARE and RHOMBUS (i.e., if SQUARE is a proper subtype, but not necessarily an immediate subtype, of both RECTANGLE and RHOMBUS). It follows that:

a. The graph shown in Fig. 14.4 isn't a valid type graph.

b. More generally, no type can have two or more distinct root types as proper supertypes.

c. Hence, the least specific type of any given value is unique, as previously stated.

---

[19] This latter part of the definition (i.e., the informal part) relies, tacitly, on the assumption that *v* is scalar. It'll need some slight extension when we get to tuple and relation types (see the final paragraph of the section "Closing Remarks" in Chapter 18).

So now I've effectively explained point 8 of the definition of the type graph concept from a couple of sections back, which (as you'll recall) reads as follows:

If nodes *T1* and *T2* are distinct root nodes, then no node is reachable from both *T1* and *T2*.

The reason is that if node *T'* were reachable from both *T1* and *T2*, then certain values of type *T'* would be values of both type *T1* and type *T2* and would thus have two distinct least specific types.

I turn now to the final sentence of IM Prescription 7: *If types T1 and T2 are distinct immediate subtypes of the same scalar type T, then there shall exist at least one value that is of type T1 and not of type T2.* Let's agree to refer to the requirement articulated in this sentence as "the noninclusion requirement." Now, if the disjointness assumption holds, then *T1* and *T2* will be disjoint, and so the noninclusion requirement will necessarily be satisfied a fortiori. But with multiple inheritance, of course, the disjointness assumption doesn't hold, and so *T1* and *T2* can certainly overlap (think of RECTANGLE and RHOMBUS, for example). But what we don't want—as the name "the noninclusion requirement" is meant to suggest—is for every value of *T1* to be a value of *T2* or the other way around; in other words, we don't want $|T1|$ to be included in $|T2|$ or the other way around. Why not? Well:

a. If $|T1| = |T2|$, then clearly *T1* and *T2* should be collapsed into a single type.

b. If $|T1| \subset |T2|$, then clearly *T1* should be a proper subtype of *T2*.

Now, if *T1* and *T2* are immediate subtypes of type *T* and we believe they overlap, then IM Prescription 8 requires us to define their intersection type *T'* (see Chapter 15); moreover, if *T1* and *T2* are regular types, then (in accordance with IM Prescription 5) the definition of *T'* will be accompanied by examples of (a) a value that's of type *T1* and not of type *T'* and (b) a value that's of type *T2* and not of type *T'*. But if $|T1| \subseteq |T2|$, then $|T'|$ will be equal to $|T1|$, and so no value will exist that's of type *T1* and not of type *T'*, and the definition of *T'* will therefore fail. So the noninclusion requirement of that final sentence of IM Prescription 7 will necessarily be satisfied in this case. However, if *T1* and *T2* do in fact overlap but we think they're disjoint, then type *T'* won't be defined; as previously noted in Chapter 3, then, the resulting type schema will be in violation of the model, and the consequences will be unpredictable. In particular, the noninclusion requirement might be violated in such a situation.

By the way, it's important to note that the noninclusion requirement has, and in fact implies, the following important generalization: No two distinct types *T1* and *T2*, neither of which is a subtype of the other, are such that $|T1| \subseteq |T2|$ or the other way around. In fact, this is easy to see. Let the least specific types (i.e., the root types) corresponding to *T1* and *T2* be *T1** and *T2**, respectively. Then:

■ If *T1** and *T2** are distinct, they're certainly disjoint, so *T1* and *T2* are disjoint too; hence, it's definitely not the case that |*T1*| ⊆ |*T2*| or the other way around.

■ Otherwise, define type *T* to be the union of all proper supertypes of *T1* and *T2*, all the way up to and including their common least specific type *T** (which is the same as both *T1** and *T2** in this case). Then *T1* and *T2* are distinct immediate subtypes of *T*, and the conditions of the noninclusion requirement apply.

TYPE DEFINITIONS

I'll close this chapter by repeating for ease of reference the definitions I'll be assuming from this point forward for types PARALLELOGRAM, RECTANGLE, RHOMBUS, and SQUARE.

```
TYPE PARALLELOGRAM    /* third and final attempt */
     POSSREP ( A POINT , B POINT , C POINT )
     CONSTRAINT NOT COLLINEAR ( A , B , C )
          AND WITH ( X1 := THE_X ( A ) , Y1 := THE_Y ( A ) ,
                     X  := THE_X ( B ) , Y  := THE_Y ( B ) ,
                     X2 := THE_X ( A ) , Y2 := THE_Y ( C ) ) :
              IF X1 = X2 THEN Y1 < Y2 ELSE X1 < X2 END IF
              AND ( X2 - X1 ) * ( Y - Y1 ) > ( Y2 - Y1 ) * ( X - X1 ) ;

TYPE RECTANGLE
     IS { PARALLELOGRAM
          CONSTRAINT LD ( PARALLELOGRAM ) = SD ( PARALLELOGRAM )
          POSSREP ( A = THE_A ( PARALLELOGRAM ) ,
                    B = THE_B ( PARALLELOGRAM ) ,
                    C = THE_C ( PARALLELOGRAM ) )
          NOT { PARALLELOGRAM ( POINT ( 0.0 , 2.0 ) ,
                                POINT ( 4.0 , 2.0 ) ,
                                POINT ( 3.0 , 0.0 ) ) } } ;

TYPE RHOMBUS
     IS { PARALLELOGRAM
          CONSTRAINT LS ( PARALLELOGRAM ) = SS ( PARALLELOGRAM )
          POSSREP ( A = THE_A ( PARALLELOGRAM ) ,
                    B = THE_B ( PARALLELOGRAM ) ,
                    C = THE_C ( PARALLELOGRAM ) )
          NOT { PARALLELOGRAM ( POINT ( 0.0 , 2.0 ) ,
                                POINT ( 4.0 , 2.0 ) ,
                                POINT ( 4.0 , 0.0 ) ) } } ;
```

```
TYPE SQUARE
      IS { RECTANGLE , RHOMBUS
            POSSREP ( A = THE_A ( RECTANGLE ) ,
                      C = THE_C ( RECTANGLE ) )
            NOT { RECTANGLE ( POINT ( 0.0 , 2.0 ) ,
                              POINT ( 4.0 , 2.0 ) ,
                              POINT ( 4.0 , 0.0 ) ) ,
                  RHOMBUS   ( POINT ( 3.0 , 4.0 ) ,
                              POINT ( 8.0 , 4.0 ) ,
                              POINT ( 5.0 , 0.0 ) ) ) } } ;
```

EXERCISES

14.1 Consider the following table:

Case	A	B	C	valid?	MST
1	(0,0)	(1,5)	(4,0)		
2	(0,0)	(2,3)	(4,0)		
3	(0,0)	(3,4)	(8,0)		
4	(2,3)	(0,0)	(4,0)		
5	(2,4)	(0,0)	(2,6)		
6	(2,4)	(0,0)	(2,2)		
7	(0,0)	(5,0)	(5,3)		
8	(0,0)	(5,0)	(5,5)		

The table is based on the type definitions from the section "Type Definitions" in the body of the chapter; it represents eight selector invocations (actually literals)—or would-be selector invocations or literals, perhaps—for type PARALLELOGRAM. Which ones are valid and which not? Also, for those that are valid, what's the most specific type of the value returned? *Note:* I haven't bothered to show those selector invocations in full syntactic detail—I've just shown the arguments, in cartesian coordinate form, corresponding to vertices A, B, and C (and for simplicity I've used literals of type INTEGER, not RATIONAL, to denote the x and y coordinates of those arguments).

14.2 Write some implementation code for operators AREA_OF, CTR_OF, CIRCUM_CIRCLE, IN_CIRCLE, and ANNULUS from the section "Operators" in the body of the chapter.

14.3 A scalene triangle is a triangle with no two equal angles (equivalently, it's one with no two equal sides). A right triangle is a triangle one of whose angles is a right angle. Obviously, some scalene triangles are right triangles and some aren't, and some right triangles are scalene and some aren't. Sketch a corresponding type graph.

14.4 What possreps do you think might be reasonable for the various types involved in Exercise 14.3? *Note:* Don't attempt to give formal **Tutorial D** type definitions—just state your thoughts in natural language prose. For example, if you think the three vertices constitute a reasonable possrep for triangles, say just that. Also, can you think of any alternative possreps? What operators do you think might be useful in connection with these types?

ANSWERS

14.1

Case	A	B	C	valid?	MST
1	(0,0)	(1,5)	(4,0)	yes	PARALLELOGRAM
2	(0,0)	(2,3)	(4,0)	yes	RHOMBUS
3	(0,0)	(3,4)	(8,0)	yes	RHOMBUS
4	(2,3)	(0,0)	(4,0)	no	n/a
5	(2,4)	(0,0)	(2,6)	yes	PARALLELOGRAM
6	(2,4)	(0,0)	(2,2)	no	n/a
7	(0,0)	(5,0)	(5,3)	no	n/a
8	(0,0)	(5,0)	(5,5)	yes	SQUARE

14.2 Instead of showing actual code, I content myself with giving definitions and explanations that will enable you to write that code yourself if you feel motivated to do so:

- The area of a parallelogram is the length of one of its sides multiplied by the perpendicular distance between that side and its opposite side.

- The center of a parallelogram is the point at which its diagonals intersect.

- Given a rectangle *r*, (a) the radius of the circumscribed circle is half the length of the diagonal of *r*, and (b) its center is the center of *r*.

- Given a rhombus *r*, (a) the radius of the inscribed circle is given by the formula

```
( ld * sd ) / ( 2 * SQRT ( ld ^ 2 + sd ^ 2 ) )
```

where *ld* and *sd* are the length of the long diagonal of *r* and the length of the short diagonal of *r*, respectively, and (b) its center is the center of *r*.

■ An annulus can be represented by a pair of concentric circles.

14.3

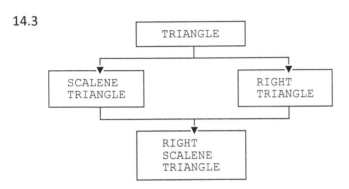

14.4 *Type TRIANGLE:* The obvious possrep consists of the three vertices *A, B, C*, with a constraint to the effect that the points in question are not collinear. A constraint that pins down which vertex is which will be needed too; perhaps we could define an ordering for points, somewhat along the lines of the one defined in the body of the chapter in connection with type PARALLELOGRAM. Another possibility would be to define an ordering based on the sizes of the interior angles at the vertices.

Type SCALENE_TRIANGLE: Same possrep as for type TRIANGLE, together with an *<is def>* to the effect that a scalene triangle "is a" triangle (and so inherits constraints and operators from that type), together with a further constraint to the effect that no two of the angles *ABC, BCA, CAB* are equal (or one to the effect that no two of the sides *AB, BC, CA* are of the same length).

Type RIGHT_TRIANGLE: Same possrep as for type TRIANGLE, together with an *<is def>* to the effect that a right triangle "is a" triangle (and so inherits constraints and operators from that type), together with a further constraint to the effect that one of the angles *ABC, BCA, CAB* is a right angle. *Subsidiary exercise:* It might be desirable to insist that the right angle be at one specific vertex, say vertex *A*. How might this effect be achieved?

Type RIGHT_SCALENE_TRIANGLE: Same possrep as for type TRIANGLE, together with an *<is def>* to the effect that a right scalene triangle "is a" scalene triangle and also "is a" right triangle (and so inherits constraints and operators from both of those types).

Alternative possreps: For triangles in general (i.e., scalene, right, or otherwise), one alternative possrep that springs to mind involves one vertex, say *A*, together with either (a) the sides *AB* and *AC* that meet at that vertex or (b) the third side *BC*. Since sides are line segments, however, to specify (say) the side *AB* is effectively to specify the begin point *A* and the end point *B*; so these possreps aren't significantly different from ones already discussed (though they might simplify that business of pinning down which vertex is which). Many other possreps might be defined also.

Operators: Some obvious operators that spring to mind are operators that return the sides of a given triangle (i.e., as line segments); operators that return the angles; operators that return the lengths of the sides; an operator that returns the area; operators that return the median corresponding to a specific vertex or specific side; an operator that returns the centroid; operators to return the unique inscribed and circumscribed circles; and so on.

Chapter 15

IM Prescriptions 8–9 Revisited

Let no one enter who is ignorant of geometry.

—Plato (c. 400 BCE)

There is no royal road to geometry.

—Euclid (c. 300 BCE)

As we know from Chapter 3, the disjointness assumption has the important consequence that every value has a unique most specific type. With multiple inheritance, however, that assumption no longer holds, and so the question is: Does that same property hold with multiple inheritance anyway?—i.e., is it still true with multiple inheritance that every value has a unique most specific type? In fact the answer to this question is *yes*, thanks to IM Prescription 8.[1] This chapter examines this issue, as well as several related issues.

First, however, let me make a preliminary point. The text of IM Prescription 8 begins thus:

Let *T1, T2, ..., Tm* (*m* ≥ 0) ... be scalar types.

Clearly, we can assume without loss of generality that types *T1, T2, ..., Tm* are all distinct. Moreover, we can also assume, thanks to the noninclusion requirement of IM Prescription 7 (see Chapter 14) that no two distinct types *Ti* and *Tj* ($1 \leq i, j \leq m$; $i \neq j$), neither of which is a subtype of the other, are such that the set of values |*Ti*| constituting *Ti* is a subset of the set of values |*Tj*| constituting *Tj*. I'll rely on these two assumptions (sometimes just tacitly) throughout this chapter.

LEAST SPECIFIC COMMON SUBTYPES

To repeat, it's my claim that the property that most specific types are unique follows from IM Prescription 8. More specifically, I claim that property follows from that portion of the prescription that has to do with common subtypes. Let me quote that portion again (the text that follows is based on the full text in Chapter 4 but is somewhat edited here):

---

[1] IM Prescription 8 was originally discussed in Chapter 6.

- Let $T1, T2, ..., Tm$ ($m \geq 0$) and T' be scalar types. Then type T' shall be a **common subtype** for, or of, types $T1, T2, ..., Tm$ if and only if, whenever a given value is of type T', it is also of each of types $T1, T2, ..., Tm$.[2] Further, that type T' shall be the **least specific** common subtype—also known as the **intersection type** or **intersection subtype**—for $T1, T2, ..., Tm$ if and only if no proper supertype of T' is also a common subtype for those types. *Note:* Given such types $T1, T2, ..., Tm$, it can be shown that a unique least specific common subtype T' always exists.

By way of illustration, type SQUARE is clearly the least specific common subtype, or intersection type, for types RECTANGLE and RHOMBUS in our running example. *Note:* For convenience, until further notice I'll take "IM Prescription 8" (or just "this prescription" or "the prescription") to refer to the foregoing reduced version, having to do with common subtypes specifically.

Now, before I try to show how this prescription does in fact guarantee the uniqueness of most specific types, I think we need to examine the question of whether the prescription is reasonable in itself (in the multiple inheritance context, that is). In other words, does it make sense to say, with multiple inheritance in particular, that every set of scalar types has a least specific common subtype? Further, does it seem reasonable to say, as the prescription claims, that the subtype in question is unique?

Well, we saw in Chapter 6 that it certainly makes sense if m, the number of scalar types in the given set of types $T1, T2, ..., Tm$, is either zero or one. Just to remind you:

- If $m = 0$, meaning the given set of types is empty, the unique least specific common subtype is the maximal scalar type, viz., type *alpha*.

- If $m = 1$, meaning the given set of types is a singleton set and contains just one type $T1$, the unique least specific common subtype is that type $T1$ itself.

What happens if $m = 2$? Tailored to this specific case, the prescription becomes:

- Let $T1$, $T2$, and T' be scalar types. Then type T' shall be a **common subtype** for, or of, types $T1$ and $T2$ if and only if, whenever a given value is of type T', it is also of types $T1$ and $T2$. Further, that type T' shall be the **least specific** common subtype—also known as the **intersection type** or **intersection subtype**—for $T1$ and $T2$ if and only if no proper supertype of T' is also a common subtype for those two types. *Note:* Given such types $T1$ and $T2$, it can be shown that a unique least specific common subtype T' always exists.

Or more colloquially (think of types RECTANGLE, RHOMBUS, and SQUARE once again):

---

[2] In other words, as we saw in the answer to Exercise 6.2 in Chapter 6, T' is a common subtype for $T1, T2, ..., Tm$ if and only if it satisfies the predicate FORALL v (IF $v \in |T'|$ THEN $v \in$ INTERSECT $\{|T1|, |T2|, ..., |Tm|\}$).

■ Any two scalar types *T1* and *T2* shall have a unique least specific common subtype.

Now, this simplified form of the prescription was effectively shown in Chapter 6 to be reasonable as well if *T1* and *T2* are either:

a. Disjoint, in which case their least specific common subtype is the minimal scalar type, viz., type *omega*, or

b. Not disjoint, but such that one is a subtype of the other. For definiteness, assume *T2* is a subtype of *T1*. Then every subtype of *T2* is a common subtype for *T1* and *T2*; of those common subtypes, moreover, the least specific is clearly *T2* itself.

So the only case not already discussed, under our current assumption that $m = 2$, is the case where *T1* and *T2* overlap and neither is a subtype of the other (a case that can't occur with single inheritance, of course, which is why it wasn't discussed in Chapter 6). For this case, the prescription becomes:

■ Let scalar types *T1* and *T2* overlap, and let neither be a subtype of the other; then they shall have at least one common subtype. *Note:* Given such types *T1* and *T2*, it can be shown that a unique least specific common subtype *T'* always exists.

Well, our various discussions of rectangles, rhombi, and squares in Chapter 14 should be sufficient to convince you that this situation is reasonable too. To be specific, we can appeal to the fact that type *T'* is the intersection type, as such, for types *T1* and *T2*; that is, the set of values $|T'|$ is the set theory intersection $|T1| \cap |T2|$ of the sets of values $|T1|$ and $|T2|$. Since the intersection of two sets is unique by definition, it follows that type *T'* is unique as well; that is, there can't be any other type *T''*, distinct from *T'*, that's also a common subtype for *T1* and *T2* but is less specific than—i.e., is a proper supertype of—*T'*. Thus, *T'* is indeed the least specific common subtype of *T1* and *T2* in this case as well, as required. Moreover, since neither of $|T1|$ and $|T2|$ is included in the other, it follows that *T'* must be distinct from both *T1* and *T2* as well.

Here's a slightly different way to say the same thing. Let types *T1* and *T2* overlap. Then there can't exist two distinct types *T'* and *T''*, both of which are common subtypes of *T1* and *T2*, and both of which are "least specific." For if they did both satisfy those conditions, then they'd both be the intersection type for *T1* and *T2*; in other words, they'd be one and the same. In other words, the situation illustrated in Fig. 15.1 below makes no sense. *Note:* That figure illustrates (but doesn't rely on) a point to be discussed later in this chapter—viz., that if types *T1* and *T2* have a common subtype *T'*, they also have a common supertype *T*.

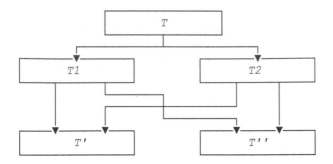

Fig. 15.1: Another graph that's not a valid type graph

To summarize to this point, then: I've shown that any two types have a unique least specific common subtype. The following statement is a rough and ready way of remembering this result (it's not so precise, but I believe it can be helpful from the standpoint of intuition nonetheless):

■ If two types overlap, they have a nonempty common subtype; conversely, if two types have a nonempty common subtype, they overlap.

See Figs. 15.2 and 15.3 later in the chapter for several illustrations of this state of affairs.

Three or More Overlapping Types

Back to IM Prescription 8 as such. I've now considered the cases where $m \leq 2$; so what about the case where $m > 2$? As it turns out, the argument in Chapter 6 regarding this case applies here unchanged, because that argument didn't rely on single inheritance as such (all it relied on was a prior demonstration to the effect that the prescription did make sense for $m \leq 2$). Thus, I claim that IM Prescription 8 does in fact make sense in all possible cases.

The foregoing paragraph notwithstanding, let's take a closer look at the case $m = 3$, just for interest. Let scalar types *T1*, *T2*, and *T3* overlap pairwise, and let the corresponding intersection types—which we now definitely know are required—be *Ta* (for *T2* and *T3*), *Tb* (for *T3* and *T1*), and *Tc* (for *T1* and *T2*).[3] Then types *Ta*, *Tb*, and *Tc* will also overlap pairwise, in general; however, it's easy to see that the three intersection types required for these types *Ta*, *Tb*, and *Tc* taken pairwise are all one and the same type, *T'* say. More specifically, it's easy to see that the set of values |*T'*| is precisely the intersection |*T1*| ∩ |*T2*| ∩ |*T3*| of the sets of values |*T1*|, |*T2*|, and |*T3*|. Hence type *T'* is obviously unique, and so it's the intersection type for *T1*, *T2*, and *T3*, and

---

[3] Of course, it's possible that types *T1*, *T2*, *T3*, *Ta*, *Tb*, *Tc* aren't all distinct, but in general they will be. See Exercise 15.6 at the end of the chapter for further discussion.

also for *Ta*, *Tb*, and *Tc*. What's more, it should be clear without going into details that the foregoing argument can readily be generalized to deal with the case of arbitrary $m > 2$.

MOST SPECIFIC TYPES

Now I can get back to my real goal: viz., showing that most specific types are unique. Despite the fact that I've already appealed to the most specific type concept many times in previous chapters, I'll begin with a definition:

> **Definition:** Let value *v* be of type *T*. If and only if no proper subtype *T'* of type *T* exists such that *v* is also of type *T'*, then *T* is the *most specific* type for, or of, *v*.

Why We Want Most Specific Types to Be Unique

Perhaps I should explain why we want most specific types to be unique anyway. In fact, the reason is easy to see. By way of illustration, suppose a given value *s* could be both a rectangle and a rhombus, and suppose further that type SQUARE hasn't yet been defined. Then that value *s* would have two distinct most specific types, RECTANGLE and RHOMBUS. And one immediate (and unpleasant) consequence of this state of affairs would appear to be as follows:

- Suppose an operator named *Op* has been defined for rectangles and another operator with the same name *Op* has been defined for rhombi.

- Suppose further for simplicity that each of these operators takes just one parameter.

- Then an invocation of *Op* with argument *s* would be ambiguous.

Note carefully, however, that I said the foregoing situation would *appear* to be a consequence (of the fact that *s* has two distinct most specific types, that is). In fact it isn't a consequence at all, and the foregoing argument is specious. To see why, suppose that (a) the expression that denotes the argument *s* to the *Op* invocation is *exp*, and hence that (b) the invocation in question looks like this: *Op(exp)*. By definition, then, *exp* has a declared type *DT(exp)*. Moreover, that declared type must be either RECTANGLE or RHOMBUS—it can't be anything else, because no operator named *Op* is defined for anything else (or let's assume as much for the sake of the discussion, at any rate)—and so the system will know at compile time which operator to invoke, and there's no ambiguity.[4]

---

[4] Note the logical difference between the situation sketched in this paragraph and the second of the two problems discussed in the section "Two Remarks on Operator Inheritance" in Chapter 14.

So the question stands: Why exactly do we insist on most specific types being unique? Well, let's stay with the same basic example; i.e., let's assume we're given just two types, RECTANGLE and RHOMBUS, neither of which is a subtype of the other. Does it make sense to say that some value exists that has both of these types as its most specific type? If it does, then:

■   First of all, there must be situations in which the value *s* of some expression *exp* of declared type RECTANGLE is to be treated as if it were a value of type RHOMBUS (or the other way around). Why must such situations exist? Because if they don't, then there's no sense in which it can possibly be of interest to say that *s* has both types. So this first point implies that the expression TREAT_AS_RHOMBUS (*exp*) must be legal. But IM Prescription 14[5] says this expression is legal only if types RECTANGLE and RHOMBUS overlap—which they do, of course, but the compiler isn't (and can't be) aware of that fact, because type SQUARE hasn't been defined. Therefore:

  a.   To repeat, given the TREAT invocation TREAT_AS_*T* (*exp*), IM Prescription 14 requires *T* and *DT(exp)* to overlap.

  b.   But if the compiler has to allow the expression TREAT_AS_RHOMBUS (*exp*) anyway, the foregoing requirement no longer applies. So we might as well drop it, since it's now effectively meaningless.

  c.   Thus, certain compile time checks now become impossible, which in turn increases the likelihood of more run time type errors.

■   By a similar argument, the expression IS_RHOMBUS (*exp*) must presumably also be legal (it'll give TRUE if and only if *s*, the current value of expression *exp*, has RHOMBUS as one of its types). Remarks similar to those above regarding IM Prescription 14 thus apply to IM Prescription 15 as well.

■   Similar remarks apply to equality comparisons also (IM Prescription 12). In this case, however, there's a little more that can usefully be said.[6] Consider the following code fragment:

```
VAR RE RECTANGLE ;
VAR RH RHOMBUS ;

IF RH = RE THEN ... ;
```

---

[5] See Chapter 16 for further discussion of IM Prescription 14 (also of IM Prescriptions 11, 12, and 15, all of which are referenced in the next few bullet items) in the multiple inheritance context.

[6] Actually I could have made an argument analogous to the one that follows in my discussions of IM Prescriptions 14 and 15 as well.

Clearly, the comparison RH = RE can give TRUE only if RH and RE both have the same current value *s*, which must be, by definition, a square. What's more, the user will certainly be aware of this fact; that is, type SQUARE must certainly exist in the user's mind, as it were, even if that type hasn't been explicitly defined. Thus, there doesn't seem to be any advantage in allowing type SQUARE not to be defined; at the same time, there do seem to be plenty of advantages in requiring such a definition.

■ It should be clear without going into details that the arguments of the previous bullet item apply to assignment also (IM Prescription 11), mutatis mutandis.

The net of all of the above is this: Not only does it seem reasonable and desirable to require most specific types to be unique, it also seems unreasonable and undesirable not to. And let me add one last point. Suppose most specific types don't have to be unique after all. Then distinct leaf types will sometimes overlap (indeed, that's exactly what happens with types RECTANGLE and RHOMBUS, if type SQUARE isn't defined). But it would surely seem a little odd to say, as *The Third Manifesto* effectively does say, that scalar leaf types have to be disjoint without inheritance but don't have to be disjoint with it; in fact, it would constitute, at least arguably, an incompatibility between the *Manifesto* as such and our inheritance model. (Without inheritance, of course, all types are leaf types.) And it would make no sense to change the *Manifesto* in this regard, for that would be to give up on static type checking altogether, contrary to one of the *Manifesto*'s explicitly stated aims.

How IM Prescription 8 Implies Most Specific Type Uniqueness

Here then is how IM Prescription 8 implies our desired result, viz., that most specific types are unique. Suppose, contrariwise, that there exists some value *v* that's of two distinct most specific types, *T1* and *T2* say. Observe that, by definition, (a) neither of *T1* and *T2* is a subtype of the other (since *T1* and *T2* are both "most specific"), and (b) neither of |*T1*| and |*T2*| is a subset of the other (since *T1* and *T2* are distinct). By IM Prescription 8, then, *v* must also be of some type *T'* that's a common subtype of *T1* and *T2*. Furthermore, *T'* must be a proper subtype of both *T1* and *T2*, since neither of these latter two types is a subtype of the other. But to say that *v* is of some proper subtype of (e.g.) *T1* is to contradict the hypothesis that *T1* was a most specific type for *v* in the first place.

By way of illustration of these ideas, consider the type graph shown in Fig. 15.2 (type EQUILATERAL in that figure consists of polygons whose sides are all the same length). Note in particular that, e.g., types QUADRILATERAL and EQUILATERAL overlap, and neither is a subtype of the other. In accordance with IM Prescription 8, then, they must have a least specific common subtype—that is, a subtype *T'* such that a polygon that's both quadrilateral and equilateral is a value of type *T'* and not of any proper supertype of *T'*—and so they do: viz., type RHOMBUS. (Note that any polygon that's both quadrilateral and equilateral is indeed a rhombus.) Of course, type SQUARE is also a common subtype for types QUADRILATERAL and EQUILATERAL; however, it's not the intersection type as such, because some polygons (which?) are both quadrilateral and equilateral but not squares.

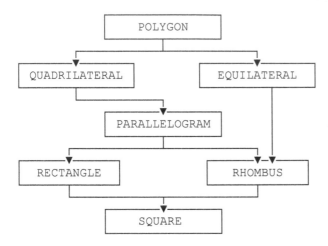

Fig. 15.2: Most specific types are unique (example)

Here for the record is a list showing the intersection types for every pair of types in Fig. 15.2 that satisfy the pertinent conditions (i.e., they overlap, and neither is a subtype of the other):

```
QUADRILATERAL    and   EQUILATERAL   :   RHOMBUS
PARALLELOGRAM    and   EQUILATERAL   :   RHOMBUS
RECTANGLE        and   EQUILATERAL   :   SQUARE
RECTANGLE        and   RHOMBUS       :   SQUARE
```

Aside: Given the foregoing, it might be thought that (e.g.) the *<is def>* for type SQUARE could specify either IS {RECTANGLE, EQUILATERAL} or IS {RECTANGLE, RHOMBUS}. However, IM Prescription 10—see Chapter 16—requires the *<is def>* in question to contain a specialization constraint for each pertinent *immediate* supertype, and the latter specification is thus the correct one. *End of aside.*

LEAF TYPES

As noted in passing earlier, IM Prescription 8 has the further consequence that (as with single inheritance) distinct scalar leaf types are disjoint. For suppose, contrariwise, that types *T1* and *T2* are distinct but overlapping scalar leaf types. In accordance with IM Prescription 8, then, *T1* and *T2* must have a common subtype *T'*. Moreover, since *T1* and *T2* are distinct and are leaf types, neither is a subtype of the other, and hence T' must be a proper subtype of both. But if they have a proper subtype, they can't have been leaf types in the first place.

MOST SPECIFIC COMMON SUPERTYPES

IM Prescription 8 has yet another important consequence: namely, not only do any two scalar types $T1$ and $T2$ have exactly one least specific common subtype, but they also have exactly one most specific common supertype. Here (lightly edited once again) is the portion of IM Prescription 8 that has to do with supertypes:

■ Let $T1$, $T2$, ..., Tm ($m \geq 0$) and T be scalar types. Then type T shall be a **common supertype** for, or of, types $T1$, $T2$, ..., Tm if and only if, whenever a given value is of at least one of types $T1$, $T2$, ..., Tm, it is also of type T.[7] Further, that type T shall be the **most specific** common supertype for $T1$, $T2$, ..., Tm if and only if no proper subtype of T is also a common supertype for those types. *Note:* Given such types $T1$, $T2$, ..., Tm, it can be shown that a unique most specific common supertype T always exists.

And here's the tailored version for the case $m = 2$:[8]

■ Let $T1$, $T2$, and T be scalar types. Then type T shall be a **common supertype** for, or of, types $T1$ and $T2$ if and only if, whenever a given value is of at least one of types $T1$ and $T2$, it is also of type T. Further, that type T shall be the **most specific** common supertype for $T1$ and $T2$ if and only if no proper subtype of T is also a common supertype for those types. *Note:* Given such types $T1$ and $T2$, it can be shown that a unique most specific common supertype T always exists.

Or more colloquially:

■ Any two scalar types $T1$ and $T2$ shall have a most specific common supertype.

As with our discussion of least specific common subtypes in an earlier section, however, this simplified form of the prescription is obviously valid—and for that reason not really very interesting—if $T1$ and $T2$ are either disjoint or such that one is a subtype of the other. So let's focus on the case where $T1$ and $T2$ overlap and neither is a subtype of the other. For this case, the prescription becomes:

---

[7] In other words, as we saw in the answer to Exercise 6.2 in Chapter 6, T is a common supertype for $T1$, $T2$, ..., Tm if and only if it satisfies the predicate FORALL v (IF $v \in$ UNION {$|T1|$, $|T2|$, ..., $|Tm|$} THEN $v \in |T|$).

[8] The cases $m = 0$ and $m = 1$ aren't worth discussing in detail. For the record, though, if $m = 0$, the most specific common supertype is *omega*; if $m = 1$, it's $T1$.

- Let scalar types *T1* and *T2* overlap, and let neither be a subtype of the other; then they shall have at least one common supertype. *Note:* Given such types *T1* and *T2*, it can be shown that a unique most specific common supertype *T* always exists.

Does this claim make sense? Let's investigate. (You might want to draw some diagrams as you work through the following explanation.)

- First of all, since they overlap, *T1* and *T2* certainly have at least one common supertype: viz., the applicable root type (which is unique, of course). *Note:* Recall that two types can overlap—and hence have a nonempty common subtype—only if they're subtypes of the same root type, thanks to IM Prescription 7.

- So suppose *T1* and *T2* have two distinct common supertypes, *Ta* and *Tb* say, neither of which is a subtype of the other.

- By virtue of IM Prescription 8, then, *Ta* and *Tb* also overlap, since they have a common subtype (actually at least two common subtypes, *T1* and *T2*).

- We can assume that *Ta* and *Tb* don't have a common proper subtype *T* that's also a common proper supertype of *T1* and *T2* (because to assume otherwise would be to assume the result we're trying to prove). In other words, *Ta* and *Tb* are both "most specific" common supertypes for *T1* and *T2*, loosely speaking.

Now rename the types as follows:

1. Rename *T1* and *T2* as *T'* and *T''*, respectively.

2. Rename *Ta* and *Tb* as *T1* and *T2*, respectively.

Then we have exactly the invalid situation shown previously in Fig. 15.1!—see the section "Least Specific Common Subtypes," earlier. It follows that our original assumption must be false; that is, the original "distinct common supertypes" *Ta* and *Tb* can't be distinct after all, and so *T1* and *T2* have precisely one most specific common supertype as claimed.[9]

It should be clear without going into details that the foregoing argument can readily be generalized to deal with the case of arbitrary $m > 2$.

---

[9] Let me remind you from Chapter 6 that, while the set of values $|T'|$ of the least specific common subtype *T'* of *T1* and *T2* is certainly the intersection $|T1| \cap |T2|$ of the sets of values $|T1|$ and $|T2|$, the set of values $|T|$ of the most specific common supertype *T* of *T1* and *T2* isn't necessarily the union $|T1| \cup |T2|$ of the sets of values $|T1|$ and $|T2|$; rather, it's some proper superset of that union, in general. For example, some parallelograms are neither rectangles nor rhombi.

The foregoing result is so important that I'd like to state it again in different words, as follows:

- If two types overlap—i.e., if they have a nonempty least specific common subtype—then they also have a most specific common supertype.

The following statement is strictly weaker than the foregoing but is nonetheless worth spelling out as an aid to intuition:

- If two types have a nonempty common subtype, they also have a common supertype.

(The converse is false, of course: Two types can have a common supertype without having a nonempty common subtype. For example, types ELLIPSE and RECTANGLE from the running example in Part II of this book have a common supertype, PLANE_FIGURE, but no common subtype other than the empty type *omega*.)

OVERLAPPING REGULAR TYPES

Suppose types *T1* and *T2* overlap and are regular types. Then their most specific common supertype, *T* say (which we now know is unique), must be a regular type also. For suppose not; i.e., suppose *T* is a dummy type. Let *T1* and *T2* have possible representations *PR1* and *PR2*, respectively. In general, then, *PR1* and *PR2* will be quite independent of one another, because (since *T* is a dummy type) there's no common source—i.e., no supertype possrep—for them to be derived from. In particular, therefore, *PR1* might have a component *C1* not present in *PR2*, and *PR2* might have a component *C2* not present in *PR1*.

Now let *T'* be the (also unique) least specific common subtype for types *T1* and *T2*. Then there's no way, in general, for an invocation of the selector corresponding to *PR1* to return a value of type *T'* (and hence of type *T2*), because that selector has no parameter corresponding to *C2*. (To put it another way, if an invocation of the selector corresponding to *PR1* returns some value *v*, then the expression THE_*C2*(*v*) is undefined.) Equivalently, specialization by constraint from type *T1* to type *T'* doesn't work (and the same goes for S by C from type *T2* to type *T'*, of course). In other words, allowing *T* to be a dummy type leads to a violation of IM Prescription 10 (see Chapters 8 and 16).

By way of an example to illustrate the foregoing discussion, consider the type graph of Fig. 14.1 from Chapter 14 once again. While type PARALLELOGRAM could possibly have a dummy type, say PLANE_FIGURE (not shown in that figure), as a proper supertype, type PARALLELOGRAM itself must be a regular type,[10] because types RECTANGLE and RHOMBUS are regular types and they overlap. Thus, every value of type RECTANGLE can be

---

[10] The fact that PARALLELOGRAM must be a regular type was previously mentioned in footnote 4 in Chapter 14.

obtained via some invocation of the PARALLELOGRAM selector, and the same goes for every value of type RHOMBUS.

AN EXTENDED EXAMPLE

The full implications of all of the points discussed in the preceding sections are far from obvious and (in my experience) not always immediately grasped. Here therefore is another example, a little more complicated than the one given in Fig. 15.2, that repays careful study. Refer to Fig. 15.3.

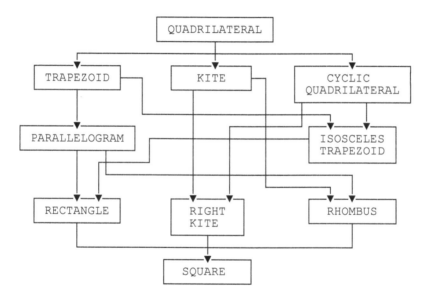

Fig. 15.3: An extended example

Perhaps I should remind you of the definitions of some of the possibly less familiar geometric terms mentioned in the figure:

■   A trapezoid is a quadrilateral with at least one pair of opposite sides parallel.[11]

---

[11] You might or might not be interested to know that a quadrilateral with at least one pair of opposite sides parallel is called a trapezoid in the U.S. and a trapezium in the U.K., while a quadrilateral with possibly no parallel sides at all is called a trapezium in the U.S. and a trapezoid in the U.K. *Caveat lector.*

- A kite is a quadrilateral with mirror symmetry about a diagonal, such that no interior angle is greater than 180°.[12] If *ABCD* is a kite that's symmetric about diagonal *AC*, then *AB* = *AD* and *CB* = *CD*.

- A cyclic quadrilateral is a quadrilateral whose vertices lie on a circle. A quadrilateral is cyclic if and only if opposite interior angles add up to 180°.

- An isosceles trapezoid is a trapezoid with mirror symmetry about the line that connects the midpoints of its parallel sides. If *ABCD* is an isosceles trapezoid with *AB* parallel to *CD*, then (a) *BC* = *AD* and (b) the interior angles at *A* and *B* are equal, as are the interior angles at *C* and *D*.

- A right kite is a kite in which the angles subtended by the diagonal of symmetry are right angles. If *ABCD* is a right kite that's symmetric about diagonal *AC*, then the angles at *B* and *D* are right angles.

One specific point illustrated by this example is the following: Suppose we delete types PARALLELOGRAM, ISOSCELES_TRAPEZOID, RECTANGLE, RIGHT_KITE, and RHOMBUS. Then type QUADRILATERAL will have three immediate subtypes TRAPEZOID, KITE, and CYCLIC_QUADRILATERAL, and the intersection type for that set of three types will be their sole immediate subtype SQUARE.

In closing this section, let me remind you of the following point from Chapter 3: Clearly—unfortunate though it might be—it will always be possible to make mistakes in setting up the type graph. For example, we might define the overlapping types RECTANGLE and RHOMBUS and forget to define the necessary intersection type SQUARE. The consequences of such mistakes will be unpredictable, in general; it's to be hoped that some kind of mechanical aid will be available in practice to help the person defining the type graph to avoid them.

MODEL OF A SCALAR VARIABLE

It follows from everything I've said in this chapter so far that the model of a scalar variable defined in IM Prescription 9—i.e., as a named ordered triple of the form <*DT,MST,v*>—is still valid (and likewise for our model of scalar expressions). It follows also that the algorithm FIND_*MST* given in Chapter 8 for computing the most specific type of a given value is still valid also.[13] For example, suppose we're given a parallelogram *p* with vertices (in clockwise

---

[12] If this latter condition isn't satisfied (i.e., if some interior angle—necessarily that at one end of the diagonal of symmetry—is greater than 180°), the figure isn't a kite but a dart.

[13] More to the point, perhaps, the algorithm TEST_*S* given in Chapter 13 for testing whether some specified value *v* is of some specified type *S* is still valid also.

sequence) *A, B, C, D*, such that *AC = BD* (so *p* is in fact a rectangle) and *AB = BC* (so *p* is a rhombus as well). First, the algorithm will examine the type constraint for (say) type RECTANGLE, since RECTANGLE is a proper subtype of PARALLELOGRAM; it will discover that *p* satisfies that constraint, and so *p* is certainly of type RECTANGLE. Next, it will examine the type constraint for type SQUARE, since SQUARE is a proper subtype of RECTANGLE; it will then discover that *p* also satisfies the type constraint for type RHOMBUS—yes, I do mean RHOMBUS—and hence that it satisfies the type constraint for type SQUARE as well. Thus, *p* is of all four types PARALLELOGRAM, RECTANGLE, RHOMBUS, and SQUARE, and *MST(p)* is SQUARE.

EXERCISES

15.1 For each pair of types in Fig. 15.3, identify the corresponding intersection type.

15.2 How many possreps can you think of for type RIGHT_KITE from Fig. 15.3?

15.3 What do you think the *<is def>* for type SQUARE from Fig. 15.3 should look like?

15.4 Give a concrete example of distinct types *T1, T2, T3, T4, T5* such that *T1* and *T2* have *T3* as an immediate subtype and *T3* has *T4* and *T5* as immediate subtypes.

15.5 Point 9 from the definition of the type graph concept in Chapter 14 reads as follows:

> If nodes *T1, T2, T'*, and *T''* are such that there exist paths from both *T1* and *T2* to both *T'* and *T''*, then there must exist a node *T* that's common to every such path.

Show that this requirement is implied by IM Prescription 8.

15.6 Let scalar types *T1, T2*, and *T3* and overlap pairwise, and let the corresponding intersection types be *Ta* (for *T2* and *T3*), *Tb* (for *T3* and *T1*), and *Tc* (for *T1* and *T2*). Give a nontrivial concrete example to illustrate this situation, and confirm that *Ta, Tb*, and *Tc* also overlap pairwise, and that the three intersection types required for these latter types considered pairwise are in fact all the same type.

ANSWERS

15.1 Since there are 10 types in the figure, there are 100 pairs of types altogether. But the interesting cases are, of course, those where the types involved overlap and neither is a subtype of the other. *Note:* It might help to make the obvious point that a given type *T'* is an intersection type in this "interesting" sense if and only if the node representing type T' in the type graph has two or more distinct incoming arcs.

Here then are the pairs of types that satisfy the foregoing conditions, together with the corresponding intersection type in each case:

```
TRAPEZOID               and KITE                  : SQUARE
TRAPEZOID               and CYCLIC_QUADRILATERAL  : ISOSCELES_TRAPEZOID
TRAPEZOID               and RIGHT_KITE            : SQUARE

KITE                    and CYCLIC_QUADRILATERAL  : RIGHT_KITE
KITE                    and PARALLELOGRAM         : RHOMBUS
KITE                    and ISOSCELES_TRAPEZOID   : SQUARE
KITE                    and RECTANGLE             : SQUARE

CYCLIC_QUADRILATERAL and PARALLELOGRAM            : RECTANGLE
CYCLIC_QUADRILATERAL and RHOMBUS                  : SQUARE

PARALLELOGRAM           and RIGHT_KITE            : SQUARE

ISOSCELES_TRAPEZOID  and RIGHT_KITE               : SQUARE
ISOSCELES_TRAPEZOID  and RHOMBUS                  : SQUARE

RECTANGLE               and RIGHT_KITE            : SQUARE
RECTANGLE               and RHOMBUS               : SQUARE

RIGHT_KITE              and RHOMBUS               : SQUARE
```

15.2 First let's consider kites in general, not just right kites (since any possrep that works for kites in general must obviously work for right kites as well, though it'll need additional constraints in the latter case). Let *ABCD* be such a kite, with vertices in clockwise sequence *A*, *B*, *C*, *D*, and let *AC* be the diagonal of symmetry. Then there are two choices as to which vertex we call *B*; for definiteness, let's choose the one with the smaller *x* coordinate (unless *BD* is parallel to the *y* axis, in which case let's choose the one with the smaller *y* coordinate). Then either of the combinations $D - A - C$, $B - A - C$ can serve as a basis for a possrep.

Now let *ABCD* be a right kite specifically. Then either of the combinations $D - A - B$, $D - C - B$ can additionally serve as a basis for a possrep, with the additional constraint that the interior angle at *B* (equivalently, at *D*) is a right angle. And here are some further possibilities:

■ *D*, *A*, and the length of side *DC* (or *BC*)

■ *A*, *B*, and the length of side *BC* (or *DC*)

■ *D*, *C*, and the length of side *DA* (or *BA*)

■ *B*, *C*, and the length of side *AB* (or *AD*)

■ The interior angle at *A* (or *C*) and the midpoint of the diagonal *BD*

And so on.

15.3 IS { RECTANGLE , RIGHT_KITE , RHOMBUS ... }

See the discussion of IM Prescription 10 in Chapter 16 for further explanation.

15.4 Here are a couple of simple examples. First, take *T1* and *T2* to be RECTANGLE and RHOMBUS, respectively; *T3* is then SQUARE. Now suppose every square is either a "large square" or a "small square," and no square is both. Then we could define *T4* and *T5* to be LARGE_SQUARE and SMALL_SQUARE, respectively, both of them immediate subtypes of T3 (i.e., SQUARE). Note, incidentally, that SQUARE is both an intersection type and a union type (but not a dummy type!) in this example.

Second, consider character strings that have at least one space at each end. Each such string is both a string with a leading space and a string with a trailing space, and so the corresponding type could well be an intersection type. Also, each such string either consists entirely of spaces or contains at least one nonspace character, and so the corresponding type could have immediate subtypes.

15.5 IM Prescription 8 requires *T1* and *T2* to have a common subtype *S* such that a given value is of each of the types *T1* and *T2* if and only if it's of type *S*. Therefore each value of *T′* must be a value of type *S*. Therefore *T′* is a subtype of *S*. By a similar argument, *T″* is also a subtype of *S*. Therefore either *T′* is *S* (and *T″* is a subtype of *T′*), or *T″* is *S* (and *T′* is a subtype of *T″*), or *S* is a proper supertype of both *T′* and *T″* as well as being a subtype of both *T1* and *T2*. In all of these cases *S* lies on each of the paths from *T1* to *T′*, from *T1* to *T″*, from *T2* to *T′*, and from *T2* to *T″*.

15.6 Consider the natural numbers. Some are divisible by 2, some by 3, and some by 5. Let *T1* be those divisible by both 2 and 3 (i.e., multiples of 6); let *T2* be those divisible by both 3 and 5 (i.e., multiples of 15); and let *T3* be those divisible by both 5 and 2 (i.e., multiples of 10). Then *Ta* is those divisible by both 15 and 10; *Tb* is those divisible by both 10 and 6; and *Tc* is those divisible by both 6 and 15. Further, a natural number is clearly an element of both *Tb* and *Tc* if and only if it's a multiple of 30; an element of both *Tc* and *Ta* if and only if (again) it's a multiple of 30; and an element of both *Ta* and *Tb* if and only if (once again) it's a multiple of 30. Thus, the three intersection types for *Ta*, *Tb*, and *Tc* taken pairwise are clearly all the same type.

Chapter 16

IM Prescriptions 10–20 Revisited

And now the fancy passes by,
And nothing will remain

—A. E. Housman:
A Shropshire Lad (1896)

Chapters 14 and 15 discussed the impact of multiple inheritance considerations on the first nine prescriptions of our inheritance model (though only for scalar types, of course). The present chapter completes the process by examining the remaining prescriptions, viz., IM Prescriptions 10-20. It's convenient to treat these prescriptions in two batches—numbers 10-15 in the section immediately following, and numbers 16-20 in the next.

IM PRESCRIPTIONS 10 - 15

IM Prescriptions 10-15 still apply 100 percent, and quite frankly there isn't much to say about them—but there is a little, as will be seen. *Note:* IM Prescriptions 10 and 11 were originally discussed in Chapter 8; IM Prescriptions 12 and 13 were originally discussed in Chapter 9; and IM Prescriptions 14 and 15 were originally discussed in Chapter 10.

IM Prescription 10: Specialization by Constraint

The only point worth mentioning explicitly here is this: If type T' is an immediate subtype for two or more regular types $T1, T2, ..., Tm$, then the type definition for type T' will include a specification—actually an *<is def>*, in **Tutorial D** terms—of the form IS $\{T1,T2,...,Tm ...\}$ (irrelevant details omitted),[1] and that specification is both necessary and sufficient to define the required specialization constraints in their entirety. For example, the definition of type SQUARE includes the following:

```
IS { RECTANGLE , RHOMBUS ... }
```

As noted in Chapter 14, this specification is effectively shorthand for the following:

---

[1] For the record, though, that *<is def>* will also contain (following the commalist of type names $T1, T2, ..., Tm$ and preceding the closing brace) at least one derived possrep definition, followed by a NOT specification.

```
IS_RECTANGLE ( s ) AND LS ( s ) = SS ( s )

AND

IS_RHOMBUS   ( s ) AND LD ( s ) = SD ( s )
```

(where *s* denotes an arbitrary value of type SQUARE). In other words, the specified *<is def>* does indeed serve to define the required specialization constraints for type SQUARE in terms of types RECTANGLE and RHOMBUS.

IM Prescription 11: Assignment with Inheritance

Given the assignment $V := X$, where V is a variable reference and X is an expression, this prescription requires the declared type $DT(X)$ of the expression X to be a subtype of the declared type $DT(V)$ of the variable V (this is a compile time check). For example, the assignment in the following code fragment will fail on a compile time type error—

```
VAR RE RECTANGLE ;
VAR RH RHOMBUS ;

RE := RH ;
```

—because type RHOMBUS isn't a subtype of type RECTANGLE. Of course, those types do overlap; so if we believe variable RH will in fact contain a rectangle at run time, then what we need to do in order to achieve what's presumably the desired effect in the example is write the assignment like this:

```
RE := TREAT_AS_RECTANGLE ( RH ) ;
```

Note: If variable RH does contain a rectangle at run time, that rectangle will in fact be a square (necessarily so), and so we could alternatively—and equally correctly—have written the assignment like this:

```
RE := TREAT_AS_SQUARE ( RH ) ;
```

See the discussion of IM Prescription 14 below.

IM Prescription 12: Equality with Inheritance

Given the comparison $X = Y$, where X and Y are expressions, this prescription requires the declared types $DT(X)$ and $DT(Y)$ of the expressions X and Y to overlap (this is a compile time check). For example, the equality comparison in the following code fragment is certainly valid:

```
VAR RE RECTANGLE ;
VAR RH RHOMBUS ;

IF RE = RH THEN ... ;
```

In fact, as we know from the previous chapter, $DT(X)$ and $DT(Y)$ overlap if and only if they have a nonempty common subtype. In the example, $DT(RE)$ is RECTANGLE and $DT(RH)$ is RHOMBUS, and types RECTANGLE and RHOMBUS do have a nonempty common subtype, viz., type SQUARE. And, of course, the comparison will give TRUE if and only if the two variables both contain the same value at run time (necessarily a value of the pertinent common subtype).

IM Prescription 13: Join etc. with Inheritance

I'll illustrate this prescription with a few examples. Let relational expressions RX and RY have declared types RELATION {P RECTANGLE} and RELATION {P RHOMBUS}, respectively. Also, let the values rx and ry currently denoted by expressions RX and RY, respectively, be as shown here:

```
rx                              ry
┌─────────────────────┐        ┌─────────────────────┐
│  P   :  RECTANGLE    │        │  P   :  RHOMBUS      │
├─────────────────────┤        ├─────────────────────┤
│ p1 :  rectangle     │        │ p2 :  square        │
│ p2 :  square        │        │ p3 :  rhombus       │
└─────────────────────┘        └─────────────────────┘
```

(Most specific types are shown in lowercase italics.) Given these sample values, then, rx UNION ry, rx INTERSECT ry, rx MINUS ry, and ry MINUS rx are as shown below (rx JOIN ry is identical to rx INTERSECT ry in this simple example):

```
rx UNION ry                rx INTERSECT ry   rx MINUS ry            ry MINUS rx
┌──────────────────────┐   ┌───────────────┐ ┌──────────────────┐  ┌──────────────────┐
│  P   : PARALLELOGRAM  │   │  P   : SQUARE │ │  P   : RECTANGLE │  │  P   : RHOMBUS   │
├──────────────────────┤   ├───────────────┤ ├──────────────────┤  ├──────────────────┤
│ p1 :  rectangle      │   │ p2 :  square  │ │ p1 :  rectangle  │  │ p3 :  rhombus    │
│ p2 :  square         │   └───────────────┘ └──────────────────┘  └──────────────────┘
│ p3 :  rhombus        │
└──────────────────────┘
```

Note the attribute declared types in particular in these pictures—especially the first one, where I'm relying on the fact that PARALLELOGRAM is the most specific common supertype of types RECTANGLE, SQUARE, and RHOMBUS. For further explanation, see the discussion of IM Prescription 24 in Chapter 18.

IM Prescription 14: TREAT

Given the TREAT invocation TREAT_AS_T(X), where X is an expression, this prescription requires T and the declared type $DT(X)$ of the expression X to overlap (this is a compile time check). Thus, for example, the following code fragment is valid:

```
VAR RE RECTANGLE ;
VAR RH RHOMBUS ;

RH := TREAT_AS_RHOMBUS ( RE ) ;
```

The TREAT invocation here is valid because types RECTANGLE and RHOMBUS do overlap (i.e., they have a nonempty common subtype, viz., type SQUARE); moreover, it will succeed if and only if the current value of variable RE is of type SQUARE (i.e., if and only if RE currently contains a value of that common subtype). As noted under IM Prescription 11 above, therefore, the assignment shown could equally well have been expressed as follows:

```
RH := TREAT_AS_SQUARE ( RE ) ;
```

Note: Perhaps you'll recall the following remarks (lightly edited here) from the discussion of TREAT in Chapter 10:

> Given the expression TREAT_AS_T(X), T would normally be a proper subtype of $DT(X)$. But there's no reason to insist on this state of affairs, and with multiple inheritance, in fact, it would be counterproductive to do so.

Now I can explain these remarks. To be specific, if we required T to be a proper subtype of $DT(X)$, then an expression such as the following wouldn't be valid:[2]

```
TREAT_AS_RHOMBUS ( RE )
```

(On the other hand, we've already seen that this particular expression could be harmlessly replaced by the following—

```
TREAT_AS_SQUARE ( RE )
```

—and this latter expression does satisfy the property that T is a proper subtype of $DT(X)$.)

---

[2] Indeed, we saw in Chapter 10 that an expression such as TREAT_AS_ELLIPSE (C), where $DT(C)$ is CIRCLE, really ought to be valid as well, even if it might not be particularly useful. (As a matter of fact, the same goes for TREAT_AS_ELLIPSE (E), where $DT(E)$ is ELLIPSE.) As we've already seen, therefore, it would be undesirable even in the single inheritance case to insist that T must always be a proper subtype of $DT(X)$.

IM Prescription 15: Type Testing

Given the IS_*T* invocation IS_*T* (*X*), where *X* is an expression, this prescription requires *T* and the declared type *DT(X)* of the expression *X* to overlap (this is a compile time check). Thus, for example, the following code fragment is valid:

```
VAR RE RECTANGLE ;

IF IS_RHOMBUS ( RE ) THEN ... ;
```

The type test here is valid because types RECTANGLE and RHOMBUS do overlap (i.e., they have a nonempty common subtype, viz., type SQUARE); moreover, it will give TRUE if and only if the current value of variable RE is of type SQUARE (i.e., if and only if RE currently contains a value of that common subtype). In other words, the IF statement shown could equally well have been expressed as follows:

```
IF IS_SQUARE ( RE ) THEN ... ;
```

Note: Perhaps you'll recall the following remarks (lightly edited here) from the discussion of IS_*T* in Chapter 10:

> Given the expression IS_*T* (*X*), *T* will often be a proper subtype of *DT(X)*. But there's no reason to insist on this state of affairs, and with multiple inheritance, in fact, it would be counterproductive to do so.

Now I can explain these remarks. To be specific, if we required *T* to be a proper subtype of *DT(X)*, then an expression such as the following wouldn't be valid:[3]

```
IS_RHOMBUS ( RE )
```

(On the other hand, we've already seen that this particular expression could be harmlessly replaced by the following—

```
IS_SQUARE ( RE )
```

—and this latter expression does satisfy the property that *T* is a proper subtype of *DT(X)*.)

---

[3] Footnote 2 applies here also, mutatis mutandis.

IM PRESCRIPTIONS 16 - 20

These prescriptions also all apply 100 percent, but there's even less to say about them than there was to say about IM Prescriptions 10-15.   So I'll content myself with simply listing the prescriptions together with their informal titles, just to remind you what they're all about. Note that numbers 16-19 all have to do with the general issue of substitutability (they were discussed in depth in Chapter 11). Number 20 has to do with union, dummy, and maximal and minimal types; it was discussed in depth in Chapter 12.

- IM Prescription 16: Value substitutability

- IM Prescription 17: Operator signatures

- IM Prescription 18: Read-only parameters to update operators

- IM Prescription 19: Variable substitutability

- IM Prescription 20: Union and dummy types etc.

EXERCISES

16.1 With reference to Fig. 15.3 in Chapter 15, is type QUADRILATERAL a union type? If it is, do you think it should be a dummy type? Justify your answers.

16.2 The answer to Exercise 12.4 in Chapter 12 showed that a union type (other than type *omega*) must have at least two immediate subtypes. But do those immediate subtypes have to be pairwise disjoint?

16.3 Can a type have more than one dummy type as an immediate subtype?

The remaining exercises all appeal to a family of types called RATIONAL_p_q ($p \geq 1$, $q \geq 0$) such that a given value is of type RATIONAL_p_q if and only if it's a number whose literal representation in decimal notation takes the form *int.frac*, where:

- *int* and *frac* are both sequences of decimal digits

- *int* consists of at most $p - q$ significant digits

- *frac* consists of at most q significant digits

Note: It's worth pointing out that this family of types is very similar, though not identical, to the SQL family of types DECIMAL(p,q). In other words, DECIMAL (like CHAR, VARCHAR, etc.) can be regarded as a type generator in SQL.

16.4 Is it true that type RATIONAL_p'_q' is a subtype of type RATIONAL_p_q if and only if $p' \leq p$ and $q' \leq q$ both hold? Do you agree that this is a case of multiple inheritance?

16.5 Does value substitutability apply?

16.6 Are there any operators that apply to values of type RATIONAL_p'_q' and not to values of type RATIONAL_p_q?

16.7 Do S by C and G by C apply?

16.8 Is there a nonempty type that's a subtype of all possible types in the family?

16.9 Consider the literal 0012.30. What's the declared type of that literal? What's the most specific type?

ANSWERS

16.1 Given that there exist quadrilaterals that aren't trapezoids, kites, or cyclic, it doesn't seem to make much sense to make QUADRILATERAL a union type. Thus, it's not a dummy type either, a fortiori.

16.2 No, they don't. For example, suppose we're interested in rectangles and rhombi but not in any other parallelograms. Then PARALLELOGRAM would be a union type, with two immediate subtypes, RECTANGLE and RHOMBUS, that overlap.

16.3 Yes, it can, but only if the type in question is itself a dummy type (see the answer to Exercise 12.6 in Chapter 12). For example, suppose, not entirely unreasonably, that type POLYGON is a dummy type. Then polygons in general might be divided into regular vs. irregular polygons, each of which might conceivably be a dummy type in turn.

16.4 First note that this exercise and the ones that follow constitute a multiple inheritance analog of the exercises in Chapter 8. Second, yes, type RATIONAL_p'_q' is a subtype of type RATIONAL_p_q if and only if $p' \leq p$ and $q' \leq q$ both hold, as the following analysis demonstrates:

- If $p' < p$, then every value of type RATIONAL_p'_q satisfies the type constraint for type RATIONAL_p_q. Likewise, if $q' < q$, then every value of type RATIONAL_p_q' satisfies the type constraint for type RATIONAL_p_q. Thus, if $p' \le p$ and $q' \le q$, then RATIONAL_p'_q' is a subtype of RATIONAL_p_q. (And if either of those "$\le$" symbols is replaced by a "$<$" symbol, then RATIONAL_p'_q' is a *proper* subtype of RATIONAL_p_q.)

- If $p' > p$, then some values of type RATIONAL_p'_q have an *int* portion of more than $p - q$ significant digits and so aren't values of type RATIONAL_p_q. Likewise, if $q' > q$, then some values of type RATIONAL_p_q have a *frac* portion of more than q significant digits and so aren't values of type RATIONAL_p_q. Thus, if $p' > p$ or $q' > q$, then RATIONAL_p'_q' isn't a subtype of RATIONAL_p_q.

Yes, this is a case of multiple inheritance. To see that this is so, consider the following specific case:

- Type RATIONAL_3_1 is a proper subtype of type RATIONAL_4_1 (every value of type RATIONAL_3_1 is a value of type RATIONAL_4_1 as well—to be specific, a value of type RATIONAL_4_1 for which the integer part consists of at most three significant digits).

- Type RATIONAL_3_1 is also a proper subtype of type RATIONAL_4_2 (every value of type RATIONAL_3_1 is a value of type RATIONAL_4_2 as well—to be specific, a value of type RATIONAL_4_2 for which the fractional part consists of at most one significant digit).

- Neither of RATIONAL_4_1 and RATIONAL_4_2 is a subtype of the other; for example, 999.9 is a value of the first type that's not a value of the second, while 99.99 is a value of the second type that's not a value of the first. Thus RATIONAL_3_1 has two distinct proper supertypes, neither of which is a subtype of the other, and so we're dealing with multiple inheritance.

16.5 Yes, by definition.

16.6 In principle, yes—for example, any operator for which some rational operand is constrained to consist of no more than p' significant digits would be such an operator—but it has to be admitted that concrete examples of such operators do tend to seem very contrived.

16.7 Yes, by definition.

16.8 Let ZERO be a type containing just the value 0.0. Then ZERO is a nonempty subtype of every type in the family. (Of course, type ZERO isn't itself a member of the RATIONAL_*p_q* family.)

16.9 We don't really have enough information to answer this question—it's a matter of how the pertinent language is defined. But it's probably reasonable to assume that the declared type of the specified literal is RATIONAL_3_1. Indeed, if it isn't, then the literal isn't very useful! Note that the declared type can't be RATIONAL_*p_q* for some $p > 3$ or some $q > 1$, for then the literal couldn't be assigned to a variable of declared type RATIONAL_3_1, even though it clearly denotes a value of that type (we'd have to assign CAST_AS_RATIONAL_3_1 (0012.30) instead— not a very user friendly state of affairs). At the same time the declared type can't be RATIONAL_*p_q* for some $p < 3$ or some $q < 1$, because the value denoted by the literal certainly has type RATIONAL_3_1 (as well as some user defined proper subtype thereof, possibly, if any such exists), and the declared type of an expression can't possibly be a proper subtype of the most specific type of the value it denotes.

Part IV

TUPLE AND

RELATION INHERITANCE

The title of this book is *Type Inheritance and Relational Theory*, but—with the exception of the preliminary material in Chapters 2 and 3 and the discussions of IM Prescription 13 in Chapters 9 and (briefly) 16, plus a few miscellaneous remarks here and there—it hasn't really had much to say so far regarding relational theory as such. But Part IV of this book, which consists of four chapters, remedies that situation somewhat. To be specific, it revisits all of the concepts introduced in Parts II and III for scalar types and considers what happens to those concepts when tuple and relation types are taken into account as well.

Chapter 17

Tuple/Relation Values

with Inheritance

Everything exists, nothing has value

—E. M. Forster:
A Passage to India (1924)

Consider the following tuple types:

```
TUPLE { E ELLIPSE , R RECTANGLE }    /* "tuple type ER" */
TUPLE { E CIRCLE  , R RECTANGLE }    /* "tuple type CR" */
TUPLE { E ELLIPSE , R SQUARE    }    /* "tuple type ES" */
TUPLE { E CIRCLE  , R SQUARE    }    /* "tuple type CS" */
```

Note the informal names ("tuple type ER," etc.) for these types as given in the comments. Now, observing with reference to the running example from Part II of this book that CIRCLE and SQUARE are subtypes of ELLIPSE and RECTANGLE, respectively, it should be clear that every tuple of type CS is also a tuple of both type CR and type ES, and further that every tuple of type CR or type ES is also a tuple of type ER. Thus, it should also be clear that tuple type CS is a subtype of both tuple type CR and tuple type ES, and further that tuple types CR and ES are both subtypes of tuple type ER. In other words, subtype / supertype relationships hold as indicated in Fig. 17.1 below.

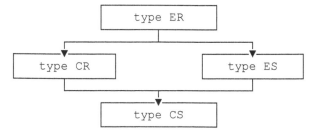

Fig. 17.1: A type graph involving tuple or relation types

Here are some further points arising in connection with this example that should be clear as well but in any case are worth spelling out explicitly:

■ All four tuple types have the same attribute names.

■ Each of the four tuple types overlaps (i.e., has values in common with) each of the other three.

■ Every pair of tuple types out of the four has at least one common subtype and at least one common supertype. In particular, the pair CR and ES, neither of which is a subtype of the other, has both (a) a common subtype (viz., type CS) that's not one of the types in question, and (b) a common supertype (viz., type ER) that's also not one of the types in question.

■ In fact, every pair of tuple types out of the four has both a least specific common subtype—i.e., an intersection type—and a most specific common supertype. In the case of the pair CR and ES in particular, CS is the least specific common subtype and ER is the most specific common supertype.

Next, all of the foregoing remarks apply to relation types also, mutatis mutandis. That is, given relation types as follows—

```
RELATION { E ELLIPSE , R RECTANGLE }    /* "relation type ER" */
RELATION { E CIRCLE  , R RECTANGLE }    /* "relation type CR" */
RELATION { E ELLIPSE , R SQUARE    }    /* "relation type ES" */
RELATION { E CIRCLE  , R SQUARE    }    /* "relation type CS" */
```

—it should be clear that:[1]

■ All four relation types have the same attribute names.

■ Each of the four relation types overlaps each of the other three.

■ Every pair of relation types out of the four has at least one common subtype and at least one common supertype. In particular, the pair CR and ES, neither of which is a subtype of the other, has both (a) a common subtype (viz., type CS) that's not one of the types in question, and (b) a common supertype (viz., type ER) that's also not one of the types in question.

■ In fact, every pair of relation types out of the four has both a least specific common subtype—i.e., an intersection type—and a most specific common supertype. In the case of

---

[1] Actually, for reasons to be discussed later in this chapter as well as in the next, these points might not be quite as clear as they seem (not as clear as their tuple counterparts, at any rate). But they're valid nonetheless.

the pair CR and ES in particular, CS is the least specific common subtype and ER is the most specific common supertype.

It follows that Fig. 17.1 can serve to depict the foregoing relation subtype / supertype relationships as well as the tuple ones discussed earlier. That being the case, I'll use it as basis for most of my examples (both tuple and relation examples) throughout this part of the book.[2] Also, for brevity, most of the time I'll refer to the types involved by those informal names ER, CR, ES, and CS. However, I must stress the point that those names are indeed informal. The correct names are as shown earlier. For example, the correct name for "tuple type ER" is:

```
TUPLE { E ELLIPSE , R RECTANGLE }
```

Similarly, the correct name for "relation type ER" is:

```
RELATION { E ELLIPSE , R RECTANGLE }
```

I'd also like to stress the fact that, regardless of whether we're talking about tuple or relation types, the type graph of Fig. 17.1 involves multiple inheritance. In fact it should be obvious that tuple and relation type inheritance will usually be multiple inheritance specifically, which is why I chose to discuss multiple inheritance first, in the previous part of the book. (It's also another reason why I claim support for type inheritance in general must include support for multiple inheritance in particular.) Now I'm in a position to discuss tuple and relation inheritance as such.

Now, you might be thinking it would be better, at least from a pedagogic point of view, to treat tuple types exclusively first, and then to extend that treatment to cover relation types as well. In practice, however, tuple and relation type inheritance are so intricately intertwined that it's virtually impossible to treat them separately. Indeed, it turns out (as you'll soon see) that many of the concepts and definitions to be discussed:

a. Come in pairs (a tuple version and a relation version), and

b. Are both recursive (meaning they refer to themselves) and mutually recursive (meaning they refer to each other). *Note:* Actually these two points shouldn't come as a surprise, given that tuples and relations can have tuple valued attributes or relation valued attributes or both.

---

[2] Note, therefore, that—again with reference to the running example from Part II of this book—I'm effectively replacing the scalar type hierarchy from that example by two separate such hierarchies, one rooted in type ELLIPSE and the other in type RECTANGLE (in other words, I'm ignoring types POLYGON and PLANE_FIGURE altogether, unless the context demands otherwise). These remarks apply throughout this chapter and the next three.

Terminology: In what follows, I'll use the abbreviation *tuple / relation* to stand for either *tuple and relation* or *tuple or relation*, as the sense demands (at least when such terms are used as a qualifier, as in, e.g., the phrase "tuple and relation types," which I'll abbreviate accordingly to just *tuple / relation types*). Also, I'll continue to use the symbols T and T' generically to refer to a pair of types such that T' is a subtype of T (equivalently, such that T is a supertype of T')—but now, of course, those types might be tuple or relation types instead of just scalar types as previously.

TUPLE / RELATION PRESCRIPTIONS

There are eight prescriptions in our model that have to do with tuple / relation inheritance specifically, and the following brief summary gives some sense of what they cover:

- IM Prescription 21: Empty types

- IM Prescription 22: Tuple / relation subtypes and supertypes

- IM Prescription 23: Proper and immediate tuple / relation subtypes and supertypes

- IM Prescription 24: Common tuple / relation subtypes and supertypes

- IM Prescription 25: Tuple / relation maximal and minimal types

- IM Prescription 26: Tuple / relation root and leaf types

- IM Prescription 27: Tuple / relation most specific types

- IM Prescription 28: Model of a tuple / relation variable

The present chapter deals with the first three from this list; the others are discussed in the next three chapters.

IM PRESCRIPTION 21: EMPTY TYPES

Type T shall be an **empty type** if and only if it is either an empty scalar type or an empty tuple type. Scalar type T shall be empty if and only if T is type *omega*. Tuple type T shall be empty if and only if T has at least one attribute that is of some empty type. An empty type shall be permitted as the type of (a) an attribute of a tuple type or relation type; (b) nothing else.

──── ♦♦♦♦♦ ────

I discuss this prescription in this part of the book because it does concern itself, mostly, with tuple types specifically and thus wouldn't have made a lot of sense prior to this point—though it does necessarily discuss the sole empty scalar type (viz., type omega) as well because, ultimately, those empty tuple types all derive from type omega. Also, the last sentence of the prescription in the Explorations version referred to declared types specifically, not to types in general, but the intrusion of that qualifier "declared" in that version seems to be unnecessarily restrictive.

The intent of this prescription is simply to provide an explicit definition for the concept of an empty type—a concept that has given rise to more than its fair share of difficulties in the past, I might add—and to say exactly where such types are permitted.

First of all, as the prescription says (and as we already know, of course), there's exactly one empty scalar type: viz., type *omega*. By contrast, there can be any number of empty tuple types (note that the definition of this latter concept as given in the prescription is recursive). Here are some examples:

```
TUPLE { E omega }

TUPLE { E ELLIPSE , R omega }

TUPLE { E ELLIPSE , X TUPLE { R omega } }
```

Now let *RT* be an arbitrary relation type, with heading *H*. By definition, then, there's always at least one relation of type *RT*—namely, the relation with heading *H* and body the empty set, or in other words the empty relation of type RELATION *H*.[3] It follows that there's no such thing as an empty relation type, which is why IM Prescription 21 makes no mention of such a thing (not explicitly, at any rate).

Now, the prescription says an empty type is permitted only in certain circumstances. In order to see how and why this restriction is reasonable, let's consider one at a time each of the various constructs in our model to which the concept of having a type applies:

■ *Scalar and tuple values and variables:* By definition, there's no value—and hence no scalar or tuple value in particular—of any empty type. It follows that an attempt to define a scalar or tuple variable with an empty declared type will certainly fail at run time if not at compile time, because there's no initial value that can be assigned to that variable.

─────────────

[3] I note in passing that "the empty relation of type RELATION *H*" (for any given heading *H*) is also the empty relation of type RELATION *H'* for all headings *H'* such that RELATION *H'* is a proper subtype of type RELATION *H* (see the discussion of IM Prescription 23, later). Another way of saying the same thing is this: Let *T* and *T'* be the relation types RELATION *H* and RELATION *H'*, respectively, and let type *T'* be a subtype of type *T*. Further, let heading *H* have an attribute of some empty type. Then the sets |*T*| and |*T'*| contain just one value, viz., the empty relation of type *T*.

For tuples, the situation is analogous but not quite the same. To be specific, let *T* and *T'* be the tuple types TUPLE *H* and TUPLE *H'*, respectively, and let type *T'* be a subtype of type *T*. Further, let heading *H* have an attribute of some empty type. Then the sets |*T*| and |*T'*| are equal—in fact, both are empty. Again, see IM Prescription 23 later for further discussion.

- *Relation values and variables:* As we saw above, there's no relation value (i.e., no relation) of any empty type, because there aren't any empty relation types. Hence, there's no way a relation variable (i.e., a relvar) can possibly be defined with an empty declared type.

- *Possible representation ("possrep") components:* An attempt to define a scalar type *T* with a possrep component of some empty declared type will certainly fail at run time if not at compile time, because there's no example value that can be specified for that type *T*.

- *Read-only operators:* Let *Op* be a read-only operator. By definition, no invocation of *Op* can return a result of any empty type. It follows that an attempt to define an invocation signature for *Op*—and, a fortiori, an attempt to define the specification signature for *Op*—with an empty declared type is illegal (if the violation isn't caught at compile time, any corresponding invocation of *Op* will certainly fail at run time).

- *Expressions:* By definition, any given expression represents an invocation of some read-only operator. It follows that no expression can be of any empty type.

- *Parameters:* Let operator *Op* have a parameter *P*. By definition, (a) *P* is replaced by an argument when *Op* is invoked and (b) no argument can be of any empty type. It follows that an attempt to define an invocation signature for *Op*—and, a fortiori, an attempt to define the specification signature for *Op*—with a parameter of some empty declared type is illegal (if the violation isn't caught at compile time, any corresponding invocation of *Op* will certainly fail at run time).

- *Attributes:* In contrast to all of the above, attributes of tuple and relation types can be of some empty type.[4] With regard to tuple types in particular, however, a tuple type *TT* with an attribute of some empty type is (as IM Prescription 21 states) necessarily empty in turn, and it can't be used as the type of anything other than some attribute of some other tuple type or some relation type.

IM PRESCRIPTION 22: TUPLE / RELATION SUBTYPES AND SUPERTYPES

Let *T* and *T'* be both tuple types or both relation types. Then type *T'* shall be a **subtype** of type *T*, and type *T* shall be a **supertype** of type *T'*, if and only if (a) *T* and *T'* have the same attribute names *A1*, *A2*, ..., *An* and (b) for all *j* (j = 1, 2, ..., *n*), the type of attribute *Aj* of *T'* is a subtype of

---

[4] This observation is true of attributes of minimal types in particular, but a type doesn't have to be a minimal type in order to have such an attribute. See Chapter 19 for further discussion.

the type of attribute *Aj* of *T*. Tuple *t* shall be of tuple type *T* if and only if *t* has a heading that is that of some subtype of *T*. Relation *r* shall be of relation type *T* if and only if *r* has a heading that is that of some subtype of *T* (in which case every tuple in the body of *r* shall also have a heading that is that of some subtype of *T*).

The third and fourth sentences of this prescription have been tightened up somewhat, compared to the corresponding sentences in the *Explorations* version. Here for example is the *Explorations* version of the third sentence:

> Tuple *t* shall be of some subtype of tuple type *T* if and only if the heading of *t* is that of some subtype of *T*.

But this sentence fails to specify just which subtypes of *T* are the ones that tuple *t* is supposed to be of! By way of example, if *t* is TUPLE {E *c*, R *r*}, where *c* and *r* are of most specific types CIRCLE and RECTANGLE, respectively, then the sentence would apparently allow *t* to be of tuple type ES and/or of tuple type CS. (After all, (a) tuple *t* in this example has heading {E CIRCLE, R RECTANGLE};[5] (b) that heading is the heading of some subtype of tuple type ER; and (c) tuple types ES and CS are each "some subtype" of tuple type ER.) By contrast, the revised version—

> Tuple *t* shall be of tuple type *T* if and only if *t* has a heading that is that of some subtype of *T*.

—states explicitly, in effect, that tuple *t* in the example is of tuple types CR and ER and no others.

Analogous remarks apply to the fourth sentence of the prescription also, regarding relation types.[6]

Tuple Subtypes, Supertypes, and Values

In the introduction to this chapter, I said the following:

---

[5] It has heading {E ELLIPSE, R RECTANGLE} as well, of course. For simplicity, however, I adopt the convention throughout the remainder of this book that to say a tuple or relation has heading *H* is to say that *H* is the heading of the *most specific* type of the tuple or relation in question (see the discussion of IM Prescription 27 in Chapter 20), unless the context demands otherwise. Analogously (somewhat), I also adopt the convention throughout the remainder of this book that to say a tuplevar or relvar has heading *H* is to say that *H* is the heading of the *declared* type of the tuplevar or relvar in question (and similarly for (a) tuplevar and relvar attributes, (b) read-only operators, (c) parameters, and (d) expressions, mutatis mutandis, unless the context demands otherwise).

[6] However, I note in passing that, perhaps a little counterintuitively, it's possible (a) for some given relation *r* to be of type RELATION *H* and not of any proper subtype of that type and yet (b) for some or even all of the tuples in that relation to be of some proper subtype of type TUPLE *H*. See the discussion of relation most specific types in Chapter 20.

[It] should ... be clear that tuple type CS is a subtype of both tuple type CR and tuple type ES, and further that tuple types CR and ES are both subtypes of tuple type ER.

Well, I do think these things should be clear, at least intuitively, but let's examine them a little more carefully. First of all, let's agree for simplicity that—as far as this subsection is concerned, at any rate—the unqualified term *type* refers to a tuple type specifically, barring explicit statements to the contrary.[7] Now let me call your attention to something I said earlier: viz., that types ER, CR, ES, and CS all have the same attribute names. Thus, if we define a tuple variable (or "tuplevar") as follows—

```
VAR TV TUPLE { E ELLIPSE , R RECTANGLE } ;
```

—then, clearly, (a) variable TV is of declared type ER; equally clearly, (b) a tuple of any of the four types ER, CR, ES, and CS can be assigned to that variable. *Note:* Recall that in **Tutorial D** tuple types are simply *available for use*, as it were (typically but not necessarily as the declared type of some tuple variable, as in the example); they don't have to be separately, explicitly defined. In fact, for reasons mentioned in passing in Chapter 2, **Tutorial D** doesn't provide any kind of explicit "define tuple type" operator anyway. Thus, all four types ER, CR, ES, and CS are certainly available for us to use as we see fit whenever and however we want to.

Now let's concentrate for a moment on the two extreme cases, types ER and CS. Does it really make sense to regard type CS as a subtype of type ER? Well, it's certainly true that:

■ Every type constraint that applies to values of type ER applies to values of type CS as well, while the converse is false. *Note:* Since **Tutorial D** doesn't provide any kind of explicit "define tuple type" operator, the only type constraints that apply to a tuple type *T* are ones implied by those that apply to the attributes of *T*. Thus, there's no way type ER could be subject to any type constraint that didn't also apply to type CS. But type CS is certainly subject to constraints that don't apply to values of type ER in general; to be specific, it's subject to the constraints that (a) values of attribute E must be of type CIRCLE and (b) values of attribute R must be of type SQUARE.

■ Every operator that applies to values of type ER applies to values of type CS as well, while the converse is false. *Note:* The operators that apply to values of type ER (and therefore to values of type CS as well) are (a) the generic tuple operators required by *The Third Manifesto* (tuple comparisons, tuple rename, tuple join, and so on), together with (b) those user defined tuple operators, if any, that have been defined for values of type ER. The operators that apply to values of type CS but not to values of type ER are (a) "compound" operators, as in, e.g., THE_R (E FROM *csx*)—where *csx* is an expression of tuple type CS—that rely on attribute E being of type CIRCLE or attribute R being of type SQUARE,

---

[7] As we'll see in the next subsection (and as you'd surely expect), everything the present subsection has to say about tuple types applies to relation types as well, mutatis mutandis.

together with (b) those user defined tuple operators, if any, that have been defined for values of type CS specifically.

Clearly, all of these observations are in accord with our usual understanding of what it means for one type to be a subtype of another, and so there does seem to be a good prima facie case for regarding CS as a subtype of ER (and ER as a supertype of CS). But is it useful to do so? The answer, of course, is *yes*. In particular, the concept of value substitutability applies, meaning that wherever the system expects a value of type ER, we can always substitute a value of type CS instead. Among other things, therefore, we can assign a value of type CS to a variable of type ER, and we can test a variable of type CS and one of type ER for equality (see Chapter 20 for further discussion).

So much for the relationship between the "extreme" cases ER and CS. Analogously, of course, it does make sense to say that types CR and ES are subtypes of type ER and supertypes of type CS, while neither of types CR and ES is a subtype of the other.

With the foregoing discussion by way of motivation, then, let's try to pin down exactly what it means for tuple type *TT'* to be a subtype of tuple type *TT*. *Note:* Here and elsewhere in this chapter I choose to depart slightly from our usual "*T'* vs. *T*" naming convention, despite the fact that the pertinent IM prescriptions themselves don't.

First of all, of course, *TT'* and *TT* must have the same attribute names, for otherwise there's no way a value of type *TT'* can possibly be a value of type *TT*. So we might attempt a definition along the following lines:

Definition: Let tuple types *TT* and *TT'* have headings

```
{ <A1,T1>  , <A2,T2>  , ... , <An,Tn>  }
{ <A1,T1'> , <A2,T2'> , ... , <An,Tn'> }
```

respectively. Then tuple type *TT'* is a *subtype* of tuple type *TT* (and tuple type *TT* is a *supertype* of tuple type *TT'*) if and only if, for all *j* (*j* = 1, 2, ..., *n*), type *Tj'* is a subtype of type *Tj* (equivalently, type *Tj* is a supertype of type *Tj'*).

And in fact this definition is perfectly acceptable, provided we understand that, for any given *j*, types *Tj* and *Tj'* might themselves be tuple types in turn or even relation types (because, as noted earlier, tuples can have tuple and relation valued attributes). In other words, the foregoing definition of what it means for one tuple type to be a subtype of another:

a. Is certainly recursive, but also

b. Relies on a definition of what it means for one relation type to be a subtype of another, a possibility I haven't yet discussed in detail.

So I need to discuss relation subtypes and supertypes. I'll do that in the next subsection. First, however, let me finish up the present subsection by stating for the record exactly what it means for a given tuple to be of a given type (note that I haven't actually done this yet—not quite, anyway). The necessary definition is straightforward, however:

Definition: Let tuple type *TT* have heading

```
{ <A1,T1> , <A2,T2> , ... , <An,Tn> }
```

Then tuple *t has*, or is *of*, type *TT* if and only if it has a heading of the form

```
{ <A1,T1'> , <A2,T2'> , ... , <An,Tn'> }
```

where, for all j ($j = 1, 2, ..., n$), type Tj' is a subtype of type Tj (equivalently, type Tj is a supertype of type Tj').

Or in other words (more simply, and relying on the notion already defined of what it means for some tuple type *TT'* to be a subtype of tuple type *TT*):

Definition: Tuple *t* is of type *TT* if and only it's of some subtype *TT'* of type *TT*.[8]

Thus, for example, the tuple returned by the "tuple type ER" selector invocation

```
TUPLE { E CIRCLE ( ... ) , R SQUARE ( ... ) }
```

is of all four of the tuple types ER, CR, ES, CS. *Note:* In particular, it's certainly of type CS. In other words, specialization by constraint has occurred in this example. To repeat something I said in Chapter 8, if S by C is performed as described in that chapter for scalar types, it'll happen automatically for tuple and relation types as well, and nothing more needs to be said about the matter.

Relation Subypes, Supertypes, and Values

I turn now to relation types. Let's agree for simplicity that (at least as far as this subsection is concerned) the unqualified term *type* refers to a relation type specifically, barring explicit statements to the contrary. By way of example, suppose we define a relation variable—i.e., a relvar—as follows:

```
VAR RV BASE RELATION { E ELLIPSE , R RECTANGLE } KEY { E , R } ;
```

---

[8] This definition might look circular, but it's not (see Exercise 17.3 at the end of the chapter).

Then it should be clear that, in accordance with the discussions of the previous subsection, the relation that's the value of relvar RV at any given time might contain tuples of any mixture of the four tuple types ER, CR, ES, and CS. It seems reasonable to suggest, therefore, that the type of that relation value might be any of the corresponding relation types ER, CR, ES, and CS. For example, if every tuple in that relation value is of tuple type CS, then it surely seems reasonable to say that the relation value is of relation type CS.

Without going through the detailed analysis, therefore—it parallels that already given for the tuple case in the previous subsection—it should be clear that we can regard relation type CS as a subtype of relation type ER, and so on. Here's the definition:

Definition: Let relation types *RT* and *RT'* have headings

```
{ <A1,T1>  , <A2,T2>  , ... , <An,Tn>  }
{ <A1,T1'> , <A2,T2'> , ... , <An,Tn'> }
```

respectively. Then relation type *RT'* is a *subtype* of relation type *RT* (and relation type *RT* is a *supertype* of relation type *RT'*) if and only if, for all j (j = 1, 2, ..., n), type Tj' is a subtype of type Tj (equivalently, type Tj is a supertype of type Tj').

Once again, however, it must be understood that, for any given j, types Tj and Tj' might themselves be tuple or relation types. As I hope you were expecting, therefore, the foregoing definition of what it means for one relation type to be a subtype of another:

a. Is recursive, and

b. Relies on a definition of what it means for one tuple type to be a subtype of another (but this latter is a possibility we've already discussed).

So what exactly does it mean for some relation to be of a given type? It turns out that the answer to this question isn't quite as straightforward as its tuple counterpart was. I'll give the definition first:

Definition: Let relation type *RT* have heading

```
{ <A1,T1>  , <A2,T2>  , ... , <An,Tn>  }
```

Then relation *r has*, or is *of*, type *RT* if and only if every tuple *t* in the body of *r* has a heading of the form

```
{ <A1,T1'> , <A2,T2'> , ... , <An,Tn'> }
```

where, for all j (j = 1, 2, ..., n), type Tj' is a subtype of type Tj (equivalently, type Tj is a supertype of type Tj').

In other words, every tuple t in the body of r is of some type TT' such that TT' is a subtype of TT, where TT in turn is that specific tuple type that has the same heading as relation type RT. Note carefully, however, that different tuples t in the body of r can be of different types TT', just so long as all of those types TT' are subtypes of that same type TT.[9]

Now, I claim that what the foregoing paragraph boils down to—as I hope you'd expect—is simply this:

Definition: Relation r is of type RT if and only it's of some subtype RT' of type RT.

However, I can't fully justify this claim yet, because ultimately it relies on a concept that I'm not yet in a position to explain properly—viz., the concept of the most specific type of a relation.[10] So I'll have to come back to this issue later (see the discussion of IM Prescription 27 in Chapter 20). Meanwhile, let's look at some examples.

Consider the relations shown below, all of which are certainly of relation type ER (but notice that the headings aren't always the heading of that type as such). Most specific types are shown in lowercase italics.[11]

E	:	ELLIPSE	R	:	RECTANGLE
e1	:	ellipse	r1	:	rectangle
c2	:	circle	r2	:	rectangle
e3	:	ellipse	s3	:	square
c4	:	circle	s4	:	square

E	:	ELLIPSE	R	:	RECTANGLE
e1	:	ellipse	r1	:	rectangle
c4	:	circle	s4	:	square

E	:	CIRCLE	R	:	RECTANGLE
c2	:	circle	r2	:	rectangle
c4	:	circle	s4	:	square

---

[9] To jump ahead of ourselves for a moment, let those various types TT' have $TT*$ as their most specific common supertype; then (a) $TT*$ must be a subtype of that tuple type that has the same heading as relation type RT, and (b) relation r is of most specific type $RT*$, where $RT*$ is that relation type that has the same heading as tuple type $TT*$. See the discussion of IM Prescription 27 in Chapter 20 for further explanation.

[10] I did touch on that concept in Chapter 9, however, when I explained our conventions for drawing pictures of relations.

[11] If you study those relations carefully, you'll see that several of them illustrate the points made in footnote 9.

E : ELLIPSE	R : RECTANGLE
c2 : circle e3 : ellipse	r2 : rectangle s3 : square

E : ELLIPSE	R : SQUARE
e3 : ellipse	s3 : square

E : CIRCLE	R : SQUARE
c4 : circle	s4 : square

E : omega	R : omega

Perhaps I should elaborate briefly on the last of these examples. By definition, no scalar value is of type *omega* and no tuple value has an attribute of type *omega*. But a relation value *can* have an attribute of type *omega*—though any such relation will necessarily be empty (as indeed it is in the case at hand).

IM PRESCRIPTION 23:
PROPER AND IMMEDIATE TUPLE / RELATION SUBTYPES AND SUPERTYPES

Let T and T' be both tuple types or both relation types, with headings

        { <A1,T1> , <A2,T2> , ... , <An,Tn> }
        { <A1,T1'> , <A2,T2'> , ... , <An,Tn'> }

respectively. Then T' shall be a **proper** subtype of T, and T shall be a **proper** supertype of T', if and only if (a) for all j ($j = 1, 2, ..., n$), type Tj' is a subtype of Tj and (b) there exists at least one j ($j = 1, 2, ..., n$) such that Tj' is a proper subtype of Tj. Also, T' shall be an **immediate** subtype of T, and T shall be an **immediate** supertype of T', if and only if (a) there exists some j ($j = 1, 2, ..., n$) such that Tj' is an immediate subtype of Tj and (b) for all k ($k = 1, 2, ..., n$, $k \neq j$), $Tk' = Tk$. If and only if T' is a proper but not an immediate subtype of T, then T' shall be a **nonimmediate** subtype of T and T shall be a **nonimmediate** supertype of T'.

——— ◆◆◆◆◆ ———

This prescription is just the tuple / relation analog of IM Prescription 5 (see Chapter 5). It wasn't included in the *Explorations* version of the prescriptions, but that was just an oversight—the concepts involved were always meant to be part of our inheritance model, and tacitly always were. Of course, the reason for the oversight was probably just that the definitions are all fairly obvious; however, I'll give a few examples for the record (most of them involving tuple types specifically, just to be definite). I'll also spell out the details of one particular implication of the prescription (a slightly unobvious implication, to my way of thinking). Here first are the examples:

- Tuple type ER is a proper supertype of each of tuple types CR, ES, and CS. It's also a supertype of itself, but of course not a proper one.

- Tuple type CS is a proper subtype of each of tuple types ER, CR, and ES. It's also a subtype of itself, but of course not a proper one.

- Tuple type ER is an immediate supertype of each of tuple types CR and ES. It's also a proper supertype of tuple type CS, but not an immediate one.

- Tuple type CS is an immediate subtype of each of tuple types CR and ES. It's also a proper subtype of tuple type ER, but not an immediate one.

There's a minor anomaly, however (this is the point I referred to above as being "slightly unobvious"). Recall that if T' and T are scalar types and T' is a proper subtype of T, then the set of values $|T'|$ is—in fact, is required to be—a proper subset of the set of values $|T|$. And the same is true if T' and T are tuple types—*unless* type T has an attribute of some empty type, in which case (as noted in footnote 3) $|T|$ and $|T'|$ are both empty and are therefore equal. By way of illustration, let T and T' be as follows:

```
TUPLE { E CIRCLE , R omega }    /* "tuple type T"  */
TUPLE { E omega  , R omega }    /* "tuple type T'" */
```

In accordance with IM Prescription 23, then, T' is clearly a proper subtype of T (as a matter of fact, it's also an immediate subtype of T); equally clearly, however, $|T'|$ isn't a proper subset of $|T|$, since as I've already said both sets, and hence both types, are in fact empty.

As for relation types, a similar but not identical situation arises. To be specific, if T' and T are relation types and T' is a proper subtype of T, then the set of values $|T'|$ is a proper subset of the set of values $|T|$—unless type T has an attribute of some empty type, in which case $|T'|$ and $|T|$ are again equal. This time, however, they're not empty; rather, they both contain exactly one value. By way of illustration, let T and T' be as follows:

```
RELATION { E CIRCLE , R omega }      /* "relation type T"  */

RELATION { E omega  , R omega }      /* "relation type T'" */
```

Here *T'* is a proper subtype of *T* but, again, the set of values |*T'*| isn't a proper subset of the set of values |*T*|—both contain just one value, viz., the following empty relation:

E : omega	R : omega

EXERCISES

17.1 In the introduction to this chapter, I said it should be obvious that tuple and relation type inheritance will *usually* be multiple inheritance specifically (italics added). When won't it be?

17.2 Identify as many ways as you can think of for a type to be empty.

17.3 In the body of the chapter, I said that tuple *t* was of type *TT* if and only if it was of some subtype of type *TT*. Why isn't this definition circular?

17.4 Is it true that (scalar, tuple, or relation) types *T1* and *T2* have a least specific common subtype and a most specific common supertype if and only if those types *T1* and *T2* belong to the same type lattice?

17.5 Is it true that two tuple types overlap if and only if they belong to the same type lattice? What about relation types?

17.6 Give an example of an operator that might be defined for relations of relation type CS and not for relations of relation type ER.

17.7 If *Op* is an operator that applies to relations of relation type ER, do you think it might make sense to define distinct implementation versions of *Op* corresponding to relation types CR, ES, and CS?

17.8 The following might be proposed as a picture of a certain relation:

E : ELLIPSE	R : RECTANGLE
e3 : ellipse	s3 : square
e5 : circle	s4 : square

Do you see anything wrong with it?

17.9 Our model of inheritance, as it applies to tuple and relation types, has been criticized on the grounds that we can't explicitly define, e.g., tuple type *TT′* to be an explicitly constrained subtype of tuple type *TT*. (In other words, all tuple and relation subtyping is implicit in our model, being based as it is purely on the types of the pertinent attributes, and there's no way to specify any explicit specialization constraint in connection with tuple or relation types.)[12] Discuss.

17.10   With reference to Fig. 15.3 in Chapter 15, let PKC be the following relation type:

```
RELATION { P PARALLELOGRAM , K KITE , C CYCLIC_QUADRILATERAL }
```

Show all immediate supertypes and all immediate subtypes of this type. How many proper subtypes does it have?

ANSWERS

17.1 By way of motivation (i.e., to show that the question is a reasonable one), let me first give a couple of examples that don't involve multiple inheritance: (a) The type TUPLE {E ELLIPSE} has just one immediate subtype, viz., TUPLE {E CIRCLE}. (b) The type TUPLE {E ELLIPSE, X INTEGER} also has just one immediate subtype, viz., TUPLE {E CIRCLE, X INTEGER}. And so on.
　　　　Now let's consider the general question. For simplicity, let's agree to ignore tuple and relation maximal and minimal types.[13] Observe next that the question really makes sense only with respect to some given tuple or relation type (i.e., it might make sense to say of some given tuple or relation type that it's either involved or not involved in multiple inheritance, but it doesn't make sense to say such a thing of tuple and relation types in general). That said, let me propose some definitions:

■ Type *T* is "involved in inheritance" if and only if it has an immediate supertype or an immediate subtype.

---

[12] According to the BNF grammar in Chapter 3, when we state, via an *<is def>* in a formal type definition, that some type *T′* is an immediate subtype of some other type *T*, *T* is required to be a scalar type specifically—but it might be more correct to say it's required to be a *nongenerated* type specifically (and hence not a tuple or relation type in particular). Of course, nongenerated types are indeed always scalar, but generated types might be scalar too.

[13] In the interest of accuracy, I note that "maximal and minimal types" here ought really to be "types with an attribute of some superroot or subleaf type" (see the discussion of IM Prescription 26 in Chapter 19).

■ Type *T* is "involved in *multiple* inheritance" if and only if it has at least two distinct immediate supertypes or at least two distinct, overlapping immediate subtypes.

Now let *T* be a tuple or relation type specifically, and let *T* have heading

```
{ <A1,T1> , <A2,T2> , ... , <An,Tn> }
```

Then type *T* will be involved in multiple inheritance if and only if (a) for some *j* (*j* = 1, 2, ..., *n*), *Tj* is involved in multiple inheritance, or (b) for some *j* (*j* =1,2, ..., *n*) and *k* (*k* = 1, 2, ..., *n*), *Tj* and *Tk* are distinct and are both involved in inheritance.

17.2 (a) There's just one way in which a scalar type can be empty, and that's if it's type *omega* (in other words, a scalar type is empty if and only if it's type *omega*). (b) Likewise, there's just one way in which a tuple type can be empty, and that's if it has at least one attribute of some empty type (in other words, a tuple type is empty if and only if it has such an attribute)—but of course this definition is recursive. (c) There's no way at all in which a relation type can be empty, because such a type always contains at least one value, viz., the pertinent empty relation.

17.3 It's not circular because it's basically just an abbreviated form of a longer, more explicit definition, and that longer definition in turn ultimately relies on the notion of what it means for one *scalar* type to be a subtype of another, a notion that has already been fully and independently defined elsewhere.

17.4 First let me define the term *type lattice* as I'm using it here (this definition is basically as given in Chapter 5 but is tightened up just slightly):

> **Definition:** Let *T* be a type, and let the corresponding maximal type be *T_alpha*; then the set of all subtypes of *T_alpha* is *the type lattice with respect to T*.

So: Is it true that types *T1* and *T2* have a least specific common subtype and a most specific common supertype if and only if those types *T1* and *T2* belong to the same type lattice? For scalar types, the answer is *yes*, albeit trivially, because all scalar types belong to the same type lattice (see Chapters 5 and 6). As for tuple and relation types, let me first note that:

■ It follows from IM Prescription 22 that if *T_alpha* is a maximal tuple or relation type, with attributes *A1, A2, ..., An*, then *T* is a subtype of *T_alpha* if and only if (a) *T* is a tuple type or a relation type accordingly; (b) the attributes of *T* have those same names *A1*,

A2, ..., An; and (c) for all *j* (*j* = 1, 2, ..., *n*), the type of attribute *Aj* of *T* is a subtype of the type of attribute *Aj* of *T_alpha*.

■ It follows from the previous point that if *T1* and *T2* are both tuple types or both relation types, then *T1* and *T2* belong to the same type lattice if and only if (a) their attributes have the same names *A1, A2, ..., An*, and (b) there exist type lattices *TL1, TL2, ..., TLj* such that, for all *j* (*j* = 1, 2, ..., *n*), attribute *Aj* of *T1* and attribute *Aj* of *T2* both belong to *TLj*.

(Note the recursive nature of the second of these points.) And yes, it does follow from these considerations that tuple or relation types *T1* and *T2* have a least specific common subtype and a most specific common supertype if and only if they belong to the same type lattice. *Note:* For further explanation, see the next three chapters—especially Chapter 18, where the issues involved in this exercise are examined in detail, and Chapter 19, where the concept of a tuple / relational maximal type is explained.

17.5   For tuple types, it's false (though it's at least true that types from different lattices are disjoint). For example, consider the following pairs of types:

```
TUPLE { E ELLIPSE , R RECTANGLE }    and    TUPLE { E omega , R omega }
TUPLE { A ELLIPSE }                  and    TUPLE { A RECTANGLE }
TUPLE { X omega }                    and    TUPLE { X omega }
```

Each of these pairs is such that the two types involved (a) belong to the same type lattice but (b) are disjoint.

For relation types, it's true: Types from the same type lattice certainly overlap because they always have the pertinent empty relation in common, and types from different lattices are disjoint.

17.6   An example might be an operator MAX_R that computes the maximum radius of the circles that are values of attribute E in a relation of type CS.

17.7   Yes, of course (but see the further remarks regarding this issue at the end of the section discussing IM Prescription 27 in Chapter 20).

17.8   The picture ignores S by C. If the body is as shown, then attribute R in the heading should be of type SQUARE (see the subsection "Pictures of Relations" in the section discussing IM Prescription 13 in Chapter 9).

17.9 I'll make just three points here:

■ *The Third Manifesto* requires tuple and relation type names to take the form they do for a very good reason: namely, that it facilitates the all important process of *type inference* (the process, that is, of determining the type of the result of evaluating an arbitrarily complex tuple or relation expression). See the *Manifesto* book for further explanation, also the answer to Exercise 21.4 in Chapter 21.

■ Another response to the criticism is that sometimes there are obvious workarounds that will achieve what seems to be the desired effect. To take a concrete example, consider the type TUPLE {N INTEGER}. Now, it's true that we can't define a type whose values are explicitly constrained to be just those tuples of that given type for which the value of attribute N is positive. But we don't need to define such a type anyway! All we need to do is define a subtype of type INTEGER, called (say) POSINT, whose values are just the positive integers; then the desired type is exactly the type TUPLE {N POSINT}.

■ By way of another example, consider the type TUPLE {X INTEGER, Y INTEGER, Z INTEGER}. Suppose we'd like to define a type whose values are just those tuples of that given type for which the Z value is equal to the sum of the X and Y values. The technique illustrated in the previous bullet item won't work here. Thus, the workaround in this case is to define an explicit constraint for every variable that we might think of, informally, as being of the desired type. For example:

```
VAR TV TUPLE { X INTEGER , Y INTEGER , Z INTEGER } ;

CONSTRAINT TC Z FROM TV = X FROM TV + Y FROM TV ;
```

Note: Constraint TC here isn't a type constraint, however; in fact, it isn't a legal constraint at all, according to **Tutorial D** as currently defined! Here's what that definition says: "The [constraint] mustn't reference any variables other than database relvars." But it does also go on to say this: "**Tutorial D** doesn't support constraints that reference any other kinds of variables, though there's no logical reason why it shouldn't."

17.10 Type PKC has three immediate supertypes, viz.:

```
RELATION { P TRAPEZOID      , K KITE          , C CYCLIC_QUADRILATERAL }
RELATION { P PARALLELOGRAM , K QUADRILATERAL , C CYCLIC_QUADRILATERAL }
RELATION { P PARALLELOGRAM , K KITE          , C QUADRILATERAL        }
```

It has six immediate subtypes, viz.:

```
RELATION { P RECTANGLE      , K KITE       , C CYCLIC_QUADRILATERAL }
RELATION { P RHOMBUS        , K KITE       , C CYCLIC_QUADRILATERAL }
RELATION { P PARALLELOGRAM , K RIGHT_KITE  , C CYCLIC_QUADRILATERAL }
RELATION { P PARALLELOGRAM , K RHOMBUS     , C CYCLIC_QUADRILATERAL }
RELATION { P PARALLELOGRAM , K KITE        , C RIGHT_KITE           }
RELATION { P PARALLELOGRAM , K KITE        , C ISOSCELES_TRAPEZOID  }
```

As for proper subtypes, believe it or not, there are 149 of them (!). *Note:* To understand why there are so many, see the discussion of IM Prescription 26 in Chapter 19.

Chapter 18

Tuple/Relation Values with

Inheritance (cont.)

I have known her continue in this a quarter of an hour
—William Shakespeare:
Macbeth (1606)

He's not such a super type
—rather a common type, really

—Anon.:
Where Bugs Go

The previous chapter explained the basic concept of tuple and relation subtypes and supertypes; in particular, it touched on the fact that every pair of tuple types and every pair of relation types has both a least specific common subtype—i.e., an intersection type—and a most specific common supertype (just so long as the types in question both belong to the same type lattice, of course, as we saw in the answer to Exercise 17.4). For example, consider the pair of (either tuple or relation) types CR and ES from Fig. 17.1. For that pair, type CS is the least specific common subtype and type ER is the most specific common supertype. This chapter explains such matters in depth.

IM PRESCRIPTION 24:
COMMON TUPLE / RELATION SUBTYPES AND SUPERTYPES

Let $T1$, $T2$, ..., Tm ($m \geq 0$), T, and T' be all tuple types or all relation types, with headings

```
{  <A1,T11>  ,  <A2,T12>  ,  ...  ,  <An,T1n>  }
{  <A1,T21>  ,  <A2,T22>  ,  ...  ,  <An,T2n>  }
......................................
```

```
{ <A1,Tm1>  , <A2,Tm2>  , ... , <An,Tmn>  }
{ <A1,T01>  , <A2,T02>  , ... , <An,T0n>  }
{ <A1,T01'> , <A2,T02'> , ... , <An,T0n'> }
```

respectively. Then:

a. Type T shall be a **common supertype** for, or of, types $T1$, $T2$, ..., Tm if and only if, for all j ($j = 1, 2, ..., n$), type $T0j$ is a common supertype for types $T1j$, $T2j$, ..., Tmj. Further, that type T shall be the **most specific** common supertype for $T1$, $T2$, ..., Tm if and only if no proper subtype of T is also a common supertype for those types.

b. Type T' shall be a **common subtype** for, or of, types $T1$, $T2$, ..., Tm if and only if, for all j ($j = 1, 2, ..., n$), type $T0j'$ is a common subtype for types $T1j$, $T2j$, ..., Tmj. Further, that type T' shall be the **least specific** common subtype—also known as the **intersection type** or **intersection subtype**—for $T1$, $T2$, ..., Tm if and only if no proper supertype of T' is also a common subtype for those types.

Note: Given types $T1$, $T2$, ..., Tm as defined above, it can be shown (thanks in particular to IM Prescription 25) that a unique most specific common supertype T and a unique least specific common subtype T' always exist. In the case of that particular common subtype T', moreover, it can also be shown that whenever a given value is of each of types $T1$, $T2$, ..., Tm, it is also of type T' (hence the alternative term *intersection type*)—in which case, for all j ($j = 1, 2, ..., n$), type $T0j'$ is the intersection type for types $T1j$, $T2j$, ..., Tmj. And it can further be shown that every tuple value and every relation value has both a unique least specific type and a unique most specific type (regarding the latter, see also IM Prescription 27).

This prescription was number 23 in the Explorations version. However, the following sentence also appeared in that version, immediately following the word "respectively": "Further, for all j (j = 1, 2, ..., n), let types T1j, T2j, ..., Tmj have a common subtype (and hence a common supertype also)." But that sentence adds nothing—it could even be argued to contradict parts a. and b. of the prescription, slightly—and is therefore omitted here.

COMMON TUPLE SUBTYPES

Once again I'll focus on tuple types specifically until further notice. Let tuple types $TT1$ and $TT2$ be such that (a) they have the same attribute names and (b) attributes with the same name have overlapping types (thus, $TT1$ and $TT2$ certainly belong to the same type lattice); then it should be clear that types *TT1* and *TT2* themselves overlap as well.[1] For example, we know from Part II of this book that scalar types ELLIPSE and CIRCLE overlap, and so do scalar types RECTANGLE and SQUARE; as a direct consequence, therefore, each of the tuple types ER, CR, ES, and CS in Fig. 17.1 overlaps each of the other three. And if tuple types *TT1* and *TT2* overlap, it seems reasonable to say they must have at least one nonempty common subtype. For completeness, moreover, it also seems reasonable to say that if tuple types *TT1* and *TT2* don't overlap, then they do still have at least one common subtype (though any such subtype will necessarily be empty), just so long as:

a. *TT1* and *TT2* have the same attribute names. (If they don't have the same attribute names, then they're from different type lattices, and the notion of having a common subtype doesn't apply.)

b. Attributes of *TT1* and *TT2* with the same name have types from the same type lattice. (If attributes with the same name don't have types from the same type lattice, then again *TT1* and *TT2* are themselves from different type lattices, and the notion of having a common subtype again doesn't apply.)

The following definition generalizes these ideas to apply to any set of tuple types from the same type lattice (actually the definition doesn't require the types in question all to be from the same type lattice, but if they're not it becomes vacuous, thanks to points a. and b. above):

Definition: Let *TT1*, *TT2*, ..., *TTm* ($m \geq 0$), and *TT'* be all tuple types, with headings

```
{ <A1,T11>  , <A2,T12>  , ... , <An,T1n>  }
{ <A1,T21>  , <A2,T22>  , ... , <An,T2n>  }
 . . . . . . . . . . . . . . . . . . . . . . . . . . . . . . . .
{ <A1,Tm1>  , <A2,Tm2>  , ... , <An,Tmn>  }
{ <A1,T01'> , <A2,T02'> , ... , <An,T0n'> }
```

respectively. Then type *TT'* is a *common subtype* for, or of, types *TT1*, *TT2*, ..., *TTm* if and only if, for all *j* (*j* = 1, 2, ..., *n*), type *T0j'* is a common subtype for types *T1j*, *T2j*, ..., *Tmj*.[2] *Note:* If *m* = 1, then *TT'* is *TT1*. If *m* = 0, then *TT'* is the tuple type with heading

---

[1] Once again, see Chapter 5 (or the answer to Exercise 17.4 in Chapter 17) for an explanation of the term *type lattice* as I'm using it here. Note in particular that the lattice in question explicitly includes the pertinent maximal and minimal types (see the discussion of IM Prescription 25 in Chapter 19); in fact, it includes all types having an attribute of some pertinent superroot or subleaf type (see the discussion of IM Prescription 26, also in Chapter 19).

[2] In other words, as we saw (in effect) in the answer to Exercise 6.2 in Chapter 6, *TT'* is a common subtype for *TT1*, *TT2*, ..., *TTm* if and only if it satisfies the predicate FORALL *t* (IF *t* ∈ |*TT'*| THEN *t* ∈ INTERSECT {|*TT1*|, |*TT2*|, ..., |*TTm*|}).

```
{ <A1,T1_alpha> , <A2,T2_alpha> , ... , <An,Tn_alpha> }
```

where, for all j ($j = 1, 2, ..., n$), type Tj_alpha is the maximal type with respect to type $T0j$ (see IM Prescription 25).

Here are some examples:

1. Each of the tuple types ER, CR, ES, and CS overlaps each of the other three, and they have CS as a common subtype. And if we limit our attention to tuple types ER and CR only, of course they overlap, and they have both CR and CS as common subtypes.

2. Scalar types ELLIPSE and RECTANGLE are disjoint. As a direct consequence, tuple types TUPLE {A ELLIPSE} and TUPLE {A RECTANGLE} are disjoint as well—even though they belong to the same type lattice—and so their sole common subtype is in fact the pertinent minimal type, viz., type TUPLE {A *omega*} (an empty type).

3. Types TUPLE {A ELLIPSE} and TUPLE {B ELLIPSE} are also disjoint (even though they have the same attribute types), because they have different attribute names. In fact, they're from distinct type lattices, and hence have no common subtype by definition.

4. Types TUPLE {X RELATION {A ELLIPSE}} and TUPLE {X RELATION {B ELLIPSE}} are also disjoint, even though they have the same attribute names, because corresponding attribute types are from distinct type lattices. As a consequence, as in the previous example, the specified tuple types are also from distinct type lattices, and hence have no common subtype by definition.

5. Let TX be the type TUPLE {X *omega*}. This type is empty (in fact, it's the minimal type for types of the form TUPLE {X T}, where T is a scalar type). Since it's empty, TX doesn't overlap with any type at all (not even itself). Thus, if TY is any type from the same type lattice—i.e., if TY is of the form TUPLE {X T} for some scalar type T—then the only subtype TX and TY have in common is TX itself.

6. Consider types TUPLE {X *omega*, Y CHAR} and TUPLE {X CHAR, Y *omega*}. These types belong to the same type lattice. They don't overlap, however, (a) because they're both empty, and (b) more specifically, because attributes X and Y are each of type *omega* in one case and CHAR in the other, and *omega* and CHAR don't overlap. So their sole common subtype is the pertinent minimal type, viz., type TUPLE {X *omega*, Y *omega*} (another empty type).

7. Let T0 be the type TUPLE { }. This type isn't empty—it contains just one tuple, viz., the empty tuple (also written TUPLE { } in **Tutorial D**). In fact, T0 is the sole type in its

lattice, and so it's the sole common subtype for every subset of the types in that lattice (!). It's also the pertinent minimal type (and the pertinent maximal type as well, come to that).

Next, not only is it intuitively obvious that any set of *m* tuple types *TT1*, *TT2*, ..., *TTm* from the same type lattice must have at least one common subtype, I think it's also intuitively obvious that (as the note attached to IM Prescription 24 in fact says) one of the common subtypes in question must be the least specific or intersection subtype in particular. Here by way of example are the least specific or intersection types corresponding to Examples 1-7 above:

1. CS (for ER, CR, ES, and CS); CR (for ER and CR).

2. TUPLE {A *omega*}.

3. *Not applicable.*

4. *Not applicable.*

5. TUPLE {X *omega*}.

6. TUPLE {X *omega*, Y *omega*}.

7. TUPLE { }.

And here's the precise definition:

> **Definition:** Let *TT1*, *TT2*, ..., *TTm* ($m \geq 0$), and *TT'* be all tuple types, with headings
>
> ```
> {  <A1,T11>   ,  <A2,T12>   ,  ...  ,  <An,T1n>   }
> {  <A1,T21>   ,  <A2,T22>   ,  ...  ,  <An,T2n>   }
>
> . . . . . . . . . . . . . . . . . . . . . . . . . . . . . . . . .
>
> {  <A1,Tm1>   ,  <A2,Tm2>   ,  ...  ,  <An,Tmn>   }
> {  <A1,T01'> ,  <A2,T02'> ,  ...  ,  <An,T0n'> }
> ```
>
> respectively. Then type *TT'* is the *least specific common subtype*—also known as the *intersection type* or *intersection subtype*—for, or of, types *TT1*, *TT2*, ..., *TTm* if and only if, for all *j* (j = 1, 2, ..., *n*), type *T0j'* is the least specific common subtype for types *T1j*, *T2j*, ..., *Tmj*. *Note:* If *m* = 1, then *TT'* is *TT1*. If *m* = 0, then *TT'* is the tuple type with heading
>
> ```
> {  <A1,T1_alpha> ,  <A2,T2_alpha> ,  ...  ,  <An,Tn_alpha> }
> ```

where, for all j (j = 1, 2, ..., n), type Tj_alpha is the maximal type with respect to type $T0j$ (see IM Prescription 25).

COMMON TUPLE SUPERTYPES

Given the discussions of the previous section, I think it's at least reasonable to expect that if tuple types $TT1$, $TT2$, ..., TTm all belong to the same type lattice, then they not only have at least one common subtype, they have at least one common supertype as well—so this time I'll just jump straight in with a definition:

Definition: Let TT, $TT1$, $TT2$, ..., and TTm ($m \geq 0$) be all tuple types, with headings

```
{  <A1,T01> ,  <A2,T02> ,  ... ,  <An,T0n> }

{  <A1,T11> ,  <A2,T12> ,  ... ,  <An,T1n> }

{  <A1,T21> ,  <A2,T22> ,  ... ,  <An,T2n> }

. . . . . . . . . . . . . . . . . . . . . . . . . . . . . .

{  <A1,Tm1> ,  <A2,Tm2> ,  ... ,  <An,Tmn> }
```

respectively. Then type TT is a *common supertype* for, or of, types $TT1$, $TT2$, ..., TTm if and only if, for all j (j = 1, 2, ..., n), type $T0j$ is a common supertype for types $T1j$, $T2j$, ..., Tmj.[3] *Note:* If m = 1, then TT is $TT1$. If m = 0, then TT is the tuple type with heading

```
{  <A1,T1_omega> ,  <A2,T2_omega> ,  ... ,  <An,Tn_omega> }
```

where, for all j (j = 1, 2, ..., n), type Tj_omega is the minimal type with respect to type $T0j$ (see IM Prescription 25).

(As with the definition of *common subtype* from the previous section, this definition doesn't actually require the types mentioned all to be from the same type lattice, but if they're not it becomes vacuous.)

Here are some examples:

1. Tuple types ER, CR, ES, and CS have ER as a common supertype. Tuple types CS and CR have both CR and ER as common supertypes.

---

[3] In other words, as we saw (in effect) in the answer to Exercise 6.2 in Chapter 6, TT is a common supertype for $TT1$, $TT2$, ..., TTm if and only if it satisfies the predicate FORALL t (IF $t \in$ UNION {$|TT1|$, $|TT2|$, ..., $|TTm|$} THEN $t \in |TT|$).

2. Tuple types TUPLE {A ELLIPSE} and TUPLE {A RECTANGLE} have TUPLE {A PLANE_FIGURE} as their sole common supertype[4] (apart from the pertinent maximal type TUPLE {A *alpha*}).

3. Types TUPLE {A ELLIPSE} and TUPLE {B ELLIPSE} are from distinct type lattices, and hence have no common supertype, by definition.

4. Types TUPLE {X RELATION {A ELLIPSE}} and TUPLE {X RELATION {B ELLIPSE}} are also from distinct type lattices and have no common supertype, by definition.

5. Let TX be the type TUPLE {X *alpha*}. This type is the maximal type for types of the form TUPLE {X *T*}, where *T* is a scalar type. Thus, if TY is any type from the same type lattice, then the only supertype TX and TY have in common is TX itself.

6. Consider types TUPLE {X CHAR, Y *alpha*} and TUPLE {X *alpha*, Y CHAR}. These types belong to the same type lattice. Neither is a supertype of the other, however, because attributes X and Y are each of type CHAR in one case and *alpha* in the other, and CHAR isn't a supertype of *alpha* (though *alpha* is a supertype of CHAR, of course). So their sole common supertype is the pertinent maximal type, viz., type TUPLE {X *alpha*, Y *alpha*}.

7. Let T0 be the type TUPLE { }. As noted in the previous section, then, this type is the sole type in its lattice, and so it's the sole common supertype for every subset of the types in that lattice (!).

Next, not only is it intuitively obvious that any set of *m* tuple types *TT1*, *TT2*, ..., *TTm* from the same type lattice must have at least one common supertype, I think it's also intuitively obvious (as the note attached to IM Prescription 24 in fact says) that one of the common supertypes in question must be the most specific common supertype in particular. Here by way of example are the most specific common supertypes corresponding to Examples 1-7 above:

1. ER (for ER, CR, ES, and CS); CR (for CS and CR).

2. TUPLE {A PLANE_FIGURE}.

3. *Not applicable.*

4. *Not applicable.*

---

[4] Here and in a few analogous contexts in this chapter I'm reinstating type PLANE_FIGURE, just for the sake of the example, as a proper supertype—in fact, the most specific common supertype—for types ELLIPSE and RECTANGLE.

5. TUPLE {X *alpha*}.

6. TUPLE {X *alpha*, Y *alpha*}.

7. TUPLE { }.

And here's the precise definition:

> **Definition:** Let *TT*, *TT1*, *TT2*, ..., and *TTm* ($m \geq 0$) be all tuple types, with headings
>
> ```
> { <A1,T01> , <A2,T02> , ... , <An,T0n> }
>
> { <A1,T11> , <A2,T12> , ... , <An,T1n> }
>
> { <A1,T21> , <A2,T22> , ... , <An,T2n> }
>
>    . . . . . . . . . . . . . . . . . . . . . . . . . . . . . . . .
>
> { <A1,Tm1> , <A2,Tm2> , ... , <An,Tmn> }
> ```
>
> respectively. Then type *TT* is the *most specific common supertype* for, or of, types *TT1*, *TT2*, ..., *TTm* if and only if, for all j ($j = 1, 2, ..., n$), type *T0j* is the most specific common supertype for types *T1j*, *T2j*, ..., *Tmj*. *Note:* If $m = 1$, then *TT* is *TT1*. If $m = 0$, then *TT* is the tuple type with heading
>
> ```
> { <A1,T1_omega> , <A2,T2_omega> , ... , <An,Tn_omega> }
> ```
>
> where, for all j ($j = 1, 2, ..., n$), type *Tj_omega* is the minimal type with respect to type *T0j* (see IM Prescription 25).

COMMON RELATION SUBTYPES

I turn now to the question of common relation subtypes and supertypes. Before we start getting into details, however, it's worth noting that the analysis that follows, in this section and the next, is similar but *not* identical to the analysis we've already been through in previous sections in connection with common tuple subtypes and supertypes—basically because a tuple type can be empty but a relation type can't.

Let relation types *RT1* and *RT2* belong to the same type lattice[5] (i.e., let them have the same attribute names, and let attributes with the same name have types that have a common subtype); then types *RT1* and *RT2* overlap.[6] Here's the definition:

Definition: Let *RT1*, *RT2*, ..., *RTm* ($m \geq 0$), and *RT'* be all relation types, with headings

```
{ <A1,T11>  , <A2,T12>  , ... , <An,T1n>  }
{ <A1,T21>  , <A2,T22>  , ... , <An,T2n>  }

. . . . . . . . . . . . . . . . . . . . . . . . . . . . . . .

{ <A1,Tm1>  , <A2,Tm2>  , ... , <An,Tmn>  }
{ <A1,T01'> , <A2,T02'> , ... , <An,T0n'> }
```

respectively. Then type *RT'* is a *common subtype* for, or of, types *RT1*, *RT2*, ..., *RTm* if and only if, for all *j* (j = 1, 2, ..., *n*), type *T0j'* is a common subtype for types *T1j*, *T2j*, ..., *Tmj*.[7] *Note:* If *m* = 1, then *RT'* is *RT1*. If *m* = 0, then *RT'* is the relation type with heading

```
{ <A1,T1_alpha> , <A2,T2_alpha> , ... , <An,Tn_alpha> }
```

where, for all *j* (j = 1, 2, ..., *n*), type *Tj_alpha* is the maximal type with respect to type *T0j* (see IM Prescription 25).

(As with the tuple analog of this definition earlier, this definition doesn't actually require the types mentioned all to be from the same type lattice, but if they're not it becomes vacuous.)
Here are some examples:

1. Each of the relation types ER, CR, ES, and CS overlaps each of the other three, and they have CS as a common subtype. Similarly, relation types ER and CR overlap, and they have both CR and CS as common subtypes.

2. Scalar types ELLIPSE and RECTANGLE are disjoint. However, relation types RELATION {A ELLIPSE} and RELATION {A RECTANGLE} *aren't* disjoint—they overlap, and have as their sole common subtype the pertinent minimal type, viz., type RELATION {A *omega*}. In other words, the sole relation of that minimal type is also of

---

[5] Footnote 1 applies here also.

[6] Note the difference here vis-à-vis the tuple case. To be specific, two relation types overlap if and only if they belong to the same type lattice, whereas two tuple types overlap if and only if they belong to the same type lattice *and* attributes with the same name have types that overlap in turn (implying among other things that the tuple types in question are both nonempty).

[7] In other words, as we saw (in effect) in the answer to Exercise 6.2 in Chapter 6, *RT'* is a common subtype for *RT1*, *RT2*, ..., *RTm* if and only if it satisfies the predicate FORALL *r* (IF *r* ∈ |*RT'*| THEN *r* ∈ INTERSECT {|*RT1*|, |*RT2*|, ..., |*RTm*|}).

types RELATION {A ELLIPSE} and RELATION {A RECTANGLE}. Of course, the relation in question contains no tuples—i.e., it's an empty relation—but type RELATION {A *omega*} as such is nonempty.

3. In contrast to the foregoing, types RELATION {A ELLIPSE} and RELATION {B ELLIPSE} are disjoint (even though they have the same attribute types), because they're from distinct type lattices, and hence have no common subtype by definition.

4. Types RELATION {X TUPLE {A ELLIPSE}} and RELATION {X TUPLE {B ELLIPSE}} are also disjoint, even though they have the same attribute names, because corresponding attribute types are from distinct type lattices. As a consequence, as in the previous example, the specified relation types are also from distinct type lattices, and thus have no common subtype by definition.

5. Let RX be the type RELATION {X *omega*}. This type is the minimal type for types of the form RELATION {X *T*}, where *T* is a scalar type, and it contains just one value, viz., the pertinent empty relation. Thus, if RY is any type from the same type lattice—i.e., if RY is of the form RELATION {X *T*} for some scalar type *T*—then the only subtype RX and RY have in common is RX itself.

6. Consider types RELATION {X *omega*, Y CHAR} and RELATION {X CHAR, Y *omega*}. These types belong to the same type lattice, and therefore they overlap. Note, however, that attributes X and Y are each of type *omega* in one case and CHAR in the other, and *omega* and CHAR don't overlap; so the sole common subtype for the two specified relation types is the pertinent minimal type, viz., type RELATION {X *omega*, Y *omega*}.

7. Let R0 be the type RELATION { }. This type isn't empty—it contains two rather important relations, viz., TABLE_DUM and TABLE_DEE (see the answer to Exercise 2.24 in Chapter 2). However, R0 is the sole type in its lattice, and so it's the sole common subtype for every subset of the types in that lattice (!). It's also the pertinent minimal type (and the pertinent maximal type as well, come to that).

Next, not only is it intuitively obvious that any set of *m* relation types *RT1*, *RT2*, ..., *RTm* from the same type lattice must have at least one common subtype, I think it's also intuitively obvious that (as the note attached to IM Prescription 24 in fact says) one of the common subtypes in question must be the least specific or intersection subtype in particular. Here by way of example are the intersection subtypes corresponding to Examples 1-7 above:

1. CS (for ER, CR, and ES); CR (for ER and CR).

2. RELATION {A *omega*}.

3. *Not applicable.*

4. *Not applicable.*

5. RELATION {X *omega*}.

6. RELATION {X *omega*, Y *omega*}.

7. RELATION { }.

And here's the definition:

> **Definition:** Let *RT1*, *RT2*, ..., *RTm* ($m \geq 0$), and *RT'* be all relation types, with headings
>
> ```
> {  <A1,T11>   ,  <A2,T12>   ,  ...  ,  <An,T1n>   }
> {  <A1,T21>   ,  <A2,T22>   ,  ...  ,  <An,T2n>   }
>
> . . . . . . . . . . . . . . . . . . . . . . . . . . . . . . . .
>
> {  <A1,Tm1>   ,  <A2,Tm2>   ,  ...  ,  <An,Tmn>   }
> {  <A1,T01'> ,  <A2,T02'> ,  ...  ,  <An,T0n'> }
> ```
>
> respectively. Then type *RT'* is the *least specific common subtype*—also known as the *intersection type* or *intersection subtype*—for, or of, types *RT1*, *RT2*, ..., *RTm* if and only if, for all *j* (*j* = 1, 2, ..., *n*), type *T0j'* is the least specific common subtype for types *T1j*, *T2j*, ..., *Tmj*. *Note:* If *m* = 1, then *RT'* is *RT1*. If *m* = 0, then *RT'* is the relation type with heading
>
> ```
> {  <A1,T1_alpha>  ,  <A2,T2_alpha> ,  ...  ,  <An,Tn_alpha> }
> ```
>
> where, for all *j* (*j* = 1, 2, ..., *n*), type *Tj_alpha* is the maximal type with respect to type *T0j* (see IM Prescription 25).

COMMON RELATION SUPERTYPES

By now the pattern should be familiar ... If relation types *RT1*, *RT2*, ..., *RTm* all belong to the same type lattice, then not only do they have at least one common subtype, they have at least one common supertype as well:

Definition: Let *RT* and *RT1*, *RT2*, ..., *RTm* ($m \geq 0$) be all relation types, with headings

```
{ <A1,T01> , <A2,T02> , ... , <An,T0n> }

{ <A1,T11> , <A2,T12> , ... , <An,T1n> }

{ <A1,T21> , <A2,T22> , ... , <An,T2n> }

. . . . . . . . . . . . . . . . . . . . . . . . . . . . . . . .

{ <A1,Tm1> , <A2,Tm2> , ... , <An,Tmn> }
```

respectively. Then type *RT* is a *common supertype* for, or of, types *RT1*, *RT2*, ..., *RTm* if and only if, for all *j* (j = 1, 2, ..., *n*), type *T0j* is a common supertype for types *T1j*, *T2j*, ..., *Tmj*.[8] *Note:* If *m* = 1, then *RT* is *RT1*. If *m* = 0, then *RT* is the relation type with heading

```
{ <A1,T1_omega> , <A2,T2_omega> , ... , <An,Tn_omega> }
```

where, for all *j* (j = 1, 2, ..., *n*), type *Tj_omega* is the minimal type with respect to type *T0j* (see IM Prescription 25).

(As with the tuple analog of this definition in the section "Common Tuple Supertypes," this definition doesn't actually require the types mentioned all to be from the same type lattice, but if they're not it becomes vacuous.)

Here are some examples:

1. Relation types ER, CR, ES, and CS have ER as a common supertype. Relation types CS and CR have both CR and ER as common supertypes.

2. Relation types RELATION {A ELLIPSE} and RELATION {A RECTANGLE} have RELATION {A PLANE_FIGURE} as their sole common supertype (apart from the pertinent maximal type RELATION {A *alpha*}).

3. Types RELATION {A ELLIPSE} and RELATION {B ELLIPSE} are from distinct type lattices, and hence have no common supertype, by definition.

4. Types RELATION {X TUPLE {A ELLIPSE}} and RELATION {X TUPLE {B ELLIPSE}} are also from distinct type lattices and have no common supertype, by definition.

---

[8] In other words, as we saw (in effect) in the answer to Exercise 6.2 in Chapter 6, *RT* is a common supertype for *RT1*, *RT2*, ..., *RTm* if and only if it satisfies the predicate FORALL *r* (IF *r* ∈ UNION {|*RT1*|, | *RT2*|, ..., |*RTm*|} THEN *r* ∈ |*RT*|).

5. Let RX be the type RELATION {X *alpha*}. This type is the maximal type for types of the form RELATION {X *T*}, where *T* is a scalar type. Thus, if RY is any type from the same type lattice, then the only supertype RX and RY have in common is RX itself.

6. Consider types RELATION {X CHAR, Y *alpha*} and RELATION {X *alpha*, Y CHAR}. These types belong to the same type lattice. Neither is a supertype of the other, however, because attributes X and Y are each of type CHAR in one case and *alpha* in the other, and CHAR isn't a supertype of *alpha*. So their sole common supertype is the pertinent maximal type, viz., type RELATION {X *alpha*, Y *alpha*}.

7. Let R0 be the type RELATION { }. As noted in the previous section, then, this type is the sole type in its lattice, and so it's the sole common supertype for every subset of the types in that lattice (!).

Next, not only is it intuitively obvious that any set of *m* relation types *RT1*, *RT2*, ..., *RTm* from the same type lattice must have at least one common supertype, I think it's also intuitively obvious that (as the note attached to IM Prescription 24 in fact says) one of the common supertypes in question must be the most specific common supertype in particular. Here by way of example are the most specific common supertypes corresponding to Examples 1-7 above:

1. ER (for ER, CR, and ES); CR (for CS and CR).

2. RELATION {A PLANE_FIGURE}.

3. *Not applicable.*

4. *Not applicable.*

5. RELATION {X *alpha*}.

6. RELATION {X *alpha*, Y *alpha*}.

7. RELATION { }.

And here's the definition:

> **Definition:** Let *RT* and *RT1*, *RT2*, ..., *RTm* ($m \geq 0$) be all relation types, with headings
>
> ```
> { <A1,T01> , <A2,T02> , ... , <An,T0n> }
> { <A1,T11> , <A2,T12> , ... , <An,T1n> }
> { <A1,T21> , <A2,T22> , ... , <An,T2n> }
> ```

```
. . . . . . . . . . . . . . . . . . . . . . . . . . . . . . . .
{ <A1,Tm1> , <A2,Tm2> , ... , <An,Tmn> }
```

respectively. Then type *RT* is the *most specific common supertype* for, or of, types *RT1*, *RT2*, ..., *RTm* if and only if, for all *j* (*j* = 1, 2, ..., *n*), type *T0j'* is the most specific common supertype for types *T1j*, *T2j*, ..., *Tmj*. *Note:* If *m* = 1, then *RT* is *RT1*. If *m* = 0, then *RT* is the relation type with heading

```
{ <A1,T1_omega> , <A2,T2_omega> , ... , <An,Tn_omega> }
```

where, for all *j* (*j* = 1, 2, ..., *n*), type *Tj_omega* is the minimal type with respect to type *T0j* (see IM Prescription 25).

CLOSING REMARKS

I showed in Chapter 15 that:

■ If two scalar types have a nonempty least specific common subtype, then they also have a most specific common supertype (moreover, that supertype is a proper subtype of type *alpha*). However, the converse is false.

The corresponding statement for tuple types is similar but not quite analogous:

■ If two tuple types have a nonempty least specific common subtype, then they also have a most specific common supertype (though that supertype might be the pertinent maximal type).[9] However, the converse is false.

However, the corresponding statement for relation types is rather different:

■ If two relation types have a—necessarily nonempty—least specific common subtype, then they also have a most specific common supertype (though that supertype might be the pertinent maximal type).[10] In this case, however, the converse is true as well.

Finally, that note attached to IM Prescription 24 says it can be shown that every tuple or relation value has a unique least specific type and a unique most specific type. The least specific type is, of course, the pertinent maximal type or, if superroot types are ignored (see the

---

[9] In the interest of accuracy, I note that "the pertinent maximal type" here ought really to be "some pertinent superroot type" (see the discussion of IM Prescription 26 in Chapter 19).

[10] The previous footnote applies here also.

discussion of Prescription 26 in Chapter 19), the pertinent root type. As for the most specific type, see the discussion of IM Prescription 27 in Chapter 20.

EXERCISES

18.1 State necessary and sufficient conditions for (a) two tuple types to overlap, (b) two relation types to overlap.

18.2 Is it true that (a) no tuple type can possibly overlap any type that's not a tuple type and (b) no relation type can possibly overlap any type that's not a relation type?

18.3 With reference to Fig. 15.3 in Chapter 15, consider tuple types defined as follows (tuple types just to be definite—they could have been relation types instead):

```
TUPLE { P PARALLELOGRAM , K KITE ,        C CYCLIC_QUADRILATERAL }
TUPLE { P RHOMBUS        , K RIGHT_KITE , C ISOSCELES_TRAPEZOID  }
TUPLE { P RECTANGLE      , K RIGHT_KITE , C RHOMBUS              }
```

What are the most specific common supertypes and least specific common subtypes for these types taken pairwise? What about the most specific common supertype and least specific common subtype for all three types taken together?

ANSWERS

18.1 (a) Two tuple types overlap—equivalently, they have a nonempty intersection type—if and only if they're from the same type lattice and so have the same attribute names, and attributes with the same name have overlapping types in turn. (b) Two relation types overlap—equivalently, they have a nonempty intersection type—if and only if they're from the same type lattice.

18.2 Yes, it is, because distinct type lattices are disjoint. In particular, therefore, every tuple type lattice is disjoint from (a) the (unique) scalar type lattice and also from (b) every relation type lattice. Hence, no tuple type can overlap with any scalar type or any relation type. Similarly for relation types, mutatis mutandis.

18.3 Let's agree to refer to the three specified types, informally, as types PKC, RRI, and RRR, respectively. For PKC and RRI, the most specific common supertype is PKC and the least specific common subtype is RRI. For RRI and RRR, the most specific common supertype is

```
    TUPLE { P PARALLELOGRAM , K RIGHT_KITE , C QUADRILATERAL        }
```

and the least specific common subtype is

```
    TUPLE { P SQUARE          , K RIGHT_KITE , C SQUARE             }
```

For RRR and PKC, the most specific common supertype is

```
    TUPLE { P PARALLELOGRAM , K KITE        , C QUADRILATERAL       }
```

and the least specific common subtype is

```
    TUPLE { P RECTANGLE       , K RIGHT_KITE , C SQUARE             }
```

For all three types taken together, the most specific common supertype is

```
    TUPLE { P PARALLELOGRAM , K KITE        , C QUADRILATERAL       }
```

and the least specific common subtype is

```
    TUPLE { P SQUARE          , K RIGHT_KITE , C SQUARE             }
```

Chapter 19

Tuple/Relation

Maximal and Minimal Types etc.

Nothing at all takes place in the universe
in which some rule of the maximum or minimum does not appear.

—Leonhard Euler:
Methodus Inveniendi Lineas Curvas (1744)

The previous chapter mentioned *T_alpha* and *T_omega* several times. Both are generic names; they denote the maximal type and the minimal type, respectively, with respect to some specified type *T*, or in other words the least upper bound and the greatest lower bound, respectively, with respect to the type lattice to which that type *T* belongs. If *T* is scalar, of course, those "*T_*" prefixes can be dropped, since all scalar types belong to the same type lattice and there's exactly one maximal and exactly one minimal scalar type: viz., *alpha* and *omega*, respectively. *Alpha* and *omega* were discussed under IM Prescription 20 in Chapter 12; the tuple / relation counterpart to that prescription is IM Prescription 25, which—along with IM Prescription 26, to which it's closely related—is the principal topic of the present chapter.

IM PRESCRIPTION 25: TUPLE / RELATION MAXIMAL AND MINIMAL TYPES

Let *T*, *T_alpha*, and *T_omega* be all tuple types or all relation types, with headings

```
{ <A1,T1>         , <A2,T2>         , ... , <An,Tn>         }
{ <A1,T1_alpha> , <A2,T2_alpha> , ... , <An,Tn_alpha> }
{ <A1,T1_omega> , <A2,T2_omega> , ... , <An,Tn_omega> }
```

respectively. Then (a) type *T_alpha* shall be the **maximal type with respect to type *T*** if and only if, for all *j* (*j* = 1, 2, ..., *n*), type *Tj_alpha* is the maximal type with respect to type *Tj*; (b) type *T_omega* shall be the **minimal type with respect to type *T*** if and only if, for all *j* (*j* = 1, 2, ..., *n*), type *Tj_omega* is the minimal type with respect to type *Tj*.

This prescription was number 24 in the Explorations version. It has been reworded slightly, however, in order to correct a logical error in that earlier formulation.

As you'll recall from Chapter 12, *alpha* and *omega* aren't just scalar types, they're union types, and indeed dummy types. Now, tuple and relation analogs of *alpha* and *omega* certainly exist (though the specifics are a little more complicated than they are in the scalar case, as you might expect), but they're not tuple / relation union or dummy types as such—in fact, there aren't any tuple / relation union or dummy types as such (not formally, at any rate). Let's take a closer look. I'll begin by considering maximal types specifically. Here are the definitions:[1]

Definition: Let tuple types *TT* and *TT_alpha* have headings

```
{ <A1,T1> ,           <A2,T2> ,          ... , <An,Tn>         }
{ <A1,T1_alpha> , <A2,T2_alpha> , ... , <An,Tn_alpha> }
```

respectively. Then tuple type *TT_alpha* is *the maximal type with respect to tuple type TT* if and only if, for all *j* ($j = 1, 2, ..., n$), type *Tj_alpha* is the maximal type with respect to type *Tj*.

Definition: Let relation types *RT* and *RT_alpha* have headings

```
{ <A1,T1> ,           <A2,T2> ,          ... , <An,Tn>         }
{ <A1,T1_alpha> , <A2,T2_alpha> , ... , <An,Tn_alpha> }
```

respectively. Then relation type *RT_alpha* is *the maximal type with respect to relation type RT* if and only if, for all *j* ($j = 1, 2, ..., n$), type *Tj_alpha* is the maximal type with respect to type *Tj*.

These definition are just as you'd expect, though it's worth pointing that once again they're both recursive and mutually recursive. Here are a couple of examples. First, the maximal type with respect to the tuple type

```
TUPLE { E ELLIPSE , R RECTANGLE }
```

is TUPLE {E *alpha*, R *alpha*}. Likewise, the maximal type with respect to the relation type

---

[1] All of the definitions in this chapter are taken more or less verbatim from the pertinent IM prescription (i.e., either IM Prescription 25 or IM Prescription 26, as applicable). I've repeated them inline in the body of the text, however, in order to keep the text flowing properly, and more particularly to save you from having to keep on referring back to the prescription in question.

```
RELATION { E ELLIPSE , R RECTANGLE }
```

is RELATION {E *alpha*, R *alpha*}. Note, therefore, that—in contrast to scalar types, where there's just one maximal type that applies to all possible scalar types—(a) distinct tuple types can correspond to distinct maximal types and (b) distinct relation types can also correspond to distinct maximal types. More specifically, note that:

■ If types *T1* and *T2* belong to distinct type lattices, then—and only then—the corresponding maximal types are distinct. (This observation applies to types in general, regardless of whether they're scalar, tuple, or relation types.)

■ Tuple type *TT_alpha* contains every tuple whose type is some subtype of some supertype of tuple type *TT* (equivalently, every tuple whose type is some supertype of some subtype of tuple type *TT*), and nothing else.[2]

■ Relation type *RT_alpha* contains every relation whose type is some subtype of some supertype of relation type *RT* (equivalently, every relation whose type is some supertype of some subtype of relation type *RT*), and nothing else.

The definitions for minimal types parallel the foregoing definitions for maximal types, of course:

Definition: Let tuple types *TT* and *TT_omega* have headings

```
{ <A1,T1> ,        <A2,T2> ,        ... , <An,Tn>        }
{ <A1,T1_omega> , <A2,T2_omega> , ... , <An,Tn_omega> }
```

respectively. Then tuple type *TT_omega* is *the minimal type with respect to tuple type TT* if and only if, for all *j* (*j* = 1, 2, ..., *n*), type *Tj_omega* is the minimal type with respect to type *Tj*.

Definition: Let relation types *RT* and *RT_omega* have headings

```
{ <A1,T1> ,        <A2,T2> ,        ... , <An,Tn>        }
{ <A1,T1_omega> , <A2,T2_omega> , ... , <An,Tn_omega> }
```

---

[2] "Type" in this sentence really means the *most specific* type of the tuple in question (see Chapter 20). An analogous remark applies to the next bullet item also.

respectively. Then relation type *RT_omega* is *the minimal type with respect to relation type RT* if and only if, for all *j* (*j* = 1, 2, ..., *n*), type *Tj_omega* is the minimal type with respect to type *Tj*.

Here are a couple of examples. First, the minimal type with respect to the tuple type

```
TUPLE { E ELLIPSE , R RECTANGLE }
```

is TUPLE {E *omega*, R *omega*}. Likewise, the minimal type with respect to the relation type

```
RELATION { E ELLIPSE , R RECTANGLE }
```

is RELATION {E *omega*, R *omega*}. Note, therefore, that—in contrast to scalar types, where there's just one minimal type that applies to all possible scalar types—(a) distinct tuple types can correspond to distinct minimal types and (b) distinct relation types can also correspond to distinct minimal types. More specifically, note that:

- If types *T1* and *T2* belong to distinct type lattices, then—and only then—the corresponding minimal types are distinct. (This observation applies to types in general, regardless of whether they're scalar, tuple, or relation types.)

- Tuple type *TT_omega* isn't necessarily empty (though in practice it usually will be; for example, the particular example shown above, TUPLE {E *omega*, R *omega*}, is certainly empty). The following conceptually important counterexample was mentioned in Chapter 18: Let T0 be the type TUPLE { }. Then T0_*omega* is equal to T0 (i.e., T0 is its own minimal type),[3] and it contains exactly one value: namely, the 0-tuple (i.e., the tuple with the empty set of attributes).

- Relation type *RT_omega* is definitely not empty; in fact, as mentioned several times previously in this book, there's no such thing as an empty relation type. To be specific, *RT_omega* contains exactly one value—viz., the empty relation of type *RT*, or in other words the sole relation whose heading is that of type *RT_omega*. A conceptually important case is as follows: Let R0 be the type RELATION { }. Then R0_*omega* is equal to R0 (i.e., R0 is its own minimal type),[4] and it contains exactly two values: namely, TABLE_DUM and TABLE_DEE (see the answer to Exercise 2.24 in Chapter 2).

---

[3] It's its own maximal type too; in fact, of course, it's the only type in its lattice, and therefore— in accordance with IM Prescription 26 as discussed later in this chapter—(a) it's also both a root type and a leaf type, and (b) that type lattice doesn't contain any superroot or subleaf types (again, see IM Prescription 26).

[4] The previous footnote applies here too (see also Exercise 19.2 at the end of the chapter).

By the way, since relation types are never empty, type *RT_omega* (unlike its scalar and tuple counterparts) can serve as a declared type. For example, the following is a legitimate relvar definition:[5]

```
VAR ERV BASE RELATION { E omega , R omega } KEY { } ;
```

Tuple / Relation Union and Dummy Types (?)

As noted earlier, the union and dummy type concepts don't apply to tuple and relation types—at least, not formally—because union and dummy types are always scalar by definition. However, those concepts do apply informally. By way of example, suppose as we did in Chapter 12 that scalar type ELLIPSE is a dummy type, with immediate regular subtypes CIRCLE and NONCIRCLE, and consider the following tuple types (tuple types only, for simplicity):

- ` TUPLE { E ELLIPSE }`

  If ELLIPSE is a dummy type, there won't be any values of this tuple type—let's call it TE—that aren't values of some proper subtype of TE; thus, TE might be implicitly regarded as a union tuple type, and indeed as a dummy tuple type as well. Now, the purpose of a scalar union or dummy type is to provide a basis for defining operators that apply to values and variables of several different types, all of them immediate subtypes of the union or dummy type in question. And the same goes for a tuple or relation "union or dummy type" such as type TE, mutatis mutandis. In other words (and as the example illustrates), the situation is analogous to the situation that arises in connection with specialization by constraint: If some scalar type happens to be a union or dummy type, then certain tuple and relation types will effectively be "union or dummy types" automatically, and nothing more needs to be said about the matter.

- ` TUPLE { E CIRCLE , X alpha }`

  This one too might be considered a tuple dummy type, if it were thought useful to do so.

- ` TUPLE { E omega }`

  This is an example of an empty tuple type. It too might be regarded as a dummy tuple type.

---

[5] Two points here: (a) First, note that relvar ERV has an empty key. Empty keys were mentioned in passing in the answer to Exercise 2.24 in Chapter 2, but for a discussion of empty keys in general see, e.g., Hugh Darwen's book *An Introduction to Relational Database Theory* (2010), available as a free download from *http://bookboon.com*. (b) Second, although relvar ERV is (by definition) a variable, its value is constant! To be specific, its value will always be the sole relation of the specified type (an empty relation, of course).

- `TUPLE { X CIRCLE , Y TUPLE { Z omega } }`

This is a more complicated example of an empty tuple type.

IM PRESCRIPTION 26: TUPLE / RELATION ROOT AND LEAF TYPES

A **root type** shall be a scalar root type (see IM Prescription 6), a tuple root type, or a relation root type. A type shall be a **tuple** root type if and only if it is a tuple type *TT* such that every attribute of *TT* is of a root type. A type shall be a **relation** root type if and only if it is a relation type *RT* such that every attribute of *RT* is of a root type.

A **leaf type** shall be a scalar leaf type (see IM Prescription 6), a tuple leaf type, or a relation leaf type. A type shall be a **tuple** leaf type if and only if it is a tuple type *TT* such that every attribute of *TT* is of a leaf type. A type shall be a **relation** leaf type if and only if it is a relation type *RT* such that every attribute of *RT* is of a leaf type.

A **superroot type** shall be a scalar superroot type, a tuple superroot type, or a relation superroot type. A type shall be a **scalar** superroot type if and only if it is type *alpha*. A type *TT* shall be a **tuple** superroot type if and only if it is a proper supertype of some tuple root type (in which case at least one attribute of *TT* must be of some superroot type). A type *RT* shall be a **relation** superroot type if and only if it is a proper supertype of some relation root type (in which case at least one attribute of *RT* must be of some superroot type).

A **subleaf type** shall be a scalar subleaf type, a tuple subleaf type, or a relation subleaf type. A type shall be a **scalar** subleaf type if and only if it is type *omega*. A type *TT* shall be a **tuple** subleaf type if and only if it is a proper subtype of some tuple leaf type (in which case at least one attribute of *TT* must be of some subleaf type). A type *RT* shall be a **relation** subleaf type if and only if it is a proper subtype of some relation leaf type (in which case at least one attribute of *RT* must be of some subleaf type).

This prescription is new—it didn't appear in the Explorations version.

Superroot Types

Here repeated from Chapters 4 and 5 (but lightly edited here) is IM Prescription 6:

> A scalar type that has type *alpha* as its sole immediate supertype shall be a **root** type; a type that has type *omega* as its sole immediate subtype shall be a **leaf** type.

As you can see, this prescription has to do with scalar types specifically. Now, tuple and relation root and leaf types exist too, of course, but once again the definitions are a little more complicated than they are in the scalar case. By way of example, consider Fig. 17.1 from

Chapter 17 once again, and assume for definiteness that types ER, CR, ES, and CS are all tuple types specifically. Clearly (?), type ER is the root type here; equally clearly, the type

```
TUPLE { E alpha , R alpha }
```

is the corresponding maximal type. But what about these two types?—

```
TUPLE { E alpha    , R RECTANGLE }
TUPLE { E ELLIPSE , R alpha      }
```

Refer to Fig. 19.1.[6]

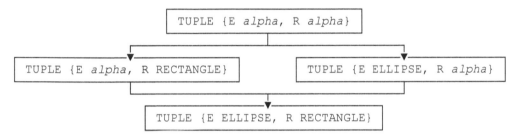

Fig. 19.1: Root, superroot, and maximal types (example)

As the figure indicates, the two types just mentioned—viz., types TUPLE {E *alpha*, R RECTANGLE} and TUPLE {E ELLIPSE, R *alpha*}—effectively act as intermediaries, coming between the root type TUPLE {E ELLIPSE, R RECTANGLE} and the corresponding maximal type TUPLE {E *alpha*, R *alpha*}. It follows that we certainly can't say that a tuple root type, like a scalar root type, has just one immediate supertype, where the supertype in question is the corresponding maximal type. To spell out the details: Every value of type TUPLE {E ELLIPSE, R RECTANGLE} is certainly a value of both of those intermediary types, and every value of either of those intermediary types is certainly a value of type TUPLE {E *alpha*, R *alpha*}.

So how exactly can we define the root type concept for tuples (or relations) in such a way as to preserve the notion that, in the case at hand, type TUPLE {E ELLIPSE, R RECTANGLE} is indeed a root type? Actually the answer is straightforward. Here it is:

Definition: A tuple or relation type *T* is a *root type* if and only if every attribute of *T* is of some root type (i.e., if and only if every proper supertype of *T* is a superroot type).

---

[6] I note in passing—for what it's worth—that the graphs in Figs. 19.1 and 19.2 (later) aren't type graphs, technically speaking, because they contravene point 3 of the type graph definition as given in Chapter 14.

Now, this definition—which is recursive, of course— makes reference to the concept of a superroot type, which can be defined as follows (again the definition is recursive):

Definition: A *superroot type* is a scalar, tuple, or relation superroot type. A scalar type is a superroot type if and only if it's type *alpha*; a tuple or relation type is a superroot type if and only if it's a proper supertype of some tuple or relation root type (in which case it must have at least one attribute of some superroot type).

Thus, all of the tuple types shown in Fig. 19.1 are superroot types apart from TUPLE {E ELLIPSE, R RECTANGLE}—i.e., tuple type ER—which is a root type but not a superroot type. As the definition states, root types as such aren't superroot types, but all proper supertypes of a root type are.[7]

Caveat: As IM Prescription 26 says, if tuple or relation type *T* is a superroot type, then *T* must have at least one attribute of some superroot type. However, the converse is false. For example, the type TUPLE {E CIRCLE, R *alpha*} does have an attribute (viz., attribute R) of some superroot type, but it's not itself a superroot type, because attribute E isn't of a root type. Similar remarks apply to subleaf types also, mutatis mutandis.

Subleaf Types

Turning now to subleaf types: Subleaf types are at the opposite extreme, as it were, from superroot types. With reference to Fig. 17.1 once again, for example, it should be obvious that the types

```
TUPLE { E CIRCLE , R omega  }
TUPLE { E omega  , R SQUARE }
```

both effectively act as intermediaries, coming between the leaf type TUPLE {E CIRCLE, R SQUARE} and the minimal type TUPLE {E *omega*, R *omega*}. (To spell out the details: Every tuple of type TUPLE {E *omega*, R *omega*} is certainly a tuple of both intermediary types—if you see what I mean—and every tuple of either of those intermediary types is certainly a tuple of type TUPLE {E CIRCLE, R SQUARE}.[8] Refer to Fig. 19.2.) It follows that we certainly can't say that a tuple leaf type, like a scalar leaf type, has just one immediate subtype, where the subtype in question is the corresponding minimal type.

---

[7] Perhaps it would be better—more consistent, at any rate, and more in accordance with mathematical convention—to introduce the term *"proper* superroot," and then define a root type to be a superroot type after all but not a proper one. For the purposes of this book, however, I'll stay with the definitions as given above. Analogous remarks apply to subleaf types also, mutatis mutandis (see the next subsection).

[8] In fact, of course, these remarks are vacuously true, because—apart from the leaf type TUPLE {E CIRCLE, R SQUARE}—the types mentioned are all empty.

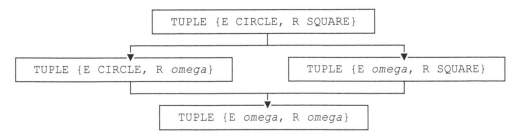

Fig. 19.2: Leaf, subleaf, and minimal types (example)

So we proceed as follows. First we define the concept of a (tuple or relation) leaf type appropriately:

Definition: A tuple or relation type *T* is a *leaf type* if and only if every attribute of *T* is of some leaf type (i.e., if and only if every proper subtype of *T* is a subleaf type).

And we define the concept of a subleaf type thus:

Definition: A *subleaf type* is a scalar, tuple, or relation subleaf type. A scalar type is a subleaf type if and only if it's type *omega*; a tuple or relation type is a subleaf type if and only if it's a proper subtype of some tuple or relation leaf type (in which case it must have at least one attribute of some subleaf type).

Thus, all of the tuple types shown in Fig. 19.2 are subleaf types except for type TUPLE {E CIRCLE, R SQUARE}—i.e., tuple type CS—which is a leaf type but not a subleaf type. As the definition says, leaf types as such aren't subleaf types, but all proper subtypes of a leaf type are.

EXERCISES

19.1 Give an example, different from the one in the body of the chapter, of a tuple type *TT* for which the corresponding minimal type *TT_omega* is nonempty.

19.2 Let R0 be the type RELATION { }. Which of the following are true statements? (a) R0 is a root type; (b) R0 is a superroot type; (c) R0 is the maximal type in its lattice; (d) R0 is a leaf type; (e) R0 is a subleaf type; (f) R0 is the minimal type in its lattice.

19.3 Consider the type RELATION {A *omega*}. This type isn't a union type, not even in the weak sense in which that notion applies to tuple and relation types. But why isn't it, exactly?

19.4 Let type T' be an immediate subtype of type T. Is it true that $|T| = |T'|$ if and only if T is a subleaf type (in which case T' is a subleaf type also, necessarily)?

19.5 If ELLIPSE is a union type, with regular immediate subtypes CIRCLE and NONCIRCLE (only), what can be said about the relation types RELATION {E ELLIPSE, S SQUARE} and RELATION {E ELLIPSE, S *omega*}?

19.6 With reference to Fig. 15.3 in Chapter 15, let PKC be the following relation type:

```
RELATION { P PARALLELOGRAM , K KITE , C CYCLIC_QUADRILATERAL }
```

What are the root and leaf types corresponding to type PKC? And given those root and leaf types, what corresponding superroot and subleaf types are there?

ANSWERS

19.1 The example in the body of the chapter was as follows: Let T0 be the type TUPLE { }. Then T0_*omega* is just T0 itself, and it contains exactly one value (viz., the 0-tuple). And the following examples build on this one:

- The tuple type

  ```
  TUPLE { Z TUPLE { } }
  ```

  is nonempty, because the tuple TUPLE {Z TUPLE { }} is a value of that type.[9] Also, that type has no immediate subtypes and is therefore minimal (in fact, it's the only type in its lattice).

- The choice of attribute name Z in the previous example is clearly arbitrary, so there are as many such tuple types as there are attribute names.

- The tuple type

  ```
  TUPLE { ZZ TUPLE { Z TUPLE { } } }
  ```

  also has no immediate subtypes and contains just one value.

---

[9] Don't be confused here—the first appearance of the expression TUPLE {Z TUPLE { }} in this bullet item is the *name* of the type, the second denotes a *value* (indeed, the sole value) of that type. *Note:* That second appearance is actually a tuple selector invocation; in fact, it's a tuple literal.

■ Moreover, types such as

```
TUPLE { ZZ1 TUPLE { Z TUPLE { } } , ZZ2 TUPLE { Z TUPLE { } } }
```

further demonstrate the existence of an indefinitely large number of nonempty minimal tuple types.

■ And then, of course, there's

```
TUPLE { ZZ RELATION { } }
```

(which contains two values). And so on.

19.2 First of all, as noted in passing in the body of the chapter (also in Chapter 18), type R0 is the only type in its lattice, from which it follows immediately that (a), (c), (d), and (f) are true and (b) and (e) are false. (Regarding these last two, incidentally, in fact there are no superroot or subleaf types in this lattice at all. Compare footnote 3.)

19.3 Because RELATION {A *omega*} { } is a value (a relation) whose most specific type is RELATION {A *omega*} (see Chapter 20). This state of affairs violates the definition of a union type, which says that no value of a union type *T* can have most specific type equal to *T*. *Note:* Since the specified type RELATION {A *omega*} is certainly a subleaf type, this exercise shows that subleaf types aren't necessarily union types (or dummy types either, a fortiori).

19.4 Yes, it is. Observe, therefore, that the notion that "proper subtypes are proper subsets" is violated *only* in the very special case where *T* and *T'* are both subleaf types.

19.5 The following discussion answers the question for both of the specified relation types:

■ RELATION {E ELLIPSE, S SQUARE} can be regarded as a regular union relation type, with three immediate subtypes (two regular and one dummy): RELATION {E CIRCLE, S SQUARE}, RELATION {E NONCIRCLE, S SQUARE}, and RELATION {E ELLIPSE, S *omega*}.

■ Each of those three types has two immediate subtypes in turn. The first has RELATION {E CIRCLE, S *omega*} and RELATION {E *omega*, S SQUARE}; the second has RELATION {E NONCIRCLE, S *omega*} and RELATION {E *omega*, S SQUARE}; and the third has RELATION {E CIRCLE, S *omega*} and RELATION {E NONCIRCLE, S *omega*}.

■ The three types RELATION {E CIRCLE, S *omega*}, RELATION {E NONCIRCLE, S *omega*}, and RELATION {E *omega*, S SQUARE}, which can all be regarded as dummy relation types,[10] have as their unique common subtype RELATION {E *omega*, S *omega*}, which is the minimal type in the lattice. (It's not a dummy type, though, for reasons explained in the answer to Exercise 19.3.)

■ Of all of these various relation types, those (and only those) with at least one attribute of type *omega* are subleaf types, and each of those subleaf types has the empty relation with heading {E *omega*, S *omega*} as its sole value.

19.6 The (necessarily unique) root type is

```
RELATION { P QUADRILATERAL , K QUADRILATERAL , C QUADRILATERAL }
```

The sole leaf type is

```
RELATION { P SQUARE        , K SQUARE        , C SQUARE        }
```

The following are all of the superroot types (the first one is the maximal type PKC_*alpha*):

```
RELATION { P alpha         , K alpha         , C alpha         }
RELATION { P alpha         , K alpha         , C QUADRILATERAL }
RELATION { P QUADRILATERAL , K alpha         , C alpha         }
RELATION { P alpha         , K QUADRILATERAL , C alpha         }
RELATION { P alpha         , K QUADRILATERAL , C QUADRILATERAL }
RELATION { P QUADRILATERAL , K alpha         , C QUADRILATERAL }
RELATION { P QUADRILATERAL , K QUADRILATERAL , C alpha         }
```

The following are all of the subleaf types (the last one is the minimal type PKC_*omega*):

```
RELATION { P omega         , K QUADRILATERAL , C QUADRILATERAL }
RELATION { P QUADRILATERAL , K omega         , C QUADRILATERAL }
RELATION { P QUADRILATERAL , K QUADRILATERAL , C omega         }
RELATION { P omega         , K omega         , C QUADRILATERAL }
RELATION { P QUADRILATERAL , K omega         , C omega         }
RELATION { P omega         , K QUADRILATERAL , C omega         }
RELATION { P omega         , K omega         , C omega         }
```

---

[10] Two points here regarding those three dummy types: First, each has just one immediate subtype; second, each has at least one regular supertype. But didn't I argue in the answers to Exercises 12.4 and 12.6 in Chapter 12 that neither of these situations could ever be the case? Well, yes, I did; but of course my arguments in those answers had to do with scalar types specifically (where "proper subtypes are proper subsets"), and they can easily be seen not to apply to relation types. Regarding the second point, moreover, my answer to Exercise 12.6 explicitly excluded what I called "the pathological case" of type *omega*, which *is* an example of a (scalar) dummy type with regular supertypes, and the second of the foregoing points is, of course, just a logical consequence of that pathological case.

Chapter 20

Tuple/Relation Variables

with Inheritance

Q: What type of inheritance do you hope for from your relations?
A: Variable—it depends on how those relations change.

—Tinley Roquot
(*with apologies to Ambrose Bierce*)

We saw in Chapter 15 that scalar values, at least, always have a unique most specific type, even with multiple inheritance. And the same goes for tuple and relation values as well, though once again the details are a little more complicated than they are in the scalar case. Such matters are the principal focus of this chapter.

IM PRESCRIPTION 27: TUPLE / RELATION MOST SPECIFIC TYPES

Let *H* be a heading defined as follows:

```
{ <A1,T1> , <A2,T2> , ... , <An,Tn> }
```

Then:

a. If *t* is a tuple of type TUPLE *H*, meaning *t* shall take the form

```
TUPLE { <A1,MST1,v1> , <A2,MST2,v2> , ... , <An,MSTn,vn> }
```

where, for all *j* ($j = 1, 2, ..., n$), type *MSTj* is a subtype of type *Tj* and is the most specific type of value *vj*, then the **most specific** type of *t* shall be

```
TUPLE { <A1,MST1> , <A2,MST2> , ... , <An,MSTn> }
```

b. If *r* is a relation of type RELATION *H*, let the body of *r* consist of tuples *t1, t2, ..., tm* ($m \geq$ 0). Tuple *ti* ($i = 1, 2, ..., m$) shall take the form

```
TUPLE { <A1,MSTi1,vi1> , <A2,MSTi2,vi2> , ... , <An,MSTin,vin> }
```

where, for all *j* (*j* = 1, 2, ..., *n*), type *MSTij* is a subtype of type *Tj* and is the most specific type of value *vij* (note that *MSTij* is different for different tuples *ti*, in general). Then the **most specific** type of *r* shall be

```
RELATION { <A1,MST1> , <A2,MST2> , ... , <An,MSTn> }
```

where, for all *j* (*j* = 1, 2, ..., *n*), type *MSTj* is the most specific common supertype of those most specific types *MSTij*, taken over all tuples *ti*.

This prescription was number 25 in the Explorations version. Several textual revisions and corrections have been made in the version given here, but the general intent of the prescription hasn't changed.

Despite what I said in the introduction to this chapter, in the tuple case the most specific type concept isn't really all that complicated; in fact, it's quite straightforward. Here's the definition:

Definition: Let tuple *t* be as follows:

```
TUPLE { <A1,v1> , <A2,v2> , ... , <An,vn> }
```

Then the *most specific type* of *t* is the tuple type with heading

```
{ <A1,MST1> , <A2,MST2> , ... , <An,MSTn> }
```

where, for all *j* (*j* = 1, 2, ..., *n*), type *MSTj* is the most specific type of value *vj*.

Once again I think this definition is more or less as you'd expect (it's recursive, of course). By way of example, consider the expression

```
TUPLE { E EX , R RX }
```

This expression represents an invocation of the selector for the tuple type TUPLE {E ELLIPSE, R RECTANGLE} ("tuple type ER"), denoting (let's say) tuple *t*. Now let the most specific types of the expressions EX and RX be CIRCLE and SQUARE, respectively. Then specialization by constraint comes into play, and the most specific type of *t* is

```
TUPLE { E CIRCLE , R SQUARE }
```

("tuple type CS").

I turn now to relations. This time, I think it's instructive to consider some examples before attempting to come up with a definition as such. Below are some examples of relations of relation type ER (actually they're the same as the ones shown in the section on IM Prescription 22—"tuple / relation subtypes and supertypes"—in Chapter 17).

```
┌─────────────────┬──────────────────┐
│ E  : ELLIPSE    │ R  : RECTANGLE   │
╞═════════════════╪══════════════════╡
│ e1 : ellipse    │ r1 : rectangle   │
│ c2 : circle     │ r2 : rectangle   │
│ e3 : ellipse    │ s3 : square      │
│ c4 : circle     │ s4 : square      │
└─────────────────┴──────────────────┘

┌─────────────────┬──────────────────┐
│ E  : ELLIPSE    │ R  : RECTANGLE   │
╞═════════════════╪══════════════════╡
│ e1 : ellipse    │ r1 : rectangle   │
│ c4 : circle     │ s4 : square      │
└─────────────────┴──────────────────┘

┌─────────────────┬──────────────────┐
│ E  : CIRCLE     │ R  : RECTANGLE   │
╞═════════════════╪══════════════════╡
│ c2 : circle     │ r2 : rectangle   │
│ c4 : circle     │ s4 : square      │
└─────────────────┴──────────────────┘

┌─────────────────┬──────────────────┐
│ E  : ELLIPSE    │ R  : RECTANGLE   │
╞═════════════════╪══════════════════╡
│ c2 : circle     │ r2 : rectangle   │
│ e3 : ellipse    │ s3 : square      │
└─────────────────┴──────────────────┘

┌─────────────────┬──────────────────┐
│ E  : ELLIPSE    │ R  : SQUARE      │
╞═════════════════╪══════════════════╡
│ e3 : ellipse    │ s3 : square      │
└─────────────────┴──────────────────┘

┌─────────────────┬──────────────────┐
│ E  : CIRCLE     │ R  : SQUARE      │
╞═════════════════╪══════════════════╡
│ c4 : circle     │ s4 : square      │
└─────────────────┴──────────────────┘

┌─────────────────┬──────────────────┐
│ E  : omega      │ R  : omega       │
╞═════════════════╪══════════════════╡
└─────────────────┴──────────────────┘
```

Now, those relations are indeed all of relation type ER as stated, but in most cases the corresponding most specific types are proper subtypes of that type (as indeed the specified headings indicate). Thus, if we define a relvar ERV as follows—

```
VAR ERV BASE RELATION { E ELLIPSE , R RECTANGLE } KEY { E , R } ;
```

—and then assign one of the relations shown to this relvar, specialization by constraint will come into play once again, and the current most specific type of relvar ERV will become the most specific type of the relation in question.

As their headings show, then, the most specific types of these relations, in order from top to bottom, are relation types ER, ER again, CR, ER again, ES, CS, and ER_*omega*, respectively. (For convenience I use the label ER_*omega* here as a shorthand name for the relation type RELATION {E *omega*, R *omega*}.) Let's focus for a moment on the first of the relations shown (let's call it *TopRel*). Relation *TopRel* has most specific type ER. What's more, it would still have most specific type ER even if we removed the only tuple—viz., the (*e1,r1*) tuple—that's actually of *tuple* type ER. (But if we removed the (*c2,r2*) tuple as well, the result would then have relation type ES as its most specific type.)

Now, you might feel something slightly counterintuitive is going on here, and so it is, in a way. For example, in the case of relation *TopRel*, I seem to be saying (rather loosely) that the most specific type is the *least* specific of the types of the tuples it contains!—and in fact that *is* what I'm saying, in that particular case. And an analogous, though *not* identical, remark applies in all of the other cases too, of course. So the obvious question is: Why? In the case of *TopRel*, for example, why didn't I define the most specific type to be relation type CS (the other "extreme" type) instead? Well, suppose I did. Then:

- Certain of the attributes in certain of the tuples in that relation would contain "values of the wrong type." The (*e1,r1*) tuple, for example, contains an E value of type ELLIPSE (not CIRCLE) and an R value of type RECTANGLE (not SQUARE), and thus certainly isn't of *tuple* type CS (in fact, it's of tuple type ER).

- But allowing a relation of relation type CS to contain a tuple of tuple type ER would be a contradiction in terms—it would mean, for example, that attribute E of such a relation, of type CIRCLE, might contain values that are "just ellipses" and not circles. Indeed, such a state of affairs would be just as bad as allowing a variable of declared type CIRCLE to contain a value that's "just an ellipse."

It follows that we must define the most specific type *MST(r)* for relation *r* in the way I've done in the examples: namely, in such a way that the type corresponding to attribute *A* of *MST(r)* is the most specific common supertype—and not, as might have been expected, the least specific common subtype—of the most specific types of all of the *A* values in *r*. (My apologies if you need to read that sentence several times in order to understand it.) Hence we have the following definition:

Definition: Let relation *r* be as follows:

```
RELATION { <A1,T1> , <A2,T2> , ... , <An,Tn> } { t1, t2, ... , tm }
```

($m \geq 0$). Further, let tuple *ti* be as follows:

```
TUPLE { <A1,MSTi1,vi1> , <A2,MSTi2,vi2> , ... , <An,MSTin,vin> }
```

($i = 1, 2, ..., m$), where, for all j ($j = 1, 2, ..., n$), type *MSTij* is a subtype of type *Tj* and is the most specific type of value *vij* (note that *MSTij* is different for different tuples *ti*, in general). Then the *most specific type* of *r* is the relation type with heading:

```
{ <A1,MST1>, <A2,MST2>, ... , <An,MSTn> }
```

where, for all j ($j = 1, 2, ..., n$), type *MSTj* is the most specific common supertype of the types *MSTij*, taken over all tuples *ti*. *Note:* If $m = 1$, then the most specific type of *r* is the relation type with heading that of the most specific type of *t1*. If $m = 0$, then the most specific type of *r* is the relation type with heading

```
{ <A1,T1_omega> , <A2,T2_omega> , ... , <An,Tn_omega> }
```

where, for all j ($j = 1, 2, ..., n$), type *Tj_omega* is the minimal type with respect to type *Tj* (see IM Prescription 25).

One final remark to close this section: It follows from all of the above that if relation *r* is of high cardinality, then testing *r* to see whether it's of some specified type might be quite time consuming, because it requires every tuple in *r* to be examined. One implication of this state of affairs is that the implementer of an operator that has a parameter of some relation type might want to avoid having special implementation versions of that operator to deal with proper subtypes of that relation type. For example, suppose operator AVG_AREA computes the average area for the ellipses appearing in attribute E of some relation *r*. Suppose further that two implementation versions of that operator exist, one for when the most specific common supertype of E values in *r* is ELLIPSE and one for when it's CIRCLE. Suppose finally that *r* contains a billion tuples, none of which contains "just an ellipse." Then the implementation will have to examine all billion tuples—at run time, please observe—in order to perform the corresponding binding process.

IM PRESCRIPTION 28: MODEL OF A TUPLE / RELATION VARIABLE

Let *V* be a tuple variable or relation variable of declared type *T*, and let *T* have attributes *A1*, *A2*, ..., *An*. Then we can model *V* as a named set of named ordered triples of the form <*DTj,MSTj,vj*> ($j = 1, 2, ..., n$), where:

a.   The name of the set is the name of the variable, *V*.

b. The name of each triple is the name of the corresponding attribute.

c. *DTj* is the name of the declared type of attribute *Aj*.

d. *MSTj* is the name of the **most specific type**—also known as the **current** most specific type—for, or of, attribute *Aj*. (If *V* is a relation variable, then the most specific type of *Aj* is the most specific common supertype of the most specific types of the *m* values in *vj*—see the explanation of *vj* below.)

e. If *V* is a tuple variable, *vj* is a value of most specific type *MSTj*—the **current value** for, or of, attribute *Aj*. If *V* is a relation variable, then let the body of the current value of *V* consist of *m* tuples (*m* ≥ 0); label those tuples (in some arbitrary sequence) "tuple 1," "tuple 2," ..., "tuple *m*"; then *vj* is a sequence of *m* values (not necessarily all distinct), being the *Aj* values from tuple 1, tuple 2, ..., tuple *m* (in that order). Note that those *Aj* values are all of type *MSTj*.

We use the notation *DT(Aj)*, *MST(Aj)*, *v(Aj)* to refer to the *DTj*, *MSTj*, *vj* components, respectively, of attribute *Aj* of this model of tuple variable or relation variable *V*. We also use the notation *DT(V)*, *MST(V)*, *v(V)* to refer to the overall declared type, overall current most specific type, and overall current value, respectively, of this model of tuple variable or relation variable *V*.

Now let *X* be a tuple expression or relation expression. By definition, *X* specifies an invocation of some tuple operator or relation operator *Op*. Thus, the notation *DTj(V)*, *MSTj(V)*, *vj(V)* just introduced can be extended in an obvious way to refer to the declared type *DTj(X)*, the current most specific type *MSTj(X)*, and the current value *vj(X)*, respectively, of the *DTj*, *MSTj*, *vj* components, respectively, of attribute *Aj* of tuple expression or relation expression *X*—where *DTj(X)* is the declared type of *Aj* for the invocation of *Op* in question (see IM Prescription 17) and is known at compile time, and *MSTj(X)* and *vj(X)* refer to the result of evaluating *X* and therefore can't be known until run time (in general).

This prescription was number 26 in the Explorations version.

IM Prescription 28 extends the model of a scalar variable from IM Prescription 9 to take tuple and relation variables into account as well. Basically, of course, a tuple variable (i.e., a tuplevar) of declared type *TT* is a variable whose permitted values are tuples of type *TT*, and a relation variable (i.e., a relvar) of declared type *RT* is a variable whose permitted values are relations of type *RT*. But there's a little more that can usefully be said.

First let's consider tuple variables specifically. Let tuple variable *TV* be of declared type *TT*, and let *TT* have attributes *A1, A2, ..., An*. Then we can model *TV* as a named set of *n* named ordered triples, each such triple being of the form *<DTj,MSTj,vj>*, where:

- The name of the set is the name of the variable, viz., *TV*.

- The name of triple *<DTj,MSTj,vj>* is the name of the corresponding attribute of *TV* (equivalently, the name of the corresponding attribute of *TT*), viz., *Aj*.

- *DTj* is the name of the declared type of attribute *Aj* of *TV* (equivalently, the name of the declared type of attribute *Aj* of *TT*).

- *vj* is the value of attribute *Aj* within the current value of *TV*.

- *MSTj* is the name of the most specific type—also known as the current most specific type—for, or of, attribute *Aj* within the current value of *TV* (in other words, it's the name of the most specific type of value *vj*).

We use the notation *DT(Aj)*, *MST(Aj)*, *v(Aj)* to refer to the *DTj*, *MSTj*, *vj* components, respectively, of attribute *Aj* of this model of tuple variable *TV*. Of course, it must always be the case that *MST(Aj)* is some subtype of *DT(Aj)*. Note that *MST(Aj)* and *v(Aj)* change with time, in general; note too that *MST(Aj)* is in fact implied by *v(Aj)*.

We also use the notation *DT(TV)*, *MST(TV)*, *v(TV)* to refer to the overall declared type, overall current most specific type, and overall current value (respectively), of tuple variable *TV*. In other words (using **Tutorial D** notation):

- `DT(TV)` $\stackrel{\text{def}}{=}$ `TUPLE { A1  DT1 , A2  DT2 , ... , An  DTn }`

- `MST(TV)` $\stackrel{\text{def}}{=}$ `TUPLE { A1 MST1 , A2 MST2 , ... , An MSTn }`

- `v(TV)` $\stackrel{\text{def}}{=}$ `TUPLE { A1  v1 , A2  v2 , ... , An  vn }`

(The symbol " $\stackrel{\text{def}}{=}$ " means "is defined as.")

Note: Since no tuple variable can have an empty declared type, it follows that the declared types *DT(TV)* and *DT1, DT2, ..., DTn* must all be nonempty. And since no tuple value can have an empty most specific type, it follows that the most specific types *MST(TV)* and *MST1, MST2, ..., MSTn* must all be nonempty as well. Also, it should be clear without going into details that the foregoing definitions can readily be extended to apply to arbitrary tuple expressions instead of just to tuple variables specifically.

Turning now to relation variables (i.e., relvars): Let relvar *RV* be of declared type *RT*, and let *RT* have attributes *A1, A2, ..., An*. Let the body of the current value of *RV* consist of *m* tuples, and let those tuples be labeled (in some arbitrary sequence) "tuple *t1*," "tuple *t2*," ..., "tuple *tm*."

Then we can model *RV* as a named set of named ordered triples, each such triple being of the form <*DTj,MSTj,vj*>, where:

- The name of the set is the name of the variable, viz., *RV*.

- The name of triple <*DTj,MSTj,vj*> is the name of the corresponding attribute of *RV* (equivalently, the name of the corresponding attribute of *RT*), viz., *Aj*.

- *DTj* is the name of the declared type of attribute *Aj* of *RV* (equivalently, the name of the declared type of attribute *Aj* of *RT*).

- *vj* is a sequence of *m* values (not necessarily all distinct), being the values of attribute *Aj* from tuples *t1*, *t2*, ..., *tm* (in that order) within the current value of *RV*.

- *MSTj* is the name of the most specific type—also known as the current most specific type—for, or of, attribute *Aj* within the current value of *RV* (that type is in fact the most specific common supertype of the most specific types of the *m* values in *vj*, and hence the most specific type of *vj* as such).

We use the notation *DT(Aj)*, *MST(Aj)*, *v(Aj)* to refer to the *DTj*, *MSTj*, *vj* components, respectively, of attribute *Aj* of this model of relvar *RV*. Of course, it must always be the case that *MST(Aj)* is some subtype of *DT(Aj)*. Note that *MST(Aj)* and *v(Aj)* change with time, in general; note too that *MST(Aj)* is in fact implied by *v(Aj)*.

We also use the notation *DT(RV)*, *MST(RV)*, *v(RV)* to refer to the overall declared type, overall current most specific type, and overall current value (respectively), of relvar *RV*. In other words (using **Tutorial D** notation):

- `DT(RV)`   ≝   `RELATION { A1  DT1 , A2  DT2 , ... , An  DTn }`

- `MST(RV)` ≝   `RELATION { A1 MST1 , A2 MST2 , ... , An MSTn }`

- `v(RV)`   ≝   `RELATION { TUPLE { A1 v11 , A2 v12 , ... , An v1n } ,`
                 `           TUPLE { A1 v21 , A2 v22 , ... , An v2n } ,`
                 `           ..............................`
                 `           TUPLE { A1 vm1 , A2 vm2 , ... , An vmn } }`

Here, of course, I'm using the symbol *vij* to denote the value of attribute *Aj* within tuple *ti* (*i* = 1, 2, ..., *m*; *j* = 1, 2, ..., *n*). By way of example, let relvar ERV be defined as follows—

```
VAR ERV BASE RELATION { E ELLIPSE , R RECTANGLE } KEY { E , R } ;
```

—and let the following relation be assigned to it:

E : ELLIPSE	R : SQUARE
e3 : ellipse c4 : circle	s3 : square s4 : square

Then:

- $DT(RV)$ $\overset{\text{def}}{=}$ RELATION { E ELLIPSE , R RECTANGLE }

- $MST(RV)$ $\overset{\text{def}}{=}$ RELATION { E ELLIPSE , R SQUARE }

- $v(RV)$ $\overset{\text{def}}{=}$ RELATION { TUPLE { E e3 , R s3 } ,
                                 TUPLE { E c4 , R s4 } }

Finally, it should be clear without going into details that the foregoing definitions can readily be extended to apply to arbitrary relational expressions instead of just to relation variables specifically.

IM PRESCRIPTIONS 11 - 15 REVISITED

All of the IM prescriptions discussed in Parts II and III of this book apply essentially unchanged to tuples and relations as well. However, IM Prescriptions 11-15 in particular do merit a little further discussion. *Note:* Despite the title of this chapter, the matters discussed in this section have little to do (for the most part) with tuple and relation variables as such, but it's convenient to deal with them here.

IM Prescription 11: Assignment with Inheritance

Given the assignment $V := X$, where V is a variable reference and X is an expression, this prescription requires the declared type $DT(X)$ of the source expression X to be a subtype of the declared type $DT(V)$ of the target variable V (this is a compile time check). Here's an example in which the target variable is a tuple variable specifically:

```
VAR TV1 TUPLE { P POINT , E ELLIPSE , R RECTANGLE } ;
VAR TV2 TUPLE { P POINT , E CIRCLE  , R SQUARE    } ;

TV2 := TUPLE { P POINT ( ... ) , E CIRCLE ( ... ) , R SQUARE ( ... ) } ;
TV1 := TV2 ;
```

After the second assignment here:

- $DT(TV1)$ is unchanged (it's the tuple type specified in the definition of TV1, of course).

- *MST*(TV1) is the same as *MST*(TV2) (in fact it's the tuple type specified in the definition of TV2, but only because that type happens to be the most specific type of the current value of TV2).[1]

- *v*(TV1) is the same as *v*(TV2).

Suppose now that TV1 had been defined slightly differently:

```
VAR TV1 TUPLE { Q POINT , E ELLIPSE , R RECTANGLE } } ;
```

(The difference is that the point valued attribute is now called Q instead of P.) The assignment of TV2 to TV1 will now fail on a compile time type error, because the declared type of TV2 is no longer a subtype of that of TV1. However, the following assignment is valid:

```
TV1 := TV2 RENAME { P AS Q } ;
```

It's only fair to point out a minor oddity here, however. Given *scalar* variables E and C of declared types ELLIPSE and CIRCLE, respectively, we can assign C to E. Yet if TE and TC are *tuple* variables, of tuple types TUPLE {E ELLIPSE} and TUPLE {C CIRCLE}, respectively, we can't assign TC to TE; we have to assign TC RENAME {C AS E} to TE instead. The reason for this seeming anomaly is, of course, that tuple types have attributes, and the attribute names are part of the type; scalar types, by contrast, have no attributes, and so the question of the names of such attributes being somehow part of the type doesn't arise.

Finally, it should be clear without going into details that relational assignment obeys the same general rules as tuple assignment does. I leave provision of examples as an exercise for you.

IM Prescription 12: Equality with Inheritance

Given the comparison $X = Y$, where X and Y are expressions, this prescription requires the declared types $DT(X)$ and $DT(Y)$ of the expressions X and Y to overlap (this is a compile time check). Here's an example to illustrate tuple comparison:

```
VAR TV1 TUPLE { E ELLIPSE , R SQUARE    } ;    /* "tuple type ES" */
VAR TV2 TUPLE { E CIRCLE  , R RECTANGLE } ;    /* "tuple type CR" */

IF TV1 = TV2 THEN ... ;
```

The comparison here is valid because tuple types ES and CR do overlap (their intersection type is tuple type CS, which is nonempty). Further, the comparison will give TRUE if and only

---

[1] As usual I'm assuming here that types POINT, CIRCLE, and SQUARE have no proper subtype other than type *omega*.

if the current values of tuple variables TV1 and TV2 are both of tuple type CS (and those current values are equal, of course).

Relational comparison is analogous. Further elaboration seems unnecessary, except to note that (as you would surely expect) the rules regarding relational comparison operators other than equality, such as "⊆", follow the same general pattern as those for equality (see Exercise 20.3 at the end of the chapter).

IM Prescription 13: Join etc. with Inheritance

This prescription applies to tuple and relation types essentially unchanged. E.g., if the declared type of attribute *A* of relational expression *RX* is tuple type ES and the declared type of attribute *A* of relational expression *RY* is tuple type CR, then the declared type of attribute *A* of (*RX*) JOIN (*RY*)—assuming the relations denoted by *RX* and *RY* are joinable, of course—is tuple type CS.

IM Prescription 14: TREAT

Given the TREAT invocation TREAT_AS_*T* (*X*), where *X* is an expression, this prescription requires *T* and the declared type *DT*(*X*) of the expression *X* to overlap (this is a compile time check). And the prescription is sufficient to cover tuples and relations as well as scalars, provided the reference within the text of that prescription to "a logical equivalent"—i.e., to an operator of the form TREAT_AS_*T* (*X*)—can be taken to include one of the more general form

```
TREAT_AS_SAME_TYPE_AS ( Y , X )
```

where *X* and *Y* are tuple or relation expressions, as applicable, and *DT*(*Y*) is *T*. Let's consider the tuple case specifically. Consider the following example:

```
VAR TV1 TUPLE { E ELLIPSE , R RECTANGLE } ;   /* "tuple type ER" */
VAR TV2 TUPLE { E CIRCLE ,  R SQUARE    } ;   /* "tuple type CR" */

TV2 := TUPLE { E CIRCLE ( ... ) , R SQUARE ( ... ) } ;
TV1 := TV2 ;
```

After the second assignment, the current value of TV1 consists of a circle and a square, not just an ellipse and a rectangle (if you see what I mean). Suppose now we want to assign that value back to TV2. Then the following assignment will *not* work:

```
TV2 := TV1 ;        /* warning: compile time type error! */
```

(It fails because *DT*(TV1) isn't a subtype of *DT*(TV2).) By contrast, the following will work:

```
TV2 := TREAT_AS_SAME_TYPE_AS ( TV2 , TV1 ) ;
```

The expression on the right side here has declared type the same as that of variable TV2, so the compile time type checking succeeds.[2] Then at run time:

- If the current value of TV1 is indeed of that type—viz., DT(TV2), or in other words TUPLE { E CIRCLE, R SQUARE}—then that TREAT invocation yields a result, *res* say, with (a) $MST(res)$ equal to MST(TV1), which is the same as DT(TV2) in the example, and (b) $v(res)$ equal to v(TV1). So that value can be assigned to TV2.

- However, if the current value of TV1 is only of the (declared) type of TV1, not of TV2, then the invocation fails on a run time type error, and no assignment occurs (variable TV2 remains unchanged).

In other words, the TREAT_AS_SAME_TYPE_AS operator as just discussed is indeed a tuple analog of TREAT as defined for scalar types in Chapter 10. The "SAME TYPE AS" format is provided primarily because our tuple type naming conventions don't lend themselves to the simpler format available in the scalar case.[3]

Without going into further details, I think it should be clear that the following operators can and should also be supported:

- A relational version of TREAT_AS_SAME_TYPE_AS

- Tuple / relation operators of the form

```
X : TREAT_AS_SAME_TYPE_AS ( Y , A )
```

where X is a tuple or relational expression, A is a tuple or relation valued attribute of the tuple or relation denoted by X, and Y is an expression such that $DT(Y)$ is some proper subtype of $DT(A)$.

IM Prescription 15: Type Testing

Given the IS_T invocation IS_T (X), where X is an expression, this prescription requires T and the declared type $DT(X)$ of the expression X to overlap (this is a compile time check). And the prescription is sufficient to cover tuples and relations as well as scalars, provided the reference within the text of that prescription to "a logical equivalent"—i.e., to an operator of the form IS_T (X)—can be taken to include one of the more general form

---

[2] It's worth pointing out explicitly that the TREAT invocation in this example is logically equivalent to the tuple selector invocation TUPLE {E TREAT_AS_CIRCLE (E FROM TV1), R TREAT_AS_SQUARE (R FROM TV1)}. *Question:* Do you think an analogous remark can always be made of tuple / relation TREAT invocations? (*Answer:* Yes, it can.)

[3] Even if all types involved are scalar, however, there are likely to be situations where this more general format will prove useful, or possibly even necessary.

```
IS_SAME_TYPE_AS ( Y , X )
```

where X and Y are tuple or relation expressions, as applicable, and $DT(Y)$ is T.[4] Without going into details, I think it should be clear that a relational operator of the following form can and should also be supported:

```
X : IS_SAME_TYPE_AS ( Y , A )
```

where X is a relational expression, A is an attribute of the relation denoted by X, and Y is an expression such that $DT(Y)$ is some subtype of $DT(A)$.[5]

EXERCISES

20.1 With reference to the type graph of Fig. 14.1 in Chapter 14, let relvar RV be defined as follows:

```
VAR RV BASE
    RELATION { PX PARALLELOGRAM , PY PARALLELOGRAM }
    KEY { PX , PY } ;
```

Here are some possible "states" (i.e., sample values) for this relvar. What are the corresponding most specific types?

PX : PARALLELOGRAM	PY : PARALLELOGRAM
x1 : rectangle	y1 : rectangle
x2 : rhombus	y2 : rectangle
x3 : rectangle	y3 : square
x4 : square	y4 : square

PX : PARALLELOGRAM	PY : PARALLELOGRAM
x2 : rhombus	y2 : rectangle
x4 : square	y4 : square

---

[4] As with TREAT, (a) this "SAME TYPE AS" format is provided primarily because our tuple type naming conventions don't lend themselves to the simpler format available with scalar types, and (b) in any case, even with scalar types, there are likely to be situations where this more general format will prove useful, or possibly even necessary.

[5] "NOT" versions of all of these operators could and probably should be provided also (see the answer to Exercise 10.8 in Chapter 10).

PX : PARALLELOGRAM	PY : PARALLELOGRAM
x3 : rectangle *x4 : square*	*y3 : square* *y4 : square*

PX : PARALLELOGRAM	PY : PARALLELOGRAM
x4 : square	*y4 : square*

PX : PARALLELOGRAM	PY : PARALLELOGRAM

20.2 Let relation *r* have attributes *A1*, *A2*, ..., *An* (only). Explain the most specific type of *r* in your own words. Give some examples.

20.3 Let *RX* and *RY* be relational expressions. Is it true that $RY \subseteq RX$ can evaluate to TRUE only if *MST(RY)* is a subtype of *MST(RX)*?

20.4 Let relvars RV1 and RV2 be defined as follows:

```
VAR RV1 BASE RELATION { E omega , C CIRCLE } KEY { } ;

VAR RV2 BASE RELATION { E omega , C omega } KEY { } ;
```

At all times, each of these relvars must necessarily have as its value the sole relation of most specific type RELATION {E *omega*, C *omega*} (right?). So is the following assignment legal?

```
RV2 := RV1 ;
```

If not, what needs to be done to it to make it legal?

20.5 As a final exercise before we move on to those other approaches to inheritance to be described in the next part of the book, can you think of any practical applications of our inheritance model, over and above its use in connection with geometric types as exhaustively discussed in chapters prior to this point?

ANSWERS

20.1 The most specific types (from top to bottom) are as follows:

- ■ RELATION { PX PARALLELOGRAM , PY RECTANGLE }

- RELATION { PX RHOMBUS   , PY RECTANGLE }
- RELATION { PX RECTANGLE   , PY SQUARE   }
- RELATION { PX SQUARE   , PY SQUARE   }
- RELATION { PX *omega*   , PY *omega*   }

20.2 First let me spell out something that might have already occurred to you but deserves to be stated explicitly anyway.[6] In Chapter 2, I said this:

> [Every] value is certainly of some type. In other words, if *v* is a value, then *v* can be thought of as carrying around with it a kind of flag that announces "I'm an integer" or "I'm a supplier number" or "I'm a rectangle" (etc., etc.).

And in a footnote I added this:

> Since tuples and relations are values, these remarks apply to tuples and relations in particular. For tuples and relations, however, the function of what I'm referring to here as "a kind of flag" is performed by the pertinent heading.

And then in Chapter 5 I said this:

> [With inheritance, a value] might have to carry around several distinct flags—e.g., "I'm an ellipse" *and* "I'm a circle." (Of course, a flag that specifies just the most specific type is all that's logically required.)

Putting these remarks together, it's clear that tuples and relations might effectively have to have several distinct headings—one corresponding to the pertinent most specific type, and one corresponding to each proper supertype of that specific type. For example, the following relation (*r*, say)—

E : CIRCLE	R : RECTANGLE
c2 : circle c4 : circle	r2 : rectangle s4 : square

—has all of the following headings:[7]

---

[6] I did touch on these matters in footnote 5 in Chapter 17, though.

[7] Of course, it would have even more if we were to reinstate types PLANE_FIGURE and POLYGON.

```
{ E CIRCLE  , R RECTANGLE }
{ E ELLIPSE , R RECTANGLE }
{ E alpha   , R RECTANGLE }
{ E CIRCLE  , R alpha     }
{ E ELLIPSE , R alpha     }
{ E alpha   , R alpha     }
```

Of these, the first one listed corresponds to relation *r*'s most specific type.

Definitions of tuple / relation most specific types were given in the body of the chapter, of course, but here's an alternative (and rather more succinct) definition for the relational case:

Definition: Let relation *r* have attributes *A1, A2, ..., An* (only). Then the most specific type of *r* is the type RELATION *H* such that each tuple of *r* is of type TUPLE *H* and there's no heading *H'* such that TUPLE *H'* is a proper subtype of TUPLE *H* and each tuple of *r* is of type TUPLE *H'*.

Here are some examples:

■ The most specific type of both TABLE_DEE and TABLE_DUM is RELATION { }.

■ Let *r* be the relation denoted by the following relation literal:

```
RELATION { TUPLE { E1 ELLIPSE ( LENGTH ( 4.0 ) ,
                                LENGTH ( 4.0 ) ,
                                POINT ( 1.0 , 2.0 ) ,
                   E2 ELLIPSE ( LENGTH ( 4.0 ) ,
                                LENGTH ( 4.0 ) ,
                                POINT ( 0.0 , 0.0 ) ) } }
```

Then the most specific type of *r* is RELATION { E1 CIRCLE, E2 CIRCLE }—or if as elsewhere in the book type CIRCLE has a proper subtype O_CIRCLE, then it's RELATION { E1 CIRCLE, E2 O_CIRCLE }.

■ By contrast, let *r* be the relation denoted by the following relation literal:

```
RELATION { TUPLE { E1 ELLIPSE ( LENGTH ( 4.0 ) ,
                                LENGTH ( 4.0 ) ,
                                POINT ( 1.0 , 2.0 ) ,
                   E2 ELLIPSE ( LENGTH ( 4.0 ) ,
                                LENGTH ( 4.0 ) ,
                                POINT ( 1.0 , 0.0 ) ) } ,
```

```
TUPLE { E1 ELLIPSE ( LENGTH ( 5.0 ) ,
                     LENGTH ( 4.0 ) ,
                     POINT  ( 1.0 , 2.0 ) ,
        E2 ELLIPSE ( LENGTH ( 3.0 ) ,
                     LENGTH ( 3.0 ) ,
                     POINT  ( 0.0 , 0.0 ) ) } }
```

Then the most specific type of *r* is RELATION { E1 ELLIPSE, E2 CIRCLE }, because the most specific type of at least one E1 value is ELLIPSE and that of at least one E2 value is CIRCLE (and the most specific type of no value of E1 is less specific than ELLIPSE and the most specific type of no value of E2 is less specific than CIRCLE).

20.3 Yes, it is. To spell out the details:

■ First, $RY \subseteq RX$ can't possibly be true if $DT(RY)$ and $DT(RX)$ (and hence $MST(RY)$ and $MST(RX)$, a fortiori) are from different type lattices. In this case, in fact, the expression "$MST(RY)$ is a subtype of $MST(RX)$" isn't even defined, and the comparison $RY \subseteq RX$ will fail on a compile time type error.

■ Second, if $DT(RY)$ and $DT(RX)$ are from the same type lattice and $MST(RY)$ is a subtype of $MST(RX)$, then $RY \subseteq RX$ might evaluate to TRUE. Such is the case, for example, if *RY* and *RX* happen to have the values *ry* and *rx* shown below:

ry

E : ELLIPSE	R : RECTANGLE
e1 : ellipse c4 : circle	r1 : rectangle s4 : square

rx

E : ELLIPSE	R : RECTANGLE
e1 : ellipse c2 : circle e3 : ellipse c4 : circle	r1 : rectangle r2 : rectangle s3 : square s4 : square

■ Third, if $DT(RY)$ and $DT(RX)$ are from the same type lattice but $MST(RY)$ isn't a subtype of $MST(RX)$, then (a) by definition, the relation *ry* denoted by *RY* must contain a tuple of type TUPLE *H* such that RELATION *H* is a proper supertype of $MST(RX)$; (b) also by definition, the tuple in question can't possibly appear in the relation *rx* denoted by *RX*; hence, (c) $RY \subseteq RX$ must evaluate to FALSE. Here's an example of this situation:

```
  ry                                              rx
┌─────────────────┬─────────────────┐    ┌─────────────────┬─────────────────┐
│ E  : ELLIPSE    │ R  : RECTANGLE  │    │ E  : CIRCLE     │ R  : RECTANGLE  │
╞═════════════════╪═════════════════╡    ╞═════════════════╪═════════════════╡
│ e1 : ellipse    │ r1 : rectangle  │    │ e1 : circle     │ r1 : rectangle  │
│ c4 : circle     │ s4 : square     │    │ c2 : circle     │ r2 : rectangle  │
└─────────────────┴─────────────────┘    │ e3 : circle     │ s3 : square     │
                                          │ c4 : circle     │ s4 : square     │
                                          └─────────────────┴─────────────────┘
```

20.4 It's not legal according to our inheritance model, because DT(RV1) isn't a subtype of DT(RV2). The legal version is:

```
RV2 := TREAT_AS_SAME_TYPE_AS ( RV2 , RV1 ) ;
```

But the fact that the TREAT is necessary is admittedly a little odd, given that (as the exercise states) the sole possible value of RV1 is in fact the sole possible value of RV2 as well.

20.5 First of all, the exercise does ask for applications "over and above its use in connection with geometric types," but I think I should point out that what some call "geometric modeling" does have wide application in such areas as geographic information systems and display graphics. Thus, I think the potential for using our inheritance model in such contexts is worth further investigation, to say the least.

Second, our model works well for any data to which the notion of *scale* applies. Examples include certain kinds of numeric data, obviously enough—see, e.g., the exercises in Chapter 16. Consider also types such as DECIMAL(5,1), which are found in SQL and many other languages. Another example, very important in practice, is the timeline, which can be divided up according to many different scales—days, weeks, business days, months, hours, milliseconds, and so on. A detailed discussion of the application of our inheritance model to this particular problem area can be found in C. J. Date, Hugh Darwen and Nikos A. Lorentzos: *Time and Relational Theory: Temporal Data in the Relational Model and SQL* (Morgan Kaufmann, 2014).

Another possible application of our model is illustrated by the exercises in Chapter 8. And—despite the remarks in the answer to Exercise 3.14 in Chapter 3—it might be used, judiciously, in connection with types like INTEGER and RATIONAL, too.

Finally, despite my criticisms of examples like those typically found in other writings on inheritance—I refer to such examples as employees vs. programmers, monthly vs. hourly employees, full time vs. part time employees, professors vs. assistant professors, circles vs. colored circles, and numerous others like them—you might be surprised to learn that our inheritance model can in fact be used in connection with such situations after all. See the section "Structural Inheritance for Scalar Types Using the *Manifesto* Model" in Chapter 21 for further details.

Part V

OTHER APPROACHES

This final part of the book contains two fairly lengthy chapters that look at some alternative approaches to the question of type inheritance. Let me apologize immediately for the fact that these chapters might both appear quite complicated, and especially for what might seem to be an excessive number of asides and footnotes. Naturally I've done my best to explain the subject matter as clearly as I can; but (as I said in the preface) it seems to me that the complexities are innate; I mean, I believe the chapters are complicated because the material they describe is complicated. Certainly I've tried hard not to introduce any additional complications, over and above ones that are intrinsic to what's being described.

Chapter 21

Structural Inheritance

Circles ain't red
Ellipses ain't blue
Lemons ain't sweet
All this is true

—Anon.:
Where Bugs Go

This chapter is based in part on Appendix G ("A Closer Look at Structural Inheritance") of the Manifesto book. However, all of the material is revised here, sometimes extensively.

The inheritance model described in Parts II-IV of this book is concerned with what's often called behavioral inheritance, on the grounds that what's inherited is "behavior" (i.e., operators). But there's another kind of inheritance as well, so called "structural" inheritance, where what's inherited is representations. Now, I claimed in Chapter 3 that those inherited representations were physical representations specifically (so long as the types involved were scalar types, at any rate); however, I did also say that some might disagree with that claim, and I'll examine it more closely in what follows (actually in the next section). I also mentioned in that same chapter something called "the EXTENDS relationship," which is a form of structural inheritance in which the representations involved are explicitly visible to the user. This chapter investigates such matters in depth.

The plan of the chapter is as follows. The section immediately following these introductory remarks takes a look at a simple example, with a view to exposing the real issues underlying the idea of structural inheritance. The next section considers what might be involved in supporting that idea. The subsequent two sections then (a) examine a particular concrete realization of the idea ("subtables and supertables") in some detail and (b) offer some thoughts on examples of a certain common kind, of which "COLORED_CIRCLE is a subtype of CIRCLE" is typical.[1] The final section shows how it might be possible to achieve some support for structural inheritance for scalar types without departing from the prescriptions of our own inheritance model as described in previous chapters. And there's a postscript, too, which offers a brief survey of the literature in connection with these matters.

---

[1] Other examples of the same general nature include "programmers are a subtype of employees" (see the next section, also Chapter 1) and "toll highways are a subtype of highways" (see Chapter 11).

AN INTRODUCTORY EXAMPLE

The following example is typical of those commonly used in connection with the concept of structural inheritance. Consider employees and programmers. Assume for the sake of the example that every programmer is an employee but some employees aren't programmers; assume further that employees and programmers are represented by types EMP and PGMR, respectively. Clearly, there's some kind of parallel here with our familiar example of ellipses and circles, where every circle is an ellipse but some ellipses aren't circles; thus, it seems reasonable, at least on the face of it, to say that PGMR is a subtype of EMP ("programmers are a subtype of employees"). But does this notion stand up to closer inspection?

Well, let's focus for a moment on employees alone and ignore programmers. Suppose every employee has an employee number (ENO), a name (ENAME), a department number (DNO), and a salary (SALARY). As the *Manifesto* book shows, then, there are two approaches we might consider for dealing with this situation (two ways, that is, in which we might choose to represent this state of affairs formally): We could define an EMP *type* (scalar by definition), or we could define an EMP *relvar* (nonscalar by definition). As I've said, however, I'm assuming for the moment that we're going with the first of these options.[2] Hence:

- To repeat, that EMP type is scalar, and so it must be "encapsulated," meaning it has no user visible structure. *Note:* I deliberately use the object term *encapsulated* here because most of the work on structural inheritance has been done in an object context specifically.

- That type will presumably have a possrep with (a) components ENO, ENAME, DNO, and SALARY, and hence (b) a set of THE_ operators for accessing those components.

Now I can go on to define type PGMR to be a proper subtype of type EMP, much as earlier in this book I defined type CIRCLE to be a proper subtype of type ELLIPSE. That PGMR type will inherit all operators (all read-only operators, at any rate) that apply to employees in general, and will additionally have certain operators of its own. For example, suppose programmers, unlike employees in general, have a certain language skill (LANG, say, where typical LANG values are "Java," "SQL," and so on);[3] then there'll be an operator to retrieve the LANG value for a given programmer. Note immediately, however, that it follows that the possrep for EMP— i.e., the *supertype*—will have to include a LANG component (of type CHAR, say), despite the fact that employees who aren't programmers don't have a language skill property:

---

[2] You might be thinking that this first option is *obviously* the wrong way to go. If so, then I would agree with you!—and as you'll soon see, the present section will very quickly be agreeing with you as well. Indeed, the *Manifesto* book agrees with you too; in fact, it argues strongly in favor of the second option (see the answer to Exercise 21.1 at the end of the chapter for a summary of the *Manifesto* arguments in this connection). Nevertheless, there are those who would argue that the first option might be reasonable too. See the answer to Exercise 1.10 in Chapter 1 for a possible explanation for this state of affairs, and/or some of the books on object orientation mentioned in the postscript to this chapter.

[3] For simplicity, I'm assuming that each programmer has just one language in which he or she is proficient. That assumption isn't very realistic, of course, but the point isn't important for present purposes.

```
TYPE EMP POSSREP
    ( ENO CHAR , ENAME CHAR , DNO CHAR , SALARY MONEY , LANG CHAR ) ;
```

Now the specialization constraint for type PGMR, required by IM Prescription 10, might specify that a value *e* of type EMP is a value of type PGMR if and only if THE_LANG (*e*) isn't the empty string. Of course, the fact that the LANG possrep component is required in the first place, even for nonprogrammers, is sufficient to show that this design isn't a very good one;[4] but at least if we did adopt it, then it would certainly be the case that PGMR is a subtype of EMP in the sense of our inheritance model. However, the kind of inheritance involved is, by definition, behavioral, not structural. *Please understand, therefore, that designs like the one just briefly discussed are **not** what I want to concentrate on in this chapter!* As indicated in footnote 2, in fact, we'd be much more likely in practice to represent employees and programmers not as types at all but as relvars, perhaps like this:

```
VAR EMP BASE RELATION
    { ENO CHAR , ENAME CHAR , DNO CHAR , SALARY MONEY }
    KEY { ENO } ;

VAR PGMR BASE RELATION
    { ENO CHAR , ENAME CHAR , DNO CHAR , SALARY MONEY , LANG CHAR }
    KEY { ENO } ;

CONSTRAINT E_AND_P_DISJOINT IS_EMPTY ( EMP { ENO } JOIN PGMR ) ;
```

Note the constraint in particular, which says in effect that employee *e* is represented in relvar PGMR if and only if *e* is a programmer, and in relvar EMP if and only if *e* isn't a programmer. (In fact, it might have been better to call this latter relvar NONPGMR rather than EMP, but I have my reasons, which I hope will become apparent later, for wanting to stay with the name EMP.) Thus, the name, department number, and salary for any given employee *e* as well as the pertinent employee number) are represented in just one of the two relvars. As for the language skill, note that the corresponding attribute (LANG) appears in relvar PGMR only, not in relvar EMP.

Now, this design involves two relation types, neither of which is a subtype of the other as far as our model is concerned. (Recall that relation type *RT'* can be a subtype of relation type *RT* in our model only if *RT'* and *RT* have the same attribute names, which isn't the case here.) Under structural inheritance, however, we might say that the type *RT'* corresponding to relvar PGMR inherits the structure of the type *RT* corresponding to relvar EMP but *extends* that structure to include an additional attribute (LANG); and then we might to go on to say—under this very different notion of inheritance!—that type *RT'* is indeed a subtype of supertype *RT* after all.[5] And if we do, then what we have is an example of "the EXTENDS relationship."

---

[4] It also serves, not incidentally, to bolster the *Manifesto* book's arguments in favor of the alternative design (see footnote 2).

[5] As noted in Chapter 7, some writers would describe *RT'* here not as a subtype but as a *derived* type.

Now, in Chapter 3 I said we don't preclude support for such inheritance; however, I also said it had nothing to do with our model. Now I can elaborate on these remarks:

- *With regard to whether it has anything to do with our model* (I deliberately consider the second remark first): It's clear that if we limit our attention to scalar or "encapsulated" types, then any structural inheritance that might apply is merely an implementation issue, because scalar types have no structure to inherit (no structure visible to the user, that is).[6] In an object system, therefore, objects, if they're properly encapsulated, ought not to be subject to structural inheritance at all as far as the model is concerned. But the picture is muddied by the fact that even "encapsulated" objects in such systems do typically expose at least part of their internal structure to the user in the form of what are called (among other things) *public instance variables*.[7] For example, an EMP object might have public— i.e., user visible—instance variables ENO, ENAME, DNO, and SALARY.

  Now, you might be thinking there's no harm in the foregoing notion—you might be thinking that public instance variables are just like possrep components in our own scalar types. But I don't think they are. For one thing, there's no guarantee, or requirement, that the public instance variables for a given object constitute a complete representation for the object in question (e.g., an EMP object might have ENO and SALARY, but no ENAME and DNO, public instance variables). For another, in a system supporting structural inheritance, public instance variables are explicitly inherited, which possrep components explicitly aren't (see the section "Scalar Types Revisited," later). Third, there's no notion of a given object being able to have two or more distinct sets of public instance variables, thereby exposing two or more distinct "possible representations." Fourth, I think there's a strong argument that public instance variables are *physical*, anyway; that is, they expose at least part of the physical representation of the objects in question (meaning, by the way, that the dividing line between model and implementation is somewhat fuzzy, to say the least, in such a system).[8] Why do I say this?—I mean, why do I claim that public instance variables expose the physical representation? Because systems that support such public instance variables typically also support *private* instance variables, which definitely aren't visible to the user—so what's the point in having public ones at all, if not to expose at least some aspects of the physical representation?

---

[6] Well, scalar types do have possreps, of course, and those possreps in turn certainly have structure that's visible to the user. As I'll explain in the section "Scalar Types Revisited," however, I don't think it's appropriate to regard the kind of inheritance that applies to possreps—such as it is—to be structural inheritance as such.

[7] An unfortunate term, in my opinion, since it lends weight to the rather suspect notion that one variable (the containing object) might contain others (the instance variables). See footnote 28 later, also Exercise 21.7 at the end of the chapter, for further discussion of that "suspect notion."

[8] This situation is perhaps not as surprising as it might be, given that object languages have their origin in the programming world, while the idea of there being a sharp distinction between model and implementation has its origin much more in the world of databases. Of course, this isn't to say the distinction in question goes unrecognized in the programming world—not at all— but it does seem to be rather less emphasized in that world (despite the fact that object languages in particular are supposed to be very much about such issues as abstraction, encapsulation, and information hiding).

Moreover, if public instance variables are indeed physical in the foregoing sense, then structural inheritance applied to such variables definitely means it's physical representations that are inherited, which is why I claim such inheritance has nothing to do with our model.[9]

■   *With regard to the question of precluding support:*   On the face of it, our model can't handle the kind of inheritance illustrated by the example of employees and programmers (relvar version).[10] Do we want it to? I mean, do we want to revise our model so that there's a way to inform the system that relvars EMP and PGMR participate in some kind of "EXTENDS relationship" (together with support for whatever that entails)? Or is there a sense in which we might say that our model can handle that kind of inheritance after all? Subsequent sections investigate these questions in detail. But first let me spell out an obvious but important point, viz.:

If we want to examine the possibility of inheriting user visible structure, then (by definition) we're talking about tuple and/or relation types, because as far as our model is concerned (again by definition) those are the only types that possess any such structure.[11]

To be absolutely precise, then, the principal question I'll be examining in the next couple of sections is this:

Can we make sense of the idea of structural inheritance for tuple or relation types?

Note: Despite everything I've said in this section so far, it still might seem intuitively reasonable to say (as I did in my opening paragraph), at least informally, that every programmer is an employee. But I think there's a better way to characterize the situation—a way, that is, that points up the logical difference between, e.g., the example of employees and programmers, on the one hand, and the example of ellipses and circles on the other—and that's to say that a programmer is an employee who ***has a*** language skill. In other words, the crucial relationship

---

[9] In case you find the arguments presented here less than fully convincing—the arguments, that is, regarding the idea that public instance variables are physical, and in particular regarding the negative impact of those variables on the goal of data independence—I'd like to refer you to Chapter 25 ("Object Databases") of my book *An Introduction to Database Systems* (8th edition, Addison-Wesley, 2004), where those arguments are spelled out in more detail. Note also the quotes in footnote 50, which I think are telling in this connection; see also Appendix A, and footnote 28 in Chapter 22.

[10] By "our model" here, of course I mean our model as such, as opposed to an implementation of our model. Obviously implementations are at liberty to make use of physical representation inheritance if there's some advantage to be gained in doing so (just so long as all such implementation concerns remain hidden from the user, of course).

[11] Two points here: First, to repeat from footnote 6, I discount the suggestion that scalar types have user visible structure too (of a kind), in the form of the applicable possreps, and that structural inheritance might thus perhaps apply to scalar types after all. (While some kind of inheritance might indeed be said to apply to possreps—again, see the section "Scalar Types Revisited," previously mentioned in footnote 6—I don't think it's helpful to regard that kind of inheritance as structural inheritance as such.) Second, when I say that tuple and relation types do have user visible structure, I don't mean to suggest that the structure in question is the physical representation of the tuples and relations in question; rather, the physical representation of tuples and relations should be hidden from the user, just as it is for scalars.

here isn't the "is a" relationship (a programmer "is a" employee) but, rather, the "has a" relationship (a programmer "has a" language skill). Contrast the situation with ellipses and circles: Although we might say a circle "has a" property (the radius) that ellipses in general don't have, *that property is really just a degenerate form of a property (a semiaxis length) that ellipses in general do have.* The situation is different with employees and programmers: A programmer's language skill doesn't correspond to *any* property that nonprogrammer employees might have.

I'll have quite a lot more to say regarding the logical difference between "is a" and "has a" in later sections of this chapter.

A Remark on Object Languages

Even if it's true as I've claimed that public instance variables do expose physical representations, the fact remains that (a) many object systems, if not all, do support "the EXTENDS relationship" for scalar types with such variables, and (b) they clearly obtain some benefits from doing so (in particular, code reuse benefits), because otherwise they wouldn't do it. Thus, I certainly don't want anything I've said so far in this chapter to be construed as implying otherwise. In such a system, then, we might define types EMP and PGMR thus (to invent some syntax on the fly):

```
TYPE EMP PUBLIC ( ENO CHAR , ENAME CHAR , DNO CHAR , SALARY MONEY ) ;

TYPE PGMR EXTENDS EMP PUBLIC ( LANG CHAR ) ;
```

But the considerations involved—or some of them, at least—in a system that supports such type definitions will necessarily be very similar to those involved, mutatis mutandis, in a system that supports "the EXTENDS relationship" in connection with relation or (perhaps more especially) tuple types. So let me quickly move on to the next section, which addresses exactly this latter issue.

TUPLE TYPES, VALUES, AND VARIABLES

For definiteness, I'll focus in this section on tuple types specifically (the arguments I'll be presenting all apply equally well to relation types, mutatis mutandis); thus, all types, values, variables, etc., mentioned in this section will be tuple types, values, variables, etc., specifically, barring explicit statements to the contrary. So the question we need to explore reduces to this: Can we make sense of the notion of structural inheritance for tuple types? Well, suppose tuple type *TT'* "extends" tuple type *TT* by adding further attributes, and suppose we want to say that *TT'* is a subtype of *TT*, therefore. For example (to invent some syntax on the fly again):

```
TYPE EMP_TT  TUPLE { ENO CHAR , ENAME CHAR , DNO CHAR , SALARY MONEY } ;

TYPE PGMR_TT TUPLE EXTENDS EMP_TT { LANG CHAR } ;
```

Well, right away we run into a syntax problem. As explained elsewhere in this book, (a) the *Manifesto* requires tuple type names to take the form TUPLE *H* (or some logical equivalent to TUPLE *H*), where *H* is the pertinent heading, and (b) in **Tutorial D** at least, there's no separate "define tuple type" operator. There are good reasons for these rules, too (see Exercise 21.3 at the end of the chapter). For present purposes, however, I'm going to have to overlook those rules and reasons and assume that syntax along the foregoing lines, involving in particular two explicit "define tuple type" statements, is valid after all. Note in particular how "the EXTENDS relationship" between the two types is manifested in that syntax.

Given those type definitions, then, we can go on to define tuple variables (i.e., tuplevars) of the types in question. For example:

```
VAR EMP_V  EMP_TT ;

VAR PGMR_V PGMR_TT ;
```

Values of variable EMP_V are tuples with four attributes (ENO, ENAME, DNO, and SALARY); values of variable PGMR_V are tuples with five attributes (the same four, plus LANG). Note in particular that the set of values constituting type PGMR_TT is the set of tuples appearing in the body of the result of the join—actually the cartesian product—of (a) the "universal relation" containing all tuples of type

```
TUPLE { ENO CHAR , ENAME CHAR , DNO CHAR , SALARY MONEY }
```

—in other words, type EMP_TT—and (b) the "universal relation" containing all tuples of type

```
TUPLE { LANG CHAR }
```

These Subtypes Aren't Subsets

In our usual example of types ELLIPSE and CIRCLE, every circle is an ellipse, and so the set |CIRCLE| of all circles is a subset of the set |ELLIPSE| of all ellipses. The situation is very different with types EMP_TT and PGMR_TT, however:

- No value of type PGMR_TT is a value of type EMP_TT; conversely, no value of type EMP_TT is a value of type PGMR_TT, either—in fact, the two types are disjoint.

- Thus, the set |PGMR_TT| of all values of type PGMR_TT isn't a subset of the set |EMP_TT| of all values of type EMP_TT; conversely, the set |EMP_TT| isn't a subset of the set |PGMR_TT|, either—in fact, the two sets are disjoint.

Now, in our own inheritance model, to say that type *T'* is a subtype of type *T* is to say that the set |*T'*| is a subset of the set |*T*| (that's IM Prescription 2). It follows that we can't say

PGMR_TT is a subtype of type EMP_TT without doing considerable violence to the commonsense notion of subtyping, and indeed to our inheritance model in general. Let's agree, therefore, to drop the terminology of subtyping, as such, in this connection; let's agree to say rather that (e.g.) PGMR_TT is an *extension* of EMP_TT.[12] Analogously, let's agree to say that EMP_TT is a *projection* of PGMR_TT, since it's obtained from PGMR_TT by (in effect) projecting away an attribute. Then we can at least say that the set of projections of all PGMR_TT tuples, taken over all attributes except LANG, is a subset of—in fact, is identical to—the set of all EMP_TT tuples.

To pursue the point a moment longer: Despite the foregoing, those who advocate the idea of structural inheritance normally do refer to EMP_TT and PGMR_TT as supertype and subtype, respectively (see the subsection immediately following). But that terminology is really bad, because the "*sub*tuples" (i.e., tuples of the "subtype") have a superset of the attributes of the "*super*tuples" (i.e., tuples of the "supertype")! A programmer tuple, for example, has all of the attributes of an employee tuple, plus one more (LANG). And, of course, this use—or abuse, rather—of terminology flies directly in the face of conventional relational usage. To spell the point out: In conventional relational usage, "*t2* is a subtuple of *t1*" means *t2* is a projection of *t1*; but in the proposed "bad" terminology, it means *t1* is a projection of *t2*.

Substitutability

In Chapter 3, I said that in many ways the whole point of inheritance is substitutability; for example, a program that works for ellipses can work for circles too, because we can always substitute a circle wherever the system expects an ellipse. So what about employees and programmers (meaning types EMP_TT and PGMR_TT, respectively)? Does substitutability apply?—i.e., can we substitute a value of type PGMR_TT for one of type EMP_TT?

Well, we've seen that no tuple of type PGMR_TT is a tuple of type EMP_TT (and vice versa). Thus, if *Op* is an operator that takes a parameter of type EMP_TT, it can't validly be invoked with an argument of type PGMR_TT instead. In other words, inclusion polymorphism doesn't apply, and so there's no value substitutability either. Of course, we can validly invoke *Op* with an argument that's *the projection over all but LANG* of some tuple of type PGMR_TT. By definition, however, that projection is of type EMP_TT, not PGMR_TT, and it hardly seems appropriate to dignify this rather trivial possibility with the grand name of substitutability.

So what can we do? There wouldn't be much point in supporting structural inheritance in the first place if it turned out to provide no substitutability. So how can we rescue the situation?

Well, one thing we might do is say that if *Op* is invoked with a tuple argument that has all of the attributes of type EMP_TT and more besides, then those additional attributes are simply ignored. (In other words, we might get the system to perform the tuple projections mentioned above automatically.)

---

[12] In connection with this terminology, Hugh Darwen has suggested that (unlike our own model, which is based on specialization by constraint or S by C) structural inheritance might be thought of as being based on *specialization by extension* or S by E.

Aside: If we did adopt such a scheme, however, there wouldn't be any need to pretend that type PGMR_T is a subtype, as such, of type EMP_T. In other words, we wouldn't be talking about inheritance as such at all, and we could therefore drop the subtype / supertype terminology entirely. Of course, if we aren't talking about inheritance, then it's not at all clear why we're even having this discussion anyway. But never mind, let's soldier on. *End of aside.*

Another thing we would probably have to do is expand our notion of what it means for variable V to be of declared type T, such that the value of V at any time could be of type any extension of T^{13} (as well as of any subtype of T as usual). Then, for example, it would be possible to assign a value of most specific type PGMR_TT to a variable of declared type EMP_TT. Indeed, if we didn't expand our notion (i.e., of what it means to declare something to be of a certain type) in such a way, then we couldn't have, e.g., a relvar RV with an attribute E of declared type EMP_TT, such that some tuples in the current value of RV contain an E value of type PGMR_TT instead of EMP_TT. So it looks as if at least part of the solution to the problem of rescuing substitutability is necessarily going to have to involve such a scheme.

However, one obvious consequence of that scheme is the pragmatic one that the implementation might now not be able to tell ahead of time, in general, how much storage to allocate for any given variable.[14] As a result, we might have to switch to an implementation in which storage is allocated at run time and variables are implemented by means of pointers to such allocated storage. Not that that's a problem in itself, of course—but then it might be tempting to have that aspect of the implementation show through to the user at the model level; that is, variables in such a system might be defined to contain pointers instead of actual data values. (Such is typically the case in object systems, for example.[15]) And you won't be surprised to hear that having pointers visible at the model level is something we're adamantly opposed to. For one thing, it violates the prescriptions of the relational model (and the prescriptions of the *Manifesto* accordingly, of course). For another, we saw in Chapter 13 that user visible pointers make specialization by constraint impossible (to quote from that chapter, object IDs and a good model of inheritance are incompatible—and object IDs are, of course, just pointers by another name).

---

[13] This seems to be what SQL does, incidentally (though not for tuple—or rather row—types as such, but instead for what it calls "structured types"). See Chapter 22 for further discussion.

[14] On the other hand, a similar remark applies to certain system defined types already (think of, e.g., type XML in SQL, or type CHAR in **Tutorial D**).

[15] As a matter of fact it's the case to some extent in SQL as well (again see Chapter 22), a state of affairs that rather seriously undermines claims to the effect that SQL conforms to the relational model or that SQL DBMSs are relational.

Another thing we'd probably have to do is use *overloading polymorphism*[16]—in which case, however, again we wouldn't need to pretend that PGMR_T is a subtype of EMP_T, and again we could drop the subtype / supertype terminology, therefore. For example, suppose we want to conduct a "what if" experiment to determine the total cost to the company of raising certain salaries by 10 percent. As part of that experiment, we presumably need to be able to compute the hypothetical new salary for certain employees, regardless of whether the employee in question is a programmer or a nonprogrammer. To that end, we could define two operators, both called RAISE, thus:

```
OPERATOR RAISE ( E EMP_TT ) RETURNS MONEY ;
   RETURN ( ( SALARY FROM E ) * 1.1 ) ;
END OPERATOR ;

OPERATOR RAISE ( P PGMR_TT ) RETURNS MONEY ;
   RETURN ( ( SALARY FROM P ) * 1.1 ) ;
END OPERATOR ;
```

Now, e.g., the expression RAISE (*e*) will cause the "programmers" or "employees" RAISE operator to be invoked depending on whether *e* is a programmer or "just an employee."

Of course, once we start down the overloading path, there's nothing to stop different operators with the same name from implementing different semantics (indeed, in many ways that's the whole point). For example, suppose the salary increase for a given employee is supposed to be 25 percent if the employee is a programmer but only 10 percent otherwise:

```
OPERATOR RAISE ( E EMP_TT ) RETURNS MONEY ;
   RETURN ( ( SALARY FROM E ) * 1.1 ) ;
END OPERATOR ;

OPERATOR RAISE ( P PGMR_TT ) RETURNS MONEY ;
   RETURN ( ( SALARY FROM P ) * 1.25 ) ;
END OPERATOR ;
```

Let me now modify the foregoing example in order to illustrate another point (the modified version is very contrived but is sufficient for my purpose). Suppose the new salary is to be computed by increasing the original salary by 10 percent and then (for programmers only) doubling the result:

```
OPERATOR RAISE ( E EMP_TT ) RETURNS MONEY ;
   RETURN ( ( SALARY FROM E ) * 1.1 ) ;
END OPERATOR ;
```

---

[16] Recall that overloading polymorphism really means overloading operator *names* (to say that *Op* is overloaded really means there are two or more distinct operators with that same name *Op*). I note in passing that the particular kind of overloading polymorphism under discussion here is also referred to in the literature as *extension* polymorphism, for obvious reasons (see, e.g., Stanley B. Zdonik and David Maier: "Fundamentals of Object-Oriented Databases," in *Readings in Object-Oriented Database Systems*, Zdonik and Maier, eds.; Morgan Kaufmann, 1990). As noted in Chapter 2, it's also referred to as ad hoc polymorphism.

```
OPERATOR RAISE ( P PGMR_TT ) RETURNS MONEY ;
   RETURN ( 2 * RAISE ( TREAT_AS_EMP_TT ( P ) ) ) ;
END OPERATOR ;
```

The first of these operators is straightforward. The second, however, involves an invocation of TREAT, which, for the purposes of this discussion, I assume has been given somewhat revised semantics.[17] To be specific, I assume that TREAT_AS_EMP_TT (P) means "treat the argument P—which is actually of type PGMR_TT, of course—as if it were of type EMP_TT instead." Thus, the second RAISE operator computes its result by (a) invoking the first RAISE operator to increase the salary by 10 percent and then (b) doubling that increased salary. In other words, we're talking here about the mechanism usually called *operator delegation*—the function of increasing the salary by 10 percent isn't implemented explicitly for type PGMR_TT but is "delegated" to type EMP_TT instead.

Observe carefully that operator delegation isn't the same thing as operator inheritance. To be specific, we can't say in the foregoing example that the operator "increase salary by 10 percent"—i.e., the RAISE operator that applies to values of type EMP_TT—is inherited by programmers from employees, because PGMR_TT isn't a subtype of EMP_TT. (At least, I showed earlier that there's no reason for it to be, and for the sake of the present discussion I'm assuming it isn't.) Now, it's true that, like inheritance, delegation might imply a certain amount of code reuse; unlike inheritance, however, delegation is really more of an implementation issue (and perhaps an optimization issue) than it is a model issue. Observe, moreover, that whereas the "is a" relationship leads naturally to inclusion polymorphism (as we know from Parts II-IV of this book), the "has a" relationship—which, let me remind you, is the fundamental issue here— seems to lead naturally to overloading polymorphism instead, which in turn seems to lead (frequently if not always) to delegation.[18]

SUBTABLES AND SUPERTABLES

Parts II-IV of this book describe a detailed model for what in relational terms might be called *domain* inheritance (since types were called domains in Codd's early papers). When approached regarding the possibility of inheritance in a relational context, however, many people—perhaps most—immediately jump to the conclusion that what's under discussion is some kind of *relation* or *table* inheritance.[19] In particular, I mentioned in Chapter 3 the fact that SQL (meaning the

---

[17] To be specific, I'm assuming that the expression TREAT_AS_EMP_TT (PX) returns the EMP_TT value that's obtained by projecting away the LANG attribute from the PGMR_TT value that's the current value of expression PX. Note that the form of TREAT used in this expression does rely on type PGMR_TT being an extension of type EMP_TT.

[18] I remark in passing that the implementation code shown in Chapter 2 for operators such as "=", "<", etc., in connection with user defined types might be regarded as constituting further examples of delegation.

[19] In this section I favor the SQL terms *table*, *row*, and *column* over their relational counterparts *relation* (and/or *relvar*), *tuple*, and *attribute* because the discussions and examples are all based on SQL—though I haven't hesitated to omit or simplify many SQL details if they're irrelevant to my purpose.

SQL standard in particular) supports something it calls "subtables and supertables," according to which some table *T'* (the subtable) inherits all of the columns of some distinct table *T* (the supertable) and then adds some more of its own. An example (employees and programmers once again) is shown in Fig. 21.1.

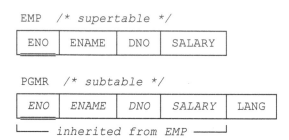

Fig. 21.1: Subtables and supertables–an example

Here are SQL definitions for this example (irrelevant details omitted, but note in particular the UNDER specifications in the CREATE TYPE for type PGMR_T and the CREATE TABLE for table PGMR):[20]

```
CREATE TYPE EMP_T
    AS ( ENO CHAR , ENAME CHAR , DNO CHAR , SALARY MONEY ) ;

CREATE TYPE PGMR_T
        UNDER EMP_T
    AS ( LANG CHAR ) ;

CREATE TABLE EMP OF EMP_T
        ( UNIQUE ( ENO ) ) ;

CREATE TABLE PGMR OF PGMR_T
        UNDER EMP ;
```

Explanation: EMP_T and PGMR_T are user defined types,[21] and PGMR_T is defined to be a "subtype" of "supertype" EMP_T ("subtype" and "supertype" in quotation marks because they're obviously not subtypes and supertypes in the sense of our model). Tables EMP and PGMR are then declared to be "of" types EMP_T and PGMR_T, respectively.[22] Observe that

---

[20] Tables EMP and PGMR are both base tables. In general, subtable and supertables in SQL can be either base tables or views. For simplicity, however, I'll assume that all SQL tables mentioned in this chapter are base tables specifically, barring explicit statements to the contrary.

[21] Actually they're what SQL calls *structured* types, which for the purposes of the present discussion you can think of as table types (but see Chapter 22).

[22] Because of this fact—the fact, that is, that they're declared to be "of" some type—each of the tables has, in addition to the columns shown in Fig. 21.1, what SQL calls a *self-referencing* column. However, self-referencing columns are irrelevant so far as the present chapter is concerned, so I'll ignore them here. For further information, see Chapter 22.

table EMP has four columns, corresponding to the four "attributes"—SQL's term—of type EMP_T. By contrast, table PGMR has just one column of its own, corresponding to the sole explicitly declared attribute of type PGMR_T; conceptually, however, it has four more (shown in Fig. 21.1 in italics) that it inherits from table EMP. Nonprogrammers have a row in EMP only, while programmers have a row in both tables—so every row in PGMR has a counterpart in EMP, but the converse is false.[23] However, the properties ENO, ENAME, DNO, and SALARY aren't recorded twice for programmers; rather, the PGMR table inherits those properties from the EMP table, as already explained. (In other words, you can think of columns ENO, ENAME, DNO, and SALARY in table PGMR as *virtual*, if you like.) Note that the uniqueness constraint UNIQUE (ENO) is also inherited by table PGMR from table EMP.

Now, it should be clear right away that subtables and supertables are basically just another example of structural inheritance (or "the EXTENDS relationship"), as it applies to the case of tables specifically. It follows that much of the discussion in the previous section applies more or less unchanged, and I won't bother to make those same points all over again. However, there are quite a few additional points that are worth calling out explicitly, and that's the purpose of the present section.

> *Aside:* What follows is the way the SQL standard works, more or less. However, I must caution you that different systems and different writers interpret the idea of subtables and supertables in different ways. By way of example, see the books (both published by Morgan Kaufmann in 1999) *Universal Database Management: A Guide to Object / Relational Technology*, by Cynthia Maro Saracco, and *Object-Relational DBMSs: Tracking the Next Great Wave* (2nd edition), by Michael Stonebraker and Paul Brown (with Dorothy Moore). Both of these books embrace the idea of inheritance. However:
>
> a.   They both assume that the kind of inheritance in question is based on "subtables and supertables" specifically.[24]
>
> b.   Moreover, their version of that notion differs significantly from the version espoused by the SQL standard. The most obvious difference is that in their version table EMP would contain rows for nonprogrammers only, whereas in the SQL standard it contains rows for all employees.

---

[23] Contrast the situation with the EMP and PGMR *relvars* (as opposed to tables) as discussed in the section "An Introductory Example" earlier. Just to remind you, (a) relvar PGMR resembled table PGMR in that it had a tuple for every programmer, but (b) relvar EMP differed from table EMP in that it had tuples for nonprogrammers only, instead of for all employees.

[24] They also assume operator overloading instead of inclusion polymorphism. What's more, they embrace (as the SQL standard does also, as we've already seen) the idea that table definitions and table type definitions should be kept separate; as a consequence, they allow several distinct tables to be of the same separately declared and explicitly named table type. (Just to remind you, **Tutorial D** by contrast explicitly does *not* support a separate "define relation type" operator, for reasons explained in Chapter 2. See also Exercise 21.3 at the end of the chapter.)

End of aside.

First of all, then, here are the implications of the design of Fig. 21.1 on the usual SQL retrieval and update operators:

- *SELECT:* Retrieval from EMP behaves normally; retrieval from PGMR behaves as if PGMR actually contained columns ENO, ENAME, DNO, and SALARY (as well as column LANG, of course). *More generally:* Retrieval from table T behaves as if T contained all of the columns of all of the proper supertables of T,[25] as well as the columns that are specific to T as such.

- *INSERT:* INSERT into EMP behaves normally; INSERT into PGMR effectively causes new rows to appear in both EMP and PGMR. *More generally:* INSERT into table T inserts (a) rows into T and (b) corresponding rows into all of the proper supertables of T.

- *DELETE:* DELETE from EMP causes rows to disappear from EMP and (if the rows in question happen to correspond to programmers) from PGMR too; DELETE from PGMR causes rows to disappear from both EMP and PGMR.[26] *More generally:* DELETE from table T deletes (a) rows from T, as well as (b) corresponding rows from all of the proper supertables of T *and* from all of the proper subtables of T.

- *UPDATE:* Updating columns ENO or ENAME or DNO or SALARY in EMP causes the same updates to be applied to corresponding rows (if any) in PGMR; updating those columns in PGMR causes the same updates to be applied to corresponding rows in EMP; updating column LANG in PGMR updates PGMR only. *More generally:* Updating columns in table T updates corresponding columns in corresponding rows in (a) all of the proper supertables of T and (b) all of the proper subtables of T.

By the way, the update behavior sketched above means we aren't just dealing with a conventional foreign key relationship from PGMR to EMP, with conventional referential actions—for if we were, then, e.g., deleting a row from PGMR couldn't possibly cause deletion of a row from EMP. The reason I mention this rather obvious point is that (a) despite what I've just said, the fact remains that ENO in table PGMR is, conceptually speaking, a foreign key

---

[25] Note that SQL does use the terminology of proper supertables and proper subtables (and every table is both a supertable and a subtable of itself, though of course not a proper one in either case). It also supports the concept of immediate supertables and immediate subtables, though it uses the adjective *direct* in place of immediate. Also, here's as good a place as any to mention that, in SQL, (a) the set of all subtables of a given table is called a *subtable family*, and (b) no table can have more than one immediate supertable. (This latter state of affairs is a consequence of two facts taken in combination—first, the fact that SQL's support for subtables and supertables is tightly bound up with its support for type inheritance, as can be seen from the interconnections between the CREATE TABLE and CREATE TYPE statements in the example; second, the fact that SQL doesn't support multiple inheritance, as we'll see in Chapter 22.)

[26] In other words, there's a more or less conventional "cascade delete" rule from EMP to PGMR, but there's also another such rule that cascades the other way, as it were. Analogous remarks apply to UPDATE also.

referencing EMP nonetheless, and (b) we can exploit that fact if we want to, as I'll show in a few moments.

Next, in addition to the conventional SQL operators described above, there are at least two further operations of an updating nature, viz., INSERT ONLY and DELETE ONLY,[27] that a system supporting subtables and supertables would seem to need (though SQL doesn't support them). To elaborate:

- *INSERT ONLY:* Suppose an existing nonprogrammer becomes a programmer. If we try to use the regular INSERT operator to insert an appropriate row into PGMR, the system will attempt to insert a corresponding row into EMP as well—an attempt that will fail on a key uniqueness violation. By contrast, INSERT ONLY would let us insert a row into PGMR only. *More generally:* If T' is a proper subtable of supertable T, then INSERT ONLY will let us insert a row into T' without simultaneously inserting a corresponding row into T.

- *DELETE ONLY:* Conversely, suppose an existing programmer becomes a nonprogrammer. If we try to use the regular DELETE operator to delete the appropriate row from PGMR, the system will delete the corresponding row from EMP as well—a side effect that presumably wasn't desired. By contrast, DELETE ONLY would let us delete a row from PGMR only. *More generally:* If T' is a proper subtable of supertable T, then DELETE ONLY will let us delete a row from T' without simultaneously deleting the corresponding row from T. (It will still cascade to delete corresponding rows from proper subtables of T', however.)

Of course, the obvious question now is: What if anything do the foregoing ideas have to do with inheritance? Well, it should be clear that they have nothing to do with the prescriptions for relation types as described in Part IV of this book. According to those prescriptions, if RT' and RT are relation types such that RT' is a subtype of supertype RT, there's no notion that RT' somehow "inherits columns"—or attributes, rather—from RT; rather, RT' and RT have the *same* columns (very loosely speaking!). So far as our model is concerned, in fact, the subtype / supertype relationship is actually implied, in part, by that very fact, viz., the fact that RT' and RT do have "the same columns" (recall once again that in **Tutorial D**, at least, we have no way of explicitly defining tuple and relation types outside of the statements that make use of those types, and hence no way of explicitly stating that one such type is a subtype of another). To repeat, then: What do subtables and supertables have to do with inheritance?

Well, the fact that our model is a model of type inheritance specifically doesn't in and of itself rule out the possibility of support for some kind of table inheritance as well. Indeed, our model should provide a framework for understanding whether some sense might be made of such a notion; after all, that model is quite general and does necessarily address the implications of type inheritance for values and variables in general—including relation values and variables in

---

[27] An UPDATE ONLY operator makes no sense, however, for reasons that should soon become obvious.

particular—and of course tables in the present context are really just relation variables (in other words, relvars), at least to a first approximation.

But therein lies the rub. Tables are indeed variables; thus, to talk of "subtables and supertables" is to talk of what might be called "subvariables and supervariables" ... whatever that might mean! (How can two distinct *variables* possibly be such that one is a "subvariable" of the other?) This state of affairs suggests immediately that:

■ First, whatever "subtables and supertables" might be all about, the one thing they're definitely not about is type inheritance; the tables in question are variables, and variables aren't types.

■ Second, the idea seems suspect right away. Inheritance applies to values, not variables! (To paraphrase a remark I made in Chapter 3: "To say a circle is an ellipse is to say that every circle *value* is an ellipse *value,* not that every circle *variable* is an ellipse *variable*.") What then can it mean to say that table (or relation variable) PGMR is a "sub" *anything* of table (or relation variable) EMP?[28]

Thus, while it might be possible to make some kind of sense out of "subtables and supertables," I claim (and I'll try to show below) that it's a completely different phenomenon, one that has essentially nothing to do with type inheritance as such.

Observe next that when we talk of PGMR being a "subtable" of "supertable" EMP (and inheriting columns from EMP), what we really mean is that each PGMR *row* inherits certain column *values* from the corresponding EMP *row*. In other words, we should really be talking about "subrows and superrows," not "subtables and supertables" at all.[29] (And then I pointed out in the previous section—though there I was talking about tuples rather than rows—that this latter terminology is really not very good, because each "subrow" is actually a superset of the corresponding "superrow.")[30]

---

[28] In Chapter 11 ("Array Variables") of his book *A Discipline of Programming* (Prentice-Hall, 1976), Edsger W. Dijkstra makes the point rather strongly that the elements of an array variable aren't themselves variables. This observation is specific to arrays as such, of course, but the point that no variable can be a "subvariable" of another is generally valid and applies to variables of all kinds. In particular, it applies to relvars; that is, a relvar is most certainly not, as has sometimes been suggested (and as SQL effectively seems to think, given its support—see Chapter 22—for tables that contain pointers to rows in other tables), a collection of tuplevars. See the answer to Exercise 21.7 at the end of the chapter for further discussion of this issue.
  Note: An apologist for the subtables and supertables idea might argue that it's only the "sub and super" terminology that's bad, and that a subtable is better thought of as being *derived from* its supertable in some way, much as a view is derived from a base table. Certainly there's no suggestion that table PGMR is somehow contained in table EMP, analogous to the way the elements of a given array variable are contained in that array variable (the specific situation discussed by Dijkstra). But this argument fails to account for columns that aren't so derived, like column LANG in table PGMR.

[29] As a matter of fact, SQL in particular does use these terms (i.e., subrow and superrow)—but it also uses the terms subtable and supertable.

[30] More precisely (or more bizarrely, depending on your point of view) each *proper* subrow is actually a *proper* superset of its immediate superrow. *Note:* In fact (and following on from the previous footnote), SQL does use these terms as well—i.e., it uses the terms *proper subrow* and *proper superrow*, in addition to the terms proper subtable and proper supertable mentioned in footnote 25.

It follows from all of the above that, whatever else they might be, "subtables and supertables" aren't an application of our inheritance ideas in which the variables are relvars specifically. Nor are they an application of our inheritance ideas in which the variables are tuplevars (or "rowvars," rather) specifically, because the only tuplevars we deal with in our model are "free standing" ones—to say it once again, there is not, nor can there be, any notion of a tuplevar somehow being contained within some relvar.

So why might subtables and supertables be a good idea? What are the advantages? Well, the only one I can see (and it's a pretty minor one) is this: Informing the system that, e.g., PGMR is a subtable of supertable EMP is shorthand for stating certain new kinds of referential actions declaratively. To be specific, it allows:

- Insertion of a row into PGMR to cause automatic insertion of the corresponding row into EMP, and

- Deletion of a row from PGMR to cause automatic deletion of the corresponding row from EMP.

(I ignore explicit UPDATEs for simplicity.)

But there's no need to pretend that columns are "inherited" by PGMR from EMP in order to achieve these effects! In fact, I believe the entire functionality—such as it is—of subtables and supertables, including INSERT ONLY and DELETE ONLY functionality, could be achieved by means of the conventional view mechanism. Let me illustrate. Suppose we were to define two regular base tables, EMP and EMP_LANG, as follows (note the foreign key constraint in particular):

```
CREATE TABLE EMP ( ENO CHAR , ENAME CHAR , DNO CHAR , SALARY MONEY ,
     UNIQUE ( ENO ) ) ;

CREATE TABLE EMP_LANG ( ENO CHAR , LANG CHAR ,
     UNIQUE ( ENO ) ,
     FOREIGN KEY ( ENO ) REFERENCES EMP ( ENO ) ) ;
```

Let's also define PGMR as a view of these two base tables, thus:

```
CREATE VIEW PGMR
   AS ( SELECT ENO , ENAME , DNO , SALARY , LANG
        FROM   EMP NATURAL JOIN EMP_LANG ) ;
```

Then tables EMP, EMP_LANG, and PGMR together not only provide all of the functionality of subtables and supertables, they also get around the need for those INSERT ONLY and DELETE ONLY operators (trivially so, in fact—the effects of those operators can now be achieved by conventional INSERTs and DELETEs on table EMP_LANG). *Note:* As a bonus, the scheme just outlined could serve as a basis for *implementing* subtables and supertables (if they're regarded as worth implementing at all, that is).

In sum, it looks as if the whole business of a subtable inheriting columns from a supertable is nothing but a syntactic shorthand. Not that there's anything wrong with syntactic shorthands in general, I hasten to add—but this particular shorthand doesn't seem to be very useful, and in any case it's already more than adequately (in my opinion, better) supported by the conventional view mechanism.

> *Aside:* Actually, I'm fairly suspicious about the whole subtables and supertables idea anyway. It seems to me likely that we're dealing with a confusion over model vs. implementation once again. To be more specific, I suspect that if table *T'* and table *T* are a subtable and corresponding supertable, respectively, then the intent is simply that (a) those tables should be implemented, for performance reasons, as a single, combined "stored table" in physical storage, and then (b) "stored rows" corresponding to those rows of table *T* that have no counterpart in table *T'* will have nulls in positions corresponding to columns that appear in table *T'* only.[31] But such implementation concerns should never show through to the model level! As I've explained at length elsewhere—see, e.g., my book *SQL and Relational Theory: How to Write Accurate SQL Code* (3rd edition, O'Reilly, 2015)—the relational model quite deliberately has nothing to say regarding physical storage matters. *End of aside.*

Finally, it's worth noting that the terminology of subtables and supertables might quite reasonably be applied "the other way around," as it were. That is, which of tables T and T' is regarded as the subtable and which the supertable might quite reasonably depend on context. For example, consider an SQL version of the suppliers-and-parts database from Chapter 1. Suppose for the sake of the example that status information can be missing for certain suppliers. Then one way we might design the database, in SQL terms, would be to have two base tables S and S' that look like this:

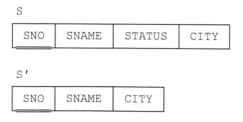

Table S corresponds to suppliers with a known status value, while table S' corresponds to suppliers for whom the status information is missing. And the point about this example—which

---

[31] I'm on record in many places as objecting to the whole idea of SQL-style nulls—rejecting them out of hand, in fact—and so you might be surprised to see me mention such a thing so casually (or at all!) here. But the nulls I'm talking about in the present context are an implementation concept merely; in other words, they're an entirely different thing from SQL-style nulls. In particular, they're explicitly not part of the model, and they explicitly don't show through as SQL-style nulls at the user level.

illustrates, incidentally, a possible basis (though not the only one) for dealing with the phenomenon of "missing information" without using nulls—is that it would be quite natural to refer to S here as the supertable and S' as the subtable; but now the supertable has a superset of the columns of the subtable, instead of the other way around as they are in the employees and programmers example.

More on INSERT ONLY and DELETE ONLY

I'd like to elaborate on those INSERT ONLY and DELETE ONLY operators briefly. Here again are the SQL definitions for the employees and programmers example:

```
CREATE TYPE EMP_T
   AS ( ENO CHAR , ENAME CHAR , DNO CHAR , SALARY MONEY ) ;

CREATE TYPE PGMR_T
         UNDER EMP_T
   AS ( LANG CHAR ) ;

CREATE TABLE EMP OF EMP_T
      ( UNIQUE ( ENO ) ) ;

CREATE TABLE PGMR OF PGMR_T
         UNDER EMP ;
```

I'll consider INSERT ONLY first. By way of example, suppose a new employee (employee Joe, with employee number E8, say) joins the company as a programmer. Then all we have to do to reflect this fact in the database is insert a row into table PGMR, as follows:

```
INSERT INTO PGMR ( ENO , ENAME , DNO , SALARY , LANG )
       VALUES ( 'E8' , 'Joe' , dx , sx , lx ) ;
```

(where dx, sx, and lx denote the pertinent DNO, SALARY, and LANG values).[32] This INSERT on table PGMR will have the side effect of inserting a corresponding row into table EMP. But suppose by contrast that Joe already exists as an employee and has only just now become a programmer. If we try to perform that same INSERT on PGMR, then, as noted earlier, the

---

[32] I note in passing that the syntax surrounding the entire "subtables and supertables" idea in SQL is hardly very user friendly, relying as it does on several levels of indirection. The INSERT statement in this example illustrates the point perfectly. To be specific, observe that that INSERT statement asserts—in effect, and among several other things—that the target table PGMR is supposed to have a column called ENO. If you want to check this, you can go to the corresponding CREATE TABLE; however, that statement just says PGMR is "of PGMR_T" and "under EMP." If now you go to the CREATE TYPE for PGMR_T, you find it just says PGMR_T is "under EMP_T"; if you go to the CREATE TABLE for EMP instead, you find it just says EMP is "of EMP_T." Either way, you then go to the CREATE TYPE for EMP_T, where (at last!) you do find there's something called ENO. However, that "something" still isn't a column as such; instead, as noted earlier in this chapter, it's what SQL rather unfortunately calls an *attribute* (see Chapter 22 for further discussion). However, SQL has a rule according to which a table that's defined to be "of" some type has columns that are derived in the obvious way from the attributes of the type in question, and so the issue is finally resolved.

implicit INSERT on EMP will fail on a key uniqueness violation. Rather, what we'd like to do is something like this (note the boldface ONLY):

```
INSERT ONLY INTO PGMR ( ENO , ENAME , DNO , SALARY , LANG )
       VALUES ( 'E8' , 'Joe' , dx , sx , lx ) ;
```

But we can't, in SQL. Instead, what we apparently have to do is first delete the existing row for Joe from table EMP:

```
DELETE FROM EMP WHERE ENO = 'E8' ;
```

And now we can do the INSERT, which will have the effect among other things of reinstating the row we just deleted:

```
INSERT INTO PGMR ( ENO , ENAME , DNO , SALARY , LANG )
       VALUES ( 'E8' , 'Joe' , dx , sx , lx ) ;
```

Now, this "solution" is bad enough on its face—but what makes it much worse is that if table EMP has any other proper subtables apart from PGMR, that DELETE we had to do on EMP will cascade to delete corresponding rows from those subtables as well, and of course the subsequent INSERT on PGMR won't reinstate those rows. Thus, it looks as if INSERT ONLY is rather more than just something that might be "nice to have."[33]

I turn now to DELETE ONLY. Suppose employee Joe used to be a programmer but has just ceased to be so. If we try to reflect this fact in the database by deleting the row for Joe from table PGMR—

```
DELETE FROM PGMR WHERE ENO = 'E8' ;
```

—then, as noted earlier, the row for Joe will be deleted from table EMP as well,[34] which presumably isn't what we wanted (after all, Joe is still an employee). Instead, what we'd like to do is something like this (again note the boldface ONLY):

```
DELETE ONLY FROM PGMR WHERE ENO = 'E8' ;
```

But we can't, in SQL. Instead, therefore, what we apparently have to do is delete the row for Joe from table PGMR—

---

[33] What makes it worse still, at least in the case of SQL specifically, is that deleting the "old" row for Joe and then inserting a "new" one will cause Joe to be assigned a brand new "REF value," with the consequence that existing references to Joe elsewhere in the database will now no longer be valid (they'll become what are sometimes called *dangling references*). A similar problem occurs in connection with SQL's lack of support for DELETE ONLY as well (see subsequent discussion). *Note:* REF values and related matters are explained in detail in Chapter 22.

[34] More generally, the row for Joe will be deleted (a) from all supertables of PGMR, including both EMP and PGMR in particular, and (b) from all subtables of any of the tables mentioned under (a) here. The full consequences of this state of affairs I leave as something for you to meditate upon.

```
DELETE FROM PGMR WHERE ENO = 'E8' ;
```

(which will have the undesirable side effect of deleting corresponding rows from proper subtables of PGMR as well, if any)[35]—and then reinsert the row for Joe into table EMP:

```
INSERT INTO EMP ( ENO , ENAME , DNO , SALARY )
        VALUES ( 'E8' , 'Joe' , dx , sx ) ;
```

Like INSERT ONLY, therefore, DELETE ONLY looks as if it's rather more than just something that would be "nice to have."

Note: As a matter of fact, SQL does support something that looks syntactically rather like DELETE ONLY (though not INSERT ONLY). However, the semantics are very different. Assume again that (a) EMP and PGMR are the only tables we have and that (b) rows for employee Joe currently appear in both. Then the SQL statement

```
DELETE FROM ONLY ( PGMR ) WHERE ENO = 'E8' ;
```

will—unlike DELETE ONLY—delete the row for Joe from table PGMR as requested, and will "cascade up" to delete the corresponding row from table EMP as well. However, it won't delete anything at all if a row for Joe also appears in some proper subtable of table PGMR (which isn't possible in the example, of course, because table PGMR doesn't have any proper subtables). That's the significance of that ONLY specification. Thus, for example, if the foregoing DELETE were addressed to table EMP instead, as follows—

```
DELETE FROM ONLY ( EMP ) WHERE ENO = 'E8' ;
```

—then nothing would happen (i.e., nothing would be deleted), because a row for employee Joe does appear in some proper subtable of table EMP (viz., table PGMR). In other words, the DELETE just shown is logically equivalent to, and can be regarded as shorthand for, the following:

```
DELETE FROM EMP
        WHERE ENO = 'E8' AND ENO NOT IN ( SELECT ENO FROM PGMR ) ;
```

ONLY can be used in SELECT expressions too. For example, the SQL expression

```
SELECT ENO FROM ONLY ( EMP )
```

---

[35] The previous footnote applies here also, of course.

returns employee numbers—or rows containing employee numbers, rather—such that the employee numbers in question appear in table EMP and not in table PGMR. In other words, the expression is logically equivalent to, and can be regarded as shorthand for, the following:

```
SELECT ENO FROM EMP
        WHERE ENO NOT IN ( SELECT ENO FROM PGMR )
```

ONLY can also be used with UPDATE. The effect is to apply the requested updates only (a) to rows in the target table *T* that have no counterpart in any proper subtable of *T*, as well as (b) to counterparts in proper supertables of *T* of those rows in *T* and (c) to counterparts in other proper subtables of the proper supertables mentioned under (b).

SCALAR TYPES REVISITED

In the section "An Introductory Example," I said, paraphrasing, that if structural inheritance is to play any part at all in our type inheritance model, then it must be in connection with tuple and relation types specifically, because those are the only types with any structure to inherit. Despite this state of affairs, discussions in the literature often begin with examples like this: "Let type COLORED_CIRCLE be a subtype of type CIRCLE," or something along similar lines.[36] Note that the types involved in this particular example are clearly scalar, and yet the inheritance involved is equally clearly structural (of some kind or another). In this section, I want to discuss examples like this one in some depth. Before I do so, however, I'd like to examine two kinds of inheritance that do apply to scalar types and might (but I think shouldn't) be regarded as examples of "structural inheritance for scalar types." Both have to do with possible representations or possreps.

■ First, recall that if scalar type *T'* is a subtype of scalar type *T*, then every possrep for *T* is necessarily, albeit implicitly, a possrep for *T'* as well; for example, every possrep for ellipses is necessarily a possrep for circles as well. As noted in Chapter 3 and elsewhere, therefore, we might regard possreps as further "properties" that are inherited, albeit silently, by subtypes from supertypes, when the types in question are scalar. And then we might go further and regard such inheritance as structural inheritance, of a kind. I'd frankly prefer not to, however, because I think to do so just muddies the issue. Note in particular that the possrep that's inherited in this way by scalar type *T'* is *identical to* the corresponding possrep for scalar type *T*; there's no notion, as there is with structural inheritance as usually understood, of that inherited structure for *T'* having—or probably having, at any rate—additional components, over and above those found in the structure for *T*. In other words, "the EXTENDS relationship" as such doesn't apply.

---

[36] I did touch on this particular example under the discussion of IM Prescription 2 in Chapter 5, as you might recall.

■ Second, if scalar type T' is a proper subtype, then every declared possrep for T' is certainly derived from some declared possrep for some immediate supertype T, and we might regard that derivation process too as structural inheritance, of a kind.[37] Here, however, the derived possrep not only has no additional components over and above those in the possrep for the supertype, it typically has fewer (think of ellipses and circles, for example). Certainly there doesn't seem any good reason for it to have more. Again, therefore, this kind of inheritance isn't structural inheritance as usually understood; in particular, "the EXTENDS relationship" as such again doesn't apply.

I turn now to the colored circles example. Now, the wording of that example clearly implies, or assumes, that colored circles are a special case of circles in general. But are they? I don't think so. By definition, surely, colored circles are images (on a display screen perhaps), whereas circles in general are not images but geometric figures in two-dimensional space. Thus, it seems to me more reasonable to regard type COLORED_CIRCLE, not as a subtype of type CIRCLE, but rather as a completely separate type. Now, that separate type might well have a possrep in which one component is of type CIRCLE, thus—

```
TYPE COLORED_CIRCLE POSSREP ( CIR CIRCLE , COL COLOR ) ... ;
```

—but it's not, to repeat, a subtype of type CIRCLE, any more than it's a subtype of the type of its other possrep component (viz., COLOR). To put it another way, a colored circle is a circle exactly as much as it is a color (which is to say, of course, that it's *not* a circle, any more than it's a color). Yet another way of saying the same thing is to say that every colored circle *has* a circle property but *is not* a circle (just as it has a color property but is not a color). As with employees and programmers, therefore, I think that what we're really talking about here is the "has a" relationship, not the "is a" relationship that I claim characterizes inheritance and subtyping as such.

I now present a series of arguments to bolster the foregoing conclusion. (Well, I say "a series of arguments," but I should probably admit up front that the arguments in question are really all just the same argument in different guises, as you'll soon see.) I'll begin by reminding you of the following remarks from Chapter 5:

> It's an obvious corollary of IM Prescription 2 that there can't be more values of type T' than there are of type T. This apparently trivial observation can be very helpful in pinpointing errors and clearing up confusions.

---

[37] In this connection, let me remind you of the following remarks from Chapter 3 (slightly paraphrased here): If T' is an immediate subtype of T, then it might be convenient to have some syntactic shorthand for declaring a possrep for T' along the lines of "same as possrep PR for T but subtracting component(s) A, B, ..., C and adding component(s) X, Y, ..., Z." As I also said in that chapter, however, the issue is a purely syntactic one, and I don't propose to discuss it any further in this book. *Note:* I'm assuming here for simplicity that T is a regular type.

In the case at hand, it's surely obvious—as I also pointed out in Chapter 5—that there are more colored circles than there are just plain circles. (I'm assuming here, reasonably enough, that two circles that differ in color but are otherwise identical are the same circle but different colored circles.) Thus, this simple test should be sufficient to show right away that it's really not reasonable to describe type COLORED_CIRCLE as a *subtype*, as such, of type CIRCLE.

> *Aside:* It's not exactly an *extension* of type CIRCLE, either (even if, despite everything I've said about such matters, we were to allow the use of such terminology in connection with possreps). However, if the language were such as to permit me to define type COLORED_CIRCLE a little differently, thus—
>
> ```
> TYPE COLORED_CIRCLE EXTENDS CIRCLE POSSREP ( COL COLOR ) ... ;
> ```
>
> —then we might perhaps more reasonably describe it as an extension, as such, of type CIRCLE (more precisely, we might describe it as having a possrep that's an extension of a possrep for type CIRCLE). *End of aside.*

Second, recall from Chapter 2 that if S is a selector for type T, then every value of type T must be produced by some invocation of S.[38] But no CIRCLE selector invocation can possibly produce a value of type COLORED_CIRCLE, since the CIRCLE selector has no color parameter; hence, a value of type COLORED_CIRCLE isn't a value of type CIRCLE, and type COLORED_CIRCLE isn't a subtype of type CIRCLE.

Third, as noted above, we might informally regard possreps as further "properties" that are inherited by subtypes from supertypes. Yet our CIRCLE possrep, with its radius and center components, can't be a possrep for colored circles, because it has no color component. Once again, therefore, type COLORED_CIRCLE can't be a subtype of type CIRCLE.

Last, there's no way to obtain a colored circle from a circle via S by C!—that is, there's no constraint we can write for type COLORED_CIRCLE that, if satisfied by a given value of type CIRCLE, means the circle in question is really a colored circle. And the reason is, of course, again basically that the CIRCLE possrep has no color component.

It should be clear, then, that CIRCLE and COLORED_CIRCLE are completely different types. However, it's probably true as suggested earlier that type COLORED_CIRCLE will have a possrep in which one component is of type CIRCLE. And it's probably also true that we'd like to be able to say that, e.g., the operator CTR which returns the center of a given colored circle is basically just the THE_CTR operator that applies to the CIRCLE component CIR of the possrep for that colored circle. Once again, then, we're talking about the concept of delegation—the responsibility for implementing the operator CTR for type COLORED_CIRCLE is delegated to the type, CIRCLE, of a certain component of one of its possreps.

---

[38] Actually, Chapter 2 makes a stronger statement—it says that every value of every type must be denotable by means of some literal. But every literal is a selector invocation, of course (it's a special case).

STRUCTURAL INHERITANCE FOR SCALAR TYPES
USING THE *MANIFESTO* MODEL

Despite everything I've said in this chapter to this point, the fact remains that it does seem very natural (even attractive) to be able to say things like "every programmer is an employee"; after all, I've said it myself more than once in this very chapter. In other words, structural inheritance—meaning, more specifically, "structural inheritance for scalar types," if that's not a contradiction in terms—might nevertheless be what people really want from an inheritance mechanism. Yet such support is likely to be problematic for various reasons, as I've tried to show in preceding sections. In the present section, therefore, I want to show how our own model can effectively be used to achieve "structural inheritance for scalar types," without having to support any such notion directly and without violating any of our IM prescriptions.

It's convenient to begin by repeating something I said in Chapter 11. In my discussion of IM Prescription 17 in that chapter, I said this:

> We reject the suggestion that changing operator semantics can ever be a good idea, and [so] we define our model to say that if a change in semantics occurs, then the implementation is in violation—i.e., it's not an implementation of the model, and the implications are unpredictable.

We're not without our critics on this issue, of course. The typical counterargument goes something like this:

> One significant advantage that's often claimed for object orientation is *code reuse*. The idea is that some existing class might be "almost right" for a new application, and that much of it can be reused by a subclass that introduces some additions and changes. For example, suppose a company has a class called EMPLOYEE, with various operators, including a PAYROLL operator that (among other things) computes the net pay for a given employee. Suppose the company now introduces a new kind of employee who is paid in a different way, perhaps at an hourly rate instead of monthly. The company might be able to reuse most of the PAYROLL code by creating a subclass, HOURLY_EMPLOYEE, with its own PAYROLL operator. The new subclass might not find the representation of the original class to be sufficient, so it will probably need to add new instance variables, such as HOURS_WORKED. Overloading the PAYROLL operator makes it possible to process a column of employees, some of whom are paid by the hour, without putting logic into the application to branch on employee type, using the principle called *polymorphism*. However, this example of code reuse and polymorphism will clearly not work under the constraint that the semantics of the PAYROLL operator mustn't change as we go from class EMPLOYEE to class HOURLY_EMPLOYEE. So a refusal to allow changes in semantics forfeits the advantage of code reuse, one of the principal advantages claimed for object orientation.

(The foregoing extract is based on a complaint from one particular critic, but I've revised the original text considerably. In particular, I've replaced the example by one of my own. Of course, I've done my best to preserve the essential nature of the original argument.)

So what's wrong with that argument? The overriding point, it seems to me, is simply that examples like the one described aren't examples of type inheritance. If employees have a monthly salary, and hourly employees are employees, then it follows as the night the day that hourly employees have a monthly salary!—for otherwise they're not employees in the first place, by definition. To put it another way, to say that hourly employees are *somewhat like* regular employees isn't the same as saying that hourly employees are *a special case of* regular employees. A mechanism that allows us to say that hourly employees are "somewhat like" regular employees might possibly be useful—it might even allow a certain amount of code reuse—but, to repeat, that mechanism isn't type inheritance. After all, if to say that type *B* is a subtype of type *A* just means that type *B* is "somewhat like" type *A* except that certain properties are added and/or dropped and/or altered, then *absolutely any type whatsoever could be regarded as a subtype of absolutely any type whatsoever!*

In fact, it seems to me that, once again, what we're really talking about here is the "has a" relationship, not the "is a" relationship at all—hourly employees "have a" certain property that employees in general don't have. (The same is true for monthly employees as well, come to that.) Note in particular that, once again, S by C doesn't apply.

A Possible Solution

Despite the foregoing analysis, it turns out that we can handle the example of monthly vs. hourly employees within the framework of our own inheritance model, if we want to; more specifically, we can handle it without having to rely on any such suspect notion as structural inheritance for scalar types. The key is to recognize that what we're talking about in that example indeed isn't the "is a" relationship and inclusion polymorphism—rather, it's the "has a" relationship and overloading. In other words, we might agree that it can be useful, *informally*, to talk as if monthly and hourly employees were both special cases of the abstract concept "employees in general," but we don't have to agree that such talk has anything to do with specialization (i.e., S by C) in the sense of our model. Thus, we proceed as follows.

First we define three relvars (actually base relvars) looking something like this:

```
VAR EMP BASE RELATION                    /* employees in general */
  { ENO ... ,
    DNO ... }
  KEY { ENO } ;

VAR MONTHLY_EMP BASE RELATION            /* monthly employees     */
  { ENO ... ,
    MONTHLY_RATE ... }
  KEY { ENO }
  FOREIGN KEY { ENO } REFERENCES EMP ;
```

```
VAR HOURLY_EMP BASE RELATION          /* hourly employees     */
   { ENO ... ,
     HOURLY_RATE ... ,
     HOURS_WORKED ... }
   KEY { ENO }
   FOREIGN KEY { ENO } REFERENCES EMP ;
```

We also define some constraints—database constraints, that is, not type constraints, in *Manifesto* terms—to ensure that every employee is either monthly or hourly and no employee is both:

```
CONSTRAINT MONTHLY_AND_HOURLY_SPAN
           ( MONTHLY_EMP { ENO }
             UNION
             HOURLY_EMP { ENO } ) = EMP { ENO } ;

CONSTRAINT MONTHLY_AND_HOURLY_DISJOINT
     IS_EMPTY ( MONTHLY_EMP { ENO }
               INTERSECT
               HOURLY_EMP { ENO } ) ;
```

We also define a couple of views (i.e., virtual relvars):

```
VAR MONTHLY_EMP_INFO VIRTUAL ( EMP JOIN MONTHLY_EMP ) KEY { ENO } ;

VAR HOURLY_EMP_INFO  VIRTUAL ( EMP JOIN HOURLY_EMP )  KEY { ENO } ;
```

Assume now that the three base relvars (and hence the two views as well, in effect) have all been appropriately "populated." Now, the object of the exercise is to be able to "[overload] the PAYROLL operator [and thus make] it possible to process a column of employees, some of whom are paid by the hour, without putting logic into the application to branch on employee type." It follows that we're going to need a relvar that includes an attribute of some *scalar* employee type, some of whose values represent monthly employees and others hourly employees.[39] To that end, then, let's define three scalar types, S_EMP, S_MONTHLY_EMP, and S_HOURLY_EMP ("S" for scalar, irrelevant details omitted), thus:

```
TYPE S_EMP UNION ;             /* dummy type    */

TYPE S_MONTHLY_EMP             /* regular type */
     IS { S_EMP
          POSSREP ( ENO ... , DNO ... ,
                              MONTHLY_RATE ... ) } ;
```

---

[39] The attribute in question can't be of a *tuple* type, because tuples from relvars EMP, MONTHLY_EMP, and HOURLY_EMP are of three different types (in fact, they belong to three different type lattices). Thus, if the attribute in question were of any of those three tuple types, it couldn't take on values of either of the other two.

```
TYPE S_HOURLY_EMP                  /* regular type */
     IS { S_EMP
          POSSREP ( ENO ... , DNO ... ,
                    HOURLY_RATE ... , HOURS_WORKED ... ) } ;
```

Every value of type S_EMP is in fact a value of either type S_MONTHLY_EMP or type S_HOURLY_EMP (and not both)—there are no values of most specific type S_EMP. However, there's no "S by C" from S_EMP to either S_MONTHLY_EMP or S_HOURLY_EMP, because S_EMP is a dummy type.[40] But value substitutability applies—we can (in fact, we must) use a value of type either S_MONTHLY_EMP or S_HOURLY_EMP wherever a value of type S_EMP is expected.

Now we can define the PAYROLL operator. Here first is the specification signature, at the S_EMP level:

```
OPERATOR PAYROLL ( E S_EMP ) RETURNS MONEY ;
   /* specification signature only */
END OPERATOR ;
```

And here are the implementation versions for monthly and hourly employees:[41]

```
OPERATOR PAYROLL VERSION M_PAYROLL ( E S_MONTHLY_EMP ) RETURNS MONEY ;
   RETURN ( some expression that computes on basis of monthly rate ) ;
END OPERATOR ;

OPERATOR PAYROLL VERSION H_PAYROLL ( E S_HOURLY_EMP ) RETURNS MONEY ;
   RETURN ( some expression that computes on basis of hourly rate ) ;
END OPERATOR ;
```

Now we define a relvar (actually a view) that contains just the desired attribute, EMP, of type S_EMP:

```
VAR REQD_VIEW VIRTUAL
    ( ( EXTEND MONTHLY_EMP_INFO :
        { EMP := S_MONTHLY_EMP ( ENO , DNO , MONTHLY_RATE ) } ) { EMP }
      UNION
      ( EXTEND HOURLY_EMP_INFO :
        { EMP := S_HOURLY_EMP ( ENO , DNO , HOURLY_RATE ,
                                HOURS_WORKED ) } ) { EMP } ) ;
```

---

[40] Despite this fact, I would still expect THE_ENO and THE_DNO (but not THE_MONTHLY_RATE, THE_HOURLY_RATE, or THE_HOURS_WORKED) operators and pseudovariables to be defined at the S_EMP level. Compare the analogous example in Chapter 12, under the discussion of IM Prescription 20, where I defined THE_CTR to apply at the ELLIPSE level even when ELLIPSE was a dummy type.

[41] I refer to them as implementation versions, and technically that's correct. Note, however, that they violate our own prohibition (mentioned near the beginning of the present section) against changing semantics! But that's because what we're doing in this example is using (a) the mechanism of inclusion polymorphism to achieve (b) the effect of overloading polymorphism, for which changing semantics isn't an issue. (On the contrary, in fact: With overloading polymorphism, changing semantics is the whole point—or a large part of the point, at any rate.)

Explanation:

■ Consider for the moment just the EXTEND operation in lines 2-3. Here it is again:

```
EXTEND MONTHLY_EMP_INFO :
      { EMP := S_MONTHLY_EMP ( ENO , DNO , MONTHLY_RATE ) }
```

The expression on the right side of the ":=" symbol inside the braces here is an invocation of the S_MONTHLY_EMP selector. Let t be a tuple in the current value of view (i.e., virtual relvar) MONTHLY_EMP_INFO. For that tuple t, then, that selector invocation returns a value v of type S_MONTHLY_EMP, with THE_ENO(v), THE_DNO(v), and THE_MONTHLY_RATE(v) equal to the ENO, DNO, and MONTHLY_RATE values from that tuple t. So the EXTEND operation effectively appends that S_MONTHLY_EMP value v to that tuple t as the value of a new attribute, called EMP. Of course, the analogous extension is performed on every MONTHLY_EMP_INFO tuple.

■ Similarly, the EXTEND in lines 5-7 effectively appends a new attribute called EMP to every HOURLY_EMP_INFO tuple.

■ Two projections are now performed, to discard all attributes of the extended forms of MONTHLY_EMP_INFO and HOURLY_EMP_INFO except the "new" attribute EMP, and the union of those two projections is then taken.

■ That union is used to define view REQD_VIEW. That view has just one attribute, EMP, whose declared type (in accordance with IM Prescription 13) is S_EMP.

So, "to process [the] column of employees, some of whom are paid by the hour, without putting logic into the application to branch on employee type":

```
EXTEND REQD_VIEW : { PAY := PAYROLL ( EMP ) }
```

Attribute PAY in the relation that results from this expression contains, for any given employee, exactly the result that's desired.

Another Example

This subsection sketches a similar (but different) solution to a similar (but different) problem. This time the problem involves multiple inheritance instead of single and inclusion polymorphism instead of overloading. It has to do with employees again; this time, however, (a) some employees are part time and some are full time; (b) some employees are managers and some are nonmanagers; and (c) I assume for the sake of the example that we want to treat part time managers differently, somehow, from the way we treat either full time managers or part time nonmanagers.

Here then is a possible approach to this problem, in outline. First of all, here's the relational design:

```
VAR EMP BASE RELATION                          /* all employees        */
   { ENO ... ,
     DNO ... }
   KEY { ENO } ;

VAR PART_TIME_EMP BASE RELATION                /* part time employees */
   { ENO ... ,
     DAY_OFF ... }
   KEY { ENO }
   FOREIGN KEY { ENO } REFERENCES EMP ;

VAR MANAGER_EMP BASE RELATION                  /* managers            */
   { ENO ... ,
     BUDGET ... }
   KEY { ENO }
   FOREIGN KEY { ENO } REFERENCES EMP ;

VAR PART_TIME_MANAGER_EMP BASE RELATION        /* part time managers  */
   { ENO ... ,
     OTHER_STUFF ... }
   KEY { ENO }
   FOREIGN KEY { ENO } REFERENCES PART_TIME_EMP
   FOREIGN KEY { ENO } REFERENCES MANAGER_EMP ;
```

Note: There are no relvars specific to full time employees, full time managers, full time nonmanagers, or part time nonmanagers (though there could be), because according to the terms of the example it's only part time managers that need special treatment of some kind.

Next we define the following scalar types (shown here in outline only—the details are tedious but straightforward—but note in particular that type S_EMP includes two BOOLEAN possrep components, PART_TIME and MANAGER, to indicate whether a given employee is part or full time and whether he or she is a manager):

```
TYPE S_EMP
     POSSREP ( ENO ... ,        DNO ... ,
               PART_TIME ... ,  DAY_OFF ... ,
               MANAGER ... ,    BUDGET ... ,
               OTHER_STUFF ... ) ;

/* If NOT ( THE_PART_TIME (e) ), then THE_DAY_OFF (e) and    */
/* THE_OTHER_STUFF (e) are both special "missing" values;    */
/* if NOT ( THE_MANAGER (e) ), then THE_BUDGET (e) and       */
/* THE_OTHER_STUFF (e) are both special "missing" values.    */
/* These constraints need to be stated formally, of course;  */
/* I omit the details here.                                  */

/* This is not a GOOD design! — but it's a possible one.     */
```

```
/* Note in particular that type S_EMP is a regular type (it   */
/* might or might not be a union type), and so subtyping       */
/* (e.g., to S_PART_TIME_EMP) can and must be done via S by   */
/* C, as indicated here:                                       */

TYPE S_PART_TIME_EMP
    IS { S_EMP
         CONSTRAINT THE_PART_TIME ( S_EMP )
         POSSREP ( ENO         = THE_ENO ( S_EMP ) ,
                   DNO         = THE_DNO ( S_EMP ) ,
                   DAY_OFF     = THE_DAY_OFF ( S_EMP ) ,
                   MANAGER     = THE_MANAGER ( S_EMP ) ,
                   BUDGET      = THE_BUDGET ( S_EMP ) ,
                   OTHER_STUFF = THE_OTHER_STUFF ( S_EMP ) } ) ;

/* Type S_MANAGER_EMP is very similar ... As for type         */
/* S_PART_TIME_MANAGER_EMP, it looks something like this:     */

TYPE S_PART_TIME_MANAGER_EMP
    IS { S_PART_TIME_EMP , S_MANAGER_EMP
         POSSREP ( ENO = ... /* etc., etc. */ ) } ;
```

Now we can define operators that apply only at the S_PART_TIME_MANAGER_EMP level (for example), define relvars with attributes of type S_EMP that contain values of any of the four types, and so on and so forth.

As the comments above suggest, the foregoing is perhaps not a very elegant solution to the problem, but at least it gets the job done, and it abides 100 percent by the prescriptions of our inheritance model.

POSTSCRIPT: A SURVEY OF THE LITERATURE

As noted near the beginning of the previous section, many people do seem to think, despite everything I've said in this chapter, that what an inheritance mechanism really needs to do is support structural inheritance specifically (meaning structural inheritance for scalar types specifically). Certainly a survey of the literature tends to support this conclusion. To put it another way, there seems to be almost universal agreement in the literature—in the object literature, at any rate, which seems to be the only place where such matters are discussed—that:

a. Scalar types have user visible structure ("public instance variables"),[42] and

b. If scalar type *T'* is a proper subtype of scalar type *T*, then *T'* has all of *T*'s public instance variables, plus (usually) some additional ones of its own.

---

[42] Which is odd when you come to think about it, because (as mentioned in an earlier footnote) the object literature also, and universally, lays strong emphasis on the notion of encapsulation—and encapsulation, if it means anything, surely means that types *don't* have any such user visible structure. Doesn't it?

To bolster these claims on my part, I now offer a few quotes from the literature, with occasional commentary by myself. By the way, I think I should say that the references I cite are far from being the only ones I consulted in carrying out this brief survey. However, I do think they constitute a sufficiently representative sample.[43] *Note:* It's telling, perhaps, that not one of the references I examined, including those cited below in particular, gives anything close to a formal definition of the term *subtype*. Most of them don't even bother to give an informal definition either. Nor do they even have an entry for *subtype* in their index, for the most part.

■ From Elisa Bertino and Lorenzo Martino: *Object-Oriented Database Systems: Concepts and Architectures* (Addison-Wesley, 1993):

[An] instance[44] of the subtype can be used in every context in which an instance of the supertype can correctly appear ... The system must only allow, in the definition of a subtype, the addition of new attributes or methods and very restricted modifications of the inherited attributes and methods.

Aside: Many publications from the object world draw a distinction, as we do not, between types and classes, and—as you might recall from Chapter 2—this book by Bertino and Martino is one that does (or at least tries to). To quote: "Object-oriented systems can be classified into two main categories—systems supporting the notion of *class* and those supporting the notion of *type* ... [Although] there are no clear lines of demarcation between them, the two concepts are fundamentally different [*sic!*] ... Often the concepts type and class are used interchangeably. However, when both are present in the same language, the type is used to indicate the specification of the interface of a set of objects, while class is an implementational notion [*so why is it "in the language" at all, if it's just "an implementational notion"?*]. Therefore ... a type is a set of objects which share the same behavior ... [and] a class is a set of objects which have exactly the same internal structure and therefore the same attributes and the same methods. [*But if all objects in a "class" have the same attributes and the same methods, isn't that class a type, by the authors' own definition?*] The class defines the implementation of a set of objects, while a type describes how such objects can be used ...With inheritance, a class called a *subclass* can be defined on the basis of the definition of another class called a *superclass*." [*But surely—in accordance with their own earlier definitions—the authors should be talking here in terms of types, not classes?*]. End of aside.

---

[43] Except, perhaps, for the fact that (I hope for obvious reasons) I tend to focus not on what might be called "pure object" writings, but rather on ones that have to do with object databases specifically.

[44] *Instance* is another term that virtually none of the sources I examined seems to define. From context, however, it generally seems to be nothing more than just another term for *object*—which reduces the question of what it does mean to a previously unsolved problem, viz., what's an object? (See the section "Values vs. Variables" in Chapter 2.) More seriously, it does seem likely that the term is supposed to cover both values and variables—in which case, of course, we run directly into another problem, viz., that none of the sources in question seems to distinguish properly (or at all?) between value substitutability and variable substitutability (etc., etc.).

■ From R. G. G. Cattell and Douglas K. Barry (eds.): *The Object Data Standard: ODMG 3.0* (Morgan Kaufmann, 2000):

[A] subtype's interface may define characteristics in addition to those defined on its supertypes. These new aspects of state or behavior apply only to instances of the subtype (and any of its subtypes). A subtype's interface also can be refined to specialize state and behavior. For example, the Employee type might have an operation for calculate_paycheck. The Salaried_Employee and Hourly_Employee class implementations might each refine that behavior to reflect their specialized needs.

Incidentally, note the switch in the last sentence here from the terminology of "types" to that of "classes" (?). Note too that the phrase "class implementations" does tend to suggest that classes as such aren't just "an implementational notion" (because if they were, then "class implementations" should be just "classes").[45]

Aside: In the section of the book containing the text just quoted, we also find this: "For example, Associate_Professor is a subtype of Professor ... an Associate_Professor instance is also logically a Professor instance." I find this example interesting, because professors surely have properties (e.g., tenure) that associate professors don't. In other words, I think an argument could be made that the example has the type hierarchy upside down. More generally, I think the example illustrates the point that it can be difficult to get the subtype / supertype relationships right, absent well defined notions of type constraints and type constraint inheritance—because these notions can serve to make it crystal clear, with respect to any such relationship, which type is the subtype and which the supertype. *End of aside.*

■ From Mary E. S. Loomis: *Object Databases: The Essentials* (Addison-Wesley, 1995):

[A] developer can use a type to define other types, which are called its subtypes ... A subtype may introduce additional characteristics (i.e., attributes, relationships, and operations) that are not part of the supertype's specification ... A subtype can be substituted for the supertype in any context where the supertype is valid.

Incidentally, note the sloppy use of *subtype* and *supertype* in the last sentence here, where what's surely meant is an "instance" (?) of the subtype or supertype in question. (Maybe

---

[45] I feel obliged to note in passing that this book also contains a number of claims that I think are (to say the least) somewhat contentious. For example, on page 3 we find this: "We go further than relational systems, as we support a unified object model for sharing data across programming languages." Also on page 3: "We have used the relational standard SQL as the basis for [the Object Query Language] OQL ... though OQL supports more powerful capabilities." And on page 10: "The ODMG Object Model ... includes significantly richer semantics than does the relational model, by declaring relationships and operations explicitly." *Your comments here.*

it's not fair to raise this criticism here; the sloppiness I refer to is actually widespread in the object literature.)

■ From R. G. G. Cattell: *Object Data Management* (revised edition, Addison-Wesley,1994):

Documents [*meaning, presumably, document types*] that have additional attributes or associated procedures ... may be declared to be subtypes of [type] document. Such objects are said to inherit the attributes, relationships, and procedures associated with documents, and may have their own attributes, relationships, or procedures as well.

■ From Jan L. Harrington: *Object-Oriented Database Design Clearly Explained* (Morgan Kaufmann, 2000):

The Animal class provides the data common to all types of animals. The subgroups—Mammals, Reptiles, and Fish—*add* the data specific to themselves ... [The] subgroups are known as *subclasses* or *derived* classes.

By the way, neither *subtype* nor *subclass* appears in the index of this book, but there's a glossary, which contains the following entries among others:

Subtype: The object-oriented database model's term for a subclass.

Subclass: A class that is a more specific example of classes above it in an inheritance hierarchy.

■ From James Martin and James J. Odell: *Object-Oriented Methods: A Foundation* (2nd edition, Prentice-Hall (1997):

This book is the only one I've found that agrees with us (albeit only partially) that type constraints in general, and S by C and G by C in particular, should be supported. Consider the following extracts:

Pages 29-30: Specifying the method of ... classification changes [*i.e., changes in most specific type of an object*] is a technique at the very heart of OO process specification ... [The] collection of concepts that applies [*sic*] to an object can change over time—a phenomenon called *dynamic classification* ... Most OO programming languages [insist that] an object can be an instance of only one ... class for life ... However, in OO analysis, we are not modeling how computer languages and databases work, we are analyzing the enterprise world as people understand it.

As far as I can tell, this extract seems to be saying that (a) S by C and G by C are what's needed in the real world but (b) object systems don't support them.

Page 128: A *classification* event is the classification of an existing object. For example, ... a PERSON object [might become] a member of the EMPLOYEE set ... A *declassification* event is the declassification of an existing object. [For example, ...] a PERSON object [might be removed from] ... the EMPLOYEE set—after which the object remains a PERSON, but is no longer an EMPLOYEE.

Unfortunately, the authors nowhere address the question of how these "classifications and declassifications" might actually be effected in practice. By contrast, our model explains these aspects in detail (we even offer some observations on how they might be efficiently implemented). Of course, since their book is really concerned with object analysis and design, not with object application programming, the authors' lack of specificity might perhaps be justified. Anyway, it's good to find a book that seems to agree that S by C is logically required. That said, however, I have to say too that several other aspects of the book do seem a little puzzling. Here are a few examples:

Page 26: An object is anything to which a concept applies. It is an instance of a type.

One implication of this definition is surely that values and variables are both objects. However, the question of values vs. variables is never discussed, although examples of objects in the book certainly include both. *Value* isn't in the glossary; *variable* is, but it's defined as "synonymous with *field*," where a *field* in turn is defined as "an implementation of a property"—and so *variable* is perhaps to be understood as a (public?) instance variable specifically, at least as far as the cited reference is concerned (?).

Page 143: All operations ... require objects as variables [*sic*].

Page 361: [An] *argument* [is] ... any object that is a parameter [*sic!*].

Page 40: A ... *relation* ... is a type whose instances are tuples.

Several comments on this one! First, of course, a relation *has* a type but *is not* a type. Second, "instances" of a relation type are surely, by definition, relations, not tuples (?). Third, it's clear—at least, I think it's clear—that *instances* here refers to values, whereas such is usually not the case at other points in the book.

Pages 33-35: [We use] the term *concept* ... to mean a notion or idea that we apply to objects in our awareness ... A recommended term for *concept* in the object-oriented analysis standards community is *type*. Therefore ... the name *type* will be used ... In [the Unified Modeling Language] UML, there is a basic concept called *class*. Here, classes used in analysis are called *types* and classes used for implementation purposes are called *implementation classes*. *Page 15:* The *extension* [of a concept] is the set of all objects to which the concept applies. *Page 27:* [A] *set* is a particular collection, or *class*, of objects ... *Class* is technically considered to be the correct word when referring to the collection of objects to which a concept applies ... Some [writers] argue that *set* and *class* mean the same thing. Since *class* has a different meaning in OO programming languages, the word *set* will be used to avoid confusion. It is worth noting, however, that the inspiration for using the term *class* in OO originally came from the centuries-old mathematical notion. *Page 386:* The extension of the concept MORTAL [is] the collection, or *set*, of things to which the definition applies ... The set of MORTAL objects, therefore is not a fixed collection. *Page 354:* [The term] *extension* [is] used interchangeably with *set*.

Sorting out what these remarks might mean I leave as an exercise for you!

EXERCISES

21.1 With reference to the section "An Introductory Example," why do you think the *Manifesto* book recommends defining EMP and PGMR as relvars rather than types?

21.2 Explain "is a" vs. "has a" in your own words.

21.3 Why does the *Manifesto* insist that tuple and relation types have names of the form TUPLE *H* and RELATION *H* (or something logically equivalent), respectively?

21.4 What's a subtuple?

21.5 Explain the semantic difference between DELETE ONLY and the use of the ONLY option on SQL's regular DELETE statement.

21.6 What do you understand by the term *delegation*?

21.7 In the body of the chapter, I claimed that the notion of "variables containing variables" makes no sense. But why doesn't it?

ANSWERS

21.1 The following answer focuses on employees specifically, but the discussion applies equally to programmers, mutatis mutandis. It consists for the most part of a lightly edited version of text from Appendix B ("A Design Dilemma?") of the *Manifesto* book.
    First, then, here are **Tutorial D** definitions for the two possible designs—i.e., employees as a type (*Design T*) vs. employees as a relvar (*Design R*):

```
TYPE EMP POSSREP              / * "Design T" */
   ( ENO CHAR , ENAME CHAR , DNO CHAR , SALARY MONEY ) ;

VAR  EMP BASE RELATION        / * "Design R" */
   { ENO CHAR , ENAME CHAR , DNO CHAR , SALARY MONEY } KEY { ENO } ;
```

Note in particular that the EMP type is scalar or "encapsulated," while the EMP relvar isn't.

Now I want to argue that the choice between these two designs is really no choice at all. Observe first that *Design T* gives us no way to hire and fire!—and so that design is clearly inadequate as it stands. The reason is that, loosely speaking, type EMP is the set of *all possible* employees (i.e., it's not just the ones who currently work for the company), and there's simply no way to insert a new employee into that set or delete an existing one. To put it another way, the set in question contains all possible values of the form

```
EMP ( eno , name , dno , sal )
```

(where *eno*, *name*, *dno*, and *sal* are values of types CHAR, CHAR, CHAR, and MONEY, respectively), regardless of whether any employee currently exists having those values as the pertinent properties. In other words: Types are *static*. *Note:* If you're having difficulty with this idea, consider the simpler example of type INTEGER. That type just *is* the set of all integers, and it's clearly not possible to insert new integers or delete existing ones.[46]

It follows from the foregoing that *Design T* additionally requires an accompanying relvar, perhaps looking like this:

```
VAR EMPV BASE RELATION { EMP EMP } KEY { EMP } ;
```

Relvar EMPV has a tuple for every employee currently of interest (meaning, presumably, every employee who currently works for the company), and now of course we do have a way to hire new employees and fire existing ones. Note carefully, however, that relvar EMPV does indeed have just one attribute, not four, thanks to encapsulation.[47] Note too that the KEY specification is almost a "no op"; in particular, note that what it *doesn't* say is that employee numbers are unique. If we wanted to say such a thing, we'd have to define a separate constraint (a database constraint, in *Manifesto* terms), perhaps along the following lines:

```
CONSTRAINT ENO_UNIQUE
          COUNT ( EMPV ) =
          COUNT ( ( EXTEND EMPV :
                        { ENO := THE_ENO ( EMP ) } ) { ENO } ) ;
```

One implication of the *Design T* approach is thus that it tends to suggest that the database will wind up containing a large number of relvars with just one attribute each, and possibly with

---

[46] After all, suppose it *were* possible to "insert a new integer." Where would that "new integer" come from?

[47] Note the difference here vis-à-vis SQL's "typed tables"! "Typed tables" in SQL are tables defined by means of a CREATE TABLE statement of the form CREATE TABLE <*table name*> OF <*type name*>. They're discussed in detail in Chapter 22, but the salient point here is that they're definitely not encapsulated. Examples were given in the section "Subtables and Supertables" in the body of the present chapter.

a large number of constraints looking like the one just shown as well: a state of affairs that should give us some pause, you might think.

Anyway, now we can at least "hire and fire." We can also perform operations analogous, though not identical, to the kinds of relational operations we would probably have performed on relvar EMP if we'd opted for *Design R* instead. Here are a couple of examples:

- (*"Restriction"*) Get employees with salary greater than $50,000:

```
EMPV WHERE THE_SALARY ( EMP ) > MONEY ( 50000 )
```

- (*"Projection"*) Get all employee name / salary pairs:

```
( EXTEND EMPV : { ENAME   := THE_ENAME  ( EMP ) ,
                  SALARY  := THE_SALARY ( EMP ) } ) { ENAME , SALARY }
```

Observe, however, that the result in this latter example has two attributes, not one! Thus, it should be clear that (a) given the single-attribute relvar EMPV required by *Design T*, we can create the four-attribute relvar EMP required by *Design R* (as a view, perhaps); furthermore, (b) we'd probably want to do exactly that in practice, because, for a variety of reasons, that four-attribute relvar is considerably more convenient than the single-attribute one.

Here to spell it out is a definition for that four-attribute view (let's call it EMPX):

```
VAR EMPX VIRTUAL
    ( ( EXTEND EMPV : { ENO    := THE_ENO    ( EMP ) ,
                        ENAME  := THE_ENAME  ( EMP ) ,
                        DNO    := THE_DNO    ( EMP ) ,
                        SALARY := THE_SALARY ( EMP ) } )
      { ENO , ENAME , DNO , SALARY } )
    KEY { ENO } ;
```

Note in particular that the KEY specification for this relvar EMPX does say that employee numbers are unique.

What the foregoing analysis seems to show is that we can start off with *Design T*, the type design, if we like, which means we also need an associated single-attribute relvar—but we'll quickly find that, in effect, we'll have to create *Design R* (the relvar design) as well. So *Design T* implies that we wind up with everything in *Design R*, plus the type EMP, plus the single-attribute relvar EMPV and constraint ENO_UNIQUE as well. So what was the point of opting for *Design T* in the first place? And what purpose is served, exactly, in *Design T* by type EMP and that single-attribute relvar EMPV and that constraint?

Given all of the above, what then is the criterion for making something a type and not a relvar? (We must have some types, of course, if only for the obvious reason that relvars can't be defined without them.) Well, here are some pertinent considerations:

■ In conventional design terms, types correspond, loosely, to *properties* and relvars to *entities* (or sets of properties and sets of entities, rather). Hence, if something is "only" a property, it should map to a type and not a relvar.

   The trouble with this idea, of course, is that "one person's property is another person's entity." For example, consider colors. We normally tend to think of the color "red," say, as a property,[48] not an entity, and thus we'd normally represent colors as a type, surely. But some users might be very interested in "red" as an entity, with further properties of its own (shade, for example, or intensity), in which case we might want to represent colors by a relvar. Perhaps this is an example of a situation where we need both a type and a relvar (the relvar representing just those colors that happen to be currently of interest for some reason).

■ Another important general point is that if the ability to "hire and fire"—or something analogous to that ability—is a requirement, then we're definitely talking about entities, not properties, and we should definitely be aiming for a relvar design.

Given such considerations, incidentally, it's odd that so many articles and presentations on object systems use employees, programmers, and so forth as examples of object classes. Of course, an object class is just a type—at least, it is as far as I'm concerned—and so those presentations are typically forced to go on to define some kind of "collection" for those employees, another such "collection" for those programmers, and so on.[49] What's more, those "collections" are collections of encapsulated objects, and they therefore effectively omit those all important (and user visible) attribute names. As a consequence, they don't lend themselves very well to the formulation of ad hoc queries, declarative integrity constraints, and so forth—a fact that advocates of the approach themselves often admit, apparently without being aware that it's precisely the lack of user visible attribute names (in effect, the encapsulation) that causes the difficulties.[50]

---

[48] As a property of some entity, that is. The concept of a property in isolation makes no sense.

[49] SQL's typed tables once again?—except that (as noted in an earlier footnote) those typed tables aren't encapsulated. Indeed, the arguments of the present paragraph might give some hint as to why that is.

[50] In fact, object systems typically support ad hoc queries (etc.) precisely by breaking encapsulation—a process that might conveniently be referred to as *decapsulation*—and exposing physical representations! Here are a couple of quotes to illustrate the point. 1. "All object DBMS products currently require that [object components] referenced in ... queries be public [*i.e., visible to the user*]" (from Mary E. S. Loomis: *Object Databases: The Essentials*, Addison-Wesley, 1995). 2. "Query management ... is one situation where violating encapsulation is almost obligatory" (from Elisa Bertino and Lorenzo Martino: *Object-Oriented Database Systems: Concepts and Architectures*, Addison-Wesley, 1993).

Overall, it's my belief that the most appropriate design approach will emerge if careful consideration is given to the distinction between (a) declarative sentences in natural language, on the one hand, and (b) the vocabulary used in the construction of such sentences, on the other. Basically, it's *unencapsulated tuples in relations* that stand for such sentences, and it's *encapsulated values in attributes in those tuples* that stand for particular elements—typically nouns—in those sentences. As I put it in my book *SQL and Relational Theory: How to Write Accurate SQL Code* (3rd edition, O'Reilly, 2015):

> Types give us our vocabulary—the things we can talk about—and relations give us the ability to say things about the things we can talk about.

Let me elaborate. First, consider the EMP relvar of *Design R* once again, and consider this tuple:

```
TUPLE { ENO 'E7' ,  ENAME 'Amy' , DNO 'D5' , SALARY MONEY ( 60000 ) }
```

Inserting this tuple into the relvar means (let's agree) that the database now contains something asserting that the following declarative sentence is true:

Employee E7, named Amy, is assigned to department D5 and earns a salary of $60,000.

By contrast, consider the EMP type of *Design T*. Where the relvar of *Design R* allowed us to insert the tuple just shown, with the interpretation just explained, the type of *Design T* merely allows us to write the following selector invocation:

```
EMP ( 'E7' , 'Amy' , 'D5' , MONEY ( 60000 ) )
```

This selector invocation doesn't of itself assert the truth of anything at all (neither does it deny it, of course). Rather, it constitutes nothing more than a certain rather heavy duty noun, something like "an E7-numbered, Amy-named, D5-assigned, $60,000-earning employee." Now, we can if we like form a tuple containing just that "noun"—i.e., that EMP value—and then insert that tuple into the single-attribute relvar EMPV that *Design T* additionally requires. Speaking a trifle loosely, however, to do what I've just described is (a) simply to place a "There exists" in front of that noun to form a declarative sentence, and then (b) to assert that the sentence in question is in fact true.

Of course, the "true fact" asserted by the four-attribute tuple in *Design R* is exactly the same as the "true fact" asserted in different words, as it were, by the one-attribute tuple in *Design T*. So which of the two ways of asserting that fact do you think is the more economical, the more communicative, and the more amenable to further reasoning?

21.2 See the body of the chapter.

21.3 So that the type of the result of evaluating an arbitrary tuple or relational expression can be pinned down precisely and understood by both the system and the user. With reference to the suppliers-and-parts database, for example (see Chapter 1), the projection of S over STATUS and CITY—i.e., S {STATUS,CITY}, in **Tutorial D** notation—is of type

```
RELATION { STATUS INTEGER , CITY CHAR }
```

And the join of S and P on CITY—S JOIN P, in **Tutorial D**—is of type

```
RELATION {SNO SNO , SNAME NAME , STATUS INTEGER , CITY CHAR ,
          PNO PNO , PNAME NAME , COLOR COLOR , WEIGHT WEIGHT }
```

21.4 It depends on context! In the relational world, a subtuple of tuple *t* is a subset (i.e., a projection) of *t*. In the world of structural inheritance, a subtuple of tuple *t* is likely to be a superset (i.e., an extension) of *t*.

21.5 Loosely, (a) DELETE ONLY deletes rows from the target table and corresponding rows from that table's subtables, but doesn't delete corresponding rows from the target table's supertables; (b) SQL's DELETE with the ONLY option deletes rows from the target table and corresponding rows from that table's supertables (and subtables of those supertables), but only if there are no corresponding rows in the target table's subtables. For more details, see the body of the chapter.

21.6 See the body of the chapter.

21.7 I'll consider the case of array variables specifically, just to be definite, but the following arguments generalize to nonscalar variables of any kind, including relvars in particular. Let *A* be an array variable, and assume for the sake of the discussion that its current contents are to be regarded as a set of element variables (not values!) $A[1]$, $A[2]$, ..., $A[m]$. Then:

a. Every assignment to *A* will have the side effect of updating some of those $A[i]$'s (for some values of *i*) as well, and every assignment to $A[i]$ (for some *i*) will have the side effect of updating *A* as well. In a sense, therefore, *A* and the $A[i]$'s are in lockstep, as it were. Certainly they're not totally independent variables.

b. Consider the following multiple assignment:

```
A := a , A[i] := ai ;
```

Note that, by our assumption, the individual assignments here have different target variables, so they can't be combined into a single assignment. So what are the semantics of this multiple assignment? In particular, do they differ from those of the following?—

```
A[i] := ai , A := a ;
```

Also, what happens if the expression *ai* takes the form *A[j]* for some *j ≠ i*?

c.   How about this one (*j ≠ i*)?—

```
A[i]:= A[j] , A[j] := aj ;
```

Again the individual assignments here have different target variables, so they can't be combined into a single assignment.

Note further that if *A* is a "variable length array," then elements can be inserted and deleted—in which case "inserting an tuple into *A*" doesn't just update variable *A*, it apparently creates a new element variable! Likewise, "deleting an element from *A*" also doesn't just update variable *A*, it apparently drops some existing element variable. Thus, there seems to be some mixing of realms—more specifically, some mixing of data operations and metadata operations—going on. Overall, in other words, the idea of "variables containing variables" does seem to confuse a variety of concepts that would much better be kept separate.

Chapter 22

Inheritance in SQL

The hardest thing of all is to find a black cat in a dark room,
especially if there is no cat.

—Confucius (551-479 BCE)

This chapter is based in part on material from (a) Chapters 5 and 20 of my book An Introduction to Database Systems *(8th edition, Addison-Wesley, 2004) and (b) Appendix H of the Manifesto book. However, all of that material is revised here, usually extensively, and there's a great deal of new material as well.*

This chapter presents an overview of SQL's type support, including of course its support for type inheritance in particular. I'd like to stress that word *overview*, however; the treatment is very far from exhaustive—many details are simplified, and some features are omitted altogether. But I hope there's enough here to give you some idea of the extent of SQL's support in this area and also, perhaps, to give you some idea of what might be missing. *Note:* As noted in the preface, all references to SQL in this book, and hence in this chapter in particular, should be understood as referring to the SQL standard specifically. The reference document is:[1]

> International Organization for Standardization (ISO): *Database Language SQL*, Document ISO/IEC 9075:2008 (2011)

In this connection, you might find the following book helpful (it's a complete tutorial reference and guide to the SQL standard as of 1997):

> C. J. Date (with Hugh Darwen): *A Guide to the SQL Standard* (4th edition, Addison-Wesley, 1997)

Although this book is now fairly old as these things are measured in the computing field, just about everything it says is still applicable to the version of the standard that's current at the time of writing (viz., "SQL:2011").

---

[1] It's interesting to note, incidentally, that although SQL is almost universally thought of (and indeed described) as a "relational" database standard, that reference document doesn't describe it as such—in fact, it never uses the term *relational* at all, nor the term *relation*.

The following books together provide a comprehensive discussion of the 1999 version of the standard ("SQL:1999"):

Jim Melton and Alan R. Simon: *SQL:1999—Understanding Relational Components* (Morgan Kaufmann, 2002)

Jim Melton: *Advanced SQL:1999—Understanding Object-Relational and Other Advanced Features* (Morgan Kaufmann, 2003)

SQL:1999 was the first version of the standard to include user defined types and type inheritance support. As a consequence, these two books do contain fairly extensive coverage of those topics, which the one mentioned above by Darwen and myself doesn't. *Note:* For the record, let me add that there have been two versions, or "editions," of the standard since SQL:1999, viz., SQL:2003 and the current version, SQL:2011. So far as I know, however, there are no books dedicated to any version more recent than SQL:1999. As a consequence, I've found in writing the present chapter that I've frequently had to refer to the second of the foregoing books in particular (and I'm pleased to be able to acknowledge that debt here). Please note, therefore, that all otherwise unattributed references to "Melton" throughout what follows should be understood as references to that specific book.

One last introductory point: There are no exercises and answers in this chapter because this isn't supposed to be a book about SQL. If you want to test your understanding of the material, however, you should be able to take many of the exercises from previous chapters and adapt them to the SQL context.

SQL SCALAR TYPES WITHOUT INHERITANCE

Before I can discuss SQL's support for type inheritance, I need to explain SQL's support for types as such (i.e., without inheritance). I'll discuss scalar types in this section and nonscalar types in the next.

System Defined Types

As we saw in Chapter 2, system defined types are necessarily scalar. SQL supports the following system defined types:

```
BOOLEAN     INTEGER              CHARACTER(n)
            SMALLINT             CHARACTER VARYING(n)
            BIGINT               CHARACTER LARGE OBJECT(n)
            NUMERIC(p,q)         BINARY(n)
            DECIMAL(p,q)         BINARY VARYING(n)
            FLOAT(p)             BINARY LARGE OBJECT(n)
```

These types should all be reasonably self-explanatory; note in particular that literals of essentially conventional format are supported in every case.[2] *Note:* SQL supports several other system defined types as well, including an "XML document" type (XML), a variety of "national character string types" (NATIONAL CHARACTER(*n*), etc.), and a variety of datetime types (DATE, TIME, TIMESTAMP, INTERVAL). However, details of these additional types are beyond the scope of this book. Points arising:

1. A number of defaults, abbreviations, and alternative spellings are also supported, including INT for INTEGER, CHAR for CHARACTER, VARCHAR for CHARACTER VARYING, VARBINARY for BINARY VARYING, CLOB for CHARACTER LARGE OBJECT, and BLOB for BINARY LARGE OBJECT.[3] *Note:* With regard to the various "binary" types here, note that BINARY doesn't mean binary numbers, it means bit strings—or, perhaps more accurately, *byte* strings, since the associated length specifications (see point 2 below) give the corresponding length in "octets." (Further evidence that this latter interpretation is correct is provided by the fact that "binary" literals take the form of a sequence of hexadecimal digits enclosed in single quotes, preceded by the letter X.)

2. As you can see, SQL, unlike **Tutorial D**, requires its various character string types (CHAR, VARCHAR, and CLOB) to have an associated length specification. In fact, as explained in Chapter 2, these "types" aren't really types at all, they're type generators. By contrast, CHAR(25), for example, is a type, and it's obtained by invoking the type generator CHAR with the value 25 as sole argument to that invocation. Analogous remarks apply to every "scalar type" in the foregoing list apart from type BOOLEAN and the various integer types (SMALLINT, INTEGER, BIGINT). For simplicity, however, I'll overlook this point in what follows—most of the time, at any rate—and continue to refer to CHAR and the rest as if they were indeed types as such, just as SQL itself does.

3. Explicit assignment and explicit equality comparisons are supported for all of these types. For assignment, the syntax is:

```
SET <scalar variable ref> = <scalar exp> ;
```

---

[2] Well ... perhaps they're not quite as self-explanatory as all that. For example (and despite that remark about literal formats being "essentially conventional"), there aren't really any NUMERIC or DECIMAL literals, as such, at all! Instead, the literal (e.g.) 123.45 is considered to be of type neither NUMERIC(p,q) nor DECIMAL(p,q) for some p and q, but rather of a type for which no specific SQL keyword exists: viz., "exact numeric." (Analogously, the literal 5E2 is considered to be of type, not FLOAT(p) for some p, but rather another type for which no specific SQL keyword exists: viz., "approximate numeric.") For the record, the difference between NUMERIC(p,q) and DECIMAL(p,q)—where $p > 0$, $q \geq 0$, and $p \geq q$—is that the former has precision *exactly* p decimal digits and the latter has precision *at least* p decimal digits. According to the standard, moreover, "digits" here means *significant* digits in both cases, which is rather surprising if true—it would surely seem more reasonable to say NUMERIC(p,q) has *at most* p significant digits and DECIMAL(p,q) has *at most* r significant digits for some $r \geq p$ (for otherwise, e.g., 3.0 wouldn't be a value either of type NUMERIC(5,1) or of type DECIMAL(5,1)).

[3] The "object" types mentioned here aren't object types in the object oriented sense.

For equality comparison, the syntax is:

```
<scalar exp> = <scalar exp>
```

4. For system defined types SQL supports a weak form of strong typing (if you see what I mean).[4] To be specific, (a) BOOLEAN values can be assigned only to BOOLEAN variables and compared only with BOOLEAN values; (b) numeric values can be assigned only to numeric variables and compared only with numeric values (where "numeric" means INTEGER, SMALLINT, BIGINT, NUMERIC, DECIMAL, or FLOAT); (c) character string values can be assigned only to character string variables and compared only with character string values (where "character string" means CHAR, VARCHAR, or CLOB);[5] and (d) bit string values can be assigned only to bit string variables and compared only with bit string values (where "bit string" means BINARY, VARBINARY, or BLOB). Thus, an attempt to compare, e.g., a number and a character string is illegal. However, an attempt to compare, e.g., two numbers is legal, even if those numbers are of different types, say DECIMAL and FLOAT, respectively (in this example, the DECIMAL value will be coerced to type FLOAT before the comparison is done).[6]

DISTINCT Types

SQL supports two kinds of user defined types, *DISTINCT* types and *structured* types,[7] both of which are defined by means of the CREATE TYPE statement. Now, DISTINCT types are scalar types, which is why I discuss them in the present section. By contrast, structured types can be regarded as either scalar or nonscalar, depending on context. (At least, that's the official story—but I don't really believe it; as far as I can see, there's essentially no context in which a structured type behaves as if it were truly scalar. For that reason, I've chosen to discuss structured types in the next section, under the general heading of nonscalar types.)

Be that as it may, for now let's focus on DISTINCT types. Here by way of example is an SQL definition for type WEIGHT as a DISTINCT type (note that, perhaps a little surprisingly, "DISTINCT" does *not* appear as a keyword in that definition):

```
CREATE TYPE WEIGHT AS DECIMAL(5,1) FINAL ;
```

---

[4] See the answer to Exercise 2.6 in Chapter 2 for a brief explanation of the notion of strong typing.

[5] The answer to that same Exercise 2.6 in Chapter 2 gives further details regarding the assignment and comparison of character strings in SQL.

[6] As explained in the answer to that same Exercise 2.6 in Chapter 2, the term *coercion* just means implicit type conversion.

[7] I depart from the standard in setting the word "DISTINCT," in the DISTINCT type context, in all caps in order to stress the point that the word isn't being used in that context in its ordinary natural language sense.

As the example suggests, in its simplest form—i.e., ignoring various optional features—the syntax for defining a DISTINCT type looks like this:

```
CREATE TYPE <type name> AS <underlying type name> FINAL ;
```

Points arising:

1. FINAL means this type can't have any proper subtypes. DISTINCT types are required to be "final" in this sense.[8]

2. The *<underlying type name>* is the name of a system defined type, and it defines the representation of values of the DISTINCT type in question. Note carefully that the representation in question is the actual representation, not just some possible representation; in fact, SQL doesn't support any kind of "possrep" notion at all.

3. There's nothing analogous to **Tutorial D**'s CONSTRAINT specification; in other words, SQL doesn't really support type constraints,[9] apart from the obvious implicit constraint that values of the type must be representable in terms of the underlying type. In the case of type WEIGHT, for example, there's no way to specify in the pertinent CREATE TYPE statement that, for any given WEIGHT value, the corresponding DECIMAL(5,1) value must be greater than zero (!) and less than 5000, say. Rather, every value d of type DECIMAL(5,1)—even if $d \leq 0$ or $d \geq 5000$—corresponds to some unique WEIGHT value w, and every WEIGHT value w corresponds to some unique DECIMAL(5,1) value d.

4. Comparison operators that apply to the DISTINCT type seem—though the standard is curiously reticent on the matter—to be those that apply to the underlying type. *Note:* Apart from assignment (see point 7 below), other operators that apply to the underlying type do *not* apply to the DISTINCT type. For example, let WT be an SQL variable of declared type WEIGHT. Then all of the following will fail on a compile time type error:

```
WT + WT
WT + 14.7
WT * 2
```

5. Selectors and THE_ operators are supported (not by those names, however). For example, if DW is an SQL variable of declared type DECIMAL(5,1), then the expression WEIGHT(DW) returns the corresponding weight value ("selector functionality"); and if WT is an SQL variable of declared type WEIGHT, then the expression DECIMAL(WT) returns the corresponding DECIMAL(5,1) value ("THE_ operator functionality"). Hence,

---

[8] Actually a DISTINCT type can't have any proper supertypes either.

[9] The justification, such as it is, for this (in my opinion, highly regrettable) omission was explained in Chapter 13.

the following examples are valid (table P in these examples is, of course, an SQL analog of relvar P from the suppliers-and-parts database in Chapter 1):

```
SELECT PNO ,
       DECIMAL ( WEIGHT )              /* "THE_ operator functionality" */
       AS DWT
FROM   P
WHERE  WEIGHT > WEIGHT ( DW )          /* "selector functionality        */

DELETE
FROM   P
WHERE  WEIGHT = WEIGHT ( 14.7 ) ;      /* "selector functionality"       */
```

(The expression WEIGHT(14.7) in the second of these examples is effectively a WEIGHT literal, though SQL doesn't use that term.)

   Note: Since the representation (i.e., the underlying type) for any given DISTINCT type always has exactly one component, these "selectors" and "THE_ operators" are really nothing more than simple CASTs (in other words, they're really just type conversion operators—see the answer to Exercise 2.6 in Chapter 2). Indeed, explicit CASTs can be used in their place.[10] For example, CAST (DW AS WEIGHT) could be used instead of, and is logically equivalent to, WEIGHT(DW), and CAST (WT AS DECIMAL(5,1)) could be used instead of, and is logically equivalent to, DECIMAL(WT). Also, if *DT1* and *DT2* are distinct DISTINCT types, then explicit CASTs can optionally be defined for mapping between values of type *DT1* and values of type *DT2*.

6. With one important exception (see point 7 below), strong typing does apply to DISTINCT types. Note in particular that comparisons between values of a DISTINCT type and values of the underlying representation type are illegal. Hence, the following are *not* valid, even if (as before) the SQL variable DW in the first example is of type DECIMAL(5,1):

```
SELECT PNO , DECIMAL ( WEIGHT ) AS DWT
FROM   P
WHERE  WEIGHT > DW                  /* warning: illegal! */

DELETE
FROM   P
WHERE  WEIGHT = 14.7 ;              /* warning: illegal! */
```

7. The sole exception to strong typing, mentioned under points 4 and 6 above, has to do with assignment. For example, if we want to retrieve some WEIGHT value into some DECIMAL(5,1) variable—DW, say—then some type conversion clearly has to occur. Now, we can certainly perform that conversion explicitly, as here:

---

[10] The CAST operators in question are system defined; that is, creating DISTINCT type *DT* with underlying type *UT* automatically causes the system to create operators for casting from *DT* to *UT* and vice versa.

```
SELECT   DECIMAL ( WEIGHT )
INTO     DW                          /* DW is of type DECIMAL(5,1) */
FROM     P
WHERE    PNO = PNO('P1') ;
```

However, the following is also legal (and an appropriate coercion will occur):

```
SELECT   WEIGHT                      /* instead of DECIMAL(WEIGHT) */
INTO     DW
FROM     P
WHERE    PNO = PNO('P1') ;
```

Coercions in the opposite direction are valid as well.[11]

8. Additional operators can be defined as required. *Note:* The SQL term for such operators is *routines*, and there are three kinds: *functions*, *procedures*, and *methods*. Functions and procedures correspond very roughly to our read-only and update operators, respectively; methods can be regarded as functions also, but unlike functions in general they're tightly associated with a particular type—necessarily a user defined type[12]—and they're invoked using a different syntactic style. Methods are discussed in the subsection "Methods" below. Here by contrast is an example of a function as such—i.e., one that's not a method[13]—called ADDWT ("add weight"), which allows two WEIGHT values to be added and returns the result as another WEIGHT value:

```
CREATE FUNCTION ADDWT ( W1 WEIGHT , W2 WEIGHT ) RETURNS WEIGHT
       RETURN ( WEIGHT ( DECIMAL ( W1 ) + DECIMAL ( W2 ) ) ) ;
```

All of the following will now be legal expressions of type WEIGHT:

```
ADDWT ( WT , WT )
ADDWT ( WT , WEIGHT ( 14.7 ) )
ADDWT ( WEIGHT ( 14.7 ) , WT )
ADDWT ( WEIGHT ( 14.7 ) , WEIGHT ( 3.0 ) )
```

Note: If we wanted, e.g., ADDWT(WT,14.7) and ADDWI(14.7,WT) to be legal expressions as well, we could define two further ADDWT functions, one taking a WEIGHT parameter and a DECIMAL(5,1) parameter in that order, and the other taking a

---

[11] Please note, however, that (to say it again) assignment as such is the *sole* exception to the strong typing rule. Thus, for example, if operator *Op* has a parameter *P* of declared type WEIGHT, then—at least according to my reading of the standard—invoking *Op* with an argument *A* corresponding to *P* of declared type DECIMAL(5,1) won't work, even though such an invocation might be thought of informally as causing *A* to be assigned to *P*.

[12] Note this point carefully! One implication is that what SQL calls the subject parameter (and corresponding subject arguments)—see the subsection "Methods" below—must necessarily be of some user defined type.

[13] For simplicity, from this point forward I'll take the unqualified term *function* to mean, specifically, a function that's not a method, unless the context demands otherwise.

DECIMAL(5,1) parameter and a WEIGHT parameter in that order. I'll leave the details as an exercise. Note, however, that an analogous remark does *not* apply to methods (see the subsection immediately following)—at least, not 100 percent (why not?).

Methods

Recall from Chapter 7 that *method* is basically just an object term for operator; in fact, methods were added to SQL in 1999 (along with user defined types) as part of an explicit attempt to make SQL more "object like."[14] By way of example, consider the function ADDWT discussed above. Suppose that for some reason we decide to use a method instead of a conventional function to provide ADDWT functionality (in order to avoid confusion with ADDWT as defined above, let's agree to call that method MADDWT). What we have to do, then, is this. First, we extend the definition of type WEIGHT to contain an appropriate signature,[15] thus:

```
CREATE TYPE WEIGHT AS DECIMAL(5,1) FINAL
        METHOD MADDWT ( W2 WEIGHT ) RETURNS WEIGHT ;
```

We also define the method as such (i.e., we provide the necessary implementation code), as follows:

```
CREATE METHOD MADDWT ( W2 WEIGHT ) RETURNS WEIGHT
        FOR WEIGHT
        RETURN ( WEIGHT ( DECIMAL ( SELF ) + DECIMAL ( W2 ) ) ) ;
```

Now all of the following are legal MADDWT invocations (WT in these examples is once again an SQL variable of type WEIGHT):

```
WT . MADDWT ( WT )
WT . MADDWT ( WEIGHT ( 14.7 ) )
WEIGHT ( 14.7 ) . MADDWT ( WT )
WEIGHT ( 14.7 ) . MADDWT ( WEIGHT ( 3.0 ) )
```

Explanation:

---

[14] It's worth noting here that, to quote Melton (page 113), "SQL's object facilities were quite consciously designed to be similar to Java's"—though in the next paragraph he also says that "it's somewhat unclear in the SQL standard exactly what an object *is*" (italics in the original).

[15] The term *signature* in SQL corresponds, more or less, to our specification signature (SQL has nothing—well, nothing explicit, at any rate—corresponding to our invocation signature). A signature in SQL consists of the operator name, a sequence of parameter declared types, and an indication of whether the operator in question is a procedure or a function (methods here counting as functions). *Note:* The foregoing is the standard's own definition of the term, but subsequent uses of "signature" in the reference document seem to suggest that—for a function, at any rate—the result declared type is part of the signature too. What definitely, but perhaps a little surprisingly, appears *not* to be part of the signature is any indication as to which parameters if any are subject to update.

1. Methods in SQL always have this kind of two-part, lockstep definition (signature in CREATE TYPE, implementation code in CREATE METHOD). By contrast, functions and procedures are defined via separate CREATE FUNCTION and CREATE PROCEDURE statements (the first of these was illustrated in the previous subsection, of course). These statements are analogous, somewhat, to the CREATE METHOD statement shown in the example, but functions and procedures aren't tightly tied to one particular type as methods are—only methods have their specification signature included in the pertinent type definition, and only methods have "FOR *<type name>*" specified as part of their definition.[16]

2. Unlike functions and procedures, methods are "selfish." Recall from Chapter 11 that what this means is that one parameter (SQL calls it the *subject* parameter) is singled out for special semantic treatment (see point 3 below), and hence special syntactic treatment also, necessarily (see point 4 below). The term *selfish method* derives from the fact that the subject parameter is typically unnamed and so has to be referenced within the method's implementation code in some ad hoc way, typically by means of the keyword SELF. *Note:* Both of these points apply to SQL specifically (note the appearance of the keyword SELF in the MADDWT code above). Note too that MADDWT has two parameters, but only one, the second, is explicitly named and mentioned inside the parentheses following the operator name in the CREATE METHOD statement. Note finally that those parentheses are required even if there's nothing for them to enclose (i.e., even if the method has no parameters other than the subject one).

3. The special semantic treatment consists in using the type—meaning, more precisely, the *most specific* type—of the argument corresponding to the subject parameter (i.e., the "subject argument"), and that type alone, to control the run time binding process.[17] *Note:* Like our own inheritance model, SQL does support the notion of most specific types, as we'll see later in this chapter. However, that notion is significant only in the context of structured types, and it's therefore not very relevant for the purposes of the present section.

4. The special syntactic treatment consists in the fact that any given method is regarded as being "for" some particular type: viz., the declared type of the subject parameter. As noted under point 1 above, this state of affairs is reflected in SQL by (a) the fact that the method

---

[16] Two points here. First, the fact that the signature for a given method has to be specified as part of the pertinent type definition means that creating a new method *M* for an existing type *T* is slightly nontrivial, involving as it does an alteration to the definition of type *T*. Second, the signature and the implementation code are both provided automatically in the special case in which (a) the type defined in the CREATE TYPE statement in question is a structured type, not a DISTINCT type, and (b) the method in question is a constructor, an observer, or a mutator function for that type (see the section "SQL Nonscalar Types without Inheritance," later). *Note:* As we'll also see later, the methods referred to in part (b) of the foregoing sentence are indeed methods, even though SQL refers to them as functions.

[17] In practice it might be possible to do some or even all of the binding at compile time, but methods in general always involve (at least conceptually) some degree of run time binding.

signature appears as part of the definition of the type in question, together with (b) the fact that the type in question is explicitly mentioned, via the FOR specification, in the definition of the method. (In other words, and indeed as already noted, the type and the method are in lockstep, as it were. See Chapter 11 if you need to remind yourself why we deliberately chose not to adopt any analogous mechanism in *The Third Manifesto*.)

5. As the examples indicate (but simplifying slightly), the syntax for a method invocation takes the form

```
<subject argument exp> . <method name> ( <argument exp commalist> )
```

Note: Such an expression has sometimes been described (at least in early object systems) as "sending a message" to the argument denoted by the *<subject argument exp>*, saying, in effect, "apply method *<method name>* to yourself, using further arguments as specified in the *<argument exp commalist>*."

SQL NONSCALAR TYPES WITHOUT INHERITANCE

Like **Tutorial D**, SQL supports certain nonscalar type generators (the SQL term is *type constructors*, but I'll call them *type generators* here for consistency with earlier chapters). The ones that are of most interest to us in the present context are (a) the ROW type generator, which is, of course, SQL's counterpart to **Tutorial D**'s TUPLE type generator,[18] and (b) the CREATE TYPE statement itself, when considered in its capacity to define what SQL calls structured types specifically. I'll deal with row types first.

Row Types

SQL's row types resemble **Tutorial D**'s tuple types in that they're simply available for use whenever they're needed (typically as the declared type of some variable); they don't have to be separately defined, and in fact they can't be. (Note that exactly the opposite is the case with structured types, as we'll see in the subsection "Structured Types" later in this section.) Here's an example of an SQL row variable definition:

```
DECLARE PRV /* "part row variable" */
        ROW ( PNO    PNO ,
              PNAME  NAME ,
              COLOR  COLOR ,
              WEIGHT WEIGHT ,
              CITY   VARCHAR(20) ) ;
```

---

[18] SQL also supports (a) two further nonscalar type generators, ARRAY and MULTISET (but SQL's array and multiset types aren't very important in the larger scheme of things, and I propose to ignore them for the purposes of this chapter), and (b) a scalar type generator called REF, which I'll be discussing later in the present section.

As you can see, the type of variable PRV is indeed a row type, and it's specified by means of an invocation of the ROW type generator (I'm assuming for the sake of the example that PNO, NAME, and COLOR are user defined types—probably DISTINCT types—that have already been defined; type WEIGHT is as defined in the previous section; and CITY has a system defined type, viz., VARCHAR(20)). *Note:* For some reason, SQL refers to the components of row types produced by invocation of the ROW type generator—also to the components of values and variables of such row types—not as columns but as *fields*. In the example, therefore, the SQL row variable PRV has five fields, called PNO, PNAME, COLOR, WEIGHT, and CITY. What's more, those fields are ordered left to right; thus, e.g., PNO is the first field of that variable, PNAME is the second, and so on.

SQL also supports row assignment. Here's a simple example:

```
SET PRV = ROW ( PNO('P1') , NAME('Nut') , COLOR('Red') ,
                               WEIGHT(12.0) , 'London' ) ;
```

The expression on the right side here is a row selector invocation (SQL would call it a *row value constructor* invocation);[19] in fact, it's a row literal, though SQL doesn't use that term.[20] *Note:* Actually, the keyword ROW in an SQL row value constructor invocation is optional, and in practice is almost always omitted (probably because earlier versions of SQL didn't support it). Thus, the foregoing example could be simplified slightly to just:

```
SET PRV = ( PNO('P1') , NAME('Nut') , COLOR('Red') ,
                          WEIGHT(12.0) , 'London' ) ;
```

The parentheses are required, though.

Here's a slightly more complicated example:

```
SET PRV = ( P WHERE PNO = PNO('P1') ) ;
```

In this case the expression on the right side isn't a row selector invocation, it's a *row subquery*— i.e., it's an SQL table expression in parentheses that's acting as a row expression. Simplifying slightly, the table *t* returned by that table expression is required to contain exactly one row *r*; so long as it does, *t* is coerced to *r*, and *r* can then be assigned to the row variable referenced on the

---

[19] SQL uses the term *constructor* in numerous contexts. However, I have to say that, at least in contexts like the one at hand, I find that term rather inappropriate, suggesting as it does that values don't simply exist as I said they did in Chapter 2 but have to be "constructed." I prefer our term *selector*.

[20] Incidentally, the example illustrates the somewhat peculiar fact that, while the fields of a given row type *RT* have names (and those field names are explicitly considered to be part of the type), literals of that type *RT don't* have such names; instead, they consist simply of a sequence of literals of the applicable field types. (In the example, the literal on the right side of the assignment denotes a value of the row type that's the type of row variable PRV.) Contrast the situation with tuple types and literals in **Tutorial D**. (Incidentally, it follows from the foregoing that, even without inheritance, the very same row literal in SQL might denote a value of any number of different row types, and "the" intended type of such a literal can't be determined in general just by looking at it. The consequences of this state of affairs are unclear.)

left side. A **Tutorial D** analog of this assignment would look like this (note the explicit extraction here of the pertinent tuple from the single-tuple relation containing it):

```
PRV := TUPLE FROM ( P WHERE PNO = PNO('P1') ) ;
```

But SQL has no explicit counterpart to **Tutorial D**'s TUPLE FROM operator as such.
I turn now to row equality comparisons.[21] Here's a simple example:

```
PRV = ( PNO('P1') , NAME('Nut') , COLOR('Red') ,
                         WEIGHT(12.0) , 'London' )
```

By way of another example, consider the following SELECT expression, which contains an explicit row equality comparison in the WHERE clause:

```
SELECT PNO
FROM   P
WHERE  ( COLOR , CITY ) = ( COLOR('Red') , 'London' )
```

This SELECT expression is logically equivalent to the following:

```
SELECT PNO
FROM   P
WHERE  COLOR = COLOR('Red') AND CITY = 'London'
```

I'll give one more example, in order to illustrate another point. Consider the following CREATE TABLE statement:

```
CREATE TABLE NADDR
       ( NAME VARCHAR(25) NOT NULL ,
         ADDR ROW ( STREET CHAR(50) ,
                    CITY   VARCHAR(20) ,
                    STATE  CHAR(2) ,
                    ZIP    CHAR(5) ) NOT NULL ,
         UNIQUE ( NAME ) ) ;
```

Observe in particular that column ADDR of table NADDR is defined to be of a certain row type, with fields STREET, CITY, STATE, and ZIP. (In general, fields of a given row type can be of any type whatsoever, including other row types in particular.) References to such fields make use of dot qualification as illustrated in the following retrieval example (the syntax is *<exp>.<field name>*, where *<exp>* is a row expression and *<field name>* is the name of a field of the row type of that expression):

---

[21] For completeness I should mention that SQL row comparisons actually support not just equality but all six of the usual comparison operators: "=", "<>" (not equals), "<", ">". "<=", and ">=". The full details are quite complicated, however (especially when coercions and nulls are taken into account), and I therefore omit them here. You can find the specifics if you're interested in the book mentioned in the introduction to this chapter, *A Guide to the SQL Standard* (4th edition, Addison-Wesley, 1997), by Hugh Darwen and myself.

```
SELECT  NT.NAME
FROM    NADDR AS NT
WHERE   NT.ADDR.STATE = 'CA'
```

NT here is a correlation name. For technical reasons, having to do with avoiding a certain syntactic ambiguity that might otherwise occur, SQL requires explicit correlation name qualifiers to be used in field references like the one in the example (NT.ADDR.STATE).[22]

Here by contrast is an update example:[23]

```
UPDATE  NADDR
SET     ADDR.STATE = 'NH'
WHERE   NAME = 'Joe' ;
```

Observe that this latter example doesn't use correlation names at all.

> *Aside:* Two points of detail here. First, since a field within a row type can itself be of some row type, field references can involve lots of dots (as in, e.g., R1.F2.F3.F4.F5). Second, observe that I've defined a column constraint (NOT NULL) on column ADDR in the CREATE TABLE statement, in order to prevent nulls from appearing as entries in the column in question. In general, however, such a constraint won't prevent nulls from appearing in *fields within* entries in the column in question. (Note that a row with nulls in some of its fields—even in all of its fields!—is logically distinct from a null row. A NOT NULL constraint on column ADDR will ensure that no entry in that column either is null or has a null in every field, but it won't prevent such an entry from having nulls in some of its fields and not in others.) If we want to prohibit nulls entirely, therefore, we'll have to specify a series of additional constraints—probably as part of the pertinent CREATE TABLE statement—along the lines of the one shown here:
>
> ```
> CHECK ( ADDR.STREET IS NOT NULL )
> ```
>
> What we can't do is attach a NOT NULL specification to the definition of field STREET as such, as part of the definition of column ADDR. *End of aside.*

---

[22] In certain contexts, at any rate, but not in others! The very next example (an UPDATE example) illustrates this point. Further details are beyond the scope of this book.

[23] Actually this example seems to be illegal, because according to the standard ADDR.STATE doesn't seem to be a legal SET clause target. However, I presume this state of affairs is just an oversight, and I choose to ignore it here.

Table Types

So much for row types; what about table types? Interestingly, SQL doesn't really support the concept of a table type at all;[24] more specifically, it doesn't support a TABLE type generator (or table type constructor, as SQL would probably call it). In other words, it has nothing directly analogous to **Tutorial D**'s RELATION type generator. Of course, it does have a mechanism, CREATE TABLE, for defining what by rights should be called table variables. Here's an example (it's an SQL analog of the **Tutorial D** definition of relvar S from the suppliers-and-parts database in Chapter 1):

```
CREATE  TABLE  S
     (  SNO      SNO                   NOT  NULL ,
        SNAME    NAME                  NOT  NULL ,
        STATUS   INTEGER               NOT  NULL ,
        CITY     VARCHAR(20)  NOT  NULL ,
        UNIQUE  (  SNO  )  )  ;
```

Note carefully, however, that there's nothing in this example—no sequence of linguistic tokens—that can logically be labeled "an invocation of the TABLE type generator." (This fact might become more apparent when you realize that the specification UNIQUE (SNO), which defines a certain integrity constraint on suppliers, doesn't have to come after the column definitions but can appear almost anywhere—e.g., between the definitions of columns SNAME and STATUS. Not to mention those NOT NULL specifications on the individual column definitions, which also define certain integrity constraints.) In fact, to the extent that the variable S can be regarded (in SQL) as having any type at all, that type is nothing more than *bag of rows*, where the rows in question have fields of types (in left to right order) SNO, NAME, INTEGER, and VARCHAR(20).

As a matter of fact, SQL's treatment of tables is really quite strange when you come to think about it. As Melton says, quite correctly, "the table is SQL's most fundamental data structure"; yet, to repeat, there's no table type generator! One consequence of this state of affairs is that no column of any table in SQL can be of a "table type"—in other words, SQL doesn't support table valued columns.[25] Further evidence that SQL doesn't really regard tables as "first class citizens" is provided by the fact that it fails to provide direct support for either table assignment or table equality comparisons. Of course, it's true that workarounds are available for such operations—but workarounds shouldn't be necessary in the first place.

---

[24] Despite the fact that it does support something it calls "typed tables." We'll be looking at these in some detail in the subsection "Typed Tables," later. The term is hardly very appropriate, however, because (as we'll see) if *TT* is a "typed table" that has been defined to be "of type *T*," then *TT* is certainly *not* of type *T*, and neither are its rows.

[25] It does support columns that contain values that are multisets [*i.e., bags*] of rows, but such values aren't tables in the SQL sense (and such columns therefore aren't table valued columns), because SQL's table operators don't apply to them.

Structured Types

Recall now that SQL supports two kinds of user defined types, DISTINCT types (discussed in the previous section) and structured types.[26] Here are a couple of examples of structured type definitions:

```
CREATE TYPE POINT
  AS ( X FLOAT , Y FLOAT ) FINAL ;

CREATE TYPE LINESEG
  AS ( BEGIN POINT , END POINT ) NOT FINAL ;
```

(Actually the second example fails because BEGIN and END are reserved words in SQL, but I choose to ignore that detail here.) In its simplest form, then—i.e., ignoring a variety of optional features—the syntax for creating a structured type is:

```
CREATE TYPE <type name>
  AS ( <attribute commalist> ) [ NOT ] FINAL ;
```

Points arising:

1. Note that "STRUCTURED" doesn't appear as a keyword in the definition. Instead, if the keyword AS is followed by an opening parenthesis,[27] then the type being defined is a structured type; otherwise it's a DISTINCT type.

2. FINAL means this type can't have any proper subtypes; NOT FINAL means it can. Purely for the sake of the example—not for any really good reason—I've specified FINAL for type POINT and NOT FINAL for type LINESEG.

3. The *<attribute commalist>*—which mustn't be empty—specifies the physical representation of values of the type being defined.[28] Each *<attribute>* consists of an *<attribute name>* followed by a *<type name>*. (Note, therefore, that in SQL tables have columns; rows have fields; and structured types have attributes.)

---

[26] According to Melton, structured types in SQL were originally called abstract data types or ADTs.

[27] Or if (a) the keyword UNDER appears following the *<type name>* (see the section "The SQL Approach to Inheritance," later), or if (b) the AS specification is omitted entirely (see the discussion of IM Prescription 20 near the end of this chapter).

[28] Some might dispute my use of the qualifier *physical* here, but I stand by it (despite the fact that the standard says, paraphrasing slightly, that "physical representations of values of user defined types are undefined"). Incidentally, Melton appears to agree with me on this point. On page 56 of his book, he gives an example of changing the representation (i.e., the attributes) of a certain type, and goes on to say "Perhaps obviously, [the] data in the database would have to be converted to [the new representation], but that's not relevant to the example." Clearly, such conversion will be necessary only if representations are physical. And on page 31 he says "the fact that [SQL's] object model doesn't allow for private attributes, but only for public attributes, makes it impossible to completely hide the implementation details of types"—implying, again, that the attributes in question constitute the physical implementation of the type in question.

4. For each attribute, the system will automatically define two operators, one *observer function* and one *mutator function* (actually they're methods, but SQL refers to them as functions), that provide functionality somewhat analogous to that of **Tutorial D**'s THE_ operators and (in effect) pseudovariables. For example, if LS, P, and Z are SQL variables of types LINESEG, POINT, and FLOAT, respectively, then all of the following assignments are valid:

```
SET Z = P.X ;                    /* "observes" X attribute of P */

SET P.X = Z ;                    /* "mutates" X attribute of P  */

SET X = LS.BEGIN.X ;             /* "observes" X attribute of   */
                                 /* BEGIN attribute of LS        */

SET LS.BEGIN.X = Z ;             /* "mutates" X attribute of     */
                                 /* BEGIN attribute of LS        */
```

Note: SQL's mutators aren't actually mutators in the conventional object sense of the term (i.e., they aren't update operators; in fact, of course, as I've already said, they're functions, and functions in general are read-only). However, they (i.e., SQL's mutators) can be used in such a way as to achieve conventional mutator functionality. For example, "SET P.X = Z"—which, believe it or not, doesn't explicitly contain a mutator invocation—is defined to be shorthand for "SET P = P.X(Z)," which does.[29] But I'll continue to talk about mutators as if they really were update operators, for simplicity.

5. No selectors are provided automatically, but somewhat analogous functionality can be achieved as follows. First of all, I need to explain that given a structured type *T*, SQL automatically provides what it calls a *constructor function* for *T*,[30] having that same name *T*. It's important to understand, however, that the constructor function for type *T* returns the same value on every invocation: namely, that value of type *T* whose attributes all have the applicable default value.[31] For example, the constructor function invocation

---

[29] To elaborate briefly: The expression P.X(Z) denotes an invocation of the mutator called X, and P and Z denote the subject argument and an additional argument, respectively, to that invocation. That invocation returns a point with x coordinate equal to the x coordinate of the point currently contained in P and y coordinate equal to Z, and the SET statement then causes that point to be assigned to P.

[30] So long as *T* is instantiable, that is (see the section "The SQL Approach to Inheritance," later). *Note:* As mentioned in footnote 16 (and despite the nomenclature), constructor functions, like observer functions and mutator functions before them, are actually methods; unlike other methods, however, they—constructor functions, that is—have no subject parameter.

[31] The default value for a given attribute can be specified along with the pertinent <*attribute*> within the definition of the pertinent structured type. If no such default value is specified explicitly, the default value—the "default default"—will be null. *Note:* For reasons beyond the scope of this book, the default must be null if the type of the attribute in question is either a row type or a user defined type. As a consequence, the constructor function invocation LINESEG( ), for example, will necessarily return a kind of "pseudo" line segment whose BEGIN and END components are both "null points."

```
POINT ( )
```

returns the point with default X and Y values. Now, however, we can invoke the X and Y mutators to replace the result of that constructor function invocation by the point we really want. Moreover, we can bundle up the initial construction and those subsequent mutations into a single expression, as in this example:

```
POINT ( ) . X ( 5.0 ) . Y ( 2.5 )
```

This expression overall returns the point with cartesian coordinates (5.0,2.5). *Explanation:* First, POINT( ) is, as we've just seen, a POINT constructor function invocation, and it returns—at least, let's agree it does for the sake of the example—what we might think of as a "pseudopoint," with x and y coordinates both null.[32] Second, the result of that invocation becomes the subject argument to the X mutator invocation, which effectively replaces that pseudopoint by another, this one having x coordinate 5.0 and y coordinate null. Third, the result of *that* invocation becomes the subject argument to the Y mutator invocation, which effectively replaces that second pseudopoint by a real point with x coordinate 5.0 and y coordinate 2.5.

Here's a more complex example (and I'll leave it to you to explain this one to yourself to your own satisfaction):

```
LINESEG ( ) . BEGIN ( POINT ( ) . X ( 5.0 ) . Y ( 2.5 ) )
            . END   ( POINT ( ) . X ( 7.3 ) . Y ( 0.8 ) )
```

Aside: Actually there's another way of obtaining "selector functionality," one that you might find a little more user friendly. First, in the definition of the pertinent type, we can give the signature for a *constructor method*,[33] having (necessarily) the same name as the type in question. For example:

```
CREATE TYPE POINT
    AS ( X FLOAT , Y FLOAT ) FINAL
        CONSTRUCTOR METHOD POINT ( X FLOAT , Y FLOAT ) RETURNS POINT
        SELF AS RESULT ;
```

(Note the required SELF AS RESULT specification.) Next we define the code for that method:

---

[32] Note that a "pseudopoint" with both coordinates null is not itself considered to be null (i.e., it's not "a null point"). Compare the remarks earlier in this chapter on the logical difference between a null row and a row all of whose fields are null.

[33] Not to be confused with a constructor function, naturally, despite the fact that (as previously noted) a constructor function is actually a method.

```
CREATE CONSTRUCTOR METHOD POINT ( X FLOAT , Y FLOAT ) RETURNS POINT
      FOR POINT
      BEGIN
         SET SELF.X = X ;
         SET SELF.Y = Y ;
         RETURN SELF ;
      END ;
```

And now the expression

```
NEW POINT ( X , Y )
```

will return the point whose *x* and *y* coordinates are equal to the values of variables X and Y (whatever those values might be), respectively. *Explanation:* The keyword NEW causes (a) the POINT constructor *function* to be invoked and then (b) the value returned by that invocation—viz., a pseudopoint with *x* and *y* coordinates both null—to be passed as the subject argument to an invocation of the POINT constructor *method*.

By the way, I hope I haven't confused you with all the different X's and Y's in the foregoing example. Just to spell the differences out, though: The X and Y in the signature and in the first line of the constructor method definition (also on the right side of the two assignments) are parameters; the X and Y in the expressions SELF.X and SELF.Y are attributes of the POINT type; and the X and Y in the NEW expression are SQL variables of type POINT. *End of aside.*

6. The comparison operators that apply to values of a given structured type are specified by means of a separate CREATE ORDERING statement.[34] Here are two examples:

```
CREATE ORDERING FOR POINT EQUALS ONLY BY STATE ;
```

```
CREATE ORDERING FOR LINESEG EQUALS ONLY BY STATE ;
```

EQUALS ONLY means that "=" and "<>" (not equals) are the only valid comparison operators for values of the type in question. The alternative to EQUALS ONLY is FULL, meaning that "<", "<=", etc., are allowed in addition to "=" and "<>". BY STATE means that two values *v1* and *v2* of the type in question are equal if and only if every attribute of *v1* has the same value as the corresponding attribute of *v2*. (Alternatives to BY STATE are possible but are beyond the scope of this book.) *Note:* If a given structured type has no associated "ordering," then no comparisons at all, *not even equality comparisons*, can be

---

[34] Note that those comparison operators, including "=" in particular, are still specified via CREATE *ORDERING*—emphasis added—even if ordering as such (meaning, basically, support for "<") doesn't apply! Note too that CREATE TYPE and CREATE ORDERING are separate statements, but it's not possible to have more than one CREATE ORDERING for a given CREATE TYPE.

performed on values of that type—a state of affairs with far reaching consequences, as you might imagine.

7. In addition to the operators already mentioned (observers, mutators, constructor functions and methods, assignments, and comparisons), other operators can be defined as required.

8. Strong typing applies to structured types.

Let's take a look at how structured types might be used. Here again, repeated from near the beginning of this subsection, is the original definition for the structured type POINT:

```
CREATE TYPE POINT
   AS ( X FLOAT , Y FLOAT ) FINAL ;
```

This type can now be used in the definitions of SQL variables and columns in SQL tables. For example, let's extend our previous definition of table NADDR from the subsection "Row Types" to include an additional column called LOCATION, whose value within a given row is the geographic point on the map corresponding to the ADDR value in that row:

```
CREATE TABLE NADDR
      ( NAME ...             NOT NULL ,    /* type omitted for simplicity   */
        ADDR ROW ( ... )     NOT NULL ,    /* fields omitted for simplicity */
        LOCATION POINT       NOT NULL ,
        UNIQUE ( NAME ) ) ;
```

Column LOCATION is of type POINT,[35] and we can access the components—i.e., values of the POINT attributes—of a given LOCATION value using dot qualification syntax, more or less as if that LOCATION value were just a simple row value. Here are a couple of examples:[36]

```
SELECT NT.LOCATION.X , NT.LOCATION.Y
FROM   NADDR AS NT
WHERE  NT.NAME = 'Joe'

UPDATE NADDR
SET    LOCATION.X = 7.3 ,      /* Note: 7.3 coerced to type FLOAT! */
       LOCATION.Y = 0.8        /* Note: 0.8 coerced to type FLOAT! */
WHERE  NAME = 'Joe' ;
```

---

[35] I'm assuming for the sake of the example, not very realistically, that "geographic points on the map"—i.e., values of column LOCATION—are represented in terms of cartesian coordinates instead of conventional map coordinates, such as latitude and longitude.

[36] Note that the SELECT example not only uses dot qualifications, it uses explicit correlation names as qualifiers (such explicit names being required in this context, at least in the SELECT clause though not necessarily in the WHERE clause). By contrast, the UPDATE example doesn't use correlation names at all. Further details of these matters are beyond the scope of this book.

When used as in these examples, therefore, an SQL structured type effectively behaves rather like a row type, as you can see. Note in particular that, at least in the context at hand, structured types certainly do seem to be nonscalar,[37] inasmuch as they certainly do have user visible components—again, just like a row type. The only differences are that:

- The components are called attributes instead of fields.

- The structured type, unlike the analogous row type, has a separately and explicitly declared name (POINT, in the example). I'll have a little more to say regarding this state of affairs at the very end of the subsection "Typed Tables" immediately following.

Typed Tables

So far, then, SQL's structured types look as if they might not be too hard to understand. But there's more to come, much more. The crucial point is this: SQL also allows a base table[38] to be defined to be "OF" some structured type, in which case all kinds of further considerations come into play. In order to illustrate and discuss some of those further considerations, let me first extend the definition of type POINT slightly, as follows (note the third line in particular):

```
CREATE TYPE POINT
   AS ( X FLOAT , Y FLOAT ) FINAL
       REF IS SYSTEM GENERATED ;
```

Now I can define a table to be "OF" this type—for example:

```
CREATE TABLE POINTS OF POINT
     ( REF IS PID SYSTEM GENERATED ) ;
```

Explanation:

1. REF is a scalar type generator, and the corresponding generated types are called reference types (loosely, "REF types"). More precisely, if a structured type T is defined with a "REF option"—e.g., REF IS SYSTEM GENERATED[39]—then the corresponding generated type is called REF(T), and values of that type (loosely, "REF values") serve as unique identifiers for rows within tables, if any, that are defined to be "OF" type T. In the example, then, the

---

[37] I.e., they're not "encapsulated," to use the jargon. In other words, as noted in footnote 50 in Chapter 21, perhaps we could say they've been "decapsulated" (assuming they were ever encapsulated in the first place, which I'm not sure I really believe).

[38] Or a view—but details of the view case are beyond the scope of this book. For simplicity, I'll take the unqualified term *table* throughout the rest of this chapter to mean a base table specifically, barring explicit statements to the contrary.

[39] Other REF options—e.g., REF IS USER GENERATED—are also available, but the details are beyond the scope of this book. *Note:* Actually, REF IS SYSTEM GENERATED is the default. In the example, therefore, I could have left the original type definition for type POINT unchanged.

system automatically generates a type called REF (POINT), whose values are references to rows within tables, if any, that are defined to be "OF" type POINT.[40]

2. In the example, table POINTS is a table that has been defined to be "OF" some structured type (type POINT, of course, in this particular case). That table is thus an example of what the standard calls, not very aptly, both a *typed table* and a *referenceable table*. To spell the point out: All typed tables are referenceable tables, and all referenceable tables are typed tables. As the standard puts it:

    A table ... whose row type is derived from a structured type is called a *typed table*. Only a base table or a view can be a typed table.

    And elsewhere:

    A referenceable table is necessarily also a *typed table* ... A typed table is called a referenceable table.

    But a "referenceable table" is actually *not* referenceable—rather, its rows are. Indeed, it's important to understand that a row in a "typed" or "referenceable" table is the *only* construct in SQL that can and does have a REF value to identify it. Thus, to say a given table is "referenceable" is to say that (a) its rows have certain identifying REF values associated with them, and (b) those REF values can then be used elsewhere—in particular, in rows in tables elsewhere in the database—as references to the rows in question.[41]

    Note: I'll show in just a few moments how the association is established between those REF values and the rows in question, and how those REF values can then be used to reference those rows.

3. Let "typed table" *TT* be "OF" type *T*. Then that keyword "OF" is really not very appropriate, because (as mentioned in footnote 24) table *TT* is actually *not* "of" type *T*, and neither are its rows.[42] To elaborate:

---

[40] There seems to be some confusion in the standard—not to say inconsistency—as to when the generation of type REF (POINT) actually occurs, but for present purposes you can take it to be when the first or only table "OF" type POINT is created.

[41] Be aware that SQL uses the terminology of referencing in two quite different senses. One is as sketched here. The other, and older, sense has to do with foreign keys—a foreign key value in one row is said to reference the row that contains the corresponding target key value. I'll have more to say about foreign keys vs. REF values later in this chapter.

[42] Which accounts for all of those quotation marks, of course, surrounding "OF" and "typed table," in the text prior to this point. I'll drop them from this point forward because I know how annoying they can be—but I do wish language designers could be a little more careful in their choice of terminology and keywords. Quite apart from anything else, poor choices make the language just that much harder to teach, learn, and understand.

a.   First of all—but please note that this first point is purely hypothetical!—if table *TT* had just one column and that column were actually of type *T*, then we might reasonably say something to the effect that the table is of type TABLE(*T*) and its rows are of type ROW(*T*). (Not in SQL, though, because "TABLE(*T*)" and "ROW(*T*)" aren't legitimate SQL constructs.)

b.   But, in general, table *TT* doesn't have just one column. Rather, it has one column for each attribute of *T*, plus one additional column (see point c. below). Thus, table POINTS in particular has columns called X and Y, both of type FLOAT and both of them explicitly visible to the user,[43] together with the additional column discussed under point c. below. What it most definitely doesn't have is a column of type POINT.

Aside: If we want to impose a NOT NULL constraint on those columns X and Y— which of course I would strongly suggest we do want to do—we can do so by extending the REF option specification within the CREATE TABLE statement for table POINTS to contain some appropriate "column options," as shown here:

```
CREATE TABLE POINTS OF POINT
    ( REF IS PID SYSTEM GENERATED
      X WITH OPTIONS NOT NULL
      Y WITH OPTIONS NOT NULL ) ;
```

And if we additionally want to say that no two rows existing in POINTS at the same time have the same X value and the same Y value:

```
CREATE TABLE POINTS OF POINT
    ( REF IS PID SYSTEM GENERATED
      X WITH OPTIONS NOT NULL
      Y WITH OPTIONS NOT NULL
      UNIQUE ( X , Y ) ) ;
```

We could even effectively bundle these NOT NULL and uniqueness specifications together into a single PRIMARY KEY specification, like this:

```
CREATE TABLE POINTS OF POINT
    ( REF IS PID SYSTEM GENERATED
      PRIMARY KEY ( X , Y ) ) ;
```

---

[43] So in this context once again, the structured type definitely seems to be nonscalar (or "decapsulated")—again, just like a row type. (In the case at hand, in other words, the user must be explicitly aware that (a) type POINT has attributes called X and Y and (b) those attributes are both of type FLOAT.)

For reasons that aren't entirely clear, however, such bundling is permitted only if the pertinent table has no proper supertable. In other words, only root tables are allowed to have primary keys as such[44] (see the section "The SQL Approach to Inheritance," later). But note the implication: A self-referencing column—see point c. below—isn't necessarily regarded as constituting the primary key as such (if any) for the pertinent table. (It is, however, automatically considered to be both UNIQUE and NOT NULL.) *End of aside.*

c. As noted under point b. above, table *TT* has another column as well: namely, a column of the applicable REF type, REF(*T*). However, the syntax for defining that column is not the normal column definition syntax but instead looks like this:

```
REF IS <column name> SYSTEM GENERATED
```

This extra column is called a *self-referencing column*, and it's used to contain those unique IDs or "references" for the rows of the table being defined.[45] The ID for a given row is assigned (and placed in that row in the self-referencing column position) when the row is first inserted into the table, and it remains associated with that row until the row is deleted. In the example, therefore, table POINTS actually has *three* columns (PID, X, and Y, in that left to right order), not just two. (Column PID is the self-referencing column, of course.) It follows that what the standard calls the "row type" of that table—see the first quote from the standard under point 2 above—is precisely this:

```
ROW ( PID REF ( POINT ) , X FLOAT , Y FLOAT )
```

d. It's worth noting in passing that the attachment of a unique ID to a given row—i.e., placing a REF value in the self-referencing column position when the row in question is inserted—is regarded by some people as transforming that row into an *object*.[46] Nothing else in SQL is regarded as an "object."

---

[44] *Root table* isn't an SQL term; rather, such tables are called *maximal supertables*. However, I'll stay with our familiar "root" terminology in this chapter.

[45] Don't be confused—the CREATE *TYPE* statement specifies REF IS SYSTEM GENERATED, the CREATE *TABLE* statement specifies REF <column name> IS SYSTEM GENERATED. Incidentally, it's not at all clear why it should be necessary to define the table to be OF some structured type in the first place, instead of just defining an appropriate column in the usual way, in order to obtain this "unique ID" functionality, but that's the way it is.

[46] For example: "Once an instance [*sic*] of a structured type has a unique identity, then it really behaves exactly as an object is expected to behave in an object-oriented environment. For all practical purposes, it *is* an object" (Melton, page 30—but see footnote 14!). Also: "[A] typed table is, in many ways, no different than an ordinary SQL table, but it has the important characteristic that its rows can be manipulated through method invocations in addition to ordinary SQL data manipulation statements" (Melton, page 109). Note, however, that these remarks of Melton's shouldn't be construed as meaning that a row from a table that has been defined to be OF type *T* can be used as an argument to an operator invocation where the corresponding parameter has declared type *T*, because it can't.

Now, I have to say I think there's something very problematic going on with all of this. Of course, the basic idea is intuitively straightforward—the idea, that is, that any given row *r* has a unique ID, and that ID never changes so long as *r* exists in the database. (It's never reused, either.) But what exactly does that phrase "any given row *r*" mean? For one thing, is *r* a value, or is it a variable? Well, it can't be a value, because then it never could change (in fact, like all values, it would be self-identifying, and it wouldn't need any form of additional ID). So it must be a variable; indeed, it *is* a variable, because as just indicated SQL allows it to be updated.[47] Moreover, when those REF values are used as references to the rows in question, then they're acting as nothing but *pointers* to those rows.[48] So we're back to that business, discussed briefly in the previous chapter, of variables containing variables: specifically, to the notion—I would say the logical absurdity—of table variables containing row variables.[49]

By the way, another good question to ponder in this connection is as follows (I touched on this question, somewhat indirectly, in the answer to Exercise 21.7 in Chapter 21): Is this notion of table variables containing row variables consistent in any way with the notion that table (or relation) assignment is the only update operator we need?

I have another question too. When someone says a certain REF value is being used to identify a certain row, I want to ask: Which row is it, exactly, that's that "certain row"? Surely, the only possible answer to this question is: It's the row identified by that particular REF value. (Certainly SQL doesn't require any other kind of "row identifier.") So it seems to me that, as well as involving a logical absurdity as noted above, there's something circular about the whole idea.

Aside: I suppose it *might* be possible to rescue the idea, in part, by inventing a scheme along the following lines: 1. Assume the existence of operations that (a) insert a single row into a table and (b) update a specific row within a table. 2. When row *r* is inserted

---

[47] Further evidence that it must be a variable is provided by the fact that those REF values are really just slightly abstract *addresses*, and values don't have addresses, variables do (recall from Chapter 2 that values don't have location, variables do).

[48] Some might dispute my claim here that those REF values are acting as pointers, but I think the discussions in the next subsection support it rather strongly, and I stand by it. (I note in passing that certain remarks of Melton's indicate his agreement with me on this issue, too.) Of course, if they *are* pointers, then the tables containing them can't possibly represent relations (or relvars) in the relational model sense. Indeed, it's not clear why such tables are supported in SQL at all; certainly there seems to be no useful functionality that can be achieved with them that can't equally well—in fact, better—be achieved without them. And in connection with *that* issue, I'd like to mention something else, too. A tutorial overview of SQL:1999 ("SQL:1999, Formerly Known as SQL3," by Andrew Eisenberg and Jim Melton) appeared in *ACM SIGMOD Record 28*, No. 1 (March 1999). Observing that, while it certainly did describe the object features of SQL, the article did nothing to justify them, Darwen and I wrote to the then editor of *SIGMOD Record* as follows: "With reference to [the subject article]—in particular, with reference to the sections *Objects ... Finally* and *Using REF Types*—we have a question: What useful purpose is served by the features described in those sections? To be more specific, what useful functionality is provided that can't be obtained via features already found in SQL:1992?" Our letter was never published, however, and to this day our question remains unanswered.

[49] What's more, those row variables (regardless of whether or not they're considered to be contained in table variables) constitute a violation of Codd's *Information Principle*; which states that the only kind of variable permitted in a relational database is the relvar (i.e., the relation variable) specifically. See Appendix B or my book *SQL and Relational Theory: How to Write Accurate SQL Code* (3rd edition, O'Reilly, 2015) for a discussion of some of the (serious!) consequences of such a violation.

into table *T*, it's given a unique identifier (perhaps the timestamp of the insertion). 3. That identifier never changes, even when the row is updated.

Given such a scheme, however, it still wouldn't really be rows as such that had unique identifiers, it would be *row insertion events*. (Note that two rows *r1* and *r2* might be identical in all respects except for the time of their insertion.) And I'm not at all comfortable with the importance such a scheme would attach to the "update row" and (more particularly) "insert row" operations—especially since there aren't any such operations in the relational model, nor is there any logical need for them. What's more, of course, the whole scheme still involves the notion of "variables containing variables," with all that that entails. *End of aside.*

Of course, in order to be able to proceed with the rest of this chapter, I'm simply going to have to overlook all of the foregoing concerns. But I'm not at all happy about it.

One final point to close this subsection: As I've had occasion to point out several times in previous chapters (see, e.g., Chapter 2), there's deliberately no explicit "define tuple type" operator in **Tutorial D**; instead, there's a TUPLE type generator, which can be invoked in (e.g.) the definition of a tuple variable. As a consequence, the only names tuple types have in **Tutorial D** are names of the form

```
TUPLE { A1 T1 , A2 T2 , ..., An Tn }
```

while tuples as such take the form

```
TUPLE { A1 v1 , A2 v2 , ..., An vn }
```

One important consequence of this discipline is that it's immediately clear in **Tutorial D** when two tuple types are one and the same, and when two tuples are of the same type.

Now, I observed in the subsection "Row Types" near the beginning of the present section that row types in SQL are similar (somewhat) to **Tutorial D**'s tuple types in the foregoing respect. But structured types are different; there *is* an explicit "define structured type" operator (viz., CREATE TYPE), and structured types do have additional and explicit names. For example, consider the following SQL definitions:

```
CREATE TYPE POINT1 AS ( X FLOAT , Y FLOAT ) FINAL ;
CREATE TYPE POINT2 AS ( X FLOAT , Y FLOAT ) FINAL ;

DECLARE V1 POINT1 ;
DECLARE V2 POINT2 ;
```

POINT1 and POINT2 are distinct (not DISTINCT!) types; thus, variables V1 and V2 are of different types, and they can't be compared with one another, and neither can be assigned to the other. *Note:* Despite the foregoing state of affairs, you might be thinking that at least every value of either type is also a value of the other. However, such thinking is erroneous. It's true that every value of either type *has the same representation* as some value of the other—but the values as such aren't the same. Rather, values of V1 are values of type POINT1, values of V2 are values of type POINT2, and no value of type POINT1 is a value of type POINT2 and no value of type POINT2 is a value of type POINT1. (Also, if we define tables T1 and T2 to be of types POINT1 and POINT2, respectively, then those two tables—even though they have "the same" columns X and Y—have different row types, because of those self-referencing columns. Thanks to Hugh Darwen for this observation.)

Operations Involving Typed Tables

Recall this definition for table NADDR from a few pages back:

```
CREATE TABLE NADDR
     ( NAME ...            NOT NULL ,    /* type omitted for simplicity    */
       ADDR ROW ( ... ) NOT NULL ,      /* fields omitted for simplicity */
       LOCATION POINT   NOT NULL ,
       UNIQUE ( NAME ) ) ;
```

Now let's revise this definition so that column LOCATION contains, not values of the structured type POINT as such, but pointers to rows in table POINTS instead:

```
CREATE TABLE NADDR
     ( NAME ...                                 NOT NULL ,
       ADDR ROW ( ... )                         NOT NULL ,
       LOCATION REF ( POINT ) SCOPE POINTS NOT NULL ,
       UNIQUE ( NAME ) ) ;
```

Explanation:

1. First of all, note that table NADDR is still a regular table, not a typed table—a table doesn't have to be a typed table in order to have a column of some REF type. (It has to be, and in fact is, a typed table if and only if the column in question is a self-referencing column.)

2. Values of column LOCATION are defined to be values of type REF (POINT).[50]

3. The specification SCOPE POINTS limits the REF values appearing in column LOCATION of table NADDR to ones appearing in column PID of table POINTS, thereby guaranteeing that the REF values in question do indeed point to rows currently appearing in table

---

[50] But this raises a question: What does the result from a query of the form SELECT LOCATION FROM NADDR look like? More specifically, if the result is displayed, what do the displayed LOCATION values look like? Are there any REF literals? (*Answer:* No, there aren't. The only thing the standard has to say about such matters is this: "In a host variable, a REF value is materialized as an *N*-octet value, where *N* is implementation defined.")

POINTS as such.[51] (The table named in a SCOPE clause must be a typed table specifically. No REF value can ever appear in the self-referencing column of two or more such tables—at least, not so long as the tables in question are root tables.) "Currently appearing" here means, of course, that if some expression involving column LOCATION is evaluated at time *t*, then every value of that column that's relevant to that specific evaluation is a value that appears in column PID of table POINTS at that same time *t*.

Now suppose we want to retrieve the *x* and *y* coordinates of the location for Joe. What we need to do, then, is (a) start with the row for Joe in table NADDR, (b) follow the pointer from Joe's LOCATION column value over to the corresponding row in table POINTS, and then (c) extract the X and Y column values from that POINTS row. So we need an operator that will "follow a pointer." In SQL, that operator is called *dereference*, and it's written in concrete syntactic form as a hyphen followed by a "greater than" symbol.[52] Here then is an SQL formulation of the specified query:

```
SELECT  LOCATION -> X , LOCATION -> Y
FROM    NADDR
WHERE   NAME = 'Joe'
```

This expression yields a result of two columns, both of type FLOAT, called X and Y, respectively. The two subexpressions in the SELECT clause might be read as "the X in the row that LOCATION points to" and "the Y in the row that LOCATION points to," respectively.

    Incidentally, note that what appears following the dereferencing symbol is, technically, an attribute name, not a column reference. Thus, the following, which might have been thought to have been an expansion or clarification of the expression shown above, will actually fail on a syntax error:[53]

```
SELECT  LOCATION -> POINTS.X , LOCATION -> POINTS.Y    /* syntax error! */
FROM    NADDR
WHERE   NAME = 'Joe'
```

And while I'm talking about syntax, let me point out another little oddity: namely, that the selected items (i.e., the ones mentioned in the SELECT clause), in expressions like the one just shown, don't actually come "from" the table mentioned in the FROM clause.

    Aside: As a matter of fact SQL also supports another dereferencing operator, explicitly called DEREF. Here's an example:

---

[51] Except that *dangling references* can occur. In SQL, a dangling reference is a REF value that points to a row that no longer exists (in the example, such a situation can arise if suitable precautions aren't taken when a row is deleted from table POINTS). The result of "dereferencing" such a reference—see further discussion in a few moments—is defined to be null.

[52] We've met this operator before, in Chapter 13, where it was called DEREF.

[53] Even though the expression SELECT POINTS.X, POINTS.Y FROM POINTS is legal!

```
SELECT DEREF ( LOCATION ) AS JOE_POINT
FROM    NADDR
WHERE   NAME = 'Joe'
```

Technically, this expression yields a result table of just one column, called JOE_POINT, of type POINT. However, the significance of this fact—the fact, that is, that the result table has just that one column, a state of affairs that appears to constitute the sole situation in SQL in which it might be argued that structured types are "encapsulated" or scalar—is unclear, to say the least, given that the observer and mutator functions associated with type POINT can and must be used to expose the X and Y coordinates of JOE_POINT values within rows in that result table. *End of aside.*

What about updates on table NADDR? Well, DELETEs are straightforward, and there's nothing special to say about them. INSERTs are another matter, though. The question is: When we insert a row into that table, what do we do about the necessary LOCATION value? Well, languages that, like SQL, support pointers and a dereferencing operator usually support a corresponding *referencing* operator as well, which, given a variable *V*, returns the address of— i.e., a pointer to—*V*.[54] But SQL doesn't. As a consequence, we can't invoke that operator in order to obtain the address of some row from table POINTS. Instead, we need to write an expression—typically a *scalar subquery*[55]—that will explicitly extract the PID value from the row in question, and then plug that value into the row we're inserting into table NADDR. For example:

```
INSERT INTO NADDR ( NAME , ADDR , LOCATION )
          VALUES ( 'Joe' ,
                   jax ,
                 ( SELECT PID
                   FROM    POINTS
                   WHERE   X = 5.0 AND Y = 2.5 ) ) ;
```

(where *jax* is some expression that evaluates to Joe's address). A similar approach can be used with UPDATE statements, if necessary.

---

[54] We met this operator in Chapter 13 as well, where it was called PTR_TO. As a matter of fact the operator is rather unusual, inasmuch as it's certainly read-only, and yet (as with an update operator) its argument—its sole argument, in fact—must be a variable specifically.

[55] A scalar subquery in SQL is, loosely, an SQL table expression in parentheses that's acting as a scalar expression. Simplifying slightly, the table *t* returned by that table expression is required to consist of one column and one row (*r*, say); so long as it does, *t* is coerced to *r*, and *r* is then coerced to the single value *v* it contains. *Note:* Despite the terminology (viz., "scalar subquery"), the value *v* itself doesn't actually have to be scalar—it might be a row, for example.

Aside: Note that, while we can certainly retrieve data from table POINTS by following pointers from table NADDR, we can't update it in the same way (i.e., we can't do what might be called "update via dereferencing"). For example, the following is illegal:

```
UPDATE NADDR
SET    LOCATION -> X = 7.3 ,     /* warning: illegal! */
       LOCATION -> Y = 0.8       /* warning: illegal! */
WHERE  NAME = 'Joe' ;
```

On the other hand, the following, which achieves the presumably intended effect, *is* legal:

```
UPDATE POINTS
SET    X = 7.3 ,
       Y = 0.8
WHERE  PID =
     ( SELECT LOCATION
       FROM   NADDR
       WHERE  NAME = 'Joe' ) ;
```

End of aside.

Now, so far I've considered only queries on, or via, a table that has pointers into another (necessarily typed) table. What about queries on a typed table as such? In fact such queries just follow SQL's normal rules.[56] For example, the following expression will return the *y* coordinates of all points currently represented in table POINTS that have *x* coordinate 5.0:

```
SELECT Y
FROM   POINTS
WHERE  X - 5.0
```

Updates are reasonably straightforward too, except for a couple of issues.[57] The first is that (of course) we can't insert into or update column PID, since values in that column are provided by the system and never change. The second is that care might be needed in connection with

---

[56] For simplicity I assume here that the tables in question have no subtables or supertables. Subtables and supertables, and queries and updates on such tables, are discussed in Chapter 21. Do note, however, that subtables and supertables in SQL must be typed tables specifically.

[57] Well, there's one point I must mention, because if it's correct it's certainly very odd (but perhaps it's not correct). On page 76 of his book, Melton says this: "You can never change the most specific type of a structured type instance to any type other than the one it had when it was created, not even to a proper supertype or a proper subtype." Now, it's true that this remark refers to instances, not values or variables (see footnote 83); but if "instance" means *value*, the remark is trivially true and wouldn't be worth making, so I have to assume it means *variable*. So let structured type *T* have an attribute E of declared type ELLIPSE; let typed table *TT* be declared to be of type *T*; and let a row *r* be inserted into *TT* in which the E value is of most specific type ELLIPSE. Then the most specific type of *r* has an E component of most specific type ELLIPSE. And if *r* is updated—I assume for the sake of the argument that *r* counts as a variable!—in such a way that it now contains a value of most specific type CIRCLE (where CIRCLE is a proper subtype of type ELLIPSE) in the E column position, the most specific type of *r* is apparently still considered to have an E component of most specific type ELLIPSE. Circular noncircles! (Noncircular circles are possible too, of course.)

deletions in order to avoid producing "dangling references" (i.e., REF values somewhere that point to a row that no longer exists).

I'll finish up this subsection with two further observations:

■ First, here's a quote from the *Manifesto* book (it's somewhat paraphrased here, however, in order to fit the present context better):

> In a relational database, no table or row has any "hidden" component that (a) can be accessed only by invocation of some special operator instead of by means of a simple column reference, or that (b) causes invocations of the usual operators on tables or rows to have irregular effects.

Do you think self-referencing columns abide by this principle? I'll leave it to you to be the judge.

■ Second, I really do think those REF values are pointers. The thing about pointers is: They *point*—I mean, they have a direction to them, and they have a single, specific target. Note the asymmetry this state of affairs gives rise to. In our example, to get from a given row in table NADDR to the corresponding row in table POINTS (or to the X and Y values in that corresponding row, rather), we can write something like this:

```
SELECT LOCATION -> X , LOCATION -> Y
FROM   NADDR
WHERE  NAME = ...
```

But to get from a given row in table POINTS to the corresponding row(s) in table NADDR (or to the NAME and ADDR values in those corresponding rows, rather), we have to write something like this:

```
SELECT NAME , ADDR
FROM   NADDR
WHERE  LOCATION =
     ( SELECT PID
       FROM   POINTS
       WHERE  X = ... AND Y = ... )
```

Contrast the situation with relational keys and foreign keys. Key and foreign key values are regular data values, and they're thus, like all data values in a relational database, what might be called "*n*-way associative." For example, the part number P1, in some tuple in relvar SP (or indeed in any tuple anywhere in the database), is simultaneously linked— speaking purely logically, of course—not just to the pertinent part tuple in relvar P but to all shipment tuples in relvar SP (and indeed to all tuples anywhere in the database) that happen to contain that same part number. As a consequence, queries like

```
SELECT *
FROM    P
WHERE   PNO IN
      ( SELECT PNO
        FROM   SP
        WHERE  ... )
```

and

```
SELECT *
FROM    SP
WHERE   PNO IN
      ( SELECT PNO
        FROM   P
        WHERE  ... )
```

are much more symmetric. So which do you think REF values more closely resemble?—pointers, or foreign keys?[58]

Structured Types and "Scalarness" Revisited

I've said I don't really think there's any context in which a structured type behaves as if it were truly scalar (or "encapsulated"). To be specific, it always seems to be the case that its attributes are, or are effectively, visible to the user—and that's more or less the definition of what it means not to be scalar. But am I being entirely fair here? Let's take a closer look.

Consider the following definition for type POINT once again:

```
CREATE TYPE POINT
   AS ( X FLOAT , Y FLOAT ) FINAL ;
```

Given this definition, the X and Y observer and mutator functions (which are provided automatically by the system, remember) allow us to refer to the cartesian coordinates of any given point P via dot qualification, thus: P.X, P.Y. But if we wanted to, we could define additional observer and mutator functions RHO and THETA for this type (where RHO and THETA correspond to polar instead of cartesian coordinates, of course).[59] And if we did, then a

---

[58] For an extensive discussion of the logical difference between pointers and foreign keys, I refer you to my paper "Inclusion Dependencies and Foreign Keys," in C. J. Date and Hugh Darwen: *Database Explorations: Essays on The Third Manifesto and Related Topics* (available free online at *www.thethirdmanifesto.com*). See also my paper "Object IDs vs. Relational Keys," in C. J. Date (with Hugh Darwen and David McGoveran): *Relational Database Writings 1994-1997* (Addison-Wesley, 1998). Here let me just note for the record the following **Tutorial D** analogs of the two SQL expressions I said were "much more symmetric": P MATCHING (SP WHERE ...) and SP MATCHING (P WHERE ...).

[59] I don't think we could define a polar constructor method, though, because, although a given structured type is allowed to have any number of such methods, they must all have different signatures. (Recall that in SQL a signature consists of the operator name, a sequence of parameter declared types, and an indication of whether the operator in question is a procedure or a function. In the case of type POINT, a cartesian constructor method and a polar constructor method would both be functions, would both have the same operator name POINT, and would both have two parameters each of declared type FLOAT, and thus would have the same signature.)

user of the type could behave more or less as if it had been defined with attributes RHO and THETA instead of X and Y. In particular, that user could refer to the polar coordinates for any given point P via dot qualification, thus: P.RHO, P.THETA. The net effect would thus be to make type POINT look rather like, in our terms, a scalar type with two distinct possreps.[60]

In contrast with our approach, however, those two "possreps" wouldn't be named; in particular, therefore, there wouldn't be a POLAR "selector" as such. Nevertheless, we'd presumably still be able to "select" a point by its polar coordinates as illustrated in this example:

```
POINT ( ) . RHO ( 2.7 ) . THETA ( 1.0 )
```

With discipline, therefore, it does seem that SQL's nonscalar structured types might be made to behave somewhat like **Tutorial D**'s scalar types with possreps. There's at least one difference, though (possibly only a minor one):

- In **Tutorial D**, specification of a given possrep implies that THE_ operators and pseudovariables *will* be defined, automatically, for each component of that possrep.

- In SQL, by contrast, the possrep notion as such doesn't exist; thus, it would be entirely possible to define, say, a RHO observer and/or mutator, but no THETA observer and/or mutator, for type POINT.

On balance, therefore, I think I still have to say that SQL's structured types are really much more nonscalar than they are scalar.

THE SQL APPROACH TO INHERITANCE

At last (not before time, you might be thinking) I come to the topic that's the real point of this chapter: SQL's approach to inheritance. First of all, SQL does allow some type *T'* to be explicitly defined as a proper subtype of some other type *T*—but only if types *T'* and *T* are structured types specifically, and even in that case it supports single inheritance only. Thus, SQL has (a) no explicit support for multiple inheritance, (b) no explicit inheritance support for generated types,[61] and (c) no inheritance support at all for either system defined types or DISTINCT types. That said, however:

---

[60] Since SQL doesn't support type constraints, however, the logical relationships between those two "possreps" wouldn't be explicitly visible to the user but would effectively be hidden inside the code implementing those observer and mutator methods. Note in particular that the RHO and THETA mutators would have to be responsible for maintaining those relationships.

[61] In fairness, it might be argued that our model doesn't have much in the way of *explicit* inheritance support for generated types either. But it does have some—think of tuple / relation maximal and minimal types, for example, also superroot and subleaf types—and it also has a very great deal of implicit support (everything, in fact, that's a logical consequence for such types of its inheritance support for nongenerated types).

■ SQL does have some implicit (and limited) inheritance support in connection with certain generated types. For example, the type VARCHAR(3) is implicitly a subtype of type VARCHAR(5).[62] As a consequence, it has some implicit (and limited) inheritance support in connection with certain row and structured types also.

■ As another consequence of the same point, SQL has some implicit (and limited) multiple inheritance support also. For example, the type NUMERIC(3,1) is implicitly a subtype of both type NUMERIC(4,1) and type NUMERIC(3,2), neither of which is a subtype of the other. Hence, it has some implicit (and limited) multiple inheritance support in connection with certain row and structured types also.

But the foregoing exceptions aren't officially considered by the SQL standard to be part of its inheritance support as such. In what follows, therefore, I'll limit my attention for the most part to SQL's explicit support only (and hence to structured types only).

Second, then, that explicit support has clearly (?) been designed on the assumption that those structured subtypes and supertypes will typically be used in connection with SQL's support for subtables and supertables.[63] Now, I described this latter support in some detail in Chapter 21; in particular, I showed in that chapter that the kind of inheritance involved in that support, whatever else it might be, is certainly not type inheritance as such, since tables aren't types.[64] Thus, I don't propose to say much more about it here. Rather—merely in order to avoid leaving any false impressions—I'll content myself with describing, albeit only in outline, a few issues that I deliberately didn't discuss at all in that previous chapter:

1. Suppose the pertinent structured types are organized into a type hierarchy *TH*. Then the pertinent subtables and supertables must be organized into a table hierarchy *BH* that corresponds one to one with the types in *DH*, where *DH* is a type hierarchy that's derived from *TH* in accordance with the rules spelled out in Exercise 3.12 in Chapter 3.

2. Every table *B* in *BH* must be defined to be OF type *BT*, where *BT* is the type that corresponds to *B* in *DH*. Thus, *B* must be a typed table specifically.

---

[62] Note, however, that I'm using "subtype" here in our sense, not SQL's (in fact, the subtyping in question relies implicitly on our own model's notion of specialization by constraint). A similar remark applies to the next bullet item also.

[63] If I'm right on this, however, then I have to say too that I don't understand why it was thought necessary, or desirable, to design the language that way. After all, Parts II-IV of this book showed how inheritance clearly makes sense without relying on any such assumption. In other words, I don't see why we shouldn't just ignore SQL's subtables and supertables altogether and simply use SQL's structured types as column types in tables (etc.), much as **Tutorial D**'s user defined types can be used as attribute types in relvars (etc.). Of course, if this approach had been adopted, then I suppose difficulties might have arisen from the fact that SQL's structured types aren't properly scalar. But isn't that putting the cart before the horse? I mean, the reason why SQL's structured types aren't properly scalar is almost certainly because it was assumed they'd be used as the basis for defining SQL's typed tables. Food for thought here, perhaps.

[64] Indeed, how could it possibly be type inheritance, when tables in SQL don't really even *have* types? (Note that, for reasons explained in detail earlier in this chapter, I reject any suggestion that SQL's so called "typed tables" might be said to have types.)

3. Every table in *BH* will therefore have a self-referencing column, *BID* say. *BID* is explicitly defined—typically via a specification of the form REF IS *BID* SYSTEM GENERATED— only for the table at the root of hierarchy *BH*; for all other tables in *BH*, it's inherited.

4. To take a concrete example, let structured types EMP_T and PGMR_T and tables EMP and PGMR be as sketched in the section "Subtables and Supertables" in Chapter 21, and let a row for employee Joe appear in both tables. Then the value of the self-referencing column will be the same in both of those rows. *Note:* "Both of those rows" is perhaps a slightly misleading way of putting it; the value in question will certainly appear in the row for Joe in table EMP and will therefore also appear, but *virtually*, in the row for Joe in table PGMR.

To repeat, SQL's support for inheritance in connection with structured types seems to have been designed on the assumption that it'll be used in connection with subtables and supertables specifically. But it doesn't have to be used that way, and in some respects it's easier to see the forest as well as the trees if we ignore subtables and supertables entirely. And so I will, from this point forward. To be more specific, what I plan to do in the remainder of this chapter is describe and analyze SQL's inheritance support in some detail, using the prescriptions of our own inheritance model (which make no mention of "subtables and supertables," of course) as an organizing principle, or basis, for such a description and analysis.

Ellipses and Circles

It's convenient to begin by giving some possible[65] SQL structured type definitions for types ELLIPSE and CIRCLE from earlier parts of the book (and let's assume until further notice that these two are the only structured types we have to deal with):

```
CREATE TYPE ELLIPSE
  AS ( A LENGTH , B LENGTH , CTR POINT )
      NOT FINAL ;

CREATE TYPE CIRCLE UNDER ELLIPSE
  AS ( R LENGTH )
      NOT FINAL ;
```

Points arising:

1. The UNDER clause in the definition of type CIRCLE identifies ELLIPSE as that type's immediate supertype (or direct supertype, in SQL terms). Thus, properties that apply to ellipses in general are inherited, unconditionally, by circles in particular (and the AS clause

---

[65] Possible but perhaps unlikely, as we'll see in the subsection "Concluding Remarks" at the very end of this chapter.

specifies additional attributes[66]—SQL's term again—that apply to circles in particular and not to ellipses in general). Note, however, that:

a.   *Properties* here doesn't mean, as it does in our model, operators and type constraints, it means operators and *structure* (i.e., attributes). In other words, SQL supports both behavioral inheritance and structural inheritance—the latter because (as we know from earlier in this chapter) the attributes that make up the internal structure of a structured type are definitely visible to the user. As for type constraints, they're not inherited because SQL doesn't support them, and so there aren't any to inherit.

b.   Following on from point a., *operators* here doesn't mean, as it does in our model, just read-only operators, it means "routines" (i.e., all procedures, all functions, and all methods). In other words, SQL fails to distinguish adequately between values and variables, and it requires unconditional inheritance of update operators as well as read-only ones—with the consequence that, e.g., circles might be noncircular, noncircles might be circular, and so on. (To pursue the point a moment longer: In our model, if some value v is of most specific type ELLIPSE, then it's definitely a noncircle, and if it's of most specific type CIRCLE, then it's definitely a circle. In SQL, by contrast, if v is of most specific type ELLIPSE, it might in fact be a circle, and if it's of most specific type CIRCLE, it might in fact be a noncircle.)

2.   Here now by way of example is AREA_OF as a method for type ELLIPSE:

```
CREATE METHOD AREA_OF ( ) RETURNS AREA
      FOR ELLIPSE
      RETURN ( 3.14159 * SELF.A * SELF.B ) ;
```

The CREATE TYPE statement for type ELLIPSE will need to be revised to include the corresponding signature, of course:

```
METHOD AREA_OF ( ) RETURNS AREA
```

3.   By default, the foregoing method will be inherited by type CIRCLE. Of course, although it doesn't make very much sense to do so in this rather simple example, we could if we wanted explicitly define another version of AREA_OF for type CIRCLE specifically:[67]

```
CREATE METHOD AREA_OF ( ) RETURNS AREA
      FOR CIRCLE
      RETURN ( 3.14159 * SELF.R * SELF.R ) ;
```

---

[66] Zero or more such additional attributes, in general. Of course, there's just one in the example.

[67] Functions and procedures can have versions too. An example (ADDWT) was mentioned earlier in the chapter—though that example really illustrated overloading, not "versions" in our sense, because it didn't involve any subtyping.

If we do, we'll also need to extend the CREATE TYPE statement for type CIRCLE to add the following:

```
METHOD AREA_OF ( ) RETURNS AREA
```

Now an invocation of AREA_OF will invoke either the ELLIPSE or the CIRCLE version of the method, depending on the most specific type of the subject argument. In other words, the AREA_OF method now has two implementation versions. Note, however, that this fact is explicitly *not* hidden from the user, and neither is the implementation code for those two versions. Now, such user visibility might make sense in the context of overloading, but it doesn't make much sense in the context of inclusion polymorphism—and in the case at hand, of course (viz., AREA_OF), inclusion polymorphism is really what we're dealing with.[68]

4. Assuming for the sake of the example that reference types REF (ELLIPSE) and REF (CIRCLE) do in fact both exist—see footnote 40—then REF (CIRCLE) will automatically be considered a proper subtype of REF (ELLIPSE).

5. Recall now that in order to be able to support even simple equality comparisons between values of some structured type, a suitable "ordering" [*sic*] needs to be defined. For example:

```
CREATE ORDERING FOR ELLIPSE EQUALS ONLY BY STATE ;
```

Now "=" and "<>" comparisons on comparands of most specific type ELLIPSE, CIRCLE, or a mixture are legitimate.[69]

So much for ellipses and circles, at least for the time being. As promised, I now propose to analyze SQL's inheritance support in detail, using our own inheritance model as a basis for that analysis and the ellipses and circles example as a basis for illustrations. Before I begin, however, I'd like to elaborate on why I think using our model in such a manner is a reasonable thing to do. Naturally, we (I mean Darwen and myself) believe our model is valuable in and of itself. However, we also believe it can be useful as a yardstick or framework—i.e., as a basis against

---

[68] I note in passing that different versions in SQL can optionally be given their own "specific name"—corresponding to what elsewhere in this book I've referred to as a version name—thereby making it possible (e.g.) to drop a specific version individually. A similar remark applies to overloaded operators such as ADDWT (see footnote 67).

[69] There are some mysteries here, though. First, according to my reading of the standard, CREATE ORDERING ... BY STATE can be specified solely at the root type level. So if as elsewhere in this book the pertinent root type is PLANE_FIGURE, not ELLIPSE, how could such a specification possibly make any sense, given that—as we'll see when we get to the discussion of IM Prescription 20 later in this section—PLANE_FIGURE probably doesn't have any "state" for comparisons to be based on? Second (again according to my reading of the standard), comparisons on values of a proper subtype are based solely on those attributes that the subtype in question inherits from the pertinent root type, which if true doesn't seem to make much sense either.

which alternative proposals, and indeed concrete implementations, can indeed be analyzed, criticized, evaluated, and perhaps judged. Please note immediately, however, that we expressly don't want our ideas to be used in connection with any kind of "checklist" evaluation (not of SQL and not of anything else, either). We do think our ideas can serve as a convenient framework for structuring discussions, but they're not meant to serve as a basis for any kind of scoring scheme. We're not interested in scoring schemes.

With the foregoing caveat in mind, let's now examine SQL to see how it measures up against our inheritance model prescriptions. For each prescription in turn, I'll give an informal statement (in the pertinent subsection heading) of what that prescription is all about, just as a reminder, and then I'll discuss SQL's support or lack thereof for the pertinent concepts. *Note:* For the sake of what follows—and despite everything I've had to say about such matters in this chapter prior to this point—I'm going to have to assume, in connection with those prescriptions that have to do with scalar types specifically, that SQL's structured types are scalar after all (or that they're meant to be scalar, at any rate).

IM Prescription 1: Types Are Sets

SQL conforms to this prescription, but it does so in a rather peculiar way, owing to its assumption that inheritance means structural inheritance specifically. For example, values of type CIRCLE have an attribute R (radius) that values that are "just of type ELLIPSE" don't have; thus, values of type CIRCLE certainly can't be considered as values that are "just of type ELLIPSE." Yet substitutability applies: A value of type CIRCLE can be used wherever a value of type ELLIPSE is expected (in which case the R attribute of the CIRCLE value in question is presumably just ignored, if the context in question isn't prepared to deal with it). It follows that—if ELLIPSE and CIRCLE are the only types we have, and speaking rather loosely—the set of values that might be thought of, in a certain sense, as constituting type ELLIPSE is the union of (a) the set of values that conform to the (a,b,ctr) structure of ellipses and (b) the set of values that conform to the (a,b,ctr,r) structure of circles.[70] And it follows further that, again in a certain sense, the set of values that can be thought of as constituting some given type T isn't fully known until all proper subtypes of T have been defined.

And yet ... If c is a value of type CIRCLE, then what we might call the *projection* of c on (a,b,ctr) will indeed be a value that's "just of type ELLIPSE." In a different sense, therefore, the set of values that are just of type ELLIPSE *is* known as soon as type ELLIPSE is defined. However, the fact remains that the set of all values that can be used where a value of type ELLIPSE is expected is indeed not fully known until all proper subtypes of type ELLIPSE have been defined.

---

[70] In case you're concerned about the fact that if c is a value of type CIRCLE, then the values of a, b, and r for c will—or at least should—all be equal, I'm going to have to ask you not to worry about it for now. I'll come back to this question in the subsection "Concluding Remarks" at the very end of the chapter (see in particular footnote 86).

IM Prescription 2: Subtypes Are Subsets

The remarks under IM Prescription 1 apply here also, mutatis mutandis (i.e., SQL conforms to this prescription too, but again in a slightly peculiar way):

- If we agree to regard a value of type CIRCLE as a value of type ELLIPSE (see the discussion above of IM Prescription 1), then the set of values constituting type CIRCLE is indeed a subset of the set of values constituting type ELLIPSE (a proper subset, in fact).

- Alternatively, if we choose not to regard a value of type CIRCLE as a value of type ELLIPSE, then at least the projection of a CIRCLE value on (a,b,ctr) is such a value, and so the set of such projections is a subset of the set of ELLIPSE values. (It's not a proper subset, though; in fact, the set of projections of those CIRCLE values on (a,b,ctr) is identical to that set of ELLIPSE values.) *Note:* In Chapter 5, I said it's an obvious corollary of IM Prescription 2 that there can't be more values of type T' than there are of type T. Under the present interpretation, however, this corollary doesn't hold, because there are—at least potentially—more, not fewer, values of type CIRCLE than there are of type ELLIPSE.[71]

IM Prescription 3: "Subtype of" Is Reflexive

SQL conforms to this prescription.

IM Prescription 4: "Subtype of" Is Transitive

SQL conforms to this prescription.

IM Prescription 5: Proper and Immediate Subtypes and Supertypes

SQL does use the terminology of proper subtypes and supertypes. As for immediate subtypes and supertypes, however, it uses the term *direct* in place of the (in my view, more apt) *immediate*. Also, it fails to support the idea that if T is an immediate supertype of T', then the definition of T' should be accompanied by a specification of an example value that's of type T and not of type T' (i.e., in order to guarantee that proper subtypes are proper subsets). See IM Prescription 2 above for further discussion of this latter point.

---

[71] There won't be more if we can guarantee that if c is a value of type CIRCLE, then the values of a, b, and r for c are all equal (see the previous footnote). But we can't—at least, not very easily, and certainly not declaratively as part of the definition of type CIRCLE—because SQL doesn't support type constraints. Again, see footnote 86 for further explanation.

IM Prescription 6: Scalar Root and Leaf Types

SQL conforms to this prescription—i.e., it does support the scalar root and leaf type concepts, though its term for *root type* is "maximal supertype" (not to be confused with maximal types in the sense of our model). If ELLIPSE and CIRCLE are the only types we have, therefore, ELLIPSE is a maximal supertype. (Oddly, SQL's term for *leaf type* isn't "minimal subtype" but "leaf type"; thus, if, again, ELLIPSE and CIRCLE are the only types we have, then CIRCLE is a leaf type.) Note, however, that SQL defines these concepts without mentioning types *alpha* and *omega*; in fact, it doesn't mention types *alpha* and *omega*, or analogs of those types, anywhere at all. It also doesn't mention the term *lattice* (but then neither does our own model, at least not explicitly). This latter omission is unsurprising, however, given that SQL's explicit inheritance support provides for scalar types only, implying among other things that the types concerned would all be part of the same type lattice anyway—just so long as the complete set of available scalar types includes some presumably user defined analog of *alpha*, at any rate.

IM Prescription 7: Disjoint and Overlapping Types

SQL conforms to this prescription, insofar as it's possible to do so—which might not be very far—while (a) supporting single inheritance only and (b) *not* supporting type constraints. For example, do you think the SQL types DECIMAL(5,1) and NUMERIC(5,1) are distinct? (Yes.) And disjoint? (No.) How about types CHAR(25) and VARCHAR(25)?

IM Prescription 8: Common Subtypes and Supertypes

SQL's conformance to this prescription is partial only, owing to its lack of support for types *alpha* and *omega*. To be specific:

- If the types in question—*T1, T2, ..., Tm*, say—don't all belong to the same type hierarchy, then they don't have any common subtypes or common supertypes at all.

- If types *T1, T2, ..., Tm* do all belong to the same type hierarchy, then (a) they certainly have a common supertype, even if it's only the pertinent root type, but (b) they don't have a common subtype unless they're all supertypes of the same leaf type (in which case, however, they do—though the common subtype in question is necessarily just the most specific of types *T1, T2, ..., Tm*).

- If types *T1, T2, ..., Tm* have a common supertype, then they have both a least specific and a most specific common supertype.

- If types *T1*, *T2*, ..., *Tm* have a common subtype, then they have both a least specific and a most specific common subtype (though those common subtypes are both necessarily just the most specific of types *T1*, *T2*, ..., *Tm*).

However, at least it's true—in fact, it's obvious (?)—that every value does at least have a unique most specific type; in other words, the "MST uniqueness" property does apply.

IM Prescription 9: Model of a Scalar Variable

SQL conforms to the spirit of this prescription, though it doesn't use the <*DT,MST,v*> notation. It does use the terms *declared type* and *most specific type*; however, it doesn't regard variables as such, or expressions, as having associated most specific types—only values have any such thing.[72] Thus, when I refer in what follows to the most specific type of some variable, what I mean is, of course, the most specific type of the current value of the variable in question. (Well, that's what it means in our model too—but in our model we explicitly state as much.)

IM Prescription 10: Specialization by Constraint

Since SQL doesn't support type constraints, it doesn't conform to this prescription either; in fact, its lack of support for both S by C and G by C is more or less total (other than as noted in footnote 62). Note, however, that this lack doesn't mean the most specific type of a variable can't change (where, as explained under IM Prescription 9, by "the most specific type of a variable" I really mean the most specific type of the value that's the current value of the variable in question). For example, consider the following SQL code fragment:

```
DECLARE E ELLIPSE ;

SET E = CX ;
SET E = EX ;
```

CX and EX here are, let's agree, expressions that return values of most specific types CIRCLE and ELLIPSE, respectively. According to my reading of the standard, then:

- After the first assignment, the variable E (which has declared type ELLIPSE) has most specific type CIRCLE.[73]

---

[72] This observation is true as far as it goes. However, what it really signifies isn't exactly clear, given that (among other things) SQL seems to be in two minds as to whether a row in a typed table is a value or a variable. In this connection, see in particular footnote 57.

[73] Which means, incidentally (just to spell the point out), that a variable of declared type ELLIPSE, with attributes A, B, and CTR, now contains a value of type CIRCLE, with attributes A, B, CTR, and R.

■ After the second, it has most specific type ELLIPSE.[74]

Note carefully, however, that these effects are *not* obtained by S by C and G by C as such (they can't be, since by definition there are no constraints available to control any such S by C or G by C process).

IM Prescription 11: Assignment with Inheritance

SQL appears to conform to this prescription, modulo the discussion under IM Prescription 10.

IM Prescription 12: Equality with Inheritance

SQL fails to conform to this prescription for several reasons. First of all, SQL's support for equality is deeply flawed anyway, even without inheritance. That is, it violates the *TTM* prescription on equality, which (as we saw in Chapter 2) reads as follows:

> **D** shall support the **equality** comparison operator "=" for every type *T*. Let *v1* and *v2* be values, and consider the equality comparison *v1* = *v2*. The values *v1* and *v2* shall be of the same type *T*. The comparison shall return TRUE if and only if *v1* and *v2* are the very same value.

Details of some but not all of SQL's deficiencies in this regard can be found in the *Manifesto* book.[75] I'll mention just one of them here, which is that, for some types (including certain system defined types in particular, such as type XML), equality isn't even defined.

Second, equality isn't necessarily defined for user defined types either. In particular, if *T* is a structured type, then *T* has an associated "=" operator if, but only if, an appropriate "ordering" has been defined for it (see the discussion of CREATE ORDERING earlier in this chapter).[76] Note that this particular criticism applies regardless of whether there's any type inheritance involved.

Third, even if "=" is defined for some given structured type, the semantics of that operator are at least potentially user defined and thus, in effect, arbitrary. (This criticism too applies

---

[74] But this conclusion is partly guesswork, I fear; I mean, it's my attempt to make sense of what the standard does have to say about such assignments, which is this: "[An] expression *E* whose declared type is some user defined type *UDT1* is assignable to a [variable] *S* whose declared type is some user defined type *UDT2* if and only if *UDT1* is a subtype of *UDT2*. The effect of the assignment ... is that the value of *S* is *V*, obtained by the evaluation of *E*. The most specific type of *V* is some subtype of *UDT1*, possibly *UDT1* itself, while the declared type of *S* remains *UDT2*." Well, I think you can see that this extract leaves a number of questions unanswered! Note in particular that it doesn't say which specific "subtype of *UDT1*" is that "most specific type of *V*" (perhaps we're supposed to read "The most specific type of *V* is some subtype of *UDT1*" as meaning "The most specific type of *V must be* some subtype of *UDT1*"?). In any case, there does seem to be some contradiction between what I think the standard is trying to say here and footnote 57, q.v.

[75] Further details can be found in *A Guide to the SQL Standard* (4th edition, Addison-Wesley, 1997), by Hugh Darwen and myself, also in my book *SQL and Relational Theory: How to Write Accurate SQL Code* (3rd edition, O'Reilly, 2015).

[76] And even then UNIQUE, DISTINCT, UNION, INTERSECT, GROUP BY, and a host of other operations of a similar nature, can't be applied to a column of the type in question, if the pertinent CREATE ORDERING specifies EQUALS ONLY! (Thanks to Hugh Darwen for this observation.)

regardless of whether there's any type inheritance involved.) In fact, SQL doesn't even require the most specific types of the comparands to be the same in order for an "=" comparison to give TRUE. Thus, for example, SQL would allow an equality comparison between, say, an ellipse and a polygon to give TRUE.

It follows from all of the above that there's no guarantee that SQL will support joins, unions, intersections, and differences properly, especially (but not exclusively) if any structured types are involved. (Yet again, this criticism applies even without type inheritance.)

IM Prescription 13: Join etc. with Inheritance

SQL conforms to this prescription insofar as it conforms to IM Prescription 12, q.v.

IM Prescription 14: TREAT

SQL conforms to this prescription inasmuch as it does support a TREAT operator (in fact, the operator in question is called TREAT). For example, the SQL analog of

```
    TREAT_AS_CIRCLE ( E )
```

is

```
    TREAT ( E AS CIRCLE )
```

But SQL has no direct counterpart to the generalized form TREAT_AS_SAME_TYPE_AS (Y,X), nor to the relational expression RX : TREAT_AS_T(A).

IM Prescription 15: Type Testing

SQL conforms to this prescription. The SQL analog of

```
    IS_T ( X )
```

is

```
    TYPE ( X ) [ IS ] OF ( T )
```

The optional IS is a noiseword. A negated form is supported too; that is, the SQL analog of

```
    IS_NOT_T ( X )
```

(see Exercise 10.8 in Chapter 10) is

```
    TYPE ( X ) [ IS ] NOT OF ( T )
```

In both cases, the expression following OF is basically just a parenthesized, nonempty commalist of type names[77] (so SQL has no support for anything corresponding to our IS_SAME_TYPE_AS (*Y,X*) and IS_NOT_SAME_TYPE_AS (*Y,X*) operators). An analogous remark applies to all of the operators discussed in the remainder of this subsection.

SQL also supports a counterpart to the relational operator *RX* : IS_*T*(*A*), but its support is clumsy. Let relvar R have attributes A, B, and C (only) Then the SQL analog of R :IS_*T* (A) looks like this:

```
SELECT  TREAT ( A AS T ) AS A , B , C
FROM    R
WHERE   TYPE ( A ) IS OF ( T )
```

For obvious reasons, such expressions become increasingly cumbersome as the degree of R increases.

Unlike **Tutorial D** (see Exercise 10.9 in Chapter 10), SQL also supports "most specific type" analogs of the foregoing operators. Here's the SQL analog of "IS_MS_*T* (*X*)" (again, see Exercise 10.9):

```
TYPE ( X ) [ IS ] OF ( ONLY T )
```

(The keyword ONLY here would seem to be rather misleading, however, except in the special case where *T* is a root type.)[78] And—under the same assumptions as before—here's the SQL analog of "R : IS_MS_*T* (A)":

```
SELECT  TREAT ( A AS T ) AS A , B , C
FROM    R
WHERE   TYPE ( A ) IS OF ( ONLY T ) )
```

SQL also provides an operator (actually a method) called SPECIFICTYPE that returns the most specific type of its sole argument as a VARCHAR string.

IM Prescription 16: Value Substitutability

SQL conforms to this prescription, though it doesn't use the term *substitutability* (value or otherwise), nor the term *polymorphism* (read-only or otherwise). It does, however, talk about both (a) overriding methods and (b) overloading functions and methods. In our terms (and to a first approximation only, probably), *overriding* here seems to refer to the idea that an operator

---

[77] The expression TYPE(*X*) IS OF (*T1,T2,...,Tm*) returns TRUE if and only if *X* is of type *T1* or type *T2* or ... or type *Tm*; the expression TYPE(*X*) IS NOT OF (*T1,T2,...,Tm*) returns TRUE if and only if *X* is not of type *T1* and not of type *T2* and ... and not of type *Tm* (in other words, if and only if TYPE(*X*) IS OF (*T1,T2,...,Tm*) returns FALSE).

[78] It might help to point out that the keyword ONLY here is playing a role analogous to the one it plays in SQL's SELECT ... FROM ONLY ... and DELETE FROM ONLY ... (see Chapter 21).

can have two or more implementation versions, and *overloading* seems to refer sometimes to overloading as defined earlier in this book and sometimes to inclusion polymorphism. But it's hard to be sure.

IM Prescription 17: Operator Signatures

It's implicit in this prescription that (a) it should at least be possible to perform the binding process at run time,[79] and also that (b) all of the arguments to a given operator invocation should participate equally in that run time binding process. In fact, SQL did conform to these requirements, more or less, when inheritance was first introduced, but it changed at the eleventh hour. The reason for the change was that C++ and Java, the two most likely host languages for applications using the object features of SQL, both perform run time binding on the basis of the first argument only. That's why SQL now supports both (a) "selfish methods," as in C++ and Java, for which the binding process is performed at run time on the basis of the most specific type of just that first argument (i.e., the subject argument),[80] and (b) "non method" operators (viz., functions and procedures), for which the binding process is performed at compile time on the basis of the declared types of all of the pertinent argument expressions.[81] Thus, SQL fails to conform to this prescription for methods, because of their "selfish" nature, and at least arguably fails for functions and procedures too, because of their lack of support for run time binding.

As for the different kinds of signatures required by IM Prescription 17, (a) SQL's methods conform insofar as they conform to the run time binding part of this prescription (see above), and (b) SQL's functions and procedures conform only partially (in effect, specification and invocation signatures are combined in this latter case).

SQL has no requirement that if "the same" operator has several distinct implementation versions, then those versions all implement the same semantics. Given the emphasis on structural inheritance, in fact, it's likely that they won't.

IM Prescription 18: Read-Only Parameters to Update Operators

SQL conforms to this prescription.

IM Prescription 19: Variable Substitutability

SQL fails to conform to this prescription, since it requires update operators to be inherited unconditionally.

---

[79] In SQL, binding is called *subject routine determination*.

[80] As mentioned in footnote 17, it might be possible to do part or even all of the binding at compile time (i.e., on the basis of the declared type of the expression denoting the subject argument), but methods in general always involve, at least conceptually, some degree of run time binding.

[81] It's not clear that all arguments participate equally in that process, though, because according to the standard the argument expressions are explicitly considered in order from left to right.

IM Prescription 20: Union and Dummy Types etc.

SQL's conformance to this prescription is partial only. To elaborate, suppose we extend our ellipses and circles example to include type PLANE_FIGURE as an immediate ("direct") supertype of type ELLIPSE (recall also from Part II of this book that PLANE_FIGURE was originally a dummy type and had no possrep):[82]

```
CREATE TYPE PLANE_FIGURE
       NOT INSTANTIABLE
       NOT FINAL ;
```

NOT INSTANTIABLE means the type being defined has no "instances," where the term *instance* means a value whose most specific type is the type in question;[83] in other words, the type in question is what our inheritance model would call a union type. Such a type must have at least one INSTANTIABLE subtype. (INSTANTIABLE means the type in question does have at least one such instance; i.e., the type in question isn't a union type, so there does exist at least one value whose most specific type is the type in question. Types ELLIPSE and CIRCLE are INSTANTIABLE. However, INSTANTIABLE is the default, which is why I didn't bother to specify it explicitly when I defined those types originally. Leaf types are required to be INSTANTIABLE.)

So NOT INSTANTIABLE types correspond to our union types (and INSTANTIABLE types correspond to our nonunion types, of course). Moreover, a NOT INSTANTIABLE type with no attributes, like PLANE_FIGURE in the example, is effectively a dummy type (though SQL doesn't use that term, nor does it have any explicit equivalent).[84] But SQL has no support for the special dummy types *alpha* and *omega*.

---

[82] Of course, we'll also have to add UNDER PLANE_FIGURE to the definition of type ELLIPSE.

[83] My interpretation here of what NOT INSTANTIABLE means—i.e., that every "instance" of the type being defined has as its most specific type some proper subtype of that type—is undeniably correct, but what exactly is meant in SQL contexts by the term *instance* is rather less clear. The 2011 version of the standard uses the phrase "instance of a value," suggesting that *instance* perhaps means what I called in Chapter 2 an *appearance* (since "appearance of a value" does make sense, while "value of a value" doesn't). By contrast, the 1999 version of the standard defines an instance to be a *physical representation* of a value. Melton's book includes the following: "Making a type INSTANTIABLE imposes no requirement on your application to actually create any instances of the type," which suggests rather strongly (to me, at any rate) that an instance is a variable—especially since these "instances" do certainly seem to be updatable. Yet elsewhere that same book states explicitly (indeed, it stresses the point) that "instances are *values*, not objects." But then on the very next page it talks about "instances of values," and elsewhere it talks about "constructing a value." Overall, there does seem to be a considerable degree of muddle surrounding this notion.

[84] It doesn't use the term "regular type" either (nor does it have anything equivalent); however, any structured type that has at least one attribute—possibly inherited—is effectively a regular type. (As noted previously, the clause AS (*<attribute commalist>*) on CREATE TYPE, if specified, must contain at least one *<attribute>*; however, it doesn't have to be specified— i.e., it can be omitted entirely—in which case, if the type being defined is a root type, then that type will have no attributes at all. See the discussion of IM Prescription 20 later in this section.)

IM Prescription 21: Empty Types

SQL fails to conform to this prescription (there are no empty types in SQL). Note in particular that PLANE_FIGURE isn't empty, even though it has no attributes, because every ellipse "is a" plane figure, and type ELLIPSE certainly isn't empty (why not?).

IM Prescription 22: Tuple / Relation Subtypes and Supertypes

If "tuples" is interpreted to mean rows, then SQL conforms to this prescription with respect to tuples. Having no relation (or table) type generator, it obviously fails to conform with respect to relations. *Note:* SQL's conformance with respect to tuples (or rows, rather) is vacuous, though, because no user defined operator can have a row valued parameter. (Actually the support is vacuous in another sense too, because implementations at the time of writing typically—perhaps universally—don't support row types anyway.)

IM Prescription 23: Proper and Immediate Tuple / Relation Subtypes and Supertypes

The remarks under IM Prescription 22 apply here also.

IM Prescription 24: Common Tuple / Relation Subtypes and Supertypes

The remarks under IM Prescription 22 apply here also, modulo the discussion under IM Prescription 8.

IM Prescription 25: Tuple / Relation Maximal and Minimal Types

SQL fails to conform to this prescription.

IM Prescription 26: Tuple / Relation Root and Leaf Types

The remarks under IM Prescription 22 apply here also, partly (but SQL has no support for superroot or subleaf types).

IM Prescription 27: Tuple / Relation Most Specific Types

The remarks under IM Prescription 22 apply here also.

IM Prescription 28: Model of a Tuple / Relation Variable

The remarks under IM Prescription 22 apply here also, modulo the discussion under IM Prescription 9.

Concluding Remarks

This brings me to the end of my analysis of SQL's support for type inheritance in terms of our own inheritance model. In conclusion, however, I need to make it clear that I think my analysis might have been unfair, or at least misleading, in one important respect. To be specific, I don't think SQL's type inheritance mechanism was ever intended for examples like our ellipses and circles example (certainly it wasn't designed to support the idea that subtypes should be obtained by constraining supertypes; indeed it couldn't have been, given that SQL doesn't support type constraints anyway).[85] Let me elaborate.

Take another look at the SQL definitions I gave earlier for ellipses and circles (irrelevant details omitted):

```
CREATE TYPE ELLIPSE ...
  AS ( A LENGTH , B LENGTH , CTR POINT ) ... ;
CREATE TYPE CIRCLE UNDER ELLIPSE
  AS ( R LENGTH ) ... ;
```

With these definitions, circles have attributes A, B, CTR (inherited from ellipses), and R (specified for circles only). And if it's true as I claimed earlier in this chapter that the specified attributes constitute the *physical* representation, then any given circle will be physically represented by a collection of four values, three of which will supposedly all be the same![86] For such reasons, it's likely that the definition of type CIRCLE will actually *not* specify any attributes of its own at all—instead, it will simply inherit the attributes specified for type ELLIPSE, like this:

```
CREATE TYPE ELLIPSE ...
  AS ( A LENGTH , B LENGTH , CTR POINT ) ... ;
CREATE TYPE CIRCLE UNDER ELLIPSE ... ;       /* no AS specification */
```

On the other hand, the representation for type CIRCLE will now not have an R ("radius") attribute, and so there won't be any automatically provided methods for "observing" and "mutating" the radius of any given circle. And then on the third hand ... If the representation does have an R attribute, and if we do "mutate" it (i.e., while leaving the A and B attributes

---

[85] As explained earlier, in fact, it seems to have been designed on the basis of an assumption that it'll be used in conjunction with SQL's support for subtables and supertables specifically (most of the time, at any rate).

[86] I say they'll *supposedly* all be the same, but of course there are no type constraints available to guarantee that they are—that's left to the user (or, perhaps more realistically, to the definer of the constructors and mutators for types ELLIPSE and CIRCLE; it would of course be possible to incorporate tests in the implementation code for those methods to ensure that ellipses have $a > b$ and circles have $a = b = r$). Note, however, that by "circles" in the foregoing I don't mean all possible values of type CIRCLE—rather, I mean only what SQL would probably call "instances" of that type that have been explicitly "constructed" (and similarly for "ellipses," of course, mutatis mutandis).

unchanged), then we'll wind up with a "noncircular circle"—i.e., a "circle" for which the A, B, and R values aren't all the same after all.

For one reason or another, therefore, it might reasonably be argued that "ellipses and circles" is a bad example to use as a basis for illustrating SQL's type inheritance functionality. Certainly SQL doesn't deal with that example very well. So let's switch to a different example:

```
CREATE TYPE CIRCLE
   AS ( R LENGTH , CTR POINT ) ... ;

CREATE TYPE COLORED_CIRCLE UNDER CIRCLE
   AS ( COL COLOR ) ... ;
```

Observe that this example is exactly the one I was deprecating in Chapter 21, where I claimed, in effect, that colored circles aren't circles in the same kind of way that, e.g., circles are ellipses. But if we're talking about inheriting, and possibly extending, *representations*, then the example begins to make a little more sense. Certainly it's reasonable to think of a colored circle as being represented as indicated—i.e., by extending the representation (radius and center) of a circle to contain an additional (color) component.[87] Moreover, if we say that type COLORED_CIRCLE is "UNDER" type CIRCLE, then it's also reasonable to think of operators that work for circles in general—for example, an operator to compute the area—as applying to colored circles in particular (thus, colored circles can be substituted for circles). But the one thing that doesn't make sense is to think of colored circles being a constrained form of circles in general, or equivalently to think of colored circles being obtained from circles via specialization by constraint. In other words, SQL's inheritance mechanism seems to be designed, not for dealing with inheritance at all in the sense in which that term is understood in our model, but rather for dealing with what in Chapter 21 I called *delegation*. Recall from that chapter that delegation means that the responsibility for implementing certain operators associated with the type in question is "delegated" to some other type (typically the type of some component of the original type's representation). For example, "compute the area" for a colored circle is effectively implemented by invoking "compute the area" on the corresponding circle. And so it might have been clearer to call the SQL mechanism a delegation mechanism in the first place, instead of pretending it had anything to do with subtypes.

---

[87] Though I would prefer to think of it (as we did in Chapter 21) as *having a circle component*—instead of explicit radius and center components—and then additionally having that color component.

APPENDIXES

The subject of type inheritance seems mostly to have been investigated in an object context specifically. By contrast, the inheritance model defined by Darwen and myself was constructed from first principles, using a combination of logic, common sense, and well established criteria for language design, and being guided by our background knowledge of relational theory. In particular, we saw no need to appeal to any concepts or mechanisms from the object world, nor did we do so. As a consequence, our solutions to certain inheritance issues differ, sometimes markedly, from approaches discussed in the object literature to those same issues. Appendixes A and B offer a little more by way of background explanation as to why we don't always agree with those object approaches. Finally, Appendix C provides for purposes of quick reference a glossary of some of the more important terms and concepts involved in our own approach.

Appendix A

Encapsulation Is a Red Herring

This appendix is based on a column that first appeared in Database Programming & Design 12, *No. 9 (September 1998). It doesn't have much to do with the principal topic of this book (i.e., type inheritance) as such—at least, not directly—but it does have certain implications for that topic, which is why I wanted to include it here.*

I mentioned the notion of *encapsulation* several times in the body of this book (mostly in Chapters 21 and 22, but also elsewhere in passing). Encapsulation is widely perceived as a key feature, or benefit, of object technology. But it seems to me that the focus on encapsulation has always been a little bit off base; rather, what's important, as I tried to explain in Chapter 2, is just to make a clear distinction between types and representations. Indeed, as the title of this appendix indicates, I feel that encapsulation per se is a little bit of a red herring, and in what follows I'd like to try to explain why I feel this way.

WHAT DOES ENCAPSULATION MEAN?

By now you should have a pretty good idea of what encapsulation means, but for the record let me take a moment to spell it out anyway. Basically, a data type is said to be encapsulated if values, and hence variables also, of the type in question have no user visible components (and then those values and variables are said to be encapsulated as well). For example, in their book on Smalltalk (*Smalltalk-80: The Language and its Implementation*, by Adele Goldberg and David Robson, Addison-Wesley, 1983),[1] the authors say this:

> An object consists of some private memory and a set of operations ... An object's *public* properties are the messages that make up its interface ... An object's *private* properties are a set of instance variables that make up its private memory.

Now, there does seem to be a slight element of confusion in this extract—does the term *object* really mean an object, or does it mean an object type?—but I think the general meaning is clear. To be more specific, I think we can reasonably take the term *message* to mean the specification signature for some operator, and the term *instance variable* to mean some

---

[1] Smalltalk is widely credited with being the first object oriented system and language (though Smalltalk in turn was surely influenced by SIMULA—see O. J. Dahl and K. Nygaard: "SIMULA: An Algol-Based Simulation Language," *CACM 9*, No. 9, September 1966), and Goldberg and Robson were two of the team responsible for its design and development.

component of the physical representation of the object(s) in question. If so, then it follows that the Smalltalk user is able to operate on values and variables of an encapsulated type solely by means of the operators that have been explicitly defined in connection with that type. For example, we might have a type CIRCLE, and we might be able to invoke operators that return the area, or the circumference, or the radius (and so on) of any given circle. However, we couldn't legitimately say that circles have an area *component*, or a circumference *component*, or a radius *component* (and so on). One important consequence is that we don't know, nor do we need to know, how circles are represented inside the system; rather, that representation is visible solely to the code that implements the operators. In other words, the type is of interest to users— it's part of the model—while the representation is of interest to the implementation only.

Here's another quote that covers more or less the same ground as the previous one but goes into a little more detail. It's from that tutorial on object databases mentioned several times in this book already (viz., Stanley B. Zdonik and David Maier: "Fundamentals of Object-Oriented Databases," in Zdonik and Maier (eds.): *Readings in Object-Oriented Database Systems*, Morgan Kaufmann, 1990):

> Encapsulation [means each type has] a set of [operations and] a representation ... that is allocated for each [object of the type in question]. This representation is used to store the state of the object. Only the methods implementing operations for the objects are allowed to access the representation, thereby making it possible to change the representation without disturbing the rest of the system. Only the methods would need to be recoded.

Observe now that—as this quote effectively suggests—encapsulation can be regarded as nothing more than the familiar database notion of data independence in another guise (I touched on this point in passing in Chapter 2). After all, if we do manage to keep type and representation properly separated, and if we also succeed in our goal of keeping the representation hidden, then we can change that representation as much as we like without having to change application programs (we only have to change the code that implements the operations).

Perhaps now you begin to see why I don't think the notion of encapsulation, as such, is all that significant. After all, it basically just means that we don't have to worry about what we shouldn't *need* to worry about: namely, physical representations (also known as actual or internal representations). In other words, encapsulation really is, as already claimed, just a logical consequence of the crucial distinction we already draw—the logical difference, in fact—between type and representation. But of course there's quite a bit more that can usefully be said on the subject; hence this appendix.

One last point on the definition of the term: While preparing this appendix, I took the trouble to look up "encapsulation" in a number of books (nearly 20 of them, in fact) on object technology and related matters. It was a pretty dispiriting exercise, I can tell you—and I was very struck by the fact that I could nowhere find a really precise definition of the concept. (The best *explanations* were in the Smalltalk book already mentioned, by Goldberg and Robson, and I think it's telling that that particular book doesn't seem to use the term "encapsulation," as such, at all. Certainly it's not in the index.) Anyway, one thing I did discover was that some writers seem to think the concept refers specifically to the physical bundling, or "packaging," of data representation definitions and operator definitions. For example, here's a quote from *The Object Database Handbook: How to Select, Implement, and Use Object-Oriented Databases*, by Douglas K. Barry (Wiley Publishing, 1996):

> Encapsulation refers to the concept of including processing or behavior with the object instances defined by the [type]. Encapsulation allows code and data to be packaged together.

But it seems to me that to interpret the term in this way is to mix model and implementation considerations. The user shouldn't care, and shouldn't need to care, whether or not code and data are "packaged together"! Thus, it's my belief that—from the user's point of view, at least, which is to say from the point of view of the model—encapsulation simply means what I said before: namely, that the data in question has no user visible components and can be operated upon only by means of the pertinent operators.[2]

BUT WHAT ABOUT AD HOC QUERY?

Now, you might be aware that the concept of encapsulation is in conflict, somewhat, with the requirement to be able to perform ad hoc queries.[3] After all, encapsulation means data can be accessed only via predefined operators, while ad hoc query means, more or less by definition, that access is required in ways that can't have been predefined. For example, suppose that (as elsewhere in this book) we have a type called POINT, denoting points in two-dimensional space. Suppose we also have a predefined operator to "get"—that is, read or retrieve—the x coordinate of any given point, but no analogous predefined operator to get the corresponding y coordinate. Then even the following simple queries—

- Get the y coordinate of point p

- Get all points on the x axis

- Get all points with y coordinate less than five

(and many others like them)—obviously can't be handled; in fact, they can't even be formulated.

---

[2] Two further points in connection with the extract quoted: First, I note that, not only does it use the deprecated term *instance*—which I've had occasion to complain about elsewhere in this book—but it does so in the phrase "object instances." Since *instance*, whatever it means, is generally taken to be a synonym for *object* (another less than fully explained term!), the extract quoted is apparently talking about "object objects." Second, it says the "processing or behavior" is included with those "object instances." I find this hard to believe. Surely it would be included with the object *type*, not with the "object instances"?

[3] I've touched on this point previously too. See footnote 50 in Chapter 21.

Now, *The Third Manifesto* deals with this issue by requiring that (at least in the case of a regular type) operators be defined that expose some possible representation for values and variables of the type in question. As you know, we call those operators "THE_ operators." In the case of type POINT, for example, operators THE_X and THE_Y might be defined, thereby allowing operations such as the following:

```
PY := THE_Y ( P ) ;
/* get y coordinate of point in variable P  and */
/* assign it to RATIONAL variable PY          */

DP := LENGTH ( SQRT ( THE_X ( P ) ^ 2 + THE_Y ( P ) ^ 2 ) ) ;
/* get distance of point in variable P from the */
/* origin and assign it to LENGTH variable DP   */
```

(and so on). Thus, THE_X and THE_Y effectively expose a possible representation—namely, cartesian coordinates *x* and *y*—for points, thereby making it possible to perform ad hoc queries involving points.[4] Note carefully, however, that this fact doesn't mean that points are physically represented by cartesian coordinates inside the system; it merely means, to repeat, that cartesian coordinates are a possible representation. The physical representation might be cartesian coordinates *x* and *y*, or it might be polar coordinates ρ and θ, or it might be something else entirely. In other words, THE_ operators don't violate encapsulation, and they don't undermine data independence.

> *Aside:* I remark in passing that DATE and TIME in SQL serve as examples of *built in* (i.e., system defined) types for which certain possible representations are effectively exposed. For example, dates have an exposed possible representation consisting of a YEAR component, a MONTH component, and a DAY component. Though I should perhaps add that those "possible" representations are likely to be rather close—in practice, they're probably identical—to the physical ones, in SQL, since (as we saw in Chapter 22) SQL doesn't really have a possrep notion, as such, at all. *End of aside*.

WE DON'T ALWAYS WANT ENCAPSULATION

Another reason why I don't think encapsulation as such is all that important has to do with another point over which there seems to be a certain amount of confusion in the literature, and that's as follows: Some types are definitely *not* encapsulated anyway, nor do we want them to be. I refer in particular to certain generated types—types, that is, that have been defined by means of certain type generators, such as ARRAY, LIST, TUPLE, and RELATION. To fix our ideas, let's focus on RELATION as a familiar example (though remarks analogous to those that

---

[4] And ad hoc updates, too, and more generally making it possible to define any further read-only and update operators that might be desired for operating on values and variables of type POINT.

follow apply to ARRAY and the rest as well, of course). So instead of the POINT type discussed in the previous section, let's consider a POINTS relvar (relation variable), defined thus:

```
VAR POINTS BASE
    RELATION { X RATIONAL , Y RATIONAL }
    KEY { X , Y } ;
```

Now, this relvar definition makes use of the RELATION type generator to specify the (generated) type of the relvar, which is, of course, a specific relation type—namely, the relation type

```
RELATION { X RATIONAL , Y RATIONAL }
```

And this type is certainly not encapsulated—it has user visible components, viz., the attributes X and Y. And, of course, it's precisely the fact that it does have those user visible components that makes it possible for us to perform ad hoc queries on relvar POINTS; for example, we can project it over attribute Y, or restrict it to just those tuples with Y value less than five.

I note in passing that the book on object / relational DBMSs by Stonebraker and others— viz., Michael Stonebraker and Paul Brown (with Dorothy Moore): *Object-Relational DBMSs: Tracking the Next Great Wave* (2nd edition, Morgan Kaufmann, 1999), mentioned in passing in Chapter 21[5]—makes essentially the same point:

> Base types are completely encapsulated. The only way to manipulate [a value of] a base type is to retrieve it or execute a function that takes [a value of] its type as an argument. In contrast, row objects are completely transparent. You can see all the fields, and they are readily available in the query language. Of course, an intermediate position is to allow some fields of a row object to be public (visible) and the remainder to be private (encapsulated). This is the approach used by C++.

I take "base types" here to mean scalar types; similarly, I take "row objects" to mean nonscalar, generated types, or rather values (and/or variables?) of such types. However, I should say too that it's not clear, when Stonebraker et al. talk about being able to "see all the fields" of a "row object," whether they properly distinguish as *The Third Manifesto* does between physical and possible representations. On the whole, it seems likely that they're considering physical representations only—in which case they seem to be agreeing with my remarks in Chapter 21, to the effect that such "fields" (at least the public ones, which I referred to in that chapter as public instance variables) definitely serve to expose the physical representation in question.

Anyway, to get back to my main argument: Please note very carefully that the fact that relation types aren't encapsulated doesn't mean we lose data independence. In the case of the POINTS relvar, for instance, there's no logical reason why that relvar can't be represented physically by polar coordinates ρ and θ instead of cartesian coordinates x and y. (I know it probably can't be represented that way in today's SQL products, but I regard that state of affairs

---

[5] See also Appendix B for further discussion of this book.

as a defect in those products. As I've had occasion to complain elsewhere—see, e.g., my book *SQL and Relational Theory: How to Write Accurate SQL Code* (3rd edition, O'Reilly, 2015)— today's SQL products provide very much less data independence than relational technology is theoretically capable of.) In other words, we still have to make a clear distinction between types and representations, even with nonencapsulated types like the relation type illustrated in the example. To say it again, the fact that some given type isn't encapsulated doesn't in and of itself necessarily mean that data independence is undermined.

SCALAR vs. NONSCALAR TYPES

In *The Third Manifesto*, we require support for both a TUPLE and a RELATION type generator; as a consequence, users are able to specify whatever tuple and relation types they want (e.g., as part of a tuplevar or relvar definition). We also require users to be able to define types that, unlike tuple and relation types, are just "simple" types—that is, types like POINT, LENGTH, ELLIPSE, CIRCLE, and so on—possibly even types like RATIONAL, if they're not provided as system defined types. And we opted for the term *scalar types* as a generic way of referring to such "simple" types (and then we naturally talked in terms of *scalar values* and *scalar variables* and *scalar operators* as well).

Now, the reason we chose the term *scalar* was because:

a. It was already available (it's been used with the meaning we had in mind for many years in the world of programming languages).

b. What's more, it did seem to be the obviously correct generic term to contrast with terms such as "tuple" and "relation" (and "array" and "list" and all the rest). In fact, we would argue that it's obviously correct even though the physical representation of those "scalar" values and variables can be as complicated as you like. For example, a given scalar value might have a physical representation consisting of an array of stacks of lists of character strings, in appropriate circumstances. (Yet again I stress the importance of not confusing types and representations.)

And now I observe that our term "scalar" means exactly the same thing as "encapsulated"! In other words, a type is encapsulated if and only if it's scalar in the foregoing sense. Thus, I feel that if the industry had opted, as we did in *The Third Manifesto*, for the already available term *scalar*, there would have been no need to invent the term *encapsulated* at all. And I further feel that we might thereby have avoided some of the confusions I've been talking about in this appendix.

Note: Because they have no user visible components, scalar types—encapsulated types, if you insist—are sometimes said to be *atomic*. I would rather not use such terminology, however, because it's led to too much misunderstanding in the past (on my own part as much as anyone else's, I hasten to add); instead, I prefer to concentrate on our "new, improved" understanding of the true nature of first normal form.

> *Aside:* The term *first normal form* (abbreviated 1NF) is due to Codd, inventor of the concept. He discusses it—though, oddly enough, not by that name—on page 6 of his book *The Relational Model for Database Management Version 2* (Addison-Wesley, 1990), where he says this:
>
> Atomic data cannot be decomposed into smaller pieces by the DBMS ... The values in the domains on which each relation is defined are required to be atomic with respect to the DBMS.
>
> (Recall from Chapter 1 that *domain* is just another word for *type*.) The crucial point about this extract as far as this appendix is concerned is simply that (a) Codd is asserting, in effect, that relations must be in 1NF, meaning their attributes must all be of some scalar—or "atomic"—type,[6] and (b) he is contrasting such "atomic" values with "compound values" such as tuples and relations. *End of aside*.

SUMMARY

In this appendix I've tried to show why, in my opinion, the term "encapsulated" is more trouble than it's worth. To summarize:

- First of all, the term "scalar" seems (at least to me) to capture the essential idea better, and it has a longer and more respectable pedigree than "encapsulated" does.

- Second, there seems to be a widespread misunderstanding to the effect that *all* data should be encapsulated. I've tried to show that this idea is mistaken, and again I think that to talk in terms of scalar vs. nonscalar types makes the true state of affairs much clearer and reduces the risk of confusion.

- Third, some people seem to think of "encapsulation" as a physical rather than a logical concept anyway (see the quote from Barry in the section "What Does Encapsulation Mean?" for an illustration of this point).

I therefore think it's worth trying to avoid the term "encapsulation" altogether—which is precisely why I didn't make much use of it in the body of this book.

---

[6] Of course, we now know that this position of Codd's (i.e., regarding the definition of 1NF) is unnecessarily restrictive; as we saw in Chapter 2 of this book, relational attributes don't have to be limited to being scalar but can be, e.g., tuple or even relation valued. For further discussion of such matters, see my paper "What First Normal Form Really Means," in the book *Date on Database: Writings 2000-2006* (Apress, 2006).

Appendix B

Persistence Not

Orthogonal to Type

This appendix is based in part on a column that first appeared on the Database Programming & Design *website **www.dbpd.com** (October 1998). Like Appendix A, it doesn't have much to do with the principal topic of this book (i.e., type inheritance) as such—at least, not directly—but it does have certain implications for that topic, which is why I wanted to include it here.*

I explained in the previous appendix why I felt the focus in the object world on encapsulation was a little off base. Now I want to turn my attention to another well known object dictum: namely, that **persistence** [*should be*] **orthogonal to type**, which I'll refer to as POTT for short. POTT means, essentially, that (a) any data structure that can be created in a conventional application program—for example, an array, or a linked list, or a stack—can be stored as an object in an object database, while at the same time (b) the structure of such an object remains exactly as user visible as it would be if it weren't "persistent." For example, let EMPS be the set of all employees in a given company. Then EMPS might be represented in an object database as either a linked list or an array—among other things, of course, but let's agree to limit our attention for now to just those two possibilities—and users will have to know which it is, because the access operators will differ accordingly.

One of the earliest papers, if not *the* earliest, to articulate the POTT position was "Types and Persistence in Database Programming Languages," by Malcolm P. Atkinson and O. Peter Buneman (*ACM Comp. Surv. 19*, No. 2, June 1987).[1] Atkinson in particular was also one of the authors of *The Object-Oriented Database System Manifesto*,[2] which proposed a set of features that the authors claimed a DBMS would have to support if it was to qualify for the label "object oriented"—and, of course, those features did include POTT. Subsequently, the *Third Generation Database System Manifesto*,[3] by Stonebraker et al., also endorsed POTT as an objective for

---

[1] This paper is a good starting point for reading in the area of database programming languages in general (such languages being regarded by many people as the sine qua non of object database systems).

[2] Malcolm Atkinson, François Bancilhon, David DeWitt, Klaus Dittrich, David Maier, and Stanley Zdonik: "The Object-Oriented Database System Manifesto," Proc. 1st International Conference on Deductive and Object-Oriented Databases (Kyoto, Japan, 1989, published by Elsevier Science in 1990).

[3] Michael Stonebraker, Lawrence A. Rowe, Bruce G. Lindsay, James Gray, Michael Carey, Michael Brodie, Philip Bernstein, and David Beech: "Third Generation Database System Manifesto," *ACM SIGMOD Record 19*, No. 3 (September 1990).

future database systems. (To quote: "Persistent X for a variety of X's is a good idea.") And the authors of *The Object Database Standard: ODMG 3.0*[4]—referred to in what follows simply as ODMG—agree also (unsurprisingly):

> [An] object DBMS [is] a DBMS that integrates database capabilities with object-oriented programming language capabilities. [It] *makes database objects appear as programming language objects* ... [It] extends the programming language with *transparently persistent data* ... and other database capabilities [*italics added for emphasis*].

The position of *The Third Manifesto* is very different. As the *Manifesto* book puts it:

> Databases (and nothing else) are persistent ... [Since] the only kind of variable we permit within a database is, very specifically, the [relation variable or] relvar, the only kind of variable that might possess the property of persistence is the relvar.

In what follows, I want to try and explain why we—that is, Hugh Darwen and I, the authors of *The Third Manifesto*—take the position we do in this regard.

POTT VIOLATES DATA INDEPENDENCE

One reason we reject POTT is that it can lead to a loss of data independence, as I now explain. As I've already said, POTT means that any data structure that can be created in a conventional application program can be stored as an object in an object database, and further that the structure of such objects is visible to the user. Now, this "anything goes" approach to what can be kept in the database is a major point of difference between the object model and the relational model, of course, so let's take a closer look at it. *Note:* I assume for the sake of the discussion that the term *object model* is well defined and well understood, though such an assumption is perhaps a little charitable to the object world.

Be that as it may, we can characterize the difference between the two approaches as follows:

- The object model says we can put anything we like in the database (any structure we can create with the usual programming language mechanisms).

- The relational model says the same thing—but then goes on to insist that whatever we do put there *must be presented to the user in pure relational form.*

More precisely, the relational model, quite rightly, says nothing whatsoever about what can be physically stored. It therefore imposes no limits on what structures are allowed at the

---

[4] R. G. G. Cattell and Douglas K. Barry (eds.), *The Object Data Standard: ODMG 3.0* (Morgan Kaufmann, 2000).

physical level; the only requirement is that whatever structures are in fact physically stored must be mapped to relations at the logical level, and hence be hidden from the user.[5] Relational DBMSs thus make a clear distinction between the logical and physical levels of the system—in other words, between the model and its implementation—and object systems don't.

As I've already said, one consequence of this state of affairs is that (contrary to claims sometimes heard elsewhere) object systems might well provide less data independence than relational systems can, or do. For example, suppose the implementation, within some object database, of the object representing that set EMPS of all employees in some given company is changed from an array to a linked list. What are the implications for existing code that accesses that object? (*Answer:* It breaks.)

I should perhaps ask the further question: Why would we *want* to change the implementation of an object in such a manner, anyway? The answer is surely performance. Ideally, therefore, such a change should not affect anything *except* performance; in practice, however, it does.

It seems to me, in fact, that the ability to have all of these different ways of representing data at the logical level is an example of what I've referred to elsewhere as *spurious generality*.[6] I would argue further that the whole idea seems to stem from a failure to make a clean separation between model and implementation (we might need lots of different representations at the physical level, but we don't need the same thing at the logical level). Indeed, I remember Codd once saying to a member of the audience at a conference (in response to a question during a panel discussion): "If you tell me that you have 50 different ways of representing data in your system—at the logical level, that is—then I'll tell you that you have 49 too many."

POTT CAUSES ADDITIONAL COMPLEXITY

It should be obvious that POTT leads to additional complexity—and by "complexity" here I mean, primarily, complexity for the user, though in certain respects life gets more complicated for the system too. For example, the relational model supports just one "collection type generator" (to use a common object term): viz., RELATION. It also supports a set of generic operators—join, project, and so forth—that apply to all "collections" of that type (in other words, to all relations). By contrast, ODMG supports four collection type generators, viz., SET, BAG, LIST, and ARRAY, each with its own set of operators that apply to collections of the type in question. And I would argue that the ODMG operators are certainly more complicated, and at

---

[5] Turning this statement around, one thing the relational model clearly *doesn't* say is that relations must be stored as such, with (e.g.) one file per relation, one record per tuple, and one field per attribute—a style of implementation that I've referred to elsewhere as "direct image," and one that's unfortunately found in most if not all of the leading SQL products today. For further discussion of such matters, I refer you to my book *Go Faster! The TransRelational™ Approach to DBMS Implementation* (2002, 2011, available free online at *http://bookboon.com*).

[6] E.g., in the paper "Database Graffiti," in C. J. Date (with Hugh Darwen and David McGoveran), *Relational Database Writings 1994-1997* (Addison-Wesley, 1998).

the same time less powerful, than their relational counterparts. Here by way of example are the ODMG operators for lists:

```
IS_EMPTY
IS_ORDERED
ALLOWS_DUPLICATES
CONTAINS_ELEMENT
INSERT_ELEMENT
REMOVE_ELEMENT
CREATE_ITERATOR
CREATE_BIDIRECTIONAL_ITERATOR
REMOVE_ELEMENT_AT
RETRIEVE_ELEMENT_AT
REPLACE_ELEMENT_AT
INSERT_ELEMENT_AFTER
INSERT_ELEMENT_BEFORE
INSERT_ELEMENT_FIRST
INSERT_ELEMENT_LAST
REMOVE_FIRST_ELEMENT
REMOVE_LAST_ELEMENT
RETRIEVE_FIRST_ELEMENT
RETRIEVE_LAST_ELEMENT
CONCAT
APPEND
```

Incidentally, it's worth pointing out in passing that the one "collection type generator" that ODMG most obviously does *not* support is RELATION! The ODMG book claims that "the ODMG data model encompasses the relational data model by defining a TABLE type,"[7] but that "TABLE type" (actually it's a type generator) is severely deficient in many respects. In particular, many of the crucial relational operators—including join in particular—are missing. (I should mention too that there are numerous additional problems with claims to the effect that "the ODMG data model" "encompasses" or "is more powerful than" the relational model, but this appendix isn't the place to go into details. A few examples of such claims were mentioned in passing in Chapter 21.)

Now, ODMG does support a query language, called OQL. OQL is a read-only language (update operators are omitted) that's loosely patterned after SQL. To be more specific:

■ OQL provides SQL-style SELECT – FROM – WHERE queries against sets, bags, lists, and arrays (though not relations).

■ It also provides analogs of the SQL GROUP BY, HAVING, and ORDER BY constructs.

---

[7] That claim appears in Section 2.4.2.1 ("Table Type") of the ODMG book, which reads in its entirety as follows: *The ODMG data model encompasses the relational data model by defining a Table type to express SQL tables. The ODMG Table type is semantically equivalent to a collection of structs.* (A "struct" can be thought of as an SQL-style row.) *Note:* The foregoing text appears in Version 2.0 of the ODMG book. Interestingly, it seems to have been dropped from Version 3.0.

- It also supports union, intersection, and difference operations, together with certain special operations for lists and arrays (for example, "get the first element").

- It also supports "path expressions" for "traversing relationships" (in other words, following pointers) between objects.

And the ODMG book makes a number of specific claims regarding OQL. Here are a couple of them (italics added in both cases):[8]

- "We have used the relational standard SQL as the basis for OQL, where possible, *though OQL supports more powerful capabilities.*"

- "[OQL] is *more powerful* [than a relational query language]."

In my opinion, by contrast, OQL illustrates very well my point that POTT leads to additional complexity. That is, I would argue that OQL isn't more *powerful*, it's more *complicated* (the computing community often seems to confuse these two notions). And the extra complication derives from the fact that so many different data structures are exposed to the user. And *that* state of affairs is a direct consequence, it seems to me, of a failure to appreciate the advantages of keeping model and implementation rigidly apart.

Let's take a moment to investigate this issue of increased complexity a little more closely. First of all, note that when we talk of lists in the database, arrays in the database, and so on, what we're really talking about is list *variables*, array *variables*, and so on—just as, when we talk of relations in the database, we really mean relation variables (relvars). Now, the only kinds of variables we find in a relational database are, of course, those relation variables specifically (that is, variables whose values are relations); relational databases don't permit list variables (variables whose values are lists), or array variables (variables whose values are arrays), or any other kinds of variables. It follows that to allow, say, list variables in the database would constitute a major departure from the classical relational model.

Why exactly would that departure be so major? Well, orthogonality would dictate, first of all, that we'd have to define a whole new query language for lists—that is, a set of list operators (a "list algebra"?), analogous to the operators we already have for relations (the relational algebra).[9] Of course, we'd certainly need to worry about the concept of closure in connection with that language. And we'd need to define a set of list update operators, analogous to the existing relational ones. We'd need to be able to define list integrity and security constraints, and list views. The catalog would need to describe list variables as well as relation variables. (And what would the catalog itself consist of?—list variables? or relation variables? or a mixture of the two?) We'd need a list design theory, analogous to the existing body of relational design

---

[8] The first of these claims is repeated from Chapter 21.

[9] Note that the ODMG operators listed on the previous page come nowhere near constituting such a "list algebra."

theory. We'd also need guidelines as to when to use list variables and when relation variables. And so on (I'm sure this list of issues—pun intended—isn't exhaustive).

The net of all this is:

- Assuming that such a "list algebra" can be defined, and all of the other questions raised in the previous paragraph answered satisfactorily, now we'll have two ways of doing things where one sufficed previously. In other words, as already noted, adding a new kind of variable certainly adds complexity, but it doesn't add any power—there's nothing (at least, nothing useful) that can be done with a mixture of list and relation variables that can't be done with relation variables alone.

- Thus, the user interface will now be more complex and involve more choices—very likely without good guidelines as to how to make such choices.

- As a direct consequence of the foregoing, database applications—including in particular general purpose applications or "front ends"—will become more difficult to write and more difficult to maintain.

- Those applications will also become more vulnerable to changes in the database structure; that is (again as noted earlier), some degree of data independence will be lost. Consider what happens, for example, if the representation of some piece of information is changed from relation variables to list variables or the other way around.

All of the foregoing is, of course, in direct conflict with Codd's *Information Principle*. Codd stated that principle in various forms and various publications over the years; indeed, I heard him refer to it on occasion as "*the* fundamental principle underlying the relational model." One way to state it is as follows:

> *At all times, all information in the database must be cast explicitly in terms of relations and in no other way.*

In his book,[10] Codd gives a number of arguments in support of this principle (arguments with which I concur, of course). In fact, the real point is this: As we've argued in the *Manifesto* book, relations are both necessary and sufficient for representing any data we like (at the logical level, of course); thus, we must have relations, and we don't need anything else.

---

[10] E. F. Codd: *The Relational Model for Database Management Version 2* (Addison-Wesley, 1990).

CONCLUDING REMARKS

So where did POTT come from? It seems to me that what we have here is (as so often) *a fundamental confusion between model and implementation*. To be specific, (a) it has been observed that certain SQL products don't perform very well on certain operations (especially joins), and (b) it has been conjectured that performance would improve if we could use, say, lists or arrays instead of relations.[11] But, of course, such thinking is seriously confused—it mixes logical and physical levels. Nobody is arguing that lists and so forth might not be useful at the physical level; the question is whether those lists and so forth should be exposed at the logical level. And it's the position of relational advocates in general, and Darwen and myself as authors of *The Third Manifesto* in particular, that the answer to that question is a very firm *no*.

POSTSCRIPT: THE FIRST AND SECOND MANIFESTOS

As I explained in Chapter 1, the reason we call our *Manifesto* "the third" is that we originally wrote it to be seen, at least in part, as a response to two earlier ones (both of which were mentioned in the introduction to this appendix); the first was *The Object-Oriented Database System Manifesto* (1989) and the second was the *Third Generation Database System Manifesto* (1990). The following notes briefly describing and analyzing these two earlier proposals are based on material from Appendix J ("References and Bibliography") of the *Manifesto* book.

Note: Throughout what follows, use of the first person plural, in the comments in particular, refers as usual to Hugh Darwen and myself. Also, I need to make it clear that those comments are based on the premise that the object of the exercise[12] is to define features of a good, genuine, general purpose DBMS. We don't deny that some of the features we object to[13] might be useful for a highly specialized DBMS, tied to some specific application area such as (e.g.) CAD/CAM, with no need for (e.g.) declarative integrity constraint support—but then we would question whether such a system is truly a DBMS as such, as that term is usually understood.[14]

---

[11] Or pointers instead of foreign keys!—which is, I believe, one major reason why object database systems support object IDs. *Note:* For some additional conjectures regarding possible origins of the POTT idea, see the extended extract from my paper "Why 'The Object Model' Is Not a Data Model," quoted in the final pages of this appendix.

[12] Pun intended.

[13] Pun intended.

[14] In this connection, again I refer you to my paper "Why 'The Object Model' Is Not a Data Model" (see footnote 11).

The Object-Oriented Database System Manifesto

The aim of this document, like that of our own *Manifesto*, is to propose a foundation for future DBMSs. As noted in Chapter 1, however, it virtually ignores the relational model; in fact, it doesn't seem to take the idea of a model, as such, very seriously at all. Here's a direct quote:

> With respect to the specification of the system, we are taking a Darwinian approach: We hope that, out of the set of experimental prototypes being built, a fit model will emerge. We also hope that viable implementation technology for that model will evolve simultaneously.

In other words, the authors are suggesting that the code should be written first, and that a model might possibly be developed later by abstracting from that code. By contrast, we believe it would be better to develop the model first (which is what happened in the relational case, of course; indeed, it's also what we're advocating in connection with our approach to inheritance, as I hope the body of this book makes clear).

Be that as it may, the paper goes on to propose the following as mandatory features—i.e., features that, it suggests, definitely must be supported if the DBMS in question is to warrant the label "object oriented":

1. Collections
2. Object IDs
3. Encapsulation
4. Types or classes
5. Inheritance
6. Late binding
7. Computational completeness
8. User defined types
9. Persistence
10. Large databases
11. Concurrency
12. Recovery
13. Ad hoc query

The paper also discusses certain optional features, including multiple inheritance and compile time type checking; certain "open" features, including language style ("we see no reason why we should impose one programming paradigm more than another: the logic programming style, the functional programming style, or the imperative programming style could all be chosen"); and certain features on which the authors could reach no consensus, including—a little surprisingly, considering their importance—views and integrity constraints.

Here now in a nutshell are our positions on the proposed mandatory features (only).

■ We agree that Number 8 is crucial and Number 5 is highly desirable (though we note that, as mentioned in Chapter 3, the authors are deliberately vague as to exactly what Number 5 might mean). Number 4 is implied by Number 8. Number 6 is more or less implied by Number 5 (and is therefore probably desirable too), but it's primarily an implementation issue, not a model issue (it's just another term for run time binding). We agree with Number 7.

■ We agree that Numbers 10-13 are important, but they're independent of whether the system is relational, an object system, or something else entirely. *Note:* The point is worth repeating from Appendix A, however, that Number 13 in particular—i.e., ad hoc query support—can be difficult to achieve in a pure object system, because it clashes with the object goal of encapsulation and the idea that all access has to be by means of predefined methods.[15] We note too that providing many different data structures at the logical level, as object systems do, inevitably makes the query interface, if any, more complicated (in fact, OQL, mentioned earlier in this appendix, provides an eloquent illustration of this point).

■ With regard to Numbers 1 and 9, the only kind of "collection" we want (and indeed the only kind we need)—and certainly the only kind of data construct we want to possess the property of "persistence"—is, very specifically, the database relvar. To repeat, we firmly reject the whole POTT idea ("persistence orthogonal to type").

■ As explained in Appendix A, we think the emphasis on encapsulation (Number 3) is a little off base. What's important is to distinguish between type and representation (and hence, in database terms, to achieve data independence). After all, unencapsulated relations can provide just as much data independence, in principle, as encapsulated objects can.

■ We reject Number 2 outright.

All of that being said, let me now add that—and it is to the credit of the authors that they recognize as much—their paper was never really intended to be more than a stake in the ground. To quote:

> We have taken a position, not so much expecting it to be the final word as to erect a provisional landmark to orient further debate.

The Third Generation Database System Manifesto

In part, this second manifesto is a response to—i.e., a counterproposal or rebuttal to—the first. Let me explain the title. Basically, first generation database systems are the old hierarchic and network (CODASYL) systems, such as IMS and IDMS, respectively; second generation systems are relational (or at least SQL) systems; and third generation systems are whatever comes next. Here's a quote:

---

[15] In connection with this point, I refer you to footnote 50 in Chapter 21 once again.

Second generation systems made a major contribution in two areas, nonprocedural data access and data independence, and these advances must not be compromised by third generation systems.

(Of course, we believe relational systems made rather more than just two "major contributions," but let that pass.) In other words, third generation systems, whatever else they might do, must certainly support the relational model. Unfortunately, the authors then go on to say that supporting the relational model really means supporting *SQL*, a position that's very close to being a contradiction in terms.

The following features are claimed as essential requirements of a third generation DBMS (I've paraphrased the original text somewhat):

1. Provide traditional database services plus richer object structures and rules

    - Rich type system
    - Inheritance
    - Functions and encapsulation
    - Optional system assigned tuple IDs
    - Rules (e.g., integrity rules), not tied to specific objects

2. Subsume second generation DBMSs

    - Navigation only as a last resort
    - Intensional and extensional set definitions (meaning collections that are maintained automatically by the system and collections that are maintained manually by the user, respectively)
    - Updatable views
    - Clustering, indexes, etc., hidden from the user

3. Support open systems

    - Multiple language support
    - Persistence orthogonal to type
    - SQL (characterized as "intergalactic dataspeak")
    - Queries and results must be the lowest level of client / server communication

Again we offer our own comments and reactions:

1. *Traditional database services and richer object structures and rules:* Of course we agree with "traditional database services." We also agree with "rich type system" and "[type] inheritance," so long as it's understood that (a) *type* is just another (and, in my opinion,

better) term for *domain*,[16] and (b) the sole use made of such types as far as the database is concerned is as the domains over which attributes of database relvars are defined[17] (in other words, we don't want those "richer object structures" to appear as variables in the database, either in place of or alongside such database relvars). "Functions"—we prefer the term *operators*—are implied by "rich type system." Regarding "encapsulation," see Appendix A. Regarding "tuple IDs," there seems to be some confusion here between tuples and "objects," a point that might be the cause for some alarm;[18] we reject object IDs, of course, but we support the idea of system keys, and such keys might possibly be thought of as (necessarily user visible) "tuple IDs." As for rules: We certainly support integrity rules specifically, of course; further, we don't preclude support for other kinds of rules (e.g., security rules), though if this latter is what the authors mean by "rules," then it seems to us something of a secondary issue.

2. *Subsume second generation DBMSs:* If by "subsume" here the authors mean it's the relational model that must be subsumed, then we reject the suggestion categorically (but perhaps they don't mean that). "Navigation only as a last resort": We take a firmer stand and reject navigation entirely; we think it's incumbent on anyone who thinks that navigation is ever necessary to show first that there's some problem for which a nonnavigational (relational) solution is logically—or at least effectively—impossible. We also reject "extensional set definitions" (in the sense meant here), because the meaning of any set thus defined is hidden in some application instead of being exposed in the database. We agree with support for updatable views.[19] Finally, we also agree that access mechanisms—indexes and the like—should be hidden from the user (they aren't always hidden in certain object systems, or indeed in certain SQL systems, but they were always supposed to be hidden in true relational systems).

3. *Support open systems:* We agree with this objective in principle (and we have no objection to "multiple language support"), but of course we reject the idea of "persistence orthogonal to type." We also reject SQL (we're in this business for the long haul). We do agree with the general sense of "queries and results being the lowest level of client / server communication"—though the term *client / server* sounds a little quaint these days—but remark that this objective seems to be in conflict with the earlier objectives concerning "extensional set definition" and "navigation."

---

[16] The reason I mention this rather obvious point will become clear in the discussion of the first book mentioned in the subsection "Related Publications," later in this section.

[17] And as the types of those database relvars themselves, of course, in the case of relation types.

[18] It turns out we were right to be alarmed, too (we originally wrote this commentary in the 1990s). See Chapter 22.

[19] In this connection I'd like to draw your attention to another recent book of mine, *View Updating and Relational Theory: Solving the View Update Problem* (O'Reilly, 2013).

To close this subsection, I'd like to draw your attention to another paper: "Comments on the Third Generation Database System Manifesto," by David Maier (Tech. Report No. CS/E 91-012, Oregon Graduate Center, Beaverton, Ore., April 1991), which is, as the title indicates, a review and analysis of the second manifesto. Maier is highly critical of just about everything in this latter document; we agree with some of his criticisms and disagree with others. However, we do find the following remarks interesting, since they bear out our own contention that "object orientation" really involves just one good idea—viz., proper type support:

> Many of us in the object-oriented database field have struggled to distill out the essence of "object orientedness" for a database system ... My own thinking about ... the most important features of OODBs has changed over time. At first I thought [the most important features were] inheritance and the message model. Later I came to think that object identity, support for complex state, and encapsulation of behavior were more important. Recently, after starting to hear from users of OODBMSs about what they most value about those systems, I think that *type extensibility* is the key. Identity, complex state, and encapsulation are still important, but [only] insomuch as they support the creation of new data types.

Related Publications

To conclude this appendix, I'd like to mention and briefly comment on a few more publications that have to do with topics raised in the first two manifestos (especially with that business of "persistence orthogonal to type" or POTT). The first is a book—one I've mentioned a couple of times already in the present book, in fact:

■ Michael Stonebraker and Paul Brown (with Dorothy Moore): *Object-Relational DBMSs: Tracking the Next Great Wave* (2nd edition, Morgan Kaufmann, 1999)[20]

This book is a tutorial on object / relational systems. It's heavily—in fact, almost exclusively—based on the Universal Data Option of Informix's Dynamic Server product.[21] That Universal Data Option was based on an earlier system called Illustra, a commercial product that Stonebraker himself was instrumental in developing. Regrettably, the authors of the book nowhere come right out in support of (a) our position that, as explained in Chapter 1, a true "object / relational" system would be nothing more nor less than a true relational system, nor (b) our position that today's "relational" systems aren't true relational systems at all, but SQL systems merely.

Be that as it may, Stonebraker et al. claim that a "good" object / relational DBMS must possess the following four "cornerstone characteristics," with features as indicated:

---

[20] This book is indeed in its second edition as stated, but most of the commentary that follows is based on the first edition. There are many cosmetic differences between the two editions, but the overall message is the same in both.

[21] Informix was acquired by IBM in 2001.

1. Base type extension

    - Dynamic linking of user defined functions
    - Client or server activation of user defined functions
    - Secure user defined functions
    - Callback in user defined functions
    - User defined access methods
    - Data types of arbitrary length

2. Complex objects

    - Type constructors
    - User defined functions
    - Data types of arbitrary length
    - SQL support

3. Inheritance

    - Data and function inheritance
    - Overloading
    - Inheritance of types, not tables
    - Multiple inheritance

4. Rule system

    - Retrievals as well as updates are events and actions
    - Integration of rules with type and inheritance extensions
    - Rich execution semantics for rules
    - No infinite loops

To elaborate:

1. *Base type extension:* The authors use this term to mean that users must be able to define their own scalar types and operators (they use the term *functions*, however, reserving *operators* for functions like "+" that make use of some special notation); they also, most unfortunately, assert that "a data type is both information and operations [whereas] the relational notion of a domain includes only the stored [*sic!*] representation, and there is no behavior associated with a domain."[22] *Dynamic linking* is self-explanatory (but it's a

---

[22] This claim is *obviously* incorrect if taken literally, because it implies there aren't any operators at all, not even "=" (and without "=" we can't even tell whether a given value is a value of the domain in question). See footnote 16.

pragmatic issue, not a logical requirement). *Client or server activation* means it must be possible to execute user defined functions in the same address space as the DBMS (at the server) and also in other address spaces (at the client); moreover, such executions must be *secure*—i.e., they mustn't be allowed to read or (worse) update anything that's supposed to be protected. (For obvious reasons, this problem is likely to be particularly severe if the execution occurs at the server.) The fancy term *callback* just means user defined functions must be allowed to perform database operations. *User defined access methods* means that type definers or implementers must be able to extend the system by introducing new storage structures and corresponding access code. *Data types of arbitrary length* just means there mustn't be any predefined limit on the amount of storage required for the physical representation of any given value.

Note: The Third Manifesto suggests that function definitions and type definitions are better kept separate, not bundled together. Stonebraker et al. agree with this position.

2. *Complex objects:* The authors use this term to mean that certain type generators—they use the term *type constructors*—must be supported. (A "complex object" is presumably either a value or a variable of such a generated type.) In particular, the following type generators "must" be supported:

   ■   Composites (records)
   ■   Sets
   ■   References

The term *composites* here corresponds, more or less, to our TUPLE type generator (though there seems to be some confusion over whether or not corresponding "composite" values and variables are encapsulated). *Sets* is self-explanatory. As for *references*, here's a quote: "An object / relational DBMS allows a column in a table to contain ... a [pointer] to a [row] ... in another table ... [The] actual value stored ... is an [object identifier or] OID." *The Third Manifesto* categorically prohibits such a state of affairs, of course;[23] in fact, we find here, regrettably, a certain amount of confusion once again over the logical difference between values and variables, also over the logical difference between model and implementation.

The *user defined functions* and *data types of arbitrary length* features just mean that (of course) generated types are indeed types; hence, users must be able to define functions that operate on values and variables of such generated types, and again there mustn't be

---

[23] In this connection, I'd like to mention the following. In 1997, I wrote a paper with the title "Don't Mix Pointers and Relations!" The purpose of that paper was to criticize efforts to do exactly that (i.e., mix pointers and relations, which is what Stonebraker et al. are proposing here) in the working draft of what became SQL:1999. Don Chamberlin (who incidentally is often described as "the father of SQL") wrote another paper in response to mine titled "Relations and References—Another Point of View" and defending those efforts. However, it seemed to me that Chamberlin's paper missed much of the point of mine, and so I wrote a rebuttal ("Don't Mix Pointers and Relations—*Please!*"). Chamberlin's paper was published alongside the first of my two papers in *InfoDB 10*, No. 6 (April 1997). Both of mine (but, sadly, not Chamberlin's) can be found in C. J. Date (with Hugh Darwen and David McGoveran), *Relational Database Writings 1994-1997* (Addison-Wesley, 1998).

any predefined limit on the amount of storage required for the physical representation of any given value.

Last, we agree with the *SQL support* feature, but only as an aid to migration,[24] not because such support is desirable in itself.[25]

3. *Inheritance:* We agree with the desirability of inheritance support. As noted in Chapter 21, however, Stonebraker et al. unfortunately use this term to refer not to type inheritance as such but rather to that business of "subtables and supertables," a very different notion. Moreover, the authors don't really address the question of an abstract inheritance model at all, nor do they mention most of the intrinsic complexities that seem to occur in connection with inheritance in general. For the record, however, we offer a few comments on the features the authors list under their "inheritance" heading. *Data and function inheritance* means a subtable inherits both columns and (user defined) functions from its supertable(s). *Overloading* means polymorphism (but it's definitely, as stated, overloading polymorphism, not inclusion polymorphism). *Inheritance of types, not tables* means—to use the terminology of *The Third Manifesto*—that relation type definitions and relvar definitions must be kept separate,[26] and hence that several relvars can be of the same separately and explicitly named relation type. (Recall that **Tutorial D** by contrast explicitly does *not* support a separate "define relation type" operator, for reasons explained in Chapter 2 and elsewhere.) *Multiple inheritance* is self-explanatory (at least, the basic idea is, though the consequences might not be).

4. *Rule system:* We agree that a rule system might be desirable in practice, but rule systems are at least arguably independent of whether the system is object / relational or something else. I therefore choose not to discuss them here.

It's noteworthy, incidentally, that Stonebraker et al. nowhere discuss the debate over the equations *domain = class* vs. *relvar = class* (see Chapter 1). Indeed, their examples suggest rather strongly that *relvar = class* is the right equation, though they never come out and say as much explicitly, and Stonebraker is on record elsewhere as stating that the opposite is the case.

---

[24] In fact the *Manifesto* book has some concrete proposals to make in this connection.

[25] One obvious difference between the first and second editions of Stonebraker et al.'s book is worth commenting on here—viz., the increased emphasis on SQL as such in the second edition. In fact, the first three of the four "cornerstone characteristics" are explicitly relabeled on page xii of the second edition thus: support for base type extension in an SQL context, support for complex objects in an SQL context, and support for inheritance in an SQL context.

[26] *Inheritance of types, not tables* would seem to contradict "subtable and supertable support," but it doesn't.

The second publication I'd like to mention in this subsection also has to do with object / relational systems specifically:

- Won Kim: "Bringing Object / Relational Down to Earth," *Database Programming & Design 10*, No. 7 (July 1997)

In this article, author Kim claims that "confusion is sure to reign" in the marketplace for object / relational DBMSs because, first, "an inordinate weight has been placed on the role of data type extensibility" and, second, "the measure of a product's object / relational completeness ... is a potentially serious area of perplexity." And he goes on to propose "a practical metric for object / relational completeness that can be used as a guideline for determining whether a product is truly [object / relational]"—an idea that inevitably invites comparison with the approach taken in *The Object-Oriented Database System Manifesto* to the question of determining whether a DBMS is truly object oriented.

Kim's scheme (*metric* is really not the mot juste, since there's nothing quantitative about it) involves the following criteria:

1. Data model
2. Query language
3. Mission critical services
4. Computational model
5. Performance and scalability
6. Database tools
7. Harnessing the power

With respect to Criterion Number 1, Kim takes the position—very different from ours—that the data model must be "the Core Object Model defined by the Object Management Group," which, he says, "comprises the relational data model as well as the core object-oriented modeling concepts of object-oriented programming languages." According to Kim, it thus includes all of the following concepts: *class* (Kim adds "or type"—?), *instance, attribute, integrity constraints, object IDs, encapsulation, (multiple) class inheritance, (multiple) ADT inheritance* (ADT = abstract data type), *data of type reference, set-valued attributes, class attributes, class methods,* and more besides. (Note that relations, which of course we regard as both crucial and fundamental, aren't even mentioned! Kim claims that the Core Object Model includes the entire relational model in addition to everything in the foregoing list, but it doesn't.)

As for Criterion Number 2 ("query language"), Kim's position—again very different from ours, in at least two major ways—is that the language must be some kind of "Object SQL" (i.e., a version of SQL that has been extended to deal with all of the various constructs just listed).

Criteria Numbers 3-6 all have to do with the implementation rather than the model. In other words, they might be important in practice; by definition, however, none of them can be a feature, or one of the features, that distinguishes a system that's object / relational from one that isn't. In other words, it's not clear exactly what Kim's metric is supposed to be measuring.

The final criterion ("harnessing the power") constitutes an interesting, and major, point of difference between Kim's position and ours. Our opinion, as explained in Chapter 1, is that user defined types constitute *the* primary justification for object / relational systems. Kim's opinion, by contrast, is that user defined types are merely a secondary feature (indeed, they've been "oversold"), and they constitute just one aspect of "harnessing the power." The other, he claims, is the ability of an object / relational DBMS to act as the basis for "heterogeneous database fusion"—i.e., to serve as a unified front end to a variety of disparate databases "including RDBs, OODBs, hierarchical databases, CODASYL databases, and even flat files." As explained my book *An Introduction to Database Systems* (8th edition, Addison-Wesley, 2004), however, such functionality is more properly ascribed to what's usually called *data access middleware*, not to a DBMS (whether it be object / relational or some other kind).

The last publication I'd like to mention—with apologies—is a paper by myself:

■ "Why 'The Object Model' Is Not a Data Model," in C. J. Date (with Hugh Darwen and David McGoveran): *Relational Database Writings 1994-1997* (Addison-Wesley, 1998)

In this paper, I argue among other things that (a) "the object model" is really a model of storage, not data, and that (b) partly because of that fact, object and relational database systems are more different than is usually realized. The following excerpt, lightly edited here, captures the essence of the argument:

> Object databases grew out of a desire on the part of object application programmers—for a variety of application specific reasons—to keep their application specific objects in persistent memory. That persistent memory might perhaps be regarded as a database, but the important point is that it was indeed application specific; it wasn't a shared, general purpose database, intended to be suitable for applications that might not have been foreseen at the time the database was defined. As a consequence, many features that database professionals regard as essential were simply not requirements in the object world, at least not originally. Thus, there was little perceived need for:
>
> ■ Data sharing across applications
> ■ Physical data independence
> ■ Ad hoc queries
> ■ Views and logical data independence
> ■ Application independent, declarative integrity constraints
> ■ Data ownership and a flexible security mechanism
> ■ Concurrency control
> ■ A general purpose catalog
> ■ Application independent database design
>
> These requirements all surfaced later, after the basic idea of storing objects in a database was first conceived, and thus all constitute add-on features to the original object model ... One important consequence is that there really is a difference in kind between an object DBMS and a relational

DBMS. In fact, it could be argued that an object DBMS isn't really a DBMS at all—at least, not in the same sense that a relational DBMS is a DBMS. For consider:

■   A relational DBMS comes ready for use. In other words, as soon as the system is installed, users (application programmers and end users) can start building databases, writing applications, running queries, and so on.

■   An object DBMS, by contrast, can be thought of as a kind of *DBMS construction kit*. When it's originally installed, it isn't available for immediate use by application programmers and end users. Instead, it must first be tailored by suitably skilled technicians, who must define the necessary classes and methods, etc. (the system provides a set of building blocks—class library maintenance tools, method compilers, etc.—for this purpose). Only when that tailoring activity is done will the system be available for use by application programmers and end users; in other words, the result of that tailoring will indeed more closely resemble a DBMS in the more familiar sense of the term.

■   Note further that the resultant "tailored" DBMS will indeed be application specific; it might, for example, be suitable for CAD/CAM applications, but be essentially useless for, e.g., medical applications. In other words, it still won't be a general purpose DBMS, in the same sense that a relational DBMS is a general purpose DBMS.

This same paper also contains a detailed examination of the object ID concept, and in that connection I'd like to quote another extended extract (also lightly edited here):

Consider the following:

■   In a traditional programming language, when a variable is declared, a *name* is typically specified for that variable, and that variable can then be referenced by that name from that point forward.

■   At the implementation level, by contrast, when an area of storage is allocated, it isn't given a name; instead, the system returns the *address* of that storage, and that storage can then be referenced by that address from that point forward.

What happens in an object system? When an object is "constructed," it isn't given a name; instead, the constructor operation returns an object ID—which is to say, an address—for the new object.[27] I conclude that an "object" in an object system is much more like an area of storage than it is like a conventional variable.

My next point is related to my previous one: Given an object type, object systems permit the construction of any number of individual objects of that type. For example, given type CIRCLE,

---

[27] I'm taking "object" here to mean a variable—sometimes called a *mutable object*—specifically. (Values, also known as *immutable* objects, are of course never "constructed" but simply exist.) As we now see, however, mutable objects lack one very important feature of a typical variable (viz., a name); in that respect, therefore, they're somewhat less than true variables. (On the other hand, they're also more than just plain storage, inasmuch as they are at least usually typed.)

the user is at liberty to construct as many CIRCLE "variables" (mutable objects) as he or she desires: one, two, a hundred, a million, possibly none at all. As a direct consequence of this state of affairs, individual CIRCLE "variables" do not—in fact, cannot—have names in the usual sense but are distinguished by address (object ID) instead, as we've already seen.

Now, it's interesting, and relevant, to note that a close parallel to the foregoing state of affairs can be found in one of the first programming languages I ever learned (viz., PL/I), in the form of what PL/I calls "based variables." Consider the following PL/I code fragment (I've numbered the lines for purposes of subsequent reference):

```
1.    DECLARE 1 CIRCLE BASED ,
2.              2 RADIUS ... ,
3.              2 CENTER ... ;
4.    DECLARE C_PTR POINTER ;

5.    ALLOCATE CIRCLE SET ( C_PTR ) ;
6.    C_PTR -> RADIUS = some radius value ;
7.    C_PTR -> CENTER = some center value ;
```

Explanation:

■ Lines 1-3 declare a "based variable"—actually a based *structure* variable—called CIRCLE, with components RADIUS and CENTER. The specification BASED means that the declaration is really just a *template*; no storage will be allocated for circles at compile time.

■ Line 4 declares a "regular" (i.e., nonbased) variable, a pointer variable called C_PTR. Storage *is* allocated by the compiler for this variable.

■ Line 5 allocates storage for an unnamed CIRCLE variable—that is, an unnamed variable whose structure conforms to the template defined in lines 1-3. It also returns a pointer to that storage—equivalently, to that unnamed variable—in the pointer variable C_PTR.

■ Lines 6-7 assign values to the RADIUS and CENTER components of the particular CIRCLE variable that the pointer variable C_PTR currently happens to point to.

The parallels to object systems are obvious: The based variable declaration for CIRCLE corresponds to an object type definition; ALLOCATE CIRCLE is an invocation of the corresponding constructor; access to a given CIRCLE variable by means of its address corresponds to access to a given object by means of its object ID; "construction" and initialization are logically distinct operations. And, of course, any number of individual unnamed CIRCLE variables can be allocated, each with its own address, just as any number of individual unnamed objects can be constructed, each with its own object ID.

Why bother with these parallels? Well, Robert Sebesta, in his book *Concepts of Programming Languages* (6th edition, Addison-Wesley, 2004), refers to variables like the allocated CIRCLE variable in the foregoing example as *explicit heap-dynamic variables:* "Explicit heap-dynamic variables are *nameless ... memory cells* that are *allocated and deallocated by explicit run-time instructions* specified by the programmer ... These variables *can only be referenced through pointer or reference variables*" (my italics). And he goes on to say: "Explicit dynamic variables [and the corresponding pointers] are often used for dynamic structures, such as linked lists and trees, which need to grow and shrink during execution. Such structures can be built conveniently using pointers and explicit heap-dynamic variables."

So the point is this: Just as pointers and explicit heap-dynamic variables can be used to build and maintain "dynamic structures" in programming languages like PL/I, so object IDs and objects can be used to build and maintain such structures in object systems. In particular, object databases can and do generally include such dynamic structures.

Observe now that relational systems can and do generally involve dynamic structures also. The difference is that in the relational case those structures are built and maintained using, not pointers, but rather the mechanisms—usually keys and and foreign keys—prescribed by the relational model. There's no *logical* need to use pointers instead of keys for such a purpose. And there are good reasons not to! To quote Sebesta again: "The disadvantages of explicit heap-dynamic variables are *the difficulty of using pointer and reference variables correctly*, along with the cost of references to the variables [and of the associated] allocations and deallocations " (my italics again). To be specific, pointers lead to pointer chasing, and pointer chasing is notoriously error prone.[28]

It's worth mentioning that Codd certainly agreed with the foregoing. When he first defined the relational model, he very deliberately excluded pointers. And in his book *The Relational Model for Database Management Version 2* (Addison-Wesley, 1990), he explained why:

> It is safe to assume that all kinds of users [including end users in particular] understand the act of comparing values, but that relatively few understand the complexities of pointers. The relational model is based on this fundamental principle ... [The] manipulation of pointers is more bug-prone than is the act of comparing values, even if the user happens to understand the complexities of pointers.

In view of the foregoing, it's curious that so many people seem to regard object IDs as the sine qua non of the object model.[29] For example, *The Object-Oriented Database System Manifesto* says "Thou shalt support object identity"—but it doesn't give any logical justification for such an edict. Likewise, in his paper "A Shift in the Landscape (Assessing SQL3's New Object Direction)," *Database Programming & Design 9*, No. 8 (August 1996), Jim Melton says "References in the form of object identifiers are the key [*sic!*] to the object oriented paradigm," but he provides no evidence in support of this strong claim. And in a useful annotated and comprehensive anthology of writings on the subject compiled by Declan Brady (a private communication dated July 1st, 1996, containing "the substance of everything I've managed to unearth on the [subject] of object IDs"), numerous similar assertions can be found. So far as I can see, however, none of those assertions is accompanied by any logical supporting arguments.

The arguments earlier in this appendix against the "persistence orthogonal to type" idea are also based in part on this paper.

---

[28] Indeed, it's this aspect of object systems that gives rise to the criticisms, sometimes heard, to the effect that such systems "look like CODASYL warmed over."

[29] Personally, I would have said user defined types were the sine qua non.

Appendix C

G l o s s a r y   o f   T e r m s

The *Manifesto* model of type inheritance involves a number of concepts that in some cases, at least, you probably weren't previously familiar with, and for that reason you might have experienced some difficulty in keeping them all straight in your head while you were reading the text. As an aide mémoire, therefore, this appendix provides a brief summary of some of the more important of those concepts. Note, however, that for ease of understanding the definitions that follow are sometimes a little rough and ready; they're accurate as far as they go, but they're not always quite as complete or precise as those in the body of the book, and in a few cases they're quite considerably reworded. Also, the full implications of certain of the definitions— *common subtype* is a case in point—for tuple and relation types are deliberately omitted.

alpha The maximal scalar type.

binding The process of determining which version of a given operator is to be executed in response to a given invocation of the operator in question.

common subtype Type T' is a common subtype for, or of, types $T1$, $T2$, ..., Tm if and only if, whenever a given value is of type T', it's also of each of types $T1$, $T2$, ..., Tm.

common supertype Type T is a common supertype for, or of, types $T1$, $T2$, ..., Tm if and only if, whenever a given value is of at least one of types $T1$, $T2$, ..., Tm, it's also of type T.

compile time binding Given an expression OpI denoting an invocation of some operator Op, the process of finding, at compile time, the invocation signature for Op for which the declared types of the parameters exactly match the declared types of the corresponding argument expressions in OpI, thereby causing the corresponding version of Op to be invoked at run time (unless the compiler's decision is overridden at run time by run time binding, q.v.).

declared type The type specified when some item (such as a variable, an attribute, a parameter, or a read-only operator) is declared. Moreover, since every expression—even if it's just a literal or a simple variable reference—consists essentially of an invocation of some read-only operator, it follows that expressions have a declared type too.

delegation   A mechanism according to which the responsibility for implementing some operator *Op* for some type *T* is delegated to some other type, typically but not necessarily the type of some component of some possrep for *T*.

derived possrep   Let *T'* be a scalar type with at least one regular immediate supertype. Then each possrep declared for *T'* is a derived possrep, explicitly defined in terms of some possrep for some regular immediate supertype of *T'*. *Contrast* inherited possrep.

disjointness assumption   A simplifying assumption, valid with single but not multiple inheritance, to the effect that types *T1* and *T2* are disjoint if and only if neither is a subtype of the other.

DT(X)   The declared type of *X*.

dummy type   A union type with no possrep.

generalization by constraint   Let types *T''*, *T'*, and *T* be such that *T''* is a proper subtype of *T'* and *T'* is a subtype of *T*, and let *v'* be a value that satisfies the type constraint for type *T'* and not for any proper subtype of *T'*. Also, let *V* be a variable of declared type *T*, and let the most specific type of *V* be *T''*. Finally, let the value *v'* be assigned to *V*. Then generalization by constraint (G by C) occurs, and the most specific type of *V* becomes *T'*.

immediate subtype   Type *T'* is an immediate subtype of type *T* if and only if it's a proper subtype of *T* and there's no type that's both a proper supertype of *T'* and a proper subtype of *T*.

immediate supertype   Type *T* is an immediate supertype of type *T'* if and only if it's a proper supertype of *T'* and there's no type that's both a proper subtype of *T* and a proper supertype of *T'*.

implementation version   Let type *T* be a proper supertype of type *T'*, and let *Op* be a read-only operator that applies to values of type *T* and hence, by definition, to values of type *T'* also (read-only just to be definite; the implementation version concept applies to update operators too, mutatis mutandis). Then it's possible, though not required, for *Op* to have two distinct implementation versions, one for values of type *T* and one for values of type *T'*. If so, however, then both versions should implement the same semantics.

inclusion polymorphism   Every read-only operator that applies to values of a given type *T* necessarily applies to values of every proper subtype *T'* of *T*. Such an operator is thus polymorphic, and the kind of polymorphism it exhibits is called inclusion polymorphism, on the grounds that the relationship between *T* and *T'* is basically that of set inclusion. As for update operators, an update operator that applies to variables of type *T* might or might not apply to variables of some proper subtype T' of T. If it does, then it too is said to exhibit inclusion polymorphism.

inherited possrep Let T' be a scalar type with at least one regular immediate supertype T. Then every possrep PR (declared or otherwise) for values of type T is necessarily, albeit implicitly, an inherited possrep for values of type T' as well. However, PR isn't considered a derived possrep (q.v.) for type T' unless it's explicitly declared.

intersection type Least specific common subtype. Also known as intersection subtype.

invocation signature *See* signature.

leaf type A scalar type T is a leaf type if and only if the only immediate subtype of T is *omega*. A tuple or relation type T is a leaf type if and only if every attribute of T is of some leaf type.

least specific common subtype Type T' is the least specific common subtype for types $T1$, $T2$, ..., Tm if and only if it's a common subtype for $T1$, $T2$, ..., Tm and no proper supertype of T' is also a common subtype for those types.

least specific common supertype The applicable maximal type.

least specific type Let value v be of type T and not of any proper supertype of T; then T is the least specific type of v. Note that T is necessarily a maximal type (e.g., if v is a scalar value in particular, the least specific type of v is *alpha*). Informally, however, least specific types are often defined to exclude superroot types, thus: Let v be of type T and let T be a root type; then T is the least specific type of v.

maximal type The least upper bound with respect to a given type lattice (i.e., the type within that lattice that contains the union of all of the sets of values in all of the types in that lattice).

minimal type The greatest lower bound with respect to a given type lattice (i.e., the type within that lattice that contains the intersection of all of the sets of values in all of the types in that lattice).

most specific common subtype The applicable minimal type.

most specific common supertype Type T is the most specific common supertype for types $T1$, $T2$, ..., Tm if and only if it's a common supertype for $T1$, $T2$, ..., Tm and no proper subtype of T is also a common supertype for those types.

most specific type   Let value v be of type T. If and only if no proper subtype T' of type T exists such that v is also of type T', then T is the most specific type for, or of, v.

MST(X)   The most specific type of X.

omega   The minimal scalar type.

overloading   Same as overloading polymorphism.

overloading polymorphism   Using the same name for two or more different operators. The operators in question must have different specification signatures (q.v.) but should preferably have similar semantics.

proper subtype   Type T' is a proper subtype of type T if and only if it's a subtype of T and T and T' are distinct.

proper supertype   Type T is a proper supertype of type T' if and only if it's a supertype of T' and T and T' are distinct.

regular type   A scalar type that's not a dummy type.

root type   A scalar type T is a root type if and only if the only immediate supertype of T is *alpha*. A tuple or relation type T is a root type if and only if every attribute of T is of some root type.

run time binding   Given some invocation OpI of some operator Op, the process of finding, at run time, the invocation signature for Op for which the declared types of the parameters exactly match the most specific types of the corresponding arguments to OpI, thereby causing the corresponding version of Op to be invoked.

signature   Let Op be a read-only operator, with parameters $P1$, $P2$, ..., Pn, and let parameter Pi have declared type DTi ($i = 1, 2, ..., n$). Then Op has a specification signature and a set of invocation signatures, where:

- The specification signature consists of the operator name, the parameter declared types $PDT1$, $PDT2$, ..., $PDTn$, and the result declared type RDT.

- Each invocation signature consists of one possible combination of argument expression declared types $ADT1$, $ADT2$, ..., $ADTn$, together with the declared type $IRDT$ of the result produced by an invocation of Op with arguments of most specific types equal to the declared types $ADT1$, $ADT2$, ..., $ADTn$, respectively, specified in the invocation signature in question. *ADT1*, *ADT2*, ..., *ADTn*, and *IRDT* are necessarily subtypes of *PDT1*, *PDT2*, ..., *PDTn*, and *RDT*, respectively.

Now let *Op* be an update operator, with parameters *P1*, *P2*, ..., *Pn*, and let parameter *Pi* have declared type *PDTi* (i = 1, 2, ..., *n*). Then (again) *Op* has a specification signature and a set of invocation signatures, where:

■ The specification signature consists of the operator name, the parameter declared types *PDT1*, *PDT2*, ..., *PDTn*, and an indication as to which parameters are subject to update.

■ Each invocation signature consists of one possible combination of argument expression declared types *ADT1*, *ADT2*, ..., *ADTn*. *ADT1*, *ADT2*, ..., *ADTn* are necessarily subtypes of *PDT1*, *PDT2*, ..., *PDTn*, respectively.

specialization by constraint   Let *S* be a selector of declared type *T*, and let *X* be an expression denoting an invocation of *S*. Let the value returned by *X* be *x*. Further, let *x* satisfy the type constraint for proper subtype *T'* of *T* and not for any proper subtype of *T'*. Then specialization by constraint (S by C) occurs, and the most specific type of *X* becomes *T'*.

specialization constraint   Let *T* be a regular type, and let *T'* be a nonempty immediate subtype of *T*. Then the type constraint for type *T'* will specify that, in order for some given value to be of type *T'*, that value must be of type *T* and must additionally satisfy some further constraint. That type constraint is the specialization constraint for type *T'*.

specification signature   *See* signature.

subleaf type   A scalar type is a subleaf type if and only if it's type *omega*. A tuple or relation type is a subleaf type if and only if it's a proper subtype of some tuple or relation leaf type (in which case it must have at least one attribute of some subleaf type).

substitutability   Value substitutability or variable substitutability or both, as the context demands.

subtype   Type *T'* is a subtype of type *T* if and only if every value of type *T'* is a value of type *T*.

superroot type   A scalar type is a superroot type if and only if it's type *alpha*. A tuple or relation type is a superroot type if and only if it's a proper supertype of some tuple or relation root type (in which case it must have at least one attribute of some superroot type).

supertype   Type *T* is a supertype of type *T'* if and only if every value of type *T'* is a value of type *T*.

__T_alpha__ The maximal type with respect to the type lattice containing type *T*.

__T_omega__ The minimal type with respect to the type lattice containing type *T*.

type constraint error The error that occurs if a selector is invoked with arguments that violate the applicable type constraint. Such errors are detected at run time. *Contrast* type error.

type error The error that occurs if an operator is invoked with argument types not matching those specified for some invocation signature for the operator in question. Such errors are detected at compile time (except, sometimes, in the context of TREAT). *Contrast* type constraint error.

type lattice Given some type *T*, the set of all subtypes of the corresponding maximal type *T_alpha* (equivalently, the set of all supertypes of the corresponding minimal type *T_omega*) is the type lattice corresponding to *T*.

union type A scalar type *T* such that every value *v* of type *T* has as its most specific type some proper subtype of *T*.

__v(X)__ The value of *X*.

value substitutability Wherever a value of type *T* is permitted, a value of any subtype of *T* can be substituted.

variable substitutability Wherever a variable of declared type *T* is permitted, a variable of declared type some nonempty subtype of *T* can be substituted—but only if such substitution makes sense.

version Same as implementation version.

Index

For alphabetization purposes (a) differences in fonts and case are ignored; (b) quotation marks are ignored; (c) other punctuation symbols—hyphens, underscores, parentheses, etc.—are treated as blanks; (d) numerals precede letters; (e) blanks precede everything else. Note: There are no index entries for the definitions in Appendix C.

Have it your way.

Milton Keynes UK
Ingram Content Group UK Ltd.
UKHW031802151123
432638UK00007B/443

9 781491 959992

Get even more for your money.

Join the O'Reilly Community, and register the O'Reilly books you own. It's free, and you'll get:

- $4.99 ebook upgrade offer
- 40% upgrade offer on O'Reilly print books
- Membership discounts on books and events
- Free lifetime updates to ebooks and videos
- Multiple ebook formats, DRM FREE
- Participation in the O'Reilly community
- Newsletters
- Account management
- 100% Satisfaction Guarantee

Signing up is easy:

1. Go to: oreilly.com/go/register
2. Create an O'Reilly login.
3. Provide your address.
4. Register your books.

Note: English-language books only

To order books online:
oreilly.com/store

For questions about products or an order:
orders@oreilly.com

To sign up to get topic-specific email announcements and/or news about upcoming books, conferences, special offers, and new technologies:
elists@oreilly.com

For technical questions about book content:
booktech@oreilly.com

To submit new book proposals to our editors:
proposals@oreilly.com

O'Reilly books are available in multiple DRM-free ebook formats. For more information:
oreilly.com/ebooks

O'REILLY®